BIOTECHNICAL
SLOPE PROTECTION
AND EROSION CONTROL

BIOTECHNICAL SLOPE PROTECTION AND EROSION CONTROL

Donald H. Gray

Dept. of Civil Engineering
The University of Michigan

Andrew T. Leiser

Dept. of Environmental Horticulture
University of California, Davis

KRIEGER PUBLISHING COMPANY
MALABAR, FLORIDA

Original Edition 1982
Reprint Edition 1989

Printed and Published by
ROBERT E. KRIEGER PUBLISHING CO., INC.
KRIEGER DRIVE
MALABAR, FLORIDA 32950

Copyright © 1982 by Van Nostrand Reinhold Company, Inc.
Reprinted by Arrangement

Library of Congress Cataloging-in-Publication Data

Gray, Donald H.
    Biotechnical slope protection and erosion control / Donald H.
    Gray, Andrew T. Leiser.
       p.   cm.
    Reprint. Originally published: New York : Van Nostrand Reinhold,
    c1982.
    Bibliography: p.
    Includes index.
    ISBN 0-89464-259-6 (alk. paper)
    1. Slopes (Soil mechanics) 2. Soil stabilization. 3. Soil
    erosion. 4. Soil-binding plants. I. Leiser, Andrew T. II. Title.
    [TA710.G6287 1989]
    624.1'51363--dc20   89-31979
                                               CIP

10   9   8   7   6   5   4   3

Preface to the Reprint Edition

Biotechnical Slope Protection was first published in 1982. Many new developments have occurred in the intervening years, particularly those related to the combined use of vegetation and geosynthetics to repair slope failures. In addition, numerous case studies can be cited now of successful applications of biotechnical techniques ranging from streambank repair to highway fill slope protection. These new developments and applications invite exposition in a new edition or version of this book. Even so, the basic core and substance of the biotechnical or "soil bioengineering" approach has not changed. The reader will still find much useful background information plus details about specific biotechnical measures in the present, interim edition.

Biotechnical Slope Protection and Erosion combines the perspectives and techniques of engineering and horticulture to achieve a common goal, namely, the retention of earth masses and the prevention of soil losses from slopes. The book explains how vegetation and structures can be used together in attractive, environmentally compatible, and cost-effective ways for this purpose. This approach, which is eclectic and interdisciplinary, forms the basis of "biotechnical slope protection."

The general principles and advantages of biotechnical slope protection systems are discussed. Low-cost biotechnical measures, such as contour wattling, brush layering, live staking, and brush matting, are described in detail. The use of slope planting in conjunction with earth-retaining structures is also discussed. This latter technique includes plantings on slopes above low toe-walls, on benches of tiered retaining walls, and in the frontal interstices, or openings, or porous retaining structures, such as crib walls, welded-wire walls, gabions, and cellular revetments.

Biotechnical Slope Protection and Erosion is intended primarily as a handbook for practicing professsionals, but is written in such a way that it can be understood and used by students, laypersons, and other interested parties. Analytical or somewhat technical material, particularly in chapters 2, 3, and 5, can be skimmed over without loss of continuity or utility. Sufficient descriptive material is contained in these chapters to convey the sense and intent of the subject matter. The contents of the book should prove of value to practitioners in such diverse fields as geotechnical engineering, geology, soil science, forestry, landscape architecture, and environmental horticulture. Detailed and comprehensive information is presented on alternative approaches to solving slope stability problems and designing slope protection systems. Both engineering design and plant material guidelines of interest to the practicing professional are included.

Property owners and land managers with either a personal stake or assigned responsibility for rehabilitation of land and protection of homes and property against slope failures and erosion should also find the book helpful. Many of the protection measures are relatively low cost and labor-skill intensive -- thus affordable to an individual. Lastly, the book can be used as a reference text in college-level courses, extension courses, and workshops whose course content includes such topics as erosion control, watershed rehabilitation, streambank repair, and land restoration.

Contents

Preface / v

1. INTRODUCTION / 1

1.1 Biotechnical or Combined Vegetative-Structural Slope Protection / 1

1.2 Reasons for Biotechnical Approach / 1
    1.2.1 Cost Effectiveness / 1
    1.2.2 Environmental Compatibility / 1
    1.2.3 Use of Indigenous, Natural Materials / 1
    1.2.4 Labor-Skill Intensiveness / 1

1.3 Extent and Severity of Soil Erosion and Slope Movement Problems / 3
    1.3.1 Soil Erosion / 3
    1.3.2 Mass-Movement / 6

1.4 Application of Biotechnical Slope Protection / 7

1.5 Scope and Organization of Book / 8

1.6 References Cited / 9

2. SOIL EROSION AND MASS-MOVEMENT / 10

2.1 Definitions / 10
    2.1.1 Soil Erosion / 10
    2.1.2 Mass-Movement / 10

2.2 Nature of Soil Erosion / 10
    2.2.1 Determinants of Rainfall Erosion / 11
    2.2.2 Determinants of Wind Erosion / 12
    2.2.3 Types of Water Erosion / 13
        2.2.3.1 Rainfall Erosion / 13
        2.2.3.2 Stream Channel Erosion / 15
        2.2.3.3 Groundwater Erosion / 16

2.3 Soil Loss Predictions / 16
    2.3.1 Rainfall Erosion / 16
        2.3.1.1 Rainfall Factor / 16
        2.3.1.2 Soil Erodibility Factor / 18
        2.3.1.3 Slope Length and Steepness Factors / 18

2.3.1.4   Cropping Management Factor / 20
2.3.1.5   Erosion Control Practice Factor / 20

2.4   Evaluation of Soil Loss Reduction Measures at Construction Sites / 23
2.4.1   Evaluation Formula / 23
2.4.2   Factor C Values for Construction Sites / 24
2.4.3   Factor P Values for Construction Sites / 25
2.4.4   Computing System Effectiveness / 25

2.5   Nature of Mass-Movement / 25
2.5.1   Types of Slope Movements / 25
2.5.2   Causes of Slope Movement / 26
2.5.3   Indicators of Slope Instability / 27

2.6   Slope Stability Predictions / 29
2.6.1   Approaches to Analysis / 29
2.6.2   Limit Equilibrium Analysis / 30
2.6.3   Shear Strength Parameters / 30
2.6.3.1   Total Stress Analysis / 31
2.6.3.2   Effective Stress Analysis / 31
2.6.4   Translational Slope Failures / 31
2.6.4.1   Selection of Soil Parameters / 33
2.6.4.2   Stability of Road Fills / 33
2.6.5   Rotational Slope Failures / 34
2.6.5.1   Critical Height of Road Cuts / 34
2.6.5.2   Stability Analysis by "Method-of-Slices" / 35

2.7   References Cited / 35

3.   ROLE OF VEGETATION IN THE STABILITY AND PROTECTION OF SLOPES / 37

3.1   Hydro-Mechanical Influences of Vegetation / 37
3.1.1   Prevention of Soil Erosion / 37
3.1.2   Prevention of Mass-Movement / 37

3.2   Root Reinforcement / 39
3.2.1   Mechanics of Root Reinforcement / 39
3.2.2   Theoretical Models of Root-Reinforced Soil / 40
3.2.3   Root Morphology and Strength / 43
3.2.4   Root and Fiber Reinforcement Tests / 47
3.2.5   Root Reinforcement in Sandy, Cohesionless Slopes / 51

3.3   Soil Moisture Modification and Depletion / 53
3.3.1   Soil Moisture Stress and Slope Movement / 53
3.3.2   Soil Moisture Stress in Forested vs. Cutover Slopes / 54

3.4   Slope Buttressing and Arching / 155
3.4.1   Mechanics of Arching and Buttressing / 55
3.4.2   Theoretical Model of Arching in Slopes / 56
3.4.3   Field Evidence for Arching Restraint / 57

3.5   Surcharge from Weight of Vegetation / 60
3.5.1   Influence of Surcharge on the Stability of "Infinite Slopes" / 60
3.5.2   Estimates of Surcharge from Weight of Trees / 60

3.6   Consequences of Vegetation Removal on Slope Stability / 61
    3.6.1   Relationship between Mass-Movement and Timber Harvesting / 61
    3.6.2   Results of Studies in the Western Cascades / 62

3.7   Summary and Conclusions / 63

3.8   References Cited / 64

4.   PRINCIPLES OF BIOTECHNICAL SLOPE PROTECTION / 66

4.1   Elements of System / 66

4.2   Role of Vegetation / 73

4.3   Role of Structure / 74
    4.3.1   Retaining Structures / 74
    4.3.2   Revetments and Grade Stabilization Structures / 76

4.4   Compatibility between Engineering and Biological Requirements / 81

4.5   References Cited / 82

5   STRUCTURAL-MECHANICAL COMPONENTS OF BIOTECHNICAL SLOPE PROTECTION / 83

5.1   Retaining Structures—General / 83
    5.1.1   Purpose and Function of Structure / 83
    5.1.2   Basic Types and Selection Criteria / 83
    5.1.3   Stability Requirements / 85
        5.1.3.1   External Stability / 88
        5.1.3.2   Internal Stability / 91
    5.1.4   Standard Designs / 91

5.2   Toe-Wall Construction / 91
    5.2.1   Rock Breast Walls / 91
    5.2.2   Gabion Walls / 93
    5.2.3   Crib Walls / 94
        5.3.2.1   Timber Cribs / 95
        5.2.3.2   Concrete Crib Walls / 97
    5.2.4   Welded-Wire Walls / 99
    5.2.5   Reinforced Earth Walls / 104

5.3   Revetments / 107
    5.3.1   Riprap / 107
    5.3.2   Gabions / 109
    5.3.3   Articulated, Precast Blocks / 112
    5.3.4   Cellular Grids / 112

5.4   Costs of Slope Protection Measures / 114
    5.4.1   Cost of Retaining Soil in Place / 116
    5.4.2   Cost Comparisons Among Methods / 116

5.5   References Cited / 120

6.   VEGETATIVE COMPONENTS AND REQUIREMENTS / 122

6.1   Introduction / 122

6.2   Constraints: Legal, Economic and Practical / 122
    6.2.1   Legal and Political Constraints / 122
    6.2.2   Economic contraints / 123

6.3   Site Analysis / 123
    6.3.1   Climate / 123
    6.3.2   Vegetation / 124
        6.3.2.1   Overall vegetation spectrum / 124
        6.3.2.2   Pioneer or Invader Species / 124
        6.3.2.3   Transitional Species / 124
        6.3.2.4   Subclimax and Climax Species / 124
        6.3.2.5   Summary / 124
    6.3.3   Microsite parameters / 124
        6.3.3.1   Microclimate / 125
        6.3.3.2   Aspect and Topography / 125
        6.3.3.3   Site Soils / 125
        6.3.3.4   Pot Tests to Estimate Fertilizer Requirements of Soils / 127
        6.3.3.5   Adjacent vegetation / 128

6.4   Species Selection / 128
    6.4.1   Desirable Plant Characteristics for Erosion Control / 129
    6.4.2   Native vs. Introduced Species / 129
        6.4.2.1   The Case for Native Species / 129
        6.4.2.2   The Case for Introduced ("Exotic") Species / 129
    6.4.3   Plant Geography, Variation and Adaptation, and Species
        Selection / 130
    6.4.4   Plant Succession / 130
    6.4.5   Nitrogen-Fixing Plants for Site Improvement / 130
    6.4.6   Grasses for Interim Erosion Control / 131
    6.4.7   Species Mix / 131
    6.4.8   Plant Lists / 131
    6.4.9   Availability / 132

6.5   Seeds and Planting Stocks / 132
    6.5.1   Seeds / 132
    6.5.2   Transplants / 133
    6.5.3   Propagation / 133
        6.5.3.1   Seed Propagation / 133
        6.5.3.2   Cutting Propagation / 134
        6.5.3.3   Growing Media / 135
        6.5.3.4   Containers / 135
        6.5.3.5   Scheduling / 136
        6.5.3.6   Hardening off / 136

6.6   Site Preparation / 138
    6.6.1   Grading and Shaping / 138
        6.6.1.1   Restoration Projects / 138
        6.6.1.2   Cut Slopes / 139
        6.6.1.3   Fill Slopes / 139

6.6.2 Water Control / 142
   6.6.2.1 Surface Water / 142
   6.6.2.2 Energy Dissipation / 144
   6.6.2.3 Seepage Control / 144
   6.6.2.4 Protecting Adjacent Areas / 145

6.7 Planting Techniques / 145
   6.7.1 Direct Seeding / 145
      6.7.1.1 Grasses and Forbs / 146
      6.7.1.2 Woody Species / 147
   6.7.2 Seed and Seedling Protection / 150
      6.7.2.1 Irrigation / 150
      6.7.2.2 Thinning Plants / 151
   6.7.3 Cuttings / 151
      6.7.3.1 Cutting Size / 151
      6.7.3.2 Preparation of Cuttings / 152
      6.7.3.3 Sticking Cuttings / 152
   6.7.4 Transplants / 152
      6.7.4.1 Time of Planting / 152
      6.7.4.2 Planting Tools / 152
      6.7.4.3 Planting Hole / 152
      6.7.4.4 Fertilizers and Amendments / 152
      6.7.4.5 Planting Procedure / 153

6.8 Special Methods for Structures / 153
   6.8.1 Crib Walls and Revetments / 153
   6.8.2 Breast Walls / 153
   6.8.3 Gabions / 154
   6.8.4 Tiered Structures / 154

6.9 Aftercare and Protection / 154
   6.9.1 Significance / 154
   6.9.2 Protection from Rodents and Browsers / 154

6.10 Summary / 154

6.11 References Cited / 154

7. QUASI-VEGETATIVE OR HYBRID SLOPE PROTECTION
     TECHNIQUES / 157

7.1 Introduction / 157

7.2 Contour-Wattling / 157
   7.2.1 Definition / 157
   7.2.2 Historical Development / 157
   7.2.3 General Principles and Description of Method / 158
      7.2.3.1 Function of Wattling / 158
      7.2.3.2 Selection of Wattling Materials / 160
      7.2.3.3 Preparation and Handling of Wattles / 160
      7.2.3.4 Stakes and Staking / 161
      7.2.3.5 Placement and Covering of Wattles / 161
      7.2.3.6 Timing of Installation / 162
      7.2.3.7 Summary / 162

7.2.4   Installation of Wattling / 162
   7.2.4.1   Site Survey / 162
   7.2.4.2   Slope Preparation / 163
   7.2.4.3   Staking and Trenching / 163
   7.2.4.4   Placement and Covering of Wattles / 163
   7.2.4.5   Planting / 165
   7.2.4.6   Maintenance / 165
7.2.5   Uses or Applications for Wattling / 165
   7.2.5.1   Road Fills / 165
   7.2.5.2   Road Cuts / 166
   7.2.5.3   Gullied or Slumped Areas / 166
   7.2.5.4   Eroded Slopes / 167

7.3   Contour Brush-Layering / 168
   7.3.1   Description of Method / 168
   7.3.2   Installation Procedure / 168
      7.3.2.1   During Embankment Construction / 168
      7.3.2.2   Remedial Treatment for Eroding Slopes / 170

7.4   Reed-Trench Terracing / 171
   7.4.1   Description of Method / 171
   7.4.2   Construction Procedure / 171
   7.4.3   Terrace Plantings / 172

7.5   Brush Matting / 172
   7.5.1   Description of Method / 172
   7.5.2   Construction Procedure / 173

7.6   Live Staking / 173
   7.6.1   Selection of Species for Live Staking / 173
   7.6.2   Preparation and Handling of Cuttings / 174
   7.6.3   Time to Plant Stakes / 175
   7.6.4   How to Plant Stakes / 175
   7.6.5   Where to Plant Stakes / 175
      7.6.5.1   Check Dam Reinforcement / 175
      7.6.5.2   Gully-Head Plug Reinforcement / 175
      7.6.5.3   Gully Erosion Control / 176
      7.6.5.4   Wattle Staking on Slopes / 176
      7.6.5.5   Revetment Staking and Reinforcement / 176
      7.6.5.6   Breast-Wall Staking / 177

7.7   References Cited / 177

8.   CHECK DAMS FOR GULLY CONTROL / 178

8.1   Introduction / 178
   8.1.1   Purpose and Function of Check Dams / 178
   8.1.2   Porous vs. Nonporous Dams / 178
   8.1.3   Biotechnical Construction Methods and Materials / 178

8.2   General Design Criteria / 179
   8.2.1   Check Dam Configuration / 179
   8.2.2   Spacing / 180

8.2.3   Height / 180
8.2.4   Spillway / 181
8.2.5   Apron / 181
8.2.6   Rock Size and Gradation / 181
8.3   Construction of Check Dams / 182
8.3.1   Single-Row Post-Brush Dam / 182
8.3.2   Double-Row Post-Brush Dam / 183
8.3.3   Brush and Rock Dam / 184
8.3.4   Brush and Wire-Netting Dam / 184
8.3.5   Loose Rock Dam / 185
8.3.6   Split Board Dam / 185

8.4   References Cited / 187

9. CASE HISTORIES AND APPLICATIONS OF BIOTECHNICAL SLOPE PROTECTION / 188

9.1   Introduction / 188

9.2   Case History No. 1—Backshore Slope Protection: Great Lakes Shoreline / 188
9.2.1   Nature of Great Lakes Shoreline and Magnitude of Erosion Problem / 188
9.2.2   Shoreline Degradation Processes / 189
9.2.3   The Rocky Gap Bluff Stabilization Project / 189
9.2.3.1   Project objectives / 189
9.2.3.2   Project location and site description / 190
9.2.4   Plot Treatments and Results / 190
9.2.4.1   Plot No. 1: Post-Brush Dam and Willow Staking / 190
9.2.4.2   Plot No. 6: Crib Wall and Contour Wattling / 192
9.2.5   Summary and Conclusions / 195

9.3   Case History No. 2—Watershed Rehabilitation: Redwood National Park / 197
9.3.1   Park Setting / 197
9.3.1.1   Geology and soils / 197
9.3.1.2   Vegetation / 197
9.3.2   Erosion and Slope Stability Problems / 197
9.3.3   Watershed Rehabilitation Program / 198
9.3.3.1   Objectives and Scope of Program / 198
9.3.3.2   Site selection / 201
9.3.4   Upper Miller Creek Rehabilitation Test Site / 203
9.3.4.1   Site Description / 203
9.3.4.2   Rehabilitation Tasks / 204
9.3.4.3   Effectiveness of Erosion Control Measures / 205

9.4   Case History No. 3—Cut Slope Stabilization: Lake Tahoe Basin / 209
9.4.1   Location of the Project and the Erosion Problem / 209
9.4.1.1   Objectives of the Project / 209
9.4.1.2   Soils of the Project Area / 209
9.4.1.3   Climate of the Project Area / 209
9.4.1.4   Vegetation of the Project Area / 209
9.4.2   Preliminary Research / 209
9.4.2.1   Site and Vegetation Analysis / 209
9.4.2.2   Propagation Research / 211

        9.4.2.3   Interim Stabilization Research / 211
        9.4.2.4   Fall vs. Spring Planting / 213
        8.4.2.5   Willow Cuttings / 213
        9.4.2.6   Fertility Studies / 213
    9.4.3   Integrated Slope Plantings / 215
        9.4.3.1   Site 1, 03–ED–89 P.M. 2.04–2.11 / 216
        9.4.3.2   Site 2, 03–ED–89 P.M. 2.93–2.99 / 216
        9.4.3.3   Sites 3 and 4, 03–ED–89 P.M. 4.30–4.45 / 217
        9.4.3.4   Grass Plantings, All Sites / 218
    9.4.4   CalTrans Cut, 03–ED–89 P.M. 2.36–2.52 / 221
    9.4.5   Costs–Benefits / 222
    9.4.6   Summary / 225

9.5   References Cited / 228

APPENDIX I.   STANDARD DESIGNS AND SPECIFICATIONS
              FOR STRUCTURAL COMPONENTS / 231

APPENDIX II. AN ANNOTATED LIST OF SELECTED REFERENCES OF
              PLANTS FOR EROSION CONTROL / 260

APPENDIX III. NOMENCLATURE AND SYMBOLS / 265

INDEX / 267

BIOTECHNICAL
SLOPE PROTECTION
AND EROSION CONTROL

1
Introduction

1.1 BIOTECHNICAL OR COMBINED VEGETATIVE–STRUCTURAL SLOPE PROTECTION

As the title suggests, biotechnical slope protection entails the use of mechanical elements (or structures) in combination with biological elements (or plants) to arrest and prevent slope failures and erosion. Both biological and mechanical elements must function together in an integrated and complementary manner. Principles of statics and mechanics are used to analyze and design biotechnical slope protection systems; so too must principles of horticulture and plant science be employed. Some knowledge and awareness of important considerations from each of these major disciplines are necessary for successful implementation. Accordingly, this book will introduce the engineer to some aspects of horticulture, and the plant specialist to some concepts from mechanics.

1.2 REASONS FOR BIOTECHNICAL APPROACH

We have already alluded to one of the main advantages of a biotechnical approach to slope protection, viz., plants and structures can function together in mutually reinforcing or complementary roles. We may cite the following additional reasons to use such systems.

1.2.1 Cost Effectiveness

Actual field studies (White, 1979) have shown that in many instances combined structural–vegetative slope protection systems are more cost-effective than the use of either vegetation or structures alone. Vegetative treatments alone are usually much less expensive than earth retaining structures or other constructed protection systems. On the other hand, their effectiveness in terms of preventing soil loss or arresting slope movement under severe conditions may also be much lower.

1.2.2 Environmental Compatibility

Biotechnical slope protection systems blend into the landscape. The structural or mechanical components, which are described in Chapter 5, do not visually intrude upon the landscape as much as conventional earth retaining structures. Examples of such structures include log or timber cribs, welded-wire walls, gabion and rock breast walls, and reinforced earth. In addition, opportunities arise to incorporate vegetation into the structure itself. This is done by planting either in the voids or interstices between structural members or upon the benches purposely designed into a structure as explained in Chapter 4.

1.2.3 Use of Indigenous, Natural Materials

Biotechnical slope protection systems emphasize the use of natural, locally available materials—earth, rock, timber, vegetation—in contrast to man-made artificial materials such as steel and concrete. The distinction here is one of emphasis. In many instances or critical situations an effective design may require the use of steel and concrete. But even in this case opportunities for biotechnical design still exist. A good example is a porous or open-face crib retaining wall whose front face can be vegetated with a variety of plants and vines. Such retaining walls not only support but also lend an attractive appearance to cut slopes and embankments, as shown in Fig. 1.1.

1.2.4 Labor-Skill Intensiveness

Biotechnical slope protection measures and systems tend to be more labor-skill-intensive than energy-capital-intensive. The nature of biotechnical slope protection systems is such that well-supervised, skilled labor can often be substituted for high-cost, energy-intensive materials. A good example would be slope protection by willow wattling (see Fig. 1.2) or brush-layering—quasi-vegetative techniques that are described in Chapter 7.

Fig. 1.1. Vegetated, open-front crib wall supporting a roadway. Colorful native shrubs and plants have become established in the openings between structural members at the face of the wall. Trinidad Beach, California.

Fig. 1.2. Slope protected by contour-wattling. Partially buried and staked willow wattles protect slope against erosion; wattles eventually root and sprout, thus further stabilizing the slope. Redwood National Park, California.

For all of the above reasons biotechnical slope protection systems merit serious consideration. There will, of course, be instances when a vegetative treatment alone (e.g., grass seeding, hydromulching, and the planting of cuttings) will work satisfactorily. In other instances, structural retaining systems may be required in which vegetation would be used primarily for landscaping (see Fig. 1.3). In any event opportunities and circumstances for effective use of biotechnical slope protection should not be overlooked.

1.3 EXTENT AND SEVERITY OF SOIL EROSION AND SLOPE MOVEMENT PROBLEMS

The twin problems of erosion and mass-movement are widespread and costly. They affect and disrupt agriculture, transportation routes, resource extraction operations, water supply and storage, and urban development sites. Damages from both these land degradation processes annually run into hundreds of millions of dollars. The conditions under which they occur, their location, and specific estimates of this damage are reviewed briefly in this chapter.

1.3.1 Soil Erosion

As a rule, regions with highly erodible soils, high relief, sparse vegetation, strong winds, and dry climate but with occasionally intense storms exhibit the highest erosion losses. Man's activities frequently intensify rates of erosion, particularly if they entail stripping or removing vegetation, tilling or otherwise disturbing the soil, and increasing or concentrating runoff.

The total amount of soil eroded from the land and delivered as sediment to waterways is very large. Estimates of annual sediment yields in the United States range up to 2 billion tons per year (Brandt, 1972). Of the total amount eroded about one-fourth to one-third is transported to the oceans, with the rest being deposited in flood plains, river channels, lakes, and reservoirs. The impact of this sediment on water quality is significant; sediment is conceded by most authorities to be the largest single stream pollutant.

The principal sources of sediment include erosion from natural or undisturbed land, cultivated land, urban construction sites, highways and roadsides, streambanks, and mining or resource extraction operations. Typical erosion rates from those sources are summarized in Table 1.1. Erosion rates range from a low of 15 tons/sq mi/year

Fig. 1.3. Reinforced concrete, counterfort retaining wall system along freeway in San Francisco, California. Specially designed tiers in the structure have been landscaped with plants and shrubs. Role of vegetation in this case is primarily ornamental. (*Photo courtesy of Caltrans*)

Table 1.1. Erosion rates associated with different land uses.

SEDIMENT SOURCE	EROSION RATE; TONS/MILE^2/YEAR	GEOGRAPHIC LOCATION	COMMENT
Natural	15–20	Potomac River Basin	Native cover
	32–192		Native cover
	200	Pennsylvania and Virginia	Natural drainage basin
	320	Mississippi River Basin	Throughout geologic history
	13–83	Northern Mississippi	Forested watershed
	25–100	Northwest New Jersey	Forested and under-developed land
	115		Soils eroding at the rate they form
Agricultural	12,800	Missouri Valley	Loess region
	13,900	Northern Mississippi	Cultivated land
	1,030	Northern Mississippi	Pasture land
	10,000–70,000		Continuous row crop without conservation practices
	200–500	Eastern U. S. piedmont	Farmland
	320–3,840		Established as tolerable erosion
Urban	50,000	Kensington, Maryland	Undergoing extensive construction
	1,000–100,000		Small urban construction area
	1,000	Washington, D.C. area	750 mile^2 area average
	500	Philadelphia area	
	146	Washington, D.C. area watersheds	As urbanization increases
	280		
	690		
	2,300		
Highway Construction	36,000	Fairfax County, Virginia	Construction on 179 acres
	50,000–150,000	Georgia	Cut slopes

(From U. S. Environmental Protection Agency, 1973)

for natural or undisturbed areas to a high of 150,000 tons/sq mi/year for highway construction sites. These erosion rates underscore the fact that man's activities (e.g., farming, mining, timber harvesting, and road building) tend to accelerate erosion rates greatly over pre-disturbance levels.

The economic costs of erosion and sedimentation are substantial. Direct costs include damage to property from either sediment accretion or loss of soil (Fig. 1.4). Sediment removal costs alone may range from $7 to $68 per cu yd (1973 dollars), depending upon whether the sediment is removed from streets, sewers, or basements (U. S. Environmental Protection Agency, 1973).

Indirect costs and damages of erosion and sedimentation probably exceed direct costs but are much harder to assess. These damages are summarized in Table 1.2. The U. S. Corps of Engineers, for example, annually dredges approximately 400 million cu yds of sediment from the nation's rivers and harbors to keep them navigable. Conservative estimates place the loss of reservoir capacity from siltation at 1.5 billion cu yd per year. This represents an annual loss of 1 million acre-ft of reservoir storage capacity per year.

The U. S. Army Corps of Engineers (1978) has estimated that out of approximately 3.5 million miles of streams (7 million bank-miles), a total of approximately 8 percent or about 575,000 bank-miles are experiencing erosion to some degree. Available data showed the total damages for all degrees of bank erosion to be about $270 million annually. Of the total bank-miles experiencing erosion,

Fig. 1.4. Erosion damage at urban construction site. (*Photo courtesy of USDA Soil Conservation Service*)

Table 1.2.   Damages caused by erosion and sedimentation.

DAMAGES ON LAND	DAMAGES IN STREAMS
• Agricultural productivity loss	• Flooding
• Roadway, sewer, basement siltation	• Eutrophication
• Drainage disruption	• Siltation of harbors and channels
• Foundation and pavement undermining	• Recreational value loss
• Gullying of roads	• Loss of reservoir storage cap
• Aesthetic impact	• Loss of wildlife habitat and disruption of stream ecology
• Dam failures due to piping or overtopping (earth dams)	• Increased water treatment costs
	• Aesthetic impact

some 142,000 bank-miles were reported to have serious erosion. While this degree of erosion occurs on only 2 percent of the 7 million bank-miles in the nation, it results in an estimated total damage of $200 million annually.

The estimated annual cost to prevent the more serious streambank erosion (based on conventional protection methods) was over $870 million. The U. S. Corps of Engineers (1978) noted the need for finding alternative, lower-cost methods for controlling streambank erosion.

Many of the Corps's streambank protection projects authorized under the Streambank Erosion Control and Demonstration Control Act [1] of 1974 are directed toward this end. Some of their demonstration measures are based on biotechnical concepts, that is, on the combined or integrated use of vegetation and structures.

_____

[1] Public Law 93-251, Section 32, March 1974.

1.3.2 Mass-Movement

Slope failures or mass movement can occur anywhere steep slopes and slide-prone or weak materials are encountered. The presence of water in the slope also plays a critical role in both increasing driving forces and reducing resistance to sliding. Slope failures affect and disrupt transportation routes, urban development, mining, and timber harvesting operations. These activities are very often themselves a causative factor in mass-movement of slopes.

Individual slope failures are usually not as spectacular as certain other natural hazards such as earthquakes, major floods, and tornadoes. On the other hand, slope failures are collectively more widespread, and total financial loss from slope movements exceeds that of most other geologic hazards (Fleming and Taylor, 1980; Alfors et al., 1973).

The costs of slope failures include both direct and indirect losses. Direct costs are associated with actual damages to installations or property (Fig. 1.5). Indirect costs may include (1) loss of tax revenues and reduced real estate values, (2) loss of productivity of agricultural or forest lands, (3) impairment or degradation of water quality, and (4) loss of industrial productivity caused by disrupted transportation systems. As with erosion costs,

indirect costs of slope failures are harder to evaluate, but they may be larger and more significant in many cases than direct costs.

Slope movement costs and damages to buildings, highways, and other facilities have been estimated on both a regional and national level for the United States. Krohn and Slosson (1976) estimated the annual landslide damage to buildings and their sites in the United States to be $400 million dollars (1971 dollars). This figure did not include other damages such as those to transportation facilities, mines, and indirect costs.

With regard to transportation routes, a survey conducted by the Federal Highway Administration indicated that approximately $50 million was spent annually to repair landslides on the federally financed portion of the national highway system (Chassie and Goughnor, 1976). Distribution of the direct costs of major landslides for 1973 by Federal Highway Administration region within the United States is shown in Fig. 1.6. The cost for an individual region was based on both landslide risk and the amount of highway construction in the area. In addition the costs represent a single year; the average cost for a particular region could vary significantly from the given costs.

These costs may represent only the tip of the iceberg. Significantly, the national highway system includes fed-

Fig. 1.5. Destruction of hillside home by mudslide. (*Photo courtesy of Los Angeles Dept. of Building and Safety*)

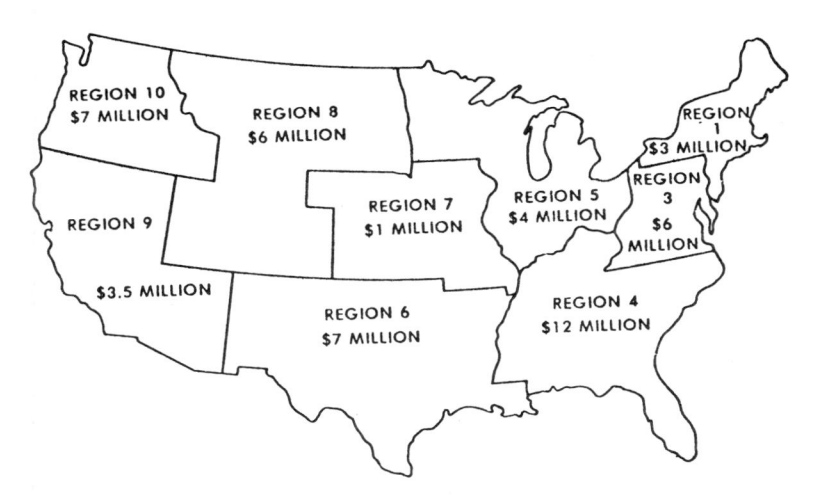

Fig. 1.6. Cost of landslide repairs to federal-aid highways in the United States for 1973. (*From Chassie and Goughnor, 1976*). Used with permission of the Transportation Research Board, Washington, D.C.

eral and state highways, but does *not* include most county and city roads, private roads, and streets or roads built by other government agencies. The U. S. Forest Service, for example, manages one of the largest transportation systems in the world. This agency authorizes the construction of some 7000 to 8000 miles of secondary or low-volume forest roads each year and has maintenance responsibility for approximately 200,000 miles of existing roads (Howlett, 1975). Most of this system is located in steep, mountainous terrain comprised of frequently unstable, erodible, and fragile soils. As a result, erosion and mass-movement pose constant problems. Costs of maintaining and repairing damage to this road system were estimated by the U. S. Forest Service at $82 million in 1975.

In this regard, even the National Park Service has been forced to allocate substantial funds for repair of slope failures and erosion largely associated with roads in sensitive terrain. In acquiring additional lands for Redwood National Park in 1978, the Park Service also inherited approximately 300 miles of old haul roads and another 3500 miles of skid or tractor trails left over from past timber harvest activities on these lands. The enabling legislation[2] for Park expansion also authorized the appropriation of $33 million as of October 1978, for watershed rehabilitation and slope repair work.

Total annual costs of landslides to highways and roads in the United States are difficult to determine precisely because of the aforementioned considerations and because of uncertainty in determining: (1) costs of smaller slides that are routinely handled by maintenance crews; (2) costs of slides on nonfederal aid routes; and (3) in-

direct costs that are related to landslide damage. If these factors had been included, Chassie and Goughnor (1976) reckoned that $100 million is a conservative estimate of total annual cost of landslide damage to highways and roads in the United States.

Based on all the preceding estimates plus indirect costs and estimated damages to facilities not classed as roads and buildings, Schuster (1978) estimated direct and indirect costs of slope failures or mass-movements in the United States in excess of one billion dollars per year.

1.4 APPLICATION OF BIOTECHNICAL SLOPE PROTECTION

Biotechnical slope protection methods can be used to correct and remedy many of the problems described in Section 1.3. Actual instances or applications of biotechnical slope protection are documented in Chapter 9. Anytime the advantages noted in Section 1.2 can be realized, biotechnical protection measures should be considered. To recapitulate, these advantages include cost effectiveness, environmental compatibility, use of locally available or natural materials, and labor-skill intensiveness.

Examples of situations and places where biotechnical slope protection methods have been used with good success include stabilization of cut and fill slopes along transportation corridors (Bowers, 1950; Schiechtl, 1978). Biotechnical slope protection methods have been employed along both major highways (Leiser et al., 1974) and secondary road systems (Kraebel, 1936). The latter include access or timber haul roads in forested regions.

Biotechnical slope protection measures can be employed in the coastal zone for relatively low-cost protection of backshore slopes against the ravages of both erosion and mass-movement. Some interesting and suc-

---

[2] Public Law 95–250, The United States Congress, 1978.

cessful examples of biotechnical protection of slopes in the coastal regions of the United States have been documented in the literature (Reid, 1969; Knutson, 1977; Whitlow et al., 1979). Biotechnical methods can also be employed to protect streambanks and channels against bank erosion primarily through use of vegetated, porous, or cellular revetments (Edminster et al., 1949; U. S. Army Corps of Engineers, 1978). Biotechnical measures have been used successfully in the past and should be considered for future use to protect slopes in housing developments and construction sites (White and Franks, 1978). Of particular interest in this regard is the applicability of biotechnical earth support and slope protection methods for earth-sheltered housing construction. Biotechnical methods could enhance the appeal and versatility of earth-sheltered construction by simultaneously providing both support and landscaping on vertical or sloping earth surfaces. Biotechnical methods can be used, for example, to stabilize and landscape: earth berms placed against structures; cuts and recesses in slopes that are designed to accommodate buildings; exterior, earth or rock fill dividing walls; and slopes leading down into sunken courtyards.

Another area of potential application lies in rehabilitation of slopes and watersheds severely damaged by resource exploitation, for example, mining or timber harvesting (Gray and Jopson, 1979; Madej et al., 1980). Severe constraints may operate in this case to limit the type of slope protection measures that can be employed, viz., cost limitations, requirements for use of labor-skill-intensive measures, prohibition against use of stark or massive retaining structures, and so on. In such cases the use of biotechnical methods may be particularly attractive.

Control of gully erosion provides yet another instance where biotechnical methods are appropriate and effective. The long-term goal of gully control is establishment of vegetative cover. This can seldom be accomplished, however, without short-term assistance from various structural–mechanical measures (Heede, 1976).

1.5 SCOPE AND ORGANIZATION OF BOOK

A brief discussion on the nature of surficial erosion and mass–soil movement is presented in Chapter 2. A clear distinction is drawn between these two slope processes and the factors that control them. A basic understanding of these processes is required in order to design systems for their prevention and control.

The role of vegetation in reinforcing soils and stabilizing slopes is described in Chapter 3. Specific mechanisms such as mechanical reinforcement from roots, soil moisture depletion from evapotranspiration in the fo-

liage, and soil arching restraint and buttressing by tree stems are all analyzed. The importance and significance of these protective mechanisms are examined for some specific slopes or geological settings.

Chapter 4 introduces the reader to the basic principles and concepts of biotechnical slope protection. The roles of the structural–mechanical and biological elements or components are discussed. Basic examples are presented to show how these components work and fit together in a complementary manner.

Specific design considerations and guidelines for the mechanical and the biological components of biotechnical slope protection are treated in Chapters 5 and 6, respectively. Types of structural measures appropriate for biotechnical slope protection are identified and described in Chapter 5; stability considerations and general design guidelines are discussed in this chapter. Standard designs for retaining structures (e.g., concrete and timber cribs, welded-wire walls, and gabion walls) are included in Appendix I.

Chapter 6 describes what type of vegetation to select, how to plant, when to plant, and how to establish and maintain vegetation for slope protection purposes. Desirable properties of plants used for erosion control work are described. Unfortunately, suitable plants tend to be very site-specific and also subject to such constraints as availability. This militates against publishing plant lists; however, sources of such lists are provided in Appendix II, which includes plants that have worked well in past applications. The circumstances and site conditions for which these lists were prepared are briefly cited there. Also included in Chapter 6 is a description of necessary modifications and/or amendments to cribfills and backfills in retaining structures in order to permit establishment of vegetation without compromising engineering performance of the structure itself.

Quasi-vegetative techniques such as contour-wattling, brush-layering, and reed-trench terracing are described in Chapter 7. In many ways these techniques epitomize the biotechnical approach in the sense that they are truly hybrid applications of mechanics and biology. Contour willow wattling was developed and used very successfully by the U. S. Forest Service (Kraebel, 1936) to stabilize steep slopes along mountain roads in California. In recent years interest in this method has revived, and it has been used quite successfully in a number of applications (Gray et al., 1980; Leiser et al., 1974).

A brief treatment of biotechnical methods for arresting and controlling gully erosion is included in Chapter 8. These methods involve constructing low, porous check dams from essentially native, locally available materials. Such structures range from dumped, loose rock dams to post and brush check dams.

It is instructive to consider some actual examples of

biotechnical slope protection. Thus Chapter 9 describes and compares results of some well-documented case histories of biotechnical slope protection. These include coastal bluff stabilization along the Great Lakes, watershed rehabilitation in Redwood National Park, and cut slope stabilization in the Lake Tahoe Basin.

1.6 REFERENCES CITED

Alfors, J. T., et al. (1973). Urban geology: master plan for California, *Calif. Div. of Mines & Geology, Bull. 198,* 112 pp.

Bowers, H. D. (1950). Erosion control on California highways, State of California, Department of Public Works, Division of Highways, Sacramento, Calif., 70 pp.

Brandt, G. H. (1972). An economic analysis of erosion and sediment control methods for watersheds undergoing urbanization, Final Rept. to Dept. of the Interior, Ofc. of Water Resources Research, Contract No. 14-31-0001-3392.

Chassie, R. G., and Goughnor, R. D. (1976). National highway landslide experience, *Highway Focus* 8(1): 1-9.

Edminster, F. C., Atkinsons, W. S., and McIntyre, A. C. (1949). Stream bank erosion control on the Winooski River, Vermont, *USDA Circular No. 837,* 54 pp.

Fleming, R. W., and Taylor, F. A. (1980). Estimating the costs of landslide damage in the United States, *U. S. Geological Circular No. 832,* 21 pp.

Gray, D. H., and Jopson, T. M. (1979). Vegetative-structural slope protection for rehabilitation of disturbed areas in Redwood National Park, Final Rept. to National Park Service, U. S. Dept. of Interior, Arcata, Calif., 204 pp.

Gray, D. H., Leiser, A. T., and White, C. A. (1980). Combined vegetative-structural slope stabilization, *Civil Engr.* (ASCE) 50(1): 82-85.

Heede, B. H. (1976). Gully development and control, *USDA Forest Service Research Paper RM-169,* Rocky Mtn. Forest and Range Exp. Stn., Fort Collins, Colo., 42 pp.

Howlett, M. R. (1975). Managing a 200,000-mile road system: Opportunity and challenge, in "Low-Volume Roads," *Trans. Res. Board Spec. Report 160,* NAS-NRC, Washington, D.C., pp. 53-61.

Knutson, P. (1977). Summary of CERC research on use of vegetation for erosion control, *Proc., Workshop on Role of Vegetation in Stabilization of the Great Lakes Shoreline,* Great Lakes Basin Commission, Ann Arbor, Mich. pp. 31-37.

Kraebel, C. J. (1936). Erosion control on mountain roads, *USDA Circular No. 380,* 43pp.

Krohn, J. P., and Slosson, J. E. (1976). Landslide potential in the United States, *Calif. Geology* 29(10): 224-231.

Leiser, A. T., et al. (1974). Revegetation of disturbed soils in the Tahoe Basin, Final Rept. to Calif. Dept. of Transportation, CA-DOT-TL-7036-1-75-24, 71 pp.

Madej, M. A., Kelsey, H., and Weaver, W. (1980). An evaluation of 1978 rehabilitation sites and erosion control techniques in Redwood National Park, U. S. National Park Service, Arcata, Calif., Tech. Rept. No. 1, 113 pp.

Reid, Georgina (1969). *How to Hold Up a Bank,* New York: A.S. Barnes & Co.

Schiechtl, H. M. (1978). Environmentally compatible slope stabilization, *Geotechnik* 1(1): 10-21 (Organ der Deutchen Gesellschaft fur Erd und Grundbau).

Schuster, R. L. (1978). Introduction, in "Landslides: Analysis and Control," ed. by Schuster, R. L., and Krizek, R. J., *Trans. Res. Board Spec. Rept. 176,* NAS-NRC, Washington, D.C., pp. 1-9.

U. S. Army Corps of Engineers (1978). The Streambank Erosion Control Evaluation and Demonstration Act of 1974, Interim Report to Congress, Dept. of the Army, Washington, D.C.

U. S. Environmental Protection Agency (1973). Comparative costs of erosion and sediment control construction activities, EPA-430/9-73-016, U. S. Govt. Printing Ofc., Washington, D.C.

White, C. A. (1979). Best management practices for the control of erosion and sedimentation due to urbanization of the Lake Tahoe Region of California, *Proc., Intl. Symposium on Urban Runoff,* Univ. of Ky., Lexington, Ky., pp. 233-245.

White, C. A., and Franks, A. L. (1978). Demonstration of erosion and sediment control technology, Lake Tahoe region of California. California State Water Resources Control Board Final Rept., 393 pp.

Whitlow, T. H., Harris, R. W., and Leiser, A. T. (1979). Use of vegetation to reduce levee erosion in the Sacramento-San Joaquin Delta, Rept. prepared for State of Calif. Dept. of Water Resources, Contract No. B-52830, by Dept. of Envl. Horticulture, Univ. of Calif., Davis, 46 pp.

2
Soil Erosion
and Mass-Movement

2.1 DEFINITIONS

2.1.1 Soil Erosion

Soil erosion is the removal of surface layers of soil by the agencies of wind, water, and ice. Soil erosion involves a process of both particle *detachment* and *transport* by these agencies. Erosion is initiated by drag, impact, or tractive forces acting on individual particles of soil at the surface.

The two most common types of erosion are rainfall and wind erosion. Rainfall erosion starts with falling raindrops themselves. When these drops impact on bare or fallow ground, they can dislodge and move soil particles a surprising distance. At the onset of runoff, water collects into small rivulets which may erode very small channels called rills. These rills may eventually coalesce into larger and deeper channels called gullies. Gullying is a complex and destructive process; once started, gullies are difficult to stop.

Erosion may also occur along streambanks where the velocity of the flowing water is high and the resistance of the bank materials low. Piping or spring sapping is yet another type of erosion, in this case caused by seepage and emergence of water from the face of an unprotected slope.

Rainfall and wind erosion are controlled by a number of soil, climatic, and topographic factors, including intensity and duration of precipitation, ground roughness, length and steepness of slope, inherent soil erodibility, and type or extent of cover. All of these factors are taken into account explicitly in the Universal Soil Loss Equation (Wischmeier and Smith, 1965). This relationship makes it possible to predict or estimate erosion losses from particular sites.

2.1.2 Mass-Movement

Mass-movement is a descriptive name for the downward and outward movement of slope-forming materials—natural rock, soils, artificial fills, or combination of these materials. The terms mass-erosion or mass-wasting are sometimes used. Mass-movements are popularly known as landslides. Strictly speaking, however, landslides or slides refer to a particular type of mass-movement.

Unlike soil erosion, mass-movement involves the sliding, toppling, falling, or spreading of fairly large and sometimes relatively intact masses. Mass movements have been classified into categories based largely on the type of movement (Varnes, 1978). Among the various types of mass-movements, only slides are amenable to quantitative stability analysis by techniques of limiting equilibrium and limit analysis. A slide is a slope movement wherein a shear failure occurs along a specific surface or combination of surfaces in the failure mass.

Many of the same slope, soil, and hydrologic factors that control erosion also control mass-movement (e.g., steepness of slope and shear strength of soil). Precipitation, a key factor directly affecting rainfall erosion, only affects mass-movement indirectly via its influence on the groundwater regime at a site. In contrast, geologic conditions such as orientation of joints and bedding planes in a slope have a profound influence on mass stability but not on surficial erosion. Vegetation has an important influence on both erosion and shallow mass-movement, as will be demonstrated in Chapter 3.

2.2 NATURE OF SOIL EROSION

Erosion is characterized by the detachment and transport of individual soil grains. The primary agents of erosion include water, wind, and ice. These agents can scour and remove soil particles as a result of flowing past, impacting upon, or exiting from the surface of a soil. The various agents and types of erosion are summarized in Table 2.1. Frost action may act in concert with wind and rainfall to initiate and facilitate downslope movement of soil particles.

In this section we review briefly the determinants of erosion, namely, the climatic, topographic, and pedalogic variables that control erosion. We also examine the various types or categories of water erosion and their significance, (i.e., rainfall, stream channel, and groundwater erosion). Unlike water erosion, wind erosion varies essentially by degree rather than type. For a more detailed treatment the reader is referred to texts on these subjects (Schwab et al., 1966).

2.2.1 Determinants of Rainfall Erosion

Rainfall erosion is controlled by four basic factors, viz., climate, soil type, topography, and vegetation. This relationship can be expressed schematically as follows:

$$\text{Rainfall Erosion} = f \begin{cases} \text{Climate—storm intensity and duration} \\ \text{Soil—inherent erodibility} \\ \text{Topography—length and steepness of slope} \\ \text{Vegetation—type and extent of cover} \end{cases}$$

The rainfall erosion factors can be expressed in terms of identifiable and measurable parameters as noted. These parameters in turn can be used to estimate or predict rainfall erosion losses from a site as explained in Section 2.3.

The most important climatic parameters controlling rainfall erosion are intensity and duration of precipitation. Wischmeier and Smith (1958) have show that the most important "single" measure of the erosion-producing power of a rainstorm is the product of rainfall energy times the maximum 30-minute rainfall intensity. Raindrops impacting on bare soil not only cause erosion; they also tend to compact the soil and decrease its infiltration capacity.

The susceptibility of a soil to erosion is known as its "erodibility." Some soils (e.g., silts) are unherently more erodible than others (e.g., well-graded sands and gravels). Soil erodibility has been the subject of numerous studies reported in the technical literature (Paaswell, 1973; Farmer, 1973; Arulanandan et al., 1975). In general, increasing the organic content and clay size fraction of a soil decreases erodibility. Erodibility also depends upon such parameters as soil texture, antecedent moisture content, void ratio, pH, and composition or

Table 2.1. Agents and types of erosion.

AGENT	TYPE OF EROSION OR DEGRADATIONAL PROCESS	
Water	1. Raindrop splash 2. Sheet erosion 3. Rilling 4. Gullying 5. Stream channel erosion 6. Wave action 7. Groundwater piping	
Ice	1. Solifluction 2. Frost action 3. Glacial scour 4. Plucking	
Wind	Wind cannot be subclassified into "types"; instead it varies only by "degree."	
Gravity	1. Creep 2. Earth flow 3. Avalanche 4. Rock fall 5. Debris slide	These are usually classified under *mass-wasting,* but they often act in conjunction with erosion.

Note: Many of the above degradational processes operate jointly or in combination. This is particularly true of mass-wasting (gravity + water) and glacio-fluvial (ice + water) processes.

ionic strength of the eroding water. The dependence of soil erodibility on all these variables is summed up in Table 2.2.

There is not yet a simple and universally accepted erodibility index for soils. Instead, various tests have been proposed for this purpose, including the SCS dispersion test (Volk, 1937), crumb test (Emerson, 1967), and pinhole test (Sherard et al., 1976). A suggested hierarchy of erodibility based on the Unified Soil classification system is:

$$\text{Most erodible} \rightarrow \text{least erodible}$$
$$ML > SM > SC > MH > OL$$
$$>>$$
$$CL > CH > GM > GP > GW$$

Table 2.2. Soil Erodibility trends.

- Is low in well-graded gravels
- Is high in uniform silts and fine sands
- Decreases with increasing clay and organic content
- Decreases with low void ratios and high antecedent moisture content
- Increases with increasing sodium adsorption ratio and decreasing ionic strength of water

This erodibility hierarchy is simple, but based on gradation and plasticity indices of remolded or disturbed soils. It fails to take into account effects of soil structure, void ratio, and antecedent moisture content. Wischmeir et al. (1971) have published an erodibility nomograph for use with the Universal Soil Loss Equation (see Section 2.3.1) which is based on easily measured soil properties.

Topographic variables influencing rainfall erosion are (a) slope angle, (b) length of slope, and (c) size and shape of watershed. The influence or importance of length tends to increase as slopes become steeper. For instance, a doubling of slope length from 100 to 200 ft will only increase soil losses by 29 percent in a 6 percent slope, whereas the same doubling of slope length in a 20 percent slope will result in a 49 percent increase in soil loss. This is one of the reasons for benching or terracing and contour wattling long, steep slopes.

Vegetation plays an extremely important role in controlling rainfall erosion. Removal or stripping of vegetation by either human or natural agencies (e.g., wildfires) often results in accelerated erosion (Fig. 2.1). The importance of vegetative cover in controlling erosion losses from watersheds was demonstrated by Anderson (1951). Statistical analyses of erosion losses (sediment yields) from several watersheds in the western United States produced the following relationship:

$$\log E_s = 3.073 - 2.430 \log C_V + 3.427 \log D.\,R. \quad (2.1)$$
$$(\text{correlation coef.} = 0.88)$$

where: E_s = ave. suspended sediment of stream, ppm

C_V = ave. cover density of watershed, %

$D.\,R.$ = dispersion ratio of soil (an erodibility index)

2.2.2 Determinants of Wind Erosion

Wind erosion is controlled by the same basic factors that control rainfall erosion. The dependence of wind erosion on these factors is expressed schematically in the following relationship:

$$\text{Wind Erosion} = f \begin{cases} \text{Climate—temperature, rainfall distribution, wind velocity and direction} \\ \text{Soil—texture, particle size, moisture content, surface roughness} \\ \text{Vegetation—type, height and density of cover, seasonal distribution} \end{cases}$$

These factors again can be expressed in terms of identifiable and measurable parameters as noted above. Unlike rainfall erosion, topographic parameters such as length and steepness of slope are relatively unimportant in wind erosion. On the other hand, surface roughness and the presence of low barriers that act as wind breaks and sediment traps can be important.

Only relatively dry soils are susceptible to wind erosion. The climatic factors that most affect soil moisture are amount and distribution of rainfall, temperature, and humidity. The most important characteristics of the wind are its velocity, duration, direction, and degree of turbulence. Wind can only pick up and carry in suspension dry soils with particle sizes primarily less than 0.1 mm (i.e., fine silt size material).

Wind erosion consists of three distinct phases: initiation of movement (detachment), transportation, and deposition. Soil movement by wind is initiated as a result of turbulence and velocity. The velocity required to start movement increases as the weight of particles increases. For many soils, this velocity is about 13 mph at a height of 1 ft above the ground. The velocity required to sustain movement, once started, is less than that required to initiate movement.

Laboratory studies by Chepil (1945) established that soil particles are transported by wind in the manner shown in Table 2.3. The major portion of soil particles

Fig. 2.1. Accelerated erosion as a result of vegetation loss following a wildfire. (*Photo courtesy of Los Angeles Dept. of Building and Safety*)

Table 2.3. Movement of soil particles by wind. (After Chepil, 1945)

MECHANICS OF MOVEMENT	SIZE OF PARTICLES MOVED, MM	PERCENT OF SOIL MOVED
Suspension	<0.1	3–38
Saltation (skipping and bouncing)	0.1–0.5	55–72
Surface creep (rolling and sliding)	0.5–1.0	7–25

transported by the wind occurs near the ground surface at heights under 3 ft (1 m). Approximately 62 to 97 percent of the total wind-eroded soil is transported in this zone near the surface, a fact that suggests the utility of installing relatively low barriers or windbreaks to filter and impede the movement of windborne soil. Vegetation partly serves this purpose in addition to its other control functions such as increasing surface roughness, slowing and deflecting the wind, and binding soil particles together.

2.2.3 Types of Water Erosion

2.2.3.1 Rainfall Erosion.
Rainfall erosion occurs in several forms; it begins with raindrop splash and ends with gullying (Table 2.1). The mechanics of erosion differs considerably from one form to another.

Raindrop Splash. Raindrop splash results from the impact of waterdrops falling directly on exposed soil particles or thin water surfaces covering the ground. Tremendous quantities of soil can be splashed into the air in this manner. On bare ground it has been estimated (Ellison, 1948) that as much as 100 tons/acre can be splashed into the air in a heavy storm. Splashed particles may move more than 2 ft vertically and 5 ft laterally on level sur-

faces. On steep slopes this splashing will cause a net downslope movement of soil.

The impact of rain on bare ground also destroys porous, open structure of soils and reduces their infiltration capacity. Increases of 15 percent in density in a 1-inch surface layer of soil have been attributed to compaction from impingement of raindrops. The erosion potential of raindrops is a function of the rainfall energy or momentum. The latter in turn is related to rainfall intensity by the following equation (Wischmeier and Smith, 1958):

$$E = 916 + 331 \log i \qquad (2.2)$$

where:

$E =$ kinetic energy of rain, ft-tons/acre-in
$i =$ rainfall intensity, iph

A summary of the kinetic energy and velocity of fall for various rainfall intensities and size of raindrops is given in Table 2.4.

Sheet Erosion. Sheet erosion is the removal of soil from sloping land in thin layers or sheets. From an energy standpoint raindrop erosion appears to be more important than sheet erosion because most raindrops have velocities of about 20 to 30 fps (Table 2.4), whereas overland flow velocities are about 1 to 2 fps. The eroding and transporting power of sheet flow are a function of the depth and velocity of runoff for a given size, shape, and density of soil particles or aggregates.

Dry ravel and slope wash are forms of sheet erosion; the former occurs when surface layers of coarse-textured soil dry out and lose their apparent cohesion. The latter occurs when rainfall erodes without causing rilling or gullying. Frost heaving may cause more or less uniform loosening of surface layers which later erode from rain or wind action. Sheetlike erosion is an important mechan-

Table 2.4. Kinetic energy and velocity of raindrops for various rainfall intensities. (From Lull, 1959)

RAINFALL	INTENSITY, IN/HR	MEDIAN DIAMETER, MM	VELOCITY OF FALL, FT/SEC	DROPS PER SQ FT PER SEC	KINETIC ENERGY, FT-LB/ SQ FT/HR
Fog	0.005	0.01	0.01	6,264,000	4.04×10^{-8}
Mist	0.002	0.1	0.7	2,510	7.94×10^{-5}
Drizzle	0.01	0.96	13.5	14	0.148
Light rain	0.04	1.24	15.7	26	0.797
Moderate rain	0.15	1.60	18.7	46	4.241
Heavy rain	0.60	2.05	22.0	46	23.47
Excessive rain	1.60	2.40	24.0	76	74.48
Cloudburst	4.00	2.85	25.9	113	216.9
Cloudburst	4.00	4.00	29.2	41	275.8
Cloudburst	4.00	6.00	30.5	12	300.7

ism of slope retreat and source of sediment in cut slopes in granitic and andesite soils. Highway cuts in these soils often give the impression of being very stable (e.g., rills and gullies are absent) yet discharge tons of soil year after year to the roadside ditches (Howell et al., 1979).

Rilling.   Rill erosion is the removal of soil by water from very small but well-defined, visible channels or streamlets where there is concentration of overland flow. An example of rill erosion at an urban construction site is shown in Fig. 2.2. Rilling is more serious than sheet erosion because runoff velocities are higher in the rills or channels. Rilling is the form of erosion during which most rainfall erosion losses occur (Schwab et al., 1966).

Rill erosion is most serious where intense storms occur in watersheds or sites with high runoff-producing characteristics and loose, shallow topsoil. Rills are sufficiently large and stable to be seen readily, but small enough to be removed easily by normal tillage and grading operations.

Gullying.   Gullies are intermittent stream channels larger than rills. These channels carry water during and immediately after rains, and, unlike rills, gullies cannot be obliterated by normal tillage.

The dynamics of gully formation are complex and not completely understood. Several statistical models for predicting gully growth and development have been proposed. Thompson (1964) chose linear advancement of gully heads, whereas Beer and Johnson (1963) selected changes in gully surface area as the dependent variable, in their respective models.

Four principal stages of gully development are generally recognized: (1) downward cutting, (2) headward erosion and enlargement, (3) healing, and (4) stabilization. Active gullies are those that continue to widen or enlarge; they may be recognized by the presence of bare soil exposed on their sides. Vegetation starts to grow in the gully channel during healing. The stabilization stage is characterized by an equilibrium gradient in the channel, stable gully sides, and vegetation sufficiently well-established to protect the soil against any further erosion.

Gully-forming processes are diverse and pervasive. Studies by Piest et al. (1975) in erodible loessial soils of western Iowa have shown that stream flow alone was not sufficient to cause gullying. Instead, mass wasting of gully banks and headcuts were the prime processes. A whole array of processes can act individually or in concert to produce gullies, including (1) waterfall erosion at the gully head, (2) piping and spring sapping at the head and sides, (3) erosion and scour along the length of the gully bottom, (4) raindrop splash and rilling on the sides, (5) freezing and thaw erosion of the gully sides, and (6) mass wasting of the gully sides and head.

Fig. 2.2.   Rill erosion at urban construction site. Ann Arbor, Michigan.

Gullies may not be as significant as rills in terms of total quantities of soil eroded, but they are more spectacular (Fig. 2.3). They are also more difficult to control and arrest. Effective gully control must stabilize both channel gradient and headcuts. Downcutting of gully bottoms leads to deepening and widening, whereas headcutting extends the channel into ungullied headwater areas, and increases the stream net and its density by developing tributaries.

2.2.3.2   Stream Channel Erosion.

Stream channel erosion consists of soil removal from stream banks and/or sediment scour along the channel bottom. Where the erosion occurs is dependent upon the type of stream. "Youthful" or lower-order (small) streams generally exhibit bed erosion, whereas "mature" or higher-order (large) streams primarily exhibit bank erosion. In either case, there is usually a balance between material eroded and material deposited along a particular reach of stream.

Stream channel erosion should be considered separately from the rainfall-associated types of erosion discussed previously. A number of hydrologic/hydraulic and geomorphic variables govern the behavior of fluvial systems. These variables include stream discharge, sediment discharge, grain size, depth of flow, channel width, channel shape, valley slope, and sinuosity. The variables are in a dynamic equilibrium with one another. Investigations by Leopold and Maddock (1953), Lane (1955), Schum (1971), and Santos-Cayudo and Simons (1972) have determined several general relationships among hydrologic-geomorphic variables that are useful in analyzing stream activity.

Like gully erosion there are several processes acting along streams that are responsible for stream channel erosion (Keown et al., 1977). These include:

1. *Toe undercutting*—attack at the toe of an underwater slope, leading to bank failure and erosion.
2. *Bank erosion*—erosion of bank material caused by current or wave action.
3. *Bank sloughing*—slumping of saturated, cohesive banks incapable of free drainage during rapid drawdown.
4. *Flow slides*—liquefaction of banks in saturated silty and sandy soil.
5. *Piping*—bank erosion by seepage of groundwater out of the bank.

It is helpful to recognize and understand these processes when designing a prevention and control system. On the other hand, this classification of erosion processes is not particularly helpful in establishing the cause of stream channel erosion. The cause can be linked or related to the

Fig. 2.3.   Gully erosion along an unsurfaced road. Ann Arbor, Michigan.

phenomenon, however, by geomorphological mechanisms. From the standpoint of fluvial geomorphology, there appear to be three main mechanisms (Keown et al., 1977) that produce stream channel erosion:

1. *Widening*—channel enlargement caused by increased stream flow and/or sediment discharges.
2. *Deepening*—degradation or scouring of channel bottom caused by increased flows and/or changes in slope.
3. *Sinuosity change*—bank loss during and upon change in stream meander configurations. Bank loss is usually accompanied by bank accretion somewhere along the affected stretch.

2.2.3.3 Groundwater Erosion.

Groundwater erosion is the removal of soil caused by groundwater seepage or movement toward a free face. Such erosion is commonly referred to as piping. The phenomenon is also known as spring sapping—literally the detachment and movement of soil particles at the point of emergence of a spring or seep in the ground. Piping occurs when seepage forces exceed intergranular stresses or forces of cohesion.

Pipes can form in the downstream side of earth dams, (Sherard et al., 1972), gully heads, streambanks, and slopes where water exits from the ground. Once a pipe or cavity forms, it enlarges quickly because flow lines are attracted to areas of lower flow resistance, and this in turn results in further concentration of flow lines or flow net density in a positive feedback cycle.

A related phenomenon, known as boiling, occurs where there is a substantial upward component of flow of water and hydraulic gradients exceeding the critical gradient near the ground surface. For most soils the critical gradient is close to unity. Upward flow of water toward the ground surface can occur in stream bottoms, marshes, the base of some slopes, and other topographic lows where the equilibrium piezometric surface is higher than the ground surface. In such cases the ground or soil may become quick or unstable (i.e., lose all its shear strength) and, if there is upwelling of water, actually appear to boil.

2.3 SOIL LOSS PREDICTIONS

2.3.1 Rainfall Erosion

A semiempirical equation for predicting rainfall erosion was developed by the Agricultural Research Service (Wischmeier and Smith, 1965). This equation was developed originally for predicting erosion losses from cropland east of the Rocky Mountains. In subsequent years the Universal Soil Loss Equation (USLE), as it is generally known, has been modified and adapted to dif-

ferent regions of the United States (USDA Soil Conservation Service, 1972, 1977) and also for use at urban or highway construction sites (U. S. Environmental Protection Agency, 1973).

The USLE takes into account all the factors known to affect rainfall erosion, viz., climate, soil, topography, and vegetation (see Section 2.2). It is based on a statistical analysis of erosion measured in the field on scores of test plots under natural and simulated rainfall. The annual soil loss from a site is predicted according to the following relationship:

$$X = RKSLCP \tag{2.3}$$

where:

X = the computed soil loss in tons (dry weight) per acre from a given storm period
R = the rainfall erosion index for the given storm period
K = the soil erodibility factor
L = the slope length factor
S = the slope gradient factor
C = cropping management (vegetation) factor
P = erosion control practice factor

In spite of its limitations, the USLE provides a simple, straightforward method of estimating soil losses and of evaluating the effectiveness of soil loss reduction measures. The latter subject is discussed in Section 2.4. The USLE is particularly well suited for estimating rainfall erosion losses from construction sites; it is in this context that we examine the relationship next.

2.3.1.1 Rainfall Factor.

The rainfall factor, R, is also known as the rainfall index. As noted previously, the "single" most important measure of the erosion producing power of a rainstorm is the product of the rainfall energy times the maximum 30-minute rainfall intensity. The rainfall index for a single storm is thus defined as:

$$R = \frac{EI}{100} \tag{2.3}$$

where:

E = total kinetic energy of a given storm in ft-tons per acre and I is the maximum 30-minute rainfall in the area in iph

The rainfall index can also be expressed as a function of rainfall intensity alone, using Equation (2.2), presented earlier.

The records of individual storms are summed over a given time interval to obtain cumulative R values for other periods of time (e.g., a month or a year). The annual R factors for approximately 2000 locations in the United States were summarized in the form of "isoerodent" maps by Wischmeier and Smith (1965). Annual R-factor values vary from a low of approximately 50 in the northern Great Plains to a high of 600 in the Gulf Coast region.

Studies by the USDA Soil Conservation Service (1972) have established a relationship between Type II, 2-year frequency, 6-hour duration rainfall and the average Annual rainfall erosion index. This particular duration and frequency storm can be considered a typical "average" storm because it can be expected to occur 50 percent of the time, and the 6-hour duration has been found by the Soil Conservation Service to be the most frequently occurring storm length. The relationship between Annual rainfall index and Type II rainfall is shown graphically in Fig. 2.4, together with a similar curve for Type I rainfall. Types I and II refer to rainfall characteristics in different regions or zones of the United States, as shown in Fig. 2.5. Type I rainfall is confined mainly to the Pacific Coast, North Cascades, and central Sierra Nevada regions. The 2-year frequency, 6-hour duration rainfall depths for various parts of the United States are also superposed on Fig. 2.5.

Thus, both the type and depth for a 2-year, 6-hour rainfall for any location under study can be obtained from the map shown in Fig. 2.5. With this information the average Annual erosion index can be determined from the curves in Fig. 2.4. Alternatively, the rainfall for a particular location can be determined from weather records published by the U. S. Weather Bureau (1963).

In order to compare the effects of different erosion control measures at construction sites, it may be desirable to estimate potential soil loss values for an entire range of periods of time, ranging from individual storms to annually. The rainfall erosion index for *individual* storms of different duration can be obtained from either Fig. 2.6 or Fig. 2.7.

Summary procedures for estimating rainfall erosion index, R, can now be stated as follows:

Example 1: *"Single Storm" Rainfall Erosion for 2-Year, 6-Hour Storm*

1. Locate the area under study in a rainfall atlas similar to Fig. 2.5 (U. S. Weather Bureau, 1963).
2. Determine the value of the 2-year, 6-hour rainfall from the chart or atlas.
3. Check the zone (rainfall type) in which the area is located.
4. Use the graph in Fig. 2.6 or Fig. 2.7 to determine the erosion index, using the 6-hour duration.

Example 2: *"Average Annual" Rainfall Erosion Index*

1. Locate the area under study in a chart or rainfall atlas similar to Fig. 2.5.
2. Determine the value of the 2-year, 6-hour rainfall from the chart or atlas.

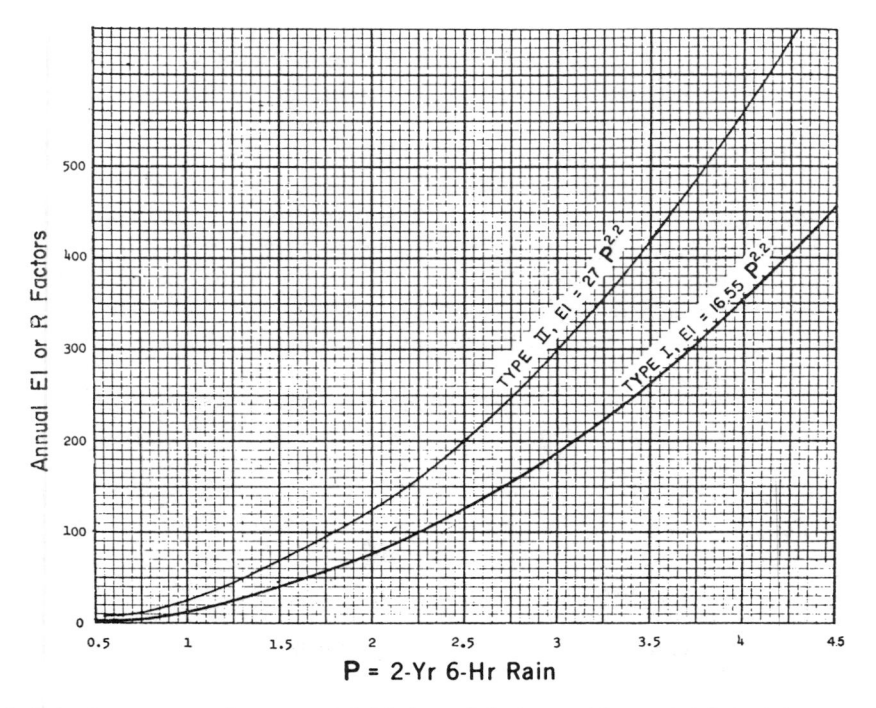

Fig. 2.4.   Relation between annual average rainfall index and the 2-year, 6-hour rainfall depth for two rainfall types.

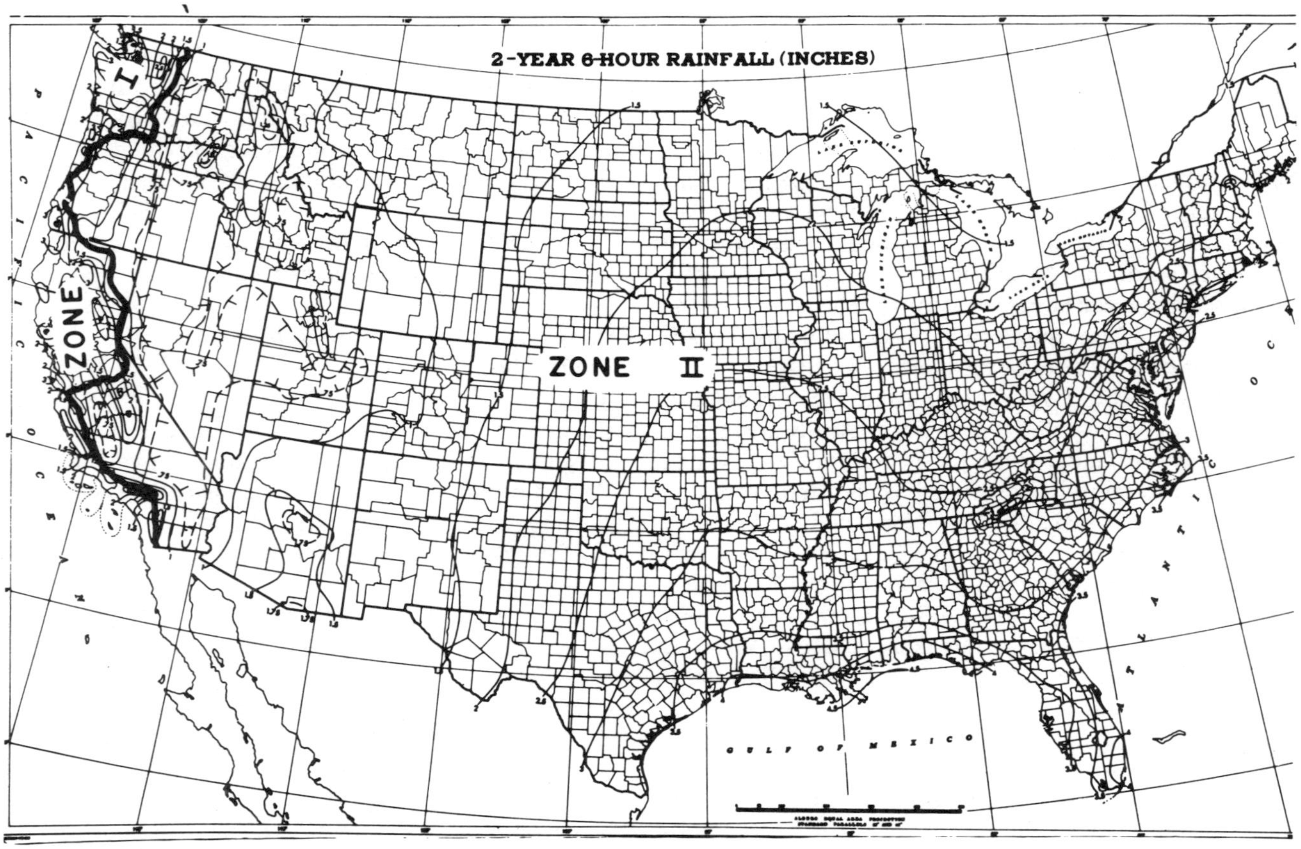

Fig. 2.5. Depths of the 2-year, 6-hour rainfall in various parts of the United States. Zones for Type I and Type II rainfall are also shown. (*Adapted from U. S. Weather Bureau, 1963*)

3. Check the zone (rainfall type).
4. Obtain the average Annual erosion index from Fig. 2.4 using the appropriate curve.

2.3.1.2 Soil Erodibility Factor. The soil erodibility factor, *K*, represents the inherent susceptibility to erosion of the soil; it is governed by textural and gradation properties of the soil, discussed previously. Erodibility factors for 23 benchmark soils, from which erosion has been experimentally measured since 1930, have been published by the Soil Conservation Service (Wischmeier and Smith, 1965). *K*-values that have been obtained experimentally range from 0.02 to 0.69.

Twelve *K*-value classes have been established by the Soil Conservation Service for ease of use. Soil series identified in Soil Conservation Service maps generally have a *K*-value assigned to them as part of the marginal information on each particular soil series.

Wischmeier et al. (1971) have also published a convenient nomograph (Fig. 2.8) that can be used to determine erodibility *K*-values of soils. The nomograph is valid for exposed subsoils at construction sites as well as farmlands. Only five soil parameters are required:

1. Percent silt and very fine sand (0.002–0.10 mm)
2. Percent sand (0.10–2.0 mm)
3. Percent organic matter
4. Structure
5. Permeability

The first three parameters will often suffice to provide a reasonable approximation of the erodibility. This approximation can be refined by including information on permeability and soil structure as indicated on the nomograph (Fig. 2.8).

2.3.1.3 Slope Length and Steepness Factors.
The effects of slope length, *L*, and steepness, *S*, on soil loss were investigated separately, but they are often combined in a single "topographic" factor, *LS*. This factor is the ratio of soil loss per unit area from a given site to that from a unit plot having a 9 percent slope and 72.6 ft length. The combined *LS* factor can be computed from an empirical equation, which is graphed in Fig. 2.9.

The topographic factor, *LS*, has been extended by the U. S. Soil Conservation Service (1972) to cover slope lengths up to 1600 ft and for slope steepness up to 100 per-

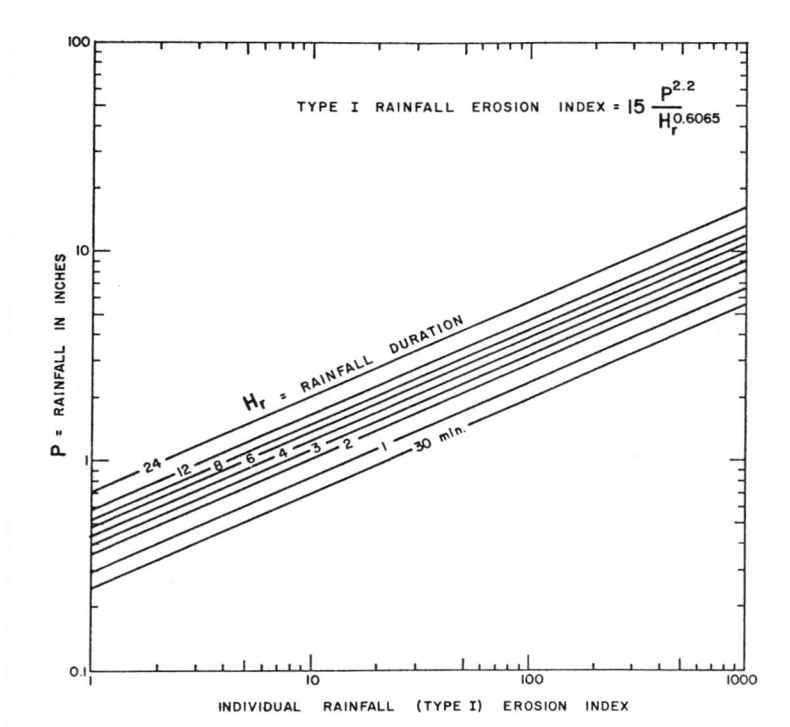

Fig. 2.6. Relation between depths and duration of Type I rainfall and single storm erosion index; 2-year frequency of occurrence.

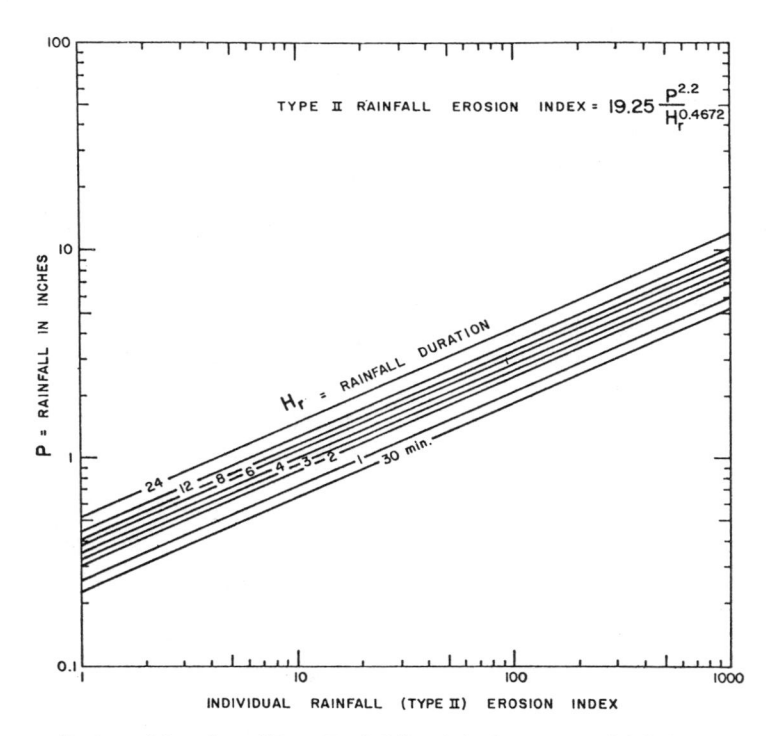

Fig. 2.7. Relation between depths and duration of Type II rainfall and single storm erosion index; 2-year frequency of occurrence.

19

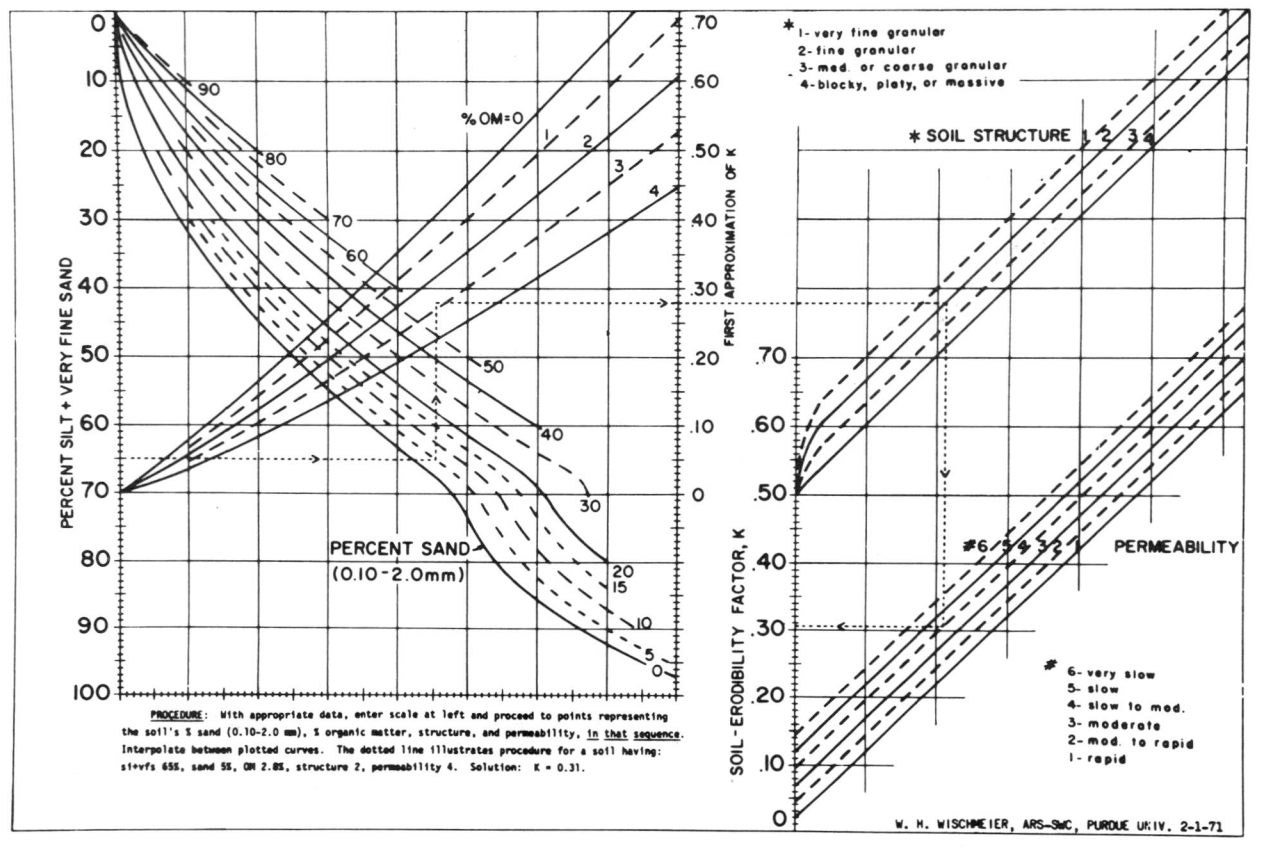

Fig. 2.8.   Soil erodibility nomograph for determining *K*-values. (*From Wischmeier et al., 1971*). Reprinted from the *Jour. of Soil and Water Conservation,* Vol. 26, No. 5. Copyright © Soil Conservation Society of America.

cent (equivalent to 1*H*:1*V*). Figure 2.9 shows extensions of the original chart beyond the 400-ft length and 20 percent slope, the extent of physical data on which the USLE was based. Slopes commonly used along roads and highways have been added to the chart shown in Fig. 2.9. These extensions and additions (shown as dashed lines) are extrapolations beyond confirmed data; therefore, they should be treated as speculative estimates.

2.3.1.4   Cropping Management Factor.
The cropping management factor, *C,* is defined as the ratio of soil loss from land cropped under specific conditions as against the corresponding loss from tilled, continuous fallow (bare) land. In physical terms it describes the protective effects of vegetation against erosion.

Vegetation or cropping mangement affects erosion via three separate and distinct, but interrelated zones of influence, viz., canopy cover, vegetative cover in direct contact with the soil, and crop residue at or beneath the surface. The effects of these three constituent influences can be defined separately, but for practical purposes are represented by a single value of the *C* factor.

For complete bare or fallow ground the *C* factor is un-

ity. Factor *C* values for pasture, range, wood land, and idle land are tabulated in Tables 2.5 and 2.6. The influence of canopy, cover type, and percent ground cover are clearly indicated in Table 2.5. Information in Table 2.5 reveals the benefit of vegetation or plant cover for reducing erosion. Factor *C* values range as low as 0.003 for well-established plant cover. This corresponds to almost a thousand-fold reduction in erosion losses over the continuous-fallow or bare-ground case. Few other variables or factors are amenable to management with such dramatic results (i.e., reduction in erosion losses) as this one.

Mulching can be considered a form of cropping management. The influence of mulching with various types of organic mulches (straw, hay, woodchips, etc.) is considered in Section 2.4.

2.3.1.5   Erosion Control Practice Factor.
The erosion control practice factor, *P,* is a parameter representing the reduction of soil loss resulting from soil conservation measures such as contour tillage, contour strip cropping, terracing, and stabilized waterways. Factor *P* values for standard erosion control practices are tabu-

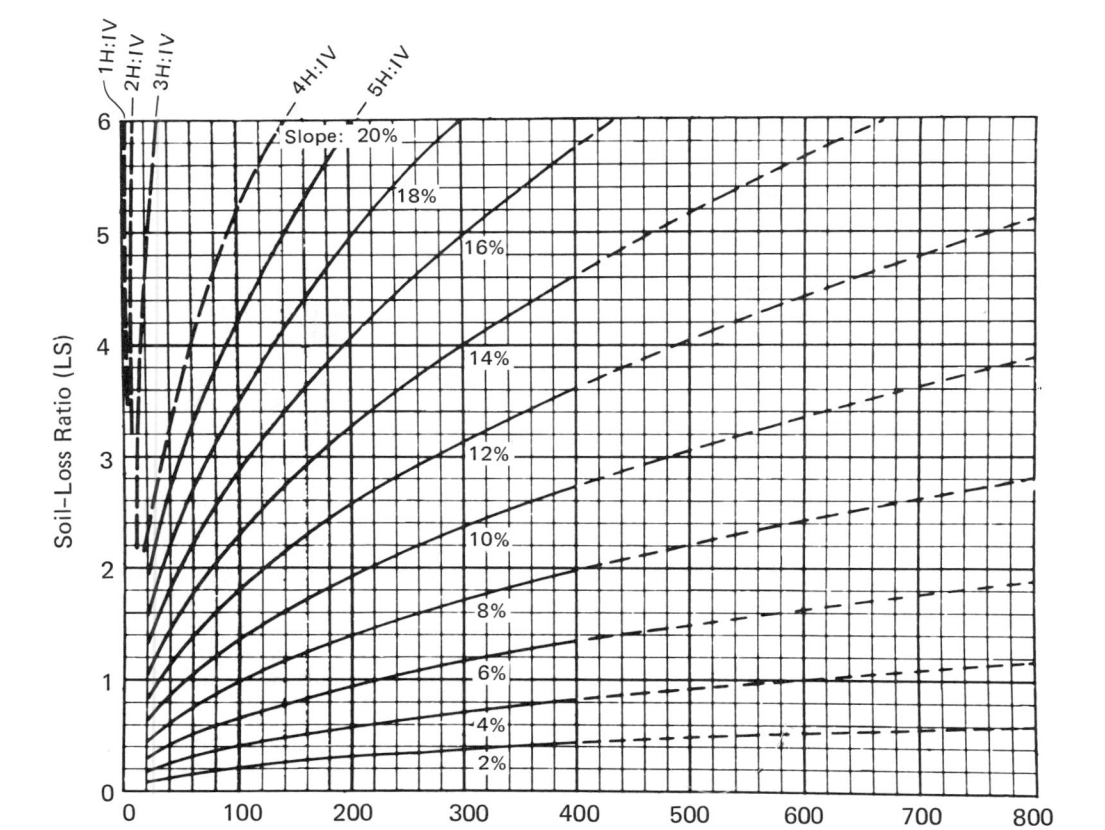

Fig. 2.9. Chart for determination of topographic factors, *LS*.

lated in Table 2.7. Values of *P* range from 0.95 for contouring on steep slopes (18 to 24 percent) to 0.25 for contour strip cropping on gentle slopes. Terracing effectively reduces the length of slope from that of the entire site to the horizontal distance between terraces. The methods of determining *P* for a given conservation practice and, alternatively, the selection of a conservation practice, using the Soil Loss Equation, have been described by Wischmeier and Smith (1965).

A number of erosion control practices—structural, mechanical, chemical, vegetative, or combinations thereof—can be used to reduce soil losses from disturbed slopes or construction sites. Methods based on the USLE for evaluating the effectiveness of these measures are described in Section 2.4.

2.3.2 Wind Erosion

Soil loss from a site by wind can also be estimated using an equation similar to the USLE, that was developed for rainfall erosion. The wind erosion equation (Skidmore and Woodruff, 1968; Woodruff and Siddoway, 1965) is an established method for predicting gross erosion from open fields. It has occasionally been used in air pollution studies to obtain estimates of fugitive dust concentrations in special areas such as tailings, piles, and dirt roads (Wilson, 1975). Its utility for predicting wind erosion losses from steep slopes of limited extent (e.g., highway cut and fills) is less certain.

The wind erosion equation can be written in the following form:

$$X' = I'K'C'L'V' \qquad (2.4)$$

where:

X' = gross annual wind erosion per unit area
K' = soil erodibility index
I' = field roughness factor
C' = climatic factor
L' = field length factor
V' = vegetative cover factor

Only a general discussion of the wind erosion equation and the controlling factors is given here. The reader is referred to references on this subject (Hayes, 1972; Skid-

Table 2.5. C factors for pasture, rangeland, and idle land.[1]

VEGETAL CANOPY			COVER THAT CONTACTS THE SURFACE					
			PERCENT GROUND COVER					
TYPE AND HEIGHT OF RAISED CANOPY[2]	CANOPY COVER[3] %	TYPE[4]	0	20	40	60	80	95–100
COLUMN NO.:	2	3	4	5	6	7	8	9
No appreciable canopy		G	.45	.20	.10	.042	.013	.003
		W	.45	.24	.15	.090	.043	.011
Canopy of tall weeds or short brush (0.5 m fall ht.)	25	G	.36	.17	.09	.038	.012	.003
	25	W	.36	.20	.13	.082	.041	.011
	50	G	.26	.13	.07	.035	.012	.003
	50	W	.26	.16	.11	.075	.039	.011
	75	G	.17	.10	.06	.031	.011	.003
	75	W	.17	.12	.09	.067	.038	.011
Appreciable brush or bushes (2 m fall ht.)	25	G	.40	.18	.09	.040	.013	.003
	25	W	.40	.22	.14	.085	.042	.011
	50	G	.34	.16	.085	.038	.012	.003
	50	W	.34	.19	.13	.081	.041	.011
	75	G	.28	.14	.08	.036	.012	.003
	75	W	.28	.17	.12	.077	.040	.011
Trees but no appreciable low brush (4 m fall ht.)	25	G	.42	.19	.10	.041	.013	.003
	25	W	.42	.23	.14	.087	.042	.011
	50	G	.39	.18	.09	.040	.013	.003
	50	W	.39	.21	.14	.085	.042	.011
	75	G	.36	.17	.09	.039	.012	.003
	75	W	.36	.20	.13	.083	.041	.011

[1]All values shown assume: (1) random distribution of mulch or vegetation, and (2) mulch of appreciable depth where it exists.

[2]Average fall height of waterdrops from canopy to soil surface: m = meters.

[3]Portion of total-area surface that would be hidden from view by canopy in a vertical projection (a bird's-eye view).

[4]G: Cover at surface is grass, grasslike plants, decaying compacted duff, or litter at least 2 inches deep.
W: Cover at surface is mostly broadleaf herbaceous plants (as weeds) with little lateral-root network near the surface, and/or undecayed residue.

Source: USDA Soil Conservation Service, 1978

Table 2.6. C factors for woodland.

TREE CANOPY[1] % OF AREA	FOREST LITTER[2] % OF AREA	UNDERGROWTH[3]	C FACTOR
100–75	100–90	Managed[4]	.001
		Unmanaged[4]	.003–.011
70–40	85–75	Managed	.002–.004
		Unmanaged	.01–.04
35–20	70–40	Managed	.003–.009
		Unmanaged	.02–.09[5]

[1]When tree canopy is less than 20%, the area will be considered as grassland, or cropland for estimating soil loss. See Table 2.5.

[2]Forest litter is assumed to be at least 2 inches deep over the percent ground surface area covered.

[3]Undergrowth is defined as shrubs, weeds, grasses, vines, etc., on the surface area not protected by forest litter. Usually found under canopy openings.

[4]Managed—grazing and fires are controlled. Unmanaged—stands are overgrazed or subjected to repeated burning.

[5]For unmanaged woodland with litter cover of less than 75%, C values should be derived by taking 0.7 of the appropriate values in Table 2.5. The factor of 0.7 adjusts for the much higher soil organic matter on permanent woodland.

(From USDA Soil Conservation Service, 1978)

Table 2.7 P factors for standard erosion control practices.

Slope, %	Up and Down Hill	Cross slope farming without strips	Contour tillage	Cross slope farming with strips	Contour stripcropping
2.0–7	1.0	.75	.50	.37	.25
7.1–12	1.0	.80	.60	.45	.30
12.1–18	1.0	.90	.80	.60	.40
18.1–24	1.0	.95	.90	.67	.45

(From USDA Soil Conservation Service, 1978)

more and Woodruff, 1968) for calculation details and design of wind erosion control systems.

Soil Erodibility. Soil erodibility, K', depends upon the ability of soil to form clods and is determined by textural and other factors. For a given site, K' is usually determined from sieve data, but it is also possible to use generalized relationships between erodibility and texture class. The Soil Conservation Service has established a series of wind erodibility ratings for all important texture classes, based on the percentage of fine material present, percentage composition of clays, and whether or not the soil is calcareous.

Surface Roughness. Surface roughness, I', inhibits erosion by absorbing and deflecting wind energy and by trapping some potentially abrasive materials. It may also exacerbate the problem by increasing wind turbulence. In many studies the I' factor is rated either 1.0 for a smooth ground or 0.5 for rough ground, with 1.0 being used when no direct information is available.

Climatic Factor. The climatic variable, C', is determined by windspeed and effective soil moisture. It can be calculated with a formula or read from maps prepared by the Agricultural Research Service (Skidmore and Woodruff, 1968).

Field Length Function. The field length function, L', is determined by graphical procedures and relates to field or area size, wind-rose characteristics, and the presence or absence of a windbreak (Skidmore and Woodruff, 1968). Use of the factor is based on observations that soil flow is zero at the upward side of a bare field and increases across the field, along the wind direction, until it reaches a maximum value equal to $K' \times I' \times C'$. If the field is too small for the maximum to be reached, then the calculated erosion rate must be reduced accordingly.

Vegetation Factor. The factor for vegetation, V', is determined from graphs that relate erosion rate to plant cover. The factor reflects reduction in gross erosion resulting from protective effects of good cover. The effects of land clearing for construction, roads, and so on,

potentially have a greater impact in humid regions than the same clearing might in arid areas. This is so because arid regions do not support as dense a plant cover and thus exhibit higher base or background erosion rates.

2.4 EVALUATION OF SOIL LOSS REDUCTION MEASURES AT CONSTRUCTION SITES

The effectiveness of individual components of erosion and sediment control can be determined from data published by the Soil Conservation Service (1972, 1977). Effectiveness factors have been derived mainly for agricultural control practices which may differ in both kind and degree from practices applied at urban and highway construction sites. Furthermore, effectiveness factors are usually published for individual components as opposed to treatment combinations. A procedure is described herein for estimating effectiveness of erosion control methods at construction sites.

2.4.1 Evaluation Formula

Individual components for reducing soil losses may be viewed as vegetation management (C) and conservation practice (P) factors respectively. Thus, the soil loss (X_1) from a given construction site having erosion and sediment control treatments is computed by the Universal Soil Loss Equation:

$$X_1 = RLSKCP \qquad (2.5)$$

If the same construction site were denuded and employed no erosion and sediment control treatments, the soil loss (X_2) would be:

$$X_2 = RLSK \qquad (2.6)$$

because factor C and P values equal 1.0 in this case. Values for $RLSK$ are equivalent in Equations (2.5) and (2.6) because the same construction site is used in both equations. The soil retained on the construction site, because erosion and sediment treatments were employed, is computed by:

$$\text{soil retained} = X_2 - X_1 \qquad (2.7)$$

Therefore, the effectiveness of the treatment in retaining soil at the construction site is:

$$\% \text{ Effectiveness} = \frac{X_2 - X_1}{X_2} \times 100$$

$$= \frac{RLSK - RLSKCP}{RLSK} \times 100$$

$$= (1 - CP) \times 100 \tag{2.8}$$

Equation (2.8) can now be used to compute effectiveness for various erosion and sediment control alternatives, provided factor C and P values can be calculated and assigned to the individual components comprising a particular system.

2.4.2 Factor C Values for Construction Sites

Factor C values for various types of natural vegetative cover were listed in Tables 2.5 and 2.6. These factor C values must be adjusted for construction sites because ground surface conditions and type of cover may differ considerably from the original cover. Cover index factors (C_c) for construction sites are listed in Table 2.8. The influence of both chemical and organic mulches on the cover index is considered in the table as well.

Two assumed construction conditions may be considered: (1) Construction is completed within 18 months of initial groundbreaking. (2) Building is started 6 months after seeding; then construction is completed within 24 months. It is further assumed that 3 months of the 18- or 24-month construction period is consumed by grading operations. During this time the ground will usually be bare or exposed, and the factor C value will be determined by the physical state of the ground surface as shown in Table 2.9.

Factor C values will change with time following surface treatment (i.e., mulching, seeding, planting, etc.). For example, factor C values for grass may decrease from 1.0 (for fallow ground) to about 0.01 between time of initial seeding and full establishment. Certain grading practices will either increase or decrease initial factor C values relative to the fallow ground condition as shown in Table 2.9. A procedure for estimating an average or weighted factor C value for an 18-month construction period is given below.

Example: Ground surface is left in a smoothed, compacted condition and then raked across the slope during initial grading (3 months). Surface treatment con-

Table 2.8 Cover index factor C_c for construction sites.

TYPE OF COVER		FACTOR C_c	%*
None (fallow ground)		1.0	0.0
Temporary seedings (90% stand):			
Ryegrass (perennial type)		0.05	95
Ryegrass (annuals)		0.1	90
Small grain		0.05	95
Millet or sudan grass		0.05	95
Field bromegrass		0.03	97
Permanent seedings (90% stand)		0.01	99
Sod (laid immediately)		0.01	99
Mulch:			
Hay rate of application, tons per acre:			
	$1\frac{1}{4}$	0.25	75
	1	0.13	87
	$1\frac{1}{2}$	0.07	93
	2	0.02	98
Small grain straw	2	0.02	98
Wood chips	6	0.06	94
Wood cellulose	$1\frac{3}{4}$	0.1	90
Fiberglass	$1\frac{1}{4}$	0.05	95
Asphalt emulsion (1250 gals/acre)		0.02	98

Fiber matting, excelsior, gravel, and stone may also be used as protective cover.

*Percent soil loss reduction as compared with fallow ground.

(From USDA Soil Conservation Service, 1978)

Table 2.9. Ground surface condition factor C_s for construction sites.

SURFACE CONDITION WITH NO COVER	FACTOR*
Compact and smooth, scraped with bulldozer or scraper up and down hill	1.3
Same condition except raked with bulldozer root rake up and down hill	1.2
Compact and smooth, scraped with bulldozer or scraper across the slope	1.2
Same condition except raked with bulldozer root rake across the slope	0.9
Loose as a disced plow layer	1.0
Rough irregular surface equipment tracks in all directions	0.9
Loose with rough surface greater than 12'' depth	0.8
Loose with smooth surface greater than 12'' depth	0.9

*Values based on estimates.

(From USDA Soil Conservation Service, 1978)

sists of temporary seeding with annual rye grass and mulching with hay at the rate of 1 ton/acre (3 months). This is followed by permanent seedings for the duration of the construction period (12 months).

Months	Representative factor C values*	Fraction of const. period	Product
0–3	1.20	3/18	0.200
3–6	0.125	3/18	0.021
6–18	0.05	12/18	0.033
	Ave. factor $\bar{C}$ value for 18-mo period		0.254

*Estimated or obtained directly from Tables 2.8 and 2.9.

2.4.3. Factor P Values for Construction Sites

Factor P values pertain to various erosion control or conservation practices. These practices consist of structural–mechanical or land management measures. On agricultural lands these measures include terracing, strip cropping, and contour tillage. Factor P values in Table 2.7 describe their relative efficiency. At construction sites, erosion control practices consist of various measures to control runoff and filter out or trap sediment. These include structural measures such as grade stabilization structures (chutes, flumes, check dams, water ladders), level spreaders, diversions, and interceptor berms—all of which can be referred to collectively as *erosion-reducing structures*. The effectiveness of erosion-reducing structures (U. S. Environmental Protection Agency, 1973) is estimated as follows:

	Factor P value
Normal rate usage (165 ft/acre)	0.50
High rate usage (over 165 ft/acre)	0.40

Thus, the overall effectiveness of erosion-reducing structures (normal rate usage) is estimated at 50 percent. For higher usage, factor P value is 0.40, which corresponds to an effectiveness of 60 percent.

Sediment basins can also be classified and evaluated as conservation measures. Basins do not stop erosion; instead, they keep eroded material from leaving a site and causing off-site damage. Methods for determining factor P values for both small sediment basins and large downstream basins are given elsewhere (U. S. Environmental Protection Agency 1973).

2.4.4 Computing System Effectiveness

The effectiveness of erosion control systems that combine both erosion-reducing structures and vegetation treatment can be computed using a variant of Equation (2.8), namely:

$$\text{System effectiveness (\%)} = (1 - \bar{C}\bar{P}) \times 100 \qquad (2.9)$$

where:

$\bar{C}$ = average or weighted vegetation management factor during construction period

$\bar{P}$ = average conservation practice factor attributable to erosion-reducing structures

The product of factors $\bar{C}$ and $\bar{P}$ represents in effect a "biotechnical erosion control factor" or combined vegetative–structural control factor.

There are at present few or no published data on values of this biotechnical erosion control factor for such integrated systems as contour-wattling (see Chapter 7). Evidence to date suggests, nevertheless, that system effectiveness for such measures is very high compared to more conventional methods. In addition, the extent to which such measures help in establishing, anchoring, or retaining vegetation on a slope will largely determine the extent to which conventional cover index factors listed in Table 2.8 apply in practice.

2.5 NATURE OF MASS-MOVEMENT

2.5.1 Types of Slopes Movements

Various schemes have been proposed over the years for classifying and describing slope movements (Sharpe, 1938; Varnes, 1958, 1978). The classification system proposed by Varnes (1958, revised 1978) is perhaps the most useful and widely adopted. His system is based on two main variables: (1) type of movement and (2) materials involved. Types of movements are divided into five main groups: falls, topples, slides, spreads, and flows. A sixth group, complex slope movements, includes combinations of two or more of the other five types. Materials are divided into two classes: rock and engineering soil; soil is further divided into debris and earth. Debris is material that is transitional in gradation between rock and earth. An abbreviated diagram of the various combinations of movements and materials is shown in Fig. 2.10.

A comprehensive description of the various types of slope movements is outside the scope of this book. The interested reader should consult the original papers by Varnes (1958, 1978) for this purpose. On the other hand, it is important to understand and to be able to identify various types of slope movements, not only for purposes of avoiding unstable slopes but also for designing prevention and control systems. Methods useful for prevention and control of one type of slope failure (e.g., shallow, translational sliding) may be ineffectual against deep-seated, rotational failures. For illustrative purposes two

Type of Movement			Type of Material		
			Bed-rock	ENGINEERING SOILS	
				Predominantly coarse	Predominantly fine
Falls			Rock fall	Debris fall	Earth fall
Topples			Rock topple	Debris topple	Earth topple
Slides	Rotational	FEW UNITS	Rock slump	Debris slump	Earth slump
	Translational		Rock block slide	Debris block slide	Earth block slide
		MANY UNITS	Rock slide	Debris slide	Earth slide
Lateral Spreads			Rock spread	Debris spread	Earth spread
Flows			Rock flow	Debris flow (soil creep)	Earth flow
Complex			Combination of two or more principal types of movement		

Fig. 2.10. Abbreviated classification of slope movements. (*From Varnes, 1978*). Used with permission of the Transportation Research Board, Washington, D.C.

prevalent types of slope movements and their geological settings are reviewed here.

Debris slides.   Debris sliding is dominantly translational, downslope movement of soil, colluvium, fractured bedrock, disrupted vegetation, and organic debris along well-defined, nearly planar failure surfaces. Debris slides occur in slopes composed of sandy, coarse-textured soils or slopes with shallow residual soils overlying an inclined bedrock contact. Debris slides are common in granitic terrain of the Idaho Batholith area (Gonsior and Gardner, 1971) and interbedded shales, siltstones, and sandstones of the Cumberland Plateau escarpment (Royster, 1973). Figure 2.11 is a schematic depiction of a translational debris slide in colluvium and shale. Movement resulted when toe support was excavated for a road. Note that the surface of failure essentially parallels or corresponds to the colluvium–shale interface.

Earth Slumps.   Slumping is the downslope movement of relatively intact masses of soil, colluvium, and vegetation along a clearly defined, concave-upward failure surface. Movement is usually deep-seated and dominantly rotational about an axis parallel to the slope. Earth

slumps tend to occur in cohesive, fine-grained soils. The failure mass may partially break up into a series of smaller, nested rotational slides upon initiation of movement, as shown in Fig. 2.12. Alternatively, the slide mass may lose all its coherence or strength after initiation of movement and deteriorate into a slump earthflow. The latter is characterized by a hummocky, lobate, and often dissected morphology. Earth slumps and slump earthflows are quite common in weathered sedimentary formations comprising the central Coast Ranges of California, particulary in areas underlain by highly sheared and fractured rock (Cleveland, 1977).

2.5.2 Causes of Slope Movement

The stability of slopes is governed by topographic, geologic, and climatic variables which control shear stress and shear resistance in a slope. Slope movements occur when shear stresses exceed shear strength of the materials forming the slope. The ratio of shear strength to shear stress along a given surface in a slope is known as a factor of safety. The surface with the lowest ratio is the critical or failure surface, and its factor of safety governs the stability of the slope. This surface also demarcates the

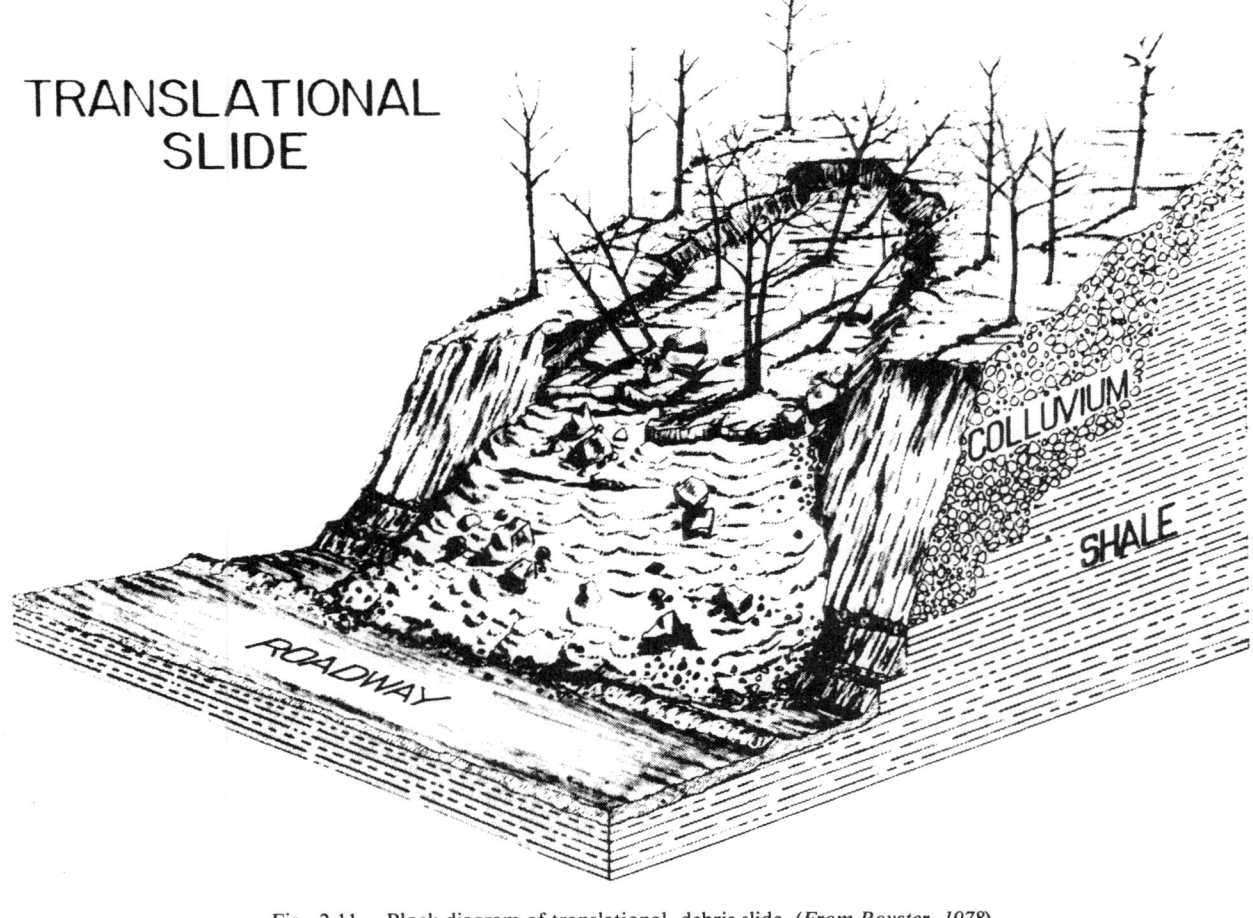

TRANSLATIONAL SLIDE

Fig. 2.11. Block diagram of translational, debris slide. (*From Royster, 1978*)

boundary between stable ground and moving ground. The term slide implicity specifies relative motion between the two. Methods for analyzing and computing the factor of safety of slopes against sliding are reviewed in Section 2.6.

Any variable or factor that increases shear stress or conversely that decreases shear strength will tend to cause slope movement. Causes of slope instability or movement have been grouped into these two categories by Varnes (1958), as illustrated in Table 2.10. Timely identification and recognition of these factors is the key to prevention and control of slope movements.

Removal of lateral support by either natural or human agencies is the most common of all factors leading to instability. This observation underscores the importance of using buttress or retaining structures at the foot of slopes as a remedial measure. The addition of water to a slope may contribute to both an increase in stress and a decrease in strength. Water in fact has been implicated as either the controlling factor or a primary controlling factor in 95 percent of all landslides (Chassie and Goughnour, 1976). Accordingly, drainage and diversion measures are

without doubt among the most effective means of preventing and/or controlling landslides. Landslide remedial measures and their effectiveness are described by Royster (1978), Zaruba and Mencl (1969), and Hutchinson (1978).

Vegetation can ameliorate many of the factors and conditions causing instability. Woody vegetation growing on a slope can increase soil shear strength by root reinforcement, decrease soil moisture stress and surcharge by evapotranspiration in the foliage, and increase overall stability as a result of buttressing and soil arching action between stems. The contribution and significance of slope vegetation to the stability of slopes are described in Chapter 3.

2.5.3 Indicators of Slope Instability

There are several visual indicators of hillside instability that are extremely useful for identifying areas of potential slope movement. These indicators, which are of a topographic, geologic, hydrologic, and botanical nature, are summarized in Table 2.11. Most of these signs of

Table 2.10. Factors contributing to instability of earth slopes. (After Varnes, 1958)

FACTORS THAT CONTRIBUTE TO *High Shear Stress*	FACTORS THAT CONTRIBUTE TO *Low Shear Strength*

A. Removal of lateral support
   1. Erosion—bank cutting by streams and rivers
   2. Human agencies—cuts, canals, pits, etc.
	A. Initial state
	   1. Composition—inherently weak materials
	   2. Texture—loose soils, metastable grain structures
	   3. Gross structure—faults, jointing, bedding, planes, varving, etc.

B. Surcharge
   1. Natural agencies—weight of snow, ice, and rainwater
   2. Human agencies, fills, buildings, etc.
	B. Changes due to weathering and other physico-Chemical reactions
	   1. Frost action and thermal expansion
	   2. Hydration of clay minerals
	   3. Drying and cracking
	   4. Leaching

C. Transitory earth stresses—earthquakes
 	
D. Regional tilting
	C. Changes in intergrannular forces due to pore water
	   1. Buoyancy in saturated state
	   2. Loss in capillary tension upon saturation
	   3. Seepage pressure of percolating groundwater

E. Removal of underlying support
   1. Subaerial weathering—solutioning by groundwater
   2. Subterranean erosion—piping
   3. Human agencies—mining
	D. Changes in structure
	   1. Fissuring of preconsolidated clays due to release of lateral restraint
	   2. Grain structure collapse upon disturbance

F. Lateral pressures
   1. Water in vertical cracks
   2. Freezing water in cracks
   3. Swelling
   4. Root wedging	

TABLE 2.11. Features indicating landslides or areas with high landslide potential.

FEATURE	SIGNIFICANCE	FEATURE	SIGNIFICANCE
1. Hummocky, dissected topography	Common feature in old and active progressive slides (slides with many individual components). Slide mass is prone to gullying.	5. Lobate slope forms	Indication of former earthflow or solifluction area.
2. Abrupt change in slope	May indicate either an old landslide area or a change in the erosion characteristics of underlying material. Portion with low slope angle is generally weaker and often has higher water content.	6. Hillside ponds	Local catchments or depressions formed as result of (4) above act as infiltration source which can exarcerbate or accelerate landsliding.
3. Scarps and cracks	Definite indication of an active or recently active landslide. Age of scarp can usually be estimated by the amount of vegetation established upon it. Width of cracks may be monitored to estimate relative rates of movement.	7. Hillside seeps	Common in landslide masses. Area with high landslide potential. Can usually be identified by associated presence of denser or phreatophyte vegetation (cattails, equisetum, alder, etc.) in vicinity of seep.
4. Grabens or "stair step" topography	Indication of progressive failure. Complex or nested series of rotational slides can also cause surface of slope to appear stepped or tiered.	8. Incongruent vegetation	Patches or areas of much younger or very different vegetation (e.g., alder thickets); may indicate recent landslides or unstable ground.
		9. "Jackstrawed" trees	Leaning or canted trees on a slope are indicators of previous episodes of slope movement or soil creep.
		10. Bedding planes and joints dipping downslope	Potential surface of sliding for translational slope movements.

ROTATIONAL SLIDE

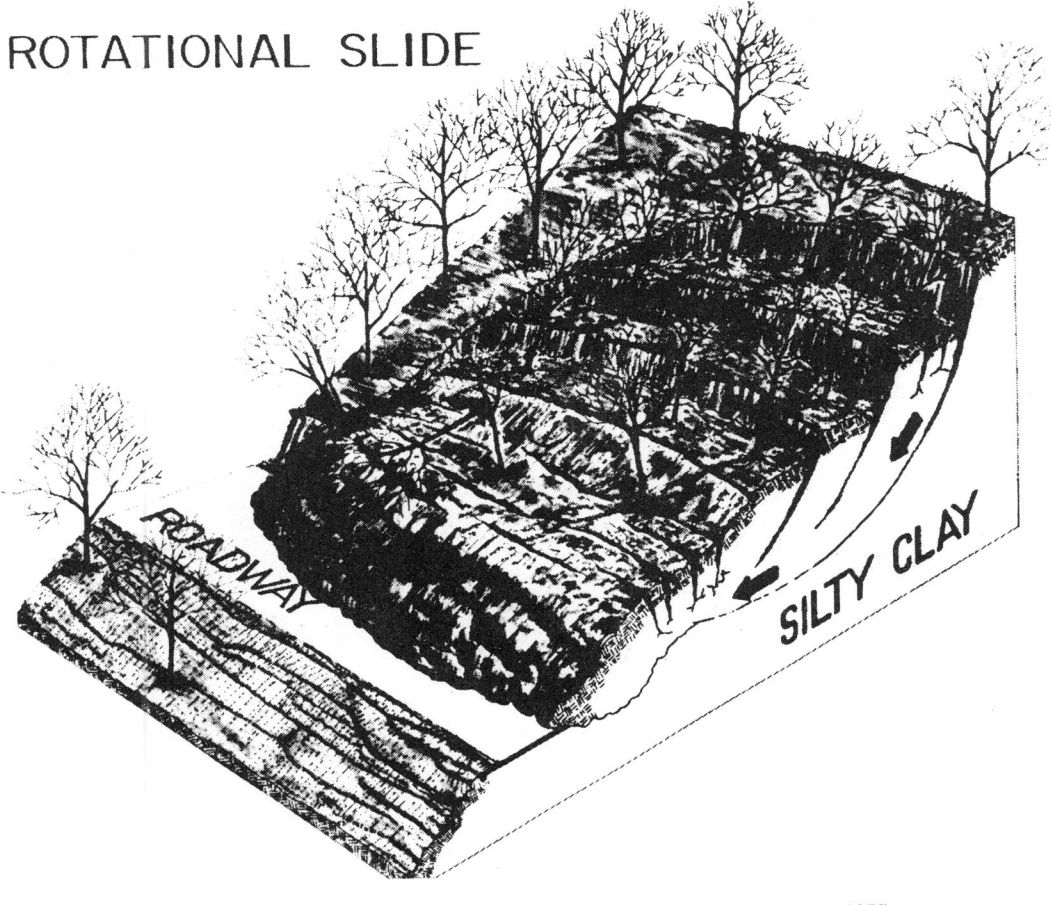

Fig. 2.12. Block diagram of rotational, earth slump. (*From Royster, 1978*)

hillside instability can be spotted by a visual reconnaissance in the field. They are signals for precautions or preventive measures which should be employed during and after slope disturbance in the area.

Peck (1967) stated a postulate that is useful for identifying potentially unstable slopes, viz., if there is not evidence of old landslides in an area, then it is fairly unlikely that moderate construction activity will start a new one. On the other hand, if old landslides abound, then it is quite likely that even minor construction operations will activate an old slide or lead to a new one.

2.6 SLOPE STABILITY PREDICTIONS

2.6.1 Approaches to Analysis

Numerous methods are available for predicting the stability of slopes and embankments. The two basic approaches are (1) limit equilibrium analysis and (2) deformation analysis. Most methods so far developed fall into the former category. Although the performance of a slope, particularly a man-made embankment, is often dictated by allowable deformations, quantitative predic-

tions of displacements are seldom undertaken routinely. Instead, the performance of a slope is evaluated in terms of its factor of safety using limit equilibrium methods. There are several reasons for this, namely, the cost and complexity plus the requirement for very accurate soil constitutive relations in deformation analysis.

Limit equilibrium methods explicitly take into account the major factors that influence the shear stress and shear resistance in a slope (Table 2.10). In addition these methods are simpler to apply than deformation analysis. Limit equilibrium methods do not result in calculation of expected slope deformations; however, there are many instances in which precise deformations are of little concern, provided the material stays in place.

A detailed treatment of slope stability analysis is outside the scope of this book. The interested reader is referred to geotechnical texts on this subject (Lambe and Whitman, 1969; Morgenstern and Sangrey, 1978; and Chowdhury, 1979). The intent here is mainly to review concepts of stability analysis and to describe a few methods that are employed in practice. This review will serve (1) to explain the combination of conditions that lead to slope movement and (2) to identify the relative importance to stability of different soil, slope, and hydrologic variables.

The methods presented satisfy the above criteria, and they are also relatively easy to apply. They make it possible to answer or evaluate the following questions about the stability of slopes:

1. The critical height for stable cut slopes
2. The critical piezometric level in a slope
3. The stability of side-cast fills along a road
4. The contribution of roots and other vegetative influences on slope stability
5. The effectiveness of drainage, buttressing, and other remedial measures

The basic features and limitations of limit equilibrium analysis are described in the next section. Several limit equilibrium stability analyses which are based on both planar and rotational slip surfaces are then presented. The former model is useful for assessing the stability of slopes susceptible to translational, debris slides (Fig. 2.11), whereas the latter is more applicable to slopes prone to rotational slides or earth slumps (Fig. 2.12).

2.6.2 Limit Equilibrium Analysis

Limit equilibrium analysis is used to determine the factor of safety for a given slope, and it can also be used to determine the effect of varying one or more parameters on the stability of a slope. A number of methods and procedures based on limit equilibrium principles have been developed for this purpose. Regardless of the specific procedure, the following principles (Morgenstern and Sangrey, 1978) are common to all methods of limit equilibrium analyses:

1. *A failure surface or mechanism is postulated.* In the simplest case, idealized slopes are assumed to fail along planes or circular sliding surfaces. More complex failure surfaces can also be proposed and analyzed when slope conditions are not uniform.
2. *The shearing resistance required to equilibrate the failure mass is calculated by means of statics.* The basic physical concepts involved here are that the potential failure mass is in a state of "limiting equilibrium" and that the failure or yield criterion of the soil or rock is satisfied everywhere along the proposed surface.
3. *The calculated shearing resistance required for equilibrium is compared with the available shear strength.* This comparison is made in terms of the factor of safety, which is generally defined as the factor by which the shear strength parameters must

be reduced in order to bring the slope into a state of limiting equilibrium along a given slip surface.
4. *The mechanism or slip surface with the lowest factor of safety is found by iteration.* The surface with the lowest computed safety factor is the critical slip surface. If the location of the slip surface is predetermined by stratigraphic control (e.g., a weak clay seam, relict jointing plane, or contact between residual soil and underlying bedrock, etc.), other trials are usually unnecessary.

Limit equilibrium analysis has some drawbacks, which should be kept in mind. Various methods that have been proposed differ in the degree to which the conditions for equilibrium are satisfied (Wright, 1973). Some common methods of analysis do not rigorously meet all requirements for static equilibrium. This is not as serious a limitation, however, as errors introduced by uncertainty in the proper choice and selection of input parameters, particularly values for shear strength of the soil (Singh, 1970). Other difficulties encountered in applying stability analyses to natural slopes (e.g., problems of progressive failure, representative sampling and testing of soil, unequal mobilization of shear strength along the failure surface, and so on) are discussed by Peck (1967). In spite of these drawbacks and problems, limit equilibrium analysis provides powerful insights into the factors and conditions governing the stability of slopes; it also provides a rational basis for assessing slope hazard and designing remedial measures.

2.6.3 Shear Strength Parameters

Determination of the factor of safety by limit equilibrium methods requires an estimate of the shear resistance that can be mobilized along the assumed failure surface. The shear strength of soil or unconsolidated rock is given by the Coulomb criterion:

$$s = c + \sigma \tan \phi \qquad (2.10)$$

where:

s = shear strength of material
σ = normal stress acting on the failure surface
ϕ = angle of internal friction
c = cohesion intercept

The angle of internal friction (ϕ) and the cohesion (c) are known as the shear strength parameters. They can be determined from various laboratory tests on representative samples of soil or, alternatively, back-calculated from analysis of a failed portion of a slope by assuming a factor of safety equal to unity.

An important consideration in slope stability analyses

is whether to employ a total or an effective stress analysis. This decision will determine what type of shear strength parameters must be used in the analysis. General rules and guidelines for selecting the appropriate type of analysis and parameters are discussed in this section and are presented also in Table 2.12.

2.6.3.1 Total Stress Analysis.
When a fully saturated soil is sheared to failure without permitting drainage, the soil behaves as though it is purely cohesive (i.e., $\phi = 0$), and the results should be interpreted in terms of total stress. It is important to note that this behavior is more a response to type of test or loading condition than it is a reflection of basic strength properties. Even so, simple, useful analyses result when $\phi = 0$ behavior is assumed, provided available shear resistance is selected with care. Undrained shear strength (c_u) can be obtained from a number of standard laboratory tests such as the unconfined compression test and vane shear test (Bowles, 1970).

Total stress analysis using undrained shear strength parameters (c, ϕ) is limited to slopes where pore pressures are governed by total (external) stress changes and in which insufficient time has elapsed for significant dissipation of pore pressures. These conditions are characteristic of the so-called end-of-construction class of problems. A temporary cut made in a cohesive, clay slope can be analyzed in this manner, provided it is not fissured and jointed (Table 2.12). A total stress analysis does not require a determination of pore pressure distribution in a slope, an important advantage of the analysis.

2.6.3.2 Effective Stress Analysis.
When pore pressures are governed by steady state seepage conditions, or if long-term stability is a consideration, then stability analysis should be performed in terms of effective stresses. This is the usual condition for natural slopes in both soil and rock. All permanent cuts or fills also should be analyzed for long-term conditions to see whether these conditions control design (Table 2.12). Some jointed and fissured clays respond to drainage along dominant discontinuities so quickly that it is doubtful that a $\phi = 0$ idealization is ever representative (Esu, 1966). These materials should be analyzed in terms of effective stress regardless of time of loading or unloading (Table 2.12).

Effective shear strength parameters (c', ϕ') may be obtained from results of either drained triaxial tests or undrained triaxial tests with pore pressure measurements (Bowles, 1970). An effective stress analysis requires that effective shear strength parameters be used and that the pore pressure distribution in the slope be known from piezometric studies. If the pore pressure is unknown or cannot be determined, there is little point to an effective stress analysis; a total stress analysis should be employed instead.

2.6.4 Translational Slope Failures

The stability of simple, natural slopes where all boundaries (ground surface, phreatic surface, base surface) are approximately parallel can be modeled and analyzed by so-called infinite slope equations. In this analysis the slip surface is assumed to be a plane roughly parallel to the ground surface. This type of analysis is appropriate when sliding takes place such that the ratio of depth to length of the sliding mass is small. The following types of slopes or slope conditions meet the aforementioned criteria:

1. Loose products of weathering (residual soil) overlying an inclined bedrock contact
2. Inclined planes of stratification dipping downslope that are underlain by stronger strata
3. Bedrock slopes mantled with glacial till or colluvium
4. Homogeneous slopes of coarse-textured, cohesionless soil (sand dunes, sandy embankments, or fills).

In the first three slopes the surface of sliding is predetermined by stratigraphic control. In the fourth, the slope failures are restricted to shallow, surface sloughing because shear strength increases with depth.

Because of the geometry of an infinite slope, overall stability can be determined by analyzing the stability of a single, vertical element in the slope as shown in Fig. 2.13.

TABLE 2.12. Parameters for clay slope stability problems (from Skempton and Hutchinson, 1969).

	CLAY TYPE	CUTTINGS		NATURAL SLOPES	
		SHORT TERM	LONG TERM	ORDER OF 100 YEARS	ORDER OF 1000 YEARS
FIRST-TIME SLIDES	Soft, normally-consolidated, intact	$x \cdot c_u$		$c' \; \phi'$	
	Lightly overconsolidated, intact		$c' \; \phi'$	$c' \; \phi'$	
	Stiff, intact			$c' \; \phi'$	
	Stiff, fissured	$f \cdot x \cdot c_u$	$r \cdot c'$, ϕ'	$c' = 0, \phi'$	$c' = 0, \phi' \rightarrow \phi'_r$
	Jointed clays	$c' = 0, \phi'$			
	Slide on preexisting	$c' \; \phi'_r$	$c'_r \phi'_r$	$c' \phi'_r$	

c_u = peak strength, undrained
$c' \phi'$ = peak strength parameters, drained
$c'_r \phi'_r$ = residual strength parameters ($c'_r = 0$)

x = reduction factor for rate of testing, anisotropy, etc.
f = reduction factor for fissures
r = time-dependent reduction factor

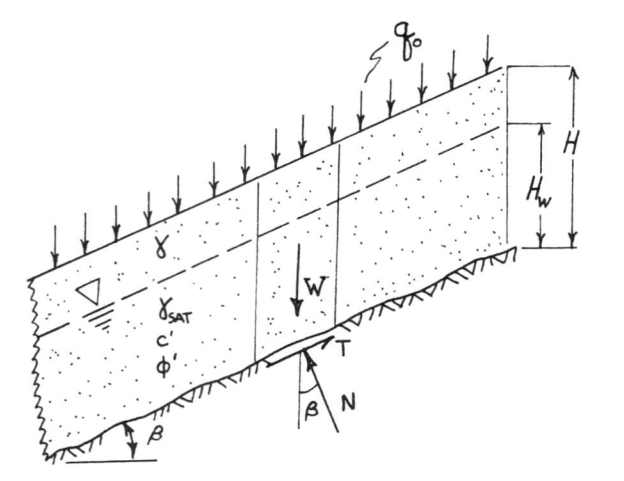

Fig. 2.13. Schematic representation of idealized "infinite" slope.

End effects in the sliding mass can be neglected, and so too can lateral forces on either side of the vertical element which are opposite and equal. The factor of safety based on an infinite slope analysis is given by the following equation:

$$F = \frac{\left[\dfrac{c'}{\cos^2 \beta \tan \phi'} + (q_o + \gamma H) + (\gamma_{BUOY} - \gamma)H_w\right]\dfrac{\tan \phi'}{\tan \beta}}{[(q_o + \gamma H) + (\gamma_{SATD} - \gamma)H_w]} \quad (2.11)$$

where:

ϕ' = effective angle of internal friction
c' = effective cohesion intercept
β = slope angle of natural ground
γ = moist density of soil
γ_{SATD} = saturated density of soil
γ_{BUOY} = buoyant density of soil $(\gamma_{BUOY} = \gamma_{SATD} - \gamma_w)$
γ_w = density of water
H = vertical thickness (or depth) of sliding mass
H_w = piezometric height above sliding surface
q_o = uniform vertical surcharge stress on slope

This expression is completely general and takes into account the influence of surcharge (q_o), the presence of a phreatic surface or groundwater table in the slope (H_w), and the existence of cohesion (c'). The influence of root reinforcement in the soil, which affects only the cohesion and not soil friction, can be accounted for by adding a "root cohesion" (c_R) to the numerator in Equation (2.11) as explained in chapter 3.

The following particular cases can be derived from the general expression:

Case i: *Cohesionless Slope, No Surcharge*
$(c' = 0, q_o = 0)$

$$F\Big|_{\substack{c'=0 \\ q_o=0 \\ H_w \neq 0}} = \frac{[\gamma(H - H_w) + \gamma_{BUOY}H_w]\tan\phi'}{[\gamma(H - H_w) + \gamma_{SATD}H_w]\tan\beta} \quad (2.12)$$

This equation shows the influence of a rise in the phreatic surface in a shallow, cohesionless soil overlying an inclined bedrock contact. Note that the controlling factor is not the absolute rise but rather the ratio (H_w/H). In other words, the same rise in phreatic surface is more serious in a "thin" soil mantle than a "thick" one.

Case ii: *Saturated, Cohesionless Slope, No Surcharge*
$(c' = 0, q_o = 0, H_w = H)$

$$F\Big|_{\substack{c'=0 \\ q_o=0 \\ H_w=H}} = \frac{\gamma_{BUOY}\tan\phi'}{\gamma_{SATD}\tan\beta} \quad (2.13)$$

But

$$\gamma_{BUOY} \approx \tfrac{1}{2}\gamma_{SATD}$$

Therefore

$$F\Big|_{\substack{c'=0 \\ q_o=0 \\ H_w=H}} \approx \frac{1}{2}\frac{\tan\phi'}{\tan\beta}$$

This equation yields the factor of safety for the worst case of complete saturation of a cohesionless infinite slope. The factor of safety is approximately one-half that of the dry case.

Case iii: *Dry, Cohesionless Slope, No Surcharge*
$(c' = 0, q_o = 0, H_w = 0)$

$$F\Big|_{\substack{c'=0 \\ q_o=0 \\ H_w \neq 0}} = \frac{\tan\phi'}{\tan\beta} \quad (2.14)$$

This equation shows that in a dry, cohesionless material the critical slope angle is equal to the angle of internal friction of the soil. If the material is end-dumped or side-cast in a loose condition, this angle will be equivalent to the angle of repose.

Case iv: *Stable Slopes with Cohesion, No Surcharge*
$(F = 1, q_o = 0)$

(a) *Dry Slope* $(H_w = 0)$

$$\frac{c_d}{\gamma H} = \cos^2 \beta \, (\tan \beta - \tan \phi') \qquad (2.15)$$

(b) *Saturated Slope* $(H_w = H)$

$$\frac{c_d}{\gamma H} = \cos^2 \beta \, (\tan \beta - \frac{\gamma_{BUOY}}{\gamma_{SATD}} \tan \phi') \qquad (2.16)$$

where c_d = the cohesion required for stability ($F = 1$).

These equations are useful for determining the amount of cohesion that must be present or develped for minimal stability ($F = 1$) for a given depth of sliding (H), slope angle (β), and friction angle (ϕ'). Note that the required cohesion is directly proportional to the thickness of sliding mass.

2.6.4.1 Selection of Soil Parameters.
Soil density should be determined in the field using standard procedures for field density testing (Bowles, 1970). Effective shear strength parameters c' and ϕ' should be used in an infinite slope analysis. These can be approximated in the laboratory by remolding samples to their in-place density and performing a triaxial test (Bowles, 1970). Shear strength parameters can also be obtained conveniently by means of an in-situ bore hole shear test (Wineland, 1975).

An approximate estimate of friction angle can be obtained from gradation and density data using the nomograph shown in Fig. 2.14. For many purposes this approximation is satisfactory in lieu of more expensive laboratory strength tests.

2.6.4.2 Stability of Road Fills.
Debris slides that originate from roadway fills are often characterized by movement along an approximately planar surface. One mode of failure is by shallow sloughing of the outside margins of a fill. This failure mode can be analyzed by the conventional infinite slope model, provided the thickness of the sliding mass is small relative to the slope length of the fill. Gonsior and Gardner (1971) suggest a minimum of 20 for the length/depth ratio.

The other mode of failure is sliding of the entire fill along the contact with the underlying ground. This mode is common in loose, side-cast fills on steep ground. The roadway in this case is supported part on cut and part on fill as depicted in Fig. 2.15. Many low-volume roads are constructed in this manner. The assumptions of the infinite slope model are not strictly observed in this mode of failure. Instead, a "sliding wedge" type of analysis seems more appropriate. Results of such an analysis show, however, that the infinite slope equations with minor modifications still yield satisfactory estimates of stability. In a dry fill, both models yield the same equation, viz., Equation (2.14). In a fill that develops a phreatic surface or thin, saturated zone along the contact (Fig. 2.15), the factor of safety will be given by an equation analogous to Equation 2.12:

$$F = \frac{(\gamma A_1 + \gamma_{BUOY} A_2)}{(\gamma A_1 + \gamma_{SATD} A_2)} \frac{\tan \phi'}{\tan \beta} \qquad (2.17)$$

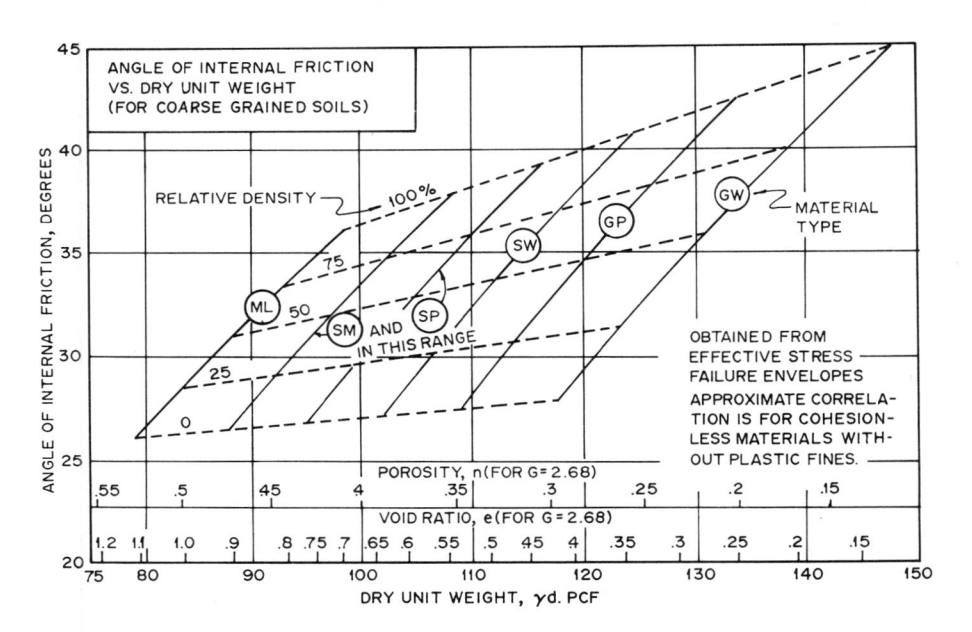

Fig. 2.14. Correlation chart for estimating soil friction angles from gradation and density data. (*From U. S. Navy Design Manual, 1971*)

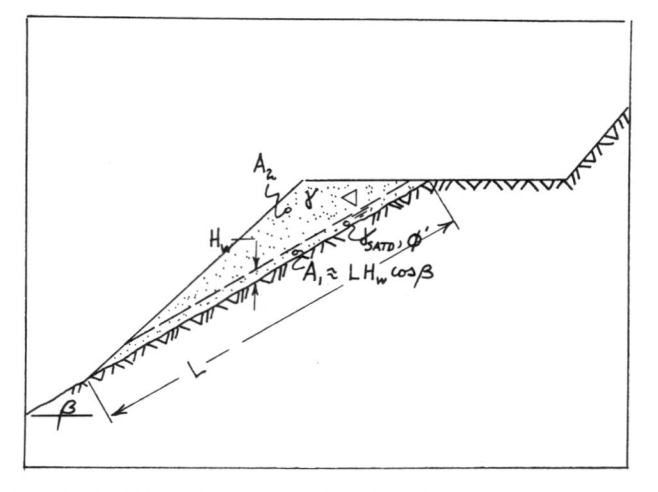

Fig. 2.15. Schematic representation of roadway supported partly on a bench cut and partly on side-cast fill. Saturated zone is shown along base of fill.

where:

A_1 = cross-sectional area of fill above phreatic surface

A_2 = saturated cross-sectional area of fill (below phreatic surface)

The areas A_1 and A_2 correspond to the heights H_w and $(H - H_w)$ in Equation (2.16).

In some cases fill failures are more complicated and involve material beneath the fill that is activated by the additional fill weight. In those cases the failure surface cuts deeper than the contact with the ground, and the failure mode may be rotational.

2.6.5 Rotational Slope Failures

Rotational slides occur in many types of soils; in these cases it is common practice to assume a circular slip surface. Several stability charts have been developed (Taylor, 1948; Chen and Giger, 1971) that can be used for computing the stability of uniform slopes characterized by both friction and cohesion. These charts are based on either a circular arc or log spiral failure surface.

2.6.5.1 Critical Height of Road Cuts. Stability

charts are useful for determining the critical height of cut for a specific combination of soil parameters (γ, c, ϕ) and slope angle of cut (α). The critical height (H_c) of a cut is the maximum height at which the slope will remain stable. This height is found from a so-called stability number (N_s), which is related to the critical height by the following expression:

$$N_s = H_c(\gamma/c) \qquad (2.18)$$

where:

N_s = stability number
H_c = critical height
γ = density of soil
c = cohesion intercept

The stability number in turn is plotted or tabulated in chart form as a function of both cut slope angle (α) and friction angle (ϕ), based on either a circular arc or log spiral failure surface. Of these charts, the one by Chen and Giger (1971) is the most useful because it takes into account the slope of the ground line (β) above the cut slope. A chart based on Chen and Giger's data is shown plotted in Fig. 2.16.

Estimation of critical height of cut and comparison with design cut heights from stability charts is useful for preliminary planning and siting. However, because these charts are in terms of total stresses, they are of limited value. Furthermore, they are not valid when seepage or groundwater is encountered in a cut. Prellwitz (1975) developed seepage correction charts that can be used in conjunction with stability charts to account for the influence of groundwater. He also developed a simple procedure known as the "center-of-gravity infinite-slope-approximation," which makes it possible to take

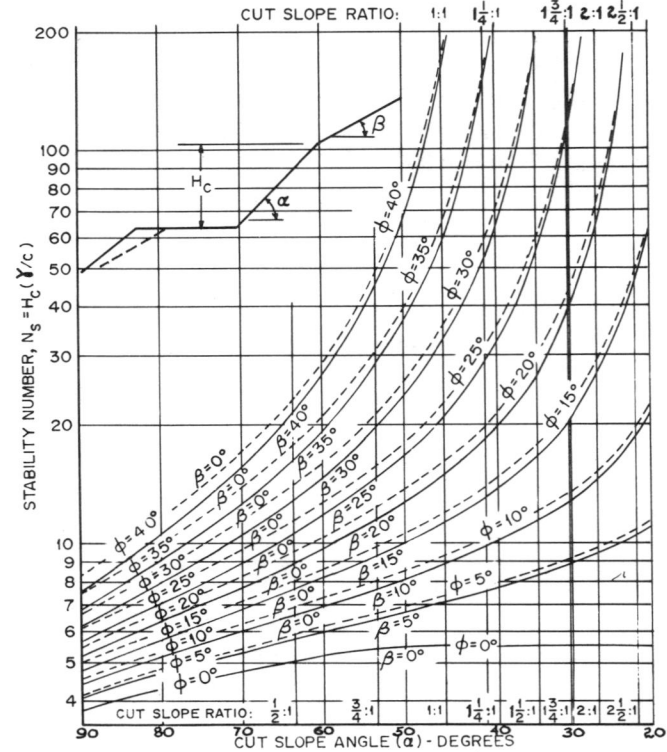

Fig. 2.16. Stability number chart for estimating the maximum stable cut height (H_c) under no seepage conditions. (*From Chen and Giger, 1971*)

into account and analyze a cut slope with a phreatic surface. This procedure is a short-cut alternative to the more exact, but more complex method-of-slices analysis.

2.6.5.2 Stability Analysis by Method-of-Slices.

Stability analyses based on the method-of-slices procedure (Bishop, 1955; Bishop and Morgenstern, 1960; and Morgenstern and Price, 1965) are the most versatile and reliable, particularly for heterogeneous slopes with irregular stratigraphy. They can be used for both total and effective stress analyses. Figure 2.17a shows the geometry of a circular surface of sliding used in the method. The forces acting on a typical slice are shown in Fig. 2.17b.

In what is usually termed the simplified Bishop method, force equilibrium of a slice in the vertical direction is taken, and the variation in X forces across a slice is ignored. This is tantamount to assuming zero shear between slices and ignoring the requirement for equilibrium in the horizontal direction. The resulting equation for the factor of safety is:

$$F = \frac{\Sigma\{ \; [c'b + (W - ub)\tan\phi'] \; \} \; 1/m_\alpha}{\Sigma \, W \sin\alpha} \qquad (2.19)$$

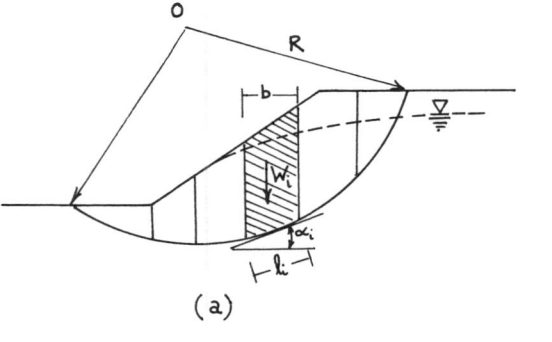

(a)

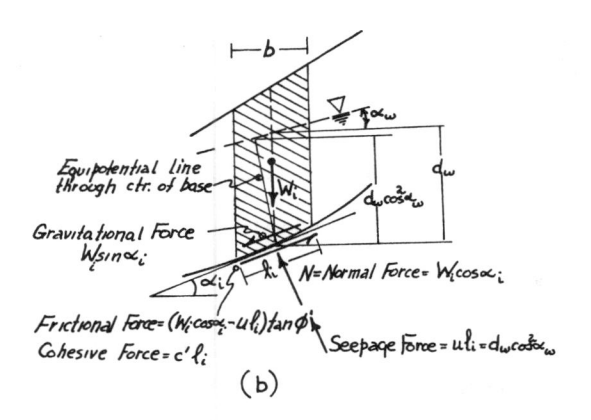

(b)

Fig. 2.17. Geometry of circular slip surface and forces on a typical slice in the method-of-slices analysis.

where:

$$m_\alpha = \cos\alpha \, [1 + (\tan\alpha \tan\frac{\phi'}{F}) \;] \qquad (2.20)$$

W = weight of individual slice
b = width of slice
α = slope angle at base of slice
u = pore water pressure at base of slice

This equation must be solved in an interative manner until the value of the safety factor (F) assumed on the right-hand side for a trial failure arc equals the value computed on the left-hand side. This procedure must be repeated for several trial failure arcs until the lowest safety factor, and hence critical failure surface, is located. Hand calculations can be made by use of tabular forms (Burroughs, et al. 1976), but solution by computer is vastly more efficient and faster. Several versions of efficient computer programs are available for solutions of Equation (2.19) (Whitman and Bailey, 1967; Little and Price, 1958).

2.7   REFERENCES CITED

Anderson, H. W. (1951). Physical characteristics of soils related to erosion, *J. Soil Water Conservation* 6(3): 129–133.

Arulanandan, K., et al. (1975). Pore and eroding fluid influences on surface erosion of soil, *J. Geotech. Engr. Div.,* ASCE, 101(GTI): 51–61.

Beer, C. E., and Johnson, H. P. (1963). Factors in gully growth in deep loess area of Western Iowa, *Trans. ASAE* 6(3): 237–240.

Bishop, A. W. (1955). Use of the slip circle in slope stability analyses, *Geotechnique* 5(1): 7–17.

Bishop, A. W., and Morgenstern, N. R. (1960). Stability coefficients for earth slopes, *Geotechnique* 10(4): 129–150.

Bowles, J. E. (1970). *Engineering Properties of Soils and Their Measurement,* New York: McGraw-Hill.

Burroughs, E. R., Chalfant, G. R., and Townsend, M. A. (1976). *Slope Stability in Road Construction,* Bur. Land Mgt., U. S. Dept. Interior, Portland, Ore., 102 pp.

Chassie, R. G., and Goughnour, R. D. (1976). National highway landslide experience, *Highway Focus* 8(1): 1–9.

Chen, W. F., and Giger, M. W. (1971). Limit analysis and stability of slopes, *J. Soil Mech. Foundations Div.,* ASCE, 97 (SMI): 19–26.

Chepil, W. S. (1945). Dynamics of wind erosion: I. Nature of movement of soil by wind, *Soil Science* 60: 305–320.

Chowdhury, R. N. (1979). *Slope Analysis,* New York: Elsevier.

Cleveland, G. B. (1977). Rapid erosion along the Eel River, California, *Calif. Geology* 30(9): 204–211.

Ellison, W. D. (1948). Erosion by raindrop, *Scientific Amer.* (Aug.): 1–7.

Emerson, W. W. (1967). A classification of soil aggregates based on their coherence in water, *Australian J. Soil Res.* 2: 211–217.

Esu, F. (1966). Short-term stability of slopes in unweathered, jointed clays, *Geotechnique* 16(4): 321–328.

Farmer, E. E. (1973). Relative detachability of soil particles by simulated rainfall, *Soil Sci. Soc. Amer. Proc.* 37(4): 629–633.

Gonsior, M. J., and Gardner, R. B. (1971). Investigation of slope failures in the Idaho Batholith, *USDA Forest Serv. Res. Paper INT-97,* 34 pp.

Hayes, W. A. (1972). Designing wind erosion control systems in the Midwest Region, *RTSC-Agron. Tech. Note LI-9,* Soil Cons. Serv., U. S. Dept. Agr., Lincoln, Neb.

Howell, R. B., et al. (1979). Analysis of short and long term effects on water quality for selected highway projects, Final Report to Calif. Dept. of Transportation, Rept. No. FHWA/CA/TL-79/17, 245 pp.

Hutchinson, J. N. (1978). Assessment of the effectiveness of corrective measures in relation to geological conditions and types of slope movement, *Bull. Intl. Assoc. Engr. Geol.* 16: 131–155.

Keown, M. P., et al. (1977). Literature survey and preliminary evaluation of streambank protection methods, *Technical Rept. H-77-9,* U. S. Army Waterways Exp. Stn., Vicksburg, Miss.

Lambe, T. W., and Whitman, R. V. (1969). *Soil Mechanics,* New York: Wiley.

Lane, E. W. (1955). The importance of fluvial morphology in hydraulic engineering, *Proc. Amer. Soc. Civil Engineers* 81(745): 1–17.

Leopold, L. B., and Maddock, T. (1954). The hydraulic geometry of stream channels and some physiographic implications, *Prof. Paper 252,* U. S. Geol. Survey, Washington, D. C.

Little, A. L., and Price, V. E. (1958). The use of an electronic computer for slope stability analysis, *Geotechnique* 8(3): 113–120.

Lull, H. W. (1959). Soil compaction on forest and range lands, *U. S. Dept. Agr. Misc. Pub. 768,* Washington, D. C.

Morgenstern, N. R., and Price, V. E. (1965). The analysis of stability of general slip surfaces, *Geotechnique* 15(1): 79–93.

Morgenstern, N. R., and Sangrey, D. A. (1978). Methods of stability analysis, in "Landslides: Analysis and Control," ed. by Schuster, R. L., and Krizek, R. J., *Trans. Res. Board Special Rept. 176,* NAS-NRC, Washington, D. C., pp. 155–171.

Paaswell, R. E. (1973). Causes and mechanisms of cohesive soil erosion: the state-of-the art, *HRB Spec. Rept. 135,* NAS-NRC, Washington, D. C., pp. 52–76.

Peck, R. (1967). Stability of natural slopes, *J. Geotech. Engr. Division,* ASCE, 93(4): 437–451.

Piest, R. F., Bradford, J. M., and Spomer, R. G. (1975). Mechanism of erosion and sediment movement from gullies, in "Present and Prospective Technology for Predicting Sediment Yields and Sources," *USDA Agric. Res. Service, ARS-S-40,* pp. 162–176.

Prellwitz, R. W. (1975). Simplified slope design for low standard roads in mountainous regions, in "Low Volume Roads," *Trans. Res. Board Spec. Rept. 160,* NAS-NRC, Washington, D. C.

Royster, D. L. (1973). Highway landslide problems along the Cumberland Plateau in Tennessee, *Bull. Assoc. Engr. Geologists* 10(4): 255–287.

Royster, D. L. (1978). Landslide remedial measures, Paper presented at 37th Annual SASHTO Convention, Nashville, Tenn.

Sandtos-Cayudo, J., and Simons, D. B. (1972). River response, in *Environmental Impacts on Rivers,* ed. by Shen, H. W., Ch. 1, Water Resource Pub., Fort Collins, Colo.

Schum, S. A. (1971). Fluvial geomorphology—the historical perspective, in *River Mechanics,* ed. by Shen, H. W., Vol. 1, Ch. 4, Water Resource Publ., Fort Collins, Colo.

Schwab, Glen O., et al. (1966). *Soil and Water Conservation Engineering,* New York: Wiley.

Sharpe, C. F. S. (1938). *Landslides and Related Phenomena: A Study of Mass Movements of Soil and Rock,* New York: Columbia University Press, 137 pp.

Sherard, J. L., Ryker, N. L., and Decker, R. S. (1972). Piping in earth dams of dispersive clay, *Proc., Spec. Conf. on Performance of Earth and Earth Supported Structures,* ASCE, Vol. 1, pp. 589–626.

Sherard, J. L., et al. (1976). Pinhole test for identifying dispersive soils, *J. Geotech. Division,* ASCE, 102(GT1): 69–85.

Singh, A. (1970). Shear strength and stability of man-made slopes, *J. Soil Mech. Foundations Div.,* ASCE, 96(SM6): 1879–1890.

Skempton, A. W., and Hutchinson, J. N. (1969). Stability of natural slopes and embankment foundations. *Proc., 7th Intl. Conf. on Soil Mech. and Foundation Engr.,* Mexico City Mexico, Vol. I, pp. 291–340.

Skidmore, E. L., and Woodruff, N. P. (1968). Wind erosion forces in the United States and their use in predicting soil loss, *Agr. Handbook 346,* U. S. Dept. Agr., Washington, D. C., 42 pp.

Taylor, D. W. (1948). *Fundamentals of Soil Mechanics,* New York: Wiley.

Thompson, J. R. (1964). Quantitative effect of watershed variables on rate of gully-head advancement, *Trans. ASAE* 7: 54–55.

U. S. Dept. of Navy (1971). *Design Manual DM-7 for Soil Mechanics, Foundations and Earth Structures,* Naval Facilities Engineering Command, Washington, D. C.

U. S. Environmental Protection Agency (1973). Comparative costs of erosion and sediment control construction activities, EPA-430/9-73-016, U. S. Govt. Printing Office, Washington, D. C.

U. S. Weather Bureau (1963). Rainfall frequency atlas for the USA for durations from 30 minutes to 24 hours and return periods from 1 to 100 years, Technical Paper No. 40, Washington, D. C.

USDA Soil Conservation Service (1972). Procedures for computing sheet and rill erosion on project areas, Technical Release No. 51, Washington, D. C., 14 pp.

USDA Soil Conservation Service (1977). Guides for erosion and sediment control in California, Misc. Publ., Davis, Calif, 32 pp.

USDA Soil Conservation Service (1978). Predicting rainfall erosion losses: a guide to conservation planning, *USDA Agric. Handbook #537,* Washington, D. C.

Varnes, D. J. (1958). Landslide types and processes, in "Landslides and Engineering Practice," ed. by Eckel, E. B., *HRB Spec. Rept. 29,* NAS-NRC, Washington, D. C., pp. 20–47.

Varnes, D. J. (1978). Slope movement types and processes, in "Landslides: Analysis and Control," ed. by Schuster, R. L., and Krizek, R. J., *Trans. Res. Board Spec. Rept. 176,* NAS-NRC, Washington, D. C., pp. 12–33.

Volk, G. M. (1937). Method of determining the degree of dispersion of the clay fraction of soils, *Proc. Soil Sci. Soc. Amer.,* pp. 432–445.

Whitman, R. V., and Bailey, W. A. (1967). Use of computers for slope stability analysis, *J. Soil Mech. Foundations Div.,* ASCE, 93(SM4): 475–498.

Wilson, L. (1975). Application of the wind erosion equation in air pollution surveys, *J. Soil Water Conservation* 30(5): 215–219.

Wineland, J. D. (1975). Borehole shear device, *Proc., GT-ASCE Speciality Conference on In-Situ Measurement of Soil Properties,* Raleigh, N.C., Vol. 1, pp. 511–522.

Wischmeier, W. H., and Smith, D. D. (1958). Rainfall energy and its relationship to soil loss, *Trans. Amer. Geophysical Union* 39(2): 285–291.

Wischmeier, W. H., and Smith, D. D. (1965). Predicting rainfall-erosion losses from cropland east of the Rocky Mountains. *Agr. Handbook No. 282,* U. S. Govt. Printing Ofc., Washington, D. C., 47 pp.

Wischmeir, W. H., Johnson, C. B., and Cross, B. V. (1971). A soil erodibility monograph for farmland and construction sites, *J. Soil Water Conservation* 26(5): 189–193.

Woodruff, N. P., and Siddoway, F. H. (1965). A wind erosion equation, *Soil Sci. Soc. Amer. Proc.* 29(5): 602–608.

Wright, S. G. (1973). Accuracy of equilibrium slope stability analysis, *J. Soil Mech. Foundations Div.,* ASCE, 99(SM10): 783–790.

Zaruba, Q., and Mencl, V. (1969). *Landslides and Their Control,* New York: Elsevier, and Prague: Academia, 205 pp.

3
Role of Vegetation in the Stability and Protection of Slopes

3.1 HYDRO-MECHANICAL INFLUENCES OF VEGETATION

3.1.1 Prevention of Soil Erosion

The use of vegetation, primarily grasses and forbs, for preventing surficial erosion on slopes is fairly common and well understood. The U. S. Soil Conservation Service and similar government agencies around the world have long advocated plantings to control both rainfall and wind erosion. The factors governing rainfall and wind erosion are discussed in detail in Chapter 2. One of the most important factors was shown to be the type and extent of vegetative cover.

Major effects of herbaceous, and to a lesser extent woody vegetation in controlling erosion include:

1. *Interception*—foliage and plant residues absorb rainfall energy and prevent soil compaction from raindrops.
2. *Restraint*—root system physically binds or restrains soil particles while above-ground residues filter sediment out of runoff.
3. *Retardation*—above-ground residues increase surface roughness and slow velocity of runoff.
4. *Infiltration*—roots and plant residues help maintain soil porosity and permeability.
5. *Transpiration*—depletion of soil moisture by plants delays onset of saturation and runoff.

3.1.2 Prevention of Mass-Movement

Vegetation, primarily woody plants, also helps to prevent mass-movement, particularly shallow sliding in slopes. This role is not so well understood and appreciated. The factors affecting slope stability were grouped by Varnes (1958) into those tending to increase shear stress and those tending to reduce shear resistance (Table 2.10). This tabulation provides a basis for examining the likely influence of vegetation on slope stability. Possible ways woody vegetation might affect the balance of forces in a slope include:

1. *Root reinforcement*—roots mechanically reinforce a soil by transfer of shear stresses in the soil to tensile resistance in the roots.
2. *Soil moisture modification*—evapotranspiration and interception in the foliage limit buildup of soil moisture stress. Vegetation also affects rate of snowmelt, which in turn affects soil moisture regime.
3. *Buttressing and arching*—anchored and embedded stems can act as buttress piles or arch abutments in a slope, counteracting shear stresses.
4. *Surcharge*—weight of vegetation on a slope exerts both a downslope (destabilizing) stress and a stress component perpendicular to the slope which tends to increase resistance to sliding.
5. *Root wedging*—alleged tendency of roots to invade cracks, fissures, and channels in a soil or rock mass and thereby cause local instability by a wedging or prying action.
6. *Windthrowing*—destabilizing influence from turning moments exerted on a slope as a result of strong winds blowing downslope through trees.

The first three effects or influences, i.e., root reinforcement, soil moisture depletion, and buttressing, enhance slope stability. The fourth, surcharge, may have either a beneficial or adverse impact depending on soil or slope conditions. These hydro-mechanical influences are examined in greater detail in the rest of the chapter.

The last two, wind throwing and root wedging, on the other hand, are likely to affect stability adversely. Strong winds blowing parallel to the ground surface will exert an overturning moment on trees. This can lead to so called wind throwing or blowdowns which create localized disturbances in the soil mantle. Wind throwing is a fairly common occurrence in some forests but it affects mainly aged or diseased trees. The total downslope force created by a wind blowing through a stand of trees, and hence its overall effect on slope stability, has never been evaluated. Brown and Sheu (1975) in their study of the effects of deforestation on slopes have outlined a theoretical framework for analyzing wind forces in trees.

The importance or significance of root wedging, an alleged tendency of roots to penetrate a soil or rock mass along cracks, fissures, and channels thereby loosening and prying it apart likewise is unknown. Root wedging was alleged to have contributed to the failure of Kelly Barnes dam in Toccoa, Georgia (Shaw, 1978). Evidence for this effect is scant and unconvincing. An equally good case can be made for the beneficial influence of roots in tying the earth dam structure together and mitigating the failure. In any event, judging by the preponderance of evidence from published field and laboratory studies, the beneficial effects of root systems far outweigh any possible adverse effects.

The neglect of the role of woody vegetation (and in some instances its outright dismissal) in stabilizing slopes and reinforcing soils is surprising. This is particularly so in light of increased interest in and successful applications of reinforced earth concepts. Literally hundreds of "reinforced earth structures" have been built around the world and are performing satisfactorily. The method, which was developed and patented by Henri Vidal (1969), basically consists of placing metallic reinforcing strips in a matrix of granular soil (Fig. 3.1). Nature of course has been reinforcing soil for ages with live roots of plants. This fact was not lost on Vidal, who was inspired to develop his reinforced earth concepts by observing the performance and behavior of sand pedestals reinforced with pine needles.

Yet another example of man emulating natural, bio-reinforcement of a soil is a system known as "reticulated root piles" (Lizzi, 1978). Reticulated root piles have been used to stabilize landslides and unsafe slopes. The system essentially consists of placing a criss-crossing array of small-diameter, cast-in-place reinforced concrete piles in a slope so that the pile–soil matrix is tied together in a unitary mass (Fig. 3.2). The analogy to tree roots is self-evident.

Tree roots are not as strong as steel strips and reinforced concrete. On the other hand, it is not simply the

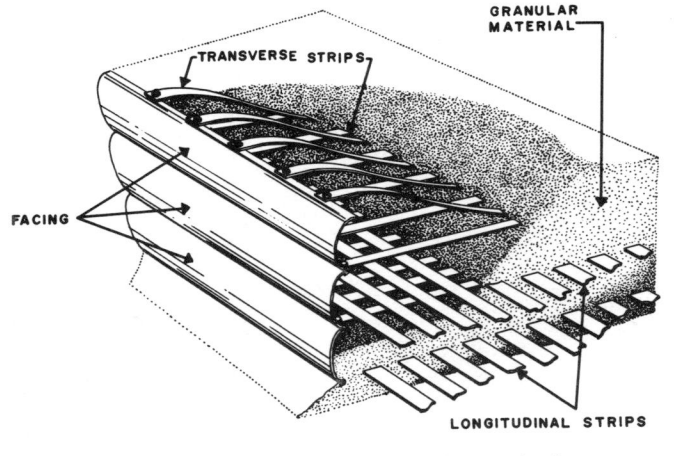

Fig. 3.1. Earth structure reinforced with metal strips.

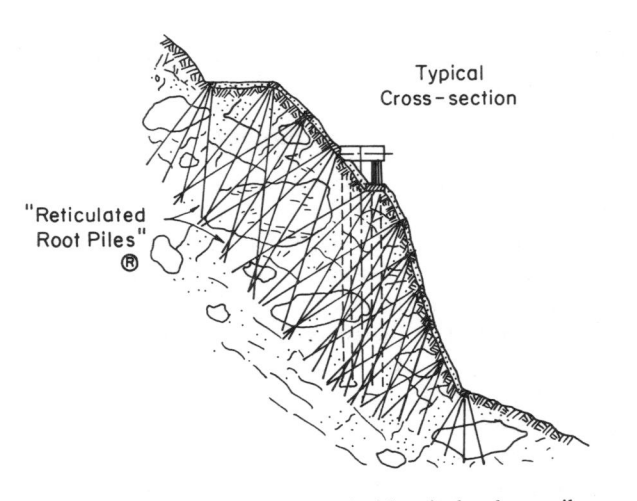

Fig. 3.2. Slope mass reinforced with reticulated root piles.

tensile strength that counts, but also the amount of friction transfer that occurs along the length of the reinforcement. In addition, plant roots do not corrode; instead they tend to be self-repairing and regenerating. Roots also tend to respond to unfavorable stress conditions at a site, either topographic or hydrologic, in a self-corrective manner through a remarkable bio-adaptive process termed "edaphoecotropism" (Vanicek, 1973). This process allows roots to escape unfavorable site conditions by a shaping or reorientation of the root system. Edaphoecotropic orientation of main root branches in trees and shrubs is important both in the safe anchoring of plants in the soil and conversely in increasing the stability of the soil or slope anchorage itself.

As noted previously, it is primarily deep-rooted, woody vegetation (trees and shrubs) that provides or contributes to slope stability. But, even herbaceous vegetation (grasses and forbs) can indirectly benefit deep-seated, mass stability by depleting soil moisture, attenuating depth of frost penetration, and stabilizing the soil against surficial erosion, thus facilitating the establishment of shrubs and trees.

To the extent that woody vegetation enhances stability of slopes, conversely its removal can trigger or increase the frequency of slope movements. The preponderance of evidence from studies from around the world convincingly demonstrates a cause-and-effect relationship between vegetation removal and increased slope failures. This evidence is reviewed briefly at the end of the chapter. Such a finding has significant implications in forestry operations, vegetation clearance for transportation routes, and other land uses that entail large-scale felling and removal of timber from unstable slopes.

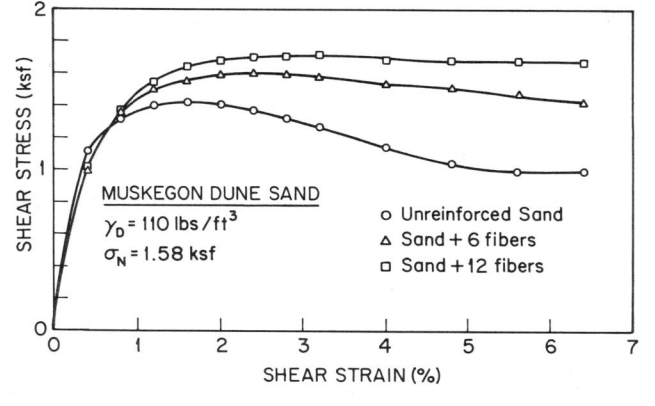

Fig. 3.3. Stress–strain response under shear of unreinforced soil vs. soil-fiber composite. Dune sand reinforced with 1.75-mm-diameter reed fibers.

3.2 ROOT REINFORCEMENT

The most obvious way in which woody vegetation stabilizes soils is by root reinforcement. The intermingled, lateral roots of plants tend to bind the soil together in a monolithic mass. On slopes, the vertical root system (i.e., the main taproot and secondary sinker roots) can penetrate through the soil mantle into firmer strata below (e.g., fractured or disintegrated bedrock), thus anchoring the soil to the slope and increasing resistance to sliding. Improved understanding about the role of roots in strengthening and reinforcing soils has come about as a result of recent theories of reinforced earth (Vidal, 1969; Schlosser and Long, 1974), as a result of theoretical models of fiber–soil reinforcement (Wu, 1976; Waldron, 1977), and as a result of field and laboratory direct shear tests of root-reinforced soil (Endo and Tsuruta, 1969; Waldron, 1977; Kassif and Kopelovitz, 1968).

3.2.1 Mechanics of Root Reinforcement

A root- or fiber-reinforced soil behaves as a composite material in which elastic fibers of relatively high tensile strength are embedded in a matrix of relatively plastic soil. Additional strength is mobilized within the composite material by the development of tractive forces between the fibers and surrounding matrix. In other words, shear stresses in the soil mobilize tensile resistance in the fibers, which in turn imparts greater strength to the soil. The net effect of fiber reinforcement on the stress–strain response of soils is to increase the shear strength of the soil, as shown by results of direct shear tests (Fig. 3.3). Another important effect is to make some soils tougher, that is, able to resist continued deformation without loss of residual strength (see also Fig. 3.3).

The increase in shear strength and stiffness of fiber-reinforced soils has been interpreted in two different ways. The first views the action of the linear reinforcing elements (fibers) in a soil as fundamentally that of anisotropic reduction of strain rate in the direction of reinforcement (Fig. 3.4). This restraint is equivalent to an increase in confining stress in the direction of reduced or suppressed strain. The increased confining stress (or "equivalent confining stress increase") in turn mobilizes additional shear resistance beyond that which would be mobilized by the externally applied confining stress alone. The *equivalent* confining stress increase is essentially proportional to the *applied* confining stress up to a limit defined as the "critical confining stress" (Yang and Singh, 1974). At that point the equivalent or mobilized confining stress levels off, and remains fairly constant. The significance of this finding is that, provided the applied confining stress exceeds a certain level, viz., the critical confining stress; the increased shear resistance from the reinforcement will be constant. The critical confining stress is a function of various properties of the

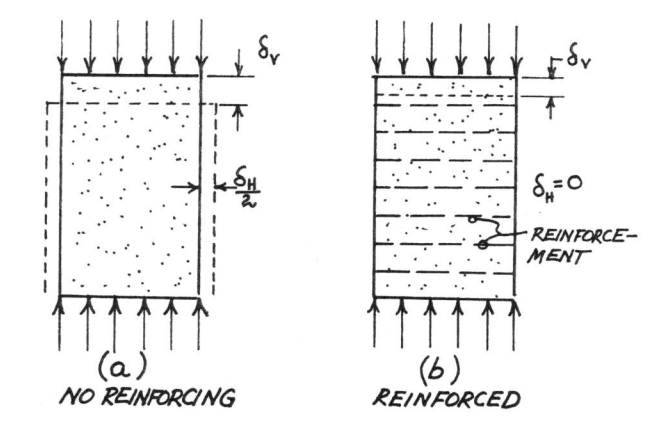

Fig. 3.4. Effect of linear reinforcement in suppressing strain in the direction of reinforcement.

soil–fiber system such as the tensile strength and modulus of the fibers, length/diameter ratio of fibers, and frictional characteristics of the fibers and soil.

A second interpretation of fiber reinforcement is that the fibers impart "pseudo-cohesion" to a soil. This view is useful but theoretically inexact in the case of unidirectional and hence anisotropic action of fibers or other reinforcement. True cohesion is not a directional property. The notion of pseudo- or apparent cohesion probably arises from the observation that fiber reinforcement appears to have little or no influence on friction angles measured in a soil during direct shear tests. The main effect is to displace the shear or failure envelope upward, thus providing additional cohesion (Fig. 3.5). But even in this case it has been observed that at low confining stress the shear envelope is either curved (Schlosser and Long, 1974) or not coincident with the failure envelope at higher confining stress. This behavior is clearly demonstrated in the results of direct shear tests on a dry, dune sand reinforced with two different lengths of a natural, palmyra fiber (Fig. 3.5). The test results in Fig. 3.5 show that a threshhold or critical confining stress must be equal or exceeded in order to mobilize the maximum contribution from fiber reinforcement. In this particular case the critical confining stress is a function of fiber length; but in the general case is also likely to be a function of other fiber properties and parameters (e.g., length/diameter ratio, tensile strength and modulus, and skin friction).

Thus, even the second interpretation of the mechanism of fiber reinforcement is incomplete without recourse to the concept of an equivalent confining stress increase.

3.2.2 Theoretical Models of Root-Reinforced Soil

Theoretical models have been proposed to predict the influence of unidirectional reinforcement of soils by both fibers and strips. A number of simplifying assumptions are invoked in these models, and they have only been tested under a limited range of conditions to date.

A simple model of a fiber-reinforced soil subject to direct shear was developed independently by Waldron (1977), Wu (1976), and Brenner and James (1977). This model assumes a flexible, elastic root extending vertically across a planar shear zone (Fig. 3.6). The model is an idealization of the case in which vertical roots (taproots and sinker roots) extend across a potential sliding surface in a slope (Fig. 3.7). The initial orientation of the roots with respect to the failure surface is assumed to be perpendicular.

According to this model, the tensile force that develops in the fibers (or roots) when the soil is sheared can be resolved into a tangential component which directly resists shear and a normal component which increases the confining stress on the shear plane. The model tacitly assumes that the tensile strength of the fibers is fully mobilized (i.e., they break in tension rather than pulling

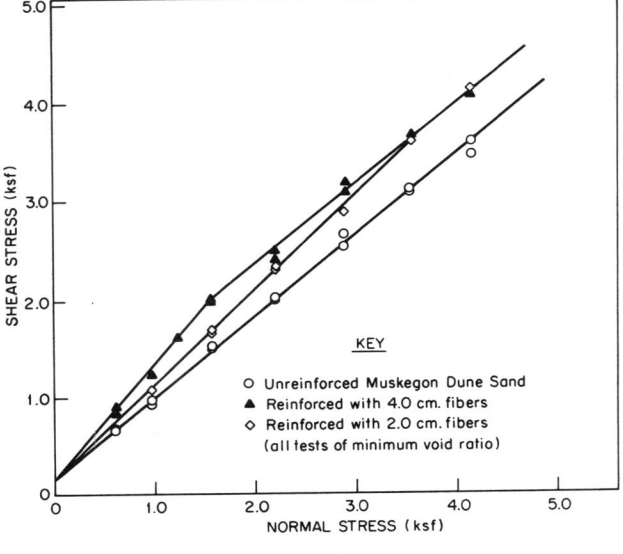

Fig. 3.5. Influence of fiber reinforcement (palmyra) on shear strength envelopes of dry, Muskegon dune sand. Fiber area ratio $(A_R/A) = 0.50\%$. Fiber orientation is initially perpendicular to shear plane.

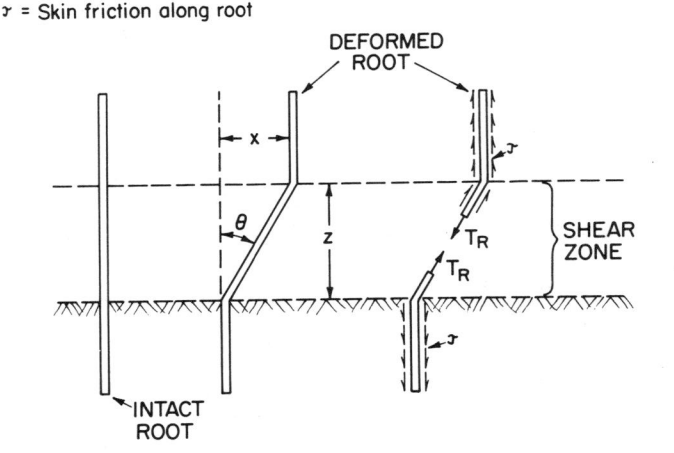

Fig. 3.6. Perpendicular root reinforcement model. Flexible elastic root is aligned perpendicularly to shear surface at start.

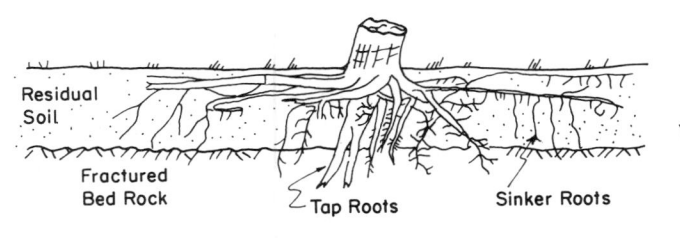

Fig. 3.7. Schematic illustration of root system of tree showing main taproots and sinker roots extending vertically downward.

$$t_R = T_R \frac{\Sigma n_i a_i}{A} \qquad (3.2b)$$

where:

n_i = number of roots in size class i

a_i = mean cross-sectional area of roots in size class i, in^2

A = area of soil in sample count, in^2

out). The soil friction angle (ϕ) is assumed to be unaffected by the reinforcement. Mathematically, this mobilization of tensile resistance in the fibers translates into a shear strength increase in the soil given by the following equation:

$$\Delta S_R = t_R [\cos\theta \tan\phi + \sin\theta] \qquad (3.1)$$

where:

ΔS_R = shear strength increase from root or fiber
reinforcement, psi

θ = angle of shear distortion

ϕ = angle of internal friction

t_R = average tensile strength of fibers (roots) *per unit area of soil*, psi

The average tensile strength of fibers or roots per unit area of soil (t_R) can be determined by multiplying the average tensile strength of the roots (T_R) by the fraction of the soil cross section filled or occupied by roots (A_R/A). Thus:

$$t_R = T_R (A_R/A) \qquad (3.2a)$$

where:

T_R = average tensile strength of roots, psi
(A_R/A) = root area ratio or fraction of soil cross-sectional area occupied by roots

This is a useful and important relationship because it states that the maximum possible root contribution to soil strength can be estimated from measuring the tensile strength of the roots (T_R) and the fraction of the soil cross-sectional area along a potential sliding surface occupied by roots (A_R/A). The root cross-sectional area (A_R) can be found by counting the number of roots in different size classes (n_i) in a given soil cross-sectional area (A) and then summing the product of the root numbers in each size class times their corresponding mean cross-sectional area (a_i) for that size class:

Actual root density studies or measurement of root area ratios for different soils and tree species have been made by Burrough and Thomas (1977), Wu (1976), and Megahan et al. (1978). The linear relationship in Equation (3.2) between root tensile strength per unit area of soil and root area ratio has been validated by Waldron (1977) for herbaceous plant roots (barley and alfalfa) and Wu (1976) for woody plants (spruce and hemlock).

In the case of natural root systems, the tensile strength tends to vary with the size or diameter of the root (see Section 3.2.3). Accordingly, the root tensile strength term should be included inside the summation sign and the average root tensile strength per unit area of soil computed from the following relationship:

$$t_r = \frac{\Sigma T_i n_i a_i}{A} \qquad (3.2c)$$

where T_i = tensile strength of roots in size class i, psi.

Equations (3.1) and (3.2) provide a basis for estimating the contribution of roots to soil strength. The only uncertain or indeterminate variable in the equations is the angle of shear distortion (θ). This angle will vary with the amount of lateral shear displacement (x) and the thickness of the shear zone (z).

From results of laboratory direct shear tests conducted by Waldron (1977) on various root-permeated soils, the angles of shear distortion varied between 40 and 50 degrees. From results of field observations by Wu (1976) of failures in root-permeated soil masses on slopes, the angle appeared to vary at most between 45 and 70 degrees. By running a parametric variation or sensitivity analysis on Equation (3.1), Wu showed that the bracketed term is relatively insensitive to all expected values of either friction angle (ϕ) or shear distortion angle (θ). The bracketed term varied only from 1.0 to 1.3 for $25° < \phi < 40°$ and $40° < \theta < 70°$ (Fig. 3.8). Thus assuming the midpoint of the range to be the most probable value for the bracketed term, the maximum shear strength increase from root or fiber reinforcement (ΔS_R) may be estimated to an average or first approximation simply by:

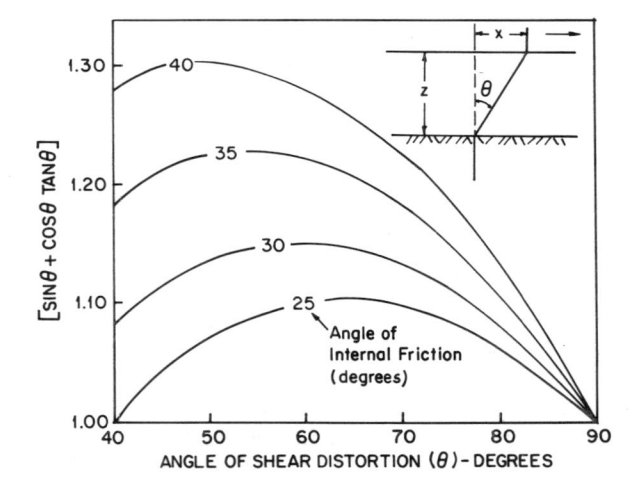

Fig. 3.8. Range in bracketed term of the perpendicular root reinforcement equation with expected variation in angle of internal friction (ϕ) and angle of shear distortion (θ).

$$\Delta S_R \approx 1.15 t_R \qquad (3.3a)$$

or
$$\Delta S_R \approx 1.15 T_R (A_R/A) \qquad (3.3b)$$

or
$$\Delta S_R \approx 1.15 \frac{\Sigma T_i n_i a_i}{A} \qquad (3.3c)$$

This relationship is employed later in this chapter (Section 3.2.5) to examine the contribution and significance of root reinforcement to the stability of actual slopes.

As noted previously, the root reinforcement model assumes that the tensile strength of the fibers or roots is fully mobilized during failure. This requires that the roots are long enough and/or frictional enough so that the frictional bond between roots and soil matrix exceeds the tensile strength of the roots. The minimum length (L_{min}) of fibers of uniform size (d_R) required to mobilize full tensile resistance and prevent pullout is given by the following expression:

$$L_{min} > \frac{T_R d_R}{2 \tau'_R} \qquad (3.4)$$

where:

L_{min} = minimum length to mobilize tensile strength of fibers during shear, in

d_R = diameter of fibers, in

T_R = tensile strength of fiber (or root), psi

τ'_R = maximum tangential shear stress or pullout resistance between fiber and soil, psi

For fiber lengths less than the value calculated in Equation (3.4), the root or fiber will slip or pull out before breaking in tension. Evidence for full mobilization of tensile resistance has been found from field examination of broken, exposed roots in shear planes of landslides (Wu, 1976; Megahan et al., 1978).

The root reinforcement model (Fig. 3.6) assumes that the roots are initially oriented perpendicular to the shear surface. In nature plant roots may be inclined at many different angles to a sliding or failure surface. What is the effect of orientations other than perpendicular?

Initial orientation of the fibers perpendicular to the shear surface does not yield the maximum strength increase. The optimal position occurs when the reinforcement is inclined initially at an angle equal to $45 + \phi/2$ degrees to the shear surface. This can be demonstrated both theoretically and experimentally.

A more generalized model of a fiber-reinforced soil is shown in Fig. 3.9. This model takes the initial inclination of the fibers (i) into account. The shear strength increase in this case is given by the following equations:

$$\Delta S_R = t_R [\sin(90 - \psi) + \cos(90 - \psi) \tan \phi] \qquad (3.5)$$

$$\psi = \tan^{-1} \frac{1}{k + (\tan i)^{-1}} \qquad (3.6)$$

where:

i = initial inclination of fibers with respect to shear plane

x = lateral displacement

z = thickness of shear zone

k = shear distortion ratio ($= x/z$)

The bracketed expression in Equation (3.5) is shown plotted in Fig. 3.10 for various values of initial inclination (i) and shear distortion ratio (k). Maximum values of the bracked expression (and hence shear strength increase) occur at fiber inclinations close to $45 + \phi/2$. This corresponds to an inclination of 60 degrees in a typical sand with friction angle (ϕ) of 30 degrees.

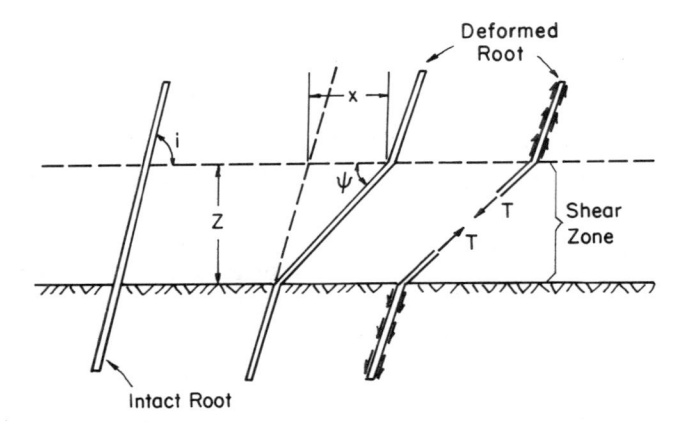

Fig. 3.9. Inclined root reinforcement model. Flexible, elastic root extends across shear surface at arbitrary angle (i) at start.

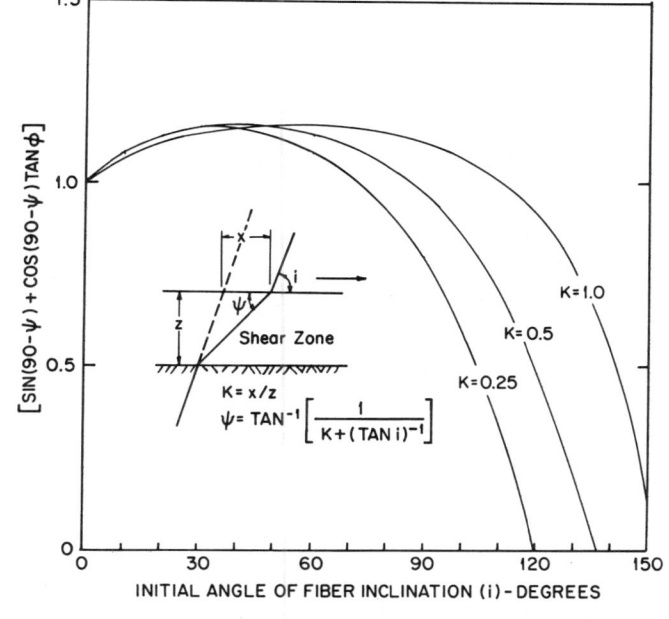

Fig. 3.10. Range in bracketed term in the inclined root reinforcement equation with variation in the angle of inclination (i) and shear distortion ratio (k). Friction angle (ϕ) is assumed to be 30°.

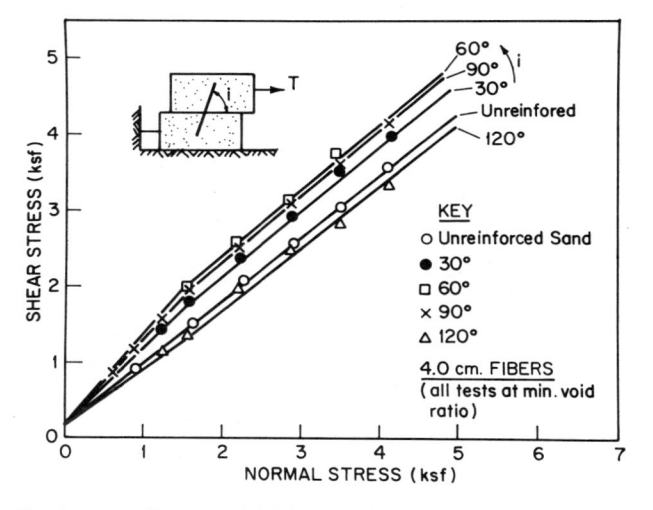

Fig. 3.11. Influence of initial fiber orientation on the shear strength envelopes of dry, Muskegon dune sand. Fiber area ratio (A_R/A) = 0.50%. Fiber length (L) = 4 cm.

When the initial angle of inclination exceeds 90 degrees, a shear strength decrease may occur, depending on the initial angle of inclination (i) and shear distortion ratio (k). This is reasonable because for inclinations greater than 90 degrees and small shear distortion ratios, the fibers may go into compression and hinder, rather than enhance, shear resistance in the soil.

These theoretical predictions are corroborated by results of direct shear tests on dry sands reinforced with fibers initially oriented at different angles to the failure plane (Fig. 3.11). Both theory and experiment indicate little difference, however, for fibers inclined at angles between 30 and 90 degrees to the shear plane. Accordingly, the simpler, vertical reinforcement model (Fig. 3.6 and Equation 3.3) should provide satisfactory estimates for root or fiber reinforcement of a soil. It must be emphasized, however, that these predictions are based on full mobilization of the tensile strength of the fibers. Even if the fibers are long enough to resist pullout, it does not follow that the full tensile strength of the fibers will be mobilized. The fibers must also be rigid enough (i.e., have a high enough tensile modulus) that maximum tensile resistance in the fiber is mobilized more or less concurrently with the peak shear resistance in the soil.

3.2.3 Root Morphology and Strength

The development and structure of root systems are controlled in general by their genetic character as well as by the rooting environment. The importance of hereditary factors in controlling root development can be seen where a number of species grow side by side in the same soil (Fig. 3.12). Some species develop taproot systems, whereas others develop fibrous root masses.

The depth and extent of branching of roots are important in choosing plants for soil stabilization and watershed cover. According to the root reinforcement model examined in the previous section, soil rooting strength is favored by a high concentration of long, flexible roots per unit volume of soil and a relatively high tensile strength in the roots. Deep-rooted species are preferable for stabilizing soil and increasing resistance to sliding on slopes.

Kozlowski (1971) observed that root structure as well as depth and rate of growth are markedly influenced by the rooting environment. Root development may be affected by local soil and site conditions such as moisture availability, temperature, nutrient status, and mechanical impedance. Differentiation in root development and structure can occur within representatives of a single species growing in different environments (Fig. 3.13).

The root system of woody plants, trees, and shrubs usually consists of both a lateral root system and a central, vertical root system (Fig. 3.7). Secondary vertical or near-vertical roots called sinkers may also grow down from the laterals. Although the lateral roots play a role in binding the soil on a slope together in a unitary mass, the main resistance to sliding on hillslopes is provided by vertical roots. Some tree species are predisposed by heredity toward development of deep, central taproots; others are not. This development can be affected by environmental factors, as noted. Trees such as ponderosa pine (*Pinus ponderosa* Doug. ex P Laws.) tend to have extensive lateral and vertical root system development as illustrated

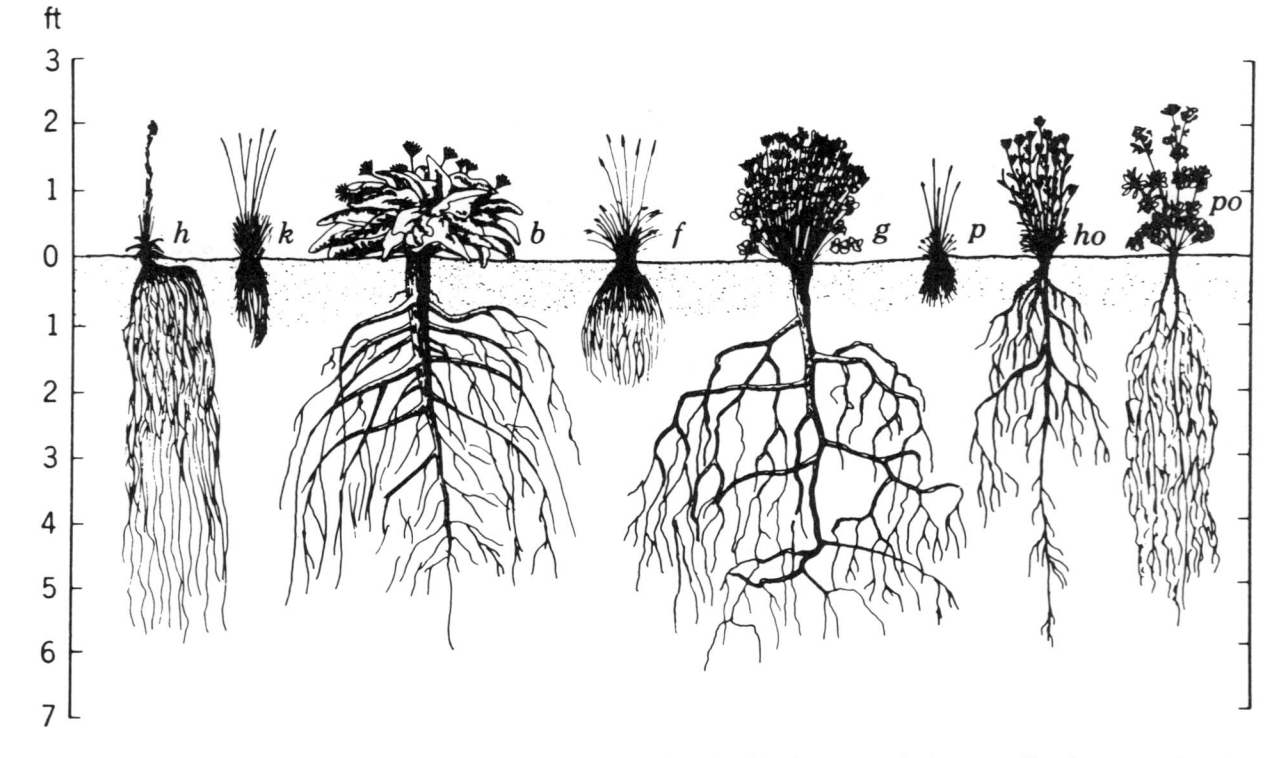

Fig. 3.12. Differences in spread and depth of root systems of various species of prairie plants grown in the same soil environment. (*From Weaver, 1919*). Reproduced from *Soil Water Plant Relationships* by Kramer. Used with the permission of McGraw-Hill Book Company.

in the photograph in Fig. 3.14 and as shown diagrammatically in Fig. 3.15.

Unfortunately, there have been few comprehensive studies of root development, structure, and *strength* for different species of trees. Root morphology studies for some tree species have been reported by Kozlowski (1971), McGinn (1963), Curtis (1964), and Sutton (1969). Techniques for studying the growth, development, and structure of tree root systems are described by Sutton (1969) and Böhm (1979). Hydraulic excavation was used by both Curtis (1964) and McGinn (1963) to determine the structure and distribution of the roots of ponderosa pine (*Pinus ponderosa*) and Douglas fir (*Pseudotsuga menziesii* (Mirb.) Franco) respectively.

Because of oxygen requirements, roots of most trees tend to be concentrated near the surface. Studies by Patric et al. (1965) in a loblolly pine plantation showed that 80–90 percent of the roots in their tests plots were concentrated in the first 3 ft. The bulk of these near-surface roots were laterals; in contrast, roots below 3 ft were oriented vertically. In a few of their plots, vertical roots were excavated at depths up to 18 ft.

In addition to oxygen requirements, plants need water. The stratigraphy and water-holding capacity of a soil are particularly important in this regard. Roots tend to avoid regions of high moisture stress and invade or permeate

moist zones. In the case of slopes characterized by shallow, coarse-textured residual soils overlying fractured bed rock (typical of slopes in granitic terrain) the most favorable region for roots to exploit from both an anchorage and a moisture standpoint is the contact between the residual soil and the underlying fractured bedrock (see Fig. 3.7). In other words, one should expect a fairly high concentration of and penetration across the contact by vertical roots. This expectation was partly confirmed by McMinn (1963) in his extensive study of the characteristics of Douglas fir root systems. Hydraulic excavation of root systems in Douglas fir stands of different ages revealed a pronounced tendency toward steeply inclined or downward root penetration not only from the central, deep-root system, but also from semivertical roots (sinkers) growing from laterals. This trend was most pronounced in older tree stands.

The tensile strength of roots for different root diameters and tree species have been investigated by Swanston and Walkotten (1970), Wu (1976), Burroughs and Thomas (1977), and Turmanina (1965). Results of these studies are summarized in Table 3.1; all show tensile strength decreasing with increasing root size for diameters up to 15 mm. Both Wu (1976) and Burroughs and Thomas (1977) measured the concentration and distribution of roots of different sizes in a soil cross sec-

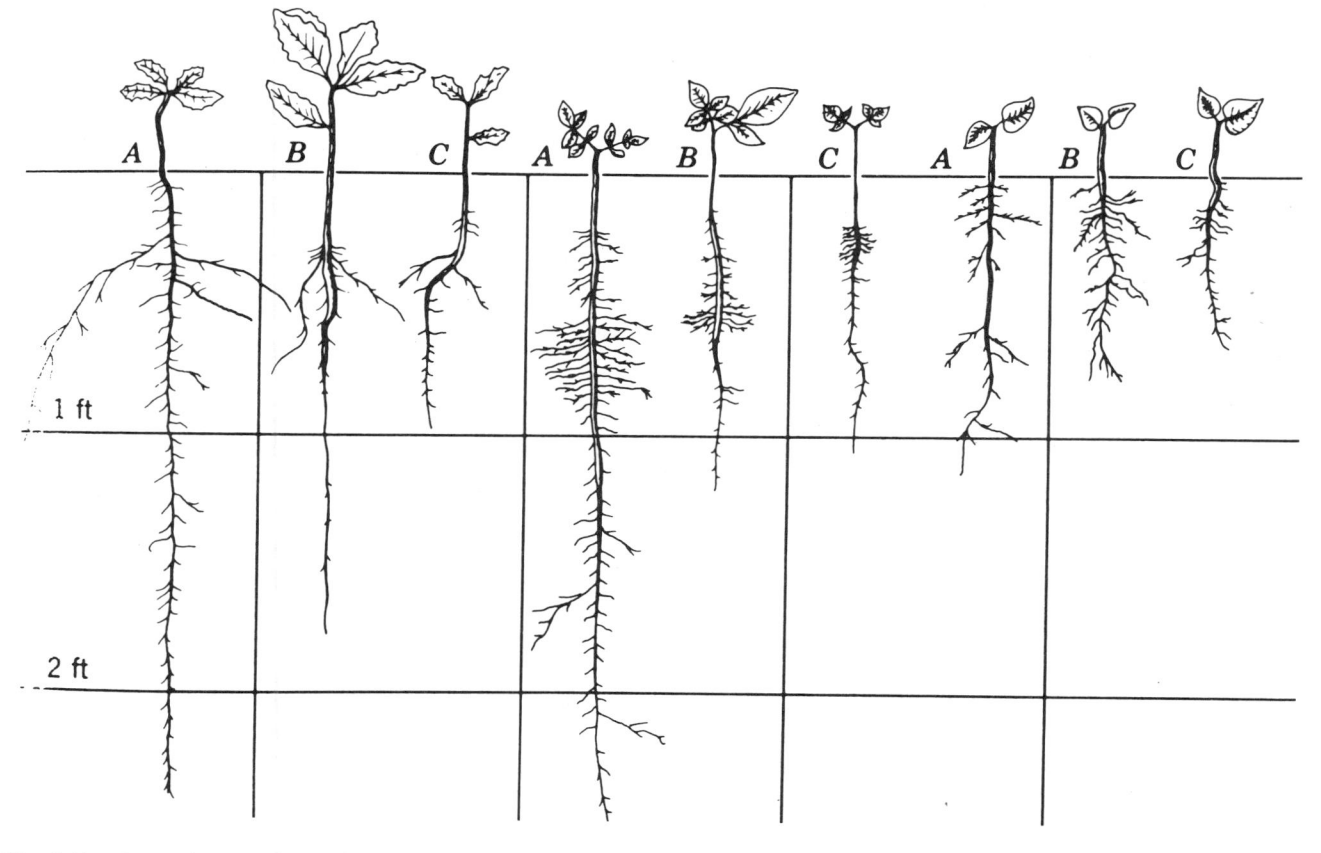

Fig. 3.13. Interaction of heredity and environment on root development by seedlings of three tree species grown in three different environments. (*From Holch, 1931*). Reproduced from *Soil Water Plant Relationships* by Kramer. Used with the permission of McGraw-Hill Book Company.

Fig. 3.14. Root system of ponderosa pine tree (*Pinus ponderosa* Laws) exposed in a road cut in granitic terrain showing development of extensive vertical and lateral root system.

tion. The former measured the distribution of vertical roots (spruce and hemlock) in a horizontal plane at a contact between the "B" and "C" soil horizons, and the latter the distribution or concentration of lateral roots

Table 3.1. Tensile strength of fresh roots of different tree species.

Tree species	Root Diam., MM	Root Tensile Strength		
		PSI	KG/CM²	Ave. all size classes, KG/CM²
Rocky Mt. Douglas fir	2	3285	231	
(from Burroughs and	4	3226	227	191
Thomas, 1977)	6	2579	181	
	8	2349	165	
	10	2152	151	
Coastal Douglas fir	2	8214	578	
(from Burroughs and	4	8504	598	510
Thomas, 1977)	6	6846	481	
	8	6482	456	
	10	6243	439	
Spruce–hemlock	2	1450	102	
(from Wu, 1976)	4	1390	98	99
	6	1380	97	
Birch	≤2	6600	464	
(from Turmanina,	2–7	3170	223	382
1965)	7–15	—	—	
	>15	6560	460	

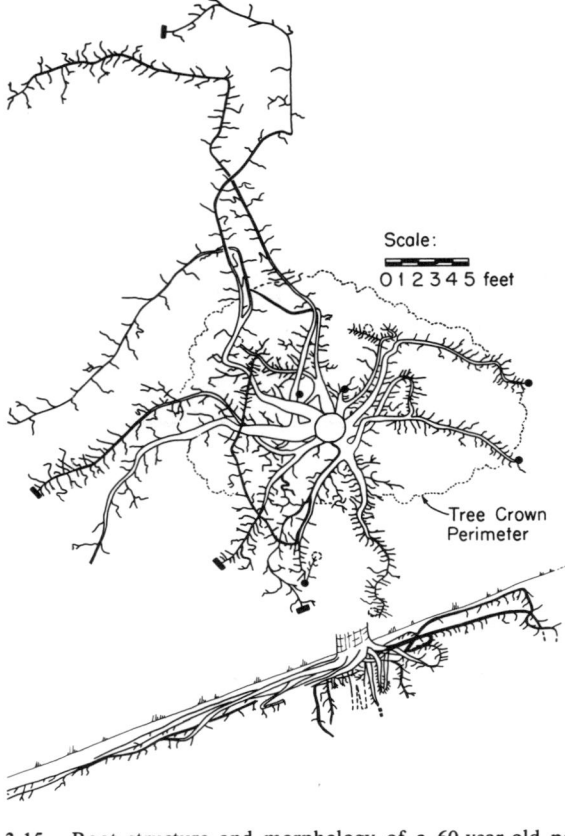

Fig. 3.15. Root structure and morphology of a 60-year-old ponderosa pine tree. (*From Curtis, 1964*)

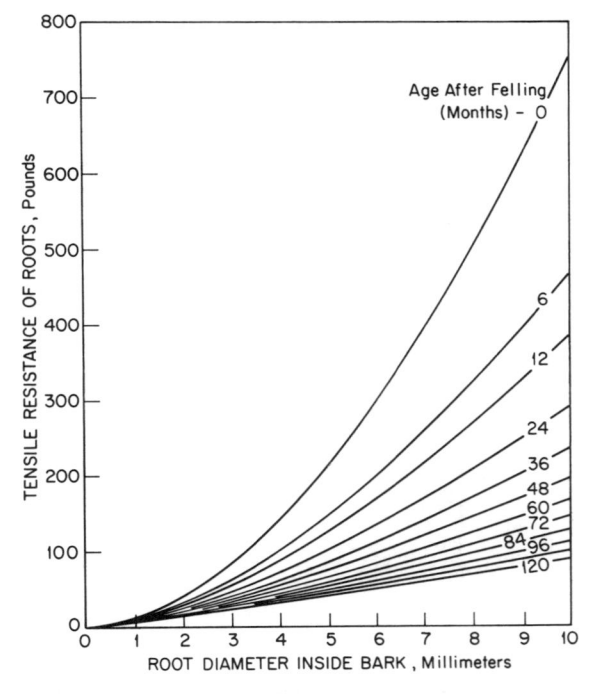

Fig. 3.16. Tensile resistance of roots of Pacific Coast Douglas fir as a function of age and size of root. (*From Burroughs and Thomas, 1977*)

(Douglas fir) in a vertical plane or trench midway between trees.

Swanston and Walkotten (1970) and more recently Burroughs and Thomas (1977) measured the decline in strength of roots with age or time after cutting. The tensile resistance of roots as a function of age and root size for both the Rocky Mountain and Pacific Coast species of Douglas fir (*Pseudotsuga menziesii*) is shown plotted in Figs. 3.16 and 3.17. A pronounced decrease in root strength with time can be observed, with the decline being more rapid in the Pacific Coast species. The results of laboratory tests by Burroughs and Thomas (1977) show that the roots of Pacific Coast Douglas fir lose 50 percent of their strength after 1 year. Four years after felling, a 1-cm root has lost 75 percent of its fresh strength. In contrast, a 1-cm-diameter Rocky Mountain Douglas fir root, which is weaker initially (see Table 3.1), lost only 10 percent of its fresh strength 4 years after felling. In addition to this loss of root strength with time after cutting of the tree, the smaller roots also tended to disappear from the soil, thus leading to a simultaneous reduction in root area ratio (A_R/A) with age. With this type of information plus the root reinforcement model previously described, it is possible to assess the impact of clear-cutting or felling of woody vegetation on slope stability, at least insofar as its effect on shear strength of the soil over time is concerned.

Several investigators have looked into the role and effectiveness of tree roots in stabilizing soil on steep slopes and the time required for root decay to cause slope failures. Bishop and Stevens (1964) and Swanston and Walkotten (1970) conclude that the effectiveness of rooting as a factor in soil shear strength decreases with age, and that soils on oversteepened slopes reach their minimum effective strength due to root anchorage approximately 5 years after cutting. This conclusion is based on observations of slopes supporting old-growth Sitka spruce–western hemlock stands of timber. Megahan et al. (1978) examined the influence of various site factors on the frequency of occurrence of landslides in the Northern Rocky Mountain region. Landslide hazard was observed to increase following vegetation removal because of root decay in direct proportion to the amount of vegetation removed. On average, landslide hazards were greatest 4 years after timber removal and remained high up to about 10 years. By the end of 20 years, landslide hazards returned to their pre-disturbance levels. Rice and Krammes (1970) suggest a more slowly deteriorating site with respect to slope failures, attributable by implication to more gradual loss of rooting strength following felling of slope vegetation. Their view is based on observations of logged areas in the north coast

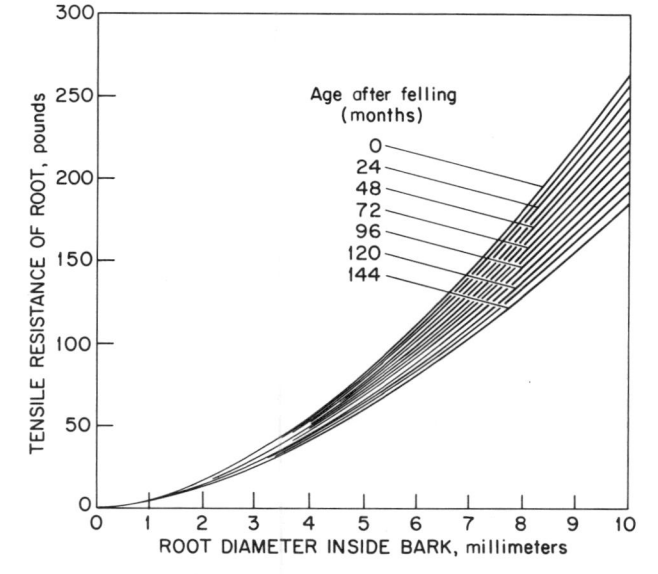

Fig. 3.17. Tensile resistance of roots of Rocky Mountain Douglas fir as a function of age and size of root. (*From Burroughs and Thomas, 1977*)

of California. They present photographic evidence of slope failures beginning and accelerating some 15 years after logging.

Root strength decline after tree felling is undoubtedly both species- and site-dependent. Whether or not slope failures result is also dependent on the rate of establishment or growth of new vegetation relative to the root strength decline of previously cut trees. This latter consideration was taken into account by Kitamura and Namba (1966) in their study of tree root contribution to soil strength and stability in plantations of *Crytomeria japonica* (L. f.) D. Don trees. Uprooting resistance of individual trees after various elapsed times, in either a tree growth mode after planting or root decay mode after cutting, were used to obtain strength growth or decay curves for individual trees. The crossover point for growth and decay curves or point of minimum net resistance was 18 to 20 years. On the other hand, for a forest stand, both the stand composition and net uprooting resistance depend upon the cutting cycle and number of new trees planted immediately after felling. By assuming a cutting cycle of 50 years and a planting of 1000 saplings/hectare immediately after cutting, Kitamura and Namba calculated that the net or minimum resistance per unit area would occur about 5 to 10 years after cutting.

Herbaceous plants—grasses and forbs—in general will not be as effective as woody plants in reinforcing soils and stabilizing slopes against mass movement. The roots of herbaceous plants tend to be weaker and penetrate less deeply than woody plant roots. A few species such as

alfalfa (*Medicago sativa* L.), on the other hand, are known to have roots that will extend downward several meters. Root reinforcement studies by Waldron (1977) showed that alfalfa roots were particularly effective in increasing the resistance to shearing. Alfalfa's large reinforcing effect was attributed mainly to vigorous permeation of the soil by roots (high A_R/A ratios) and a good frictional bond between roots and soil (high τ') because of taproots with many branches. These characteristics make alfalfa a possible candidate for reinforcing a soil and stabilizing a slope against shallow sliding and sloughing. Other properties of the plant would have to be evaluated as well, however, before its use could be recommended.

In the case of dune or beach stabilization, among the most effective plants are beach grasses such as European beach grass or marram grass (*Ammophila arenaria* (L.) Link) or American beach grass (*Ammophila breviligulata* Fern.). These pioneer plants have strong, widespreading rootstocks or rhizomes underground that send up new shoots from nodes along their length. They have the capacity to permeate sand vigorously with an extensive root network in both a lateral and a vertical direction (Fig. 3.18). They only thrive in a high-stress environment of drifting sand and limited nutrient availability.

3.2.4 Root and Fiber Reinforcement Tests

A number of investigators have determined the influence of fiber or root reinforcement on the shear strength of soils by direct shear tests in both the field and the laboratory. Endo and Tsuruta (1969) determined the reinforcing effect of tree roots on soil shear strength by running large scale in-situ direct shear tests on soil pedestals of a clay loam containing live tree roots of young European alder trees (*Alnus glutinosa* (L.) Gaertn.). A schematic diagram of their test procedure is shown in Fig. 3.19. The shear strength of the soils they tested was found to increase directly with the bulk weight of roots per unit volume of soil. An empirical relation of the following form was obtained:

$$\Delta S_R = a(R + b) \tag{3.7}$$

where:

$$\Delta S_R = \text{increase in shear resistance, kg/cm}^2$$
$$R = \text{concentration or density of roots in the soil, g/m}^3$$
$$a \text{ and } b = \text{empirical constants } (a = .93 \times 10^{-5}, b = 53 \text{ g/m}^3)$$

This relationship is similar to the strength increase predicted by the theoretical model (Equation 3.3). The root area ratio (A_R/A) can be substituted for the root concentration in the soil (R), provided the former is multiplied by the unit weight of the roots (γ_R). Equation (3.7) thus may be written:

$$\Delta S_R = a\gamma_R(A_R/A) + ab \qquad (3.8a)$$

or:

$$\Delta S_R = k_1(A_R/A) + k_2 \qquad (3.8b)$$

According to data from the study by Endo and Tsuruta, the second term in Equation (3.8b) can be neglected with little error for all root area ratios exceeding 0.1 percent. Equation (3.8b) is thus virtually identical in form to Equation (3.3), which was developed from a simple theoretical model.

Waldron (1977) likewise investigated the effect of plant roots on the shear strength of soil. His tests were made in the laboratory on 25-cm-diameter root-permeated soil columns using a specially constructed direct shear advice. Waldron investigated the reinforcing effect of alfalfa (*Medicago sativa*), barley (*Hordeum vulgare* L.), and yellow pine (*Pinus ponderosa*) at various depths and shear displacements in both a homogeneous silty clay loam and stratified soil profiles. Roots of each species increased the shear resistance of homogeneous and compacted layers of silty clay loam at a 30-cm depth. Alfalfa roots were in general more effective than either pine or

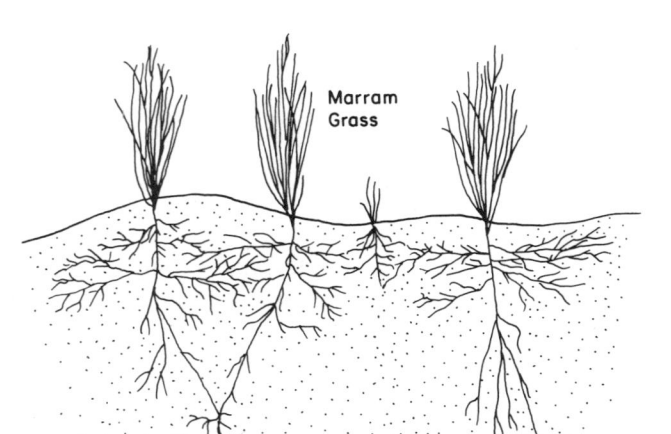

Fig. 3.18a. Root development and structure of European beach or marram grass (*Ammophila arenaria*), a dune-building plant.

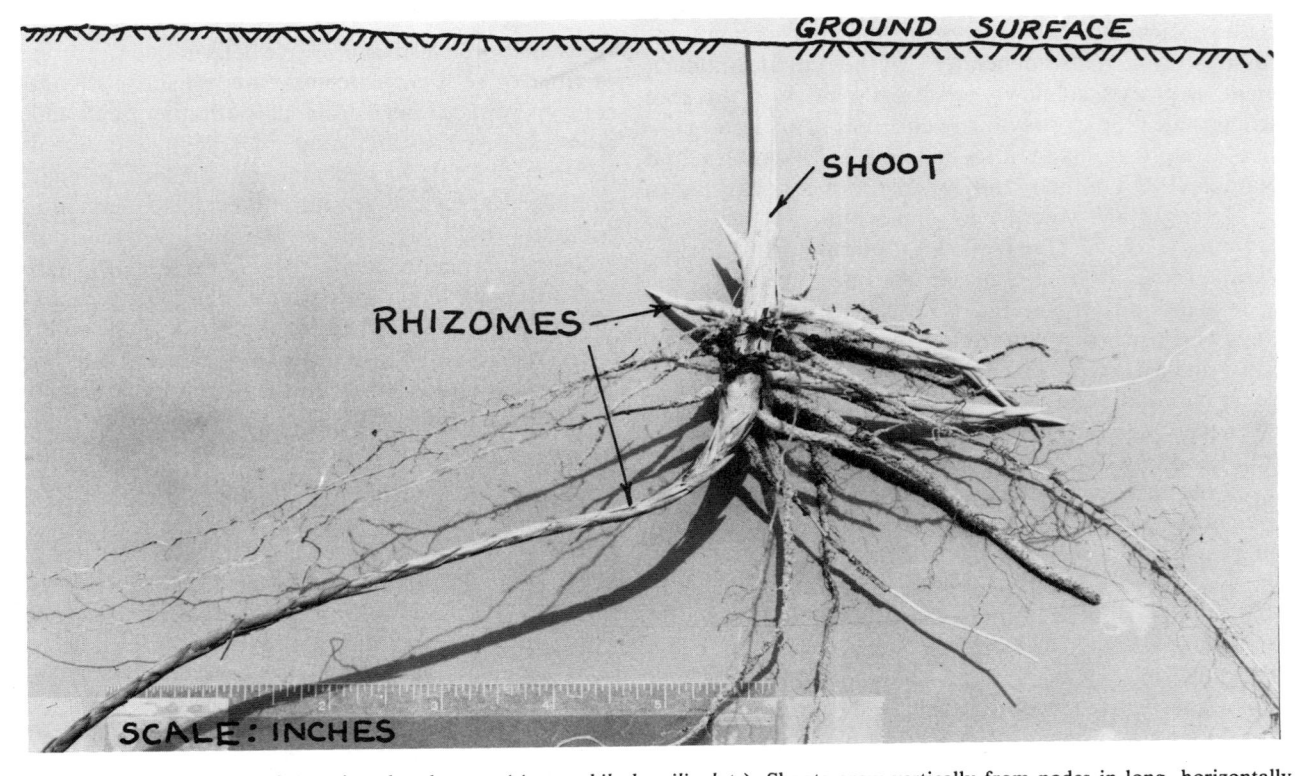

Fig. 3.18b. Root structure of American beach grass (*Ammophila breviligulata*). Shoots grow vertically from nodes in long, horizontally spreading rhizomes or rootstocks.

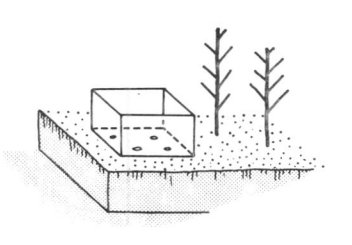

A. Soil Pedestal Guide Box in Place

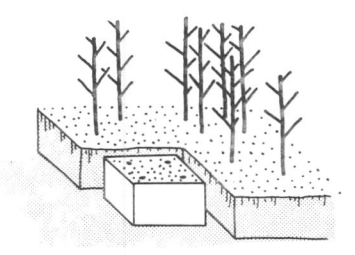

B. Soil Pedestal Excavated and Exposed

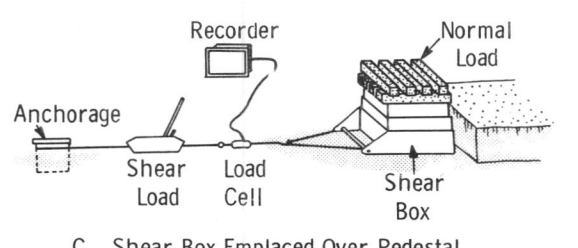

C. Shear Box Emplaced Over Pedestal

Fig. 3.19.   Schematic diagram of in-situ shear tests on soil pedestals containing roots of young nursery trees. (*From Endo and Tsuruta, 1969*)

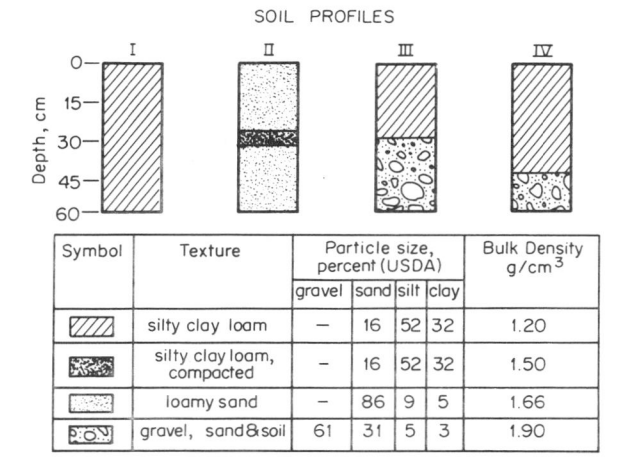

SOIL PROFILES

Symbol	Texture	Particle size, percent (USDA)				Bulk Density g/cm³
		gravel	sand	silt	clay	
▨	silty clay loam	—	16	52	32	1.20
▓	silty clay loam, compacted	—	16	52	32	1.50
░	loamy sand	—	86	9	5	1.66
▩	gravel, sand & soil	61	31	5	3	1.90

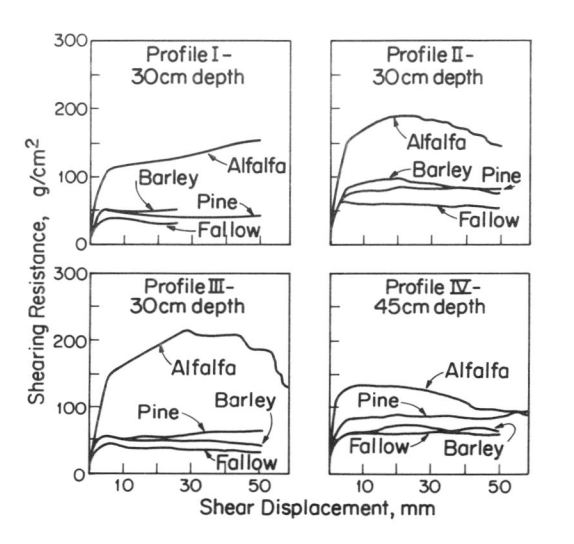

Fig. 3.20.   Experimental soil profiles and results of direct shear tests on root-permeated and fallow soils. (*After Waldron, 1977*)

barley roots in all soil profiles, as shown in Fig. 3.20. Alfalfa was particularly effective in increasing the resistance to shearing between a dense gravel–sand layer (simulating weathered rock) and an overlying silty clay loam soil.

Alfalfa roots in the homogeneous clay loam also had a larger reinforcing effect than the European alder saplings that Endo and Tsuruta (1969) sheared in situ in a forest nursery. The alder roots increased soil shear resistance at a 20-cm depth by 1.15 psi (0.084 kg/cm²) compared to 1.39 psi (0.10 kg/cm²) for alfalfa at a 30-cm depth. The relative strength increase $(\triangle S_R/(S_t)_{R=0})$ was also far greater for alfalfa (290 percent) than for alders (98 percent). Unfortunately, no data were provided, or at least reported, by Waldron (1977) as to the root concentration or root area ratio of alfalfa. Accordingly, it is not known with certainty whether the improved strength increases reported for alfalfa are due to higher root area ratios relative to the other plants or to higher tensile strength

and more favorable structure of the alfalfa roots. Waldron did provide data on shear resistance increase $(\triangle S_R)$ vs. root area ratio (A_R/A) for barley-root-permeated soils. A unique linear relationship between $(\triangle S_R)$ and (A_R/A) was observed as shown in Fig. 3.21 and as predicted by the theoretical model (Equation 3.3), irrespective of the fact the data were obtained from both homogeneous and stratified soil profiles. Also worthy of note in Fig. 3.21 is the relatively small root cross-sectional area $(A_R/A \le 0.1\%)$ required to mobilize increased shear resistance. A view of the apparatus used by Waldron to shear root-permeated soil columns is shown in Fig. 3.22.

The results of direct shear tests on a dry, uniform medium sand reinforced with two different lengths of fibers were presented previously (Fig. 3.5). The fibers (palmyra) were placed in a random pattern perpendicular to the shear surface at a fiber area ratio of 0.5 percent.

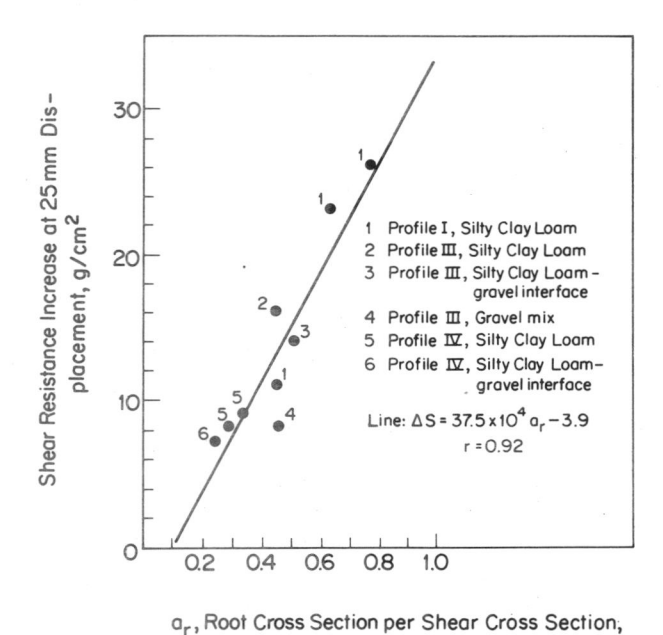

1 Profile I, Silty Clay Loam
2 Profile III, Silty Clay Loam
3 Profile III, Silty Clay Loam – gravel interface
4 Profile III, Gravel mix
5 Profile IV, Silty Clay Loam
6 Profile IV, Silty Clay Loam – gravel interface

Line: $\Delta S = 37.5 \times 10^4 \, a_r - 3.9$
$r = 0.92$

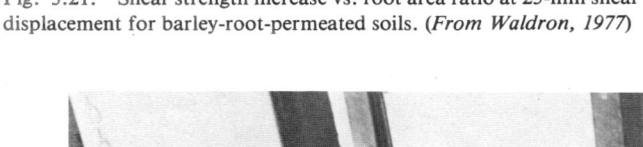

Fig. 3.21. Shear strength increase vs. root area ratio at 25-mm shear displacement for barley-root-permeated soils. (*From Waldron, 1977*)

The apparent cohesion or induced shear strength increase ($\triangle S_R$) from reinforcement (without pullout) was 530 psf (0.26 kg/cm²) for this sand–fiber system. The test results shown in Fig. 3.5 clearly illustrate one of the requirements for efficient mobilization of fiber reinforcement discussed earlier, viz., the fibers must be long enough or "frictional" enough to resist pullout, or conversely that the confining stress must be great enough to develop sufficient traction along the fiber. This threshold or limiting stress is a function of fiber length for a given sand–fiber system. For the shorter (2-cm) fibers this stress was 3.5 ksf (1.75 kg/cm²); for the longer (4-cm) fibers the stress dropped to 1.7 ksf (0.85 kg/cm²).

Kassif and Kopelovitz (1968) determined the effect of plastic-fiber reinforcement of compacted samples of both a clayey sand and loess in direct shear tests. The plastic fibers (80% polyvinyl chloride + 20% di-octyl-phtalate) were oriented normal to the shearing plane at fiber area densities up to 2.5 percent. Half the tests were run with the fibers fixed to the shear box at their ends to minimize if not prevent slippage and pullout. The reinforcement or shear strength increase was similar for both soils. Maximum reinforcement occurred at optimum water content for the clayey sand and dry of optimum for

Fig. 3.22. View of root-permeated, cylindrical column of soil being tested in direct shear. (*From Waldron, 1977*)

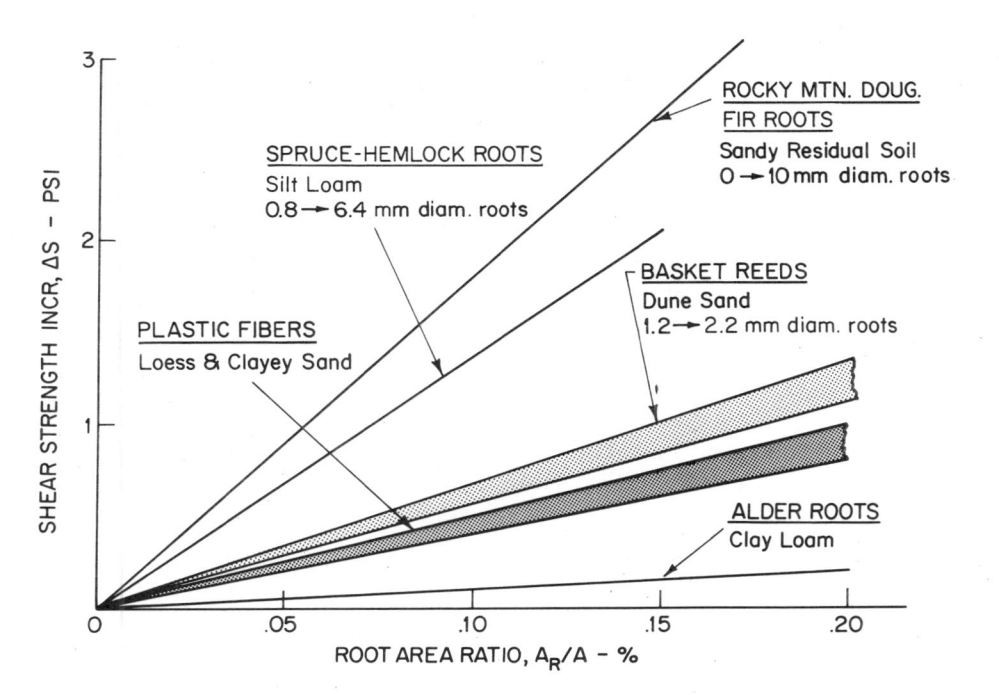

Fig. 3.23. Examples of shear strength increases resulting from root or fiber reinforcement of various soils.

the loess. Higher water contents definitely had a more deleterious effect on reinforced strength of the loess. Fixity of the fibers at their ends also produced slightly higher strengths.

The results of various root or fiber reinforcement studies are shown plotted in Fig. 3.23. The variation in shear strength increase ($\triangle S_R$) with root area ratio (A_R/A) is essentially linear for most soil–fiber systems for values of (A_R/A) less than 1 or 2 percent. With the exception of the Douglas fir and spruce–hemlock data, all curves were plotted from the results of direct shear tests. The former were calculated and plotted from root area ratio data and root tensile strength data using the theoretical fiber reinforcement model and Equation (3.3). Accordingly, the curves for Douglas fir and spruce hemlock should be regarded as theoretical upper limits based on full mobilization of tensile strength of the roots.

3.2.5 Root Reinforcement in Sandy, Cohesionless Slopes

It is instructive to examine a specific case where root reinforcement plays a demonstrable role in stabilizing a slope. Slopes with relatively shallow, cohesionless soils underlain by an inclined bedrock contact provide a good example. In such slopes root reinforcement and buttressing by trees can be very important to stability.

Slopes underlain by granitic rocks are characterized by just these conditions. Typically they have a thin mantle of coarse-textured, largely cohesionless residual soil (Fig.

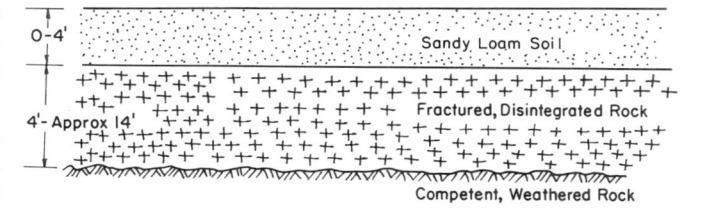

Fig. 3.24. Tyical soil profile and slope geometry in granitic slopes of the Idaho Batholith (excluding swales, depressions, and other topographic lows).

3.24). This residual soil in turn is underlain by fractured, disintegrated bedrock. When slope failures occur, the sliding surface usually lies along this contact. The most common types of slope failures are debris flows, debris avalanches, and debris slides. Most people may not associate slope movements with granitic rocks; nevertheless, huge and numerous slides have occurred in granitic areas all around the world (Durgin, 1977; Jones, 1973; Gonsior and Gardner, 1971).

A saturated, residual soil mantle derived from granitic rock has little or no intrinsic cohesion and very low bulk density. Its angle of internal friction depends on the grain size distribution and void ratio, but appears to average close to 35 degrees for a medium-grained, undisturbed granitic soil (Lumb, 1962; Gonsior and Gardner, 1971). Slopes in granitic terrain are often marginally stable because of extreme topographic relief and absence of intrinsic cohesion. Instability increases when a temporary groundwater table develops in the granitic soil mantle after an intense and prolonged storm.

The influence of both friction and cohesion on the factor of safety of a typical slope in granitic terrain is graphed in Figs. 3.25 and 3.26. The calculations are based on the "infinite slope" stability analysis discussed in Chapter 2. As shown in the figures, the stability of the soil mantle is very sensitive to cohesion, particularly when the slope becomes saturated. It is also clear that some form of cohesion must exist in steep slopes in order to provide the critical margin for stability, particularly when the soil mantle becomes saturated ($H_w = H$). Actually, not much cohesion is required to maintain a stable slope. As little as 1 to 2 psi (0.07 to 0.14 kg/cm^2) will suffice for the slope conditions illustrated schematically in Fig. 3.26, even for the worst case of full saturation ($H_w = H$) and low friction angle ($\phi = 20°$). The crucial question is what is the origin or source of this required cohesion?

The required cohesion or "apparent cohesion" in these coarse-textured, granitic soils may arise from the following sources: (1) capillary action, (2) cohesion from clays derived from weathering of feldspars, (3) cementation from precipitation of oxides, and (4) root reinforcement. Contributions from all these sources were examined in detail by Gray and Megahan (1980). They showed that

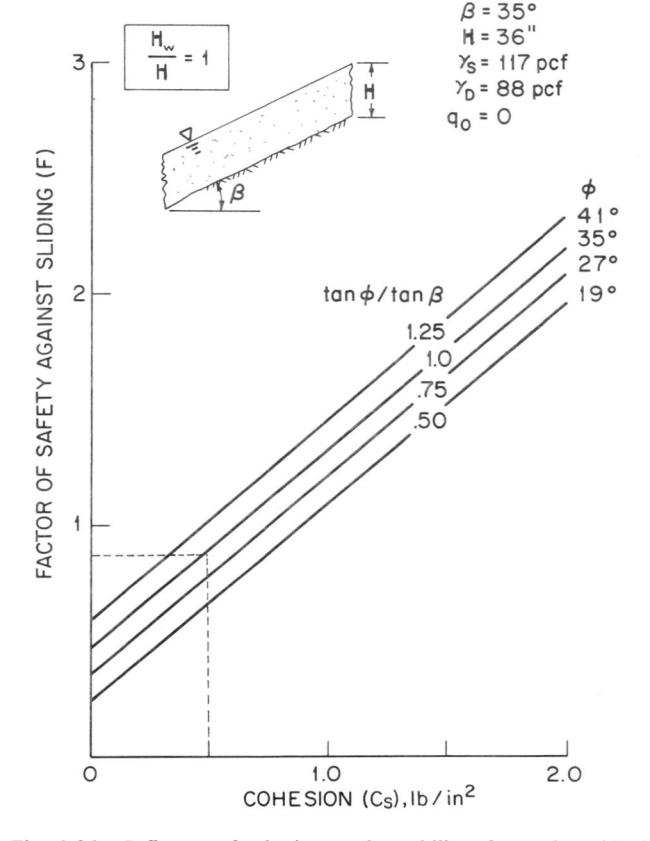

Fig. 3.26.   Influence of cohesion on the stability of a sandy residual soil resting on an inclined bedrock contact. $H_w = H$.

root reinforcement was a potential, if not the most likely, source of required cohesion for stability of steep slopes in granitic terrain.

Estimates of the contribution of root reinforcement to shear strength increase or apparent cohesion in granitic slopes can be made from the root reinforcement studies described previously in Section 3.2.4. In order to do this, some data are required on root distribution and concentrations in granitic soils. These data have been obtained, in a landslide study by Megahan et al. (1978) in the Idaho Batholith region of Idaho. They determined the size and frequency of roots exposed in the shearing surface of landslides. The dominant size class (modal value) of roots in the shear surface was 0.51 to 1.02 cm in diameter. The dominant value in the root concentration class was 70 to 113 roots/m^2. This information yields root area ratios (A_R/A) ranging from 0.14 to 0.93 percent using the data from the modal class.

Burroughs and Thomas (1977) found the same size class to be dominant for Rocky Mountain Douglas fir in their study (i.e., most of the roots they counted fell into the size range 0–1 cm). In contrast, the root area ratio (0.045 percent) calculated from their data for this size class was much lower than those computed from the data

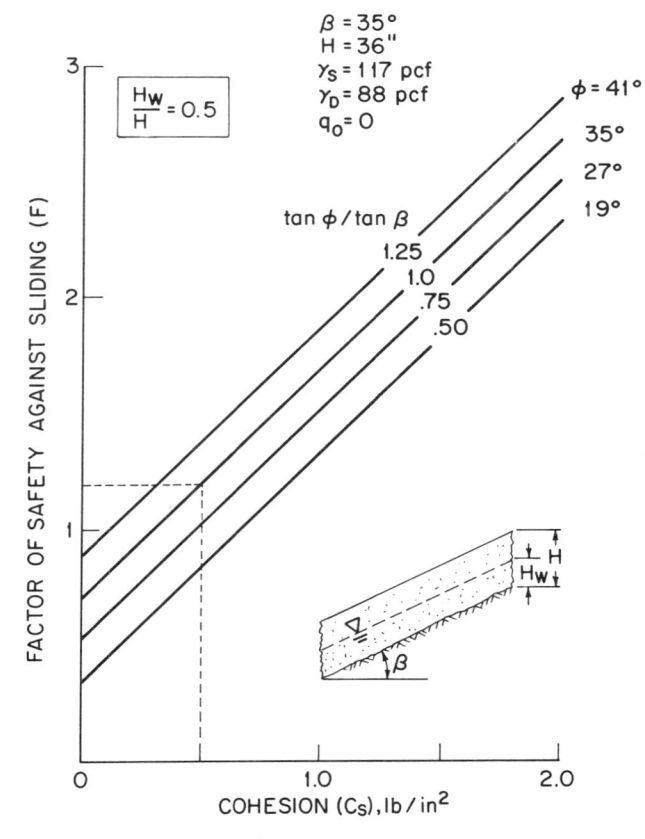

Fig. 3.25.   Influence of cohesion on the stability of a sandy residual soil resting on an inclined bedrock contact. $H_w = 0.5H$.

of Megahan et al. (1978). The difference is most likely caused by the fact that Burroughs and Thomas counted only Douglas fir roots in *vertical planes* midway between tree stumps, whereas in the other study all roots were counted in shear planes parallel to the slope regardless of species. For comparison purposes it is interesting to note that Wu (1976) measured root area ratios ranging from 0.05 to 0.17 and averaging 0.08 percent in his study of vegetative influence on landslide occurrence in southeast Alaska. His root area ratios were measured at the contact between the "B" and "C" soil horizons in soils developed on glacial till slopes supporting a spruce–hemlock forest.

From all of these studies a root area ratio in the range 0.05 to 0.10 percent can be considered as a reasonable lower bound estimate in a granitic slope. This root area ratio translates to a potential (maximum) shear strength increase of 1–2 psi based on the curves graphed in Fig. 3.23. This estimate assumes a tensile strength of roots intermediate between that of spruce–hemlock and Rocky Mountain Douglas fir. The shear strength increase ($\triangle S_R$) from root reinforcement is simply added to the cohesion (c) when computing the factor of safety of the slope using Equation (2.11). As noted previously, a shear strength increase or apparent cohesion of 1–2 psi is sufficient to provide the critical margin of stability in steep, granitic slopes. The contribution of root reinforcement to stability of these slopes is thus evaluated.

3.3 SOIL MOISTURE MODIFICATION AND DEPLETION

Vegetation can affect the stability of slopes by modifying the hydrologic regime in the soil. Trees transpire water through their leaves, and this in turn depletes soil moisture. A forest can also intercept and adsorb moisture in the crowns of trees or in the ground litter. Interception and transpiration by trees in a forest would thus tend to maintain drier soils and mitigate or delay the onset of waterlogged or saturated conditions in the soil. Conversely, clear-cutting or felling of trees tends to produce wetter soils and faster recharge times following intense rainstorms (Fig. 3.27).

3.3.1 Soil Moisture Stress and Slope Movement

The ability of trees to deplete soil moisture to considerable depth and develop large moisture deficits in the soil is well established (Hoover et al., 1953; Patric et al., 1965; Bethlahmy, 1962; Brenner, 1973). On the other hand, the consequences or significance of this process vis-à-vis slope stability has been subject to differing opinions. Landsliding and other catastrophic mass-wasting events in steep slopes are strongly correlated with high precipitation and storm activity (Fredriksen, 1970; Flaccus, 1959; Swanston, 1967). Creep movement in slopes is also influenced significantly by precipitation (Wilson, 1970; Gray, 1974, 1978; Swanston and Swanson, 1976). The influence of precipitation on both creep movement and landslide occurrence derives from its relation to groundwater movement and soil moisture stress (Swanston, 1967; Bailey and Rice, 1969; Gray, 1970; Brenner, 1973). The higher or the more prolonged the periods of elevated moisture stress in a slope, the higher will be the creep rates or accumulated creep movement (Fig. 3.28), and the greater the danger of landslides. The crucial question thus is does slope vegetation attenuate pore pressures or limit rise in piezometric levels during a major and prolonged rainstorm sufficiently to make any difference? Likewise, does slope vegetation decrease pore

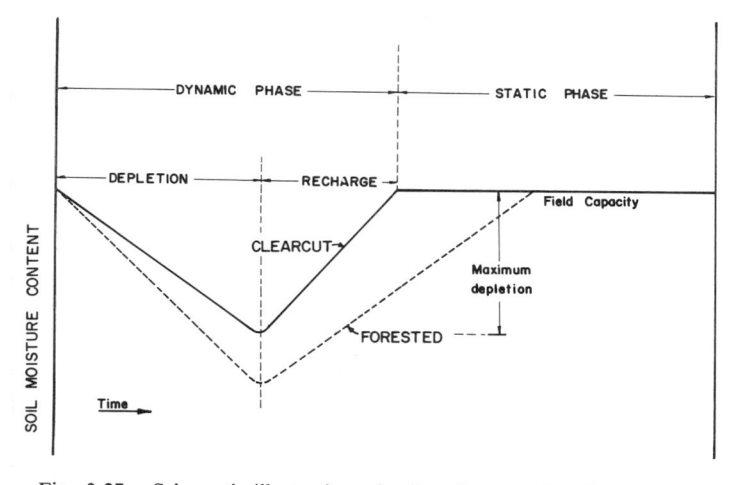

Fig. 3.27. Schematic illustration of soil moisture regime in a forested vs. cutover slope.

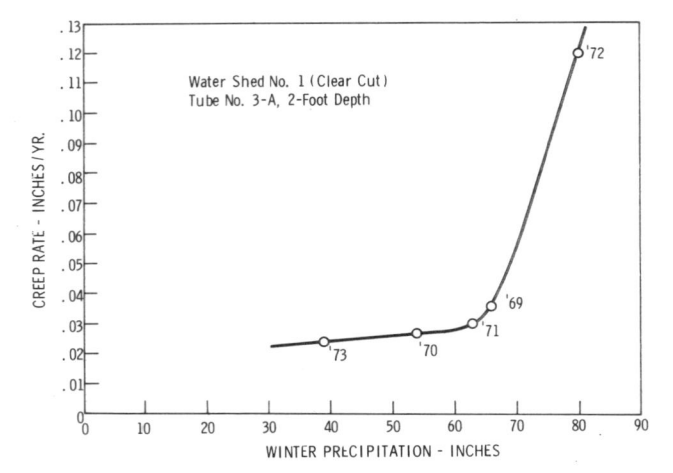

Fig. 3.28. Annual creep rate vs. winter precipitation. Cutover slope at H. J. Andrews Experimental Forest, Oregon.

pressures sufficiently over the entire year to reduce creep rates in a forested slope relative to a bare or denuded slope?

3.3.2 Soil Moisture Stress in Forested vs. Cutover Slopes

Results of a model study by Brenner (1973) showed that a forest cover accelerates soil moisture depletion in a shallow soil mantle regardless of the steepness of slope. For a simulated storm of given intensity and duration, the recharge phase for the bare or denuded slope was therefore much shorter than for the forested one. A view of the tilting-bed, experimental slope used by Brenner with adjustable slope angle and tensiometers for measuring piezometric response following simulated rainfall is shown in Fig. 3.29. Typical results from an experimental run in this study are shown in Fig. 3.30. Field studies by Bethlahmy (1962) of soil moisture content in a clear-cut plot vs. adjacent forested plot in a virgin, Douglas fir–hemlock forest in the Cascade Range of Oregon generally support these findings. It is important to point out, however, that Bethlahmy only studied first-year effects of timber removal on soil moisture. Studies by Hallin (1967) showed that, after 3 years, low vegetation that invades a cutover site is nearly as effective as old-growth timber in depleting moisture. It appears, therefore, that the first year after cutting is likely to be the most critical as far as soil moisture and its effects on slope stability are concerned.

A different view of the role of transpiring vegetation in maintaining more secure slopes was advanced by Rice and Krammes (1970). They suggest that the importance of the contribution of transpiration and vegetation modification of soil moisture to prevention of landslides

Fig. 3.29. View of tilting soil bed employed in experimental study to determine influence of slope vegetation on hydrologic regime. Piezometers and tensiometers used to measure soil moisture stress are visible in photo. (*From Brenner, 1973*)

depends upon climate. They believe that this contribution is probably negligible in climates where precipitation greatly exceeds potential evapotranspiration. On the other hand, in more arid climates, where substantial moisture deficits develop each summer, differential use of water by different types of plant cover may significantly affect the occurrence of landslides.

Some insights into the influence of tree cover on the soil moisture regime and hence on slope stability are provided by results of a soil moisture monitoring study (Gray, 1977) conducted in a forested site in central Oregon that was subsequently clear-cut. Soil moisture stress was measured by means of tensiometers installed with their tips at a depth of 5 ft in a silty clay loam derived from weathered tuff. Typical results of the tensiometer monitoring study, shown plotted in Fig. 3.31, indicate that the forest cover has little effect on the soil moisture regime once precipitation of sufficient duration and intensity falls on the slope and eliminates soil moisture suction. Tree cover at this site at least does not appear to have

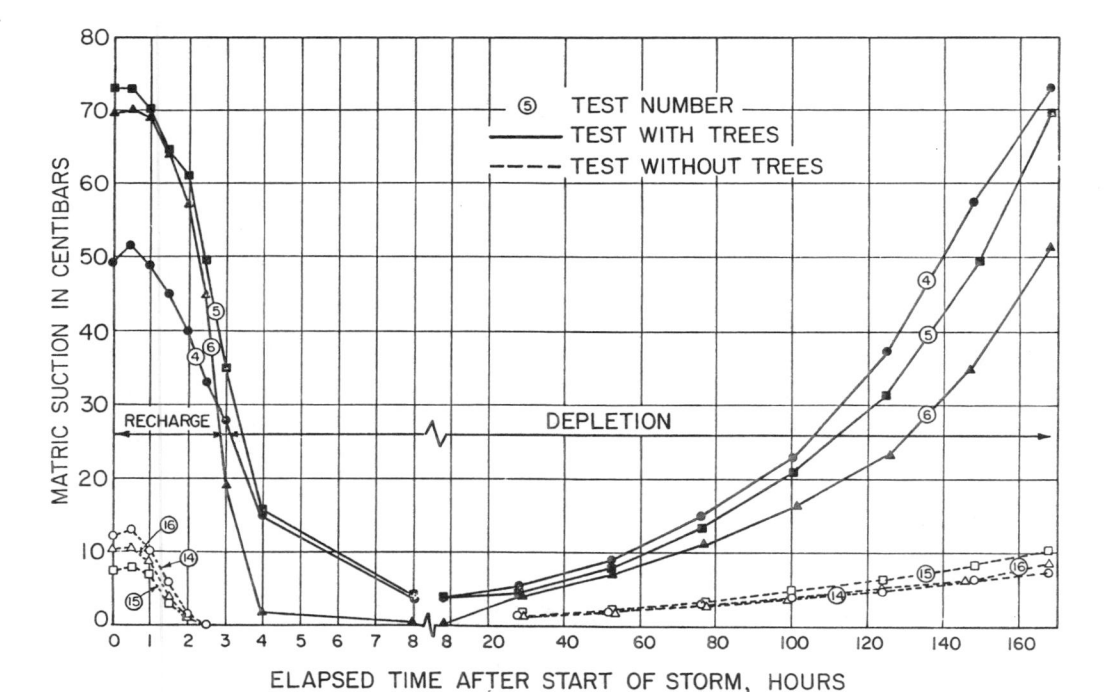

Fig. 3.30. Soil moisture stress (matric suction) during recharge and depletion in a model slope. Slope angle = 20°. (*From Brenner, 1973*)

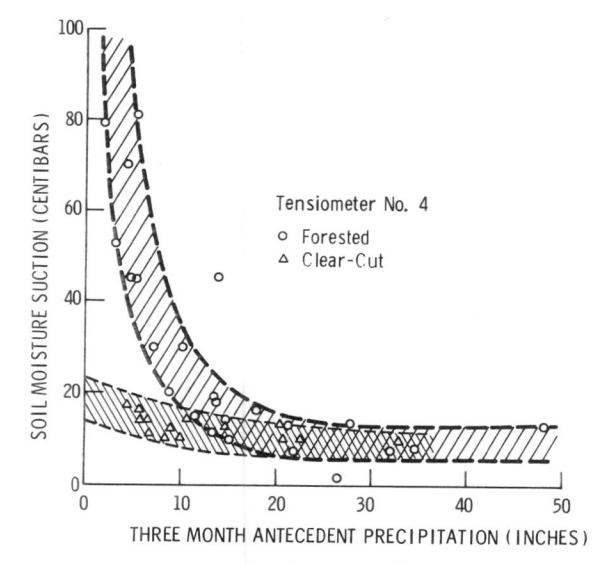

Fig. 3.31. Comparison of soil moisture tension vs. 3-month antecedent precipitation in a forested and cutover slope. H. J. Andrews Forest, Oregon.

much influence on the probability of catastrophic sliding during intense storms. On the other hand, the soil moisture suction is definitely lower during the drier season of the year. Accordingly, creep movement and its destabilizing influence could extend over a longer period

if vegetation removal results in substantially decreased soil moisture tension or suction over a large part of the year. In such cases the shear resistance may be lowered sufficiently to permit creep movement to occur when it otherwise might not (Ter Stepanian, 1965).

Wu (1976) has developed a simulation model for predicting the groundwater regime (pore pressure) of slopes based on precipitation history, evapotranspiration, and infiltration characteristics of a site. The influence of vegetation is accounted for in the evapotranspiration term. This model was used in conjunction with a stability analysis to predict statistically the probability of slope failure for a site—forested or cutover—on the basis of past rainfall records.

3.4 SLOPE BUTTRESSING AND ARCHING

3.4.1 Mechanics of Arching and Buttressing

Buttressing and soil arching action by the trunks of trees growing in slopes can also play an important role in slope stability. Buttressing or lateral restraint against shallow slope movement is provided by firmly anchored, rigid tree trunks. A good example of buttressing action by a tree that is restraining an earth mass above it is shown in Fig. 3.32.

Arching in slopes occurs when soil attempts to move

Fig. 3.32. Slope buttressing by ponderosa pine tree. Unbuttressed part of slope on left has failed. Mendocino National Forest, California.

through and around a row of piles (or trees) firmly embedded or anchored in an unyielding layer. Under the right conditions the trees in effect behave as both cantilever piles and as the abutments of "soil arches" that form in the ground upslope of the trees. The firm anchoring or embedment of trees in a nonyielding layer of a slope can occur: (1) in shallow residual soils or glacial till overlying on inclined bedrock contact; or (2) in sandy slopes where the base of tree stems are deeply buried as the result of sand accretion. An instance of deep embedment of a tree stem in a sandy coastal bluff caused by sand accretion is illustrated in Fig. 3.33.

Other conditions pertaining to spacing and diameter of the tree trunks, thickness and inclination of the yielding portion of the soil profile, and shear strength properties of the soil also determine arching effectiveness. These requirements plus evidence for the existence of arching action by trees in slopes are reviewed next.

3.4.2 Theoretical Model of Arching in Slopes

Different theoretical models have been developed to describe and predict the magnitude of lateral forces that develop against a row of rigid, embedded piles as soil moves through the piles. One theory, developed by Wang and Yen (1974), is based on a semi-infinite slope model and rigid–plastic–solid soil behavior. Their theory was developed for a single row of embedded piles (of diameter

d) spaced a distance B apart across a slope, as shown schematically in Fig. 3.34. According to this theory, the total force (P) developed against a pile of diameter (d) embedded in a slope with a thickness or depth of yielding soil H is given by:

$$P = \frac{K_o}{2} d\gamma H^2 + \left(\frac{K_o}{2} \gamma H - p \; BH \right) \quad (3.9)$$

where:

P = total force developed against a fixed, rigid pile (tree) embedded in a slope
B = clear spacing or opening between piles
H = thickness of the yielding soil layer in the vertical direction
d = diameter of the embedded pile
K_o = coefficient of lateral earth pressure at rest
p = average lateral pressure or arching pressure in openings between fixed piles
γ = unit weight of soil

The load on each pile embedded in a slope is thus the summation of two loads, one from the pressure at rest of the soil immediately uphill of the pile, similar to the lateral pressure on a retaining wall, and the other the soil arching pressure transferred to the adjacent piles as if each pile is an abutment of an arch dam (Fig. 3.35). When the average lateral pressure (p) approaches zero, arching action is a maximum. On the other hand, as the lateral

Fig. 3.33. Deep embedment of trunk of beech tree in sandy coastal bluff as result of sand accretion. Note development of second tier of roots at higher elevation to compensate for burial.

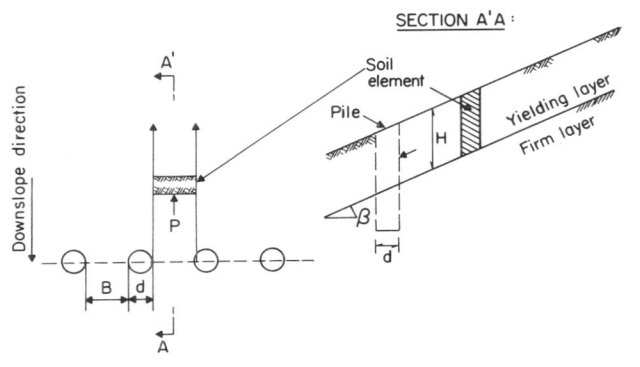

Fig. 3.34. State of plastic deformation and soil arching action around a row of piles embedded in a slope according to Wang–Yen theory.

The Wang–Yen theory of soil arching (Equations 3.9 and 3.10) provide a means of evaluating the likelihood of arching restraint from trees growing in a slope.

3.4.3 Field Evidence for Arching Restraint

The same sandy slopes that were used to investigate the contribution of root reinforcement to slope stability (Section 3.2.5) can be examined for soil arching action between trees. Analyses of field data obtained from forested, sandy slopes on the Idaho batholith indicate that these slopes meet theoretical criteria for arching restraint between trees. Tree spacings, or more importantly the width of openings between "vertical root cylinders," are of the right order of magnitude for soil arching to manifest itself according to the Wang–Yen theory. The tree trunks and their associated vertical root cylinders which are firmly anchored to bedrock behave as potential abutments of soil arches which form upslope of the trees. The relationship between tree spacing (S) and width of opening (B) between vertical root cylinders is shown schematically in Fig. 3.36. Field observations and published data (Wu, 1976; Curtis, 1964) suggest that the diameter of the vertical root cylinders (D_R) is approximately five times the stem diameter (D_T) at breast height.

Openings between vertical root cylinders average around 30 ft for the Idaho batholith (Gray and Megahan, 1980). The Idaho data were obtained from large survey units that include some unforested areas in streams,

or arching pressure (p) increases, arching is less and less effective. If the arching pressure approaches a limiting value $\frac{K_o}{2} \gamma h$, the second term in Equation (3.9) goes to zero, and arching or stress transfer to the adjacent fixed piles does not occur. The maximum allowable or critical spacing (B_{CRIT}) for the existence of arching in a slope is given by the following equation:

$$B_{CRIT} = \frac{HK_o(K_o + 1)\tan\phi + \dfrac{2c}{\gamma}}{\cos\beta(\tan\beta - \tan\phi_1) - \dfrac{c_1}{\gamma H \cos\beta}} \qquad (3.10)$$

where:

B_{CRIT} = critical clear spacing between fixed, embedded piles

c = cohesion in soil

c_1 = cohesion along basal sliding surface

β = slope angle

ϕ and ϕ_1 = angle of internal friction in soil and along basal sliding surface respectively

Fig. 3.35. Soil arches forming around openings upslope of a row of fixed gates in a tilted bed of dry sand.

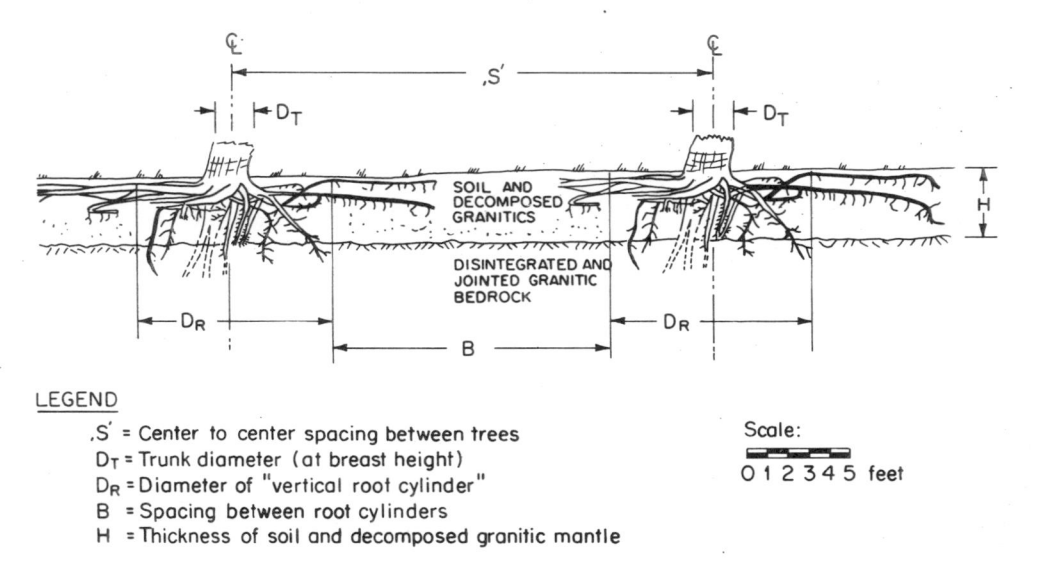

LEGEND

,S' = Center to center spacing between trees
D_T = Trunk diameter (at breast height)
D_R = Diameter of "vertical root cylinder"
B = Spacing between root cylinders
H = Thickness of soil and decomposed granitic mantle

Scale:

0 1 2 3 4 5 feet

Fig. 3.36. Schematic diagram of spacing relationships between tree trunks and their vertical root cylinders in granitic slopes.

brush, and rock outcrop. On a smaller more localized scale, spacings are considerably less, particularly in groves of trees, as illustrated in the photograph in Fig. 3.37. Based on these latter field observations, the width of openings between vertical root cylinders in the slopes averages about 6 to 7 ft.

The maximum allowable opening or critical distance (B_{CRIT}) between piles (or trees) embedded in a slope can be calculated from soil arching theory. This critical distance is shown plotted in Fig. 3.38 using the soil arching theory for slopes derived by Wang and Yen (1974). The critical distance is plotted vs. cohesion for various assumed

Fig. 3.37.   Row of ponderosa pine trees at spacings sufficiently close to manifest soil arching restraint between trees. Boise National Forest, Idaho.

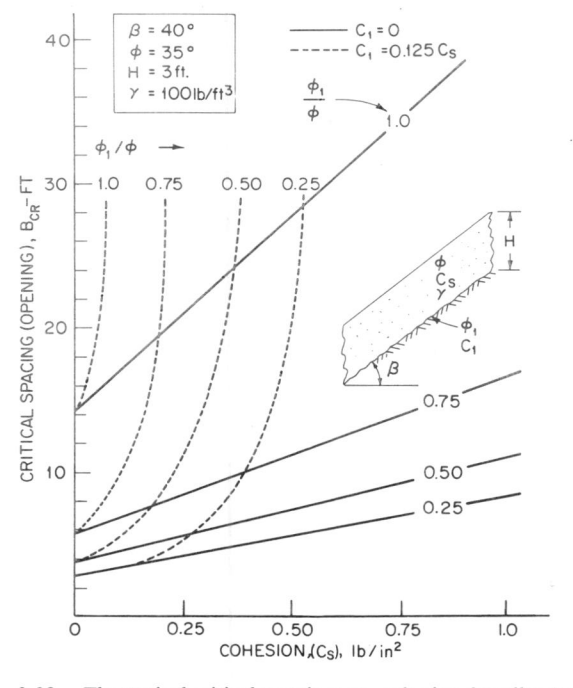

Fig. 3.38.   Theoretical critical openings vs. cohesion for piles (trees) embedded in steep, sandy slopes.

values of residual friction and cohesion (ϕ_1, c_1) along the basal sliding surface. Other soil and slope parameters used in the analysis are typical of shallow coarse-textured, granitic soils overlying a steep bedrock contact ($\beta = 40°$, $\phi = 35°$, $H = 3$ ft, $\gamma = 100$ pcf).

The soil arching analyses show that the critical distance in a shallow mantle is very sensitive to cohesion—particularly cohesion along the basal sliding surface (c_1). If no cohesion is assumed, and the residual friction (ϕ_1) along the basal sliding surface is one-half the peak friction (ϕ), then the critical spacing is 4 ft. On the other hand, if a cohesion (c) of only 50 psf is assumed with the residual cohesion (c_1) a mere 12 percent of this value, then the critical spacing increases to 21 ft. This distance exceeds the size of openings between vertical root cylinders observed in the field—particularly in groves of trees as shown in Fig. 3.37. With slightly higher values of cohesion, the critical distance increases, thus ensuring that soil arching effects will be manifest. These values of cohesion in granitic soils are well within reason. Possible sources of cohesion or "apparent cohesion" include root reinforcement, cementation, clay binder, and capillary effects. The contribution of root reinforcement was discussed previously in Section 3.2.5.

3.5 SURCHARGE FROM VEGETATION

Surcharge from the weight of trees is widely believed to have an adverse influence on the stability of slopes. This view is not generally correct; it is only true in special cases. In some instances surcharge can actually improve stability.

3.5.1 Influence of Surcharge on the Stability of "Infinite Slopes"

As noted previously, forested slopes comprised of a relatively thin layer of residual soil, coluvium, or glacial till overlying an inclined bedrock contact can be modeled by ''infinite slope'' theory (Section 2.6.4). The stability of such slopes and the influence of a vertical surcharge (q_o) can be determined by computing a factor of safety against sliding (Equation 2.11).

The safety factor of a hypothetical slope (F) vs. the ratio H_w/H for both loaded and unloaded ($q_o = 0$) slopes under various conditions is shown plotted in Fig. 3.39.

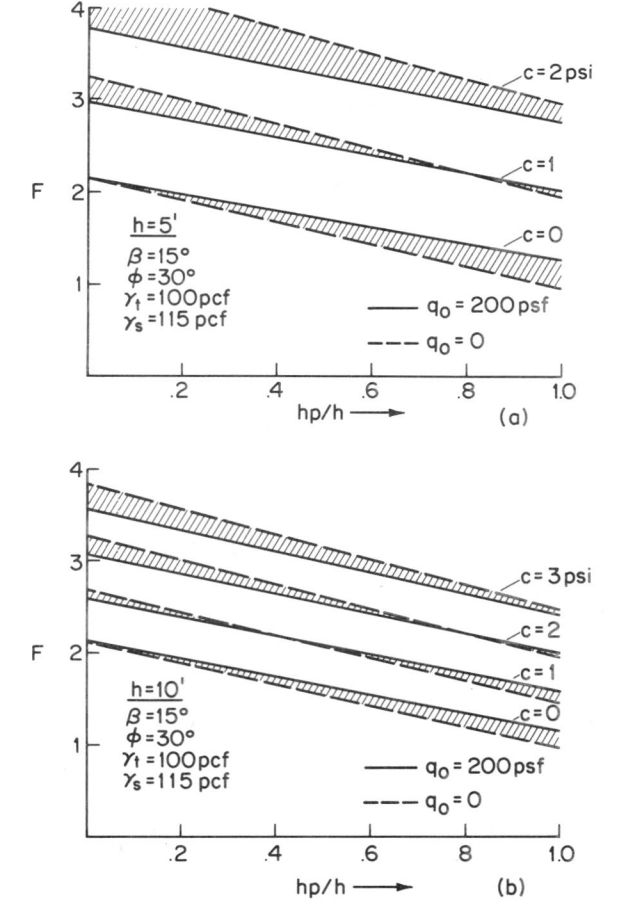

Fig. 3.39. Effect of surcharge (q_o) on safety factor of infinite slopes for various slope conditions: (a) ''thin'' slope ($H = 5'$); (b) ''thick'' slope ($H = 10'$).

Surcharge appears to have a beneficial influence on the safety factor under certain conditions, most noticeably as critical saturated conditions develop in the slope.

The results shown in Fig. 3.39 are somewhat misleading because a gentle slope angle ($\beta = 15°$) was purposely chosen in the analysis. This was done to demonstrate, however, that surcharge due to weight of vegetation is not necessarily detrimental to stability.

The conditions under which surcharge is beneficial to the stability of infinite slopes occur when:

$$c < \gamma_w H_w \tan\phi \cos^2 \beta \qquad (3.11)$$

where:

H_w = height of piezometric rise in the slope
ϕ = angle of internal friction of the soil
c = cohesion of soil
β = slope angle

This relationship shows that surcharge is beneficial for low cohesion values, high friction, high piezometric levels, and relatively gentle slopes. Assuming the worst case of maximum rise in piezometric surface ($H_w = H$) and substituting typical values for the other parameters in granitic slopes ($\beta = 30°$, $\phi = 35°$, $H = 2.5'$) results in a limiting or allowable cohesion of 0.57 psi. This cohesion is quite possible as an upper, limiting value in many granitic slopes. In such slopes, surcharge from the weight of trees would have at best a beneficial influence and at worst, a negligible effect as critical, saturated conditions develop in the soil.

3.5.2 Estimates of Surcharge from Weight of Trees

A surcharge (q_o) of 200 psf (0.1 kg/cm²) was used for the comparisons illustrated in Fig. 3.39. In general, surcharge caused by the weight of trees will neither be uniform nor this high (except perhaps locally immediately beneath a tree). As an example consider the surcharge from the weight of Douglas fir trees growing on slopes of experimental watersheds in the Cascade Range of central Oregon (Rothacher et al., 1967). Merchantable volumes of timber in these watersheds average 50,000 to 65,000 board ft/acre, and basal areas of all stems 2 inches and over range from 300–500 sq ft/acre. When the weight of the trees is spread out over the entire slope, the surcharge is only 12–15 psf. On the other hand, based on the average stem area and board feet per acre, and assuming 10 lb/board ft the surface loading stress under a tree is 1400 psf. If the trees are each assumed to distribute their weight over a circular area of 75 sq ft and are spaced approximately 30 ft apart in a simple cubic array, this surface loading stress (1400 psf) will produce a stress increase varying from 20 to 75 psf midway between trees at depths of 5 and 20 ft respectively. Thus, the influence of surcharge from the weight of trees on either creep rates or safety factors in long slopes is not likely to be very significant one way or another.

3.6   CONSEQUENCES OF VEGETATION REMOVAL ON SLOPE STABILITY

3.6.1   Relationship Between Mass-Movement and Timber Harvesting

To the extent that woody vegetation growing on slopes reinforces soils and enhances stability, conversely its removal should weaken soils and destabilize slopes. The practice of clear-cutting in particular warrants scrutiny in this regard. Clear-cutting is a silvicultural or tree-harvesting procedure in which all timber over a certain minimum diameter is felled and removed. The method is commonly employed to harvest timber in many parts of the world. Clear-cutting can result in denuded sites, vulnerable to both erosion and mass-movement (Fig. 3.40).

The evidence for a cause-and-effect relationship between vegetation removal and mass-movement is reviewed briefly in this section. One of the earliest studies on this question was conducted by Bishop and Stevens (1964) in logged areas in southeast Alaska. Bishop and Stevens noted a significant increase in both frequency of slides and size of area affected by slides after logging, as shown in Fig. 3.41. They concluded that the destruction and gradual decay of the interconnected root system were the principal cause of increased sliding. A later study by Wu (1976) on Prince of Wales Island in southeast Alaska tends to corroborate these earlier findings. Wu calculated the factor of safety against sliding of both forested and adjacent cutover slopes. The latter had lower factors of safety and in general were less stable because of loss of rooting strength and higher piezometric levels.

Studies by Bailey (1971), Rice and Krammes (1970), Megahan and Kidd, 1972; O'Loughlin (1974), Swanston (1974), Brown and Sheu (1975), Dodge et al. (1976), and Swanston and Swanson (1976) all show a cause-and-effect relationship between timber harvesting and slope instability. Steep, metastable slopes underlain by weak rock and soils are particularly sensitive to disturbances by man such as road building, clear-cutting, and vegetation manipulation. Many investigators (Dyrness, 1967; Gonsior and Gardner, 1971; and USDA, 1971) maintain that road building associated with logging plays the dominant

Fig. 3.40.   View of clear-cut sites. Klamath National Forest, California.

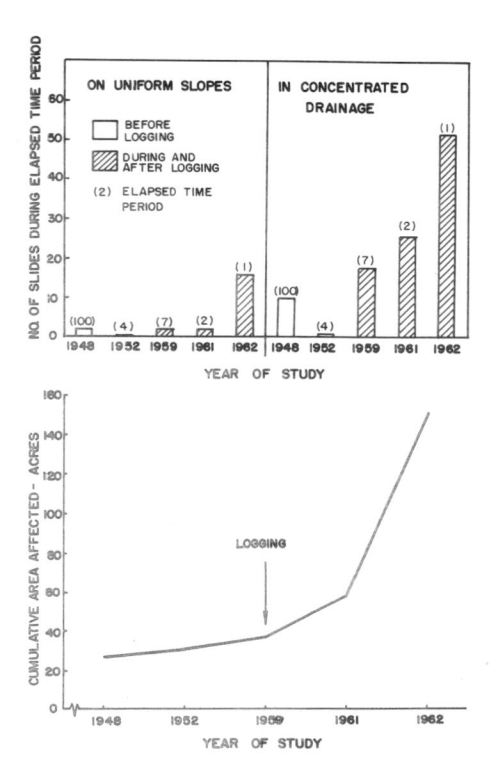

Fig. 3.41. Frequency and cumulative area of slides before and after logging. Hollis, Alaska. (*From Bishop and Stevens, 1964*)

rocks, which in many areas have been extensively altered and weathered to form clay-rich soil and saprolite. The soils developed on the volcaniclastic materials (tuffs and breccias) tend to be deep, fine-textured, and poorly drained on the gentler slopes. These conditions are particularly conducive to both creep and earth flow activity as measured and reported by Swanson and Swanston (1977). The western Cascades have a maritime climate consisting of wet, mild winters and dry summers. Precipitation ranges from 40 to 100 in/yr with 75–80 percent falling between October 1 and March 31. Principal woody vegetation growing on the slopes, except at higher altitudes, is Douglas fir and western hemlock (*Tsuga heterophylla* (Raf.) Sarg.) with lesser amounts of western red cedar (*Thuja plicata* J. Donn ex D. Don) and sugar pine (*Pinus lambertiana*).

Slope instability is endemic to the area. The rate and occurrence of mass-movement events are controlled by geologic, hydrologic, and vegetative factors. Road construction and modification of the forest cover by either cutting or burning can lead to accelerated or increased

role in slope stability problems. These same investigators concede, however, that timber harvesting per se on steep slopes, with subsequent destruction of stabilizing root systems, can contribute to occurrence of shallow landslides. After analyzing past data on relative impacts of clear-cutting as opposed to road construction, Swanston and Swanson (1976) conclude that in many instances both activities contribute about equally to the total level of accelerated mass wasting.

3.6.2 Results of Field Studies in the Western Cascades

A number of field studies have been undertaken in the western Cascade Range of Oregon in order to study the effect of clear-cutting and timber-harvesting operations on mass-movement. Only brief highlights of these studies are reported herein; the interested reader is referred elsewhere for complete details (see Dyrness, 1967; Fredriksen, 1970; Swanson and Dyrness, 1975; Swanston, 1974; Swanston and Swanson, 1976; Gray, 1977).

A detailed description of the geology, soils, climate, and vegetation of the study sites in the western Cascade Range of Oregon has been assembled by Swanson and Swanston (1977). In brief the region is generally composed of Tertiary lava flows, volcaniclastic and intrusive

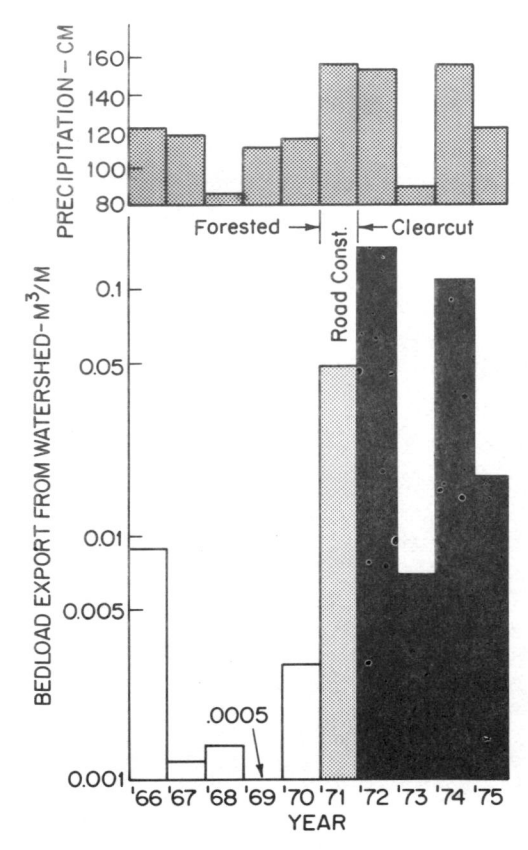

Fig. 3.42. Annual bedload export before and after clear-cutting. Coyote Creek Watersheds, Oregon. (*From Swanson and Swanston, 1977*)

Table 3.2   Debris-avalanche erosion in forest, clear-cut, and roaded areas
(from Swanston and Swanson, 1976)*

SITE	PERIOD OF RECORD YR	AREA		NO. OF SLIDES	DEBRIS-AVAL. EROSION, M³/KM²/YR	RATE OF DEBRIS-AVAL. EROSION RELATIVE TO FORESTED AREAS
		%	KM²			
Stequaleho Creek, Olympic Peninsula:						
Forest	84	79	19.3	25	71.8	× 1.0
Clear-cut	6	18	4.4	0	0	0
Road R/W	6	3	0.7	83	11,825	× 165
			24.4	108		
Alder Creek, western Cascade Range, Oregon:						
Forest	25	70.5	12.3	7	45.3	× 1.0
Clear-cut	15	26.0	4.5	18	117.1	× 2.6
Road R/W	15	3.5	0.6	75	15,565	× 344
			17.4	100		
Selected Drainages, Coast Mountains, S.W. British Columbia:						
Forest	32	88.9	246.1	29	11.2	× 1.0
Clear-cut	32	9.5	26.4	18	24.5	× 2.2
Road R/W	32	1.5	4.2	11	282.5	× 25.2
			276.7	58		
H. J. Andrews Experimental Forest, western Cascade Range, Oregon:						
Forest	25	77.5	49.8	31	35.9	× 1.0
Clear-cut	25	19.3	12.4	30	132.2	× 3.7
Road R/W	25	3.2	2.0	69	1,772	× 49
			64.2	130		

*Used by permission of Allen & Unwin, Inc.

mass-movement as documented by Swanson and Swanston (1977).

The impact of man's activities in these slopes in terms of a single mass wasting process, viz., debris-avalanche erosion, is shown in Table 3.2. This analysis shows that clear-cutting commonly results in acceleration by a factor of 2 to 4 of debris-avalanche erosion. Roads appear to have a much more profound impact (on a per-unit-area basis) because road rights-of-way cover much less area of the forest than do clear-cut units. However, when roads and clear-cutting impacts are weighted by percent of the total area ultimately influenced by the two activities, they contribute about equally to the total (absolute) level of accelerated debris-avalanche erosion.

The impact of clear-cutting on all mass-movement processes is summarized for several experimental watersheds in Fig. 3.42. The impact in this case is expressed in terms of annual bedload export from the watersheds under both forested and cutover conditions. As shown in Fig. 3.42, significant increases in sedimentation from combined slumping, creep, and debris-avalanching have occurred as a result of both road construction and vegetation removal. Bedload exports from the watersheds are con-siderably higher even when weighted for generally higher precipitation during the post-cutting period.

3.7   SUMMARY AND CONCLUSIONS

Woody vegetation increases the shear resistance of soils and enhances the stability of slopes. Both theoretical and experimental studies show that increased shear strength from root permeation is a function mainly of the tensile strength of the roots and the cross-sectional area occupied by root fibers. The roots must be long enough and frictional enough, however, to resist pullout.

Soil moisture depletion and interception by vegetation also increase soil strength and in some cases improve stability. Restraint provided by buttressing and soil arching action of trees embedded in relatively shallow slopes also enhances stability.

Both a theoretical basis and field evidence for soil arching effects in slopes are shown. Contrary to widely held beliefs, even surcharge caused by the weight of trees on a slope can have a beneficial influence. All these hydrome-chanical influences of woody vegetation play a particularly important role in stabilizing shallow, largely cohesionless soils typical of granitic slopes.

Large-scale removal or clear-cutting of trees on slopes exacerbates stability problems. A preponderance of evidence from studies all around the world supports this conclusion, as do the results of specific field studies described in this chapter.

3.8 REFERENCES CITED

Bailey, R. G. (1971). Landslide hazards related to land use planning in the Teton National Forest, Northwest Wyoming, *USDA Forest Service Report,* Intermountain Region, Ogden, Utah, 131 pp.

Bailey, R. G., and Rice, R. M. (1969). Soil slippage, an indicator of slope instability on chapparal watersheds in Southern California, *Professional Geographer* 21(3): 172–177.

Bethlahmy, N. (1962). First year effects of timber removal on soil moisture, *Intl. Assoc. Sci. Hydrol. Bull.* 7(2): 34–38.

Bishop, D. M., and Stevens, M. E. (1964). Landslides on logged areas in Southeast Alaska, *USDA Forest Service Research Paper NOR-1,* 18 pp.

Böhm, W. (1979). *Methods of Studying Root Systems,* Ecological Series No. 33, Berlin: Springer-Verlag.

Brenner, R. P. (1973). A hydrological model study of a forested and a cutover slope, *Bull. Hydrol. Sci.* 18(26): 125–143.

Brenner, R. P., and James, S. M. (1977). Effect of roots on the shear strength of a colluvial soil, *Proc., 5th Danube European Conf. Soil Mech. and Foundation Engr.,* CSSR, Bratislava, pp. 77–78.

Brown, C. B., and Sheu, M. S. (1975). Effects of deforestation on slopes, *J. Geotech. Engr. Div.* ASCE, 101(GT1): 147–165.

Burroughs, E. R., and Thomas, B. R. (1977). Declining root strength in Douglas-fir after felling as a factor in slope stability, *USDA Forest Service Research Paper INT-190,* 27 pp.

Curtis, J. D. (1964). Roots of a Ponderosa pine, *USDA Forest Service Research Paper INT-9,* 10 pp.

Dodge, M., et al. (1976). An investigation of soil characteristics and erosion rates on California forest lands, State of California Resources Agency, Department of Forestry, 105 pp.

Durgin, P. B. (1977). Landslides and the weathering of granitic rocks, *Geol. Soc. Amer. Rev. Engr. Geol.* 3: 127–131.

Dyrness, C. T. (1967). Mass-soil movements in the H. J. Andrews Experimental Forest, *USDA Forest Service Res. Paper PNW-42,* 12 pp.

Endo, T., and Tsuruta, T. (1969). The effect of tree roots upon the shearing strength of soil, *Annual Rept. of the Hokkaido Branch,* Tokyo Forest Experiment Station, 18: 168–179.

Flaccus, E. (1959). Landslides and their revegetation in the White Mountains of New Hampshire, Ph. D. Thesis, Duke University, Dept. of Botany.

Fredriksen, R. L. (1970). Erosion and sedimentation following road construction and timber harvest on unstable soils in three small western Oregon watersheds, *USDA Forest Service Research Paper PNW-104,* 15 pp.

Gonsior, M. J., and Gardner, R. B. (1971). Investigation of slope failures in the Idaho batholith, *USDA Forest Service Research Paper INT-97,* 34 pp.

Gray, D. H. (1970). Effects of forest clear-cutting on the stability of natural slopes, *Assoc. Engr. Geologists Bull.* 7: 45–67.

Gray, D. H. (1974). Reinforcement and stabilization of soil by vegetation, *J. Geotech. Engr. Div.,* ASCE, 100(GT6): 695–699.

Gray, D. H. (1977). Creep movement and soil moisture stress in forested vs. cutover slopes: results of field studes, *Final Report Submitted to National Science Foundation,* Grant No. ENG 74-02427, 141 pp.

Gray, D. H. (1978). Role of woody vegetation in reinforcing soils and stabilizing slopes, *Proc., Symp. Soil Reinforcing and Stablilizing Techniques in Engr. Practice,* New South Wales Institute of Technology, Sydney, Australia, Oct. 16–19, 1978, pp. 253–306.

Gray, D. H., and Megahan, W. F. (1980). Forest vegetation removal and slope stability in the Idaho Batholith, *USDA Research Paper INT-271,* 23 pp.

Hallin, W. E. (1967). Soil-moisture and temperature trends in cutover and adjacent old growth Douglas-fir timber, *USDA Forest Service Research Note PNW-56,* 11 pp.

Holch, A. E. (1931). Development of roots and shoots of certain deciduous tree seedlings in different forest sites, *Ecology* 12: 259–298.

Hoover, M. D., et al. (1953). Soil moisture under a young loblolly pine plantation, *Soil Sci. Soc. Amer. Proc.* 17: 147–150.

Jones, F. O. (1973). Landslides of Rio de Janeiro and the Serra das Arras escarpment, Brazil, *U.S. Geol. Survey Prof. Paper 697,* 42 pp.

Kassif, G., and Kopelovitz, A. (1968). Strength properties of soil–root systems, Technion Institute of Technology, Haifa, 44 pp.

Kitamura, Y., and Namba, S. (1966). A field experiment on the uprooting resistance of tree roots, *Proc. 77th Meet. Japan. Forestry Soc.,* pp. 568–590.

Kozlowski, T. (1971). *Growth and Development of Trees,* Vol. 2, New York: Academic Press.

Lizzi, F. (1978). Reticulated root piles to correct landslides, paper presented to ASCE Natl. Meeting, Chicago, Oct. 16–18, 1978.

Lumb, P. (1962). The properties of decomposed granite, *Geotechnique* 12: 226–243.

McGinn, R. G. (1963). Characteristics of Douglas-fir root systems, *Canad. J. Botany* 41: 105–122.

Megahan, W. F., Day, N. F., and Bliss, T. M. (1978). Landslide occurrence in the western and central Northern Rocky Mountain Physiographic Province in Idaho, paper prepared for Fifth North American Forest Soils Conference, Colorado State University, Fort Collins, Colo.

Megahan, W. F., and Kidd, W. J. (1972). Effect of logging and logging roads on erosion and sediment deposition from steep terrain, *J. Forestry* 70: 136–141.

O'Loughlin, C. L. (1974). The effects of timber removal on the stability of forest soils, *J. Hydrology (NZ)* 13: 121–134.

Patric, J. H., et al. (1965). Soil water absorption by mountain and piedmont forests, *Soil Sci. Soc. Amer. Proc.* 29: 303–308.

Rice, R. M., and Krammes, J. S. (1970). Mass-wasting processes in watershed management, *Proc. Symp. Interdisciplinary Aspects of Watershed Management,* ASCE, pp. 231–260.

Rothacher, J., et al. (1967). Hydrologic and related characteristics of three small watersheds in the Oregon Cascades, *Spec. Publ. U.S. Forest Service,* Pacific Northwest Range and Forest Experiment Station, Corvallis, Ore., 54 pp.

Schlosser, F., and Long, N. T. (1974). Recent results in French research on reinforced earth, *J. Const. Div.,* ASCE, 100(CO3): 223–237.

Shaw, G. (1978). The search for dangerous dams, *Smithsonian* 9(1): 36–45.

Sutton, R. F. (1969). Form and development of conifer root systems, Tech. Comm. No. 7, Commonwealth Agric. Bureau.

Swanson, F. J., and Swanston, D. N. (1977). Complex mass-movement terrains in the Western Cascade Range, Oregon, *Reviews in Engineering Geology,* Geol. Soc. of America, Vol. III, pp. 113–124.

Swanston, D. N. (1967). Soil water piezometry in a southeast Alaska landslide area, *USDA Forest Service Research Note PNW-68,* 17 pp.

Swanston, D. N. (1974). Slope stability problems associated with timber harvesting in mountainous regions of the western United States, *USDA Forest Service General Technical Report PNW-21,* 14 pp.

Swanston, D. N., and Swanson, F. J. (1976). Timber harvesting, mass erosion and steepland forest geomorphology in the Pacific Northwest, in *Geomorphology and Engineering,* ed. by Coates, D. R., Stroudsburg, Pa.: Dowden, Hutchinson and Ross, pp. 199–221.

Swanston, D. N., and Walkotten, W. J. (1970). The effectiveness of rooting as a factor in shear strength of Karta soil, *USDA Progress Rept.* Study No. FS-PNW-1604: 26, Portland, Ore.

Ter Stephanian, G. (1965). In-situ determination of the rheological characteristics of soils on slopes, *Proc. 6th Intl. Conf. Soil Mech. and Foundation Engr.*, Montreal, Canada, Vol. II, pp. 575-577.

Turmanina, V. I. (1965). The strength of tree roots, *Bull. Moscow Soc. Naturalists, Biol. Section* 70(5): 36-45.

USDA Forest Service (1971). Erosional effects of timber harvest, in *Clear-Cutting Practices on National Timberlands-Part 3,* Record of Hearings, U. S. Senate Subcommittee on Public Lands, Washington, D.C., pp. 1202-1223.

Vanicek, V. (1973). The soil protective role of specially shaped plant roots, *Biol. Conservation* 5(3): 175-180.

Varnes, D. J. (1958). Landslide types and processes, in "Landslides and Engineering Practice," ed. by Eckel, E. B., *HRB Spec. Rept. 29,* NAS-NRC, Washington, D.C., pp. 20-47.

Vidal, H. (1969). The principle of reinforced earth, *Highway Research Record No. 282,* pp. 1-16.

Waldron, L. J. (1977). Shear resistance of root-permeated homoegeneous and stratified soil, *Soil Sci. Soc. Amer. J.* 41: 843-849.

Wang, W. L., and Yen, B. C. (1974). Soil arching in slopes, *J. Geotech. Engr. Division,* ASCE, 100(GT1): 61-78.

Weaver, J. E. (1919). The ecological relations of roots, *Carnegie Inst. Washington Publ.,* 286.

Wilson, S. D. (1970). Observational data on ground movements related to slope instability, *J. Soil Mechanics Foundation Engr.,* ASCE, 96 (SM5): 1521-1544.

Wu, T. H. (1976). Investigation of landslides on Prince of Wales Island, Alaska, *Geotechnical Engr. Report No. 5,* Dept. of Civil Engr., Ohio State University, Columbus, Ohio, 94 pp.

Yang, Z., and Singh, A. (1974). Strength and deformation charcteristics of reinforced sand, ASCE National Meeting, Preprint 2189, January 1974.

4

Principles of Biotechnical
Slope Protection

4.1 ELEMENTS OF SYSTEM

Biotechnical slope protection systems consist of both structural–mechanical and vegetative elements working together in a complementary or integrated manner. The vegetative element should not be regarded as a cosmetic adjunct to the structure. Vegetation has an important functional role as well in terms of preventing both surficial erosion and shallow mass-movement.

The vegetation may be planted on the face of a slope above a low retaining structure or toe wall (Figs. 4.1 and 4.2). Alternatively, the interstices of the structure may be planted with vegetation whose roots ultimately will permeate and bind together the soil or backfill within or behind the structure. Vegetated rock breast walls, crib walls, gabion walls, and welded-wire walls fall into this category (Figs. 4.3 and 4.4), as do vegetated grid or cellular revetments (Figs. 4.5 and 4.6). Procedures for designing, constructing, and vegetating these structures are described in Chapters 5 and 6.

Another combination consists of planting vegetation on the steps of a tiered, retaining-wall system (Figs. 4.7 and 4.8). A variation of this approach consists of terracing a slope and planting vegetation on the steps. There is no structural component in this case, only the mechanical procedure of benching or terracing (Fig. 4.9).

Contour-wattling and brush-layering can be viewed as either quasi-vegetative or quasi-mechanical means of slope stabilization (Figs. 4.10 and 4.11). In both cases parts of woody shrubs are used as the soil-stabilizing and reinforcing material. Although natural vegetation is used for the most part, the stabilizing mechanism is largely of a mechanical nature.

Wattling consists of tied bundles of plant stems or branches, usually willow or other easy-to-root species. The bundles are laid in trenches on contour along the slope face and staked into position; then the trenches are backfilled. Construction stakes are commonly used for this purpose; these are driven through the wattles into the ground. The stakes act as "dowels" and help anchor the soil to the slope, thereby minimizing shallow debris slides. Alternatively, live willow stakes may be used. These are more difficult to drive in hard ground but provide the additional advantage of rooting and sprouting (Fig. 4.11), which will further enhance stability of the slope. Live willow cuttings can also be used by inserting them in a staggered pattern on a slope, after which they will root and sprout (Fig. 4.12). Contour-wattling, planting willow cuttings, brush-layering, and other hybrid or quasi-vegetative stabilization techniques are described in detail in Chapter 7.

A summary or taxonomy of approaches to slope protection and erosion control is presented in Table 4.1. Basic approaches are divided into three major categories according to type of construction involved, viz., live, mixed, or inert construction. Live construction entails the use of conventional plantings alone (e.g., grasses and shrubs). Vegetation in this case is used mainly to prevent surficial erosion by providing a good ground cover. At the other extreme is inert construction, which entails the use of conventional structures alone (e.g., gravity and cantilever retaining walls). These types of structures are required when slope movement is deeper-seated, or lateral earth stresses are high. The role of vegetation in this case would be mainly decorative.

Biotechnical methods fall into the middle category of mixed construction. In this case plants have multiple and important functional roles to play. Examples of biotechnical approaches were described briefly at the beginning of this chapter. They include the use of slope plantings in conjunction with low toe walls, the use of live plants as structural reinforcement or barriers to earth movement,

Fig. 4.1.   Low toe wall at base of slope with plantings, grass and trees, on face of slope. Wall is reinforced concrete, cantilever design.

Fig. 4.2.   Breast wall defense at toe of slope adjacent to roadway. Contour wattling and slope plantings are visible through holdown netting used on face of slope.

Fig. 4.3. Vegetated concrete, crib wall. Vegetation was planted in openings between headers at face of wall.

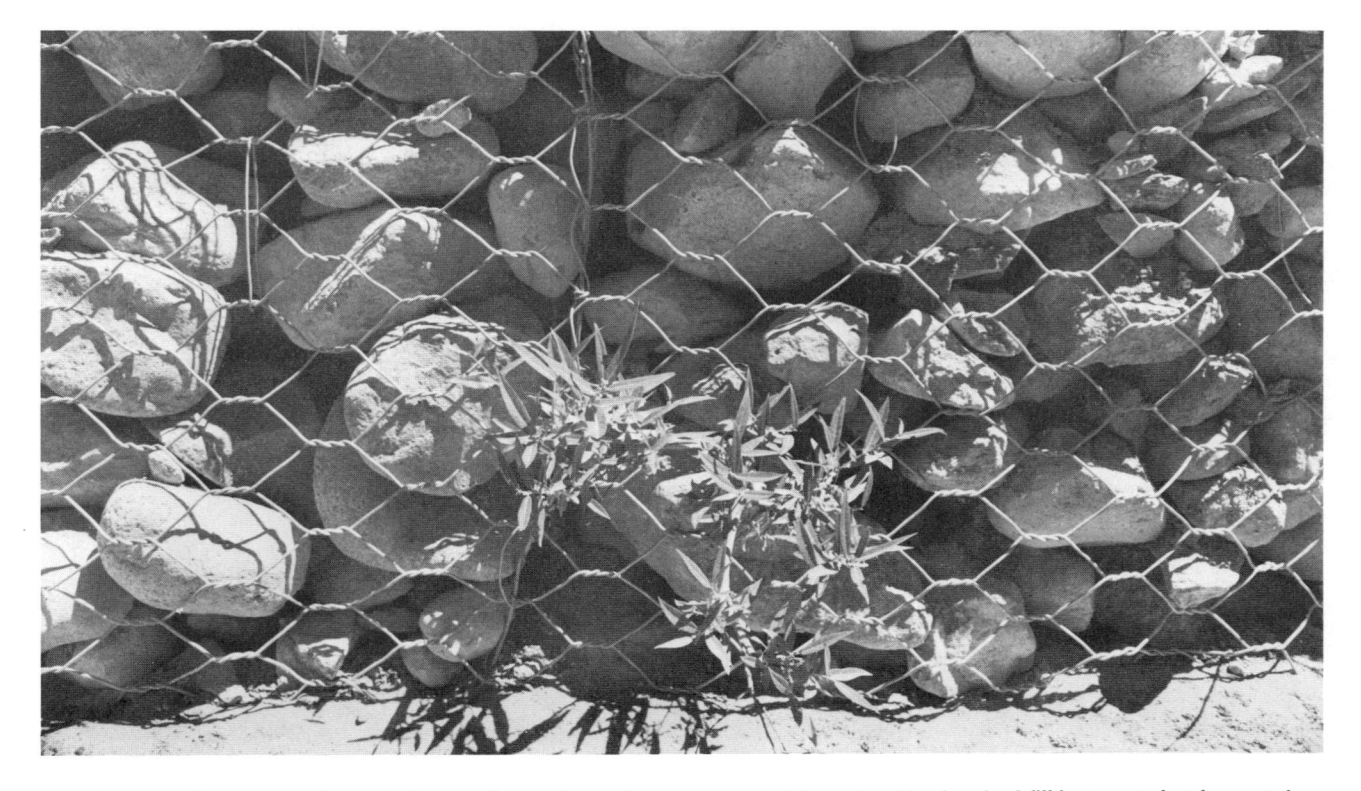

Fig. 4.4. Vegetated gabion wall. Green willow cuttings which were inserted through gabion into backfill have rooted and sprouted.

Fig. 4.5. Vegetated concrete block revetment along drainage channel. Revetment consists of slotted, concrete blocks laid on the slope. Vegetation is volunteer or naturally occurring.

Fig. 4.6. Vegetated cellular grid revetment along a highway. Openings in concrete gridwork have been planted with herbaceous vegetation.

Fig. 4.7. Highway cut stabilized by stepped-back, timber retaining wall. Woody shrubs (*Forsythia* spp.) have been planted on the benches.

Fig. 4.8. Tiered retaining wall with pedestrian path and vegetation on the horizontal benches.

Fig. 4.9.   Terraced, cut slope adjacent to highway aids in erosion control. Horizontal steps were seeded with native grasses. Interstate Highway, #80, near Colfax, California.

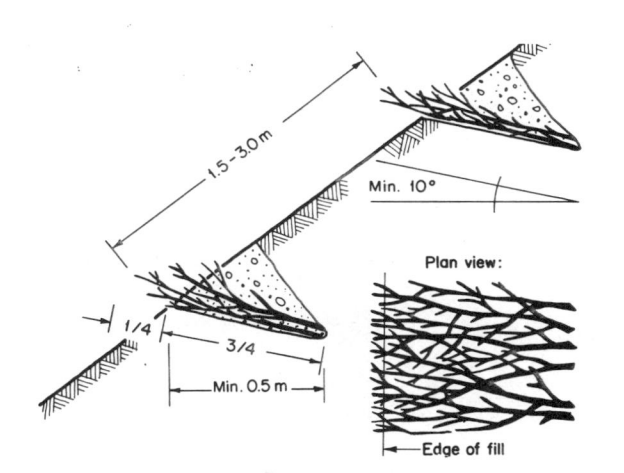

Fig. 4.10.   Slope stabilization by brush-layering method. Cut brush or green branches of easy-to-root species such as willows are placed on contour benches across a slope as shown in the diagram.

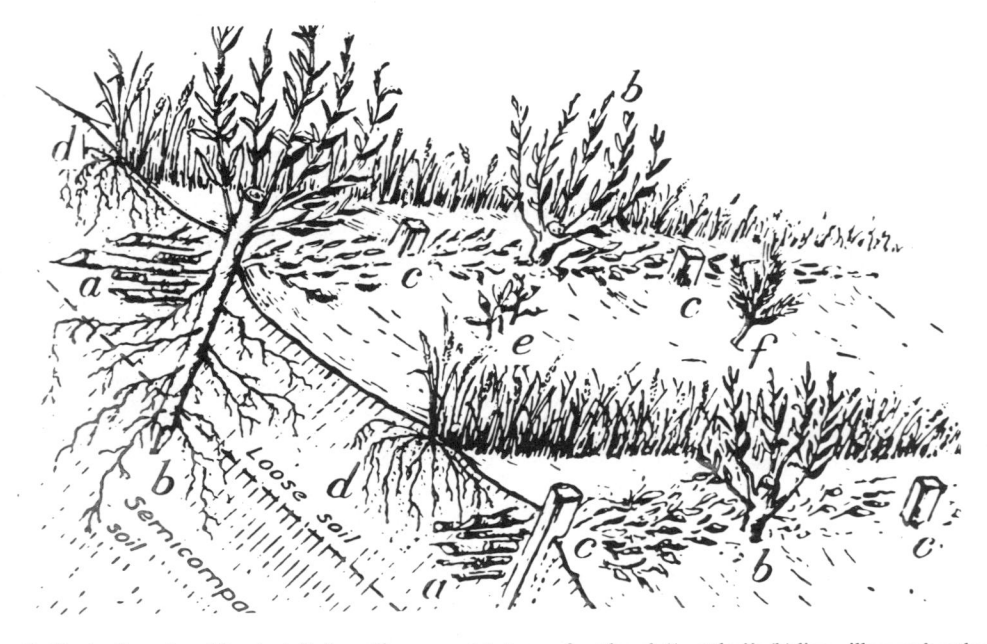

Fig. 4.11. Schematic illustration of wattling installation. Shown are (a) stems of cut brush "wattles"; (b) live willow stakes that have rooted and sprouted; (c) inert construction stakes driven through wattles; (d), (e), and (f) vegetation (grasses, shrubs, and trees) established on benches between wattles.

Fig. 4.12. Steep slope stabilized by willow staking and wattling. This previously denuded highway cut, about 1 acre in area, was producing over 100 cu yd of erosion per year. Unrooted willow cuttings were planted on 2-ft centers, and about 1100 lineal ft of willow wattling were also installed. The stuck cuttings and willow wattles have rooted and sprouted vigorously as shown. Erosion and bank sloughing problems have been virtually eliminated at this site. State Highway #89, near Luther Pass, California.

Table 4.1. Approaches to slope protection and erosion control.

Category	Examples	Appropriate uses	Stabilizing mechanism or role of vegetation
Live construction Conventional plantings	—Grass seeding —Transplants	—Control of surficial rainfall & wind erosion —To minimize frost effects	—To bind & restrain soil particles —To filter soil from runoff —To intercept raindrops —To maintain infiltration —To change thermal character of ground surface
Mixed construction Woody plants used as reinforcement & as barriers to soil movement	—Live staking —Contour-wattling —Brush-layering —Reed-trench-terracing —Brush mats	—Control of surficial rainfall erosion (rilling & gullying) —Control of shallow (translational) mass movement	Same as above, but also to reinforce soil & resist downslope movement of earth masses by buttressing & soil arching action
Woody plants grown in interstices of low, porous structures or benches of tiered structures	—Vegetated *revetments* (riprap, grids, gabion mats, blocks) —Vegetated *retaining walls* (open cribs, gabions, stepped-back walls, & welded-wire walls)	—Control of shallow mass movements & resistance to low–mod. earth forces —Improvement of appearance & performance of structures	—To reinforce & indurate soil or fill behind structure into monolithic mass. —To deplete & remove moisture from soil or fill behind structure.
Toe walls at foot of slope used in conjunction w/ plantings on the face	Low, breast walls (stone, masonry, etc.) with vegetated slope above (grasses and shrubs)	Control of erosion on cut & fill slopes subject to undermining at the toe	To stop or prevent erosion on slope face above retaining wall
Inert Construction Conventional structures	—Gravity walls —Cantilever walls —Pile walls —Reinforced earth walls	—Control of deep-seated mass-movement & restraint of high lat. earth forces —Retention of toxic or aggressive fills & soil	Mainly decorative role

and the use of plants growing in the interstices of porous revetments and retaining walls. The categorization of approaches in Table 4.1 provides a context for studying and describing biotechnical slope protection systems and understanding the role of both vegetation and structures in such systems.

4.2 ROLE OF VEGETATION

Vegetation offers the best long-term protection against surficial erosion on slopes and provides some degree of protection against shallow mass-movement. Vegetation tends to prevent surficial (rainfall) erosion by:

1. Binding and restraining soil particles in place
2. Filtering soil particles out of runoff
3. Intercepting raindrops
4. Retarding velocity of runoff
5. Maintaining infiltration

Wattling installed in a slope provides many of these protective functions. It serves as an energy dissipator for water and soil moving down the slope; it filters and traps downward moving detritus (soil and small rocks); and it provides a series of areas with reduced slope angle on which vegetation (grasses, native seedlings, and transplants) can be established (Fig. 4.10). Portions of the wattling also root and become part of the permanent stabilizing cover.

Deeper, rooted woody vegetation helps to prevent shallow mass-movements by:

1. Mechanical reinforcement from the root system
2. Soil water depletion through transpiration and interception
3. Buttressing and soil arching action from embedded stems

The role of woody vegetation in reinforcing soils and stabilizing slopes is treated in detail in Chapter 3.

Vegetation is self-regulating and self-repairing to a certain extent. Vegetative slope protection measures are also less costly per se than structural measures (White and Franks, 1978). On the other hand, vegetation suffers from several limitations and disadvantages. It is of little use for preventing deep-seated, rotational slope failures, and it is vulnerable to disease, drought, browsing, trampling, and erosion from wave action or streambank scour. Vegetation may also be difficult to establish on steep slopes. Many of these limitations can be overcome, however, by (1) selecting the right type of vegetation, (2) planting and maintaining the vegetation correctly, and (3) using the vegetation in combination with structural–mechanical elements. Procedures for the selection, establishment, and maintenance of vegetation are described in Chapter 6.

4.3 ROLE OF STRUCTURE

Properly designed structures help to stabilize a slope against mass-movement, and they protect the toe or face of a slope against scour and erosion by running water. Structures are generally capable of resisting much higher lateral earth pressures and shear stresses than vegetation. Structures can also be used to divert and convey running water away from critical areas or dissipate the energy of flowing water in a defended area within the structure.

Structures can be built from a number of materials, both natural and artificial. Natural materials include earth, rock, stone, and timber. These materials normally cost less, are environmentally more compatible, and are better suited to vegetative treatment or modification than man-made ones. Artificial materials include steel and cement. Structures made from these materials are stronger and generally more durable than natural structures, but also more energy- and capital- intensive. Some structures are comprised of both natural and artificial materials; examples include concrete crib walls, steel bin walls, gabion walls or revetments, welded-wire walls, and reinforced earth. Steel and concrete in this case mostly provide the rigidity, strength, and reinforcement, while stone, rock, and soil provide the mass. These type of structures can often be planted or vegetated using techniques alluded to previously.

4.3.1 Retaining Structures

A retaining structure of some type will usually be required to protect and stabilize oversteepened slopes. A low toe wall or retaining structure at the foot of a slope permits oversteepening of the slope at its base and flattening above. The latter makes it possible to establish vegetation on the slope, and the former reduces the amount of

clearance required between the base of a slope and an adjacent right-of-way or existing use. This advantage and other applications of retaining structures and toe walls are illustrated schematically in Fig. 4.13.

A particularly graphic example of the advantages of a structure used to support a portion of roadway on a slope is shown in Fig. 4.14. An open-faced crib structure resting on a small bench cut has been used in this case to support a fill that in turn is carrying one-third of the roadway. Advantages of this system include:

1. Considerable reduction in amount of cut necessary
2. Accommodation of the cut material in the crib
3. Limitation of side-cast material to the small excavation necessary for the crib foundation
4. Achievement of stable side slopes on the fill
5. Provisions for growing vegetation in openings between headers at the face of the crib

Slope flattening (i.e., reworking an oversteepened slope to form a less severely sloping area) followed by planting with grass and shrubs is frequently employed as a slope stabilization measure. In many instances slope flattening alone may be impractical. Figure 4.15 depicts two slope profiles that illustrate this point. In Case A the previous steeply cut slope (dashed line) is located in an area where the natural, undisturbed terrain is gently sloping. Thus, by constructing a low toe wall or retaining structure at the slope toe and reworking the face to a $1\frac{1}{2}$:1 slope, the total slope length is only slightly increased. Case B differs only in the slope of the natural terrain above the cut slope face. If the same small retaining structure is provided, and the cut face is reworked to a $1\frac{1}{2}$:1 slope, the overall slope length will be increased by 300 percent. This will greatly increase the amount of ground disturbance and surficial erosion hazard on the reworked face. The alternatives are to:

1. Construct a higher retaining structure.
2. Move the slope toe farther out into the roadway.
3. Rework the cut face to an angle somewhat steeper than $1\frac{1}{2}$:1.
4. Use an anchored, ladder grid revetment (see Chapter 5).
5. Use a combination of the above.

Many different types of retaining structures can be used to meet these objectives. Completely new wall concepts, along with improvement of existing designs, have resulted in a wide offering of structures, one to fit nearly any condition. The design and construction of appropriate retaining structures are described in Chapter 5.

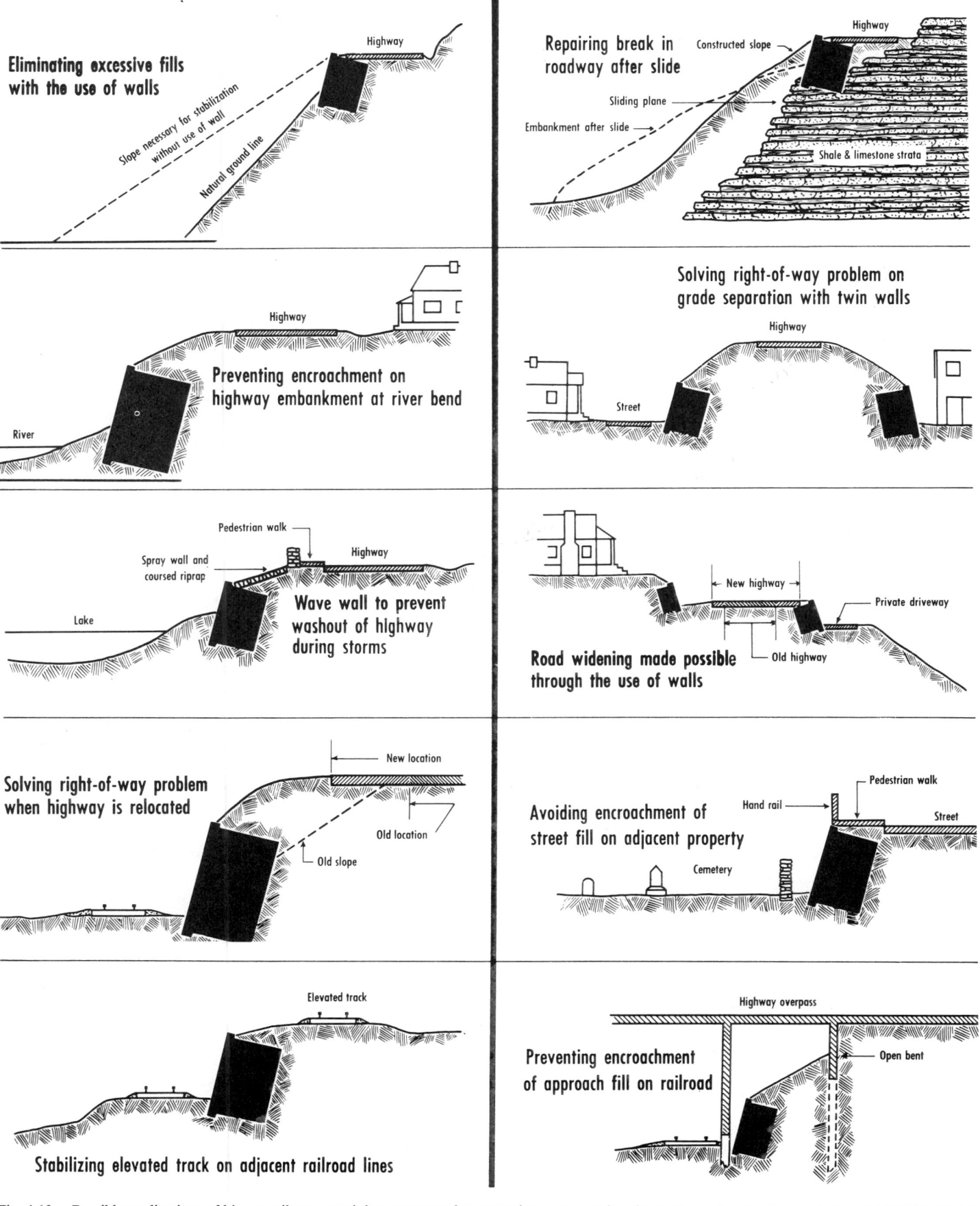

Eliminating excessive fills with the use of walls

Highway

Slope necessary for stabilization without use of wall

Natural ground line

Repairing break in roadway after slide

Highway

Constructed slope

Sliding plane

Embankment after slide

Shale & limestone strata

Preventing encroachment on highway embankment at river bend

Highway

River

Solving right-of-way problem on grade separation with twin walls

Highway

Street

Wave wall to prevent washout of highway during storms

Pedestrian walk

Spray wall and coursed riprap

Highway

Lake

Road widening made possible through the use of walls

New highway

Private driveway

Old highway

Solving right-of-way problem when highway is relocated

New location

Old location

Old slope

Avoiding encroachment of street fill on adjacent property

Pedestrian walk

Hand rail

Street

Cemetery

Stabilizing elevated track on adjacent railroad lines

Elevated track

Preventing encroachment of approach fill on railroad

Highway overpass

Open bent

Fig. 4.13.   Possible applications of bin- or crib-type retaining structures for protecting or supporting slopes. Reproduced with permission of ARMCO, Metal Products Division.

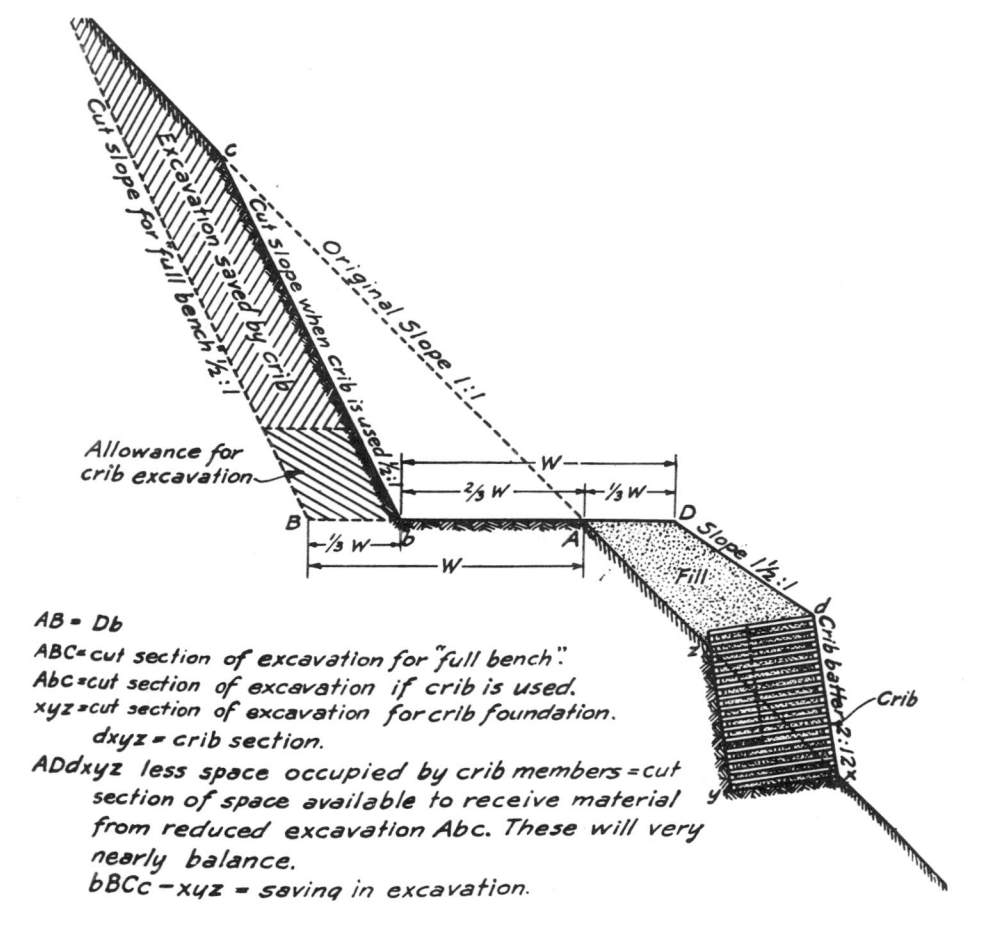

AB = Db
ABC = cut section of excavation for "full bench".
Abc = cut section of excavation if crib is used.
xyz = cut section of excavation for crib foundation.
dxyz = crib section.
ADdxyz less space occupied by crib members = cut
   section of space available to receive material
   from reduced excavation Abc. These will very
   nearly balance.
bBCc − xyz = saving in excavation.

Fig. 4.14.   Illustration of reduction in excavation made possible on a steep slope by use of cribbing. (*From Kraebel, 1936*)

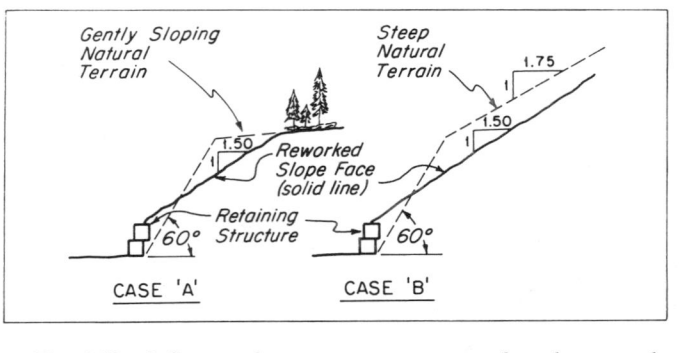

Fig. 4.15.   Influence of toe structure on amount of cut slope reworking. (*From White and Franks, 1978*)

4.3.2   Revetments and Grade Stabilization Structures

Revetments and grade stabilization structures are used where protection is required against scour and erosion by running water. A revetment is a structural armoring on a slope. The weight or mass of the revetment may also buttress the slope to some extent and increase its resistance to mass-movement. Revetments may consist of a variety of different materials, including dumped rubble rock, concrete facings, slotted or cellular concrete grids, articulated blocks, rubber-tire mats, or gabion mattresses. Revetments are commonly used to protect streambanks and channels where water velocities are high and bank materials weak.

A grade stabilization structure is used to reduce grade and dissipate the energy of flowing water within the structure itself or nearby defended area. Debris and sediment tend to be deposited and trapped upstream of the structure. This in turn permits establishment of vegetation behind the structure, which further stabilizes the ground. Grade stabilization structures may range from a series of simple, board check dams to earth embankments with pipe spillways. Mechanical box structures of concrete, masonry, steel, treated wood, or gabions have also been used. Grade stabilization structures or check dams, as they are commonly known, are often employed in gully

(a)

(b)

Fig. 4.16.   Gabion check dam used to control serious channel scour and erosion. Porretta Terme, Italy. (a) After construction in 1930; (b) after 29 years. Vegetation has become established in the channel and structure itself. (*Photos courtesy of Maccaferi Gabions, Inc.*)

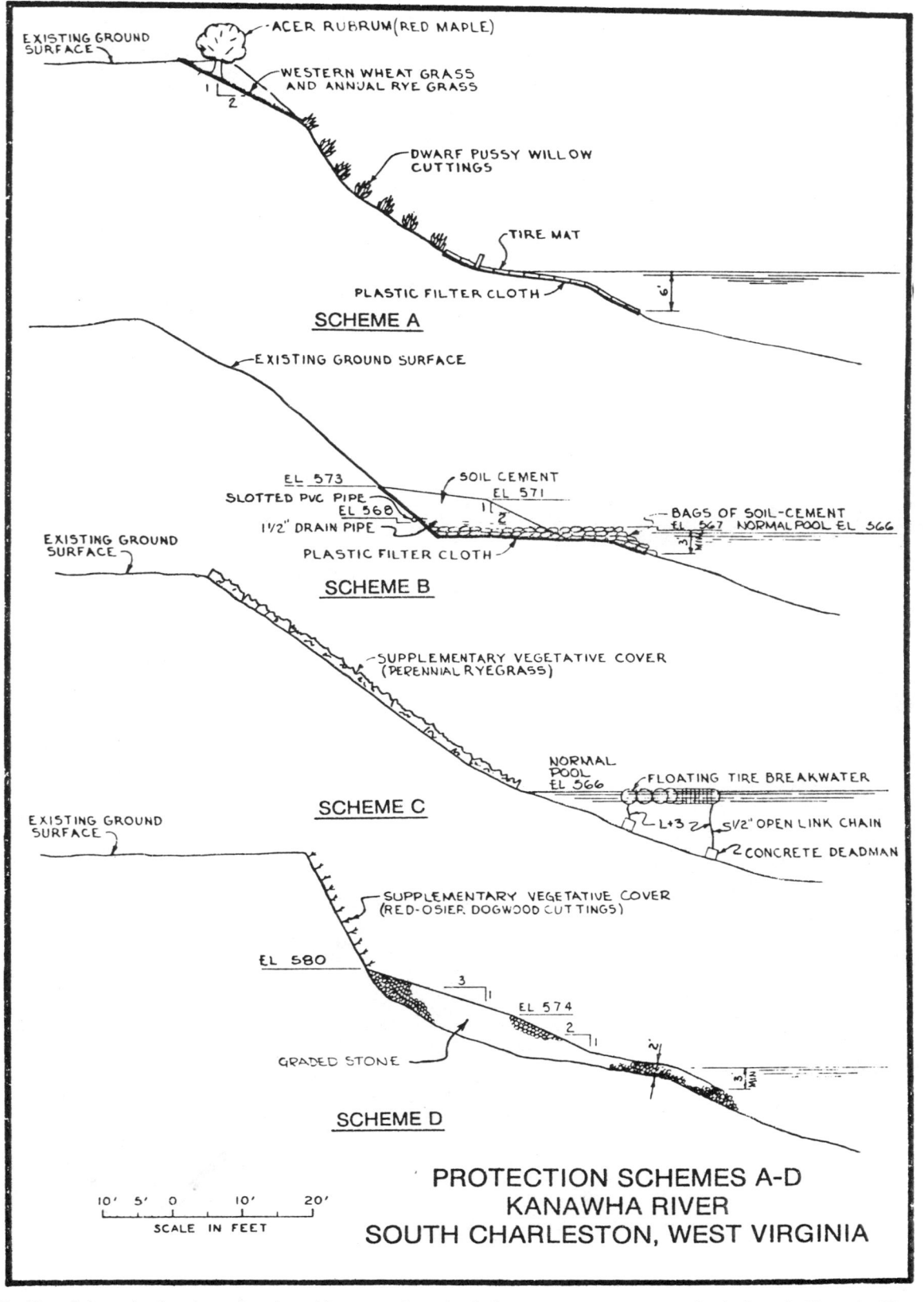

EXISTING GROUND SURFACE

ACER RUBRUM (RED MAPLE)

WESTERN WHEAT GRASS AND ANNUAL RYE GRASS

DWARF PUSSY WILLOW CUTTINGS

TIRE MAT

PLASTIC FILTER CLOTH

6'

SCHEME A

EXISTING GROUND SURFACE

EL 573
SLOTTED PVC PIPE
EL 568
1½" DRAIN PIPE
PLASTIC FILTER CLOTH

SOIL CEMENT
EL 571

BAGS OF SOIL-CEMENT
EL 567 NORMAL POOL EL 566

EXISTING GROUND SURFACE

3

SCHEME B

SUPPLEMENTARY VEGETATIVE COVER (PERENNIAL RYEGRASS)

NORMAL POOL EL 566

FLOATING TIRE BREAKWATER

SCHEME C

L+3
5½" OPEN LINK CHAIN
CONCRETE DEADMAN

EXISTING GROUND SURFACE

SUPPLEMENTARY VEGETATIVE COVER (RED-OSIER DOGWOOD CUTTINGS)

EL 580

3
1

EL 574

2
1

GRADED STONE

2

3 MIN

SCHEME D

**PROTECTION SCHEMES A-D
KANAWHA RIVER
SOUTH CHARLESTON, WEST VIRGINIA**

10' 5' 0   10'   20'
SCALE IN FEET

Fig. 4.17. Use of slope plantings in conjunction with structural–mechanical measures to protect streambank along the Kanawha River. (*From U. S. Army Corps of Engineers, 1978*)

78

(a)

(b)

Fig. 4.18. Gabion groin and revetment system used to stabilize streambank. Sasso Marconi, Bologna, Italy. (a) After construction in 1939; (b) 20 years later, vegetation established in the porous defense works; (c) 30 years later, vegetation completely obscuring structures. (*Photos courtesy of Maccaferi Gabions, Inc.*)

(c)

Fig. 4.18. (*continued*)

control work. Effective and inexpensive check dams can be constructed from loose rock in combination with wire mesh fencing and steel posts (Heede, 1976). Design and construction guidelines for check dams that make maximum use of indigenous, natural materials (rocks, brush, wood posts, and ground litter) are described in Chapter 8.

Gully control provides a good example of the combined use of structures and vegetation. The long-term goal of gully control is establishment of a vegetative cover. This goal can seldom be realized unless severe gully conditions can be altered first. Vegetation alone, for example, will rarely stabilize headcuts because of active piping and concentrated flow of water there. The immediate or short-term objective, therefore, is to stabilize critical locations with structural or mechanical measures. Critical locations where structural measures may be required include nickpoints on the gully bed, headcuts, and gully reaches close to the gully where deepening, widening, and deposition alternate frequently with differing flows. The ultimate function of these structural—mechanical measures, however, is to help establish and rehabilitate vegetation which provides long-term control and protec-

tion. Effective gully control requires, in short, a biotechnical solution to the problem. Various gully control systems and structures are described in considerable detail by Heede (1976). An interesting example of a grade stabilization structure that has revegetated naturally is shown in Fig. 4.16. In this example native vegetation has become established over the years not only in the channel and gully banks upstream but also in the voids and openings of the gabion check dam itself.

The control of stream channel erosion requires engineering measures (i.e., structural bank protection and channel armoring). Structural measures that regulate and direct stream flow (e.g., dams, weirs, groins, etc.) may also be required. Detailed descriptions and examples of streambank protection measures and systems from a nationwide demonstration program have been published by the U. S. Army Corps of Engineers (1978).

Vegetation will likely play a subsidiary role in stream channel erosion control because of its limited ability to withstand continuous inundation and high velocities. Vegetation still has an important role, nevertheless, in stabilizing the upper portions of streambanks and floodplain areas (Fig. 4.17). In many instances vegetation can be incorporated directly into the structural protection by using porous or cellular revetments that can be seeded and planted. A remarkable series of photos is presented in Fig. 4.18, showing the gradual establishment of natural vegetation in a gabion groin and revetment system along a river in Italy.

4.4 COMPATIBILITY BETWEEN ENGINEERING AND BIOLOGICAL REQUIREMENTS

At first glance biotechnical construction methods may seem unworkable because of compatibility problems (i.e., engineering requirements or conditions imposed by the structure may clash with biological requirements of the vegetation). While indeed some difficulty with incompatibility does exist, much of this concern is either misplaced or can be mitigated. Part of the problem arises from a lack of understanding on the part of both engineers who design the structure and horticulture specialists who design plantings, as to each other's design requirements and constraints. An example will serve to illustrate these points.

The backfill or cribfill behind a retaining structure should have certain specified mechanical and hydraulic properties if the structure is to perform properly. Ideally the fill should be coarse-grained, free-draining, granular material. The presence of excessive amount of clay, silt, and organic matter is not desirable. Gabions should be filled with rock no smaller than 4 inches in diameter. Reinforced earth structures have very tight specifications on allowable amount of fines in the backfill; the pH is also of concern because of possible corrosion problems with the ties.

The requirement of free drainage—so essential to the mechanical stability of an earth retaining structure—is also important to vegetation, which cannot tolerate waterlogged soil conditions. Establishment of vegetation, on the other hand, usually requires the presence of fines in the soil in order to provide some moisture and nutrient retention. In many instances these biological requirements can be satisfied without compromising engineering performance by incorporating minor amounts of fines or other amendments in the backfill. These fines or soil amendments can be put in the backfill either in a surface layer at the top or in small scattered pockets near the face. The former approach would be used in the case of a tiered or bench structure where the objective is to vegetate the horizontal steps; the latter in an open crib structure (timber or concrete) where the objective is to vegetate the face. In the case of gabions, soil can be drifted into the gabions after they are already filled with

rock in order to facilitate growth of vegetation. Conversely, cuttings of sprouting plant species (e.g., *Salix*) can be inserted through the baskets during filling into the soil or backfill beyond.

A frequently voiced concern or fear about the use of plants in conjunction with structures is that the roots will pry and tear the structure apart. The evidence for this is scant. The opposite is more likely. Over time the roots will permeate and bind the fill together into a monolithic mass, thereby improving its internal stability. Furthermore, plant roots exhibit a property termed "edaphoecotropism" (Vanicek, 1973) or simply stress avoidance. This means that plant roots will tend to avoid the face of a porous, open retaining structure because of phototropic response in the roots and because of high soil moisture tensions (moisture deficiencies) in this zone. The main danger from prying or wedging would most likely arise instead from species with trunks or stem sizes that exceed the diameter or size of openings in the face of structures or revetments. It is important, therefore, not to plant seedlings that will mature into large-diameter trees in the frontal interstices of a structure.

In regard to groundwater or hydrologic conditions in a slope, it is important to note that in some cases supplementary drainage measures may be required. In these cases structural and conventional vegetative measures (e.g., sodding or hydroseeding) either alone or in combination may not suffice to prevent slope failure (Fig. 4.19). The significance of groundwater and its potential impact on both erosion and mass stability of slopes was discussed in Chapter 2.

Erosion and slope instability caused by groundwater can be prevented or mitigated in several ways. Drains (trenches, vertical wells and horizontal drains, etc.) can be installed to relieve pore pressures in the slope or to intercept and divert groundwater before it can emerge at the slope face. Descriptions and design recommendations for horizontal drain installations have been published by Smith and Stafford (1957) and Royster (1977). Drains in saturated slopes improve not only the performance of structural retaining systems but also the establishment of a vegetative cover and its success in stabilizing a slope.

Phreatophyte vegetation such as willows and cottonwoods can play some role in maintaining a more secure slope by depleting soil moisture via transpiration in the foliage (Fig. 4.19). Slope vegetation may also play a role in arresting seepage erosion by binding and restraining soil in the root system. Vegetation with a thick, fibrous interconnected root mat that permits egress of water but restrains soil particles would be most useful. This same function can be performed by vegetation growing in the openings or voids of a porous structure such as a crib wall or gabion wall.

Fig. 4.19.   Slope failure caused by excessive moisture and groundwater seepage. Slope was graded back and sodded, but this did not prevent slope failure. Note vigorous growth of willow tree beyond failure zone. Planting of willow, a phreatophyte species, on slope might have averted the problem shown here.

4.5   REFERENCES CITED

Heede, B. H. (1976). Gulley development and control, *USDA Forest Service Research Paper RM–169,* Rocky Mtn. Forest and Range Exp. Stn., Fort Collins, Colo., 42 pp.

Kraebel, C. J. (1936). Erosion control on mountain roads, *USDA Circular No. 380.*

Royster, D. L. (1979). Some observations on the use of horizontal drains in the correction and prevention of landslides, *Bull. Assoc. Engr. Geologists,* 16(2): 301–352.

Smith, T. W., and Stafford, G. V. (1957). Horizontal drains on California highways, *J. Soil Mech. Foundations Div.,* ASCE, 83(3): 1301–1326.

U. S. Army Corps of Engineers (1978). The Streambank Erosion Control Evaluation and Demonstration Act of 1974, Interim Report to Congress, Dept. of the Army, Washington, D.C., 137 pp.

Vanicek, V. (1973). The soil protective role of specially shaped plant roots, *Biol. Conservation* 5(3): 175–180.

White, C. A., and Franks, A. L. (1978). Demonstration of erosion control technology, Lake Tahoe region of California. California State Water Resources Control Board Final Rept., 393 pp.

5.
Structural-Mechanical Components of Biotechnical Slope Protection

In this chapter we describe various structural measures that are appropriate and integral to biotechnical slope protection systems. These structural measures include various types of retaining walls and slope revetments. The purpose here is not to catalog and describe all such structural measures, but rather to focus on those that have inherent advantages with respect to economy, ease of fabrication, utilization of natural materials, appearance, and opportunities for incorporation of vegetation or plantings in the structure.

5.1 RETAINING STRUCTURES—GENERAL

5.1.1 Purpose and Function of Structure

The role of structures in biotechnical slope protection systems was discussed briefly in Chapter 4. We elaborate further on the purpose and function of a structure in this section. As noted previously, a structure placed at the foot of a slope helps to stabilize the slope against mass-movement and protects the toe and face against scour and erosion.

A toe wall at the foot of a slope permits local oversteepening of the slope at its base and flattening of the slope above (see Fig. 5.1). The latter makes it possible to establish vegetation on the slope and reduces erosion potential; the former reduces the amount of clearance required between the base of the slope and an adjacent right-of-way or existing use. If an open-face or porous structure is employed, the structure itself can be vegetated as well.

If the slope above the wall is flattened or graded back, the scaled material can often be used as backfill behind the structure. The possibility may also exist of using the scaled material within the structure itself

(e.g., as cribfill), provided it meets gradation and other requirements for such usage. Ideally it is desirable to balance the cut and fill requirements along a reach of slope in order to avoid undue soil disposal or borrow problems.

A toe-bench structure is similar to a toe wall. The two differ mostly in detail and degree in the respect that the toe-bench structure (1) is constructed farther away from the foot of the slope (hence requires little or no excavation at the toe), (2) entails no flattening or regrading of the slope above, and (3) incorporates a level or gently sloping backfill. These differences are depicted schematically in Figs 5.1 and 5.2. Toe benches can be used to provide a fairly level bench at the foot of a slope on which vegetation can be readily established to eventually screen the slope above. They also buttress the base of the slope and catch debris coming off or rolling down the slope.

Toe-bench structures are suitable for vegetative screening of high, steep rocky slopes that themselves cannot be vegetated because of lack of soil or excessive steepness of slope (Fig. 5.2). Toe-bench structures require more clearance than toe walls at the base of a slope (to avoid excavation at the toe). This may constrain their use somewhat along cut slopes adjacent to a roadway where the foot of the cut is next to the road.

5.1.2 Basic Types and Selection Criteria

Selection of a suitable retaining structure entails a wide variety of choices. Several basic types are available, each with its particular advantages, requirements, and limitations. Selection of a suitable retaining wall for biotechnical slope protection will depend upon such considerations as site constraints, availability of materials, appearance

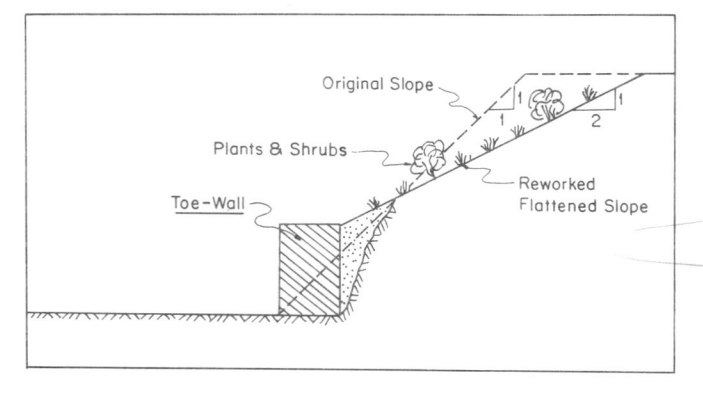

Fig. 5.1. Low toe wall which permits slope flattening and establishment of vegetation on slope above. Encroachment on land use or right-of-way at foot of slope is minimized.

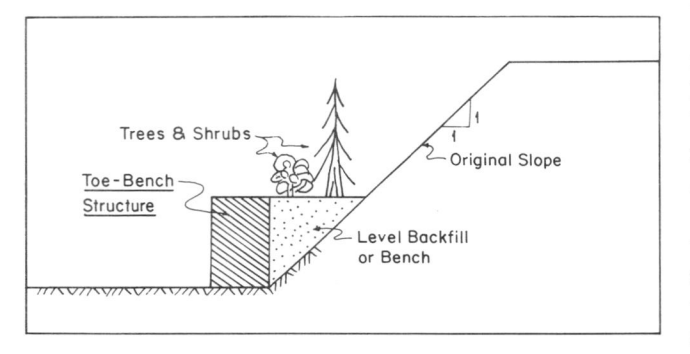

Fig. 5.2. Toe-bench structure which buttresses base of slope and creates level bench on which to establish vegetative screen. Bench also catches debris coming off the slope above.

of wall, ease of construction, opportunities for incorporation of vegetation into structure, and cost.

With regard to basic types, retaining structures can be classified into one of the following categories:

1. Gravity walls
2. Crib or bin walls
3. Reinforced earth
4. Cantilever and counterfort walls
5. Gabions and welded-wire walls
6. Pile walls
7. Tie-back walls

Schematic illustrations of these basic retaining-wall types are shown in Fig. 5.3.

Gravity walls resist earth pressure by their weight or mass. They are constructed conventionally from stone or concrete that can resist compression and shear but no appreciable tension. When constructed from masonry and cement, gravity walls are essentially monolithic. Gravity walls, like all earth-retaining structures, must be capable

of resisting external forces, viz., overturning and sliding. These stability requirements are treated in Section 5.1.3.

Breast walls can be considered as a type of gravity wall constructed with irregularly shaped rock. They are erected on firm ground and placed against a slope with only a small amount of fill behind them. Breast walls are not designed or intended to resist large lateral earth pressures; in this regard they behave more like a revetment than a retaining wall. Breast walls are quite porous; this characteristic provides opportunities for incorporating plants in the voids and interstices of the wall.

Cantilever and counterfort walls are constructed from reinforced concrete and can be built to greater heights with a greater economy of materials than conventional gravity walls. Cantilever walls are used for heights up to 30 ft (9 m), and counterfort walls are commonly used for heights greater than 25 ft (8 m). The cantilever wall is reinforced in the vertical direction to withstand bending moments (a maximum at the base of the stem) and in the horizontal direction to prevent cracking. The buttresses behind a counterfort wall are also heavily reinforced to resist tension. Both types are relatively expensive and require careful design and formwork.

A crib retaining wall consists of a hollow, boxlike, interlocking arrangement of logs, timbers, reinforced concrete beams, or steel beams filled with soil or rock. A variation on this theme, known as a bin wall, consists of steel boxes or bins that are bolted together and filled to form a wall. The cribwork can be vertical or tilted backward for greater stability. The crib members can be designed to have openings between them at the front face where plants can be established. Crib walls are relatively cheap and are usually flexible enough to tolerate some differential settlement. Structurally, cribs and bins are gravity walls and are designed accordingly. In addition, the crib itself must be analyzed for internal stability (i.e., the structural members must be capable of resisting stresses caused by the cribfill and backfill).

Gabions are wire baskets made of coarse wire mesh. These baskets are filled with stone and rock and stacked atop one another to form a gravity-type wall. Gabions depend mainly on the shear strength of the fill for internal stability, and their mass or weight to resist lateral earth forces. Gabions too are a porous type of structure that can be vegetated. Gabions are very flexible, easy to erect, and relatively inexpensive.

Welded-wire walls (Hilfiker, 1978) are a composite wire and granular soil structure. L-shaped, wire mesh sections are placed and connected between successive lifts of coarse granular backfill. The wire mesh provides both reinforcement in the backfill and containment at the face of the wall. Welded-wire walls are essentially gravity structures; they have features of both gabions and reinforced earth walls. Welded-wire walls are relatively low-cost, easy to erect, flexible, and well adapted to vegetative treatment.

Reinforced Earth® walls (Vidal, 1969) consist of a granular matrix or fill reinforced with successive layers of metal strips. The strips are connected to facing elements that conventionally are either metal or concrete panels stacked atop one another. If lightweight, porous facings are used, vegetation can be established in the face of the structure. The reinforced volume can be regarded and analyzed as a coherent gravity structure (McKittrick, 1978). Internal stability requires in addition that the metal strips or ties be designed to resist breaking in tension or failing by pullout. The depth or length of reinforcement to prevent pullout typically ranges from 0.8 to 1.0 times the wall height. Reinforced Earth offers several advantages in terms of flexibility, ease of construction, versatility, and appearance.

Pile walls have occassionally been used as retaining structures. These may consist of a row of bored, cast-in-place concrete cylinder piles or, more typically, driven, steel H-piles (Fig. 5.3). Driven pile walls have been used to support low-volume roads (Schwarzhoff, 1975) where they traverse steep terrain characterized by weak but shallow residual soils underlain by a zone of weathered rock that increases in competency with depth. The use of driven piles in this situation avoids excessive bench excavation that would be required for a bearing-type wall.

Tie-back walls essentially consist of a relatively thin flexible facing connected to a dense network of anchored tie rods. Two possible designs are shown in Fig. 5.3. One consists of light-gage steel sheeting held in place by horizontal $\frac{5}{8}$-inch diameter (16-mm) steel rods installed perpendicular to the sheeting with 8-inch (203-mm) square anchors welded on the far end. The other is made with U-shaped annular panels (similar to half round culverts) for facing with steel tie backs connected to a continuous strap anchor.

A variety of different systems plus possible modifications results in a wide offering of retaining structures—one or even several to fit nearly any condition. Schwarzhoff (1975) has presented a good review of retaining-wall practice and selection procedures for low-volume forest roads. Although any one of several types of retaining walls is often adequate, specified criteria wiln usually lead to the selection of one wall that is best suited for the job. These criteria may include environmental concerns, construction problems, management implications, site constraints, esthetics, and economics. Schwarzhoff (1975) discusses each of these criteria and outlines a systematic selection process for choosing among alternatives.

In the case of biotechnical slope protection systems there are certain criteria that are especially important, paramount among them the requirement that the struc-

ture blend in harmoniously with its surroundings. Examples of what can be done in this regard include the following:

1. Treatment of timber with preservatives that create surface texture and colorations that blend with the surroundings.
2. Use of timber and log crib walls in areas such as forests where materials are natural to their surroundings.
3. Filling gabions with native stone that draws attention away from the wire to the native materials.
4. Utilizing wall structures that minimize disturbance of existing or nearby vegetation so it can be retained to provide a screening effect.
5. Use of facing elements in walls that blend with the surroundings or lend themselves to insertion of vegetation in the wall (e.g., textured wood or lightweight, wire mesh panels for reinforced earth wall facing).
6. Planting vegetation on steps of tiered wall systems or interstices of porous structures (e.g., breast, welded-wire, gabion, and crib walls) or cellular revetments.

The ability to incorporate vegetation into a retaining structure is a particularly important attribute for biotechnical slope protection. This characteristic plus the requirements of ease of construction, flexibility, and low cost restrict initial consideration to the following types of retaining structures: (1) rock breast walls, (2) gabions, (3) crib walls, (4) welded-wire walls, and (5) Reinforced Earth.

The design and construction of the above walls are treated in great detail in this chapter. Other types of walls (e.g., concrete cantilever or counterfort walls) may be suitable in some situations; design of these walls is treated elsewhere (Bowles, 1977; Gupta and Friel, 1977).

5.1.3 Stability Requirements

All of the retaining structures listed at the end of Section 5.1.2 can be designed as gravity walls. Gravity walls resist earth forces chiefly by their weight or mass. In addition to external stability, some of the aforementioned walls must be designed for internal stability as well. Examples of stabilizing elements include ties in reinforced earth walls and structural members (e.g., stretchers and headers) in crib walls that must be capable of withstanding stresses placed on them.

Design criteria for gravity walls are described in general in this section. In the case of low toe walls or toe-bench

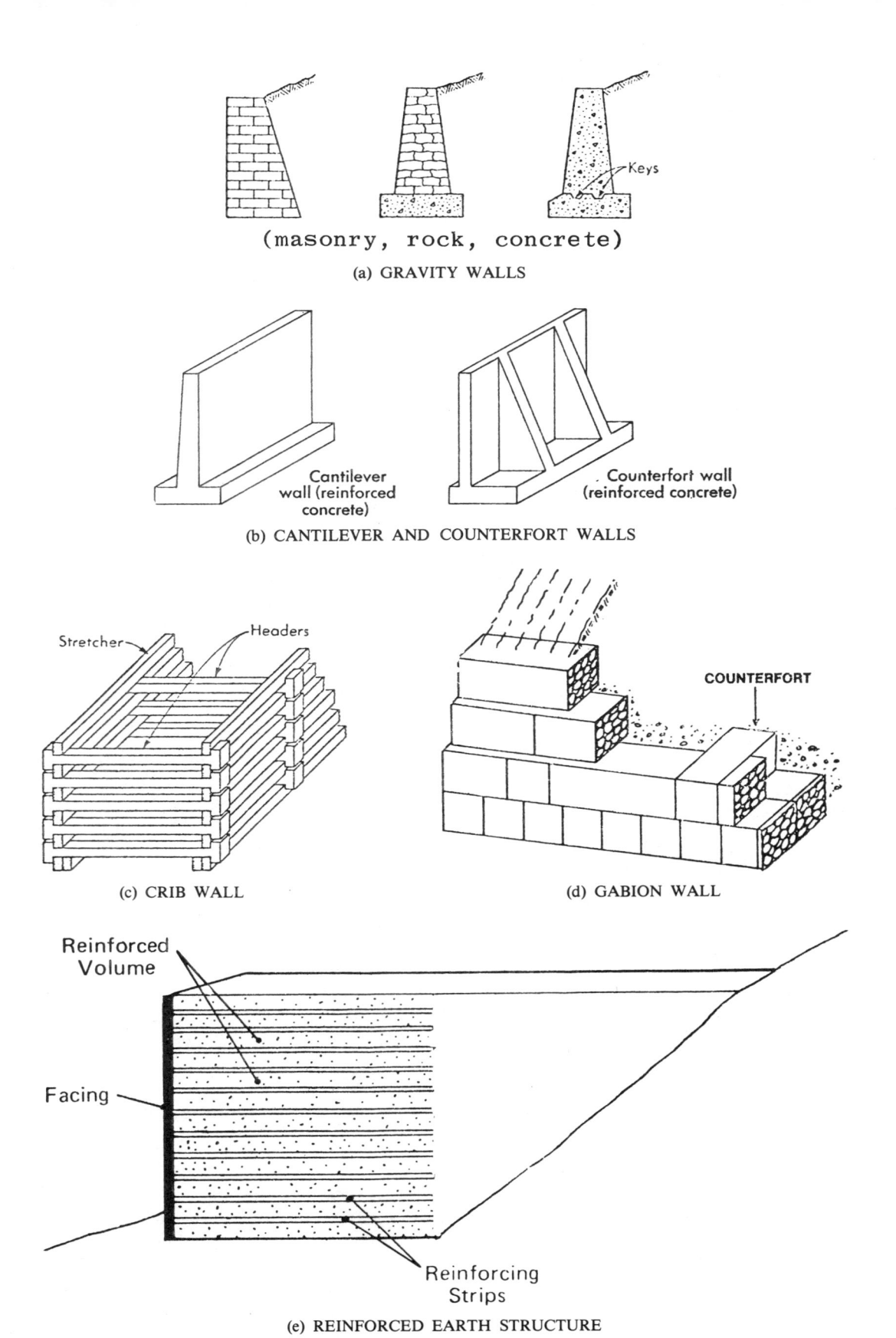

(masonry, rock, concrete)

(a) GRAVITY WALLS

Cantilever wall (reinforced concrete)

Counterfort wall (reinforced concrete)

(b) CANTILEVER AND COUNTERFORT WALLS

Stretcher

Headers

(c) CRIB WALL

COUNTERFORT

(d) GABION WALL

Reinforced Volume

Facing

Reinforcing Strips

(e) REINFORCED EARTH STRUCTURE

Fig. 5.3. Basic types of retaining structures. (a) Gravity walls. (b) Cantilever and counterfort walls. (c) Crib wall. (d) Gabion wall. (e) Reinforced earth wall. (f) Welded-wire walls. (g) Pile walls. (h) Tie-back or anchored walls.

WIRE MAT

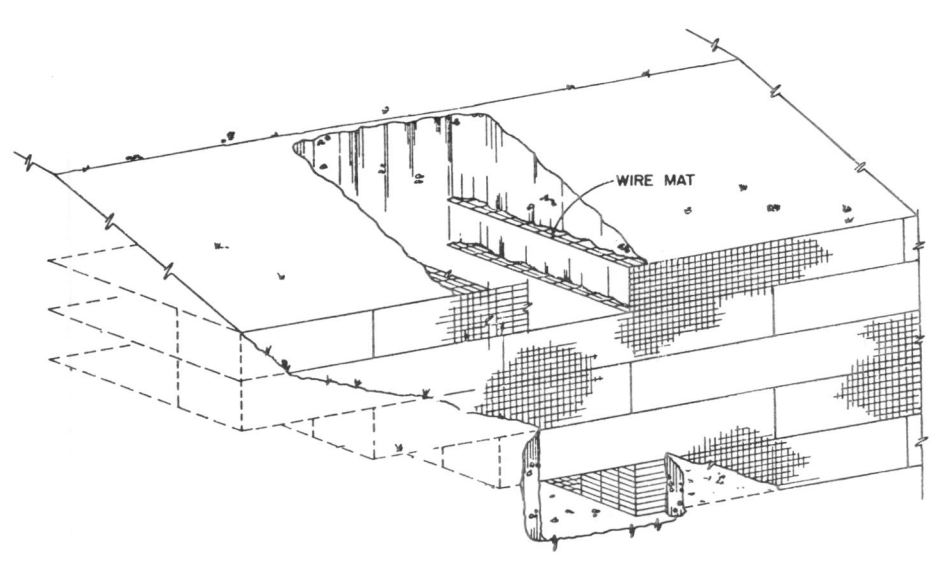

(f) WELDED-WIRE WALL

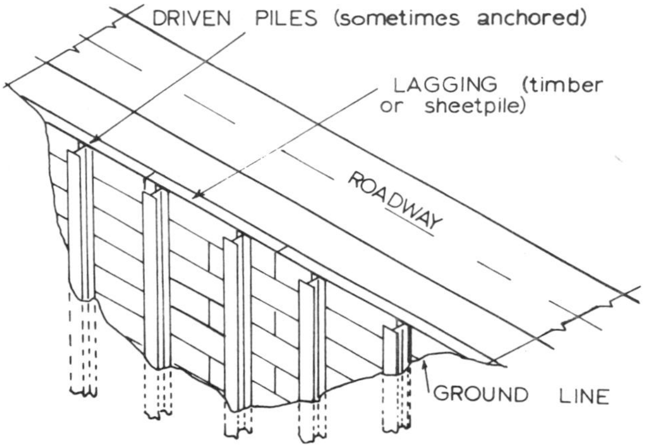

DRIVEN PILES (sometimes anchored)
LAGGING (timber or sheetpile)
ROADWAY
GROUND LINE

(g)

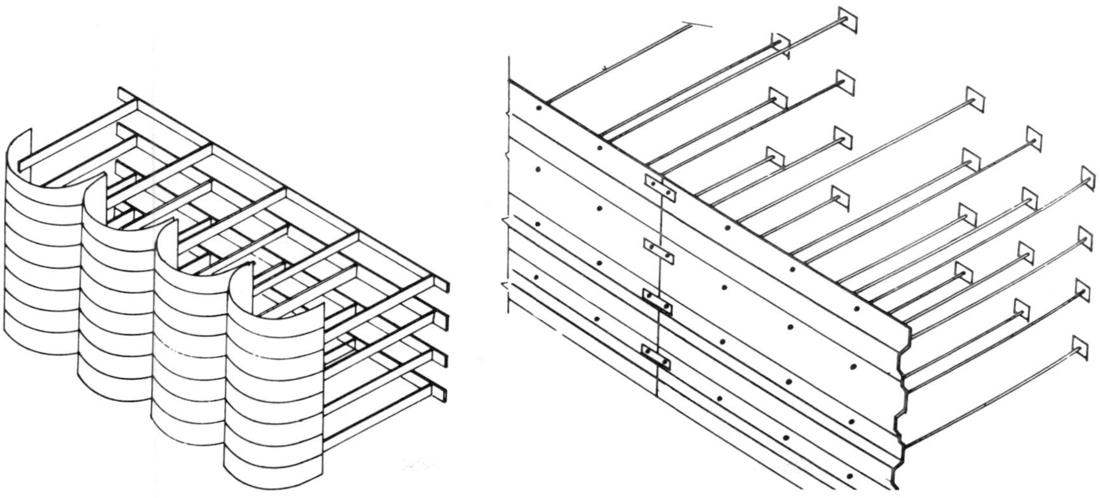

(h)

structures it is usually possible to use standard designs. These designs have been developed for different retaining-wall systems on the basis of both principles of soil mechanics and past performance or experience. Many of these standard designs are included in Appendix I.

5.1.3.1 External Stability.

Gravity wall design requires computations to determine stability of the wall against (1) overturning, (2) sliding along the base, and (3) bearing capacity failure. Essential steps in these computations include determination of the weight of the wall (W) and the lateral force (P) exerted against the wall by the retained earth and surcharge. The computations described herein assume soil construction and backfill conditions in which no buildup of hydrostatic pressure against the wall can occur. The use of permeable structures essentially precludes this possibility—another advantage of the porous structural walls described here.

The forces acting on a hypothetical gravity retaining wall are illustrated schematically in Fig. 5.4. The magnitude of the lateral earth force (P) acting against a gravity retaining wall can be computed by Coulomb's formula:

$$P_A = \frac{1}{2} \gamma H^2 K_A \qquad (5.1)$$

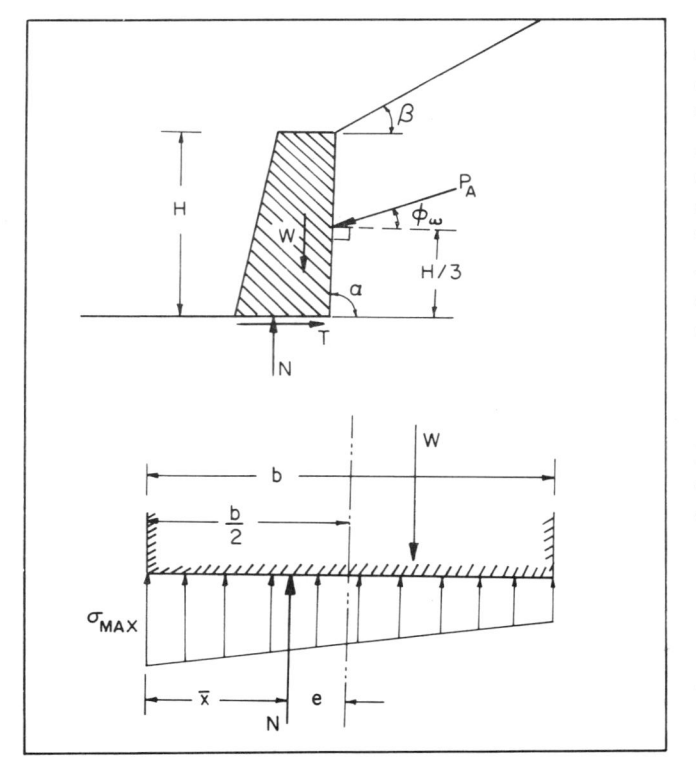

Fig. 5.4. Schematic diagram of forces and stresses acting on gravity retaining wall.

where:

P_A = active earth force per unit length of wall
γ = unit weight of the retained soil
H = height of the wall
K_A = coefficient of active earth pressure

Coulomb's formula is based on so-called active earth pressure conditions; that is, sufficient yielding on movement occurs in the wall to mobilize shear resistance in the backfill itself. This condition is usually met in the case of free-standing gravity walls.

The coefficient of active earth pressure (K_A) is a function of a number of wall, slope, and soil parameters:

$$K_A = \left[\frac{\csc \alpha \sin (\alpha - \phi)}{\left[\sin (\alpha + \phi_w) \right]^{\frac{1}{2}} + \left[\dfrac{\sin (\phi + \phi_w) \sin (\phi - \beta)}{\sin (\alpha - \beta)} \right]^{\frac{1}{2}}} \right]^2 \qquad (5.2)$$

where:

β = angle of inclination of backfill or slope
α = batter angle of wall
ϕ = angle of internal friction of retained soil
ϕ_w = angle of wall friction

Values of K_A are tabulated in Table 5.1 for various values of angle of internal friction, wall batter angle, and inclination of backfill for the special case of zero wall friction ($\phi_w = 0$). The assumption of zero wall friction yields slightly conservative estimates of the coefficient of active earth pressures; that is, lateral earth pressures may be overestimated up to 8 percent. Equation (5.2) can be used to compute more precise values assuming a wall friction approximately 0.8–0.9 times the angle of internal friction of the retained soil. Approximate estimates of the angle of internal friction of the retained soil may be obtained from the chart (Fig. 2.14) in Chapter 2.

Overturning. The resultant of the weight of the wall and lateral earth thrust should pass through the middle third of the base. The coefficient or safety factor against overturning should equal or exceed 1.5. Mathematically,

$$\bar{x} > \frac{b}{3} \qquad (5.3)$$

$$\Sigma M_R / \Sigma M_o \geq 1.5 \qquad (5.4)$$

where:

ΣM_o = overturning moment due to horizontal component of lateral earth force about toe of wall

Table 5.1. Coefficient of active earth pressure as a function of wall and backfill inclination, for $\alpha' = \alpha - 90°$, and $\phi_{\hat{w}} = 0$ (from Lambe and Whitman, 1969).*

$\beta =$		−30°	−12°	±0	+12° 1:4.7	+30° 1.1:7
$\phi = 20°$	$\alpha' = +20°$		0.57	0.65	0.81	
	$\alpha' = +10°$		0.50	0.55	0.68	
	$\alpha' = ±0°$		0.44	0.49	0.60	
	$\alpha' = -10°$		0.38	0.42	0.50	
	$\alpha' = -20°$		0.32	0.35	0.40	
$\phi = 30°$	$\alpha' = +20°$	0.34	0.43	0.50	0.59	1.17
	$\alpha' = +10°$	0.30	0.36	0.41	0.48	0.92
	$\alpha' = ±0°$	0.26	0.30	0.33	0.38	0.75
	$\alpha' = -10°$	0.22	0.25	0.27	0.31	0.61
	$= -20°$	0.18	0.20	0.21	0.24	0.50
$\phi = 40°$	$\alpha' = +20°$	0.27	0.33	0.38	0.43	0.59
	$\alpha' = +10°$	0.22	0.26	0.29	0.32	0.43
	$\alpha' = ±0°$	0.18	0.20	0.22	0.24	0.32
	$\alpha' = -10°$	0.13	0.15	0.16	0.17	0.24
	$\alpha' = -20°$	0.10	0.10	0.11	0.12	0.16

*Used with permission of John Wiley & Sons, Inc.

ΣM_R = resisting moment due to weight of wall and vertical component of lateral earth force

$\bar{x}$ = distance from toe to point of application of resultant on base

b = width of wall at its base

Sliding. The summation of the vertical forces times the tangent of the angle of internal friction of the soil at the base of the wall over the summation of the horizontal forces should equal or exceed 1.5. Mathematically,

$$\frac{\Sigma F_v \tan \phi}{\Sigma F_H} \geq 1.5 \qquad (5.5)$$

where:

ΣF_v = summation of vertical forces due to weight of wall plus vertical component of lateral earth force

ΣF_H = summation of horizontal forces against wall

Additional safety against sliding of the wall along its base is provided by embedment. A passive earth resistance can be computed from the depth of embedment and type of soil. This additional margin of safety vanishes, however, if the toe of the wall is ever excavated; therefore, it is not included in the above computations.

Pressure at Base. The ratio of the ultimate bearing capacity should equal or exceed the average bearing stress at the base by 2.5. Mathematically,

$$q_{ULT}/\sigma_{AVE} \geq 2.5 \qquad (5.6)$$

where:

q_{ULT} = ultimate bearing capacity of soil or ground beneath wall

σ_{AVE} = average bearing stress exerted by wall on soil

The ultimate bearing capacity of the ground beneath a loaded foundation or wall can be computed from various formulae given in standard textbooks in geotechnical engineering (Bowles, 1977). Bearing capacity is governed by the width of the foundation, friction angle and density of the soil, inclination and eccentricity of load, and slope of the ground surface.

Local building codes frequently list allowable bearing stresses or capacities for different types of soils which can be used to check a retaining-wall design. Alternatively, recommended or allowable bearing capacities from handbooks such as the U. S. Navy *Design Manual* (1971) can be used for this purpose (Table 5.2). In the case of rigid retaining walls there will be an uneven or trapezoidal stress distribution on the base (see Fig. 5.4) with the greatest stress intensity usually occurring at the toe. The stress intensity at the edges (toe and heel) can be calculated from the following simple expression:

$$\sigma = \frac{\Sigma F_v}{b} \left(1 \pm \frac{6e}{b}\right) \qquad (5.7)$$

where e = eccentricity or distance from center to point of application of resultant on base.

In the case of a flexible foundation such as a gabion wall the contact stress at the base will not be distributed in a planar, trapezoidal fashion as shown in Fig. 5.4. Instead the stress will decrease from a maximum at the point of application of the resultant at the base to lesser values at the edges. The pressure at the toe of a gabion wall is, therefore, generally less than for a rigid wall. Accordingly, the error of assuming a planar, trapezoidal distribution and using Equation (5.7) will yield a conservative or safer estimate of the critical stress at the toe of a flexible retaining wall, compared to a rigid wall.

Safety against overturning is only assured if the pressure under the toe does not exceed the bearing capacity of the soil. Toe pressures for standard designs should be checked in this regard. In the case of standard designs for timber cribs (Appendix IB) these toe pressures are plotted as a function of wall height on the specification sheets. Standard designs for gabion walls, on the other hand, do not include toe pressures but are safe for soils having a bearing capacity of 2 TSF. If computed pressures exceed the allowable bearing capacity for a foundation soil at a site, either the wall height must be reduced, or the heel or toe or both must be extended.

Table 5.2.   Allowable bearing capacities for different types of soils and soil conditions.*

TYPE OF BEARING MATERIAL	CONSISTENCY IN PLACE	RECOMMENDED VALUE OF ALLOWABLE BEARING CAPACITY, TONS PER SQ FT
Well-graded mixture of fine and coarse-grained soil: glacial till, hardpan, boulder clay (GW—GC, GC, SC)	Very compact	10
Gravel, gravel–sand mixtures, boulder–gravel mixtures (GW, GP, SW, SP)	Very compact Medium to compact Loose	8 6 4
Coarse to medium sand, sand with little gravel (SW, SP)	Very compact Medium to compact Loose	4 3 2
Fine to medium sand, silty or clayey medium to coarse sand (SW, SM, SC)	Very compact Medium to compact Loose	3 2.5 1.5
Fine sand, silty or clayey medium to fine sand (SP, SM, SC)	Very compact Medium to compact Loose	3 2 1.5
Homogeneous inorganic clay, sandy or silty clay (CL, CH)	Very stiff to hard Medium to stiff Soft	4 2 0.5
Inorganic silt, sandy or clayey silt, varved silt—clay—fine sand (ML, MH)	Very stiff to hard Medium to stiff Soft	3 1.5 0.5

*Adapted from *Design Manual DM-7,* Dept. of the Navy, Bureau of Yards and Docks, Washington, D.C.

5.1.2.3 Internal Stability.

In addition to withstanding external forces, structural components or members of retaining walls must be capable of safely resisting stresses to which they will be subjected. In the case of crib walls the internal stresses consist of (1) pressures exerted by earth confined in the crib and (2) stresses in crib members and connectors resulting from earth pressures exerted by both cribfill and backfill. The former can be estimated from theories developed to predict internal pressures exerted by granular materials on the walls of bins or silos (Caughey et al., 1951). In the case of member stresses, critical considerations include joint bearing stress, header flexural stress, stretcher flexural stress, and stretcher torsional shearing stress. Schuster et al. (1973) outlined procedures for calculating these stresses. They also analyzed standard designs for timber cribs to detect either overstress of the crib members or potential failure of the entire crib due to external stability problems. In general they found that standard designs for timber cribs were adequate (see Section 5.2.3.1), with the most critical or governing criteria being external stability criteria.

Internal stability requirements are also important in reinforced earth and welded-wire walls. The ties in reinforced earth walls must have a sufficiently large cross-sectional area and/or be placed in sufficient numbers to resist breaking in tension. The ties must also be sufficiently long and "frictional" enough to resist failure by pullout. Tie design criteria for reinforced earth walls are discussed by Lee et al. (1973) and McKittrick (1978). There are at present no standard tie designs for reinforced earth walls. Instead each wall system must be analyzed and designed separately. This design is provided as part of the "reinforced earth package" by the Reinforced Earth Company or licensee in the contract to erect a retaining wall (see Section 5.2.5).

Protection of structural components or members against weathering, rot, and corrosion is essential to the integrity and internal stability of many wall systems. Some control can be exercised by drainage provisions and constraints on the type of cribfill and backfill used. Members can also be made oversize or thicker to provide a margin of safety against deterioration. Alternatively, the members can be coated or impregnated to improve resistance to deterioration. Procedures for improving durability of structural members are discussed in subsequent sections describing different retaining-wall systems.

5.1.4   Standard Designs

Many retaining walls can be constructed for specified slope-loading conditions and heights from standard designs. These designs have evolved over the years on the basis of both theory and practical experience with a given retaining-wall system. Standard designs have been developed by and are available from a number of sources; these include manufacturers of retaining-wall systems (e.g., gabions, crib walls, welded-wire walls), trade associations (e.g., American Wood Preservers Institute), and state and federal agencies (e.g., U. S. Forest Service, Federal Highway Administration).

Many of these standard designs have been collected for ready reference in Appendix I. Standard designs can be used safely provided the stated conditions on which the designs are based also pertain at the site in question. It is advisable to read carefully the caveats and general notes associated with each design. In general the factors or conditions to consider include the following:

1. The maximum wall height
2. Surcharge conditions
3. Strength and finish of the structural members
4. Inclination of the wall
5. Erection and assembly sequence
6. Type of fasteners or connectors
7. Gradation and compaction requirements on cribfill and backfill
8. Conditions of foundation soil beneath wall
9. Groundwater conditions

Battered or inclined walls require less volume for the same height than vertical walls. Battering shifts the center of gravity away from the toe, into the slope, and increases the resisting moment against overturning. Choice of a particular design will depend upon the purposes of the wall, site constraints, desired height, and cost. All of the designs in Appendix I lend themselves to vegetative treatment and landscaping.

5.2   TOE-WALL CONSTRUCTION

5.2.1   Rock Breast Walls

A combination of rock and vegetation can be used to stabilize and protect the toe of steep slopes. Breast walls differ from conventional retaining structures in that they are placed against relatively undisturbed earth and are *not* intended to resist large lateral earth pressures.

Breast walls are normally 3 to 4 ft high and are usually constructed from rock 10 inches to 3 ft in diameter. They should be laid on a firm foundation of undisturbed or well-tamped earth and constructed with a 6:1 external batter angle.

The breast wall can be constructed with a sloping bench behind the wall. This bench provides a transition slope on which vegetation can be readily planted afterward. The backfill behind the wall should be well tamped. Live willow branches or green cuttings can be placed in the interstices of the rock wall as it is constructed. The butt ends of the willow branches should extend into the backfill behind the wall.

Figure 5.5 shows a typical construction profile of a breast wall using large rocks. A photograph of a rock breast wall constructed at the base of a cut slope along a roadway is shown in Fig. 5.6. Specifications and guidelines suggested for use in constructing this type of structure are listed below:

1. Rock breast walls shall be 1.0 to 1.5 m high. Rock used should normally range from 0.25 to 1.0 m in diameter. Larger boulders can be used in the base course if available.
2. The rock breast wall shall be laid upon solid foundation materials or undisturbed earth.
3. A minimum amount of excavation into the slope shall be performed to provide a foundation for the rock breast wall. The breast wall should not be placed such that it reduces an adjacent road right-of-way to less than the minimum required dimensions.
4. The rocks shall be laid with at least a three-point bearing on the foundation material or on previously laid rocks. The rocks shall be placed such that their

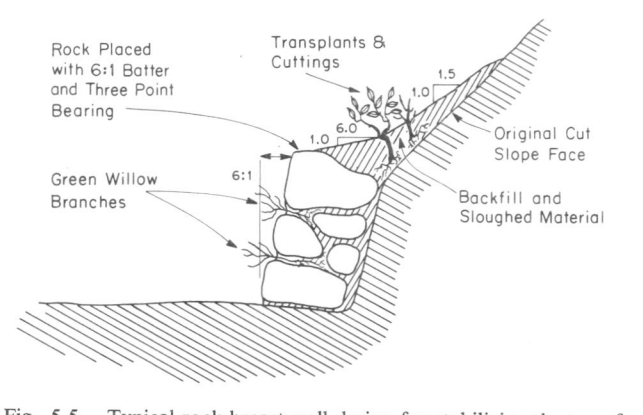

Fig. 5.5. Typical rock breast wall design for stabilizing the toe of a steep, eroding slope.

centers of gravity are as low as possible, with the bedding planes sloping inward toward the slope toe.
5. The rock breast wall shall be constructed such that the external wall face has a 6:1 batter. As the rocks are placed, fill shall be laid behind and around the rocks and tamped thoroughly.
6. In addition to fill, live willow branches may be placed in the interstices of the rock wall as it is constructed. The basal ends of the willow branches

Fig. 5.6. Rock breast wall protecting toe of road cut. Slope above was scaled, wattled, and seeded with grass. Rocks from slope scaling were used in construction of wall.

shall extend into the backfill behind the rock breast wall. The top layer of rocks must be placed in a closely adjacent and continuous manner to minimize gaps.

7. In the case of a rock breast wall constructed adjacent to a paved or impervious surface, a drainage system shall be placed at the outside toe of the rock breast wall, directing drainage waters to an appropriate disposal area and preventing erosion of the foundation material and undercutting of the rock breast wall.

The above sample specifications are intended only as a guide, and must be modified to fit the particular situation.

5.2.2 Gabion Walls

Gabions are rectangular containers fabricated from a triple twisted hexagonal mesh of heavily galvanized steel wire. Figure 5.7 depicts schematically typical one-tier and two-tier gabion breast wall installations. Photographs of typical gabion retaining wall installations are shown in Figs. 5.8 and 5.9. The use of vegetation (viz., willow cuttings) purposely introduced into gabion walls was il-

lustrated previously in Fig. 4.4. The establishment and growth of volunteer vegetation in gabion structures over time were illustrated as well in Figs. 4.16 and 4.18.

Excavation of the site for the placement of the gabions is similar to the procedure described for rock breast walls. For easy handling and shipping, gabions are supplied folded into a flat position and bundled together. Each gabion is readily assembled by unfolding and binding together all vertical edges with lengths of connecting wire stitched around the vertical edges. The empty gabions are placed in position and wired to adjoining gabions. They are then filled with cobblestone-size rock (10–30 cm in diameter) to one-third their depth. Two connecting wires are then placed in each direction, bracing opposing gabion walls together. The connecting wires prevent the gabion baskets from "bulging" as they are filled. This operation is repeated until the gabion is filled. After filling, the top is folded shut and wired to the ends, sides, and diaphragms. During the filling operation live rooting plant species, such as willow, may be placed among the rocks in a manner similar to that described for rock breast walls. If this is done, some soil should be placed in the gabions with the branches, and the basal ends of the plants should extend well into the backfill area behind the gabion breast wall.

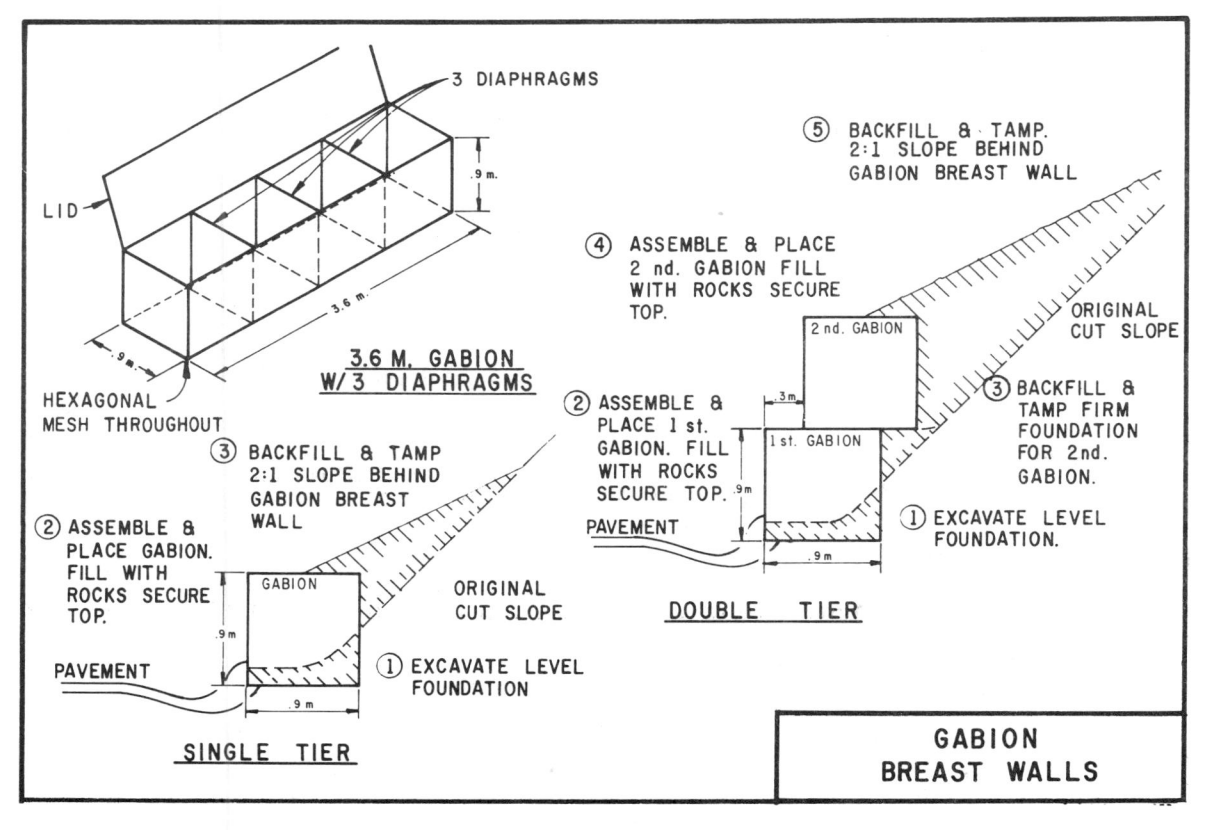

Fig. 5.7. Low gabion breast walls showing sequence of excavation, assembly, and filling. (*From White and Franks, 1978*)

Fig. 5.8. Stepped-front, gabion retaining wall following construction. Vegetation will eventually invade and grow in the interstices of the structure.

The simplest gabion structure is 3-ft-high wall using one tier of gabions. A second tier of gabions can be placed on top of the first tier and set back 18 inches (i.e., stepped back) without any significant design constraints. Gabion walls that are higher than two tiers (6 ft) usually require significant additional design constraints. As higher tiered walls are designed and used, the basal foundation of the wall must be increased, and/or counterforts must be used to brace the wall against overturning moments from the backfill.

Several different design configurations are possible with gabions. They may have either a battered or a stepped-back front. The choice of type depends upon application although the stepped-back type is generally easier to build when the wall is more than 10 ft high. The number and arrangement of gabion units also depend upon whether a level or an inclined backfill is used behind the wall. Various design configurations and guidelines can be found in Appendix IA and in gabion manufacturers' literature. Walls higher than three tiers (9 ft) should be designed under the supervision of a registered civil engineer.

Some advantages of gabion walls are:

1. Ease of handling and transportation
2. Speed of erection
3. Flexibility (thus tolerance to substantial differential movement and avoidance of extensive foundation preparation)
4. Permeability to water (hence good drainage)

Low gabion walls and rock breast walls are comparable alternatives. Hand-placed, rock breast walls are more limited in height. Gabions are sometimes criticized as being unsightly; however, use of attractive facing stone toward the front of the wall plus establishment of vegetation in the gabions can ameliorate this problem. If large rocks are readily accessible, inexpensive, and near the proposed site, then their use in construction of a rock breast wall might be preferable. If, on the other hand, rock must be imported or is only available in small sizes, it is likely that the gabion wall would be preferable.

5.2.3 Crib Walls

A crib is basically a structure formed by joining a number of cells together and filling them with soil or rocks to give them strength and weight so as to form a gravity retaining

Fig. 5.9.   Close-up view of gabion wall showing stone-filled wire baskets. Appearance of wall is enhanced by careful selection and placement of stones next to the wire.

wall. In crib structures the members are essentially assembled "log cabin" fashion. The frontal, horizontal members are termed stretchers; the lateral members, headers. Forces are transferred between the members at the corner joints. Small blocks called pillow blocks are also placed at critical locations between members to relieve compressive stresses at the joints and reduce bending and torsional stresses in the stretchers and headers.

5.2.3.1 Timber Cribs.

Components and configurations of a typical timber crib retaining wall are shown in Fig. 5.10. In modern designs, mechanical connectors such as drift pins or split rings are used at the joints; however, some old timber crib walls in mining areas of northern Idaho have dapped (i.e., notched) joints to transfer forces.

Schuster et al. (1973) have prepared a comprehensive study and analysis of timber crib retaining walls including an evaluation of existing walls and a performance comparison of different timber crib designs. Most of the information herein is extracted from their publication.

A great number of timber walls were built in the early 1900s by the mining industry in the Rocky Mountain states. Many of these walls are still standing, some in various states of disrepair. Others, particularly those with well-drained backfill, are 50 to 60 years old and still serviceable. The primary use of timber cribs today is to retain road cuts and embankments, particularly in mountainous areas and for low-volume roads.

A large percentage of timber crib walls being designed and built today are constructed of dimensioned, structural-grade timber (either $6'' \times 6''$ or $8'' \times 8''$ stock). Most commonly the members are rough-cut, structural-grade Douglas fir, although some specifications allow other species.

Log crib walls are not subject to exact engineering design and analysis; nevertheless, many have been built. Both the Washington State Department of Highways (1973) and the Federal Highway Administration have published design standards for log cribbing. These design plans can be found in Appendix IB.

A number of standard designs for timber crib retaining

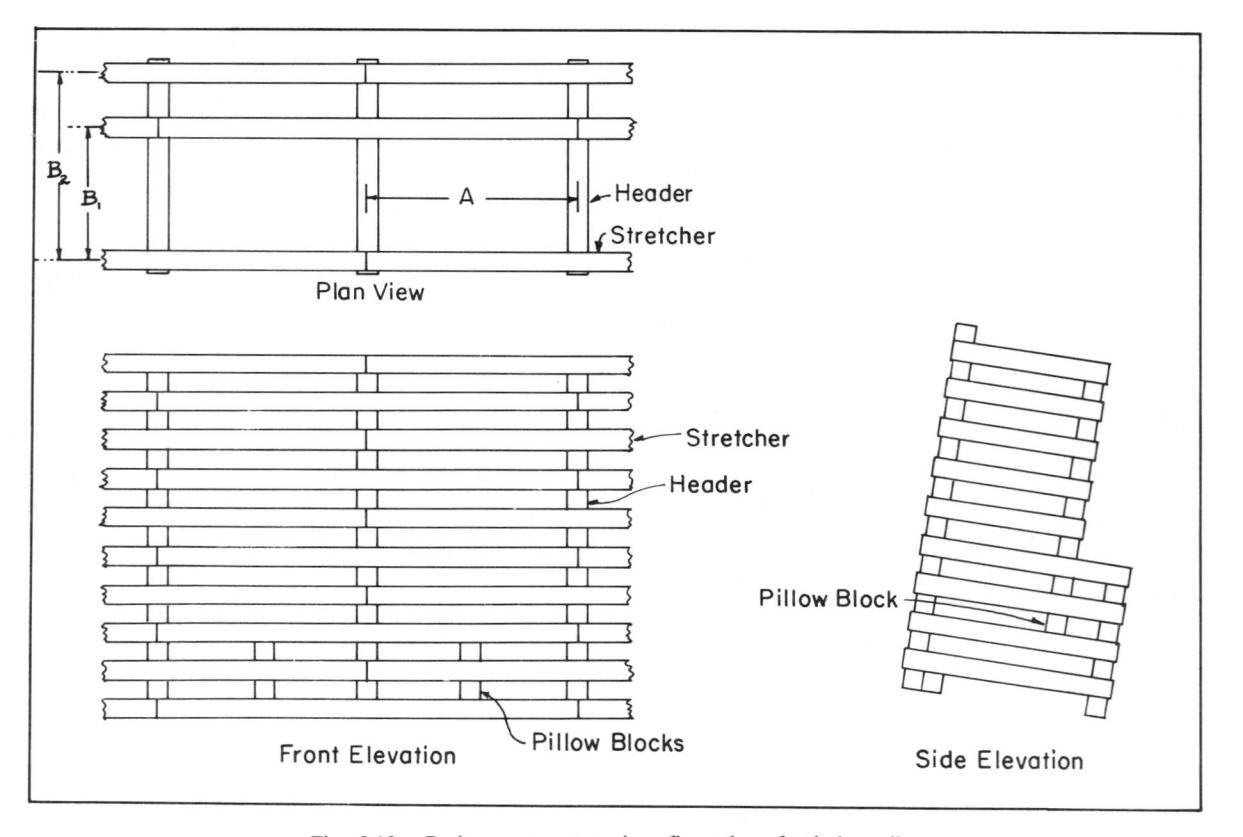

Fig. 5.10. Basic components and configuration of a timber crib.

walls are commonly used in the United States. Standard designs for timber crib retaining walls have been developed by the following organizations:

1. American Wood Preservers Institute, Washington, D.C.
2. California Division of Highways (currently designated California Department of Transportation), Sacramento, California
3. Permapost products Co., Hillsboro, Oregon
4. Bureau of Public Roads (currently designated Federal Highway Administration), Region 10, Vancouver, Washington
5. U. S. Forest Service, Region 6, Portland, Oregon
6. U. S. Forest Service, Region 1, Missoula, Montana
7. U. S. Forest Service, Region 4, Ogden, Utah

Complete discussion, design details, and evaluation of each of these standard wall designs have been provided by Schuster et al. (1973). The authors conclude that for level backfills, crib walls formed of treated, dimensional timber and constructed in accord with any of the standard designs can be safely built to the design heights. They note, however, that in a few cases additional blocking may be necessary at critical points. Timber crib walls are also moderately flexible and can withstand differential

settlements without a significant effect on the retaining action or gross stability of the wall, even with noticeable crushing of individual members or weakening of the joints.

Details of standard, treated timber cribbing designs developed by both the American Wood Preservers Institute (AWPI) and Permapost Products Company can be found in Appendix IB. The AWPI designs all use vertical members in a header–stretcher joint that is different from those used in other designs. The horizontal stretcher forces are transmitted to the header by the vertical members bolted to the sides of the projecting headers. These vertical members are also designed to act as a column in resisting the cumulative vertical reactions from the headers.

By using various combinations of base widths and either vertical or battered crib sections (see AWPI Basic Designs A through H in Appendix IB), the AWPI wall is suitable to a maximum height of 30 ft for a variety of surcharge conditions. Although the battered front face configuration is slightly more difficult to construct, it offers several advantages:

1. Less structure (timbers and cribfill) is required than for a vertical wall the same height.

2. The cribfill is less likely to ravel out the front face of the structure.
3. Vegetation is more easily planted and established in the interstices between stretchers.

The Permapost Products wall is a simpler basic design than the AWPI wall. Four types (see Permapost Basic Designs A through D in Appendix IB) are available to cover various heights up to 22 ft.

Drainage characteristics of backfill and cribfill materials have a noticeable effect on crib performance and longevity. This is particularly important in mountainous, high-precipitation areas where most timber walls are built. Use of free-draining, granular materials generally ensures that there will not be buildup of seepage pressures in the fill material. These materials also help to keep the crib members relatively dry, prolonging the life of the wood. The AWPI of other crib-wall designs assume the use of a free-draining sand or gravel fill.

Timber treatment or preservation is important for prolonging the life of a timber crib wall. Most modern timber crib members are pressure-treated with preservatives such as pentachlorophenol in heavy oil (brown), pentachlorophenol in liquid petroleum gas or mineral spirits (natural), or water-borne salts such as copper arsenate (green). Pressure treatment is commonly performed at a central plant where crib members are individually cut and drilled ready for assembly. Timbers also may be wholly or partly treated in the field by dipping, swabbing, or brushing using these same preservatives. These methods are not as effective as pressure treatment, and cannot be expected to provide the same degree of preservation of treated members.

5.2.3.2 Concrete Crib Walls.

Crib walls can also be constructed from reinforced concrete structural members. Most crib walls in use today are constructed in this fashion. Concrete crib walls are more durable and can be built to greater heights than timber cribs. The basic principle of construction remains the same, viz., a cribbing is formed of interlocking structural units, the internal spaces of which are filled with suitable free-draining material that adds to the stability of the wall.

There are several concrete crib wall systems or designs available. These systems differ in the shape of structural members (stretchers and headers), wall configuration, structural connections, and erection procedure. Two good examples of the range of designs available are (1) the Hilfiker Concrib wall and (2) the Humes Pincrib and Minicrib walls.

The Concrib wall (Hilfiker, 1972) is constructed with "dog-bone"-shaped headers that help to keep the stretchers in place (Fig. 5.11). A schematic diagram of this crib wall system showing different arrangements and

Fig. 5.11.   View of open-front, concrete crib wall utilizing "dog-bone" header design. Note establishment of vegetation in cribbing.

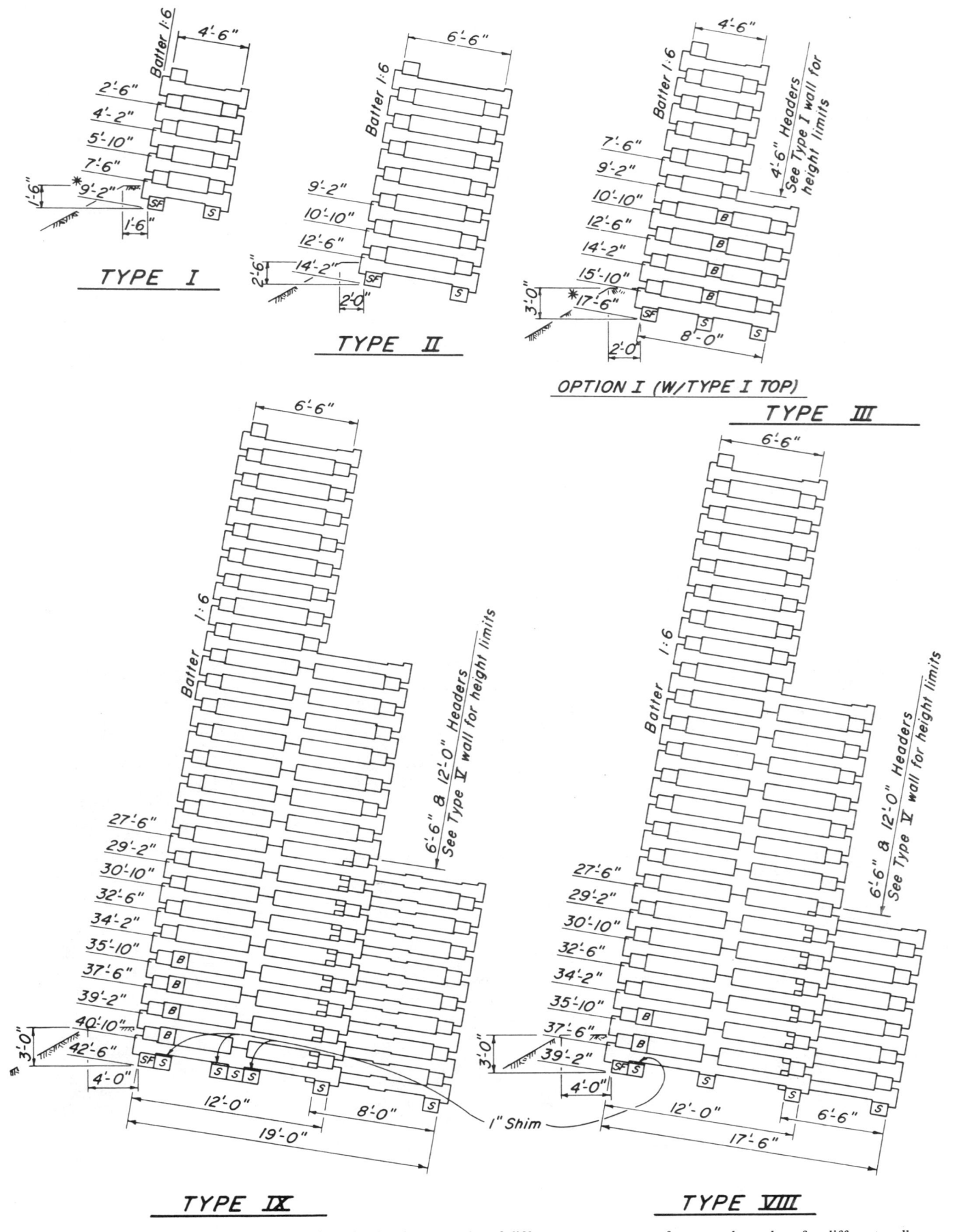

Fig. 5.12.   Reinforced concrete crib Concrib walls showing examples of different arrangements of structural members for different wall heights. (*From Hilfiker, 1972*). Reproduced by permission of the Hilfiker Pipe Company, Eureka, California.

configurations of structural members for different wall heights is presented in Fig. 5.12. The walls are usually constructed with a batter of 1:6 to improve stability, although vertical walls can also be specified. The stretchers at the front may be of either the closed-face or open-face design; the latter permits establishment of plants and shrubs in the face of the wall. An exposed aggregate finish may also be specified in order to blend the wall in more harmoniously with its surroundings.

Concrib retaining walls can be constructed to heights up to 54 ft. The unique design of the stretchers and headers in Concrib walls results in a savings in steel and cement. The stretchers are chamfered along outwardly disposed edges and incorporate primary steel reinforcing rods only on the outwardly disposed sides. The headers are necked down between their ends but can be provided with integral middle supports or enlargements that act as pillow blocks when the headers are stacked one above another in the cribwork (Fig. 5.12). Additionally, the headers are chamfered in such a way as to provide a mating bearing surface for the chamfered edges of the stretchers. The configuration of walls for other heights along with foundation pressures and other design specifications for this wall system are listed in Appendix IC.

The Humes Pincrib and Minicrib walls (Humes Ltd., Melbourne, Australia) differ considerably in the shape of the headers and structural connections (Figs. 5.13 and 5.14). The Pincrib wall is designed for large-scale retention projects. Pins in headers and false headers (Fig. 5.13) fit into holes in stretchers to facilitate erection of the wall. Minicribs were developed to minimize the cost of low-to-medium-height walls. Header design with Minicrib walls (Fig. 5.14) avoids the need for stretchers at the rear of the wall.

Both the Pincrib and the Minicrib wall have an open

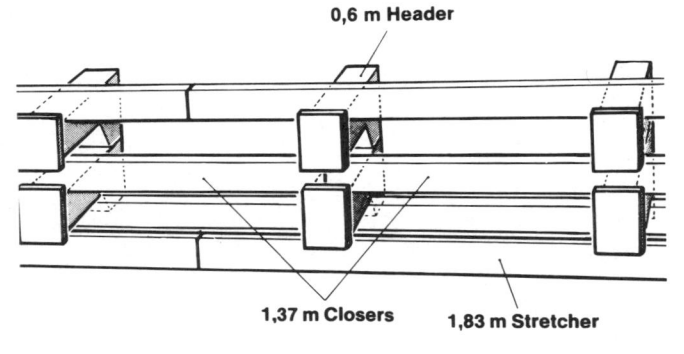

Fig. 5.14. Reinforced concrete crib Humes Minicrib wall system. Designed for lower heights than Pincrib wall. Header design avoids need for stretchers at rear of wall. (Developed and marketed by Humes Ltd., Melbourne, Australia.)

front face design (Fig. 5.13). This honeycomb or cellular face prevents buildup of hydrostatic pressure behind the wall and eliminates the need for weep holes. It also permits establishment of suitable plants and shrubs in the face of the wall (Figs. 5.15 and 5.16). Plants that have been grown successfully in these walls in Australia include snowgrass (*Poa australis*), Australian violet (*Viola hederacea* Labill.), ivys (*Hedera* spp.), dwarf daisies (*Brachycome multifida*), and climbing geraniums (*P. peltatum* (L.)).

Where the cribfill material or soil is patently unsuitable for planting, the recommended procedure is to excavate a small pocket in each open-fronted bay of the wall, and plant a seedling or cutting complete with its own pocket of suitable soil. Further details on recommended procedures for planting interstices of crib structures are given in Chapter 6.

The open-faced, Concrib retaining-wall system also provides opportunites for imaginative landscaping. By erecting the walls in a tiered fashion it is possible to vegetate not only the face of the wall, but also the intervening steps or benches as well. A good example is the tiered, retaining-wall system shown in Figs. 5.17 and 5.18, which is supporting a highway embankment.

5.2.4 Welded-Wire Walls

The welded-wire wall (Hilfiker, 1978) is a composite wire and granular soil structure. The wall is constructed from 9-gage, welded steel wire fabric. The wire fabric or matting is placed between successive lifts of granular fill. The L-shaped form of the mats is designed to both reinforce the granular fill and contain the face of the structure. Exposed vertical ends of the facing portion of each mat are bent over the horizontal wire of the mat above to form a connection between mats at the face. A backing mat and

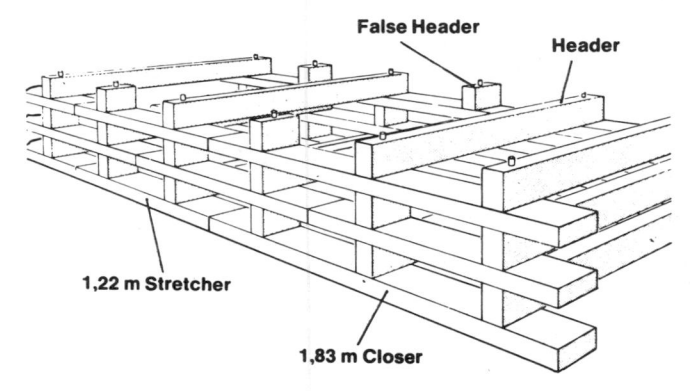

Fig. 5.13. Reinforced concrete crib Humes Pincrib wall system. Pins in headers fit into holes in stretchers to facilitate erection of wall. (Developed and marketed by Humes Ltd., Melbourne, Australia.)

Fig. 5.15. Openings between headers in a Humes Minicrib wall planted with flowering plants.

Fig. 5.16. Concrete crib wall landscaped with flowering shrubs and plants. (*Photo courtesy of Humes Ltd.*)

Fig. 5.17. View of tiered, concrete crib Concrib retaining wall system. Benches between successive tiers have been planted and landscaped with native shrubs and trees. Oakland, California.

Fig. 5.18. Highway embankment supported by retaining walls. Concrete cantilever wall is visible in foreground with landscaped concrete crib wall above. Vegetation is growing both on the bench between walls and in the open bays of the cribbing. Oakland, California.

CONSTRUCTION SEQUENCE

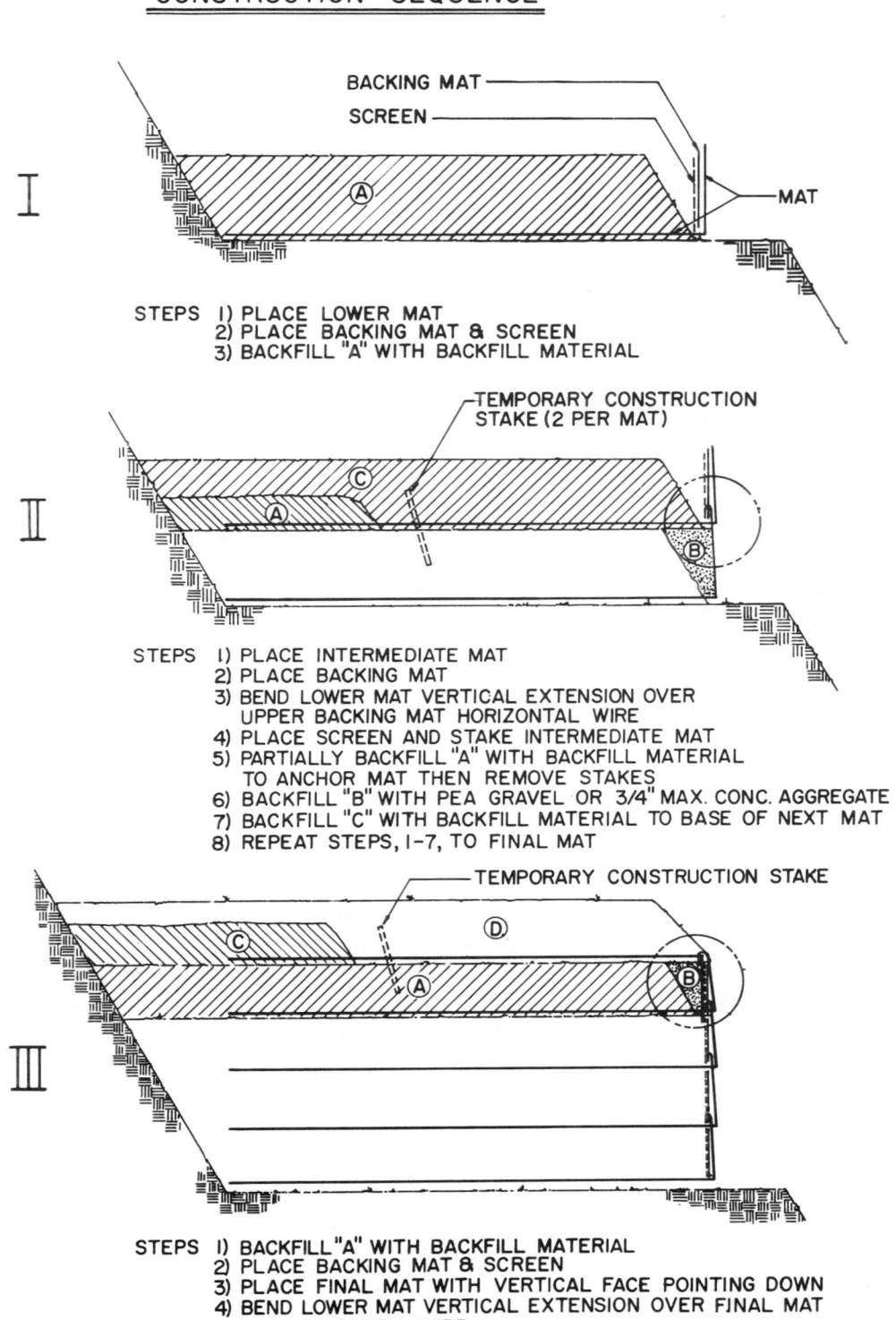

BACKING MAT
SCREEN
MAT

I

STEPS 1) PLACE LOWER MAT
2) PLACE BACKING MAT & SCREEN
3) BACKFILL "A" WITH BACKFILL MATERIAL

TEMPORARY CONSTRUCTION
STAKE (2 PER MAT)

II

STEPS 1) PLACE INTERMEDIATE MAT
2) PLACE BACKING MAT
3) BEND LOWER MAT VERTICAL EXTENSION OVER
UPPER BACKING MAT HORIZONTAL WIRE
4) PLACE SCREEN AND STAKE INTERMEDIATE MAT
5) PARTIALLY BACKFILL "A" WITH BACKFILL MATERIAL
TO ANCHOR MAT THEN REMOVE STAKES
6) BACKFILL "B" WITH PEA GRAVEL OR 3/4" MAX. CONC. AGGREGATE
7) BACKFILL "C" WITH BACKFILL MATERIAL TO BASE OF NEXT MAT
8) REPEAT STEPS, 1-7, TO FINAL MAT

TEMPORARY CONSTRUCTION STAKE

III

STEPS 1) BACKFILL "A" WITH BACKFILL MATERIAL
2) PLACE BACKING MAT & SCREEN
3) PLACE FINAL MAT WITH VERTICAL FACE POINTING DOWN
4) BEND LOWER MAT VERTICAL EXTENSION OVER FINAL MAT
TOP HORIZONTAL WIRE
5) STAKE MAT AND BACKFILL "C"
6) BACKFILL "B" WITH PEA GRAVEL OR 3/4" MAX. CONC. AGGREGATE
7) REMOVE STAKE AND BACKFILL "D" - MIN. ONE MAT SPACING

Fig. 5.19. Construction sequence for assembly and erection of a welded-wire wall. (*From Hilfiker, 1978*). Reproduced by permission of the Hilfiker Pipe Company, Eureka, California.

screen (optional) are also inserted to prevent raveling of the fill at the face. A typical construction sequence for a welded-wire wall is shown in Fig. 5.19.

The wire mats are lightweight, easy to transport to and handle at the job site. Typically these mats are fabricated from 2-inch by 6-inch welded wire mesh that is 4 to 8 ft wide and sufficiently long to provide stability to the fill, which is sandwiched between the wire. The wire mats are folded L-shaped-fashion to provide a face that is at right angles to the floor of the mat. The face is typically about 16 inches high, and the floor length is equal to approximately 80 percent of the composite height of the wall.

Welded-wire walls have fewer constraints on the material or soil that can be used in the structural or reinforced volume than other wall systems. Free-draining, coarse granular soils are preferable, but any backfill material classified as GW to SC in conformance with ASTM designation D2487 may be used in the standard designs (Appendix ID). The structural fill should be compacted to 90 percent relative compaction in conformance with ASTM method D698. Both placement and compaction of the fill can be done mechanically with motorized equipment.

Views of completed, welded-wire walls are shown in

Figs. 5.20 and 5.21. In addition to their low cost, flexibility, and ease of construction, welded-wire walls can be planted with vegetation that will grow through the wire mesh. This allows the wall to blend harmoniously with

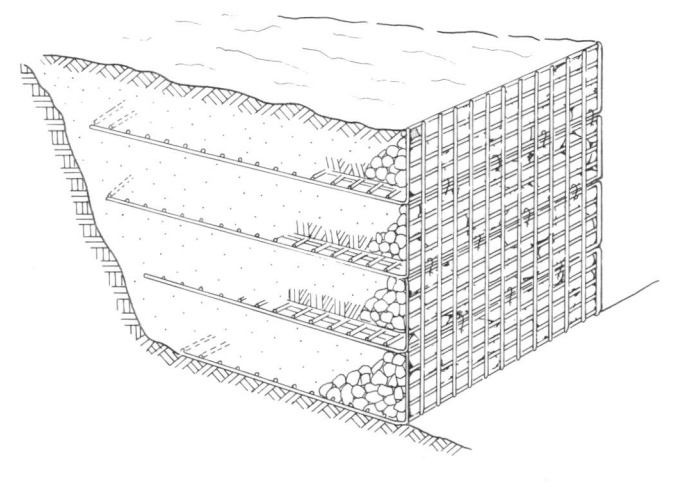

Fig. 5.20. Schematic illustration of welded-wire wall. Wire mesh mats are placed between successive lifts of fill and connected together at the front face. Raveling or loss of backfill is prevented by placing gravel behind fine wire mesh backing mats at the face.

Fig. 5.21. View of completed welded-wire wall showing porous front face which permits vegetation to grow through the wire. (*Photo courtesy of Hilfiker Pipe Company*)

the landscape. Plant roots can also permeate the structure and help bind it together in a monolithic mass.

5.2.5 Reinforced Earth® Walls

Reinforced Earth® is a system for constructing structural fills, vertically faced or sloping, that do not require massive lateral support at the face of the fill. This fill, which is internally reinforced with flexible metal strips or ties, can be employed as a retaining or load-supporting structure in a variety of different ways. The system was developed by Vidal (1969) during the 1960s and patented in France under the name "Terre Armee." The system was introduced into the United States in 1969.[1] Since then many structures using this concept have been built in the United States and have performed satisfactorily.

Walkinshaw (1975) has compiled a useful review of Reinforced Earth construction practice in the United States. His report describes the basic principle of Reinforced Earth, some highway projects that have employed the system, and construction techniques unique to the system. McKittrick (1978) has described the application of Reinforced Earth theory and research to practice in a recent state-of-the art paper.

Reinforced Earth is a composite material formed by the association of earth and linear reinforcements. Ironically, the principle of Reinforced Earth is much the same as that of natural, soil–root systems alluded to earlier in Chapter 3 in which the reinforcement resists tension in the matrix. In Reinforced Earth structures, the reinforcing consists of horizontal layers of metal strips within an earth mass as illustrated in Fig. 5.22. This is the most common use of Reinforced Earth, although other configurations are possible.

The three principal elements of Reinforced Earth shown in Fig. 5.22 are defined as:

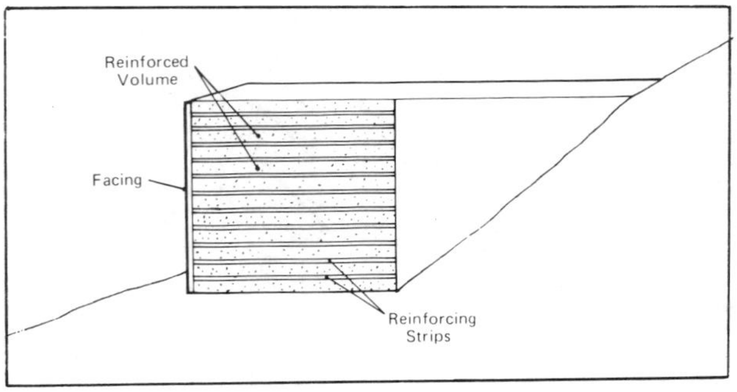

1. *The backfill material:* This extends from the facing to the end of the reinforcing strips, and is commonly called the "reinforced volume." This material must be granular and well drained. Present FHWA specifications for Reinforced Earth are given in Table 5.3.
2. *The reinforcing strips:* These are fastened *only* to the facing. The dimensions of the strips (length, width thickness, and spacing) will depend on the external loading and the height of the structure. The metal strips are usually made of either smooth or ribbed galvanized steel.
3. *The facing elements:* These may be constructed from sections of galvanized steel having an elliptical cross section or, more frequently, concrete in the form of precast panels. The latter allows for a variety of finishes or textures to be incorporated into the facing, thus providing better esthetic compatibility between the structure and its surrounding environment.

There are no standard or basic designs for Reinforced Earth walls. The length of the reinforcing strips is dependent upon the height of the wall, external loadings, and site conditions. As a general rule the length of strips is approximately 80 percent of the wall height for routine retaining applications. However, a minimum strip length or basal width of reinforced volume of 14 ft is presently required regardless of wall height. This requirement somewhat constrains the applicability of Reinforced Earth structures for low toe walls.

The internal design of a Reinforced Earth wall also includes the determination of strip spacing, width, and thickness. All these parameters are considered in the internal design prepared by the Reinforced Earth Company for each project. This design is part of the "Reinforced

Fig. 5.22. Reinforced Earth structure showing principal elements.

---

[1] "Reinforced Earth" is a registered trade mark of the Reinforced Earth Company

Table 5.3. Minimum specifications for select backfill in Reinforced Earth walls (Adopted by FHWA, 1978).

SIEVE SIZE	PERCENT PASSING
6″	100
3″	75–100
No. 200	0–25

and P.I. < 6

Or, if percent passing No. 200 is greater than 25 percent, and percent finer than 15 microns is less than 15 percent, material is acceptable if

ϕ = 30° as determined by AASHTO T-236
P.I. < 6

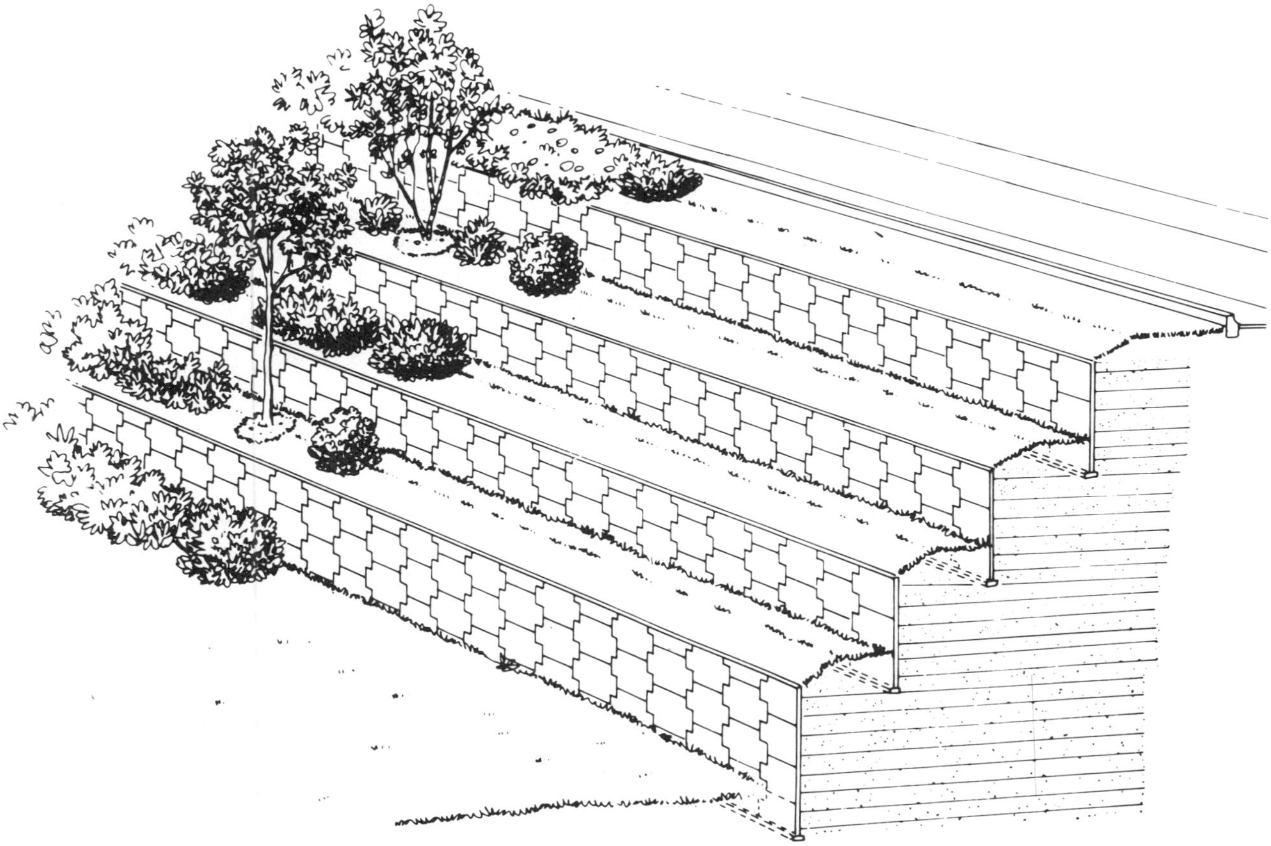

Fig. 5.23. Schematic illustration of stepped-back, Reinforced Earth wall with landscaped benches. (*From Walkinshaw, 1975*)

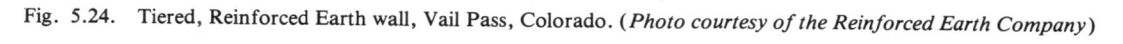

Fig. 5.24. Tiered, Reinforced Earth wall, Vail Pass, Colorado. (*Photo courtesy of the Reinforced Earth Company*)

Fig. 5.25. Tiered, Reinforced Earth wall, Heart O' The Hills Road, Olympic National Park, Washington. (*Photo courtesy of the Reinforced Earth Company*)

Fig. 5.26. Experimental steel channel-wire fabric facing for a Reinforced Earth wall. Ties are connected to 4-inch, 10-gage channel modules or panels. Wire mesh retains coarse backfill placed immediately behind the panels.

Earth package'' (i.e., technical services and/or materials supplied to the project by the Reinforced Earth Company). This aspect and other construction procedures unique to Reinforced Earth structures are described by Walkinshaw (1975).

Opportunities for vegetating Reinforced Earth structures arise in two ways. The first is by planting vegetation on the horizontal steps of tiered or stepped-back walls as illustrated schematically in Fig. 5.23. Two landscaped Reinforced Earth retaining-wall systems are shown in Figs. 5.24 and 5.25. The other approach is to plant or insert vegetation in or through porous facing elements. The Reinforced Earth Company is presently testing designs for low-cost, lightweight facings that could be adapted for this purpose. A photograph of an experimental steel channel-wire fabric facing is shown in Fig. 5.26. Besides providing a locus for establishment of vegetation, these lighweight facings are expected to cost considerably less and be easier to erect than the conventional concrete panels.

5.3   REVETMENTS

A revetment is a facing placed on a slope to armor it and prevent scour and erosion. Revetments are typically used along stream channels, waterways, or inland lakes to prevent or control bank erosion. A revetment offers some resistance (or buttressing) against mass-movement; however, its primary purpose is to prevent loss of bank material by wave action, ice scour, and fluvial erosion. Revetments are normally placed on slopes no steeper than 1½:1 (30 degrees or 57 percent). Steeper slopes require a retaining wall or other structure.

Bank armoring with structural coverage is required for erosion control where bank materials are weak and water velocities high, or in areas subject to wave action and ice scour. In curved channels the highest velocity is close to the outer edge of the channel and near the center of water depth. Erosion is caused here by a rolling spiral (helicoidal) action in which the erosive force is mostly downward, causing undercutting and caving of the bank. Because of this additional force, a more substantial and permanent type of construction is required for outside bends of curving channels.

In the past, revetments have typically been constructed from hand-placed, dumped, or derrick-placed rock (riprap). Today many types of structural facings are in use; these include:

1. Riprap
2. Gabion mattresses
3. Rubber tire networks
4. Sand-cement sacks

5. Articulated, precast concrete blocks
6. Cellular grids

A good review of streambank protection systems including most of these measures is contained in a U. S. Army Corps of Engineers (1978b) Interim Report on its streambank erosion control evaluation and demonstration program. The Corps demonstration project has tended to focus, however, on structural measures with a minor or secondary role reserved for vegetation.

The objective herein is not to describe all revetment systems but rather to concentrate on revetments that can be vegetated. Natural vegetation will often invade and establish itself in riprap and other porous structural facings (Fig. 5.27). Alternatively, vegetation can be introduced by spot seeding and insertion of cuttings. Vegetation can also be established in gabion revetments; articulated, precast block paving; and cellular grid revetments. Volunteer vegetation tends to come in naturally with time. A particularly striking example of this was shown earlier, in Chapter 4 (see Fig. 4.18), in which riparian vegetation ultimately invaded and completely obscured a gabion revetment. The "greening" process can also be speeded up by purposely drifting soil into the interstices of a porous revetment and planting shrubs or seeding the surface (Figs. 5.28 and 5.29). The vegetation not only screens the structure or facing, but the roots permeate and bind the soil underneath the revetment, thus helping to prevent sloughing and washout of the soil.

5.2.1   Riprap

A carefully placed layer of stones and boulders, generally known as riprap, is one of the most common and effective methods of bank protection. It is applicable under most conditions where bank erosion occurs. Riprap can settle and conform to the final streambed contour if scour should occur, and vegetation can become established in areas above the waterline. The limiting factors in the use of riprap are availability of suitable-size rocks; difficulty and expense of quarrying, transporting, and placing stone; and the large amount of material needed where streams are deep.[2]

Riprap revetments are particularly effective in the following situations: (1) sharp bends with a less than 300-ft radius, (2) constrictions, such as bridges, where velocities are increased, (3) along the opposite bank at the confluence of two streams, and (4) on large streams, particularly if ice damage may occur.

---

[2]The weight of the rocks may also pose a problem in some cases. Riprap used as levee protection has sunk out of sight when placed on the soft, organic muds that often comprise much of the levee system in river delta or estuarine areas (U. S. Army Corps of Engineers, 1978b).

Fig. 5.27. Stone armoring or revetment protecting cut slope along a highway. Vegetation has naturally invaded and established itself in this porous revetment. State Highway 27, Nevada.

Fig. 5.28. Gabion revetment protecting streambank along Carmel River, Monterey County, California. Picture taken January 8, 1979 during construction. (*Photo courtesy of Bekaert Gabions–Terra Aqua Conservation Co.*)

Fig. 5.29.   Same gabion revetment (Fig. 5. 28) after establishment of vegetation. Picture taken approximately 3 months later. (*Photo courtesy of Bekaert Gabions–Terra Aqua Conservation Co.*)

The bank should be graded to a 1½:1 side slope or flatter. The bottom of the revetment should be keyed into the channel slightly below the anticipated scour line. Failure to observe this precaution is a common cause of failure. The riprap should extend up the bank far enough to give adequate protection against scour by ice, running water, or wave action. This point is usually 2 to 5 ft above the normal waterline or the low point where vegetation naturally grows (Fig. 5.30). The thickness and gradation requirements for a riprap revetment can be determined from standard specifications in Appendix IE.

The method of placing riprap is important. Riprap may be either hand-placed, end-dumped, or placed by derrick crane. Most riprap is placed on a filter blanket of smaller-size material having the gradation requirements noted in Appendix IE. The purpose of the filter blanket is to prevent washout of fines or bank material through the riprap. The area to be covered with a filter blanket should be reasonably smooth. An even thickness of filter material should be placed on the prepared surface. Care must be exercised when placing the riprap to ensure that the blanket is not ruptured or displaced.

In designing riprap protection for large inland lakes that may be subjected to freezing, special problems arise. Riprap protection can become expensive when designed for ice protection initially and then increased in thickness for wave protection. If one layer is used for both wave and ice protection, the undesirable situation can arise of having a single stone thickness which does not provide sufficient protection against waves. Wave protection requires a total thickness of at least 1½ times the maximum stone size.

A way around this dilemma, where protection against ice must be provided, is to use two layers. The bottom layer should be designed for wave action, and face blocks (single layer) should be used for protection against ice as depicted in Fig. 5.31. The gradation for the bottom layer of riprap should still conform to the same criteria established for revetment riprap. The recommended size in this case will be a function of wave height rather than velocity. A chart and guidelines are presented in Appendix IE for this purpose.

5.3.2   Gabions

Gabions, which are wire mesh baskets wired together and filled with rock in place on a slope, can also be used as revetments. The baskets in this case are much flatter than gabions used in retaining walls and resemble mattresses, which they are sometimes called. A gabion revetment is normally made up of two distinct parts: a flexible apron and upper bank paving (Fig. 5.32). Alternatively, the apron can be replaced by a single-course gabion toe wall (Fig. 5.33), which not only helps to support the revetment

Fig. 5.30. Riprap revetment protecting streambanks and levee along Redwood Creek, California. Volunteer vegetation has become established in the riprap and covers much of the structural bank facing.

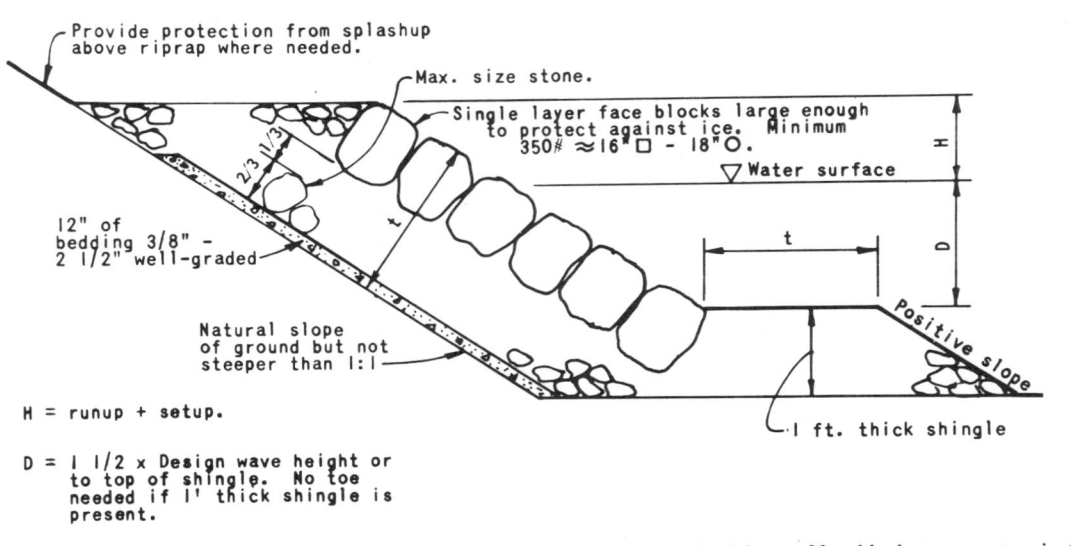

Fig. 5.31. Recommended riprap design for inland lakes. Riprap consists of two layers: a single layer of face blocks to protect against ice, and a bottom layer of stone for wave protection. See Fig. 2, Appendix IE for required stone size.

but also prevents undermining. Unlike the apron, bank paving is subjected to only intermittent attack by stream currents, and it can often be installed in the dry season during periods of low water. Since it is not subjected to continuous abrasive action and flooding, it can support

vegetation (see Figs. 5.28 and 5.29). This helps the wire mesh bond the stone fill into a monolithic mass. Gabion revetments are flexible and can conform to irregularities of a river bank and its bed.

The thickness of the upper portion of a gabion revet-

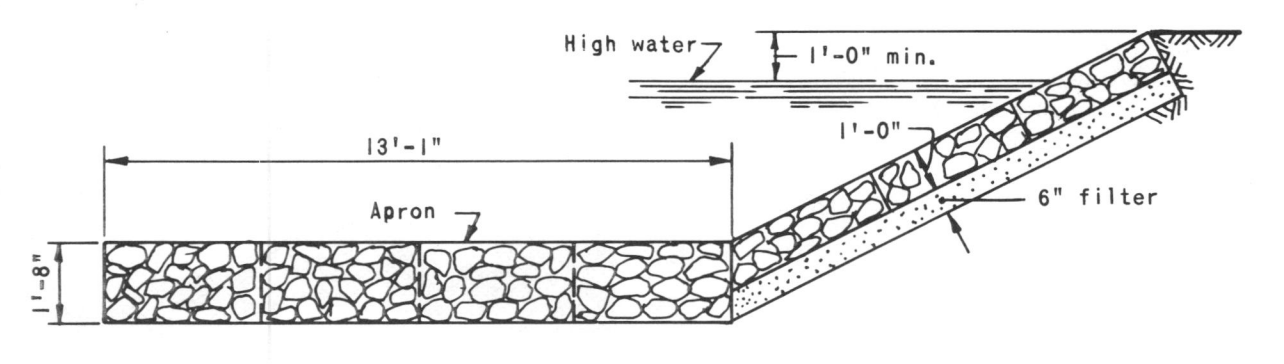

HALF SECTION

Fig. 5.32. Gabion revetment with full apron.

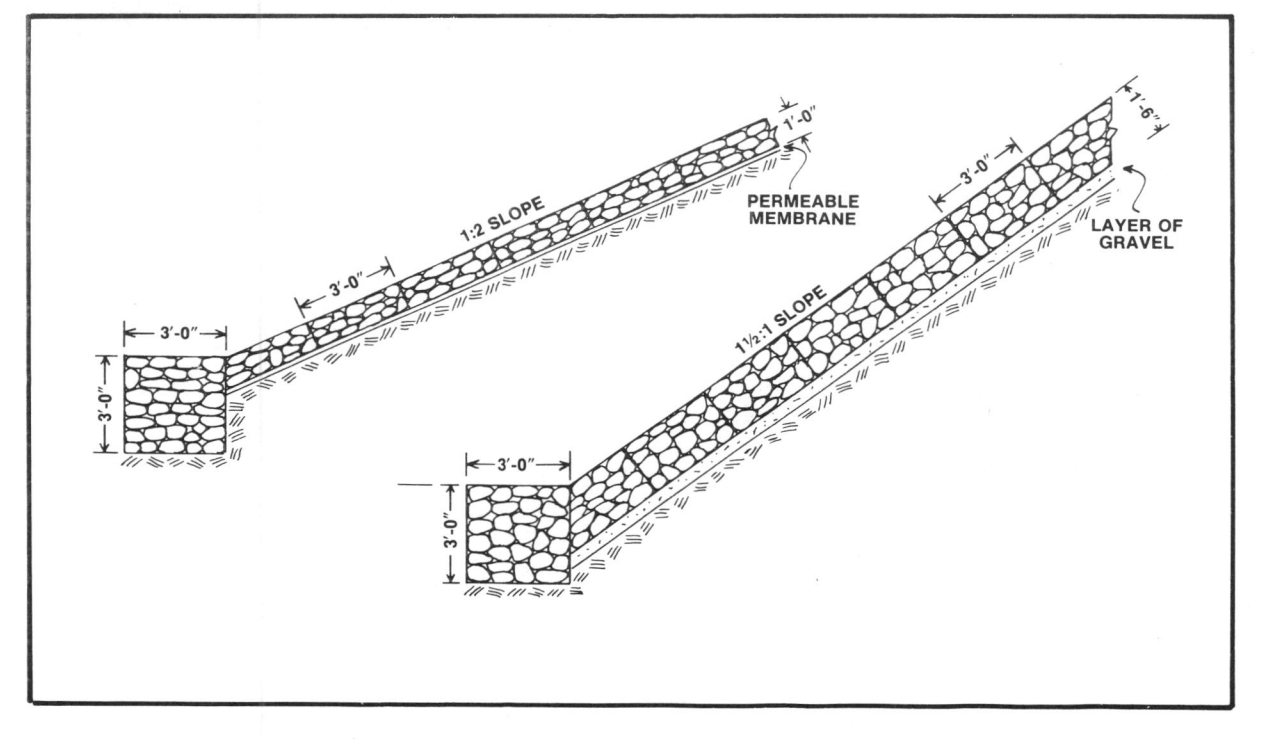

Fig. 5.33. Gabion revetments with toe walls in lieu of apron.

ment or bank paving should be that of at least two overlapping layers of stone in each cell. This thickness will prevent all bank materials except very fine sand or silt from leaching through. If fine sand or silt is present, a 4–6-inch layer of gravel or permeable membrane of cloth woven from synthetic fibers should be placed between the silty bank and the gabion paving to inhibit washout of fines.

Normally, a 12-inches-thick paving will be adequate for banks having slide slopes no steeper than 1 on 2, provided there is no possibility of rapid drawdown. If side slopes are steeper than 1 on 2 (50 percent slope), then

other measures must be taken. These include: (1) grading the bank, (2) using counterforts, (3) using thicker gabions, or (4) a combination of the first three measures. Generally, it has been found through experience that gabions 12 inches deep work well on slopes up to 1 on 2. Units 18 inches deep can be used on slopes to 1 on 1. A revetment can also be varied in thickness by using different depths of gabions up the slope. This technique is often used in areas where wave action occurs and, hence, where greater thickness or protection is required in the zone of breaking waves.

The foundation or bed for a gabion revetment should

be smoothed, and filter material, if required, should be properly placed under the gabions. The baskets should be assembled in accordance with the manufacturer's recommendations. All construction proceeds from the bottom to the top of the installation. The baskets should be stretched slightly while fitting to ensure tight packing and to maintain desired alignment.

5.3.3 Articulated, Precast Blocks

Articulated, precast concrete block revetments are a fairly recent development. The concrete blocks that have been developed and patented differ in shape and method of articulation, but share certain common features. These features include flexibility, rapid installation, and provisions for establishment of vegetation within the revetment. Examples of patented systems that have been or are being used include:

1. Ercomats (Erosion Control Systems, Inc., Metairie, Louisiana)
2. Naue Blocks (Naue Fasertechnick, Fiestel, West Germany)
3. Monoslabs (Mono Concrete Ltd., Croydon, England)

The Ercomat system consists of cellular, cobble-top blocks, bonded to a hydraulic filter cloth, which can be simply hoisted by a small crane and laid like a blanket on a bank. The tapered shape of the blocks allows the Ercomat revetment to conform to the shape of the channel. After placement the interstices in or between blocks can be backfilled with soil and planted with vegetation.

The Naue block or Terrafix revetment system employs a special design that permits flexible interlocking between blocks (Fig. 5.34). Two pivot points in each block fit into corresponding holes in two adjacent blocks. Individual blocks, therefore, cannot be detached from the system. The Naue block articulation allows both rotary and tilting motions, permitting the revetment to conform to possible settlement. The blocks are laid on a filter cloth to prevent washout of bank material through the revetment. Vegetation can be planted in the checkerboard openings between blocks (Fig. 5.35).

Monoslabs are slotted concrete blocks with a gridiron-like top surface (Fig. 5.36). Unlike the other systems, Monoslabs are not truly articulated, but are shaped so that the blocks can form a continuous mat which conforms reasonably well to a smooth bank profile. When used for streambank or levee protection, Monoslabs should be laid on a filter course or filter cloth. Monoslabs also can be vegetated readily (Fig. 5.37).

The Achilles heel of a slab or mat-type revetment is its edges. Edges are the part most susceptible to scour and undermining. If one block is removed from the revet-

Fig. 5.34. Naue concrete blocks. The blocks are interlocked by means of double mortise and tenon connections that provide a continuous articulated system (*Photo courtesy of Naue Fasertechnik*)

ment, the edges and corners of the remaining blocks are exposed, and the revetment is compromised. Flood waters impinging on these exposed corners create forces capable of rapidly destroying the entire system. For this reason, all boundaries and outside edges must be protected.

5.3.4 Cellular Grids

A cellular grid is essentially a lattice-like array of structural members that is fastened or anchored to a slope. The structural members may be either concrete or timber, and the spaces within the grid are planted with suitable vegetation. The grid structure itself does little to armor or buttress the slope (i.e., it is not a true revetment); instead it facilitates the establishment of vegetation on steep, barren slopes.

A ladder grid offers several advantages over other methods:

1. It requires little excavation and clearance at the foot of the slope.
2. It permits establishment of vegetation on very steep slopes (up to 1:1) without the need for slope flattening.
3. It does not require importation of select backfill and cribfill.

A ladder grid structure, on the other hand, cannot be placed on a rough, broken, or severely rilled slope. The slope must be relatively smooth beforehand, or it must be scaled to this condition.

A grid can be constructed from rough, sawn timber, and dimension mill brought to the site can be used for this

Fig. 5.35.   Naue concrete block or Terrafix revetment system protecting a slope. Vegetation has been planted in the open spaces between blocks. (*Photo courtesy of Naue Fasertechnik*)

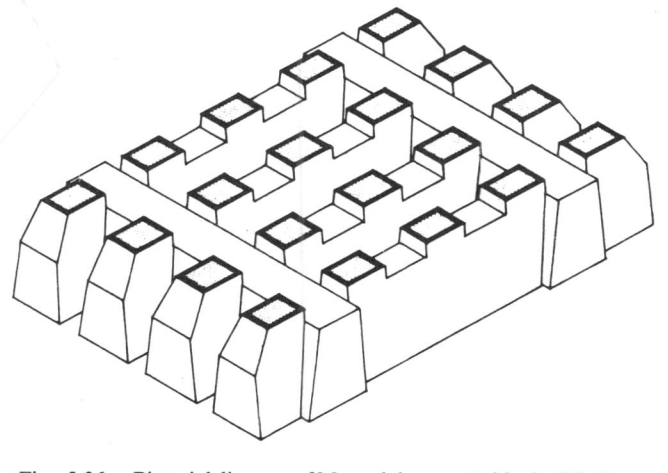

Fig. 5.36.   Pictorial diagram of Monoslab concrete blocks. Blocks are slotted and have a gridiron-like top surface.

purpose. A timber grid is schematically illustrated in Fig. 5.38. The vertical risers consist of 4″ × 4″ timbers, and the horizontal steps are 2″ × 6″ boards. The first row of vertical timbers is placed on and anchored to the slope.

The horizontal boards are then installed between the vertical timbers, and should be embedded slightly to prevent rilling and soil loss beneath them. The boards should be installed approximately on 5-ft centers up and down the slope to form a rectangular grid pattern. Very steep slopes (greater than 40 degrees) may require close spacings (e.g., 4-ft centers) in order to keep the internal slope within the grid spaces to a noneroding gradient (less than 34 degrees). The boards are installed from bottom to top; each successive row of boards provides a step for workers to stand upon while installing the next.

The spaces in the grid can be filled with soil scaled from above or removed from slope overhangs. The spaces should be banked with soil as shown in Fig. 5.38. Amendments may be added as necessary, but care should be taken not to enrich the soil too much and thereby discourage root penetration into the substrate below. Once the grid spaces have been partially filled with soil, as shown, they may be planted with shrubs and/or seeded with grasses.

A cellular, timber grid (Bowers, 1950) was used to stabilize steep (1:1) cut slopes along the Arroyo Seco Parkway in Los Angeles. In spite of the fact that no

Fig. 5.37. Storm drain channel protected by Monoslab revetment. Note establishment of volunteer vegetation in the revetment.

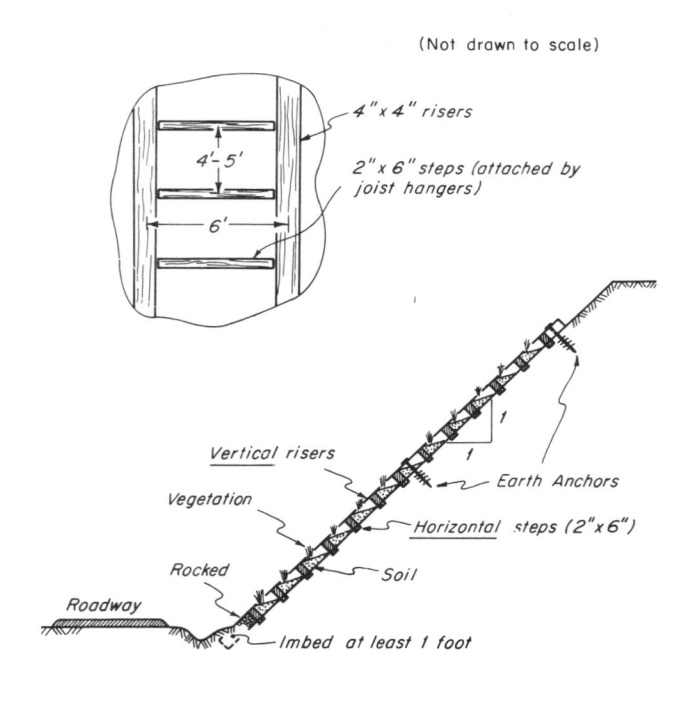

LADDER GRID

Fig. 5.38. Schematic diagram of ladder-grid structure.

preservative treatment was applied to the frame members, the system has been in use since 1940 without any observed failures caused by rotting or weakening of the grid. The most likely explanation is that ground cover plant roots have so permeated and indurated the underlying soil that the supporting effect of the wooden frames is no longer required.

The timber grid system used to stabilize cut slopes along freeways in Los Angeles differs in design from the grid shown in Fig. 5.39. The structural members were constructed from smaller-dimension lumber, and the grid spaces were also smaller. Horizontal members were cut from $1'' \times 4''$ stock, and vertical members from $2'' \times 4''$ stock; grid spaces were $2' \times 3'$ (Fig. 5.39). In addition, topsoil was cast in the grid spaces so as to completely cover the framework. The surface was then covered with straw, which was held down by a wire mesh. The latter was secured tightly to the grid with tie wires, as shown schematically in Fig. 5.39.

5.4 COSTS OF SLOPE PROTECTION MEASURES

The costs of different slope protection systems will greatly influence selection of one over another. Thus some idea of the relative costs of different structural and vegetative measures is important. However, it is not

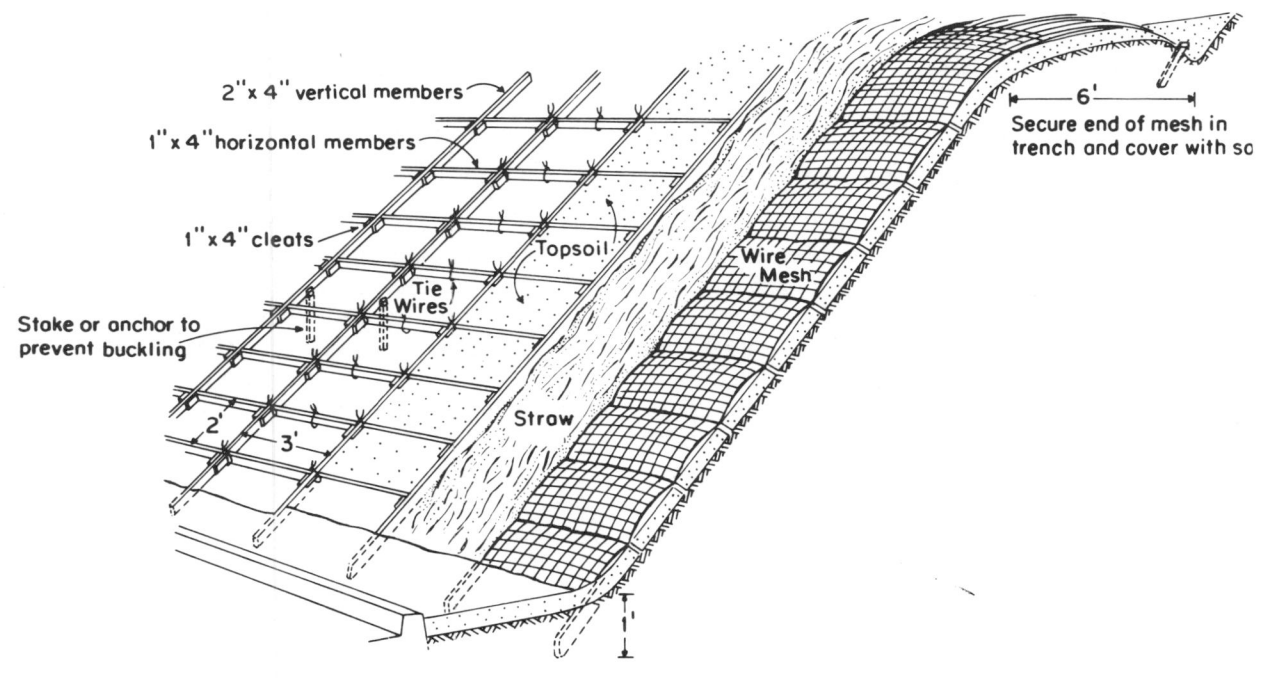

Fig. 5.39. Cut slope stabilization using anchored timber grid to hold topsoil and slope plantings in place. (*From Bowers, 1950*).

115

possible, nor is it the purpose of this book, to provide current and exact cost data. Too many factors militate against such a presentation, most notably inflation in prices with time plus site-specific effects which affect costs such as haul distances and site preparation. On the other hand, it is possible to give approximate cost estimates based on past job experience, and these estimates can be used to make at least rough comparisons.

It is also useful to have some way of computing the cost/benefits of slope protection and erosion control. A procedure is presented here for doing this (i.e., for computing the annual cost of retaining a ton of soil in place as a result of a particular measure or practice vs. the cost of removing, disposing of, or treating sediment after it leaves the site).

The costs presented are a distillation of information obtained from manufacturers' literature, published case studies, and cost-estimating guides for low-volume road construction in national forests.[3] The last is an excellent source of information on unit price data and costing procedures. Another good source of information on costs is a report published by the U. S. Environmental Protection Agnecy (1973) on comparative costs of erosion and sediment control facilities at construction sites. This report provides detailed initial or capital cost data on individual measures. The report also describes how the annual cost of retaining a unit of sediment on a site can be computed by taking into account the amortized cost of the capital investment together with the annual costs of maintaining a protective structure or practice.

5.4.1 Cost of Retaining Soil in Place

The cost of retaining or conserving a ton of soil as a result of a control measure or practice can be determined from the nomograph shown in Fig. 5.40. For example, Fig. 5.40 shows that if $4,000 has been invested initially to conserve 200 tons of soil per year, and it is required that another $1,000 per year be spent, perhaps to irrigate and fertilize an area protected against erosion, and the life of the practice, before having to be completely redone to be fully effective, is 5 years, then the cost of conserving each ton in place is $10 per ton. If only 40 tons per year are saved, then the cost is $50 per ton. The amount of soil retained or conserved by a particular practice can be computed from its effectiveness using Equation (2.9) as described previously in Chapter 2.

---

[3] Each of the eight administrative zones of the U. S. Forest Service publishes its own cost guide. These are periodically updated to reflect current costs.

The scale of the graph as shown in Fig. 5.40 is not convenient for capital costs under $2,000, and the lower-cost vegetative measures such as hydromulching fall in the latter category. A new graph can be drawn, or, alternatively, the graph shown can be used by dividing all values shown on the graph by 10, *except* the value for "Soil Retained in Tons/Year." The dashed-line example would then be for an initial cost of $400 and an annual maintenance cost of $100/year, and for 200 tons/year retained the annual cost in dollars per ton per year would be $1/ton. Should a different interest rate be considered applicable, only the lines in the lower left quadrant of the figure need be redrawn.

Once the annual costs of retention are known, these can then be compared to the direct costs of sediment removal from basements, streets, sewers, and so forth, plus any indirect costs that can also be included, such as disruption of business and transportation facilities.

5.4.2 Cost Comparisons Among Methods

Cost estimates and comparisons are shown in Table 5.4 for the retaining walls described previously in this chapter, viz., rock breast walls, gabions, cribs, welded wire, and reinforced earth. The cost estimates are only approximate to allow overall comparisons. The estimates include the cost of materials (e.g., crib members and fasteners, gabion wire baskets, reinforcements and facings, etc.) and erection or assembly (including labor for filling of crib or gabion and placement of select fill in the reinforced volume). The cost estimates *do not* include the cost of foundation excavation and preparation or of backfilling. Excavation and foundation preparation costs also may vary widely from site to site for different types of structures. Accordingly, individual sites may show considerably different costs.

The cost data summarized in Table 5.4 are based on 1978–79 prices. A cost comparison (subject to the qualifications noted previously) indicates that costs of different retaining-wall systems are comparable. Rock breast, gabion, and welded-wire walls are the least costly. At low heights (under 20 ft) Reinforced Earth walls tend to be more expensive than the others. Construction of higher walls and/or the use of lighweight, low-cost facing elements in lieu of the standard concrete or steel panels would tend to eliminate this cost disadvantage.

All the walls listed in Table 5.4 are moderately flexible, with the gabion, welded-wire, and rock breast walls perhaps having a slight advantage over the others. This advantage would tend to reduce foundation preparation costs. Materials availability and reduction of haul and shipping costs could affect cost comparisons substan-

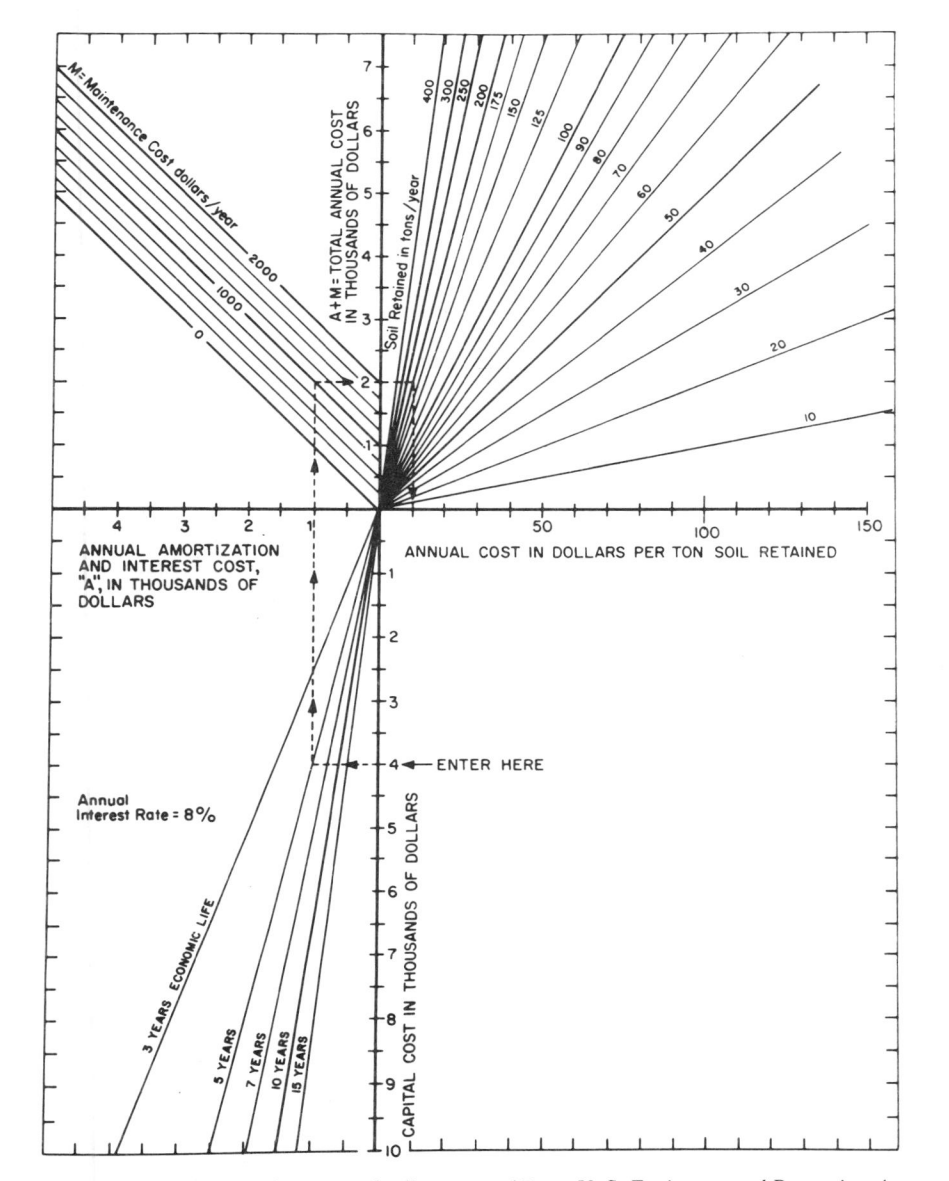

Fig. 5.40. Economic cost of conserving a ton of soil per year. (*From U. S. Environmental Protection Agency, 1973*)

tially. Timber crib walls, for example, might be attractive in forested areas from both an economic (first cost basis) and esthetic standpoint if logs were available and could be sawed on site in a dimension mill.

Comparative costs of bank-protection methods along waterways have been reported by the U. S. Army Corps of Engineers (1978a) in their Sacramento District. Their report provides detailed descriptions and costs for 20 bank-protection methods. A cost summary is provided in Table 5.5, which includes most of the structural revetment systems described in this chapter. The category "intermittent protection" applies specifically to high-velocity channels. It is instructive to note from Table 5.5 that use of vegetation (without a berm) and rock revetments offers the least expensive alternatives. It is also interesting to discover that the cost of vegetative treatment also involved initial clearing of existing vegetation on the bank and stripping of topsoil to retard weed growth.[4]

A comparison of costs of both structural and vegeta-

---

[4] A preferable alternative to stripping topsoil might be the use of pre-emergent weed killers which may be used at the time of planting woody perennials.

Table 5.4. Approximate cost comparisons for low toe walls or retaining structures.

WALL TYPE	HEIGHT RANGE, FT	UNIT COST,[1] $/SQ FT	REMARKS
1. Rock breast	0–3 3–6	4–5 5–6	Use ltd. to very low walls. Availability of large rocks on site may reduce costs 15–20%.
2. Gabion	3–9 10–15 16–21	7–9 9–11 11–13	Costs range from $40–70/cu yd on unit volume basis. Higher walls require more gabions in the basal courses.
3. Welded-wire	6–9 9–12 12–18 18–24	6.25 6.75 7.00–7.50 7.50–8.75	Cost estimate exclusive of accessibility to wall site, excavation, and backfill. Welded-wire wall is designed to use native materials (soil and rock) found at 90% of the job sites.
4. Timber cribs	6–9 10–15 16–21	8–10 10–12 12–14	AWPI designs are more expensive. Higher walls require successively wider bases (longer headers).
5. Concrete cribs (Concrib wall)	6–9 10–15 16–27	13 13–14 14–15	Cost estimate exclusive of accessibility to wall site excavation and backfill.
6. Reinforced Earth	< 20	15–17	Costs are for conventional steel or concrete panels. Use of lightweight, wire-mesh facings could decrease costs by 50–60%.

[1] Cost per square foot of front face based on 1978–79 unit price data. Costs shown are for materials, structural fill or cribfill, and assembly. Costs do not include excavation, foundation preparation, and backfilling.

tive control measures is available as a result of erosion control demonstration projects carried out by both the California Department of Transportation (Leiser et al., 1974) and the California State Water Resources Control Board (White and Franks, 1978) in the Lake Tahoe Basin.

A spectrum of erosion control measures were field-tested either separately or in combination in the Lake Tahoe Basin. Details and results of this project are discussed later, in Chapter 9. Only the cost data are presented here. Particular attention was paid in this regard to identifying the most cost-effective methods for erosion control on oversteepened slopes in and around the Lake Tahoe Basin of California. Where possible, individual breakdowns of unit materials, equipment, and labor costs were compiled for each method. In general wages and equipment costs were based upon data published by CalTrans (1976) as of June 30, 1976, plus an additional 10 percent allowance for profit. Material costs are in general equivalent to retail costs quoted by the various manufacturers, distributors, or suppliers of materials used at the project sites including estimated shipping costs as of June 30, 1976. Details of the cost estimating procedure can be found in the publication by White and Franks (1978). Rampant price and wage inflation in recent years has made their published costs ob-

solete, but the relative cost comparison between methods should still be valid.

A "hypothetical" eroding cut slope was used for the purpose of cost comparison. Such a hypothetical 1.0-hectare cut slope is illustrated in Fig. 5.41. The slope has an average slope length of 10 m and runs for 1000 m adjacent to a paved roadway. It was further assumed that the cut had an average slope angle of 1.25:1 (80 percent) and was continually sloughing eroded material to the ditch along the slope toe.

Table 5.6 summarizes the unit costs and the total costs of selected erosion control techniques if applied to the hypothetical 1.0-hectare road cut. The column entitled "% Labor" refers to the percentage of the total unit cost that is devoted to labor costs reckoned at $16.25 per person-hour. Those percentages that are followed by an asterisk indicate those tasks where a majority, if not all, of the labor could be performed by unskilled conservation corps workers. In this instance total erosion control costs may be reduced significantly because labor costs for unskilled conservation corps workers are considerably less.

As can be seen in Table 5.6, erosion control costs vary considerably. Vegetation stabilization techniques were considerably less expensive, but not necessarily effective

Table 5.5. Comparative costs of bank-protection measures.

PROTECTION MEASURE	COSTS, $1000/1000 LINEAR FT OF BANK[1]							
	PROTECTION TO TOP OF BANK (FILL)		PROTECTION TO SUS-TAINED HIGH WATER + 3' (FILL)		PROTECTION TO TOP OF BANK (CUT)		PROTECTION TO SUS-TAINED HIGH WATER + 3' (CUT)	
CONTINUOUS PROTECTION	First cost	Annual[2] cost	First cost	Annual[2] cost	First cost	Annual[2] cost	First cost	Annual[2] cost
1. Cellular concrete blocks	630	46	370	27	365	27	320	23
2. Reinforced asphalt concrete paving	600	44	565	41	330	25	295	22
3. Asbestos bulkhead	565	40	520	37	—	—	—	—
4. Sacked concrete revetment	560	41	305	22	395	29	310	23
5. Used tire mattress	550	40	305	22	300	22	270	20
6. Vegetation with berm	535	40	—	—	305	23	—	—
7. Aluminum bulkhead	525	38	485	35	—	—	—	—
8. Rock and wire mattress	500	37	280	21	340	26	295	22
9. Synthetic mattress	490	35	235	17	335	24	250	18
10. Concrete slope paving	480	35	265	19	315	23	265	19
11. Articulated concrete mattress	470	35	260	19	290	21	260	19
12. Soil cement revetment	420	31	210	15	250	18	220	16
13. Vegetation without berm	400	30	275	21	215	16	305	16
14. Rock revetment	390	28	210	15	215	16	200	15
INTERMITTENT PROTECTION								
15. Gabion hard-point	520	38	290	21	310	23	245	18
16. Grouted hard-point	465	35	250	19	260	19	220	19
17. Parallel grouted groins	455	33	265	19	180	13	155	12
18. Chemical grouted soil piles	400	29	—	—	—	—	—	—
19. Soil cement trench	350	25	—	—	—	—	—	—
20. Kellner Jack Field (placed on natural place)	315	23	315	23	—	—	—	—

[1]Cost data adapted from Sacramento District U. S. Army Corps of Engineers, 1978.
[2]Includes preparation, maintenance, and replacement plus first costs amortized at $6\frac{7}{8}\%$ over a 50-year project life.

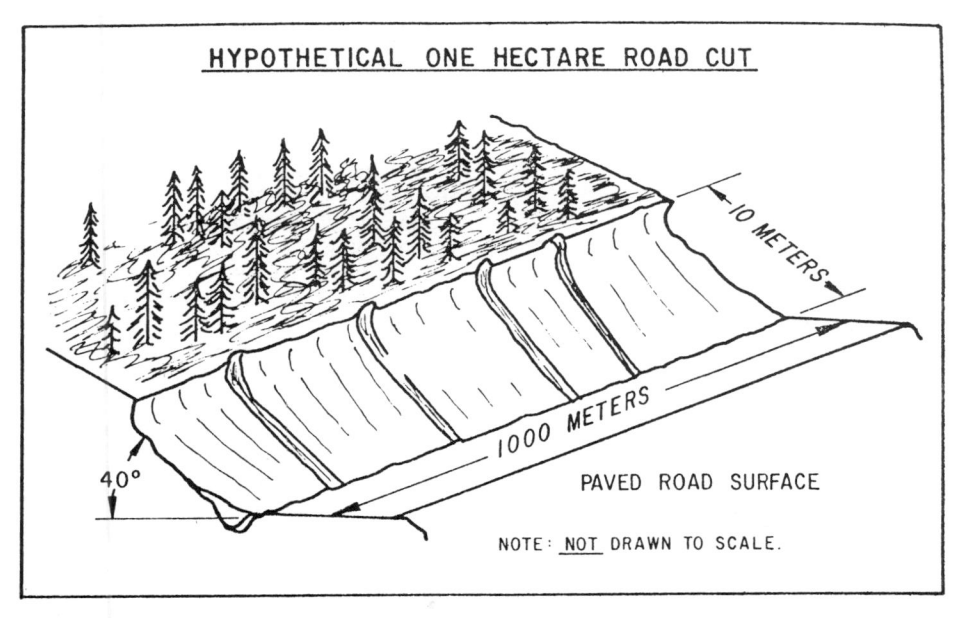

Fig. 5.41. Hypothetical 1-hectare, eroding cut slope adjacent to a road surface used in comparative cost analysis. (*From White and Franks, 1978*)

Table 5.6.   Comparative equivalent unit costs for selected
erosion control methods used on oversteepened slopes.

Mechanical stabilization	Unit cost	% Labor	Cost per Hypothetical Hectare
Curbs and dikes	$ 15.62/m	50	$ 15,620
1.00 m Rock breast wall	61.16/m	45	61,160
0.90 m Gabion breast wall*	58.61/m	52*	58,610
2.70 m Gabion retaining wall*	190.48/m	52*	190,480
Manual slope scaling*	42.68/m²	96*	9,644
Cleanup & debris removal*	0.41/m²	96*	4,086
Contour wattling*	6.14/m	82*	18,420
Gabion revetments*	27.68/m²	40*	277,800
Concrete anti-erosion grids	24.67/m²	48	246,700
Gunite revetments	10.76/m²	27	107,600
Revegetation			
+ Unrooted willow cuttings	$ 0.30/cutting	95*	$ 12,000§
+ Shrub transplants	1.36/plant	60*	54,400
+ Bare-root seedlings*	0.63/plant	86*	26,080
Seed w/2800 kg/ha hydromulch	0.18/m²	30	1,800
Seed w/5600 kg/ha hydromulch	0.27/m²	30	2,700
Seed w/4500 kg/ha tacked straw	0.22/m²	30	2,200
Seed w/jute*	1.84/m²	70*	18,400
Seed w/paper fabric*	1.92/m²	68*	19,200
Seed w/excelsior*	2.16/m²	79*	21,600
Seed w/straw & plastic net*	1.07/m²	73*	10,700
Seed w/fiberglass roving	0.80/m²	N/A	8,000

* Those tasks where a large portion of the work may be performed by unskilled conservation corps laborers.
+ 40,000/ha, 0.5 m on center
§ When more than one type of planting is used, costs should be averaged.

if used alone. Experience in the Lake Tahoe Basin strongly suggests that effective control of severely eroding slopes requires a combination of vegetative and structural treatments. This finding is discussed further in the analysis of case studies in Chapter 9.

5.5   REFERENCES CITED

ASTM (1979). Standard method for "Moisture–Density Relations of Soils Using 5.5-lb (2.5-kg) Rammer," ASTM Designation D698-70, Annual Book of ASTM Standards, American Society for Testing and Materials.

ASTM (1979). Standard method for "Classification of Soils by Unified System," ASTM Designation D2487, Annual Book of ASTM Standards, American Society for Testing and Materials.

Bowers, H. D. (1950). Erosion control on California highways, State of California, Department of Public Works, Division of Highways, Sacramento, Calif., 70 pp.

Bowles, J. E. (1970). Engineering Properties of Soils and Their Measurement, New York: McGraw-Hill.

Bowles, J. E. (1977). Foundation Analysis and Design, New York: McGraw-Hill.

CalTrans (1976). Equipment rental rates and general prevailing wage rates, publ. by State of California, Dept. of Transportation, June 1976.

Caughey, R. A., Tooles, C. W., and Scheer, A. C. (1951). Lateral and vertical pressures of granular materials in deep bins, Engr. Experiment Station, Iowa State University, Bulletin 172.

Federal Highway Administration (1974). Standard specifications for construction of roads and bridges on Federal highway projects, FP 74, Washington, D. C.

Gupta, M. M., and Friel, L. L. (1977). Design aids for cantilever retaining walls, J. Structural Div., ASCE, (103): 1113–1127.

Hilfiker, W. K. (1972). Reinforced Concrete Cribbing, U. S. Patent 3,631,682 (January 4, 1972).

Hilfiker, W. K. (1978). Fabric Structures for Earth Retaining Walls, U. S. Patent 4,117,686 (October 3, 1978).

Lambe, T. W. and Whitman, R. V. (1969). Soil Mechanics, New York: Wiley.

Lee, K., Adams, R. D., and Vagneron, J. J. (1973). Reinforced earth retaining walls, J. Soil Mech. Foundations Div., ASCE, 99(10): 745–764.

Leiser, R. T., et al. (1974). Revegetation of disturbed soils in the Tahoe Basin, Calif. Dept. of Transportation Final Rept. CA-DOT-TL-7036-1-75-24, 71 pp.

McKittrick, D. (1978). Reinforced earth: application of theory and research to practice, Proc., Symp. Soil Reinforcement and Stabilizing Techniques in Engineering Practice, The New South Wales Institute of Technology, Sydney, Australia, Oct. 16–18, 1978.

Schuster, R. L., et al. (1973). A study and analysis of timber crib retaining walls, USDA Forest Service Final Rept. No. PB-221-427, 186 pp.

Schwarzhoff, J. C. (1975). Retaining wall practice and selection for low-volume forest roads, *Trans. Res. Board Spec. Report 160,* pp. 128–140.

U. S. Army Corps of Engineers (1978a). Reconnaissance report: Sacramento River and tributaries bank protection and erosion control investigation, Sacramento District Office, Sacramento, Calif.

U. S. Army Corps of Engineers (1978b). The Streambank Erosion Control Evaluation and Demonstration Act of 1974, Interim Report to Congress, Dept. of the Army, Washington, D. C.

U. S. Dept. of the Navy (1971). *Design Manual DM-7 for Soil Mechanics, Foundations and Earth Structures,* Naval Facilities Engineering Command, Washington, D. C.

U. S. Environmental Protection Agency (1973). Comparative costs of erosion and sediment control construction activities, Rept. No. EPA-430/9-73-o16, U. S. Govt. Printing Office, Washington, D. C.

Vidal, H. (1969). U. S. Patent 3,421,326 (January 14, 1969).

Walkinshaw, J. L. (1975). Reinforced earth construction, U. S. Dept. of Transportation, Federal Highway Administration Final Report No. FHWA-DP-18, 70 pp.

Washington State Dept. of Hwys. (1973). Standard Plans for Bridge and Road Construction—1973, Olympia, Washington.

White, C. A., and Franks, A. L. (1978). Demonstration of erosion and sediment control technology, Lake Tahoe region of California, State Water Resources Control Board Final Report, 393 pp.

6
Vegetative Components
and Requirements

6.1 INTRODUCTION

Successful revegetation of sites subject to erosion requires consideration and coordination of a number of factors. Plants are living organisms that are influenced by climate, soils, and other site conditions, and by methods of handling, planting, and aftercare. The choice of plant material is governed not only by biological considerations of plant adaptation but by legal, political, and economic constraints in many cases. This choice is also affected by availability of seed or propagation materials, knowledge of cultural practices, and commercial availability of plants. Successful plant establishment is dependent on preparation of sites so that they have reasonable stability, to allow time for germination and growth or root development into site soils. Planting techniques may be critical, especially on difficult sites. Care and follow-up replanting will often be required for good vegetation control of erosion.

This chapter will address these factors, discussing principles and specific techniques when they are generally applicable. Sites, environments, and potential plant spectrum vary so widely that individual cookbook solutions are inappropriate. The information in this chapter is designed to give broad guidelines to assist in the decision-making processes for designing a revegetation project. Chapter 9 discusses case histories where applications of these principles have resulted in successful revegetation and erosion control.

6.2 CONSTRAINTS: LEGAL, ECONOMIC, AND PRACTICAL

A number of constraints beyond the control of the project designer exist for any revegetation project. Legal and political constraints include those imposed by the Endangered Species Act, limitations by governmen-

tal agencies or public pressure on plants used, and restriction on the uses of pesticides or fertilizers due to laws or pressures. Economic constraints are often important in project design. Compromises may need to be made to fit budgets; funds may not be available to buy sufficient lands for proper laying-back of slopes or extending areas of fills, or for aftercare and maintenance. The practical constraints include the climate and soils of the project area and the available plant spectrum. The project design must fit within these constraints.

6.2.1 Legal and Political Constraints

The Endangered Species Act may limit project design in several ways. As a rule, natural habitats of endangered species may not be altered. It is difficult or impossible to get permission to collect seed from or propagate plants on the endangered species list; therefore their use should not be contemplated.

Government agencies may impose limitations on the plant materials used. Native plants will be specified in many areas: national parks, roads traversing scenic areas, state and regional parks, and so on. The California Coastal Commission has attempted to limit plants in areas under its jurisdiction to those that are native to the area (Gankin, 1979; Brown, 1979). Objections may be raised to the use of native plants if the seed source or propagation material does not come from the immediate site area, because of the possible mixing of gene pools.

The use of some plants may not be allowed because they may be alternate hosts of diseases, or they may become noxious weeds. The use of certain barberry and mahonia species is limited because they are alternate hosts to wheat rust. Many junipers are alternate hosts to cedar apple rust, which occurs on apple and hawthorn. Both the host and alternate host are banned in some areas. Other plants may be prohibited because they are noxious weeds or may become noxious weeds in agricultural areas and grazing lands. Even if they are not prohibited, caution should be exercised to avoid plants that may become noxious weeds. A plant from Russia, *Halimodendron halodendron* (L.) Voss (salt tree), had been introduced to the United States as early as 1779 (Rehder, 1947). It was introduced to California in the mid-1960s because of its potential usefulness for revegetation of saline soils. The aggressive spread of this plant soon made it obvious that it might become a noxious weed, and it was eradicated by the introducer even though it was not prohibited by law. State or other governmental agriculture departments can supply information on those plants prohibited.

Aesthetic consideration may place constraints on the choice of plant materials. A highly manicured landscape may be inappropriate in rural or natural areas, and a dry nonirrigated planting may be inappropriate in a highly urbanized area. The erosion control project should blend with the surrounding landscape whenever possible.

The use of chemicals for small-animal, insect, or weed control may be limited or prohibited by governmental agencies or by public opinion. This limitation may affect the choice of plant materials and management strategies. In some areas even the use of fertilizers may be curtailed. In the Lake Tahoe Basin the use of fertilizers is discouraged, although not banned, because of the possibility of contributing to the eutrophication of the lake.

6.2.2 Economic Constraints

Dollars are always in short supply. Hence every revegetation project should be designed to yield maximum results from minimum costs. Money for additional rights-of-way acquisition to lay back existing slopes may not be available. Alternatives such as breast walls, gabions, and so on, should be considered to reduce slope angle. The costs of installation and operation of irrigation systems may be more than those of the alternatives such as closer spacing of plants, use of mulches, and the use of more mechanical methods to increase slope stability and hence achieve adequate plant establishment. Small plants are less expensive to buy and plant than large plants. Relative costs increase in a geometric rather than linear manner as plant sizes increase; three of four times as many plants in 3-inch peat pots can be purchased and planted for a given cost as those in gallon cans. Planting only twice as many small plants may be more economical than planting larger sizes, and the results in terms of plant cover and erosion control may be similar. In many cases the survival of smaller transplants may be superior because of more favorable root:top ratios.

The practical constraints on revegetation are numerous. Moreover, it is not an exact science; much needs to be learned. Some of the research that can be done on actual revegetation projects is discussed in the following sections of this chapter. Study of the existing literature on plants and revegetation will supply answers to many of our questions.

Time is often cited as a constraint on a project. It is not uncommon to hear it said that planting must be done while construction of a project is in progress, regardless of whether it is the proper season for successful plant establishment, or, conversely, that plant materials cannot be custom-grown because the planting contract cannot be let until construction is completed. The latter argument is used against the selection of the most suitable plant species in some cases. Neither argument is valid. Most construction projects take time in the planning stages, and this time could be used to do preliminary research on choices of plant materials. It is analogous to the engineering studies done on soils, subsoils, and construction materials in the course of planning projects. Contracts are let early for major structural components (e.g., bridge girders). Contracts could also be let for plant materials. Actual construction has its time constraints based on weather, proper conditions for working soils, and timing of bridge and culvert construction to avoid fish spawning seasons. There is no valid reason not to limit time of planting of revegetation projects to the proper season of the year.

Physical constraints on a project may occur. In mountainous regions the steepness of terrain above or below construction projects may make it impossible to construct or modify cuts and fills to ideal configurations. Lack of adjacent land rights-of-way may limit the modification that may be made on cuts, fills, or the spreading of mine spoils. The diversion of excess water from revegetation projects may also be limited by rights of adjacent properties.

6.3 SITE ANALYSIS

Development of a revegetation plan requires a thorough site analysis. This analysis includes compilation of available information on the climate and vegetation of the general area and analysis of the specific site. This specific analysis should include the microclimate, soils and site conditions, and the vegetation immediately adjacent to the site.

6.3.1 Climate

Climatic parameters that influence the revegetation of an area include: rainfall, total and seasonal distribution; temperatures, minimums and maximums and their duration; length of growing season; and the relative constancy of these parameters. The most readily available source of information covering the United States (Hambidge, 1941) is the 1941 USDA Yearbook, *Climate and Man*. It has not been updated since its publication but is still useful as a general guide. It lists, by state and county, the long-term records of many weather stations and gives details on all the parameters mentioned above. These data can be supplemented with more recent weather records from the governmental weather services (in the United States, the National Weather Service). In the case where weather stations are some distance from the project site, extrapolation between two or more stations may be helpful. Other data may be obtained from local sources, forest ranger districts, district highway stations, and so on. On-site stations may give data that can be correlated with the nearest official weather station on projects with a year or two of lead time. This was done for studies in the Lake Tahoe Basin discussed in Section 9.4.1.3.

The future occurrences of drought or unseasonably cold cycles cannot be predicted, but their expected frequency should be used in the planning. New plantings will not be as drought- or cold-tolerant as established plantings. If drought and cold cycles are common, only the most tolerant plants should be chosen for initial plantings, or contingencies should be made for heavier planting rates or a replant program.

6.3.2 Vegetation

6.3.2.1 Overall Vegetation Spectrum.
The major components of the vegetation should be inventoried on any project. In urban situations this will enable the planner to choose those introduced or native plants with proven performance for the area. This may be done by field work or by consultation with knowledgeable horticulturists of the area. In rural and wildland areas the native vegetation survey is important both for possible selection of plant materials and for interpreting the overall growing conditions if it becomes necessary to match these conditions with suitable introduced plants.

The native plant survey should note the particular soils, microsites, and aspects in which different species grow. Plants can then be matched to these microsites on the actual project site. If the plant spectrum is relatively unknown to the planner, much can be learned from these observations. Which plants do well in a wide variety of conditions? Which are limited to small ecological niches? Which set good seed crops? Which have the best attributes for erosion control? Which root readily when partially buried, or which resprout from roots severed during construction activity? These observations will suggest the best plants for a revegetation project.

6.3.2.2 Pioneer or Invader Species.
Pioneer species are those that first invade a newly disturbed site. These species are particularly important from the standpoint of revegetation because they can grow on poor and disturbed soils. They are aggressive, and they often contribute to the improvement of such soils (see Sections 6.4.4 and 6.4.5). These species may be identified for a given area by field observations on natural and man-disturbed areas. These plants contribute some of the best revegetation candidates. Examples of such plants that were used successfully in the case histories (Sections 9.3 and 9.4) were Oregon alder and willows in the Redwood National Park study, and Newberry penstemon, squaw carpet ceanothus, and willow in the Lake Tahoe Basin study.

6.3.2.3 Transitional Species.
Transitional species are those that follow the pioneer species on a site and persist until the subclimax or climax vegetation dominates. They may coexist with the pioneer and climax vegetation, and they may consist of more than one wave in the plant succession process. Many of these species are useful for revegetation of disturbed sites, particularly when planted as transplants and/or given a microenvironment modified by mulches, fertilizers, or a herbaceous nurse crop.

6.3.2.4 Subclimax and Climax Species.
Climax species are those that, at least in man's perception of time, are the final stage in plant succession. These species often are best suited to soils that have been modified by earlier plant communities. Many conifers that are normally considered subclimax or climax vegetation will establish themselves quite well on the relatively poor soils found in disturbed areas, however. They may grow more rapidly on better soils, but they are capable of surviving on these poor sites. Examples in the Sierra Nevada and Cascade Mountains of the western United States include most species of pine, some firs, incense cedar, and Douglas fir. Some of these species will germinate well only on bare mineral soils.

6.3.2.5 Summary.
A clear-cut distinction among pioneer, transition, and climax vegetation does not always exist. Nature is a continuum, and these are man-made classifications to describe the general situation. Field observations remain one of the best ways to select potential candidate species for revegetation.

6.3.3 Microsite Parameters

The conditions on the actual project site should be observed carefully. These conditions may vary considerably from the conditions prevailing in the general area, and differences may be critical in the final selection of plant species.

6.3.3.1 Microclimate.

The microclimate of a particular site is strongly affected by aspect (direction in which it faces), slope, and surrounding terrain.

In some areas there is little difference in rainfall among sites in a general area. In others, differences can be great. For example, rainfall on the east side of Lake Tahoe is about half that of the west side, just 15 miles distant. Rainfall patterns in Clallam County, Washington (north end of the Olympic Peninsula) vary dramatically. Average annual rainfall (Hambidge, 1941) at Forks in the western end of the county is over 117 inches. It drops to about 24.7 inches at Port Angeles, located about 45 airline miles to the east, and to about 16.4 inches at Sequim, another 18 miles eastward. It rises to over 37 inches at Bremerton (Kitsap County) about 43 miles southeast of Sequim. Some areas in the Olympic National Park just south of this transect have upwards of 200 inches of rain. The vegetation and management practices required would vary greatly among these sites.

The aspect of a site affects plant response in at least two ways. Temperatures are lower on north- and northeast-facing slopes than on south- and west-facing slopes in the Northern Hemisphere. In the Southern Hemisphere the coldest aspect is on south- and southeast-facing slopes. Colder temperatures lead to lower evapotranspiration values which result in more available water for plant growth. However, the effective growing season is reduced somewhat, soil temperatures are lower, affecting seed germination, and the possibility of frost damage is greater.

Valleys, draws, and low spots will have different microclimates from immediately adjacent higher areas. They will tend to have higher soil moisture because of higher water tables. They will be colder than adjacent higher ground. These conditions will affect plant performance in the same way that they do on slopes of different aspects.

Exposure to winds will vary from site to site in a general area. The winds may occur in either summer or winter or both. In both cases, wind increases evapotranspiration and thus reduces the effective water availability. Summer winds will make plant establishment more difficult, and winter winds may increase winter damage or kill.

6.3.3.2 Aspect and Topography.

A careful inventory of the physical characteristics of the site is necessary for planning site preparation work, identifying areas needing special treatment, selecting the final plant list, and developing planting strategies and maintenance plans.

The severity of past erosion will indicate the degree of mechanical stabilization and slope preparation necessary to allow plant establishment. Presence of bedding and jointing planes more or less parallel to the slope surface and evidences of slumping will indicate the need for special treatment. Shallow surface erosion will indicate the need for maximum surface plant cover, while more deep-seated erosion will indicate the need for a high percentage of deep-rooted species. Deep gullies may need filling (see Section 7.2.5.3). Relatively small rills and gullies will be smoothed during scaling, whereas large and severe gullies may dictate the need for reworking the slope with heavy equipment.

Slope angles steeper than 30–34 percent ($1\frac{1}{2}$–$1\frac{1}{4}$:1) are often difficult to revegetate. Exceptions sometimes occur (e.g., where subsoils are more or less uniformly rocky or consist of decomposing bedrock). Steep slopes should be laid back whenever possible (see Section 6.6.1.2). Vegetation establishment is difficult at best on the tops of cuts. Rounding improves the chances of successful revegetation and minimizes chances of future undercutting.

Wet and dry areas should be mapped at the time of maximum wetness and when the dry areas can be differentiated from the wet ones. Information obtained during the wet season will indicate the need for dewatering treatments, either mechanical (e.g., horizontal drains) or vegetative (use of phreatophytes, those plants that use large quantities of water). Mapping at the time wet and dry areas can be differentiated will make it possible to place plants in the microsites for which they are best adapted. It often will allow a greater variety in plant selection than otherwise might be thought possible.

6.3.3.3 Site Soils.

Several parameters of site soils should be determined. These parameters are soil type, pH, electrical conductivity (salinity), and presence of potentially toxic ions.

Information on the soil type is useful in selecting the plant spectrum to be used. Native plants growing on similar soils will be good candidates for revegetation. This information will also be helpful in selecting introduced species. Information on native habitat soils of these introduced species is sometimes available in the botanical literature (Floras). This information is usually limited to such comments as "sandy," "loam," or "clay" (heavy) and "dry" or "wet." Additional information may be gleaned from horticultural literature or from observations on plants in cultivation. Extremely light sandy soils may need special treatment with mulches or tackifiers to stabilize them sufficiently to allow plant establishment (see Section 9.4.2.3). Certain excessively gravel soils may have inadequate water retention. Others may be so badly cemented (e.g., Redding soil series in California) that water and root penetration is almost nonexistent.

Soil pH may limit choices of plant species. Some require acid soils, some alkaline, and some are tolerant of a wide range of pH. High soil pH (7.5 and above) or low pH (4.5 or below) may restrict availability of plant nutrients or may make toxic ions available. Extremely low pH levels will increase availability of aluminum, and manganese and other metal ions that are toxic to plants. Such areas are common in, but not limited to, mine spoils. The pH in surface soils may be satisfactory for plant growth, but highway cuts may expose strata with abnormally high or low pH levels. A cut on highway I-80 about halfway between San Francisco and Sacramento exposed layers of lignite. The pH is so low that few if any plants have been established naturally. Another cut on State Route 104 near Ione, California in the Sierra Nevada foothills was in a substrate of blue shale with the pH above 8. Further analysis showed high salinity. Water analyses of a well in an area with similar geology gave similar readings. This area had adequate rainfall (25–30") for good plant growth and normal leaching. A possible explanation for the salinity is that these strata tapped geologic water from old marine sediments. (Geologic water can vary greatly in quality.) The conditions on these two sites were totally unexpected based on surface soils. Planting on them would be futile unless remedial treatments could be designed to correct these adverse conditions. Acid soil infertility is summarized by Williams and Vlamis (1978).

Salinity may limit plant establishment. This problem is most common in arid and semiarid areas but is not limited to them. Cuts have been found where seepage from long-established dairies or cattle feeding operations (sometimes no longer in operation) have created highly saline conditions. Areas where high levels of deicing salts have been used may also be too saline for good plant growth (Hanes et al., 1970). Electrical conductivity measurements of the soil are easily made with a solu-bridge. Levels of 4 millimhos (mmhos)/cm or less (saturation paste extract) are satisfactory for all but the most sensitive plants. Levels of 8–10 mmhos/cm are severely toxic to some plants and reduce most plant growth severely. Solutions to the problem are the selection of the most salinity-tolerant plants, or in some cases, if sufficient water is available, leaching may be possible. In some mine spoil situations, interceptor drains may allow leaching. Salinity problems, analyses, and remedies are treated in "Diagnosis and Improvement of Saline and Alkaline Soil" (Richards, 1954).

Certain unique soils or soil conditions may be found. In deep highway cuts and mining operations very heavy clays may be encountered (e.g., "blue" clays are extremely plastic when wet and cementlike when dry).

Serpentine soils occur in scattered areas throughout much of the world. There are scattered outcrops in the Appalachian chain from Massachusetts to Georgia in the eastern United States. More extensive areas occur in the Pacific Coast states. Formations in the Sierra Nevada, Cascades, and Coast ranges in California total several thousand square miles. In Oregon they occupy much of the Siskiyou Range, and in Washington parts of the Northern Cascades and San Juan Islands (see Whittaker et al., 1954).

These soils are derived from magnesium iron silicates and have several features in common: (1) they are sterile and unproductive, (2) they possess unusual floras with narrowly endemic species or edaphic races, and (3) the vegetation is in striking contrast to that on surrounding soils (Fig. 6.1). Vegetation is often sparse, and these soils

Fig. 6.1. Vegetation on serpentine soils is in striking contrast to the neighboring vegetation. The hill on the right is serpentine with sparse scrub vegetation, and the nonserpentine soil on the left supports a grass-oak woodland vegetation. Lake County, California.

are often unstable. Several hypotheses have been advanced for the infertility of these soils (Walker, 1954; Whittaker et al., 1954, pp. 262–264). The critical factor in this infertility is the low levels of calcium (Whittaker et al., 1954, pp. 264–265; Martin et al., 1953). Response to calcium should be tested when dealing with serpentine soils.

The pH of the soil may not be indicative of the calcium status of these soils. Walker (in Whittaker, 1954) cites pH values mostly between 5.5 and 7.0, including samples from Lake County, California. The pH of other samples from Lake County (Leiser, 1957) was from 7.2 to 8.1. These latter levels would not suggest calcium deficiencies, but research by Walker and Kruckeberg (Whittaker et al., 1954), Martin et al. (1953), and Leiser (1957) indicated that calcium-supplying power was low. Nitrogen supply was also low (Martin et al., 1953).

Establishment of grasses and forbs on serpentines would probably benefit by additions of calcium and nitrogen. Forbs of native species should be planted from seed collected on serpentines because of the demonstration of edaphic races therein by Kruckeberg (Whittaker et al., 1954). The evidence of endemism or edaphic races in woody species is less well documented, but it does exist (Kruckeberg, 1967); therefore seeds and propagation material should be collected from serpentine sites.

6.3.3.4 Pot Tests to Estimate Fertilizer Requirements of Soils.

Nutrient (fertilizer) requirements of soils may be determined in three ways: chemical analyses of soils, field tests, and pot tests. Chemical soil analyses are the most economical method of determining fertilizer needs. A disadvantage of chemical tests is that if proper extraction techniques are not used, erroneous results may be obtained. Because of interactions among nutrients, soil pH, moisture relations, and so on, fertilizer applications based on these tests may not always give expected growth responses. Qualified testing laboratories may not always be available, and field tests are very expensive and time-consuming. Pot tests represent a compromise between chemical analyses and field testing. They are more expensive than chemical analyses but sometimes more reliable in that they use plants to assess the nutrient status of the soil. They are much more rapid and less expensive than field trials, and, with greenhouse facilities, they may be conducted throughout much of the year, as long as light intensities and duration are adequate.

Pot tests are conducted by growing plants in the soil to be tested and adding chemically pure salts in a series of six treatments: (1) complete fertilizer (nitrogen, N; phosphorus, P; potassium, K; and sulfur, S); partial treatments containing (2) PKS, (3) NKS, (4) NPS, (5) NPK, and a control (6) no fertilizer, to test the native fertility of the soil. This has been called the subtractive method. It permits determination of the nutrient-supplying power of the soil for one element in the presence of adequate amounts of the others.

Six-inch pots are preferred, but 4-inch pots may be used. Clay pots should be lined with plastic bags to prevent contamination. The bag should be turned over the rim of the pot, drawn through the drainage hole, and cut off to allow drainage. Plastic pots do not require painting. Air-dried soil is added, 1600 g per 6-inch pot. The fertilizers are added in solution and mixed with the soil just before the seeds are planted. The amounts of fertilizers to add are given in Table 6.1. Several replicates should be used. Nine or ten barley seeds (common rye grass may be used) are added per pot and thinned 10 days later to the

Table 6.1. Rates of nutrients added to soil for pot tests of nutrient deficiencies.[1]

COMPOUND	MILLIGRAMS PER 6″ POT (1600 G SOIL)		LB PER ACRE	
	COMPOUND	ELEMENT	COMPOUND	ELEMENT
Ammonium nitrate (NH_4NO_3)	686	240	857	300
Monobasic calcium phosphate ($Ca(H_2PO_4)_2 \cdot H_2O$)	427	105	532	131
Potassium chloride (KCl)	254	133	317	166
Sodium sulfate, anhydrous (Na_2SO_4)	240	54	302	68

After Vlamis, James (1966). Testing the fertility of soils in California, *Agronomia Lusitana* 25(3): 249.

CHECK   PKS   NKS   NPS   NPK   NPKS
(−N)   (−P)   (−K)   (−S)

Fig. 6.2. Pot tests may be used to assess soil fertility. Rye grass grown on this soil from a highway cut in California shows a very large requirement for nitrogen, moderate requirement for phosphorus and sulfur, and a slight requirement for potassium.

five most uniform plants. Irrigation is with distilled water as needed. Plants are grown for 7 weeks, harvested, and dried at 70°C for 24 hours, and dry weights are recorded. Dry weights are used to calculate yields relative to the complete (NPKS) treatment, these comparisons indicating the nutrient needs of the soil. Visual comparisons at the time of harvest are often sufficient for evaluation (Fig. 6.2).

If micronutrient deficiencies are suspected, a second series should be planted using the NPKS basic treatment, adding the micronutrients given in Table 6.2. Subtraction of compounds, one at a time, and growth comparisons are made as for the major nutrients. When soils are highly acid (low pH), lime should be added to raise the pH to about 7.0. Rates required may be determined experimentally by adding a series and allowing the soils to equilibrate about 1 week. Rates of 80 mg / 1600 g of soil equal 100 lb of compound per acre, 1.6 g equals 1 ton per acre, and 3.2 g equals 2 tons per acre. The lime should be added to a complete fertilizer (NPKS) series.

6.3.3.5 Adjacent Vegetation.

The vegetation immediately adjacent to the site will usually be more limited than the vegetation spectrum of the general area. An inventory will help interpret microsite conditions. The final plant selection should not necessarily be limited to these plants, but this inventory helps decide which, of the total plant spectrum available, will be the most promising candidates for revegetation. Species that are not present on the immediate site but which, in other areas, grow with those plants adjacent to the site are likely prospects.

6.4 SPECIES SELECTION

The selection of species adapted to the climate and soils of the vegetation project is one of the most important steps in achieving success. Some of the factors involved in the selection process are discussed here.

Table 6.2 Rates of micronutrient added to soil for pot tests of nutrient deficiencies.[1,2]

| | Milligrams per 6″ pot (1600 g soil) | | Lb per acre | |
COMPOUND	COMPOUND	ELEMENT	COMPOUND	ELEMENT
Manganese sulfate (MnSO$_4$·H$_2$O)	48.8	16.0	61	20.0
Sodium borate (Na$_2$B$_4$O$_7$·10H$_2$0)	35.2	4.0	44	5.0
Zinc sulfate (ZnSO$_4$·7H$_2$O)	35.2	8.0	44	10.0
Copper sulfate (CuSO$_4$·5H$_2$O)	32.0	8.0	40	10.0
Sodium chloride (NaCl)	20.0	12.0	25	12.0
Sodium molybdate (Na$_2$MoO$_4$·2H$_2$O)	0.252	0.1	5 oz	0.1

1. After Vlamis, James (1966). Testing the fertility of soils in California, *Agronomia Lusitana*. 25(3): 247–264.
2. Averages for California soils and conditions. Higher rates may be needed where fixation takes place or unfavorable pH renders nutrients unavailable. Acidification may be accomplished with ferric sulfate, or liming used to raise the pH.

6.4.1 Desirable Plant Characteristics for Erosion Control

The most important plant characteristic in selecting for erosion control is adaptation to the environment. The plants should be tough, competitive against less desirable plants, and trouble-free. Some species used along California freeways, for example, have been excellent plants when young but have developed problems at maturity. *Eucalyptus lehmannii* (Preiss ex Schauer) Benth., bushy yate, planted on highway cuts has become overgrown and in time literally "falls apart" because of splitting of the multiple stems at ground level. The removal and replanting process is costly. Species potentially prone to serious disease should be avoided even though the disease is not yet in the project area. At one time it was believed that Dutch elm disease would not spread west of the Rocky Mountains. It is now present in Idaho and California. There are other potentially devastating diseases of certain species that should be considered in making plant selection.

The root growth habits of plants should be considered when making plant selections, and the nature of the erosion problem (i.e., deep-seated vs. shallow erosion) should also be considered. Unfortunately, comprehensive and reliable information on the rooting characteristics of plants is not available. Oaks and many conifers are deep-rooted when young. They are often described as having tap and sinker roots. As these species mature, they often develop a secondary, shallow root system, and the original tap and sinker root system dies and decomposes. However, those species known to have deep root systems when young should be used when the site requires control of this type of erosion. Plants with matted root systems in the surface layers might dominate the plant list when erosion is largely surficial.

The nature of the top growth of plants should also be considered. Evergreen plants with dense growth are always good. Deciduous plants also should not be overlooked. Some have a sufficiently dense habit to intercept the impact of rain at any season. If the season of intense rainfall occurs during the summer, deciduous plants will give protection equal to that of evergreens. There may have to be a compromise between top and root growth. Shrubs, with their limited weight and exposure to wind may be more desirable than trees on areas subject to very deep-seated failure when this depth is below that which might be penetrated by tree roots.

6.4.2 Native vs. Introduced Species

The choice must be made between native and introduced ("exotic") plant species on biotechnical erosion control projects. Each type has practical and aesthetic advantages. In fact, the choice is being dictated with increasing frequency by the regulatory and political constraints discussed in Section 6.2.1. In some cases, "native" is interpreted in the very narrow sense of using propagating sources from the immediate site area.

6.4.2.1 The Case for Native Species.
Native plants have evolved under local soil and climatic conditions and are mostly well adapted to microsites similar to those on which they grow. They are, once established, adapted to annual fluctuations in rainfall and temperatures. Natives often have minimal fungous and insect problems or exist in reasonable balance with such pests. When properly matched to microsites, they will become established, reproduce, and perform satisfactorily without supplementary irrigation or maintenance. Native plants blend aesthetically with the surrounding vegetation.

There are some limitations to the use of native plant species. The availability of native planting stock, seeds or transplants, is sometimes limited because of lack of demand or limited knowledge about propagation methods and cultural requirements. Solution of these problems requires research time and money. The number of plant species suitable for revegetation may be limited in some geographic areas (e.g., desert areas and grassland communities). There may be limited numbers of species adapted to artificially altered or disturbed sites. For example, the number of species adapted to the highly acid soils of mine spoil sites, and the number available for planting reservoir draw-down sites subjected to periodic flooding, are often limited. The use of introduced species may be necessary when the numbers of suitable plant species is limited.

6.4.2.2 The Case for Introduced ("Exotic") Species.
The number of introduced species with potential for revegetation of any particular site is usually greater than the number of native species. This is so because we can draw from worldwide flora, with climatic conditions similar to those of the site. The commercial availability of introduced species is usually greater because these are the plants of our cultivated landscapes; more information is usually available about their propagation and cultural requirements. The consumer, landscape architect, and nurseryman, at least in the United States, have dismissed native plants as being "common" and hardly worthy of attention. However, this situation is rapidly changing.

Introduced plants may sometimes be better adapted to an area than native plants. This may be so because of random chance in evolution or because evolutionary changes in the native plant spectrum have not occurred as rapidly as climatic changes. *Robinia pseudoacacia* L., black locust, has been so well adapted in parts of Russia that the uninformed consider it a native there, although it is native in the eastern United States. Introduced plants sometimes have fewer problems than natives because diseases and pests have been "left behind" (e.g., *Eucalyptus* and some *Acacia* and *Cotoneaster* species).

Introduced species may be more pleasing, aesthetically, than many natives in urbanized areas because they blend with the surroundings.

The arguments against introduced species are largely the reverse of those in favor of using natives.

6.4.3 Plant Geography, Variation and Adaptation, and Species Selection

Much can be learned about the potential of a given plant species for revegetation from a knowledge of plant geography and infraspecific variation. Selection of introduced species can often be made by matching the climate of the project area with similar climates elsewhere in the world. For revegetation projects in the eastern and midwestern United States many suitable candidates may be found from Japan and much of eastern China where similar climatic conditions occur. Areas in parts of California have a Mediterranean climate. Suitable plants for these areas may come from other areas of the world, the Mediterranean Basin, the tip of South Africa, southern Chile, and two areas in Australia, which have a Mediterranean-type climate.

Within a species, native or introduced, it is useful to know the degree to which variation occurs (infraspecific variation). Variation in the adaptation to differences in microenvironments and soils is called ecotypic variation. As a rule, species with wide distribution will have more potential for variation than those with a narrow range. Identification of ecotypes requires research plantings where plants from different areas are grown in one or more locations. Foresters refer to these plantings as provenance trials. Seed sources from nearby or similar habitats are usually better adapted to a site than ecotypes, but sometimes sources from harsher sites are best. An example of the value of testing ecotypes is illustrated by *Acer macrophyllum* Pursh. This species has a wide geographic range on the west coast of North America, from British Columbia to southern California. It grows in areas with widely differing rainfall and temperatures. The species is generally not regarded as being adapted to growth in the Great Central Valley of California. An ecotypic study conducted at the University of California, Davis, included collections from the nearest geographic location, the foothills of the Sierras about 40 miles east of Davis, California, and from Marin County, about 60 miles to the southwest. These plants did not perform well. Plants grown from seed collected in the San Bernardino

Mountains at a 5,000-ft elevation, 450 miles to the south, were outstanding (Langhart, 1972); Leiser, unpub. data). Information on variation should be used whenever it is available. Much is known on the rangeland plants of the West, and more of this type of research is being done in other areas (e.g., Henderson et al., 1979). Ecotypic variation occurs in grasses and forbs as well as in woody plants.

6.4.4 Plant Succession

The concept of plant succession enters into vegetation planting. It is based on the fact that, in natural ecosystems, there is a change in the vegetation component on a given site with time (see Sections 6.3.2.2–6.3.2.4). The pioneer species may only be the grasses for temporary stabilization until the more permanent woody component becomes established in projects using introduced plant materials, or, as in the case of many urban freeway plantings, there may be no pioneer species. The concept is much more important in projects using native plants. In grassland areas (e.g., the Great Plains), grasses may be both the pioneer and the climax vegetation. In most other areas a recognizable change can be observed (sometimes over hundreds of years) in the vegetation patterns among recently disturbed sites, sites of intermediate age, and old mature sites.

The plant selection process should consider plant succession in areas where it occurs. Plantings may be mixed, using species of different successional levels. Such a mix will hasten the establishment of a stable, permanent vegetation. The pioneer or invader species will contribute to immediate cover and site improvement. The species of later successional communities will provide the more permanent vegetation and aesthetic blending with adjacent plant communities.

6.4.5 Nitrogen-Fixing Plants for Site Improvement

Legumes should be incorporated into the plant lists when available because of their ability to improve sites by adding nitrogen. The seeds or plants should be inoculated with the appropriate bacteria. Commercial inoculants are available for many species, particularly those used for forage. Inoculation of native species for which no commercial inoculant is available should be accomplished by incorporating soil from native stands in the soils in which transplants are grown or by topdressing raw sites with native soils when possible. Subsoils of highway cuts have been shown to be essentially devoid of the nitrifying bacteria even though there were legumes growing nearby.

Plants other than legumes may be capable of fixing nitrogen. A list of the genera involved is given in Table 6.3. The inoculants for these plants are not available com-

Table 6.3. Number of species in genera forming *Alnus*-type nitrogen-fixing root nodules.[1]

GENUS	SPECIES COMPLEMENT[2]	SPECIES WITH NODULES
Alnus	35	32
Arctostaphylos	70	1
Casuarina	45	24
Ceanothus	55	31
Cercocarpus	20	4
Chamaebatia[3]	2	1
Coriaria	15	13
Discaria	10	2
Dryas	4	2
Elaeagnus	45	16
Hippophaë	3	1
Myrica	35	26
Purshia	2	2
Shepherdia	3	2

[1] After Bond (1976).
[2] After Willis (1966).
[3] After Heisey et al. (1980).

mercially, but inoculation as described for legumes may be employed. The importance of some of these plants in improving site quality may not be known. Research on these plants lags behind that on legumes.

6.4.6   Grasses for Interim Erosion Control

Woody plants require time to develop sufficient size to control erosion adequately, and the quick cover that can be obtained with grasses is usually needed in the interim. The principles for the selection of grasses are partly the same as those for selection of woody plants, and partly unique. Species, cultivars, and ecotypes should be adaptable to the site. Testing may be required in the absence of information in the literature. Fertility requirements should be minimal to allow the grasses to persist after the initial fertilization at planting time. The ideal species should have strong root development and minimal top growth. Excessive top growth is undesirable for several reasons. It will mat and crowd out the more permanent species, harbor rodents which may be destructive to the woody species, and constitute a fire hazard. Grasses that may become agricultural pests should be avoided. A mix of grasses should be used. Some of the best long-term species may be slow to develop and spread, and quick, short-lived species will give short-term protection. The short-lived species should be picked from those that are not overly aggressive. Perennial grasses should dominate the mix. A good mixture also increases the assurance of a stand because it is difficult to anticipate all of the variables that will affect germination and establishment on any given site.

Legumes and other forbs may be seeded with the grass mix for soil improvement and for aesthetics.

6.4.7   Species Mix

A mix of plant species should be used in most vegetation programs. The need for quick cover and permanent plants can often be met best by such mixes. It is impossible to predict with certainty the success of any one species on plantings that are to receive little or no maintenance. Microsite conditions vary from place to place on a given site. By using an adequate mix of species the chances of successful vegetation are greatly increased. A monoculture is always more susceptible to diseases or losses from abnormal weather conditions than is a planting with a good species mix. A species mix is also desirable from the standpoint of aesthetics.

6.4.8   Plant Lists

Lists of plants used in past revegetation projects are helpful in selecting suitable species. These lists should be used with some caution, however. The plants listed may be for a general geographic area, and not all the plants may be suitable for a specific site. Where possible, supplement the use of the lists with information on applications to particular sites. Lists only reflect past experience and may overlook species of potential value. Some lists are relatively large and complex, and may require considerable effort to use them wisely. Such lists, however, are valuable references (e.g., Schiechtl, 1980).

Recent increased concern for the environment has resulted in an increase in the research on revegetation. This research is resulting in much new information on plants suitable for this work. A person working in the area of biotechnical erosion control should keep abreast of this research. Much good information is being developed, for example, by the Surface Environment and Mining (SEAM) research projects. Some of the methodology developed in this research will be useful in other areas.

A comprehensive list of sources of plant lists would be voluminous. A few of the good sources currently available are given here as examples.[1] Plants suitable for erosion control or revegetation of difficult sites in a wide range of geographical locations are listed by Schiechtl (1980) for general use, by Kaul (1970) and McKell et al. (1971) for dry-land situations, and by Whitlow and Harris (1979) for wetlands and waterways. Plant lists for a number of locations in the United States are contained in the U. S. Environmental Protection Agency references (1975 and 1972). Hall and Ludgwig (1975) list plants suitable for revegetation around the Great Lakes. Numerous lists are available for the arid and semiarid areas of the West, as given by Monsen and Plummer (1978), Plummer et al. (1968), and Stark (1966). Lists for California by Horton (1949), Edmunson (1976), and Chan et al. (1971) are also applicable to some adjacent areas.

6.4.9 Availability

The availability of plant materials, seeds or plants, is often a limiting factor in developing the planting list. Introduced plants are often readily available from commercial nurseries. Forest trees and some native shrub species are sometimes available from government agencies, state and national forest service and USDA Soil Conservation Service nurseries. Supply of native plants may be limited, but there are increasing numbers of commercial nurseries specializing in their production.

There are numerous dealers in seeds of both native and introduced plants. Addresses may be obtained from nursery trade magazines and state divisions of forestry. The USDA Forest Service publishes, from time to time, a list of seedmen and nurseries dealing in species used in forest and conservation plantings.

Collection of seeds and production of planting stock may have to be an integral part of the revegetation project if commercial sources are not available.

6.5 SEEDS AND PLANTING STOCKS

The availability and quality of seeds and planting stocks are an important part of the revegetation program. When they are available from commercial sources, it is necessary to specify standards of quality when writing

specifications. Quality standards for grasses will vary among political jurisdictions; they are usually available from state departments of agriculture or seed testing laboratories. Standards for nursery crops have been developed by the American Association of Nurserymen (1980). These standards cover bare-root, balled and burlapped, container-grown plants and the smaller sizes of plant materials (liners) often used for revegetation projects.

When seeds of planting stocks are not available, or when it is desirable to collect or grow them as part of the project, the following guidelines will be helpful. These are intended only as general guidelines because quite comprehensive information is available on detailed procedures.

6.5.1 Seeds

Good seed production of wild plants varies from year to year. Some of this variation is due to alternate bearing (i.e., alternate years of heavy bearing and accumulation of food reserves for another crop), and some is due to variation in the weather. Species that bear flowers on the previous season's growth usually bear good seed crops the year after a season with average or above average rainfall. Unseasonal frosts, at flowering time or before seeds are mature, may reduce or eliminate seed crops.

The establishment of seed orchards where plants may be fertilized and irrigated may be justified for long-term projects such as mine spoil revegetation. Such seed blocks are maintained for some species by the USDA Soil Conservation Service.

Seed collection from wildland plants must be timed carefully. Seed collected too early will have low viability. Fruits of many of these plants dehisce or fall very soon after maturity, and the crop may be lost if collection is delayed unduly. Information on the ripening dates of many seeds of woody plants grown in the United States is contained in "Seeds of Woody Plants in the United States" (Schopmeyer, 1974). Additional information of a regional nature is contained in publications by Mirov and Kraebel (1939), Mirov (1940), Plummer et al. (1968), and Emery (1964). Ripening dates given are approximate and vary with location, especially with latitude and altitude. The timing of seed collection for any particular area may be estimated by observing the phenology or seasonal sequence of development of the plant. If these data are recorded for a particular species and location, it will be easier to time collection in subsequent years, adjusting for differences in the start of the growing season.

Note the time of anthesis (shedding of pollen). The next stage of development is the soft dough stage when the developing embryo is soft and watery or milky. Seeds in this stage will rarely germinate. The hard dough stage oc-

---

[1] Appendix II contains a more complete, annotated summary of plant list sources according to geographic-climatic region and primary intended use.

curs as the seed becomes fully mature. Conditions vary with species, but the embryo is usually hard or firm, and often the seed coat begins to take on its mature color. Seed collection can begin when this stage is reached. Seeds collected with part of the plant and allowed to dry naturally will increase in maturity as they dry, in some cases. The ideal time to collect seed would be at full maturity for most species, but if collection is delayed too long, seeds will be shed or gathered by wildlife.

Seeds should be cleaned after collection. Detailed cleaning methods are listed in Schopmeyer (1974) and Young et al. (1978). Small quantities of seed for experimental purposes may be cleaned sufficiently by hand. Fleshy fruits or seeds may be macerated for a period in water and then rubbed through screens of appropriate size. Dry seeds may be separated from capsules and chaff by a series of soil analysis screens, or, if very large, sorted from chaff by hand. Commercial seed-cleaning equipment should be used for larger quantities of seeds (see Young et al., 1978). Air-screen and air-separator cleaning machines are widely used and relatively inexpensive.

Proper storage of seed will prolong seed life. Detailed information is available in the previous references in this section and in Hartman and Kester (1975). Optimum storage conditions vary for different species. Seed should be dried to a low moisture content, usually 5–6 percent and stored at 0–5°C in moisture-proof containers. There are exceptions to this general rule, however. Many seeds have moderate to long storage life, but fleshy seeds often have a short storage life (e.g., oak and horsechestnut species). Some species have a very short life, often a matter of days. Members of the willow family, willows, and poplars (including cottonwood) are examples of these species.

Seeds of some species have no dormancy and will germinate readily whenever the microenvironment (moisture, temperature, oxygen, and light) is favorable. Seeds of many other species are in a state of dormancy (i.e., germination can be prevented or delayed by an impermeable seed coat, immature embryo, or chemical inhibitors, or a combination of these factors).

Seeds with dormancy due to an impermeable seed coat require treatment regardless of time of planting. Seeds with dormancy due to immature embryos or chemical inhibitors will germinate if planted out-of-doors in the fall but require treatment if sown in the spring or sown in greenhouses.

Dormancy due to impermeable seed coats may be broken by mechanical scarification, soaking in hot water at temperatures of 77–100°C (170–212°F) for a few seconds to several minutes, or soaking in concentrated sulfuric acid for varying lengths of time.

Embryo dormancy can be broken by stratification (storage in a moist medium like sand or vermiculite) at 0–10°C (32–50°F), or by treatment with various chemicals.

Dormancy due to inhibitors may be overcome by leaching with water, treating with various chemicals, or exposing the seed to red light of 6400–6700 Å). Specific treatments are detailed in Schopmeyer (1974), Mirov and Kraebel (1937), Mirov (1940), and Hartman and Kester (1975).

6.5.2 Transplants

The use of transplants has been very successful for revegetation of disturbed sites. It has allowed plant establishment on sites where direct seeding failed (see Section 9.4). Use of good-quality planting stock increases the chances of success. Quality control requires attention to details of propagation, growing, and care at the planting site.

6.5.3 Propagation

Seeds or cuttings may be used for propagation of transplants. Seed propagation has the advantages of economy in the collection of propagating materials, and minimum space requirements in the early stages of propagation. Some species that are difficult to root will grow readily from seed. Cuttings usually produce suitable-size plants more rapidly and are also used when seeds are not available or when seed dormancy problems make germination difficult. They are more expensive to collect than seed and initially require more space for propagation.

Sanitation is of paramount importance in all the propagation procedures. The subject is often neglected in literature on methodology but is well covered by Baker (1957). Seeds and cuttings should be surface-sterilized before planting. Workbenches, growing containers (flats, pots), and propagation benches should be steam-sterilized or treated with suitable fungicides. Growing media, except peat, vermiculite, and perlite, should be sterilized. Ultimately plants will be grown on or in the ground, but the most susceptible period in the life cycle, the seedling or rooting stage, will be past. When native soils must be used to inoculate with nitrogen-fixing bacteria or mychorriza in the absence of prepared inoculum, they should not be sterilized of course.

6.5.3.1 Seed Propagation. Seeds are sown after any necessary pretreatments (see Section 6.5.1). Research may be needed for species on which information is lacking. This may involve a series of stratification times and temperatures, or series or chemical treatments at different concentrations and times.

Seeds may be sown directly in the containers in which

they will be grown if they are to be outplanted as relatively small plants, and if expected germination is high and pretreatments are known. Two to several seeds are sown per container and thinned to one seedling after germination.

Seeds may be sown in flats or outdoor beds when germination is questionable, space is limited, or plants are to be grown in large containers. Outdoor beds are used when raising bare-root planting stock. The spacing used in flats or beds will be based on seed and seedling size, expected germination, and ultimate handling. The seeds should never be allowed to dry after planting. After germination, watering should be sufficient to keep seedlings moist but not overly wet to discourage the growth of pathogens.

Transplanting should take place as soon as the plants are large enough to be handled and before crowding takes place. Crowding produces spindly plants, and when seedlings are in flats, the roots may be severely damaged if transplanting is delayed. Roots should be pinched during transplanting to induce banching and to prevent the development of twisted, kinked, or girdling roots. Root pruning can be accomplished in the seed flat by painting the bottom with copper naphthenate (Nussbaum, 1969). Poor root systems may reduce growth and ultimately field survival (Harris et al., 1967, 1971). The planting hole should be deep enough that the roots are straight when planted. If a second transplanting is needed, any circling roots at the sides or bottom of the rootball should be cut.

6.5.3.2 Cutting Propagation.

Stock for cuttings is often wild-collected. Supplies are usually plentiful, and the source of the plants is known. Quality of cutting wood may be variable because of drought or other factors. Sometimes there is considerable delay between collecting and processing time, and the quality of the cuttings may be diminished unless they are properly handled.

The care of cuttings during collection and handling is important. Care must be used to keep them cool and turgid until they are in the propagation bench. Collections made in the wild in the summer should be placed in ice chests as rapidly as bundles are made or small polyethylene collection bags are filled. If they are not cooled, they will "sweat" and deteriorate. Collections made from stock blocks adjacent to the propagation facility should be placed in cold storage if they are not going to be placed in the propagation bench immediately.

Stock blocks may be established for the supply of cuttings of wild or introduced species when there is enough lead time. For long-term rehabilitation projects this procedure is an attractive method of ensuring a supply of good-quality propagation material (Van Kraayenoord, 1968). Stock blocks may also be used to produce cuttings to be planted directly on site (e.g., willow, baccharis,

tamarisk, etc.). Stock blocks may be pruned, fertilized, and irrigated to produce uniform cuttings of high quality.

Two types of cuttings are commonly used: softwood and hardwood. Softwood cuttings consist of young growth and are taken during the growing season, often in late May or June. Hardwood cuttings are fully matured growth taken in the fall or winter. The choice depends partly on when the species roots best, and, with species that root well in either season, on the availability of propagation facilities and labor.

Cuttings should be surface-fertilized, recut to uniform length, and treated with rooting hormone. The size will vary with the species but 4–6 inches is common. Rooting hormones commonly used are indolebutyric acid (IBA), naphthalene acetic acid (NAA), and indoleacetic acid (IAA). They are applied by dipping the stems in a talc powder containing the hormone, by a ± 5-second dip in a solution containing the hormone (usually in a concentration range of 1000–4000 ppm), or less commonly by soaking them for 24 hours in a more dilute solution. Softwood cuttings are usually treated with lower concentrations than are hardwood cuttings. Recommended concentrations vary with the species, and often, for native plants, this information is lacking so that tests must be run.

The best propagation medium will vary with species and the nature of the propagation environment. Sphagnum peat moss, which is often used for acid-loving plants, is too wet and poorly aerated for many plants, particularly plants from dry environments. Sand is often used, but it is variable in quality and is losing favor with many propagators. Perlite is used to some extent, but many plants do not root well in it. Vermiculite of medium to coarse grade is one of the best all-around mediums. Rooting of some plants is improved by mixing it with sphagnum peat moss or perlite. There are no completely satisfactory guidelines, and research should be done with the plant spectrum and propagation environment being used. The cycling time of an intermittent mist system will have some effect on the choice of the most suitable medium.

The development of intermittent mist systems has simplified propagation of many species. These systems may be located in a growing structure or out-of-doors. The use of mist permits rooting of many plants in the summer, even in very hot and dry climates. These systems are also useful for winter propagation in greenhouses. Information on construction is available from university experiment stations and standard works on propagation (e.g., Hartmann and Kester, 1975). Closed cases (Wardian or "sweat boxes") may be useful for winter propagation of species intolerant of the amount of water applied by mist systems. One must carefully attend them, venting them in the daytime when the sun is out, and watching for signs of disease. Bottom heat from electric cables or heating pipes under benches is usually beneficial. The ideal rooting environment is one in which tops can be kept cool and bottoms of the cuttings warm.

6.5.3.3 Growing Media.

Plants in containers are now usually grown in synthetic mixes; soils are rarely used. The two most common types of mixes in use are modifications of the U.C. System mixes (Baker, 1957) and sphagnum peat–vermiculite mixes (Tinus and Mc-Donald, 1979). The U.C. System mixes consist of various proportions of suitable sands and organic matter (e.g., ⅓ each, or other proportions, of sand:spagnum peat:ammoniated redwood sawdust). The peat–vermiculite mix is usually equal proportions of sphagnum peat and horticultural grade vermiculite. Each has its advantages. The former mix is cheaper but weighs more than the latter. Weight is an important consideration in transportation and field planting. Transition of roots from the synthetic mix to the soil in which they are planted can be a problem, particularly with the peat–vermiculite mixes.

Lime and phosphorus are usually added at the time of mixing and other nutrients supplied in liquid form or by topdressing with slow-release fertilizers. Some organic forms of nitrogen (e.g., ureaformaldehyde) may not become available because of lack of soil organisms to convert the nitrogen to an available form.

Details on the use and management of these mixes may be found in the publications by Baker (1957) and Tinus and McDonald (1979).

Inoculation with Nitrogen-Fixing Bacteria and Mycorrhiza. The benefits of nitrifying bacteria in the field performance of legumes are well documented. Legumes should be inoculated with the appropriate bacteria. Legume species for which these bacteria have not been identified or prepared commercially may be inoculated with soil from root systems of the same species. Benefits of inoculation with nonleguminous plants that form nitrogen-fixing nodules are not well documented. A list of genera is given in Table 6.3 (above).

Research on mycorrhiza suggests that proper inoculation may enhance growth in plantings, particularly those on poor soils. Research on specific mycorrhizal organisms and inoculation methods is relatively recent (Tinus and McDonald, 1979). Developments in this area should be followed, and used when proved beneficial.

6.5.3.4. Containers.

Containers for production of transplants are of many kinds and sizes. A comprehensive disucssion of containers and lists of suppliers is presented in the publication by Tinus and McDonald (1979).

Older types include peat, plastic, and clay pots and metal containers. These have been used in conventional nursery production and were not specifically designed for production of plants for wildland planting. Circling roots often develop in them. The usual container has a diameter equaling its depth, and a relatively shallow root system results. Containers developed especially for growing forest tree seedlings are deeper than wide and are often designed to minimize the formation of circling roots. The greater depth also results in improved drainage.

Circling roots will not develop in peat pots if they are properly handled. They should be bedded in, and the interstices between them filled with the planting medium. The roots then grow through the pots and are pruned at planting time. A special-size peat pot, deeper than wide (2½″ dia. × 3¼″ deep, 6.5 × 8.5 cm.), has given excellent results in work done at Lake Tahoe (see Section 9.4.2.2) when handled this way.

Containers gaining wide acceptance include planting books, tubes, both paper and plastic, and planting blocks of a number of materials. Available in numerous sizes and shapes, they have been specially designed for handling and planting on revegetation projects. There are two general types, those planted with the plant and those removed at planting time. The latter are either reusable or disposable (Fig. 6.3).

Most containers designed for planting with the plant are biodegradable. Those that are not degradable may interfere with root growth. When the biogradable container remains dry during the production phase, it will restrict root growth when outplanted because it will form a barrier between the root system and the surrounding soil. Roots growing from one container to another may be damaged when containers are separated. This damage may be serious when container diameter is small and a large proportion of the root system is lost. It is not serious with peat pots with their relatively large diameter unless plants are grossly overgrown. Because breakdown of biodegradable containers may be slow without adequate moisture, they are often unsatisfactory on dry sites. If peat pots have been handled as described earlier, and the roots are penetrating the walls of the pot well, they will perform well on dry sites.

Rigid wall containers have several advantages. Roots are confined to the container, which may be shaped to direct roots downward and discourage circling. At planting time the roots are placed in intimate contact with the surrounding soil because the container is removed. The container can be reusable, reducing unit costs. Disadvantages of the rigid container are the possibility of disturbing the root system when removing the plant and the costs of collecting and returning or disposing of the containers.

A deep container theoretically has two advantages over a shallow one. Drainage will be better in the deeper container. This provides better root growth because of the increased aeration. Dry-land species generally are intoler-

Fig. 6.3. Containers for growing plants for erosion control projects are available in numerous sizes and styles. (a) paperpot; (b) styrofoam blocks; (c) single cell tubes with ponderosa pine, bundled for packing; (d) Spencer-Lemaire Rootrainer unit ("book planter") as shipped; and (e) opened for inspection or to remove plants.

ant of poorly drained growing media. The second advantage is that the root system will be deeper at planting time and be less subject to drought. In practice this second advantage does not always exist, for two reasons. Roots may not always fill the soil mass sufficiently to form a cohesive unit. These deep containers have been used mostly for conifers which, when young, have a strong taproot. These species fill the soil mass well, forming a cohesive unit that can be planted without disturbing the roots. Many shrub species do not have a taproot and when grown in very deep containers may not develop this cohesive root system. The growing medium may fall apart when such plants are removed from the container, and the roots will be disturbed or even lost as a result. This was the case with many of the shrub species grown in deep containers for the Lake Tahoe Basin research discussed in Section 9.4.

A second situation in which the very deep pots may not be advantageous occurs when planting sites are steep and unstable. The use of these containers in the Lake Tahoe Basin study (Section 9.4) often resulted in excessive disturbance of the steep cuts involved. This accelerated erosion, and the root systems of the plants were often seriously exposed before plant establishment could occur.

Another consideration in the choice of containers is the habit of the top growth of the plant. Most conifers have a central leader and narrow growth habit when young. Containers as small as 1 inch in diameter may be satisfactory for such plants. Many shrubs used for revegetation have a spreading or even prostrate habit and require greater spacing for good growth and development. Such species may produce the best quality plants when spacing is at least $1\frac{1}{2}$ to 2 or even 3 inches on center.

The choice of container should be based on the space needed for good top growth and the size and shape of soil mass that will be adequately filled with roots by planting time. Several container types and sizes were satisfactory for the production of shrub species for the Lake Tahoe Basin revegetation reported in Section 9.4, including the larger sizes of planter books and $2\frac{1}{2} \times 3\frac{1}{4}$-inch peat pots. Poor results were obtained with deep tarpaper tubes because roots did not penetrate them; removal of the tarpaper resulted in root loss. Expandable paper tubes also were unsatisfactory because of root loss when they were separated.

Rooted cuttings usually require a container with a minimum diameter of $1\frac{1}{2}$ to 2 inches and often 3 inches to accomodate the root system as it comes from the propagation bench. Cuttings may be rooted directly in containers as small as 1 inch in diameter, however. Rooting directly in the container is only economical when a very high percentage of rooting can be expected.

6.5.3.5. Scheduling. Proper scheduling or timing of plant production is one of the more difficult parts of the revegetation process. Good-quality planting stock should be of the proper size for the container, neither too small nor too overgrown. Roots should fill the medium thouroughly but should not be potbound. The literature is particularly deficient in information on the subject of scheduling plant production. Tinus and McDonald (1979) discuss examples for a few tree species.

Growth rates of plants are influenced by the environment in which they are grown: light intensities, daylength, day and night temperatures, nutrition, and media. The interactions of these parameters on growth rates are complex. Experience must be gained with each species. Adequate records will help plan scheduling for a given species, but unpredictable changes in variables such as the amount of sunlight from year to year will alter the schedule somewhat. Growth rates of plants grown out-of-doors will be strongly influenced by annual variations in length of growing season and temperatures during the growing season.

The lead time for production of small-size plants (up to 3-inch-diameter containers) will be 12 to 24 months for most species, including time for seed collection. Most species will attain adequate size in one growing season after germination or rooting. Those that grow rapidly may only require 2 to 3 months of actual growing time. Lead time must be determined for each species if this information is available in the literature.

The time to start a crop is estimated by working backward from the date the crop is needed. It will include the time from the end of the growing season to time of planting, time for hardening off, the growing period, time required for stratification and germination of seeds or rooting of cuttings, and the time between seed collection and seed sowing. Availability of seed from commercial sources and of growing structures with supplemental light during the winter can reduce the time required. The production of larger-size plants will often require a second growing season. Bare-root tree planting stock is often 2 or 3 years old.

6.5.3.6 Hardening Off. Plants grown in greenhouses must be hardened off before planting on the site in most cases. These plants will be relatively soft or succulent, having been grown at relatively high humidities, with good levels of nutrition and uniform temperatures. Hardening-off procedures will vary according to the time of production in relation to the time of planting, and the differences in climate between the growing area and the planting site. Moving the plants out-of-doors in the late summer will be sufficient when growing and planting areas have similar climate and when planting is to be done in the spring. The shorter days and cooler nights will harden the plants naturally, and they will be ready for spring planting. Outdoor bare-root stock is often dug in the late fall or early winter and either heeled-in or placed in cold storage until planting time.

Difficulties arise in two situations: when the production or growing period does not coincide with the natural seasonal cycle, and when the environment of the growing area and that of the planting area differ markedly in temperatures or length of growing season. These situations may occur simultaneously, particularly in western North America where growing areas are frequently at lower elevations than the erosion control projects. Several strategies may be employed, depending on the circumstances.

Plants may be moved from the production area to the site area in late summer or early fall for hardening when the production cycle coincides with the natural seasons. After finishing their growth and hardening naturally, they may be planted in the fall or overwintered for spring planting. Some winter protection may be necessary (e.g., mulching or covering with snow). Rodent protection is advisable. Hardening off may be accomplished at the growing site in some cases, followed by moving the plants to the planting area for overwintering.

Plants that must be kept at the growing site late in the year to attain desired size should be hardened where grown and moved to the planting site while still fully dormant. This move should be delayed as long as possible. Mulching with straw or snow over the tops of the plants may be helpful in protecting them from abnormally cold air temperatures. This method was satisfactory when plants were moved from Davis, California (elev. 50′) to Minden, Nevada (elev. 5000′) for an early March planting. There was a minimum of frost damage in this instance.

The most difficult situation occurs when the production cycle does not coincide with the natural seasons. This situation may arise in revegetation research projects when scheduling of plant production is miscalculated, or where the critical nature of a revegetation project does not permit scheduling plant production during the natural growing season. In the Lake Tahoe Basin study (Section 9.4) time was a limiting factor. It was possible to grow some species from seed or root cuttings in the fall or winter and have plants of suitable size by the April and May planting dates. The strategies employed were quite successful, namely, a reduction in water and nutrients in the greenhouse to check growth, moving out-of-doors to expose the plants to lower night temperatures for 1 to 3 weeks, and moving to the planting site area 1 to 3 weeks prior to planting when possible. At the site area, plants were given some protection against frost by covering them lightly with straw mulch. Covering with polyethyl-

ene plastic at night may be substituted for straw, but the plastic should be removed in the daytime. Attempts to harden the plants in cold storage were unsuccessful.

6.6 SITE PREPARATION

Sites must be reasonably stable for at least one growing season to permit plant establishment. Major engineering methods have been discussed in previous sections and should be used as required. This section considers minor but very important measures that may be necessary before planting to provide the best possible conditions for planting. Some of these measures may not be needed on new work. Good general treatments of this subject are contained in a number of sources, including "Erosion Control on Mountain Roads" (Kraebel, 1936), "Erosion Control on California Highways" (Bowers, 1950); "Methods of Quickly Vegetating Soils of Low Productivity, Construction Activities" (U. S. Environmental Protection Agency, 1975), and "Erosion and Sediment Control Handbook" (Amimoto, 1978).

6.6.1 Grading and Shaping

Grading and shaping in erosion control projects should always have the goals of providing maximum stability and blending into the surroundings.

6.6.1.1 Restoration Projects.
Restoration projects include the removal of roads (e.g., logging roads and landings), construction scars (temporary roads, utilities installations, etc.), spoil bank storage areas, mining scars, and damage from grazing or other activities in areas being converted to parks or natural areas. Each project will require remedies according to the kinds of disturbance and damage.

Case history 2, described in Section 9.3, details the methods applicable to renovation of damage caused by logging activities. These methods may be applied to other situations. Roads were removed by placing part of the fill material against the toe of cuts and outsloping. Stream channels were reshaped as nearly as possible to original configuration, and various measures were used to control runoff and reduce stream flow velocity.

Construction scars should be revegetated promptly by returning the site to the original configuration and revegetating as described in this chapter. Sites damaged by misuse (overgrazing, off-road vehicles, etc.) will often need special attention to gully control (see Sections 8.2–8.3).

Some aspects of mine spoils treatments are treated in "User Guide to Soils, Mining and Reclamation in the West (USDA Forest Service, 1979a), and elsewhere (see "Reclamation of Drastically Disturbed Land," Schaller and Sutton, 1978).

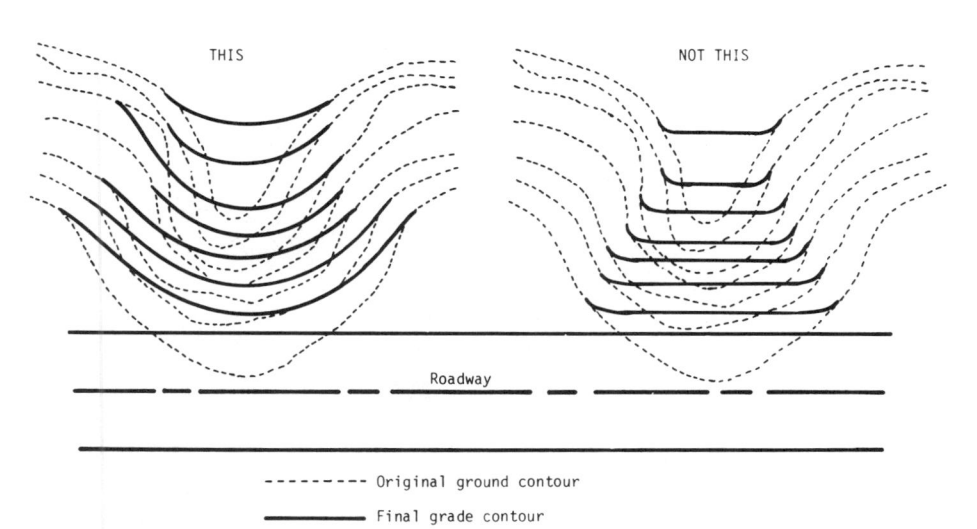

THIS NOT THIS

Roadway

- - - - - - - - Original ground contour
——————— Final grade contour

Fig. 6.4. Cut slopes should be rounded at the top and sides to blend with the surroundings and to provide the best possible environment for plant establishment. Rounding at the top of cut is especially important for slope stability and plant establishment. (*After Animoto, 1978*)

Spoil fills that are to remain in place should be graded for proper drainage. Steep slopes should be treated as for fills (see Section 6.6.1.3). Relatively gentle slopes or level areas may need to be ripped to improve drainage of water infiltration. Leaching may be necessary to reduce levels of toxic ions. Lime may be beneficial to reduce acidity (USDA Forest Service, 1979b).

Soils replaced on mined areas will not require ripping if they are not compacted during replacement. Furrowing on contour may increase infiltration for leaching and plant growth. Contouring should blend with the surrounding topography.

6.6.1.2 Cut Slopes.

Preparation of cut slopes is similar whether they are old or new construction. Those in soils should usually not exceed $1\frac{1}{2}$:1, and 2 or 3:1 is better for vegetation establishment. Exceptions exist when soils are exceptionally stable or when cuts are in decomposed rock. Cuts should be rounded at tops and sides (Fig. 6.4) to blend with surroundings and to provide the best possible environment for plant establishment. Terracing may be beneficial on steep, stable cuts. Terraces may be relatively small serrations or benches (Figs. 6.5 and 6.6).

Scaling is almost always necessary on old cuts and may be needed on new cuts if planting is delayed after construction. Overhang at the top-of-cut and all loose rocks should be removed, working from top to bottom. Large boulders should be broken by blasting to avoid damage to the cut below. Large rocks may be used for breast wall construction. Scaled material may be used for backfill behind breast walls, gabions, and so on, or removed from the site.

Rills and small gullies will be filled or obliterated during the scaling. Larger gullies may need filling and treatment with wattling (Section 7.2) or brush-layering (Section 7.3).

6.6.1.3 Fill Slopes.

New fill slopes may be treated with brush-layering, wattling, or other treatments as con-

(a)

Fig. 6.5. Small serrations improve catchment of seeds and water infiltration on slopes. (a) Scarifying blade; (b) scarifying operation; (c) plant establishment. (*After Animoto, 1978*)

(b)

(c)

Fig. 6.5 (*continued*)

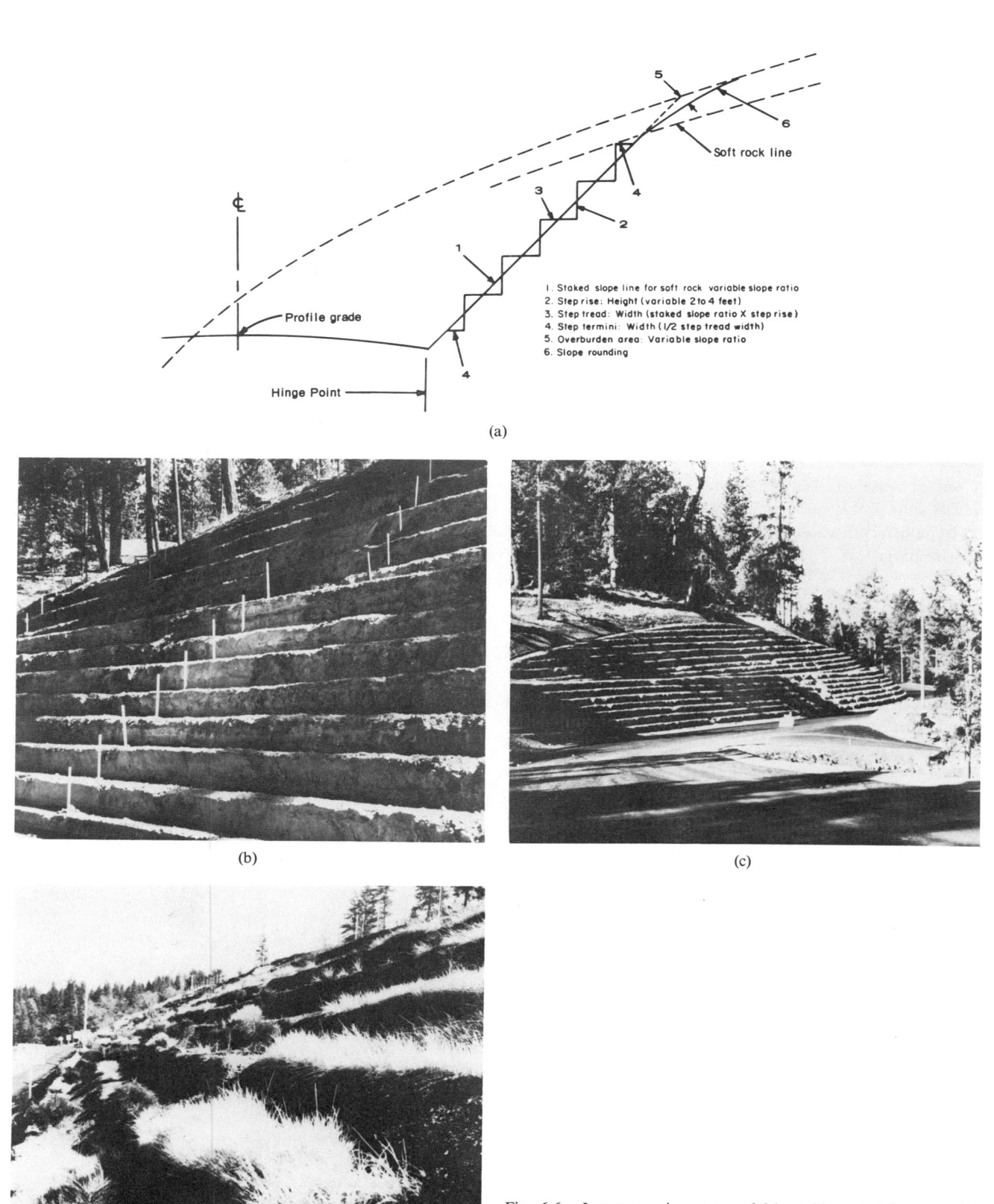

1. Staked slope line for soft rock: variable slope ratio
2. Step rise: Height (variable 2 to 4 feet)
3. Step tread: Width (staked slope ratio X step rise)
4. Step termini: Width (1/2 step tread width)
5. Overburden area: Variable slope ratio
6. Slope rounding

Soft rock line

Profile grade

Hinge Point

(a)

(b)

(c)

(d)

Fig. 6.6. Large serrations are useful in stable materials to provide favorable microsites for plant establishment. Their usefulness is limited to quite stable soils or decomposed rock. (a) Typical section in soft rock; (b) views of newly completed construction; (c) view of newly completed construction detail; (d) plant establishment. (*After Animoto, 1978*)

141

struction progresses, or with wattling after construction. Wattling and interplanting should be done at the proper season, fall or spring in most areas.

Old fill slopes may need preparation similar to that used on old cuts: scaling, smoothing of rills and minor gullies, and filling of large gullies. Major failures may require major reconstruction (Kraebel, 1936; Bowers, 1950). Brush-layering has been used successfully in repairing partial fill slope failures. Slope angle may have to be decreased to the angle of repose, and the slope toe may need reinforcing with breast walls, gabions, and so forth (see Section 5.2).

Failure of old fills due to compacted layers or improper tying to adjacent undisturbed areas must be properly corrected before revegetation begins.

6.6.2 Water Control

Control of runoff and seepage water will be required on many sites. Treatments will vary according to the source and quantity of water and must be determined on a site-to-site basis.

6.6.2.1 Surface Water.
Water flowing over cuts and fills is a common cause of erosion. Ditches, diversions, dike interceptors, and roadway berms will often control this source of water. An interceptor dike (Fig. 6.7) is a temporary ridge of compacted soil constructed at the top of cut or fill slopes. It intercepts and diverts overland flow away from unstabilized, unprotected, or newly constructed slopes. Dike interceptors are normally used as temporary or interim measures, but are sometimes appropriate as permanent installations. Formal design of an interceptor dike is usually not required. It is generally no higher than 1.5 ft with a top width of 2 ft and side slopes of 2:1 or flatter.

A diversion is a channel, with or without a supporting ridge on the lower side, constructed across the top of a slope or across any sloping land surface. A diversion is a relatively permanent structure whose purpose is to divert surface runoff away from critical areas and to transfer sediment-laden runoff to sites where it can be safely disposed of (e.g., sediment basins).

Ditches or channels should be designed and sized to handle maximum expected flows and also be stable against the erosive force of the flow. Vegetation (sod) can provide this needed protection if flow velocity is not excessive (Fig. 6.8); otherwise, structural coverage such as rock lining or riprap must be used. Table 6.4 gives permissible velocities for channels lined with vegetation. Velocity in a ditch or channel is controlled by limiting the ditch gradient and by selecting an appropriate cross section. Design criteria for diversions and ditches are given

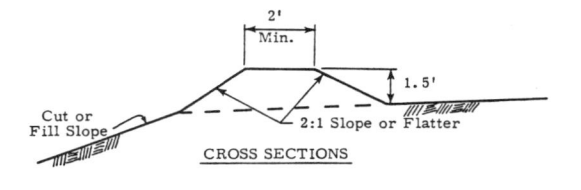

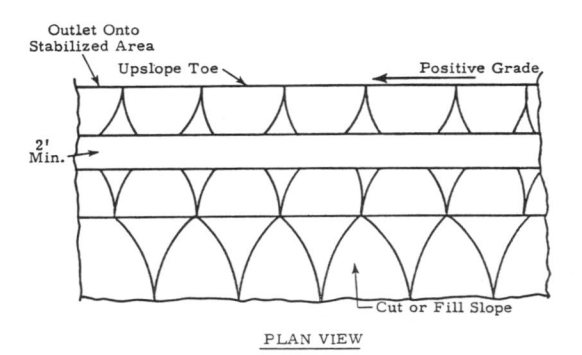

General Notes:
    a. Drawings not to scale.
    b. Outlet to stabilized area.

Fig. 6.7. Dike interceptor protecting cut or fill slope from surface runoff.

Fig. 6.8. Sod-covered drainage channels protect against erosion if they are adequately sized for maximum flows, and water velocities are not excessive. (*From Animoto, 1978*)

in engineering field manuals published by the USDA Soil Conservation Service (1975).

Fills are frequently damaged by runoff from roadways. This damage may be from overflow, sidecutting of the fill, or undercutting of the fill toe. Overflow damage occurs when berms are inadequate, culverts become plugged, or drainage ditches overflow. Proper installa-

Table 6.4. Permissible velocities for vegetative protection.

COVER	SLOPE RANGE, %	PERMISSIBLE VELOCITY[1]	
		EROSION-RESISTANT SOILS, FPS	EASILY ERODED SOILS, FPS
Reed canarygrass	0–5	7	5
Tall fescue	5–10	6	4
Kentucky bluegrass	Over 10	5	3
Grass–legume mixtures[2]	0–5	5	4
	5–10	4	3
Red fescue	0–5[3]	3.5	2.5
Annuals[4] Sudangrass, small grain (rye, oats, barley)	0–5	3.5	2.5

[1] Velocities may exceed 5 fps only where good vegetative cover and proper maintenance can be obtained.
[2] Do not use on slopes steeper than 10 percent, except for side slopes in a combination channel.
[3] Do not use on slopes steeper than 5 percent, except for side slopes in a combination channel.
[4] Annuals are used as temporary protection until permanent covers are established.
Source: USDA Soil Conservation Service (1975).

tion of AC (asphaltic–concrete) berms, maintenance of culvert openings, and sizing of ditches will minimize this problem. Berms diverting appreciable quantities of water should have adequate culverts at the point of discharge to avoid eroding adjacent areas (Fig. 6.9). Inadequate sizing or plugging of culvert entrances will result in water overflow. Ice and snow may divert pavement runoff to culverts not designed to handle the increased water volume (Fig. 6.10). Plugging of culvert entrances can be minimized by controlling the erosion above them and by adequate maintenance.

Fig. 6.9. Erosion resulting from improper culvert design at the point of discharge of pavement runoff controlled by a long AC (asphaltic-concrete) dike on California Route 44, southeast of Redding, California.

Fig. 6.10. Pavement runoff diverted from an ice-plugged culvert crosses highway where super elevation of road grade changes. The increased flow through an inadequately sized culvert downslope caused erosion in an off-highway area. Highway US 50 at foot of Myer's grade, Lake Tahoe, California.

Sidecutting of fills often occurs when drainage ditches or culverts do not have sufficient capacity for maximum flows. Undercutting of fill slopes and gully formation below them may occur when energy dissipators at culvert outlets are lacking or inadequate, or where dissipation of water is not properly managed. These deficiencies should be remedied before revegetation is attempted.

6.6.2.2 Energy Dissipation.

Energy dissipation is required where the velocity of overland flow is excessive, or where flow of water is concentrated in erodible areas. The latter is sometimes a problem near the outlet or discharge point of ditches and diversions. Energy dissipation on slopes may be accomplished in a variety of ways. Straw mulch punched into a slope with a sheep-foot roller or by hand will slow surface runoff. Control to a greater degree may be obtained with willow wattling (Section 7.2), brush-layering (Sec. 7.3), erosion checks, baffle boards, logs, or various kinds of grid work. Rigid materials must be installed deep enough to avoid undercutting, or the problem may be intensified.

A level spreader (Fig. 6.11) is an outlet constructed at zero grade across a slope where concentrated runoff may be spread at noneroding flow velocity over slope areas already stabilized by vegetation.

6.6.2.3 Seepage Control.

Seepage on cut slopes may be a major cause of slumping and gullying. The seepage is usually from groundwater strata. Many seepage areas may be controlled by willow wattling or brush-layering (Sections 7.2 and 7.3). The developing vegetation from these sources and interplanted phreatophytes (willows, alders, poplars, dogwood, etc.) will partially dry the areas and promote stabilization. The presence of free-flowing water during the wet season may indicate where plants alone will not give adequate control, and other means of water control may be needed.

Shallow seepage can be controlled by using trench drains. A relatively simple design known as a French drain or infiltration trench consists of a trench backfilled with coarse aggregate (Fig. 6.12A). These trenches are typically 2–4 ft deep and 18–24 inches wide. Greater drain efficiency can be achieved by laying a 6-inch, perforated collector pipe in the bottom and backfilling with a graded aggregate (Fig. 6.12B). Alternatively, a filter fabric and coarse open-stone combination can be used (Fig. 6.12C). French drains may be used in some situations to intercept the water and percolate it over a wider area. The water thus dissipated can be of value in aiding plant establishment or preservation of the habitat for downslope vegetation that has been dependent on this water.

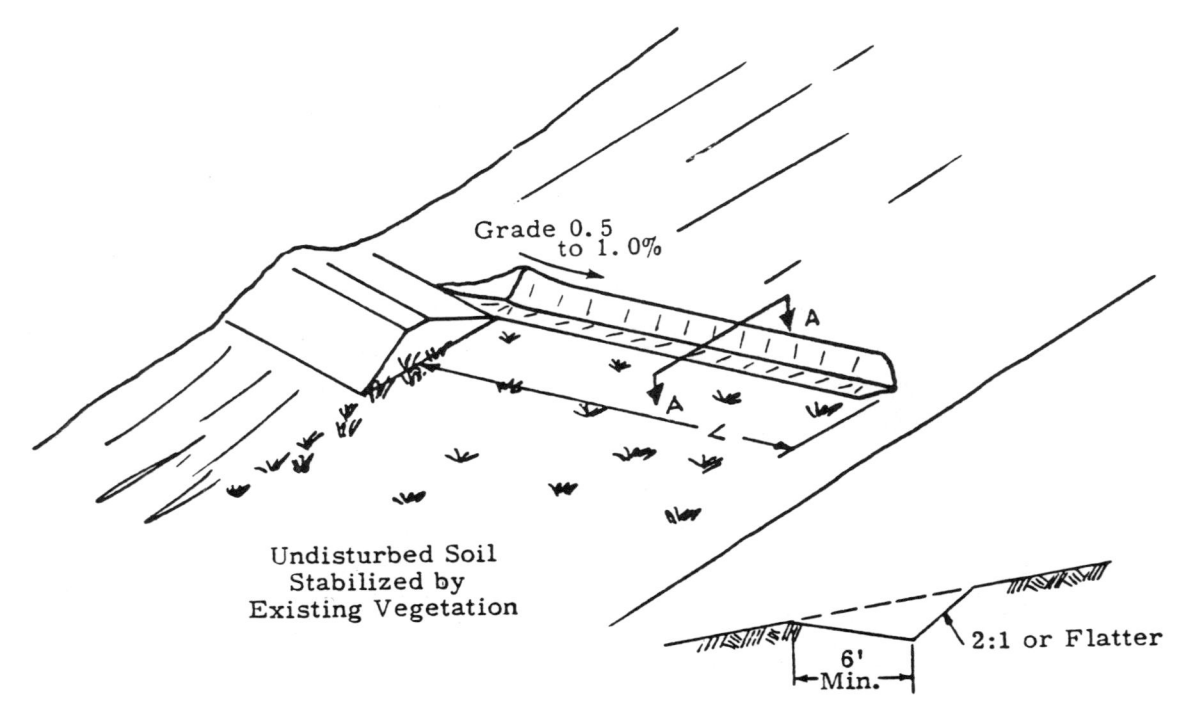

Drawing not to scale.

Fig. 6.11.   Level spreader used to convert concentrated flow to noneroding sheet flow which is discharged over slope already stabilized by vegetation.

(A)

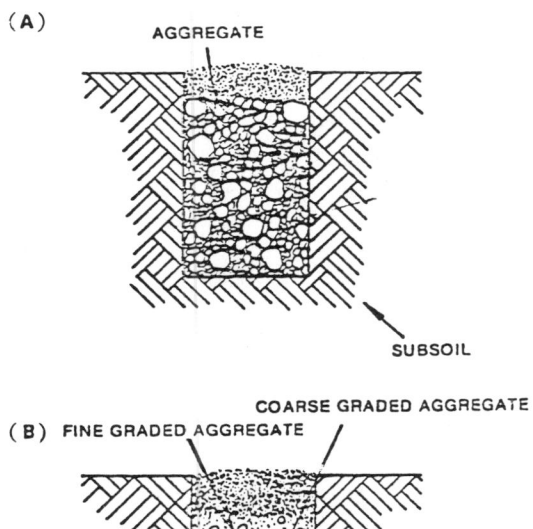

(B)

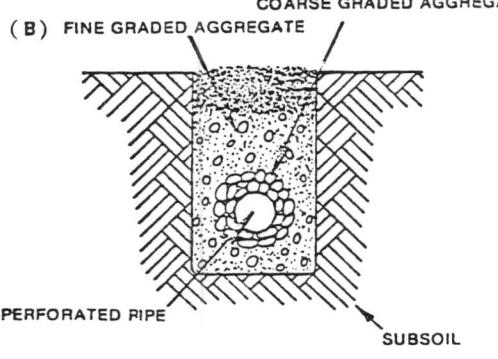

(C)

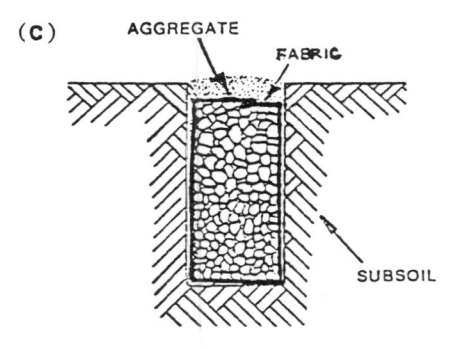

Fig. 6.12. Cross sections of a conventional French drain (a), a conventional trench drain (b), and a drain using a filter fabric (c).

Deep-seated seepage can be intercepted and diverted by using a horizontal drain (a slotted or perforated pipe driven or jetted into a slope). Horizontal drains also improve the mass stability of a slope by relieving pockets of hydrostatic pressure. Outlets of horizontal drains should extend to protected areas such as gutters or culverts. Information on the planning and layout (spacing, depth, grade, etc.) of horizontal drain installations has been published by Smith and Stafford (1957) and Royster (1977).

6.6.2.4 Protecting Adjacent Areas.

The areas adjacent to the site must be considered during site prepara-

tion work. Scaling should not destroy vegetation downslope. Material scaled from cuts is deposited on the road right-of-way and should be hauled to suitable spoil dumps or used where new or replacement fill is needed rather than being side-cast indiscriminately. Breast walls or other protective measures should be constructed at the toe of fills before scaling to avoid disturbance of vegetation below the fills. Drainage or dewatering systems constructed above the roadway should be designed with the downslope vegetation in mind. Initial design plans for a proposed improvement of the Mammoth Mountain–Devil's Postpile National Monument road in California called for a drain collector system above the highway in two areas where year-round seepage occurred. These areas were stable and well vegetated with quaking aspen, willows, rushes, and other species of plants adapted to the wet conditions. The water was to be concentrated in downslope culverts or drains. This plan would have dewatered the areas below the highway, each several hundred yards wide, and would probably have resulted in loss of much of the downslope vegetation. An alternate plan was adopted, to move the water under the road with French drains. The estimated savings in construction costs were substantial, and the microsite below was not impacted.

Rounding of cuts will destroy some adjacent vegetation, but the advantages of a more stable cut and a better microenvironment for plant establishment on the cut more than offset this loss.

6.7 PLANTING TECHNIQUES

Planting techniques will vary according to the kind of propagule (seed, stolon, cutting, or transplant) used, climate, and planting site conditions. No cookbook approach will be applicable to all situations. This section will discuss general principles and guidelines to assist in planting erosion control projects.

6.7.1 Direct Seeding

Techniques that are satisfactory for direct seeding of herbaceous species (grasses and forbs) differ from those that are most successful for woody species. Herbaceous species usually germinate rapidly compared to woody species after any pre-germination requirements (after-ripening, stratification, etc.) are fulfilled and will emerge before the soil dries to any great depth. Woody species must be planted at a greater depth, and they may need special care in mulching to keep them from drying before germination takes place. Protection from rodents is often required for woody plants because of their relatively slow rate of growth after germination.

6.7.1.1 Grasses and Forbs.

Drilling is the most satisfactory method of seeding herbaceous plants because the seeds are placed in the ground at the proper depth and covered (Kay, 1979a). Drilling is more economical of seed and fertilizer than is broadcast seeding. Drill seeding may be used on level and gently sloping sites that are not too rocky (Fig. 6.13), and range drills may be used on moderately rough sites. This method of seeding is not satisfactory on very rocky sites or cuts and steep fills.

Broadcast seeding (scattering the seed on the surface of the ground) is used on most erosion control projects. Seeds may be scattered by hand, with mechanical spreaders, in a water slurry (hydroseeding), or by air. Scarification of the site will give a better seedbed regardless of the method of broadcasting, but this is often impractical because of the area involved or the steepness of the site. Small areas may be seeded quite effectively by hand broadcasting. Broadcasting seed with centrifugal spreaders ("belly grinders") is more economical than hydroseeding and is quite satisfactory for many situations. Traversing the site in two directions, or on very steep slopes, twice using overlapping paths, will aid in achieving uniform coverage.

Hydroseeding is the application of seed in water, often with fertilizer and mulching material. This method is particularly suited to steep cuts and fills and when mulching materials other than straw are used. It is labor- and equipment-intensive and much more expensive as a rule than the former methods. Equipment with gear-type pumps and paddle agitation is superior to that with centrifugal pumps and bypass agitation. The latter-type

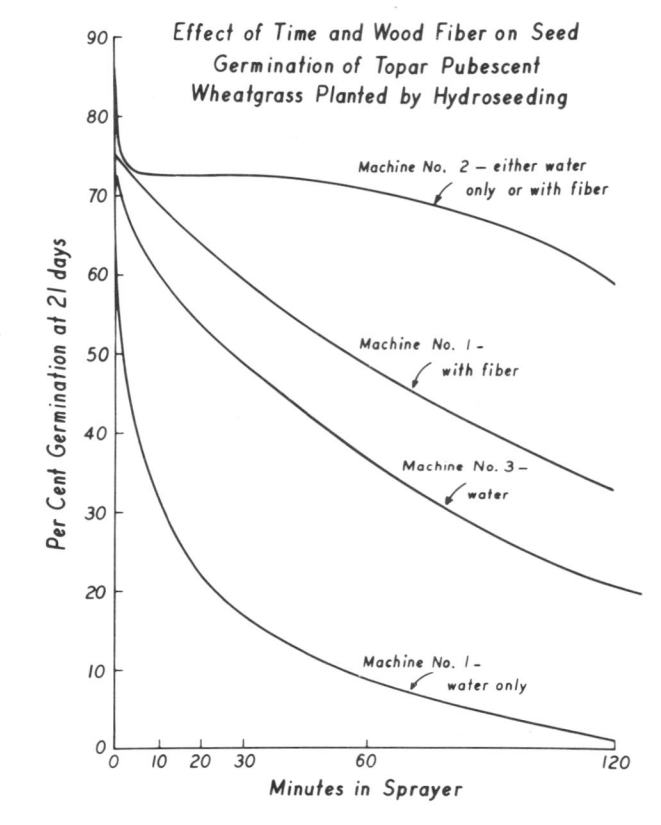

Fig. 6.14. Seed damage as a function of retention time and wood fiber in three types of hydroseeders. Machine No. 1 had centrifugal pump and bypass (through the pump) agitation, No. 2 had a gear pump and paddle agitation (see passed through the pump a single time), and No. 3 had a combination of paddle and pump bypass agitation. Seed damage was measured by percent germination of Topar pubescent wheatgrass. (*From Kay, 1972b*)

Fig. 6.13. A modified range drill is useful for seeding many sites. (*From Kay, 1972a*)

pumps damage a large percentage of the seed, the damage increasing rapidly with increase in retention time in the sprayer (Fig. 6.14) (Kay, 1972b).

Aerial seeding has been used extensively for emergency treatment of extensive areas where vegetation has been destroyed by fire in the western United States. The object is to obtain quick cover before the heavy winter rains cause serious erosion. Annual ryegrass is usually used because the native vegetation either resprouts or is regenerated from residual seeds.

The advisability of using seed mixes is discussed in Section 6.4.6. The mix used and rate of application should be tailored to the local area (Kay, 1972a).

Fertilization is usually required in order to obtain a satisfactory stand of grass. Section 6.3.3.4 discusses methods of assessing the nutrient needs of site soils. Fertilizers may be applied with a range drill at time of seeding, broadcast by hand, or applied in the hydroseeding operation. Overfertilization should be avoided because it may interfere with germination (particularly on saline soils), and it will promote excessive top growth. Excessive top growth of annual grasses in the mix will interfere with the development of the perennial grasses, forbs, and any woody species planted on the site.

The single most important practice in establishment of grasses and forbs is to cover them with soil. This is done when drill seeding is employed and sometimes when the site has been scarified.

Straw and hay are the most suitable mulching materials if weeds and fire hazards are not a problem. They are applied by hand or with blowers at 1 to 2 tons/acre and held in place by crimping or punching into the surface with special machines, or by application of a tackifier such as asphalt emulsion at 200–500 gal/acre.

Wood fiber mulches applied by hydroseeding, either with the seed or following seeding, have given excellent results but are more expensive than straw or hay. They are especially useful on steep slopes and hard ground where straw cannot be punched in. They present no fire hazard, are weed-free, and do not blow off the slope. Rates of application are usually 1000 to 3000 lb/acre. Less than 1000 lb gives an inconsistent mulch effect, and more than 3000 lb may interfere with seedling emergence. Other fibers, recycled paper, and so forth, have usually not been as satisfactory as wood fiber because of the shorter fiber length of the substitutes.

Synthetic materials such as plastic polymers have given variable results but are satisfactory under some conditions.

Comparisons of some mulch materials are given in Table 6.5. An excellent brief discussion of mulches is given by Kay in "Mulches for Erosion Control and Plant Establishment on Disturbed Sites" (May 1978).

6.7.1.2 Woody Species.

Woody species may be seeded in several ways. Broadcast seeding has been found to be relatively ineffective in most situations. Exceptions may occur when the site is adequately scarified, and the seeds lodge in the rills and are covered by soil. More effective methods are the spreading of native topsoil containing the native seed crop, drill planting, and spot seeding (sometimes referred to as direct seeding).

Topsoiling. An example of effective plant establishment of native species by spreading native topsoil is shown in Fig. 6.15. The use of this method requires the careful removal and stockpiling of soil during the construction process. Only the top 1–3 inches of soil is used. Information on using this method is somewhat limited, but the following precautions should be observed. Stockpiles should be relatively shallow to avoid anaerobic conditions or the heating of any organic matter in the soil which may damage seeds. Weed control should be practiced on the stockpiles to avoid building up large

Fig. 6.15.   Cut slope at North Star near Lake Tahoe, California, was revegetated by using a thin top dressing of native top soil after construction. The woody plants are all native species that germinated from seed contained in the top soil. Photographed in 1980, about 8 years after topsoiling.

amounts of weed or grass seeds which will compete with the native seeds. The topsoil should not be spread more than 1 or 2 inches deep on the site. Excessive depth will increase the possibility of slippage from the slope when the topsoil becomes wet. Steep slopes should be scarified on contour before spreading the topsoil to minimize this sloughing erosion.

Drill planting of woody seeds has been used (Kay, 1979a) in the Mojave desert. The same limitations apply as for seeding grasses and forbs. A major disadvantage is that the resulting plants are in rows which may not give as thorough erosion control as staggered plantings and which may not be aesthetically pleasing.

Spot Seeding. Many woody plants can be successfully established by spot seeding (Chan et al., 1971). The advantage of this method over broadcast or drill seeding is that a higher percentage of stocking may be obtained with relatively few seeds. This is so because of the more intensive preparation and care of each seeding spot. This preparation is labor-intensive, however. Results may not be as satisfactory as results of using transplants on some sites (see Section 9.4).

Plant selection is based on the general principles discussed earlier (Sections 6.2 and 6.3). A species may germinate and grow well when spot-seeded in an environment in which it would not produce viable seed. If natural regeneration is desired, care should be taken to select species native to habitats similar to the planting area. This usually means using species native to the adjacent area. The favorable microenvironment created allows the

Table 6.5. Water-holding capacity and stability of some hydromulching materials.

COMMERCIAL NAME	RAW MATERIAL	% MOISTURE[1]	WATER-HOLDING CAPACITY (WHC) CAL-TRANS[2]	USFS[3]	STABILITY[4]	COMMENTS
1. Conwed hydromulch-Minnesota	Virginia aspen wood fiber	—	14.7	13.9	Good	Long-time standard in the industry
2. Conwed hydromulch 2000 Minnesota	Virgin aspen with organic tackifier	—	14.2	—	Good	Pumps easier. No improvement in stability or WHC
3. Silva-Fiber—Washington	Virgin alder wood fiber	15.6	14.7	15.4	Good	Long-time standard in the industry
4. Grass Mulch Oregon	Defibrated ryegrass straw	23.0	10.0	6.2	Fair	High moisture. Not all defibrated. WHC low
6. Jacklin Mulch Washington	Grass seed screening		4.5		Very poor	WHC low, no fiber
7. Fibron—Oregon	Chipstock cardboard	7.4	14.5	13.7	Good	No longer available
8. Agrifiber—California	Corrugated paper	7.1	15.8	17.1	Good	High WHC
9. Cal-Fiber—California	Selected newsprint	12.4	14.6	13.5	Excellent	
10. Cal-Fiber—California	Selected newsprint	5.4	13.5	11.8	Excellent	
11. Astromulch—California	50:50 newsprint and corrugated	8.8	13.9	10.8	Excellent	
12. Fibercel—Texas	Unknown	17.7	10.2	9.6	Poor	Moisture high and WHC marginal
13. Necco—California	Waste paper	7.6	11.6	9.8	Very poor	No longer available
14. Tinex—California	Waste paper	20–70	7.7	—	Very poor	No longer available
15. Spra-Mulch—Illinois	Magazines	7.4	7.7	4.0	Very poor	WHC low, ash high
16. Verdyol—Switzerland	Raw cotton and cellulose pulp	—	11.1	7.6	Fair–good	WHC below USFS specifications
17. Experimental	50/50 news & Silva-Fiber	14.0	14.9	15.4	Excellent	
18. Experimental	50/50 corrug & Silva-Fbr.	11.4	16.5	17.8	Good	

[1] Moisture was determined by oven-drying. If sample was small or a long time in storage, no value is given.
[2] Water-holding capacity for hydromulch. 1976. Thomas Hoover. Calif. DOT ICA–DOT–7L–2167–1–76–36.
[3] Method for determining water holding capacity of hydromulch. 1976. Vance C. Setterholm. U.S.F.S., Region Two.
[4] Observed on decomposed granite surface inclined at 1:1 and subjected to the impact of 3-mm water drops at 6 in/hr.
Source: Kay, 1978.

selection of a greater variety of plant species than might otherwise be available. Irrigation for 1 or 2 years will permit the establishment of an even greater variety of plants.

Attention to detail in spot-seeding techniques is critical. Planting must be done in the fall or very early spring to take maximum advantage of prevailing soil moisture. Relative advantages of fall and spring planting are discussed in Sections 6.7.4.1 and 9.4. Stratification will be required for seeds sown in the spring for some species, whereas species sown in the fall will receive natural stratification. Planting procedures are as follows. Dig a 4-inch hole using a hand pick or trowel. (The basic planting hole is diagrammed in Fig. 6.16). Pulverize compacted soils to 8–12 inches with a shovel or auger for better water and root penetration. Firm the loosened soil before planting. Locate the seeding hole in a depression, crevice, or fissured area for best results in areas of decomposing or "rotten" rock. Construct planting holes on slopes with a slight backslope (Fig. 6.17). This backslope reduces erosion and chance of seeds being buried too deep and helps accumulate water.

Place a controlled-release fertilizer containing 1 g (0.03 oz) of nitrogen in the bottom of the hole. The nitrogen

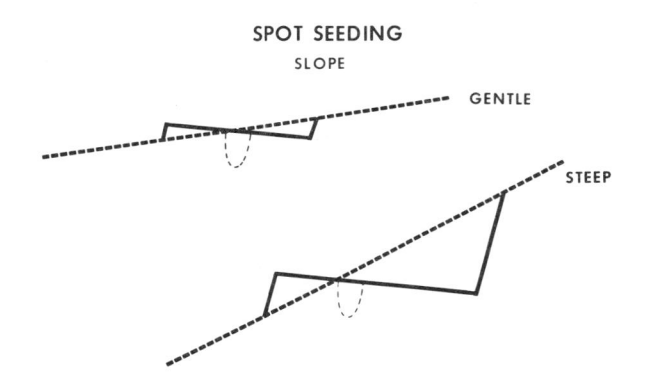

Fig. 6.17. Method of forming pockets on slopes to accumulate moisture and to prevent any loose soil from covering the seed hole.

should be in inorganic form (ammonium or nitrate ion) because organic forms may not be available in relatively sterile soils (see Table 6.6). Many soils may be deficient in sulfur or other elements. Such elements should be added if not already a component of the fertilizer used. Potassium sulfate may be used to supply 0.3 g (0.01 oz) of sulfur by adding $\frac{1}{4}$ teaspoon (0.07 oz) per planting hole. Fertilization is more important for revegetation with woody plants grown from seed than those from transplants because of the relatively slow growth of seedlings.

Replace and firm soil in the planting hole, leaving a slight depression for sowing seed. Place 3 to 20 seeds in the hole, and cover them with additional soil. The depth of the seeding surface, number of seeds, and depth of soil over the seeds are given in Table 6.7. The number of seeds in Table 6.7 is based on an estimated 50 percent germinability. This number should be adjusted for expected germinability.

Weed control is essential to success. Weeds compete for water, nutrients, and growing space. They may also harbor rodents and insects. Contact herbicides or mulches provide this control. Contact herbicides are applied after seeding but before seedling emergence and when

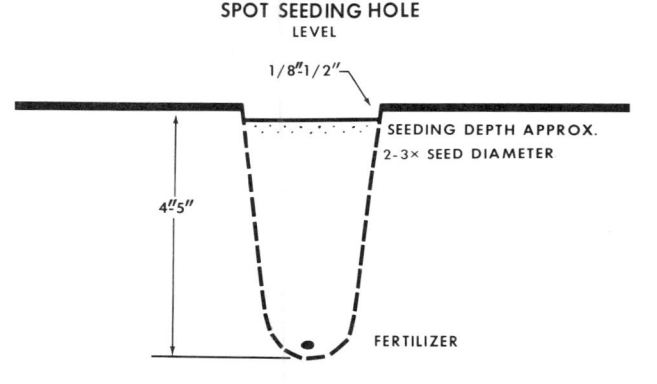

Fig. 6.16. Spot planting of seeds in a hole. This provides for good fertilizer placement, seeding depth, and depression for water accumulation.

Table 6.6. Slow-release fertilizers to give 1 g (0.03 oz) of nitrogen.

| | | AMOUNT FOR 1 G (0.03 OZ) OF NITROGEN | | | SULFUR CONTENT |
| | | WEIGHT | | VOLUME | |
FERTILIZER*	N-P-K†	(G)	(OZ)	(TEASPOONS)	(G)
MagAmp®	7–40–6	15	0.5	3	0.0
Osmocote®	18–9–9	5	0.16	1	0.09

* Organic materials, like fish meal, blood meal, and hoof and horn, might be suitable. Urea-formaldehyde does not always give good response on sterile subsoils.
† N–P–K: nitrogen expressed as percent N; phosphorus as P_2O_5; and potassium as K_2O.
® Registered trade name.
Source: Chan et al., 1971

Table 6.7 Number of seeds per hole, depth of seeding depression, soil depth over seed, and depth of depression for moisture accumulation.

Seed Diameter	Seeds* Per Hole	Depth of Seeding Depression Below Surface	Depth of Soil Over Seed	Depth of Depression for Water
(INCH)	(NUMBER)	(INCH)	(INCH)	(INCH)
$< \frac{1}{16}$	20	$\frac{1}{4}$ to $\frac{3}{8}$	$\frac{1}{8}$	$\frac{1}{8}$ to $\frac{1}{4}$
$\frac{1}{16}$ to $\frac{1}{8}$	10	$\frac{3}{8}$ to $\frac{1}{2}$	$\frac{1}{8}$ to $\frac{1}{4}$	$\frac{1}{4}$
$\frac{1}{8}$ to $\frac{1}{4}$	5	$\frac{1}{2}$ to $\frac{3}{4}$	$\frac{1}{4}$ to $\frac{3}{8}$	$\frac{1}{4}$ to $\frac{3}{8}$
$\frac{1}{4}$ to $\frac{1}{2}$	3	$\frac{7}{8}$ to 1	$\frac{1}{2}$	$\frac{3}{8}$ to $\frac{1}{2}$

* Based on approximately 50 percent germinability.
Source: Chan et al., 1971

weeds are less than 3 inches high. A circle 3 to 4 ft in diameter should be sprayed around each seed spot. If seedlings have emerged, an inverted can will protect them. Hand weeding may be necessary around the seedlings. After contact herbicides are used, long-lasting control may be obtained by using simazine (Princep®) or trifluralin (Treflan®). Use according to manufacturers recommendations.

Mulches will help control weeds, moderate soil temperatures, and conserve moisture. The mulch must not interfere with seedling emergence or growth.

The planting spot may be modified for mulching with coarse organic matter (bark or wood chips) as shown in Fig. 6.18. A collar (#2½ tin can, milk or cottage cheese carton, or cylinder made from heavy asphalt or kraft paper) should be placed in the seed hole before sowing the seed to prevent the mulch from covering the seeds. Place 2–3½ inches of mulch in a 30-inch to 3-ft-diameter circle around the seedlings (Fig. 6.18). Reduce the circle to 24–30 inches if irrigation is available. The collar also may

increase soil temperature, encouraging germination. It will also confine water applied to the seed spot.

Sheet materials also make good mulches. These include uncoated and polycoated mulching paper, black polyethylene film, asphalt roofing paper, and kraft building paper. Clear or white polyethylene should not be used because of adverse temperature effects. Soil temperatures will be too high under clear polyethylene, and reflection from white polyethylene may damage tender plants. Seed holes are prepared as described earlier. A 3-ft square of sheet mulch with a 3-inch hole in the center for the seed hole is used. The corners, and on windy sites the edges, of the sheet are anchored in slits in the ground (Fig. 6.19). Hand weeding of the planting hole may be necessary.

6.7.2 Seed and Seedling Protection

Small wire cages (Fig. 6.20A) may be needed to protect seeds and seedlings from rodents and birds. Hardware cloth ($\frac{1}{2}$-inch mesh) is suitable but must be removed when plants are 3–5 inches high. A large cylinder of wire (e.g., hog wire) may then be used for deer protection until the plants no longer need to be protected (Fig. 6.20B). Both cages are reusable.

6.7.2.1 Irrigation.
Plants can be selected that will grow from seed without irrigation on many sites with as little as 10–12 inches of rainfall. Seedling emergence, survival, and growth may be increased with irrigation, particularly on sandy or shallow soils. The decision to irrigate should be made on the basis of expected benefits and the availability of water and labor.

To irrigate seed spots, install a collar as described under mulching. Carefully fill the collar twice with water after the seeds are planted. If prolonged drought occurs, additional watering may be needed.

Monthly irrigations should begin in May or when

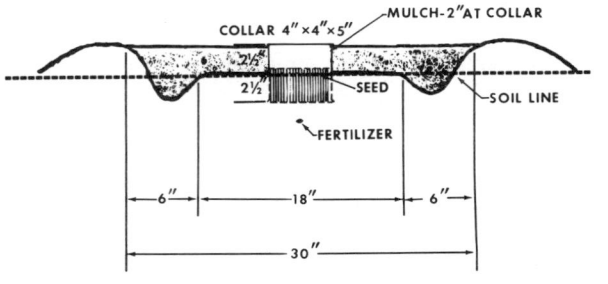

Fig. 6.18. Weed control by use of collar and mulch. The collar prevents mulch from covering the seeding hole, encourages germination by increasing soil temperature, and provides a technique for watering the seed spot for germination and initial growth.

PAPER MULCH-FLAT SURFACE

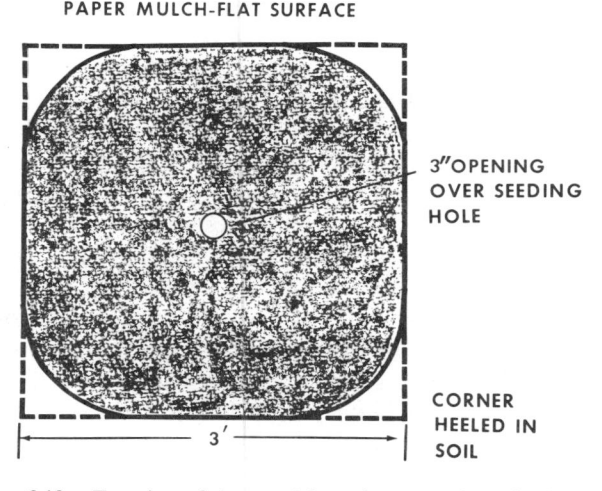

3" OPENING OVER SEEDING HOLE

CORNER HEELED IN SOIL

3'

Fig. 6.19. Top view of sheet mulch used to control weeds. Corners are heeled in to stabilize mulch and to help prevent tearing by winds.

plants first begin to wilt. Use about 1.5 liters (1.5 quarts) per irrigation. As plants grow, the amount of water and basin size should be increased.

6.7.2.2 Thinning Plants.
Plants should be thinned soon after germination. Leave two or three seedlings per hole initially to give some insurance against future hazards. During the second winter the seedlings may be thinned to one per hole. Thin by cutting the plants off at or just below soil level to avoid disturbing root systems of the plants left.

6.7.3 Cuttings

The use of cuttings is an economical method of plant establishment of certain species on many erosion control projects. Thousands of acres of California freeways have been planted with unrooted cuttings of ice plant. Kraebel (1936) described the use of cuttings of willow and baccharis on fill slopes in the relatively dry southern California mountains. Numerous others (e.g., Schiechtl, 1980; Plummer et al., 1968) have used them successfully.

6.7.3.1 Cutting Size.
Some species suitable for cuttings are discussed in Section 7.2. Any species that root readily may be used. The optimum size of cutting varies with the species and site. Poplar cuttings, called "poles," as large as 8–9 ft long and 3–4 inches in diameter have been used in New Zealand (Van Kraayenoord, 1968). Athel *Tamarisk aphylla* (L.) Karst. cuttings as long as 3 or 4 ft have been used in desert areas. The size of willow cuttings recommended varies. Some workers have had best results from cuttings larger than 1 inch in diameter. *Salix lemmonii* used in the Lake Tahoe Basin study (Section 9.4) gave best results with cuttings $\frac{1}{2}$ to $\frac{3}{4}$ inch in diameter.

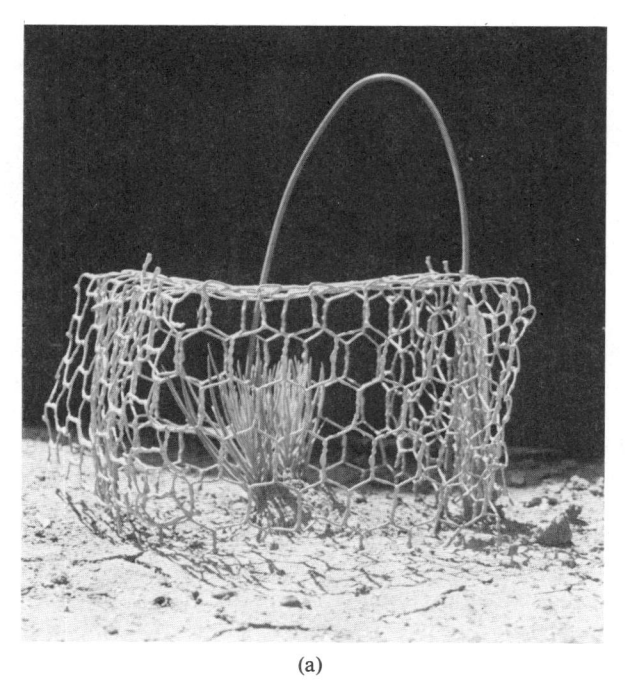

(a)

(b)

Fig. 6.20. Seed and plant protection. (a) Young pine seeds and seedlings protected by a $\frac{1}{2}$-inch mesh chicken wire cage ($2\frac{1}{2}'' \times 4'' \times 4''$); (b) a pine seedling protected by a 15-inch-diameter hog wire cylinder 3 ft high.

The length of cutting may be limited by site conditions. Cuttings over 6–8 inches long are difficult to stick in compacted soils. Longer cuttings should be used on dry sites with sandy soils.

Cuttings should be stuck in the fall or early spring when soil moisture is high in most instances. Summer plantings may be successful in areas with summer rainfall or where they can be irrigated (e.g., freeway plantings of iceplant), if they are handled carefully.

6.7.3.2 Preparation of Cuttings.

Cuttings should be cut to desired lengths, bundled, and stored under wet burlap or in water. Soaking in running water sometimes increases rootability. Two methods may be used to identify the tops vs. bottoms of the cuttings. One end may be cut square and the other at an angle. This requires two cuts when more than one cutting is made from a stem. A more efficient method is to spray-paint the top ends of cuttings after bundling. Cutting material should be examined for presence of lateral buds. In some willow species, large-diameter wood may have few live buds.

6.7.3.3 Sticking Cuttings.

Cuttings should be kept moist until stuck. They may be pushed directly into soft soils, but in hard, cemented, or rocky soils a hole will need to be made with a dibble or even a star drill. Holes should be no deeper than the length of the cutting, which should be placed in the bottom of the hole to avoid an air pocket. This would allow the base of the cutting to dry. The soil around the cutting should be tamped firmly to eliminate any air pockets. After planting, the cutting should be held firmly by the soil.

No more than an inch or two of the cutting should be exposed after planting, as a rule. Any excess should be cut with pruning shears.

Work should proceed from top to bottom on cuts and fills to avoid burying the cuttings completely. Rows of cuttings across a slope should be staggered for best erosion control.

6.7.4 Transplants

6.7.4.1 Time of Planting.

Grasses, forbs, and woody plants may be established by transplanting, which is one of the best methods of revegetating difficult sites. Plants do not go through the critical seed germination stage on site. Planting should be limited to seasons in which adequate moisture is available. Projects with adequate irrigation may be planted with plants grown in containers at any season, although establishment will usually be higher with spring or fall plantings. Establishment of irrigated plantings in wildland or reclamation projects may be variable because of limitations on available water or inconsistencies in applications of water. This was a fac-

tor in the poor survival of plantings in the Tahoe Basin reported by White and Franks (1978).

6.7.4.2 Planting Tools.

Tools used in planting include dibbles, spades, spuds, and small hand picks (see illustrations in Fig. 6.21). The choice of tools depends on the size plant to be planted and site soils. Dibbles are useful for small plants in soft but cohesive soils, but are not satisfactory in very sandy or hard soils. Spuds are useful for small plants in hard rocky soils. Small hand picks are particularly useful on steep sites where footing is difficult, and have worked well in decomposed granite and very sandy sites. Spades or shovels will be needed for larger plants. On relatively level sites, power augers may be used.

6.7.4.3 Planting Hole.

The hole should be of sufficient size and depth that root systems of containerized plants are not disturbed, and those of bare-root plants are not folded or bent in planting. Holes on steep slopes should be constructed in a similar manner to that described for spot seeding to avoid burying and to collect rainfall. Berms may be constructed as shown in Fig. 6.18 when individual plants will be irrigated.

6.7.4.4 Fertilizers and Amendments.

Fertilizers should be placed well below the plant roots if they are used (see Section 6.7.1.2). Slow-release fertilizers are probably preferable to soluble fertilizers because of the

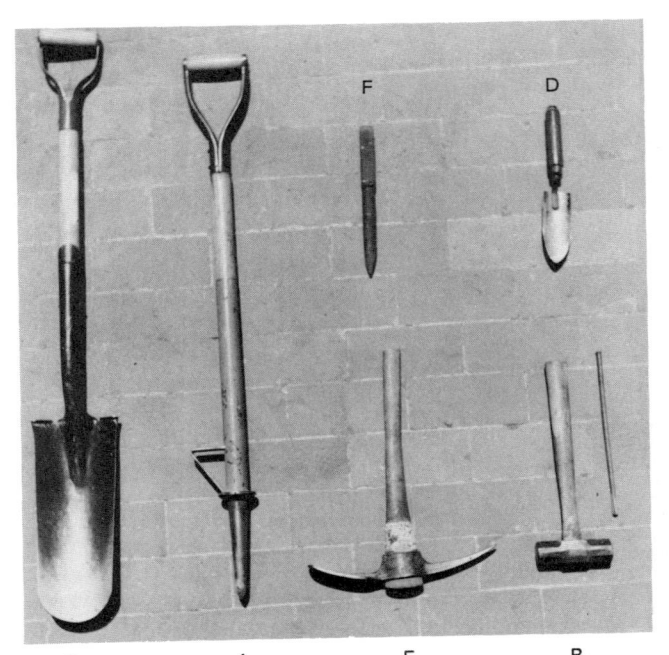

Fig. 6.21. Various tools are used for planting. The choice of tool depends upon the size and type of plant materials and the nature of the soil. A and F—two types of dibbles. B—Star drill and hammer. C— Tile or planting spade. D—Hand trowel. E—Short handled mattock.

lower solubility of the former. The value of soil amendments (organic matter) in the planting hole is questionable. Under most conditions in erosion control planting, they may be detrimental. They may form an additional interface through which roots must penetrate. If soil moisture is limiting, they may dry and be resistant to rewetting. The value of these amendments in holding water may not apply if they are not wet initially, and if rainfall is insufficient to rewet them after drying.

6.7.4.5 Planting Procedure.
Work should proceed rapidly so that planting holes do not dry out before planting and refilling. Roots of bare-root plants should be kept moist at all times, and containerized plants should be placed in the planting hole and the roots covered immediately. Planting should be an individual or at most a two-man operation; a three-man operation, as sometimes observed (one digging holes, one laying out plants, and a third planting), should be avoided. Planting holes and plant roots often dry in the process.

Plants should be handled carefully to avoid breakage and damage to the root systems. Plants grown in cans may have to be removed by cutting the cans. The tops or "shoulder" of peat pots and other biodegradable containers should be removed to well below the soil line so that the container does not act as a "wick" and remove water from the root zone.

Plants should be tamped firmly in place and the planting hole shaped as required. If water is available, they should be watered immediately.

Set plants somewhat below the level at which they were grown. This is contrary to garden practice where ample water is available. The extra soil will act as a mulch and prevent the top of the root system from drying.

6.8 SPECIAL METHODS FOR STRUCTURES

The general principles of plant selection, quality, planting times, and handling apply whether plants are used on cuts and fills or are used to vegetate engineering structures. Plant establishment in special structures requires that soil material be located in, between, or immediately behind them. When construction occurs during the dry season, planting should be delayed unless backfill soils are thoroughly wet. Planting stock will usually be cuttings or small transplants. Low-growing species or vines are the most satisfactory types of plants. Large shrubs or trees are usually inappropriate.

6.8.1 Crib Walls and Revetments

Methods for vegetating the open-fronted bays of crib walls (see Figs. 5.15 and 5.16) will depend somewhat on the nature of the cribfill and the timing of construction. Cribfill is often too coarse and granular for optimal plant

growth. Nevertheless, this does not seem to deter the eventual establishment of some plants, which may even be seen to flourish (see Fig. 1.1). When the cribfill contains sufficient fines (clay and silt-size material), planting holes may be dug in the open bays and transplants or cuttings inserted directly. If construction coincides with the proper planting season, both planting and cribfilling may be done simultaneously. If not, the plants should be inserted during a more favorable time of year.

If the cribfill is patently unsuitable for planting (i.e., too granular and droughty to support plant growth), then one of two alternative approaches may be adopted. The first is to add amendments (e.g., topsoil) in designated pockets or zones near the face of the cribwall *during* backfilling operations. These pockets should be spaced far enough apart that interconnected zones or bands of free-draining cribfill remain between them. The location of these pockets can be flagged for later planting if desired. The second approach is to hand-excavate small holes in each open-fronted bay *after* backfilling. A seedling or rooted cutting complete with its own pocket of suitable soil is then inserted in the hole. This latter operation can be carried out after construction of the cribwall during the optimal planting season. If excavation proves too difficult, open-ended planting tubes may be placed at preselected locations in the cribwall bays during construction. Transplants can be inserted into these tubes, which are then pulled out.

Slotted or cellular revetments can be vegetated in a variety of ways. These structures are generally placed directly against natural ground that is capable of supporting plant growth. Transplants or cuttings can be placed or inserted through the openings or interstices of the revetment. Alternatively, topsoil containing seeds of native plants can be drifted into the openings. Care must be exercised in this instance to remove emergent woody plants (e.g., tree species) whose basal stem diameter will ultimately exceed the size of the openings in the revetment. In some cases volunteer vegetation will come in naturally in a porous revetment over time without any direct action (see Figs. 5.30, 5.35, and 5.37).

In the case of a timber grid revetment (see Section 5.3.4 and Fig. 5.39), the open spaces in the frame should be filled with moist topsoil and lightly compacted. Straw is then spread about 6 inches deep over the structure and covered with 14-gage, 4-inch wire mesh, which is tacked to the frame. Selected ground-cover plants are then planted through the straw into the topsoil. Care must be taken not to make the topsoil too unlike the subsoil so that plant roots fail to penetrate the natural soil beneath.

6.8.2 Breast Walls

Soil should be placed behind and in the interstices of breast walls as they are constructed if plants are to be grown in them (see Fig. 5.5). Plants and unrooted cuttings may be placed during construction if construction occurs when soil moisture is high. However, planting should be delayed until the proper season if construction takes place during the dry season.

6.8.3 Gabions

Gabions must have soil mixed with the rocks during filling if plants are to be grown in them. Alternatively, soil can be drifted into the gabions after construction (see Fig. 5.29). This latter technique is more applicable, however, to gabion mattress revetments than retaining walls. It is difficult to plant or stick cuttings in gabions after construction. The ideal method is to use soil at field capacity and place long, unrooted cuttings at planting time (see Fig. 4.4). Extra care in handling the gabions will be required to avoid damage to the cuttings. When planting must be done after construction, use of unrooted cuttings will probably be the only planting method that is satisfactory.

6.8.4 Tiered Structures

The benches at set-backs of tiered structures make ideal planting sites if the backfill contains sufficient soil. It is not necessary that the entire structural backfill contain soil in this case. A relatively thin top cover of soil (about 1 ft) would be sufficient for plant establishment. The flat areas or steps between rises are stable and will collect the maximum available water. Tiered structures provide opportunities for attractive and imaginative landscaping (see Figs. 5.17 and 5.18).

6.9 AFTERCARE AND PROTECTION

6.9.1 Significance

Follow-up inspection and maintenance are often crucial to successful revegetation. All projects should have provisions for follow-up care, particularly in the first few years. Any failures of structural components, drainage measures, wattling, or brush-layering, or areas of the slope should be repaired promptly. Some replanting of grasses or woody plants may be required to give adequate cover. Grasses may need refertilization to ensure adequate cover.

6.9.2 Protection from Rodents and Browsers

Protection from rodents and browsing animals may be required in some areas. Grazing by domesticated animals in the vicinity of any project should be eliminated. Deer fencing may be justified in critical areas. Rodent protection may be accomplished by poison baits if this is permitted. Poisoning is often restricted on projects under governmental control, however. Use of wire cages around individual plants may be necessary (see Section 6.7.2, Fig. 6.20A,B). Use of individual cages is expensive but may be justified in critical problem areas.

6.10 Summary

Vegetation is a critical and fundamental part of the biotechnical erosion control process. The vegetation component is a living system with amazing adaptability, but attention to detail in handling is vital. Plants have been successfully established on sites with as little as 10 inches of natural rainfall distributed in a 3- or 4-month season without supplemental irrigation, when this attention to detail has been followed. The revegetation process is increasingly easy as amount and length of rainy season increase.

6.11 REFERENCES CITED

American Association of Nurserymen (1980). American standards for nursery stock, American Association of Nurserymen, Washington, D.C., 33 pp.

Amimoto, P. Y. (1978). Erosion and sediment control handbook, WPA 440/3-7-003, Department of Conservation, Resources Agency, State of California, 198 pp.

Baker, Kenneth F., ed. (1957). The U.C. system for producing healthy container grown plants, Division of Agricultural Sciences, University of California, Berkeley, Calif. 23:331 pp.

Bond, G. (1976). The results of the IBP survey of root-nodule formation in non-leguminous angiosperms, in *Symbiotic Nitrogen Fixation in Plants,* edited by Nutman, R. S., London: Cambridge University Press, pp. 443–475.

Bowers, H. D. (1950). Erosion control on California highways, State of California, Department of Public Works, Division of Highways. Sacramento, Calif. (Reprint of a series of articles published in *California Highways and Public Works.*)

Brown, E. Y. (1979). Personal communication to Roman Gankin, April 19, 1979. (California Control Commission, Central Region)

Chan, F. J., Harris, R. W., and Leiser, A. T., (1971). Direct seeding woody plants in the landscape, AXT-n27, Agricultural Extension Service, University of California, Berkeley, Calif., 12 pp. (Reprinted as Leaflet 2577, 1979.)

Edmunson, G. C. (1976). Plant materials study. A search for drought tolerant plant materials for erosion control vegetation and landscaping along California highways, Final Report, Research Project USDA SCS LPMC-1 USDA Soil Conservation Service, Davis, Calif., 257 pp.

Emery, D. (1964). Seed propagation of native California plants, Santa Barbara Botanical Garden Leaflet, 1(10), Santa Barbara Botanical Gardens, Santa Barbara, Calif., pp. 81–96.

Franks, A. L., and White, C. A. (1977). Demonstration of erosion and sediment control technology, California State Water Resources Control Board, Sacramento, Calif. 364 pp.

Gankin, Roman (1979). Personal communication to California Central Coastal Regional Commission (to E. Y. Brown, Jan. 24, 1979). (Senior Environmental Planner, San Mateo County, Calif.)

Hall, V. L., and Ludgwig, J. D. (1975). Evaluation of potential use of vegetation for erosion abatement along the Great Lakes shoreline, Misc. Paper 7-75, Coastal Eng. Res. Ctr., U.S. Army Corps of Engineers, Ft. Belvoir, Va., 35 pp.

Hambidge, G., ed. (1941). *Climate and Man,* USDA 1941 Yearbook of Agriculture, Washington, D.C., 1248 pp.

Hanes, E., Zelazny, L. W. and Blaser, R. E. (1970). Effects of deicing salts on water quality and biota, Natl. Coop. Hwy. Res. Program Report No. 91, NAS-NRC, Washington, D.C.

Harris, R. W., Long, D., and Davis, W. B. (1967). Root problems in nursery liner production, AXT-244, Agricultural Extension Service. University of California, Berkeley, Calif.

Harris, R. W., Davis, W. B., Stice, N. W., and Long, D. (1971). Root pruning improves nursery tree quality, *J. Amer. Soc. Hort. Sci.* 96(1): 105-118.

Hartmann, H. T., and Kester, D. (1975). *Plant Propagation, Principles and Practices,* 3rd ed., Englewood Cliffs, N.J.: Prentice-Hall, 662 pp.

Heisey, R. M., Delwiche, C. C., Virginia, R. A., Wrona, A. F., and Bryan, B. A. (1980). A new nitrogen-fixing non-legume: chamaebatia foliolosa (Rosaceae), *Amer. J. Bot.* 67 (3): 429-431.

Henderson, L. T., Koppe, T. F., and Schoenike, R. E. (1979). Ten-year evaluation of a seed source study of eastern redcedar in South Carolina, *Tree Planters Notes,* USDA Forestry Service, Washington, D.C. (Summer), pp. 3-6.

Horton, J. S. (1949). Trees and shrubs for erosion control in Southern California mountains, California Division of Forestry in Cooperation with California Forestry and Range Experimental Station, USDA Forestry Service, 72 pp.

Kaul, R. N., ed. (1970). *Afforestation in Arid Zones,* The Hague: Dr. W. Junk N. V., 435 pp.

Kay, B. L. (1972a). Revegetation of ski slopes and other disturbed mountain sites in California, Agronomy Progress Report No. 42, Department of Agronomy and Range Science, University of California, Davis, Calif. 3 pp.

Kay, B. L. (1972b). Hydroseeding: limitations and alternatives, Agronomy Progress Report No. 43, Department of Agronomy and Range Science, University of California, Davis, Calif., 3 pp.

Kay, B. L. (1979a). Hydraulic seeding is not the only way, Int. Erosion Control Assoc., Conference X, Seattle, Wash., 5 pp.

Kay, B. L. (1979b). Fibers: What's new? Int. Erosion Control Assoc., Conference X, Seattle, Wash., 7 pp.

Kay, B. (1978). Mulches for erosion control and plant establishment on disturbed sites, in *Reclamation of Drastically Disturbed Lands,* edited by Schaller & Sutton, ASA-SCSA-SSSA, Madison, Wisconsin.

Kraebel, C. J. (1936). Erosion control on mountain roads, *USDA Circular No. 380,* USDA, Washington, D.C., 44 pp.

Kruckeberg, A. R. (1967). Ecotypic response to ultramafic soils by some plant species of Northwestern United States, *Brittonia* 19(2): 133-151.

Langhart, W. C. (1972). An ecological study of big leaf maple, M.S. thesis, University of California, Davis, Calif., 123 pp.

Leiser, A. T. Unpublished data, *Acer macrophyllum* ecotype trials, University of California, Davis, Calif.

Leiser, A. T. (1957). *Rhododendron occidentale* on alkaline soil, *Rhododendron and Camellia Yearbook 1957,* London: The Royal Hort. Soc. pp. 47-51.

Martin, W. E., Vlamis, J., and Stice, N. W. (1953). Field correction of calcium deficiency on a serpentine soil, *J. Agronomy,* pp. 204-208.

McKell, C. M., Blaisdell, J. P., and Goodin, J. R., eds. (1971). Wild land shrubs. Their biology and utilization, *USDA Forestry Service Gen. Tech. Rept. INT-1,* Intermountain Forestry and Range Experimental Station, USDA Forest Service, Ogden, Utah.

Mirov, N. T. (1940). Additional data on collecting and propagating the seeds of California wild plants, For. Res. Notes No. 21, California Forestry and Range Experimental Station, USDA Forestry Service, Berkeley, Calif., 17 pp.

Mirov, N. T., and Kraebel, C. J. Collecting and propagating the seeds of California wild plants, For. Res. Notes No. 18, California Forestry and Range Experimental Station, USDA Forest Service, Berkeley, Calif., 27 pp.

Monsen, S. B. and Plummer, A. P. (1978). Plants and treatment for revegetation of disturbed sites in the intermountain area, in *The Reclamation of Disturbed Arid Lands,* ed. by Wright, R. A., Albuquerque, N. M.: University of New Mexico Press, pp. 155-173.

Nussbaum, J. J. (1969). Chemical pinching for roots of container plants, *California Agr.* 23(10): 16-18, University of California, Berkeley, Calif.

Plummer, A. P., Christensen, D. R., and Monsen, S. B. (1968). Restoring big game range in Utah, Pub. No. 68-3, Utah Division of Fish and Game, 183 pp.

Rehder, A. (1947). *Manual of Cultivated Trees and Shrubs Hardy in North America,* New York: Macmillan, 996 pp.

Richards, L. A., ed. (1954). Diagnosis and improvement of saline and alkaline soil, *Agronomy Handbook No. 60,* USDA Regional Salinity Lab., Riverside, Calif.

Royster, D. L. (1977). Some observations on the use of horizontal drains in the correction and prevention of landslides, Tennessee Department of Highways, Division of Soils and Geology, Nashville, Tenn.

Schaller, F. W., and Sutton, P., eds. (1978). Reclamation of drastically disturbed land, *Proc. Symp. Amer. Soc. Agron.,* Madison Wisc.

Schiechtl, H. (1980). *Bioengineering for Land Reclamation and Conservation,* Edmonton, Alberta: University of Alberta Press, 400 pp.

Schopmeyer, C. S., ed. (1974). Seeds of woody plants in the United States, *USDA Agronomy Handbook 450,* USDA Forestry Service, Washington, D.C., 883 pp.

Smith, T. W., and Stafford, G. V. (1957). Horizontal drains on California highways, *J. Soil Mech. Foundations Div.,* ASCE, 83: 1301-1326.

Stark, N. (1966). Review of highway planting information appropriate to Nevada, Bull. B-7, Desert Reg. Inst., University of Nevada, Reno, Nev., 207 pp.

Tinus, R. W., and McDonald, S. E. (1979). How to grow tree seedlings in containers in greenhouses, *Gen. Tech. Rpt. RM-80,* Rocky Mountain Forestry and Range Experimental Station, USDA Forest Service, Fort Collins, Colo.

USDA Forest Service (1979a). User guide to vegetation, *USDA Forest Service Gen. Tech. Rept. INT-64,* Intermountain Forest and Range Experimental Station, Ogden, Utah, 85 pp.

USDA Forest Service (1979b). User guide to soils, *USDA Forest Service Gen. Tech. Rept. INT-68,* Intermount Forest and Range Experimental Station, Ogden, Utah, 80 pp.

USDA Soil Conservation Service (1975). Engineering field manual for conservation practices, USDA Soil Conservation Service Engr. Div., Washington, D.C.

U. S. Environmental Protection Agency (1972). Guidelines for erosion and sediment control planning and implementation, EPA-R2-72-015, U. S. Environmental Protection Agency, Washington, D.C., 227 pp.

U. S. Environmental Protection Agency (1975). Methods of quickly vegetating soils of low productivity, construction activities, EPA-440/9-75-006, U. S. Environmental Protection Agency, Washington, D.C.

Van Kraayenoord, C. W. S. (1968). Poplars and willows in New Zealand with particular reference to their use in erosion control, Intl. Poplar Commission, 13th Session, Montreal, Canada

Vlamis, J. (1966). Testing the fertility of soils in California, *Agronomia Lusitana* 25(3): 247–264.

Walker, R. B. (1954). Factors affecting plant growth on serpentine soils, *Ecology* 35(2): 259–266.

Whitlow, T. H., and Harris, R. W. (1979). Flood tolerance in plants, A state-of-the art review, Department of Environment Horticulture, University of California Davis Tech. Rept. E–79-2 for U. S. Army Waterways Exp. Stat., Env. Lab., Vicksburg, Miss., 257 pp.

Whittaker, R. H., Walker, R. D., Kruckeberg, A. R. (1954). The ecology of serpentine soils: A symposium, *Ecology* 35(2): 258–288.

Williams, D. E., and Vlamis, J. (1978). Acid soil infertility, in "Soil and Plant Tissue Testing in California," ed. by Reisenauer, H. M., Bull. 1879, Division of Agr. Sci., University of California, Berkeley, Calif., pp. 46–48.

Willis, J. C. (1966). *Dictionary of Flowering Plants and Ferns,* 7th ed., Rev. by H. K. Airy Shaw, London: Cambridge University Press.

Young, J. A., Evans, R. A., Kay, B. L., Owen, R. E., and Jurak, F. L. (1978). Collection processing and germinating seeds of western wildlands plants, USDA Science and Education Adm. Agr. Reviews and Manuals ARM–10–3/July 1978.

White, C. A. and Franks, A. L. (1978). Demonstration of erosion and sediment control technology, Lake Tahoe Region of California, State Water Resources Control Board Final Report, 393 pp.

7

Quasi–Vegetative or Hybrid Slope Protection Techniques

7.1 INTRODUCTION

Quasi-vegetative methods fall under the category of "mixed construction" approaches to slope protection and erosion control discussed in Chapter 4 (see Table 4.1). These methods entail the use of live and/or dead plant parts (stems and branches) which are inserted, driven, buried, or otherwise placed on the ground in specified ways to control erosion, minimize shallow sliding, protect erosion control structures, and provide a favorable environment for the establishment of a permanent vegetative cover.

Quasi-vegetative methods are good examples of truly integrated, biotechnical slope protection. These methods are hybrid in the sense that they may require special earthwork construction procedures (e.g., slope grading, terracing, and trenching) or require the use of some non-plant materials (e.g., wire, boards, rock, stakes). On the other hand, native, locally available plant materials are used for the most part.

Quasi-vegetative slope protection techniques described in this chapter include contour-wattling, contour brush-layering, reed-trench terracing, brush matting, and live staking. All of these methods are relatively labor-skill intensive; they can be implemented without the use of heavy equipment.

7.2 CONTOUR-WATTLING

7.2.1 Definition

The word wattle is derived from the Anglo-Saxon *watel, watul, watol,* meaning interwoven twigs. It is defined as a twig, withe, or flexible rod, hence a framework or hurdle made of such rods. It has come to mean material consisting of wattled twigs used for walls, fences, and so on. Kraebel (1936, pp. 12–13) used the term in a similar but slightly different manner, viz.:

"contour-wattling" is an expression that has been adopted as a convenient name for a process somewhat different from that suggested by the dictionary definition of wattling. In this circular, wattling does not signify the weaving of twigs and withes between upright stakes, as in the customary wattle, but rather the packing of lengths of brush into continuous thick "cables" partially buried across a slope at regular contour intervals and supported on the lower side by stakes.

7.2.2 Historical Development

Kraebel reported details of numerous wattling installations on fill slopes in southern California (the Angeles and San Bernadino National Forests and other locations) and in the hills behind Berkeley, California on Grizzly Boulevard. Some slopes were as steep as 77 percent (1.3:1 slope angle). Little information is available about the extent of the use of wattling for erosion control in subsequent years. Horton (1949, p. 20) described it as "especially adapted to use on newly built road slopes, and it has been found equally useful on other eroding areas with loose, ravelling soils." He further noted, as did Kraebel, that "occasionally slippages result from the saturation, during heavy rains, of masses of road fill material resting on clay patches or on old eroded surfaces." This slippage was attributed to increased infiltration through the wattling, causing saturation of the surface layer.

Contour-wattling was employed by the USDA Soil Conservation Service (1940) as part of a demonstration project on lake bluff erosion control along Lake Michigan. Contour-wattling was employed in this case to help stabilize the face of a denuded clay till bluff that had been eroding and retreating under the combined action of both terrestrial and marine slope processes. This project is discussed further in Chapter 9 as one of several case studies in biotechnical slope protection.

In a later publication by the State of California, Department of Public Works, Division of Highways (Bowers, 1950 p. 48), the value of wattling was dismissed. Bowers stated in his article that

Fair control was obtained with this method, but it has several disadvantages. All operations must be done by hand labor. . . . Wattles installed in trenches intercept and hold runoff water. No further runoff can take place until the trench is filled with water to the overflow point. This condition cannot help but result in saturation of the uncompacted soil around and below the wattle, with consequent undermining or slumping and failure during storms of high intensity.

Apparently, little use was made of wattling following the appearance of these publications.

Kraebel had pointed out that failures could occur under such circumstances. However, he had pointed out the necessity of following placement specifications rigorously. These specifications included thorough working of soil into the wattling and the placement of stakes into the firm or compacted layers of the slope. There should be no "trench" remaining to be filled with water if soil is worked thoroughly into the wattling bundle.

More recent installations of wattling (discussed in Chapter 9) indicate that these failures need not occur when wattling is properly installed. Under conditions even of moderate rainfall, much of the runoff water is slowed and trickles through and over the wattling, proceeding downslope rather than into the slope. Thorough tamping of soil into the wattling bundles makes this possible. The importance of deep staking cannot be overemphasized. Some mechanization of wattling preparation is possible (e.g., the use of chain saws or power brush cutter in preparing wattling materials, and the use of pneumatic hammers for driving stakes). These recent installations have indicated that the use of wattling can still be cost-effective at present labor costs.

All of the early descriptions of the application of wattling were to highway fill slopes. Recent work (Leiser et al., 1974) has applied the wattling process to cut slopes with equally useful results (see Fig. 7.1 and Chapter 9, Section 9.4).

Fig. 7.1. Badly eroding roadcut in sandy, granitic soil in the Lake Tahoe basin, California, which was stabilized by contour wattling. (a) Before erosion control measures; (b) after stabilization. Slope treatment consisted of scaling top of cut and constructing a low breast wall at the toe in addition to wattling the face.

7.2.3 General Principles and Description of Method

Wattling consists of placing bundles of suitable plant materials in shallow trenches, on contour, on either cut or fill slopes (see Fig. 7.2). The bundles consist of woody plant stems, preferably of species that will root easily. When the supply of live stems of easily rooting species is limited, a portion of each bundle may be of material that will not root easily or of dead material. The material should be in leaf, or if not, material such as straw or forest litter should be incorporated into the bundles to add to the filtering properties of the wattles.

7.2.3.1 Function of Wattling. Wattling functions as an erosion control mechanism in several ways.

Fig. 7.2. Wattling consists of bundles of woody stems laid in shallow trenches, on contour, staked, and covered with soil. Species that root easily should be used when possible. Live stakes were used in this installation.

Fig. 7.3. Wattling reduces a long slope to a series of short slopes that dissipates the energy of detritus and water movement downslope. Four rows of wattling placed about 6 ft on center have begun to stabilize this cut slope at Chamberland on Highway 89, Lake Tahoe, California. Wattling rows were interplanted with native woody species and overseeded with a grass mix. Slope treatment was done in October 1972 and May 1973, and photographed in June 1974.

1. Stabilization of the surface layers of the slope from wind, gravitational, and hydraulic forces is accomplished. This stabilization, which results from the combined effects of the wattle bundles and the stakes, reduces gullying and surficial sliding.

2. Energy dissipation is achieved by slowing the movement of water and detritus downslope. A long slope effectively becomes a series of short slopes as downward-moving materials are slowed at each wattling contour (Fig. 7.3).

3. Entrapment of sediments occurs because of the filtering action of the wattling. Water reaching the bottom of the slope will have greatly reduced sediment load if the wattling has been properly installed (see Fig. 7.4 and Section 7.2.3.5).

4. Infiltration is increased as downslope surface runoff is slowed. On dry sites this increases the water available for plant establishment. It also reduces gullying by reducing surface water flow. The increased infiltration has been cited as an objection to the use of wattling on some sites. Increasing the number of stakes and the depth

Fig. 7.4. Wattling installed in a gully caused by seepage traps sediments and slows downhill water movement. Runoff water is essentially free of sediment as it trickles over the wattling. This permits the establishment of vegetation and eventual slope stabilization. Work was installed in May 1973 on Luther Pass Highway 89, Lake Tahoe, and photographed in June 1974.

to which they are driven will minimize or overcome this problem. Thorough packing of soil into and around the wattling bundles will also help to eliminate the problem.

5. Vegetation establishment is enhanced because wattling provides a suitable microsite for plants by stabilization of surface soils, increase in water infiltration, and the formation of terraces with lower slope angles. Seeds, whether planted or from natural dispersal, tend to remain in place, and seedlings have a chance to develop in the stabilized surface areas. The temporary vegetation resulting from the wattling acts as a pioneer species, allowing time for transplants or natural succession to form a more permanent vegetation cover. The physical barrier of the wattling itself traps naturally distributed seeds (see Fig. 7.5).

7.2.3.2 Selection of Wattling Materials.
The ideal plant materials for wattling are those that: (1) root easily; (2) are long, straight, and flexible; and (3) are in plentiful supply near the job site. Willow (*Salix* spp.) makes ideal wattling material. The genus consists of over 300 species with widespread distribution in the temperate and cool temperate regions of the Northern Hemisphere. However, few species occur in the Southern Hemisphere. Species of *Baccharis*—*B. viminea* DC., mule fat; *B. pilularis* subsp. *consanguinea* (DC.) O. Kuntze, chapar-

ral broom or coyote brush—are useful subjects in California. Another species, *B. glutinosa* Pers., waterwally, is found from southern California east to Texas and Mexico, and in Chile. There are about 350 species of *Baccharis* in North and South America. Others may have promise as wattling materials. Some species of elderberry (*Sambucus* spp.) root readily. There are about 20 species widespread in temperate and subtropical areas of both hemispheres. The better-known species are usually tolerant of both wet and dry soils. In dry areas where winter temperatures do not fall below 18–20°F, athel—*Tamarix aphylla* (L.) Karst., which is a native of North Africa and the eastern Mediterranean region—is an excellent material. Athel stems up to 2 inches in diameter and 3 ft long have been used to plant windbreaks and dry washes in desert regions. It could easily be grown in nursery rows in dry regions. Other species of *Tamarix* may also be useful. The genus has minute leaves, and supplementary organic matter should be added to wattling bundles to increase the filtering capacity. Some species of *Populus* (poplars, cottonwoods) root readily; others do not. More research is necessary to identify those species suitable for wattling.

Plantations may be established when materials are in short supply if enough lead time is available. Many of the suitable species will supply materials on a 2–4-year rotation.

7.2.3.3 Preparation and Handling of Wattles.
Suitable materials may be cut with loping shears, chain saws, or power brush cutting saws. It is desirable to cut whole clumps near ground level for appearance and ease of operation. A two-man operation is efficient, one cutting and one removing material. Additional trimming of stems over 1½ inches in diameter may be done by a third man. These trimmings may be used for live stakes. Stems may be any length over 3 ft—the longer the better. A two-man crew makes and ties the bundles. This crew places the required number of stems in the bundle, randomly alternating butt ends. The number of stems varies with the size and kind of plant material. When compressed and tightly tied, the bundles should be 8–10 inches in diameter. When completed, the bundles should taper at each end, and maximum length should be 1½ to 2 ft longer than the maximum stem length (i.e., be cigar-shaped) (Figs. 7.6 and 7.10).

Wattling bundles described by Kraebel had all the butt ends of stems together. This resulted in a narrow conical bundle. The bundles had to be "tied" together by interlacing the thin ends of one bundle with the butt ends of the next. The modification described above, that of alternating the butt ends of the stems, results in "cigar-shaped" bundles with slender tips extending beyond the large stem butts. These tapered ends are easily tied

Fig. 7.5. Wattling provides microsites for plant establishment. Grass establishment is good in and below the wattling rows, and woody plants have been planted between the wattling rows. Slope treatment was done in October 1972 and May 1973, and photographed in June 1974.

Fig. 7.6.   A two-man crew prepares wattling bundles by laying brush in bundles with butt ends alternating. Bundles are then compressed and tied tightly. The resulting cigar-shaped bundles (foreground) are laid in trenches with the tapered ends overlapping.

together with a stake, a simpler procedure than lacing the stem of the two bundles.

Tying is accomplished by one man holding and compressing the bundle while the second man ties with two or more loops of binder's twine or heavier material. A nonslipping knot must be used. Ties are spaced 12–15 inches apart.

Bundles should be stored until used, where they will remain alive—in a pile, in the shade, and covered, or in water or under sprinklers. Normally they should not be prepared more than 1 or 2 days before placing. The ideal situation is to place them as rapidly as they are prepared. At no time should they be spread out on the slope, exposed to sun and wind. They are live material and should be treated as such.

7.2.3.4 Stakes and Staking.   Proper staking is essential to successful wattling. The wattles are held in place by stakes placed on the downslope side of the trenches. Stabilization of the wattles was increased in research installations made in the early 1970s (Leiser et al., 1974) by driving additional stakes through the bundles to hold them down and to tie bundle ends together. This supplementary staking was done at one to two times the spacing of the downslope stakes, and before backfilling was done.

Stakes may be made of several materials. Live stakes of the same species as the wattling have the advantage that they will root and add to the plant cover. They also have

several disadvantages. The supply of suitable straight material of adequate diameter may be limited. It is difficult to "point" them uniformly for ready driving. They are softer and more flexible than stakes made of lumber and are therefore more difficult to drive into undisturbed soils in cut slopes.

Stakes cut from lumber (e.g., "construction" stakes) are available in several lengths. The construction stakes are cut from 2 × 4's and yield a stake about 2 × 3 inches on one end, tapering to 2 × ¼ inches at the point. This wedge shape does a superior job of anchoring when driven through the bundles of wattling (see Fig. 7.7). These stakes are strong, and the choice of lengths may facilitate adjustment of stake length to site conditions for firm staking.

Steel reinforcing bars may be used for staking where subsoils are very hard or cemented. When they are used, their ends should be bent over to hold the wattling down, or the wattling should be wired to the bars. A reinforcing bar will not readily decompose, and this may be an objection to its use.

7.2.3.5 Placement and Covering of Wattles. Proper placement and covering of wattles is a critical part of a successful wattling operation. Wattling is placed in trenches and staked as described in Section 7.2.4.3. Soil is brought down from the slope above and worked into the interstices of the wattling. After completion of the work, wattling should be almost but not wholly buried. A fringe of material, perhaps 10 percent of the bundle volume, should remain exposed (Fig. 7.8). Because of the natural irregularities of the bundles it is difficult to define this parameter exactly. Bundles 8–10 inches in diameter

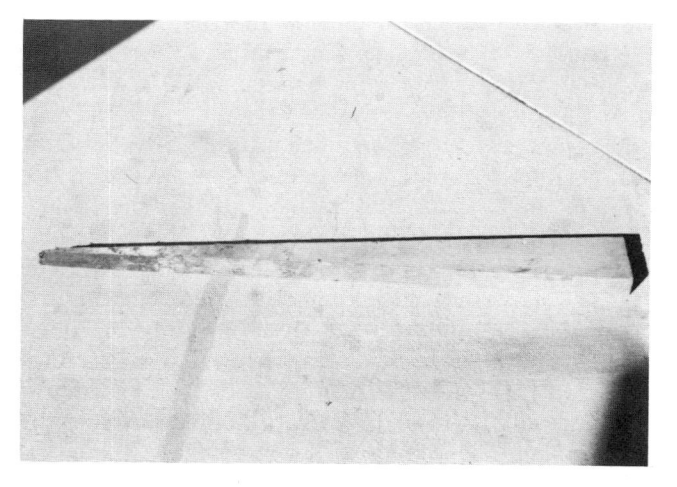

Fig. 7.7.   Construction ("con") stakes, 2 × 4's cut on the diagonal, are available in a number of lengths. They have the advantage over "live" stakes of being easily driven, and the wedge shape gives a firmer hold.

Fig. 7.9. A wattling bundle that was not covered sufficiently has dried out and not sprouted. Although it is trapping sediments quite well, there is danger that it will be undermined, resulting in increased gullying.

Fig. 7.8. A fringe of the wattling should be exposed when work is completed. This exposed wattling slows runoff and traps sediments moving downslope.

should have about 1 inch of the diameter exposed when measured perpendicular to the slope face. Twigs and loose branch ends may extend 3 or 4 inches. This would expose at least 10 percent and not more than 20 percent of the bundle circumference. If too little of the wattling is exposed, the advantages of energy dissipation, filtration of sediments, infiltration of water, and entrapment of seed are largely lost. If too much wattling is exposed, the bundles will dry excessively and not sprout. The risk of undermining the bundles with resulting gullying and slope failure are greatly increased (Fig. 7.9). Kraebel stated that in addition to the soil covering, workmen should walk on the wattling contours when preparing and laying the contour row above. Counting individual man-tasks, he stated that a wattling contour would be traversed six times if this were done. In dry soils, sufficient soil material may more or less work downward into the wattling contour. When soils are wet, care should be taken to pull enough soil down to cover the wattling to the extent required.

The vertical distance between wattling rows is varied to suit the site requirements. The distance should be as small

as 3 ft under severe erosion conditions (e.g., unstable soils and gullies), and may become greater as susceptibility to erosion decreases. Spacing as great as 20 ft has been effective in some circumstances.

7.2.3.6 Timing of Installation. Timing of wattling installation is vital to success. Placement should be done in the fall after soil moisture is near field capacity. During the winter, or early spring when the wattling is deciduous, additional materials, forest duff, straw, and so forth, should be incorporated into the wattling bundles to increase infiltration. Placement of wattling in the summer should be avoided if maximum benefits are to be attained. It can only be successful in this season if the utmost care is used to prevent the wattles from drying, and if soil moisture levels are suitable for plant growth. It may be successful in areas of adequate summer rainfall or if artificial irrigation is available.

7.2.3.7 Summary. When properly installed, wattling plant material will root, binding the soil with roots and protecting the surface with the above-ground parts. When the stakes are of live, easily rooting plant materials, they will add additional vegetation to the slope.

7.2.4 Installation of Wattling

7.2.4.1 Site Survey. A thorough survey should be made of each site. The survey should determine the need for site preparation such as scaling, smoothing, top-of-cut protection (e.g., water diversion), construction of breast walls, or other protective features to prevent undercutting of the slope toe. The depth of the loose surface layer should be determined in order to estimate the length of stakes needed. The depth may vary in different areas on the slope, and stakes of several lengths may be needed. The degree of compaction of the subsurface layers should be determined in order to select suitable staking materials. If compaction or cementing is severe, it may be impossible to drive live stakes because of their flexibility, and dry wood or reinforcing bar stakes may be needed.

The location of gullies should be mapped on old cuts and fills. Seepage areas should also be identified on old or new cuts. These areas will frequently require closer spacing of wattling contours.

The degree of erosion or potential erosion should be estimated to determine the vertical spacing of contours. Spacing should be as close as 3 ft on severe sites subject to gully formation and as much as 20 ft on sites subject to moderate, uniform sheet or dry ravel erosion. Spacing should usually be from 3 to 8 or 10 ft. Spacing may be varied on a single slope to meet particular erosion problems (see Section 9.4). In some cases only the more unstable portions of a slope need wattling.

The wattling materials should be located before the final plan of work is prepared. Limited availability of easy-to-root material may make it advisable to plan to use live stakes or at least a portion of live stakes on the project. The availability of materials may dictate a compromise between desirable and practical contour spacing. Ease of access and hauling distance will affect the distribution of work crews. The collection of plant materials should not degrade the quality of one site at the expense of another. Collection of materials may improve site quality because the cutting of material may invigorate or renew growth in the stands cut, or may reduce encroachment on streams, meadows, or pastures.

Estimates of the manpower and material requirements may be made and a plan of work developed from the site plan.

7.2.4.2 Slope Preparation.

Corrective measures, top-of-cut ditches, improvement or construction of culverts, breast-wall or gabion construction, laying back of the slope, and scaling must be done before the wattling procedure is started. Any top-of-slope overhang must be removed. If possible, slope angle must be reduced to 1:1 or less. Occasional deep gullies (3 or more ft) may be treated by wattling following the contour of the gully and placement of additional short rows of wattling between the main contours. Presence of many deep gullies or slide areas may require filling before wattling begins (see Section 7.2.5.3). Shallow gullies (less than 1 ft) can be smoothed as work progresses. Intermediate gullying (1–3 ft deep) may be eliminated by more thorough scaling, working from the top of the slope downward. This work

should be done just before the wattling operation to minimize additional erosion or gully formation.

7.2.4.3 Staking and Trenching.

Staking the slope and trenching should begin while the first bundles are being prepared. All work proceeds from the bottom of the slope to the top (see Fig. 7.10). The contours should be staked using an Abney level or similar device to keep them absolutely horizontal. Stakes must be driven to a firm hold with the tops about 6 inches above grade. Stakes should be 12–18 inches o.c. (Fig. 7.11).

Trenching should not preceed laying of the bundles by more than 1 hour to minimize drying of soil (Fig. 7.12). The trench should be shallow, about half the diameter of the bundles. It is dug immediately upslope from the stakes. Excavation may be wasted down-slope to cover lower wattles. On fill slopes the trenches should extend at least one-half the bundle length into the undisturbed soil adjacent to the fill.

7.2.4.4 Placement and Covering of Wattles.

Immediately following trenching the wattles are placed in the trench. Care must be taken to overlap the tapered ends of bundles so the overall bundle thickness is uniform. Additional stakes are driven through the bundles at a maximum spacing of 18 inches o.c. Two stakes should be used at each bundle overlap. The holding action of the stakes is usually best if they are placed near the bundle ties. These operations are best done with three persons, one to supply bundles, one to pack, and one to stake.

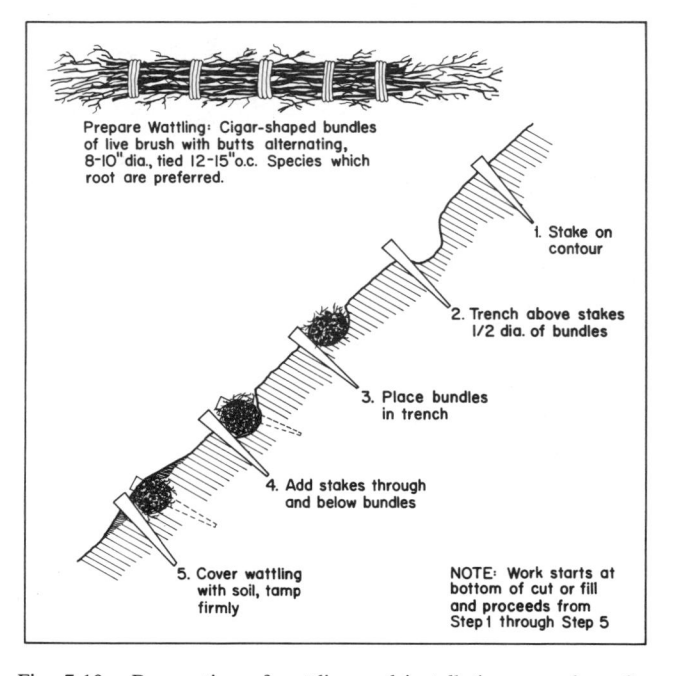

Prepare Wattling: Cigar-shaped bundles of live brush with butts alternating, 8–10" dia., tied 12–15" o.c. Species which root are preferred.

1. Stake on contour
2. Trench above stakes 1/2 dia. of bundles
3. Place bundles in trench
4. Add stakes through and below bundles
5. Cover wattling with soil, tamp firmly

NOTE: Work starts at bottom of cut or fill and proceeds from Step 1 through Step 5

Fig. 7.10. Preparation of wattling and installation procedure. Sequence of operations is shown schematically in the diagram.

Fig. 7.11. Stakes are set on contour with an Abney level or similar device and driven to a firm hold with tops about 6 inches above grade.

Fig. 7.13. Wattling is placed in trenches and immediately covered. The soil is worked into the interstices of the bundles. Workmen walking on the covered bundles while preparing and laying wattling rows above and planting between the rows facilitate firm packing of the soil.

Fig. 7.12. Trenches are dug upslope from the stakes. Trenching should be done just before laying of wattling to minimize drying of the soil.

A fourth worker should follow immediately, partially covering the wattling from the slope or from the trench above. The soil should be worked into the interstices of the wattles. This packing action is aided by the worker walking on the wattling being covered. Workers should walk on the wattling bundles as much as possible in performing all these operations. This results in maximum compaction and working of soil into the bundles (see Fig. 7.13).

As wattling contours are completed, one workman should check the work. Some stakes may need to be driven to a firmer hold. Stakes that could not be driven to their full depth because of compacted subsoil should be cut off 2–3 inches above the wattling. Additional soil should be added where needed, and excess soil should be removed so that a uniform fringe of wattling is exposed. Any weak spots in the wattling installation may result in failures.

Kraebel (1936) summarized the process as follows:

A completed contour wattle should resemble a slight terrace, from the lower edge of which protrudes a windrow of twigs and leaves, 3 to 4 inches long. As has been explained, this unburied portion of the brush is the safety factor. On a properly constructed contour the brush is neither so exposed as to encourage under-cutting by the runoff or the first storm, nor so completely buried as to be overrun by water and silt. Construction of good contour wattles is by no means a difficult or delicate feat, but if it is not correctly done much, if not all the benefit desired therefrom will be lost.

7.2.4.5 Planting.

Upon completion of the wattling installation the planting of temporary and permanent vegetation should be done (see Fig. 7.5). The planting should be delayed until the proper season if the wattling is not placed at that time. Woody vegetation, unrooted or rooted cuttings, and transplants should be planted first. Planting crews should be encouraged to walk on the wattling contours when possible. This will further work soil into the bundles and compact them. Grass and forb seeding, by hand or hydroseeding, should follow. Planting procedures were discussed in Chapter 6.

7.2.4.6 Maintenance.

Regular inspection and maintenance of wattling installations should be conducted, particularly during the first year. Stakes that were originally driven to a firm hold may loosen because of saturation of the slope or frost action. Blocked culverts or top-of-cut ditches may cause gully formation. Some areas of the slope may slump. Prompt correction of these failures is essential to prevent major problems from developing (see Fig. 7.14). Correction of slumps or gullies is discussed in Section 7.2.5.3.

7.2.5   Uses or Applications for Wattling

Wattling may be used to stabilize whole slopes or localized gully areas of slopes. It may be installed during construction or as a remedial action on old slopes. As a remedial action, wattling has the advantage of minimizing slope disturbance during placement compared to contour brush-layering (Section 7.3).

7.2.5.1 Road Fills.

The original work with wattling by Kraebel was apparently limited to treatment of old eroding or newly constructed fill slopes. The results were highly successful in both cases. The only difference in procedures between installations on old and new fills is that in the former, considerable slope preparation may need to be done (see Section 7.2.4.2). Kraebel worked on slopes that needed minimal preparation where the wattling installation itself smoothed minor gulies and on slopes that had failed to the point that major rebuilding

Fig. 7.14.   Failures in the wattling installation should be repaired promptly. This bundle has worked out of the ground, probably because of frost action and improper staking and covering. It should be replaced with a new bundle. The remainder of the installation is intact and sprouting.

was required. The slopes on Grizzly Peak Boulevard in the Berkeley (California) hills show no signs of failure or even of the original wattling installation over 50 years later. They are covered either with native chaparral or with Monterey pine plantings that were made a part of the slope treatment program (see Fig. 7.15).

Fig. 7.15.   Fill slope treated with wattling by Kraebel in the mid-1930s, and photographed in June 1974. There is no evidence of slope failure or of the original wattling. The native chaparral has completely occupied the site.

On new construction the choice between wattling and brush-layering should be based on economics, the potential stability of the fill, and the availability of suitable plant materials. Good comparative cost estimates are not available, but the consensus in the literature is that brush-layering is less expensive than wattling. It also stabilizes a fill to greater depths. However, because brush-layers extend a greater distance into the fill, they require more plant material than does a comparable wattling installation. The choice between the two methods may become one of value judgment.

Wattling may be preferable to brush-layering on old fills for several reasons. There will be less disturbance of stabilized subsurface areas of the fill. Also, the surface layers are disturbed less in a wattling installation. This is especially important in areas with high or intensive rainfall or where frost heaving is severe. The labor cost of wattling should be lower because of the rather large amount of excavation required for brush-layering. If fill slopes are so badly eroded that reconstruction is necessary, brush-layering may be the better alternative.

7.2.5.2 Road Cuts.

The first use of wattling on cut slopes may have been that in the Lake Tahoe Basin in 1972–73 (Leiser et al., 1974; see Chapter 9). Kraebel (1936), Horton (1949), and Bowers (1950) did not mention this use. Wattling may be used to treat a complete slope or parts of slopes. It is useful to stabilize newly filled areas behind breast walls or gabions and gullied areas from natural seeps or disturbed areas such as those resulting from the installation of utilities. It has the advantage over brush-layering of minimizing the disturbance of underlying or nearby more-or-less stable areas because of the placement in shallow trenches. On cut slopes it performs all the functions listed in Section 7.2.3.1. Installation procedures are exactly the same whether the wattling is on cuts or fills. More installations are needed to demonstrate the effectiveness of this biotechnical procedure for the stabilization and revegetation of cut slopes.

7.2.5.3 Gullied or Slumped Areas.

Wattling is particularly useful in the stabilization of certain types of gullies or slumps, whether on highway slopes or other areas. It would be effective for gullies on steep slopes, which are not amenable to treatment with check dams. Individual gullies may be treated without disturbing stabilized areas of a slope. Gullies caused by seepage areas are particularly suitable for wattling treatment. They are moist enough to assure rooting and sprouting of the plant material, which in turn draws much of the moisture from the seep when the plants become large enough. The gullies formed by construction activities

(a)

(b)

Fig. 7.16. Repair of sewer lateral washout in a highway cut slope by contour wattling. (a) After washout: Sediment in highway gutter is from one storm. Photograph October 1972. (b) After repair: Washout was repaired with four bundles of wattles interplanted with woody species and overseeded with grass. Photograph June 1974. No further erosion had occurred at this site by July 1980.

such as digging of trenches for utilities or drainage lines are readily controlled by wattling (see Fig. 7.16).

Gullies or slumps may be controlled either by filling and installing wattling or by installing the wattling on the existing surface. When it is desirable to fill a gully, the bottom should be scarified or trenched, especially if it is hard or smooth, to provide a more stable bond with the fill. Fill should be thoroughly compacted and then heavily staked and wattled. The stakes must be long enough to extend into the compact bottom. If the gully is more than 2 or 3 ft deep, double staking should be done. Stakes are driven into the bottom of the gully before or during filling, on contour, at the spacing that will be used for the wattling. The wattling stakes should then be driven in slightly upslope of the first row and overlap the first row at least 12 inches vertically.

When wattling is installed on existing surfaces without filling, care should be taken to keep the contours exactly level (horizontal). Unless an Abney level or similar device is used, it is easy to allow the stakes and trenches to drop at the deepest part of the gully. This tends to concentrate runoff in the deepest part of the gully.

The wattling should extend at least half a bundle length beyond the gully on each side for additional anchoring. If a slope is already treated with wattling, the bundles in the gully should be firmly anchored to existing bundles. When wattling is being placed on an entire slope at more than the minimum spacing, it is advisable to place additional contours in those areas that are deeply gullied (see Fig. 7.17).

7.2.5.4 Eroded Slopes. Contour wattling may be effective in halting further erosion and permitting revegetation of eroded slopes. The principles and methodology used on road cuts and fills apply equally to any slopes. However, wattling alone will probably not control erosion on slopes steeper than 1:1. Steeper slopes should first be laid back or the slope angle reduced by breast walls, gabions, or other structural methods.

7.3   CONTOUR BRUSH-LAYERING

7.31   Description of Method

Contour brush-layering consists of embedding green branches of shrub or tree species, preferably those that will root, on successive horizontal rows or contours in the

(a)

(b)

Fig. 7.17 Gully repair on steep slope by contour wattling. (a) Gully repair work in progress: This gully was about 6 ft deep and 15 ft wide. Wattling was placed on contour at about 7-ft intervals in May 1973, interplanted with unrooted willow cuttings, and overseeded with grass. (b) Fully repaired gully: Complete erosion control was attained during the first year. A good stand of grass, wattling sprouts, and willow cuttings has been established. The willow had not yet leafed out when photographed in April 1974.

face of a slope. Rooted cuttings have also been used in lieu of branches. The method is schematically illustrated in Fig. 7.18. Brush-layering may be incorporated for slope protection purposes during construction of a fill or embankment, or alternatively used as a rehabilitation measure for seriously eroded and barren slopes. Schiechtl (1978) describes the use of contour brush-layering (or "Busch lagenbau") for stabilizing the downstream face of an earth dam in Austria. The method, known locally as faggoting, has been used to stabilize levees in low-lying areas of fen districts in England (Doran, 1948). Brush-layering was also developed for use during construction to stabilize fill slopes of very erodible soils along highways in California (Bowers, 1950; Horton, 1949; Howell et al., 1979). The function of the brush-layer in the latter case was primarily to minimize formation of gullies, in the event that the surface protection on the slope face should fail.

Contour brush-layering is related to contour wattling (Kraebel, 1936; Leiser et al., 1974), but there are some important differences and advantages of contour brush-layering, viz.:

1. It lends itself more readily to partial mechanization. There are no willow bundles to tie, and the benches can be excavated with a small tractor. When it is installed on fills as construction progresses, regular grading equipment can be used for hauling and placing the brush.
2. The branches are inserted into the slope (perpendicular to the strike) rather than parallel. The reinforcement is better oriented, therefore, to resist shallow shear failures or slipouts.
3. The need for staking is eliminated.
4. It may be reinforced with wire mesh or other materials.

Contour brush-layering is similar in principle to a sloping Reinforced Earth revetment (Bartos, 1979). In both cases the reinforcement (metal strips and branches) is placed essentially horizontally in successive layers up the face of a slope. In a Reinforced Earth revetment it is common practice to make the strip length (or width of reinforced volume) about one-third the slope height. This is an important difference because in contour brush-layering the branches would normally not exceed 6–8 ft in length. Hence, to behave in a truly "Reinforced Earth" mode, the slope height should not exceed 18–24 ft. On the other hand metal strips do not sprout and develop root laterals as will branches of species that will root. Thus rooting provides an additional coherence and reinforcement to the face of the slope that tends to offset the limitations of branch length.

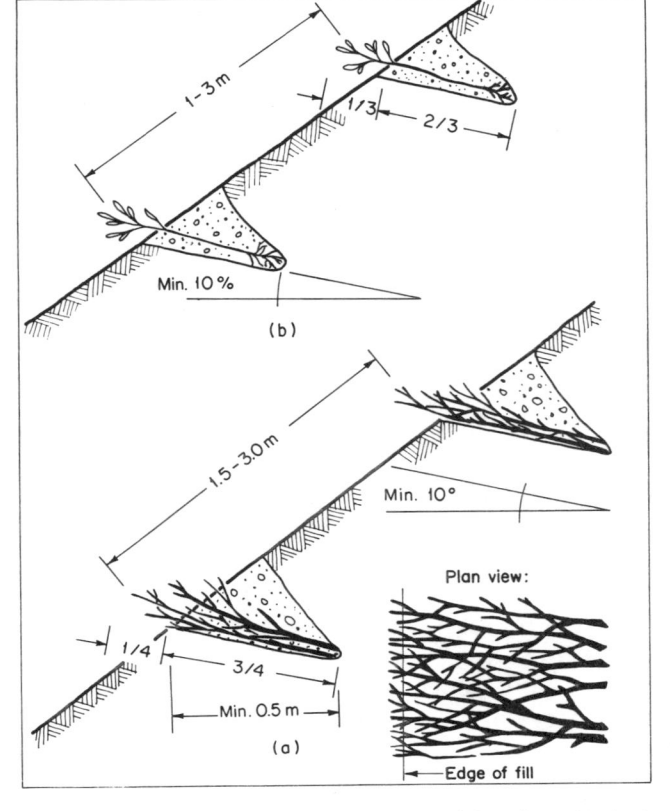

Fig. 7.18. Slope stabilization by contour brush-layering using both green willow cuttings (a) and rooted plants (b). (*After Schiechtl, 1978*)

7.3.2 Installation Procedure

7.3.2.1 During Embankment Construction. If used concurrently with construction of a fill or embankment, cuttings and branches of tree species that will root, such as willow (*Salix*), are layered between successive lifts of fill. The branches should be 3–4 ft long, ¾–2 inches in diameter, and spaced 8–12 inches apart (maximum). The branches should be placed more or less randomly with some crisscrossing of stems (Fig. 7.18). The butt ends should angle down slightly into the slope, and the tips should be allowed to protrude slightly beyond the face of the slope as shown in Fig. 7.18.

Vertical spacing between brush-layers will be dictated by the erosion potential of the slope (i.e., the soil type, rainfall, and length and steepness of the cut or fill slope). It may be as little as 1 m or as much as 3 or more m. On long slopes, spacing should be closer at the bottom and increase as one moves up the slope. Brush-layering specifications adopted by the California Division of Highways (Bowers, 1950) recommend vertical spacings of 4 ft near the bottom increasing to 8 ft at the top (Fig. 7.19). These same specifications also recommend a brush

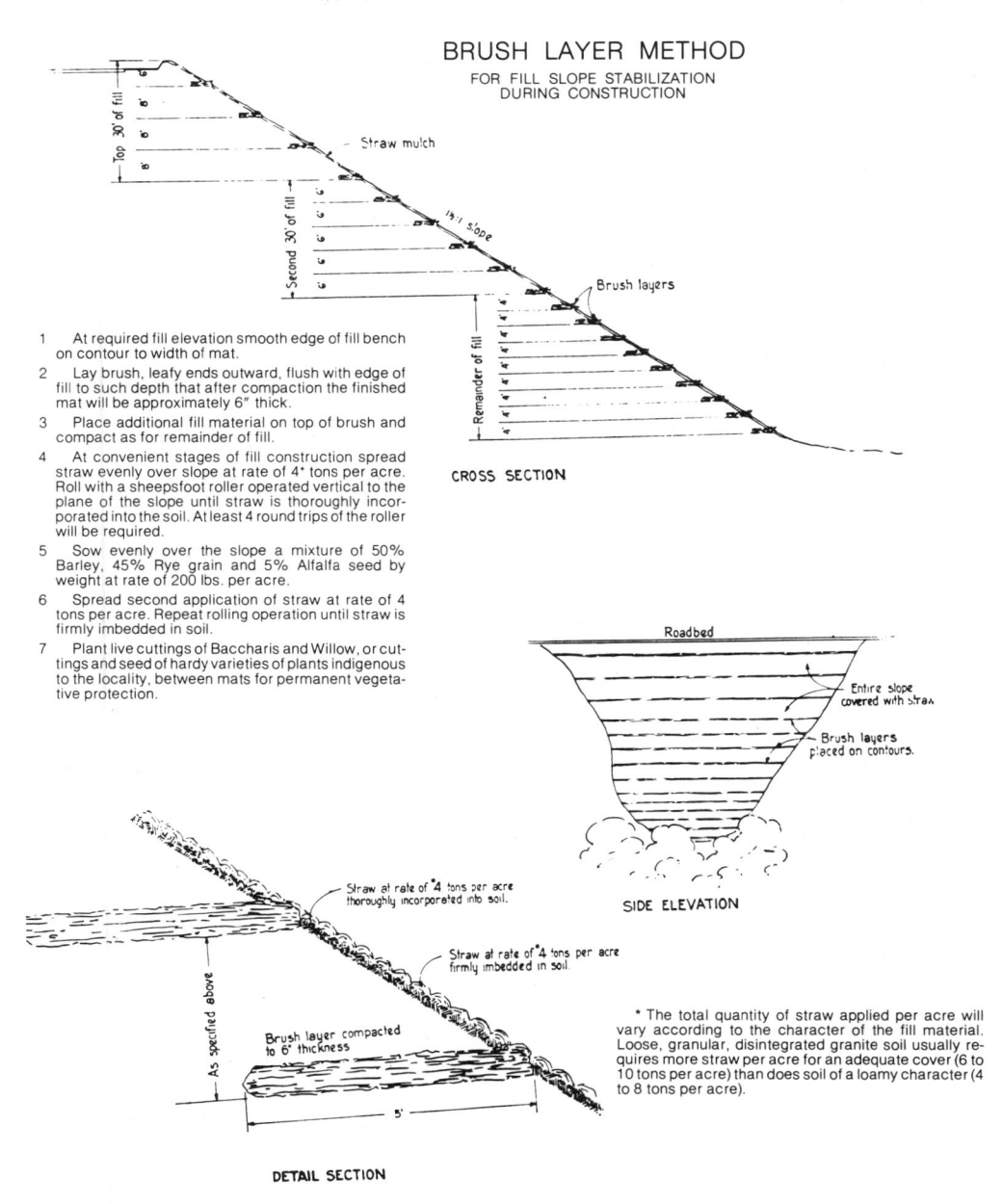

BRUSH LAYER METHOD
FOR FILL SLOPE STABILIZATION
DURING CONSTRUCTION

1 At required fill elevation smooth edge of fill bench on contour to width of mat.

2 Lay brush, leafy ends outward, flush with edge of fill to such depth that after compaction the finished mat will be approximately 6″ thick.

3 Place additional fill material on top of brush and compact as for remainder of fill.

4 At convenient stages of fill construction spread straw evenly over slope at rate of 4* tons per acre. Roll with a sheepsfoot roller operated vertical to the plane of the slope until straw is thoroughly incorporated into the soil. At least 4 round trips of the roller will be required.

5 Sow evenly over the slope a mixture of 50% Barley, 45% Rye grain and 5% Alfalfa seed by weight at rate of 200 lbs. per acre.

6 Spread second application of straw at rate of 4 tons per acre. Repeat rolling operation until straw is firmly imbedded in soil.

7 Plant live cuttings of Baccharis and Willow, or cuttings and seed of hardy varieties of plants indigenous to the locality, between mats for permanent vegetative protection.

CROSS SECTION

Roadbed

Entire slope covered with straw

Brush layers placed on contours.

SIDE ELEVATION

Straw at rate of 4 tons per acre thoroughly incorporated into soil.

Straw at rate of 4 tons per acre firmly imbedded in soil.

Brush layer compacted to 6′ thickness

As specified above

5′

DETAIL SECTION

* The total quantity of straw applied per acre will vary according to the character of the fill material. Loose, granular, disintegrated granite soil usually requires more straw per acre for an adequate cover (6 to 10 tons per acre) than does soil of a loamy character (4 to 8 tons per acre).

Fig. 7.19.   Specifications for fill slope stabilization using brush-layer method. (*From Bowers, 1950*)

branch length of 5 ft. It should also be noted that the California specifications recommend placement of brush tips flush with the edge of the fill (see Fig. 7.19). The purpose of this is to limit excessive buildup of sediment upslope of the brush-layer and danger of scour downslope. Some protrusion of brush tips is advisable, on the other hand, to filter sediment from slope runoff and hold it on the slope. Examples of brush-layer stabilization of roadway fills in California both during construction and for repair of a failed section of an existing fill are shown in Figs. 7.20 and 7.21 respectively.

The California specifications sometimes used wire reinforcement of the brush mat. This was achieved by laying 5-ft-wide, 2 × 4-inch galvanized wire mesh fencing on the prepared fill bench surface. Brush is placed on the wire, leafy ends outward, to such a depth that after compaction the finished mat will be from 4 to 6 inches thick. Wire mesh is also laid on top of the brush, and the edges are tied together at 1-ft intervals with 16-gage galvanized wire. The wire mesh is further tied along its center and at quarter points at 3-ft intervals.

Wire-reinforced brush mats have been used in loca-

Fig. 7.20. Brush-layers and wire-reinforced brush mats installed in a fill during construction. City Creek Road, San Bernardino County, California. (*From Bowers, 1950*)

Fig. 7.21. Brush-layers installed during repair of failed section of fill slope. Bulldozer is being used to rework fill slope face and prepare benches for brush. Near Weaverville, Trinity County, California. (*From Bowers, 1950*)

tions where embankment stability and erosion problems are extreme. On low embankments and upper portions of high slopes, every fourth brush layer is replaced by a wire-reinforced brush mat; and as the distance from the top of the fill becomes greater, this interval is reduced until every third and, finally, every second layer consists of a reinforced mat.

7.3.2.2 Remedial Treatment for Eroding Slopes.

In the case of remedial action on existing slopes, contour brush-layering consists of excavating a bench on contour, placing brush or green cuttings on the bench, backfilling and tamping soil on top of the brush, and repeating this procedure up the slope. This process or sequence of oper-

ations is illustrated schematically in Fig. 7.22. Spoil from the bench above is used to backfill the bench below. The uppermost bench may be covered with spoil from the top-of-slope rounding. Contour brush-layering should be limited to existing slopes no steeper than 75 percent (37 degrees) because of difficulty of maintaining stable slopes above the benches during their excavation. If the benches are made 5 ft wide, and slopes are restricted to 1:1, then the vertical spacing between benches must increase as the slope becomes steeper. This vertical spacing ranges from 10 ft on a 57 percent (30 degrees) slope to 15 ft on a 75 percent (37 degrees) slope, as shown in Fig. 7.22. Use of narrower benches would make it possible to reduce this vertical spacing and still maintain the 1:1 slope above the bench during excavation.

It is advisable to construct a low toe wall or bench structure at the base of an existing slope in advance of contour brush-layering as shown in Fig. 7.22. This wall helps to protect the toe of the slope and retain spoil from the first bench excavation. Willow branches should be used on the bottom half of the slope, where conditions are usually wetter than above. More drought-tolerant cuttings—for

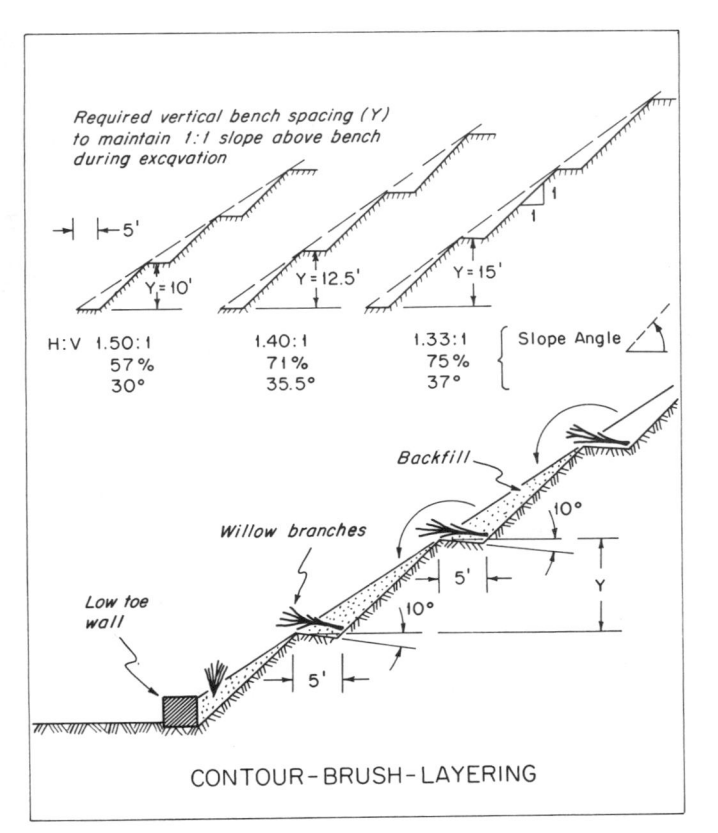

Fig. 7.22. Schematic diagram of contour brush-layering, showing sequence of operations and vertical spacing between benches for different slope angles.

example, in northern California chapparal broom (*Baccharis pilularis* subsp. *consanguinea* (DC.) O. Kuntze) or in sourthern California mulefat (*B. viminea* DC.)—can be considered for use at the top. In other areas, different species might be used (e.g., *Tamarix aphylla*). Irrigation may be necessary during dry summer months of the first growing season in order to ensure good rooting and survival of plants.

7.4   REED-TRENCH TERRACING

7.4.1   Description of Method

Reed-trench terracing is a method that was developed to stabilize sandy banks and coastal bluffs. It has been used successfully by homeowners along the shores of Long Island, New York to protect shorefront properties against surface erosion and shallow bank sliding (Reid, 1969).

Reed-trench terracing basically consists of staking a series of wooden barriers (or checkboards) on contour, digging a trench behind (upslope) and extending slightly deeper than the barrier, and backfilling the trench with common reed grass (*Phragmites communis*). The reeds are then covered with sand that was removed when the trench was dug. This procedure starts from the bottom and continues up the slope as shown schematically in Fig. 7.23. A series of benches or level terraces is thus created on the slope which tends to arrest downward movement of sand and also provides a locus for establishment of vegetation.

The reeds perform important mechanical and organic functions. They prevent the sand from drifting or washing out through the bottom of the checkboards; they absorb and retain water where it falls, preventing rilling and gullying; they serve as an underground irrigation system by collecting water, spreading it laterally, and gradually releasing it by capillary action to nourish plant-

ings above; they provide the necessary aeration for good root growth and allow soil microflora to flourish, which in turn leads to accumulation of topsoil and permanent vegetation. Adapted grasses, trees, shrubs, and vines are planted which in this well-aerated environment send down deep roots that go several feet into the slope, forming a root network that firmly anchors the soil, absorbs moisture during periods of excessive precipitation, and retains moisture to protect slope plantings during long periods of drought.

7.4.2   Construction Procedure

The first step in reed-trench terracing is placing the checkboards on contour and staking them in place. Two fence pickets are driven into the slope to support the board, which is then itself embedded or driven into the sand a couple of inches. The recommended lumber for the checkboards is 6 ft long, 1″ × 8″ cedar or other decay-resistant wood siding—for economy, durability, and ease of handling. For vertical supports or stakes, cedar fence pickets 3 or 3½ ft long spaced about 3 ft apart are recommended. The fence pickets may be coated with a water-resistant wood preservative for longer life.

The lumber used for maintenance levels (Fig. 7.24) and for steps, both of which must bear traffic, should be sturdier than that used for vegetation terraces. In this case either 2″ × 8″ or 2″ × 10″ planks are recommended, depending on the steepness of the slope. Winged steel fence posts, 6 ft high, should also be used to support the horizontal barriers of the walking levels (Fig. 7.24). These fence posts should be driven down to the top of the barrier and spaced no less than 4 ft apart for stability.

The next step is to dig a narrow trench behind and

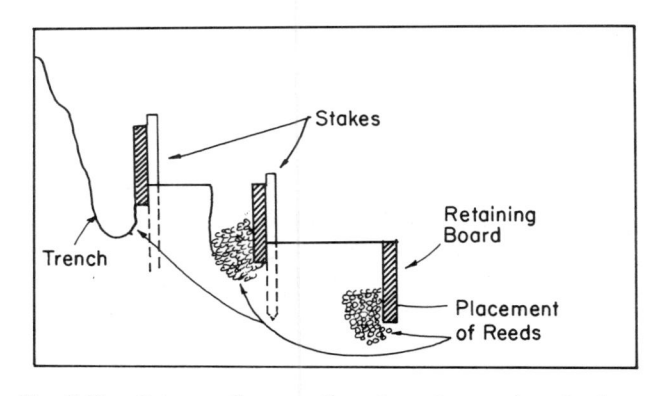

Fig. 7.23.   Cutaway diagram of reed-trench terracing. Reeds are placed in narrow trenches dug behind retaining boards. Center-of-mass of reeds should be at juncture where wood meets sand.

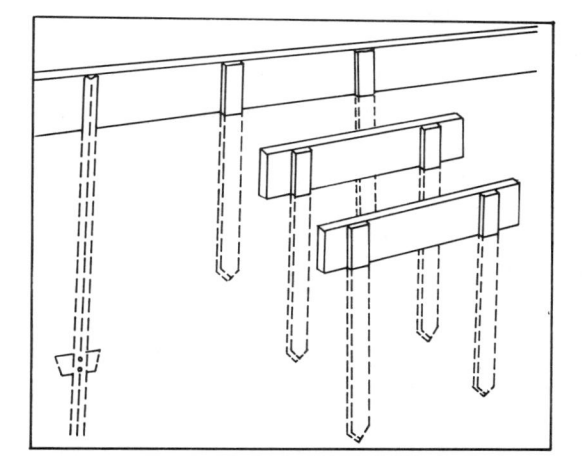

Fig. 7.24.   Schematic diagram of maintenance levels and steps to service a reed-trench layout on a slope. Lumber used for this construction must be sturdier than that used for vegetation terraces. (*Adapted from Reid, 1969*)

slightly lower than the checkboard. The trench can be hand-dug with a gardening spade, and it may be necessary to wet the ground slightly in very sandy slopes in order to keep the trench from collapsing. The reeds are then collected, and a bundle of reeds at least 6 inches in diameter when compressed should be deposited along the full length of the trench. The reeds are wedged and tamped into the trench with their center of mass at the point where wood meets sand (Fig. 7.23) in order to form a protective seal or filter at this junction.

The entrenched reeds should be wetted down thoroughly using spray from a garden hose. The reeds are next covered with sand that was removed when digging the trench. This sand should be firmed and leveled for subsequent seeding or planting. It is important that each terrace be level to catch any debris coming downslope and to catch and hold rainfall.

The maximum slope on which reed-trench terracing has been successfully carried out is 1:1 or 45 degrees. Some cohesion must have been present in such steep slopes in order to carry out the construction work. Slopes steeper than 45 degrees must be graded back before attempting this method, preferably to a gradient not exceeding 1½:1 even though this may entail loss of frontage at the top of a bluff. The gradient of the slope determines the spacing between terraces or boards; as the slope gets steeper, the boards are placed closer together. As a general rule, the boards should be placed close enough for level or nearly level terraces to be constructed between them.

Fencing and a stairway are useful adjuncts to a reed-trench stabilization program. The former keeps away trespassers and would-be bank climbers, who can quickly undo the best efforts of this type of slope stabilization. The latter provides access not only from the top of a bluff to the beach below, but also to the maintenance levels in the reed-trench terrace system. Protection at the toe of the slope is also essential. A reed-trench system cannot withstand scour and erosion by wave action at the base of a slope. If this is likely to occur, a beachfill protected by a bulkhead or offshore groin system is a possible countermeasure.

7.4.3 Terrace Plantings

The final step in a reed-trench terrace system is to establish vegetation on the terraces. Among grasses best-fitted for sandy soils in the coastal zone of the United States are American beachgrass (*Ammophila brevil-igulata*) and European beachgrass (*A. arenaria*). Both have extensive and tenacious root systems that are very effective in permeating and binding sand. These pioneer plants have strong, wide-spreading rootstocks or rhizomes underground, and runners or stolons near or over the surface. They have the capacity to vigorously permeate sand with an extensive root network in both a lateral and a vertical direction. They also thrive on a high-stress environment of drifting sand and limited nutrient availability.

Another candidate grass for southern states is weeping lovegrass (*Eragrostis curvula* (Schrad.) Nees). This grass, a native of South Africa, is well suited to loose sandy soils, is fairly resistant to drought, is not affected by salt spray, grows as tall as 6 ft, and sends down correspondingly long soil-binding roots. Other faster-growing grass seeds such as perennial rye can be added to lovegrass seed to provide a quick, but less permanent and durable, ground cover.

Other vegetation with good soil-holding properties and minimal maintenance needs can be planted among the grasses on sandy bluffs. Suitable candidates include black locust (*Robinia pseudoacacia* L.), Japanese black pine (*Pinus thunbergiana* Franco), honeysuckle (*Lonicera* spp.), woodbine or Virginia creeper (*Parthenocissus quinquefolia* (L.) Planch), beach pea (*Lathyrus japonicus* Willd.), beach plum (*Prunus maritima* Marsh), sedum (*Sedum* spp.), bayberry (*Myrica pensylvanica* Loisel), and autumn olive (*Elaeagnus umbellata* Thunb).

7.5 BRUSH MATTING

7.5.1 Description of Method

Brush matting is essentially a mulch of hardwood brush fastened down with stakes and wire. It is employed primarily in conjunction with other streambank protection measures. Used alone it provides a certain amount of bank protection and erosion control; it can resist temporary inundation, but not scour and undercutting. Structural measures such as groins and revetments are necessary if bank undercutting is a problem.

Brush matting was employed very effectively for streambank erosion control work along the Winooski River in Vermont (Edminster et al., 1949). It was an integral component of the most successful combination of measures used on the Winooski project. These measures included bank sloping, riprapping at the toe, brush matting, and planting.

Hardwood brush convenient to the site was used for mulch material on the bank above the riprap in the Winooski project. The brush consisted mainly of willow and speckled alder (*Alnus incana* (L.) Moench) with some elm, maple, and other hardwoods. In some cases, planting was done first, followed by the brush matting. In others, cuttings were inserted through matting installed immediately following grading. Before and after views of a typical reach of riverbank stabilized in this fashion are shown in Fig. 7.25.

(a)

(b)

Fig. 7.25.   Severely eroded riverbank. (A) Prior to treatment in 1937. (B) Same bank in 1938 after it was sloped, brush-matted, and planted with purple-osier willows, and toe of slope riprapped. Willows are in second growing season. (*From Edminster et al., 1949*)

Both the seasonal requirements for planting and the mechanical difficulties of planting through the brush after the mat is placed need to be considered. Only unrooted, heavy cuttings can be used because seedlings, rooted cuttings, and small raw cuttings can be planted through the brush only with great difficulty.

7.5.2   Construction Procedure

A mulch of hardwood brush should be placed over exposed soil following bank grading as soon as possible. It is preferable to plant first and then mulch to avoid difficulties of trying to plant through a dense, brush mat. Speckled alder and purple-osier willow are ideal species,

but any convenient brush may be used. Stems should be cut with a thickness of about 1 inch or less and laid to form a tight mat.

The brush is laid shingle-fashion with the butt ends pointed upstream (Fig. 7.26). It should be trimmed, if necessary, to lie flat on the bank. The mat should be 4 to 18 inches thick, depending on the size of stream and quantity of ice and bed load.

A brush mat must be secured so that it will not float away. Stakes driven in at an angle and crossing each other in pairs may be all that is needed on small streams. The stakes used should be 3 ft long, placed at about 3-ft centers. On larger rivers with high velocities or rivers carrying ice floes in winter, a more secure tie-down system is required. In this case the stakes should be driven straight in and the mulch held in place by lacing no. 9 galvanized wire between the stakes in a diamond pattern (Fig. 7.26). A tight lacing will be assured if the stakes protrude a few inches above the brush before the wire is attached. The stakes are later driven in deeper; this tightens the wire and binds the mat firmly.

Applying alder brush in the matting between mid-September and the time the ground freezes gives the ripe seeds that fall on the bank opportunity to grow into plants that will be a desirable part of the living cover.

7.6   LIVE STAKING

A quick and effective means of securing a vegetative cover for control of soil erosion and shallow sliding is planting or driving unrooted cuttings. This method is also known as sprigging or willow staking. A sprig is a shoot, cane, pole, or cutting from a live tree or bush. Cuttings from plant species that will root easily will grow if planted in the ground under certain conditions.

It is well known that most willows, many poplars, and cottonwoods will grow readily from cuttings when they are set in moist soil (e.g., streamsides and wet meadows). Several species of willow will also grow from cuttings in much less favorable soils such as road fills and gullies in bare, denuded land. Even in very unfavorable sites willow cuttings will often grow vigorously for a few years before they die out. In the meantime they will have performed the important function of stabilizing and modifying the soil, serving as pioneer species until other plants become started.

7.6.1   Selection of Species for Live Staking

Wherever possible native tree and brush species that root readily from cuttings should be used. Species with long straight stems are much easier to cut and drive than those with crooked stems.

Willows have been used extensively for this purpose.

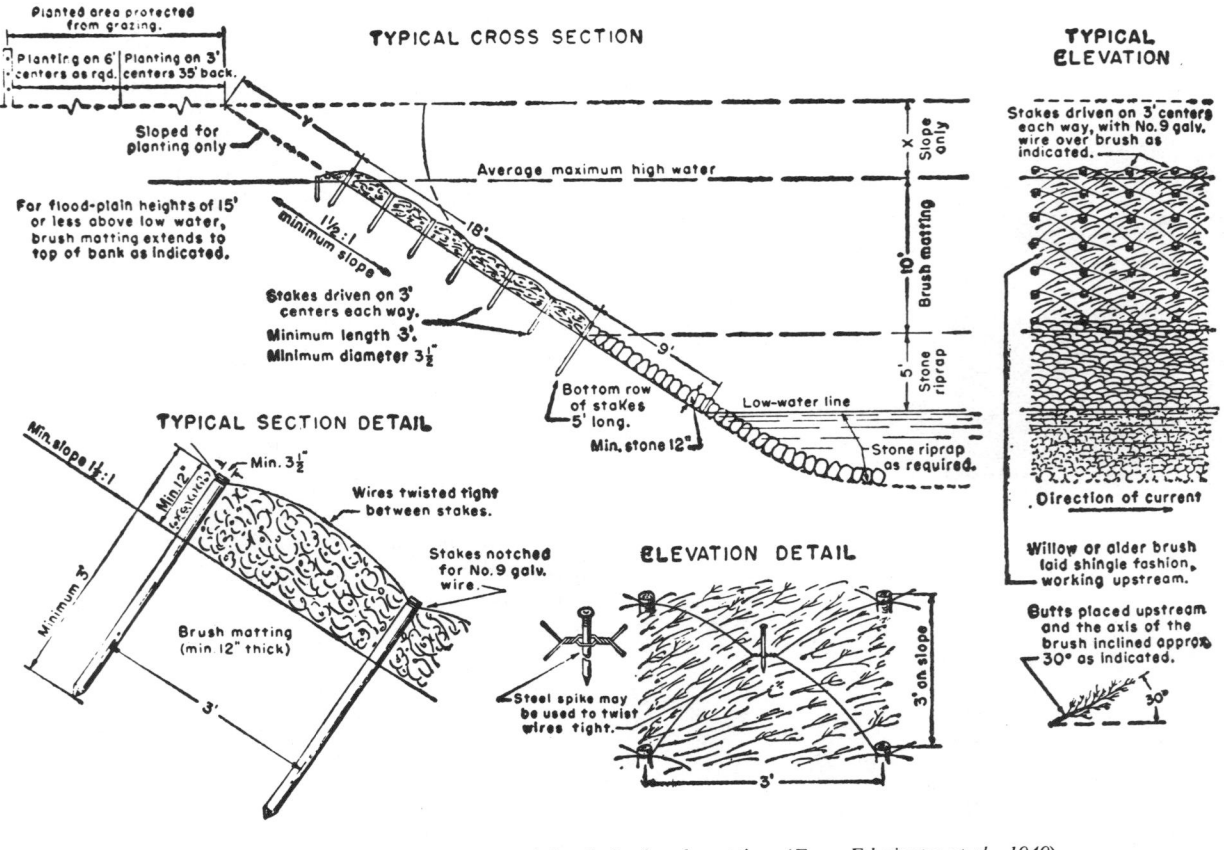

Fig. 7.26. Construction procedure and details for brush matting. (*From Edminster et al., 1949*)

The genus is so widely distributed that in every locality one or more species can usually be found that are suitable for this work. Species most commonly used in California, where live staking has been employed most widely, include the arroyo willow (*Salix lasiolepis* Benth), red willow (*S. laevigata* Bebb.), and Hinds willow (*S. hindsiana*). At high elevations the Sierra meadow or Lemmon willow (*S. lemmonii*), a shrubby species, has been used.

Plants other than willow have also been used successfully for live staking. One species of baccharis, variously known as mulefat, water moat, or motie (*Baccharis viminea* DC.), has proved to be well suited for live staking on road fills in California (Kraebel, 1936). Sprouts from planted cuttings of this species have been observed to make prodigious growth in one season, with as many as three sprouts from 7 to 10 ft high from a single cutting not being unusual. Another species, *B. pilularis* subsp. *consanguinea* (DC.) O. Kuntze, one of the most abundant and widespread shrubs in the Coast Ranges of California, is well adapted to that locality. This plant is locally called coyote brush and chaparral broom. Although the old-wood cuttings sprout less vigorously than those of *B. viminea,* their growth is ample to make

them useful in erosion control. In semiarid regions, desert aphyll has been used to control erosion in streams and washes and as wind breaks.

7.6.2 Preparation and Handling of Cuttings

In preparing and handling cuttings prior to planting, the following guidelines will increase the chances for success:

1. Select healthy wood of reasonable straightness from plant species that root easily and are native to the planting site.
2. Make clear cuts with unsplit ends. Stems up to 1½ inches in diameter can best be cut with two-handled brush pruning shears. Several stems of small diameter may be cut at a time with a carpenter's hatchet. Larger branches can be cut with chain saws. The butt end of cuttings may be pointed to facilitate driving.
3. Trim branches from cuttings as close as possible.
4. *Length:* Cuttings of small diameter (up to 1½ inches) should be at least 18 inches long. Thicker and longer cuttings (up to 3 or 4 ft) are desirable for staking wattling on slopes.

5. *Diameter:* The minimum diameter is ¼ inch; the thicker the cutting, the greater the food reserves. Cuttings greater than 1 inch are desirable, although their numbers may be limited by the supply.

6. *Location of buds and bud scars:* Cuttings put out their greatest concentration of shoots and their strongest ones just below an annual ring (formed from a terminal bud scar). Cuttings should be cut so that a terminal bud scar is within 1 to 4 inches of the top. At least two buds and/or bud scars should be above the ground after planting.

7. *Handling of stakes between cutting and planting:* Cuttings must not be allowed to dry out. They are best planted the same day as prepared. They must be kept covered and moist during transport, storage, and during the planting operation. Cuttings may also be kept submerged in water for one to several days after preparation to ensure that they remain moist. At no time should cuttings be left exposed to the air to dry out prior to planting.

7.6.3 Time to Plant Stakes

Stakes should be cut and planted when willows or other suitable species used are dormant. This period extends from the time the leaves start to turn yellow in the autumn until the time growth starts in the spring. In moist soils, willow stakes can sometimes be planted successfully during the summer season, but usually this should not be attempted. When this procedure is attempted, the cuttings should be defoliated. Additional soaking of cuttings prior to planting may be required for late plantings.

7.6.4 How to Plant Stakes

In addition to the way in which stakes are prepared and stored, the way in which they are set in the ground is also crucial for success. The following guidelines should be observed:

1. Plant the cuttings right side up (i.e., with the butt ends in the ground). It is not always easy to tell the top from the butt of a leafless cutting. A good rule is to have the butt end of all stakes pointed or marked immediately by the cutting crew at the time they are made. Alternatively, the tops of bundles of cuttings may be painted with a water-soluble latex paint. The paint also seals the ends and reduces dessication of the cuttings.

2. Set the cutting as deep as possible. Most of the sprig length should be planted in the ground. It is preferable that at least 80 percent of the sprig length be in the ground. Two reasons for deep planting are to minimize water loss due to transpiration, and to lessen the problem of root breakage caused by relative movement between the cutting and the ground.

3. Avoid stripping the bark or needless bruising of the stakes when setting them in the ground. In fairly soft soil the stakes can be driven with a wooden maul. Do not use an ax or sledge. In hard ground use an iron bar or star drill to prepare the holes for the cuttings.

4. Tamp the soil around the cutting. The cutting must be firm in the ground so that it cannot be readily moved or pulled out.

7.6.5 Where to Plant Stakes

Live stakes can be planted in a number of areas and situations where they will be helpful for minimizing erosion and arresting shallow slope movement until more permanent vegetation has had a chance to take hold. General locations include bare soil areas on slopes that show evidence of recent movement or active erosion. Especially suited for live staking are persistent wet areas, road cut and road fill slopes where soil conditions permit, and raw soil areas on slumps.

Gullies and stream channel banks can also be live-staked. Areas best-suited to staking are the floors and banks of small incipient gullies, sediment fills behind check dams, raw gully banks, berms of water bars, and the area just below water bar outlets. Live stakes can also be incorporated into contour wattling protection systems, porous revetments, breast walls, and brush mulches. Specific examples of these applications are described next.

7.6.5.1 Check Dam Reinforcement.

For strengthening check dams, willow cuttings should be planted around the dam as shown in Fig. 7.27. Normally, the stakes should be spaced 1 ft to 18 inches apart. On large dams willows should also be planted at additional points marked "secondary" in Fig. 7.27. This secondary planting consists in extending the willows part way around the upstream face of the dams, and in planting another row about 2 ft downstream from the apron.

7.6.5.2 Gully-Head Plug Reinforcement.

The head of a gully is a particularly vulnerable location. Brush

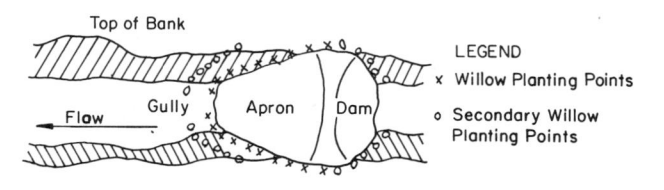

Fig. 7.27. Plan of gully check-dam showing points for planting willows.

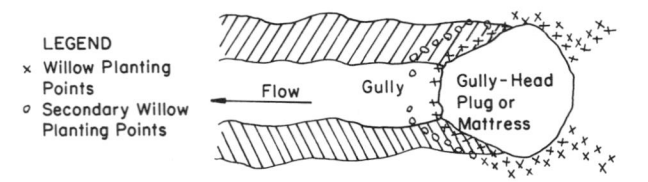

Fig. 7.28. Plan of gully-head plug or mattress showing points for planting willows.

and rock plugs can be placed at these locations to stop headward erosion of the gully. A plug is more effective if vegetation can become established in and around it as soon as possible. In order to strengthen gully-head plugs, willow stakes should be planted in the pattern shown in Fig. 7.28. The stakes should be spaced 1 ft to 18 inches apart.

7.6.5.3 Gully Erosion Control.
Some gullies cannot be satisfactorily controlled by the construction of dams. Either the gully is relatively shallow, or the slope is too great for the safe use of check dams, or both. In any case, the planting of willows in clusters along a gully may be beneficial (Fig. 7.29). The distance between willow clusters normally depends upon the gradient of the gully bottom. The steeper the gully grade, the closer together the clusters. Usually the spacing can vary from 500 ft with a gully gradient of 1 percent, to 25 ft with a gully gradient of 20 percent.

In the rows of willows in a cluster (Fig. 7.29), the stakes should be set 1 ft to 18 inches apart in the rows, and the rows themselves should be spaced about 4 ft apart. The rows should extend from the top of the bank downstream to the toe.

7.6.5.4 Wattle Staking on Slopes.
One of the principal uses of live staking is to hold down or support wattles of cut brush. Inert stakes of lumber or construction stakes may be cheaper and more convenient for this purpose than live stakes. On the other hand, if the soil is relatively loose and moist, and if the supply of live-wood stakes is both abundant and conveniently situated, the live staking may be advantageous.

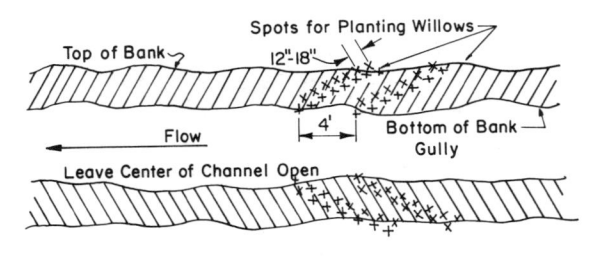

Fig. 7.29. Plan of gully showing planting points for a willow cluster.

Live stakes are driven through the brush wattles which are placed in shallow trenches on contour (see Section 7.2). The stakes should be at least 18 inches long; on very loose slopes longer lengths are preferable. The stakes should be driven at least 80–90 percent of their length and spaced about 12–18 inches apart. If willows or other suitable sprouting species are scarce, construction stakes can be substituted. Ideally, however, there should be a live stakes at least every 4 or 5 ft along each contour wattle. The live stakes, wattles, and contour plantings of mixed grain and shrubs act together to provide protection against erosion and shallow sliding (Fig. 7.30).

7.6.5.5 Revetment Staking and Reinforcement.
Live staking can also be employed in conjunction with porous revetments (see Section 5.3). Willow cuttings can be inserted or driven through interstices or openings in gabions (see Figs. 5.28 and 5.29), riprap, articulated blocks, and rubber-tire revetments. Live stakes provide initial mechanical restraint and anchorage. In time they will root and sprout, thus permeating and binding the soil beneath the revetment into a monolithic mass.

Small plants of suitable species may be planted in interstices of many of these construction structures as long as planting methods meet those described in Chapter 6. Planting should be done in spring or fall, and when soil moisture levels are adequate. Roots must be in soil backfill or in soil in interstices. The advantage of long cut-

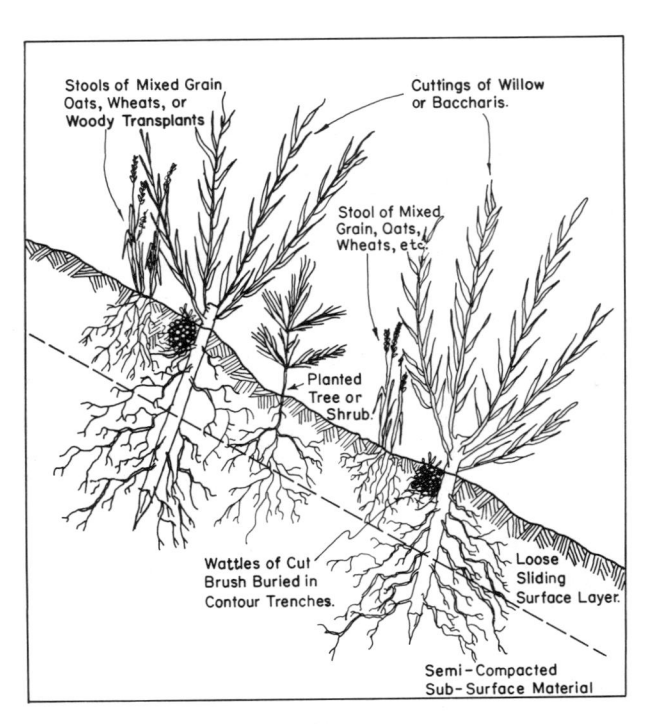

Fig. 7.30. Cross-sectional view of brush wattles and live, willow stake control systems. (*From Kraebel, 1936*)

tings is that the base of the cutting is placed in the soil materials.

7.6.5.6 Breast-Wall Staking.

Live staking or planting of rooted plants may be done during construction of breast walls if construction occurs during the proper season. Care must be taken to fill the interstices with the available soil, and cuttings should be long enough to reach into soil if a portion of the backfill consists of small rocks or gravel. If construction is done during the dry season, it may be possible to drive stout cuttings between the rocks of the breast wall at a later date. Such plantings reinforce the fill behind the breast wall and help blend the wall into the surroundings.

7.7 REFERENCES CITED

Bartos, M. J. (1979). 101 uses for earth reinforcement, *Civil Engr.* 49(1): 51–57.

Bowers, H. D., (1950). Erosion control on California highways, State of California, Department of Public Works, Division of Highways, Sacramento, Calif., 70 pp.

Doran, W. E. (1948). Stabilization of river banks, *Proc., 2nd Intl. Conf. on Soil Mech. and Foundation Eng.,* London, Vol. 2, pp. 60–63.

Edminster, F. C., Atkinson, W. S., and McIntyre, A. C. (1949). Streambank erosion control on the Winooski River, Vermont, *USDA Circular No. 837,* 54 pp.

Horton, J. S. (1949). Trees and shrubs for erosion control in Southern California mountains, publ. by USDA Forest Service, California Forest and Range Experiment Station, 68 pp.

Howell, R. B. et al. (1979). Analysis of short and long term effects on water quality for selected highway projects, Final Report to Calif. Dept. of Trans., Rept. No. FHWA/CA/TL-79/17, 245 pp.

Kraebel, C. J. (1936). Erosion control on mountain roads, *USDA Circular No. 380,* 43 pp.

Leiser, A. T., Nussbaum, J. J., Kay, B., Paul, J. and Thornhill, W. (1974). Revegetation of disturbed soils in the Tahoe Basin, Final Rept. to Calif. Dept. of Trans., CA-DOT-TL-7036-1-75-24, 71 pp. University of California, Davis, Ca.

Reid, G. (1969). *How to Hold Up a Bank,* A. S. Barnes and Co., New York.

Schiechtl, H. M. (1978). Environmentally compatible slope stabilization, *Geotechnik* 1(1): 10–12 (Organ der Deutchen Gesellschaft fur Erd und Grundbau).

USDA Soil Conservation Service (1940). Lake bluff erosion control, Rept. prepared by U. S. Soil Conservation Service, Lansing, Mich., 81 pp.

8
Check Dams for Gully control

8.1 INTRODUCTION

8.1.1 Purpose and Function of Check Dams

The chief purpose of check dams in gullies, from the standpoint of erosion control, is to decrease the velocity of the water moving down the gully. By decreasing the velocity, silt and debris are deposited in the gully instead of additional material being eroded away.

The velocity of flowing water is decreased by lessening the effective gradient (i.e., the slope of the channel down which the water flows). When the dam is first built, the flow of water is impeded or slowed immediately upstream. This causes suspended material to be deposited in the catch basin behind the dam (Fig. 8.1). When the catch basin is filled, a relatively level surface or delta is formed over which the water flows at a noneroding gradient. The water then cascades over the dam through a spillway onto a defended area or apron. By constructing a series of such check dams along the gully, a stream channel of comparatively steep slope or gradient is replaced by a "stair-stepped" channel consisting of a succession of gentle slopes with "cushioned" cascades in between.

8.1.2 Porous vs. Nonporous Dams

There are innumerable check dam designs, but most can be classified into one of two categories. Solid, nonporous dams, such as those built from concrete, sheet steel, or wet masonry, receive a strong impact from the dynamic and hydrostatic forces of flow. These dams are not only relatively expensive to construct but also require strong anchoring into gully banks. They are durable and permanent but sometimes visually intrusive in the landscape.

In contrast, porous dams release part of the flow through the structure, and thereby decrease the head of flow over the spillway and the dynamic and hydrostatic forces against the dam. Porous dams are simpler and more economical to construct. Natural, indigenous

materials—rock, brush, and posts—can be used in lieu of steel and concrete. For most gully control work where large torrents are not a factor and where life and high-cost property are not endangered, these simpler porous dams are appropriate. The check dams described in this chapter are all of the porous type. They also meet the criteria for biotechnical construction methods discussed in Chapter 1.

8.1.3 Biotechnical Construction Methods and Materials

As noted earlier (Chapter 1), biotechnical construction methods are characterized by use of natural, indigenous materials; incorporation of vegetation into and around a structure; low cost; and labor-skill-intensive work. Heede (1976), in his treatise on gully development and control, describes the design and construction of porous check dams meeting many of these criteria. His designs include loose rock, wire-bound rock, single fence, double fence, and gabion check dams. Kraebel and Pillsbury (1934) likewise employed native, readily available materials for use in check dam construction and gully control in mountain meadows. Many of the methods cited here are adapted from their work.

In this chapter we describe low-cost check dams constructed almost entirely from natural, indigenous materials, viz., rock, brush, forest litter, wooden posts, and rough boards. Selection of one design over another rests in large part on availability of these materials at a particular site. In order to clarify the nature or character of each of these materials, they are defined below.

Dam Brush. Either chaparral or tree branches are satisfactory, although the latter are usually easier to handle. Brush should be somewhat flexible, green, and heavily leaved. Brush that is dry and brittle is difficult to handle, and does not make a satisfactory dam. Branches should be cut into small enough lengths that they are easy to pile into a dense mass; usually 3 or 4 ft is the maximum

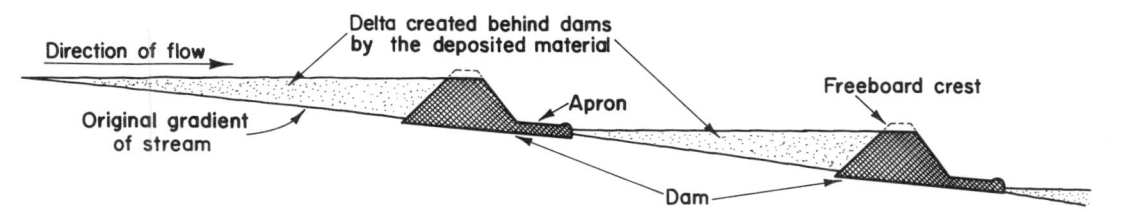

Fig. 8.1.   Cross-sectional view of gully check dam showing upstream deltas formed by deposited sediment. Check dams are constructed so that sediment fill behind downstream dam (after filling to spillway level) abuts base of upstream check dam.

convenient length. All of the following have been used with success in the past: pine, fir, cedar, live oak, willow, and orchard prunings.

Apron Brush.   The requirements for apron brush are the same as for dam brush, except that apron brush must be long and flexible. For this reason the chaparral types are not so desirable, because long, straight, and flexible branches 5 to 10 ft long are seldom found. Willow and branches of various evergreen trees are excellent.

Litter.   This may be fine-textured vegetative material to be used under aprons and against the upstream faces of dams. In mountain areas the best and most readily available material is forest litter or duff (e.g., pine needles) that can be raked up from under trees. Straw is an excellent material when available. If none of the above can be obtained, any fine, dense brush such as sage may be used.

Posts.   Any good fence-post material is satisfactory. Use of live willow is recommended where possible because it will root and grow. Dead-wood posts can be treated with wood preservatives to extend their life.

Rock.   The quality, shape, size, and gradation of rock used in construction of check dams substantially affect the success and life of the structure. Obviously, rock that disintegrates rapidly when exposed to water and atmosphere will have a short structural life. Flat and round rock, such as river cobbles, should be avoided. Both types tend to slip out of a structure more easily than broken or quarried rocks, which anchor well with each other.

If only small rocks are used in a dam, they may be moved by the impact of the first large water flow. In contrast, a check dam constructed of only large rocks that leave large voids in the structure will offer resistance to flow, but may allow destructive piping through the voids. Large voids prevent the accumulation of sediment above the structures. In general, this accumulation is a desirable goal because it increases the stability of the structures, reduces effective gradient, permits establishment of vegetation, and enhances stabilization of the gully.

Required size and gradation of rock for check dams depend on the type and size of dam and the magnitude of expected flows. Large voids will not occur if the rock is well graded. The majority of the rock should be large enough, however, to resist expected flows. See Section 8.2.6 for guidelines on rock size and gradation.

Wire Netting.   Wire mesh used in check dams should be resistant to corrosion and of sufficient strength to resist pressure exerted by flow and rocks, and should have openings not larger than the average rock size in the dam.

Wire.   No. 9 to no. 12 galvanized iron wire is satisfactory.

Boards.   Split boards from on-site materials such as downed timber or cull logs may be used. Board widths may vary from 8 to 14 inches, depending on the log being split. Rot-resistant wood such as redwood and cedar is preferable.

8.2   GENERAL DESIGN CRITERIA

8.2.1   Check Dam Configuration

The spacing, height, and dam configuration are important design considerations regardless of what type of structure is built. In general, numerous low dams along a gully are preferred to a few high dams. A "low" check dam is considered to be one not over 4 ft in height. There is less danger of such structures washing out in time of flood, and if they should wash out, less damage will result. Furthermore, low dams are less expensive than higher ones and lend themselves to biotechnical construction methods.

Check dams may have different cross sections and be constructed from different materials, but all should have a spillway and apron. A spillway is simply a provision to pass flood flows safely over the dam. This requires a low center or notch (Fig. 8.2), which draws the overflow toward the middle of the channel, so that there is no tendency to cut around the dam. An apron is a protected area below the downstream face of the dam which is

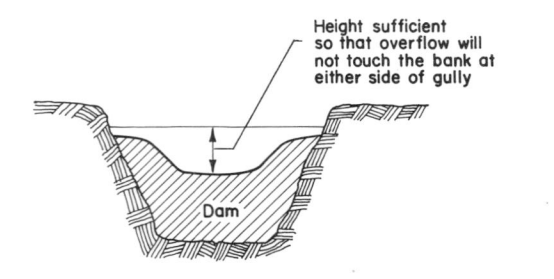

Fig. 8.2. Elevation view of gully showing low center or notched spillway in a check dam.

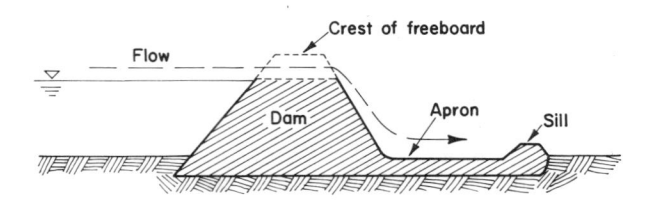

Fig. 8.3. Cross-sectional view of check dam showing downstream apron and sill.

essential to prevent falling water from undercutting the dam (Fig. 8.3). The apron may be constructed to dissipate the energy of the falling water in addition to armoring or protecting the ground beneath.

8.2.2 Spacing

In general, the most efficient and most economical spacing is obtained if a check dam is placed at the upstream toe of the final sediment deposits of the next dam downstream (Heede, 1976). Determination of this spacing requires knowledge of the relationship between the original gradient of the gully channel and that of sediment deposits above check dams placed in the gully. Relationships developed so far have been empirical. Heede and Mufich (1973) developed the following equation to simplify the calculation of spacing as follows:

$$S = \frac{H_E}{KG \cos \psi} \qquad (8.1)$$

where:

S = spacing between dams
H_E = effective dam height as measured from gully bottom to spillway crest
G = gully gradient as a ratio ($G = \tan \psi$)
ψ = angle corresponding to the gully gradient
K = an empirical constant

The equation is based on the assumption that the gradient of the sediment deposits or delta is $(1 - K)G$. In dams examined by Heede (1966), values for K were:

$$K = 0.3 \text{ for } G \leq 0.20 \qquad (8.2)$$

$$K = 0.5 \text{ for } G > 0.20 \qquad (8.3)$$

The generalized equation (8.1) can be used by the designer, after the applicable K value has been ascertained for the treatment area, or alternatively the values given above can be used as preliminary estimates. Figure 8.4 illustrates the relationship between dam spacing, height, and gully gradient based on Equations (8.1) through (8.3). For a given gully, the required number of dams decreases with increasing spacing or increasing effective dam height, and increases with increasing gully gradient.

8.2.3 Height

The effective height of a check dam (H_E) is the elevation of the crest of the spillway above the original gully bottom. The height not only influences spacing (see Equation 8.1) but also volume of sediment deposits.

Heede and Mufich (1973) developed an equation that

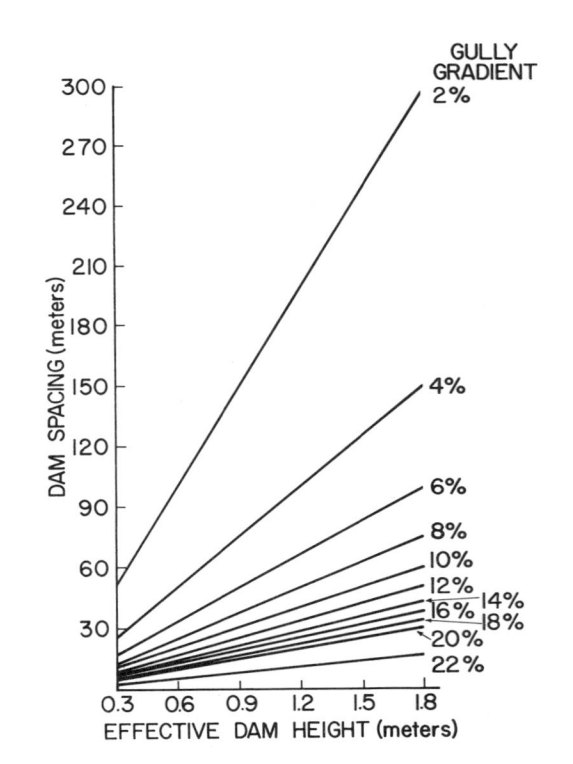

Fig. 8.4. Spacing of check dams, installed in gullies with different gradients, as a function of effective dam height. (*From Heede, 1976*)

relates the volume of sediment deposits to spacing and effective height of dam:

$$V_S = \tfrac{1}{2} \, H_E \, L_{HE} \, S \cos \psi \qquad (8.4)$$

where:

V_S = sediment volume
L_{HE} = average length of dam
S = spacing between dams
ψ = angle corresponding to gully gradient

The average length of dam (L_{HE}) may be calculated by the equation;

$$L_{HE} = L_B + \frac{L_U - L_B}{2D_B} H_E \qquad (8.5)$$

where:

L_B = bottom width of gully
L_U = bank width of gully
D_B = depth to bottom of gully

If S from Equation (8.1) is substituted into Equation (8.4), then:

$$V_S = \frac{H_E^2}{2KG} L_{HE} \qquad (8.5)$$

Equation (8.5) indicates that sediment deposits increase as the square of effective dam height increases.

8.2.4 Spillway

The depth, length, and shape of spillways greatly affect check dam performance. As a minimum spillways should accomodate expected peak flows from a design storm with a 25-year return period. Spillway depth and length must be sufficient to prevent flows from reaching the banks on either side of the dam crest. Most gullies have either trapezoidal, rectangular, or V-shaped cross sections. Heede and Mufich (1973) developed equations for the calculation of spillway dimensions for check dams placed in these gully shapes.

The shape of the spillway is also important for several reasons. Spillways with perpendicular sides retain debris easier than those with sloping sides; hence, trapezoidal cross sections are preferable to rectangular ones. The length of the spillway relative to the width of the gully bottom is also important for the protection of the channel and structure. Normally, it is desirable to design spillways with a length not greater than the available gully bottom width so that the waterfall from the dam will strike the gully bottom. This avoids the problem of the water first

striking the gully banks where erosion is more difficult to control.

8.2.5 Apron

Aprons are installed on the gully bottom immediately downstream of the check dam to prevent flows from undercutting the structures. Required apron lengths depend upon whether the structure has a sloping downstream face as in a loose rock dam or is a straight-drop structure such as a steel sheet or fence-type dam.

Rigorous calculation of apron length for the former requires field and laboratory investigation of prototypes. Heede (1976) has presented a simplified design procedure or rule of thumb. The length of the apron is made 1.5 times the height of the structure in channels where the gradient does not exceed 15 percent, and 1.75 times where the gradient is steeper than 15 percent. The resulting apron lengths include a sufficient margin of safety to prevent the waterfall from hitting the unprotected gully bottom.

In addition, the apron should be embedded into the channel floor so that its surface is roughly level and about 0.45 ft (0.15 m) below the original bottom elevation. At the downstream end of the apron, a loose-rock sill can be built 0.45 ft (0.15 m) high, measured from channel bottom elevation to the crest of the sill. This end sill creates a pool or tailwater pond that cushions the impact of the waterfall from the dam spillway.

8.2.6 Rock Size and Gradation

Proper size and gradation of rock is required when used in porous dams to resist both displacement and piping problems. Because required size and gradation of rock depend upon size and type of dam plus magnitude of flow, strict rules for effective rock gradation cannot be provided. On the other hand, there has been sufficient experience with gully control structures to establish some general rules. The following recommendations are based on empirical values derived from gully treatments in the Colorado Rocky Mountains (Heede, 1976).

As a general rule, rock diameters should not be less than 10 cm, and 25 percent of all rocks should fall into the 10- to 14-cm size class. The upper size limit will be determined by the size of the dam; large dams can include larger rock than small ones. Likewise, large design peak flows will require larger rock sizes than small flows. As an example, assume that the designed total dam height ranges between 1 and 2 m, where total height is measured from the bottom of the dam to the crest of the freeboard. The type of dam is loose rock without reinforcement. Design peak flow is estimated not to exceed 1 m³/sec. An effective rock gradation would call for a distribution of size classes as follows:

Size	Percent
10–14 cm	25
15–19 cm	20
20–30 cm	25
31–45 cm	30

If, on the other hand, dam height were increased to 3 m, rock up to 1 m diameter, constituting 15 percent of the volume, could be placed into the base of the dam and the second largest size class decreased by this portion. If peak flow were estimated not to exceed 0.75 m³/sec, the 31- to 45-cm size class could be eliminated, and 55 percent of the volume could be in the 20- to 30-cm class.

8.3 CONSTRUCTION OF CHECK DAMS

Check dams described herein all utilize native, natural materials (with the exception of wire) that can be obtained at the site. Selection of one design over another is governed largely by local availability of these materials. Readers should refer to material specifications (Section 8.1.3) for description of materials cited herein.

8.3.1 Single-Row Post-Brush Dam

Location and Use: This dam is suitable for gullies up to 5 ft deep and up to 15 ft wide as shown in Fig. 8.5. It is used where brush, and trees suitable for posts and poles, are readily available.

Materials Required:

1. Posts: two to four, 4-inch diameter × 6 ft long.
2. Stakes: two to four, 3-inch diameter × 3 ft long.
3. Poles: two, 3–4 inch diameter × 6 ft long.
4. Wire: about 15 ft of no. 9 galvanized wire.
5. "Dam brush," "apron brush," and "litter."

Construction Procedure:
1. Slope back the banks, if too steep, as shown in Fig. 8.5. Throw the fresh dirt upstream from the dam.
2. Set posts of sound wood with 4-inch tops. The

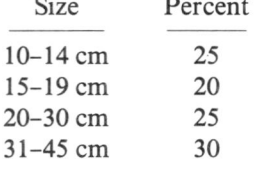

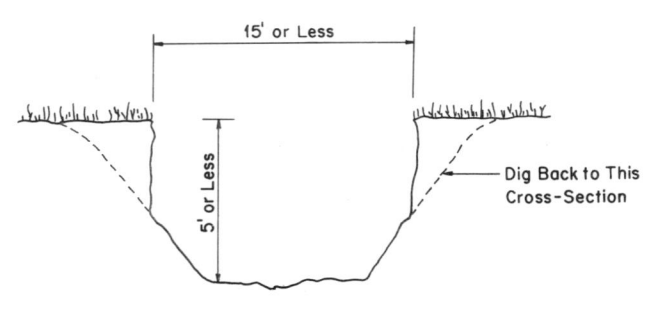

Fig. 8.5. Cross section of gully showing maximum gully size for best use of single-row post-brush dam.

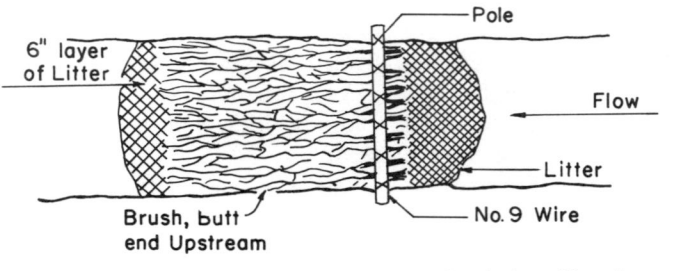

Fig. 8.6. Elevation of gully after banks have been dug back. The posts have been set, and the layer of litter has been placed.

center posts should be long enough that they can be buried 3 to 3½ ft, and extend up to within 1 or 2 ft of the top of the gully bank. The outer posts need not be set quite so deep but should extend higher, as shown in Fig. 8.6. Space the posts 2 ft apart. Willow posts are recommended.

3. Set two to four stakes 3 inches in diameter and 3 ft long, as shown in Fig. 8.6. Use willow, if possible, and plant right side up so they will sprout.

4. Place a 6-inch layer of litter between the posts, and on the gully bottom and sides downstream from the posts for about 6 ft, as shown in Fig. 8.7.

5. Place brush or green tree branches as shown in Figs. 8.8 and 8.9. The long, straight limbs, apron brush, should be placed in a layer across the bottom. For the rest of the dam, the shorter dam brush should be used. The butt ends should be placed upstream. Usually, the gully can be almost filled with brush, and when the cross poles are placed, the brush will be forced down into a compact mass.

6. Place the cross poles on the upstream side of the posts. One or two men should stand on these poles to

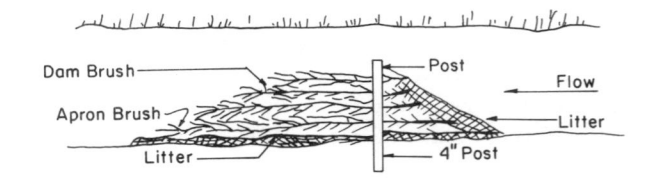

Fig. 8.7. Side section of completed dam. Note that the longer brush is on the bottom to form an apron.

Fig. 8.8. Plan of completed single-row, post-brush dam. Note that the brush is carefully piled and tramped, with the butt ends laid upstream between the posts.

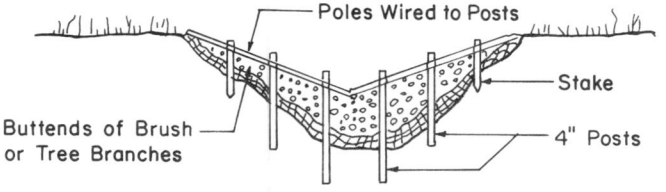

Fig. 8.9. Elevation view of single-row, post-brush dam, looking downstream; complete except for litter against upstream face.

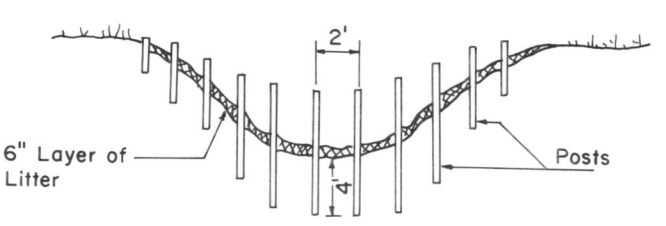

Fig. 8.11. Sectional elevation of gully showing posts and litter in place for dam. Note that the posts are lower in the center.

compress the brush properly while the poles are being wired to the posts and stakes with no. 9 galvanized wire.

7. Place a layer of litter against the upstream face of the dam, and carefully pack into the openings between the butt ends of the brush.

8.3.2 Double-Row Post-Brush Dam

Location and Use: This type of dam has been used most on gullies 15 to 20 ft wide and 5 to 7 ft deep. However, it may safely be used on much larger mountain meadow gullies, provided the center height of the dam does not exceed about 4 ft.

Materials Required:

1. Posts: The center posts should be 8 to $8\frac{1}{2}$ ft long and 6 to 8 inches in diameter, but shorter posts may be used at the side of the ditch and may be only 4 to 6 inches in diameter. Willow posts are excellent.
2. Wire: About $3\frac{1}{4}$ feet of no. 9, soft, galvanized wire is required for each foot of width of the gully from bank to bank.
3. "Apron brush," "dam brush," and "litter."
4. Stakes: 2 to 3 ft long. Use willow if possible.

Construction Procedure:

1. Slope banks back, if too steep, as shown in Fig. 8.10. Throw the loose dirt upstream from the dam.
2. Set posts as shown in Fig. 8.11.
3. Place a 6-inch layer of litter on the gully bottom and banks extending about 10 ft downstream from the posts, as shown in Figs. 8.11 and 8.12.

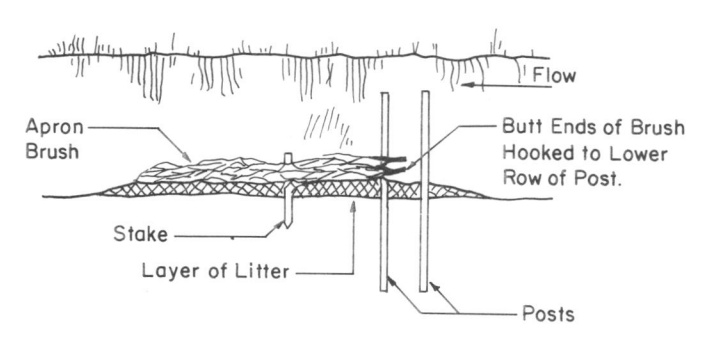

Fig. 8.12. Side section of double-row, post-brush dam after apron brush has been placed.

4. Place about a 1-foot layer of apron brush, butts upstream and hooked to the lower row of posts, as shown in Fig. 8.12. This brush should extend downstream about 10 ft or more.

5. Drive a row of stakes across the gully through the middle of the apron and wire the limbs down to form a dense mat. Willow stakes are preferable.

6. Entirely fill the space between the two lines of posts with dam brush laid crossways of the gully. Thoroughly pack it, and pile it above the tops of the posts for a foot or more.

7. Staple wire to a post at one end, stretch it tight, and thread it back and forth as shown in Fig. 8.13. It is usually necessary to have one or more men stand on the brush while wiring to help force the brush into a compact mass.

8. Place litter against the upstream face of the dam, as shown in Figs. 8.13 and 8.14.

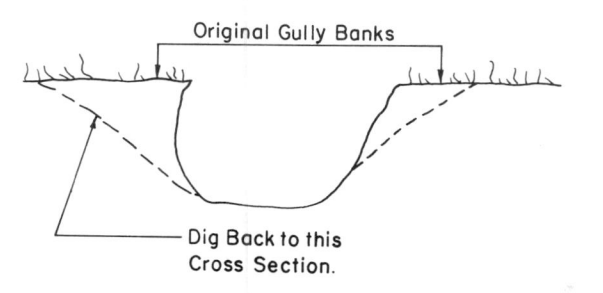

Fig. 8.10. Sectional elevation of gully showing how banks should be sloped back prior to constructing a double-row, post-brush dam.

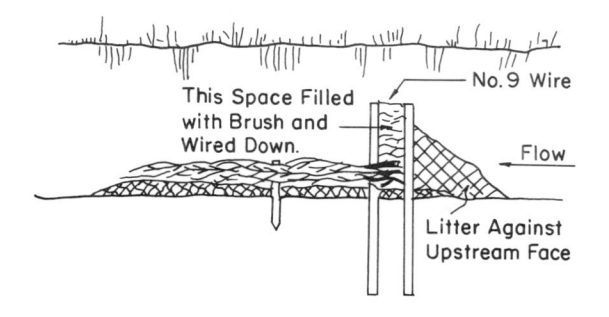

Fig. 8.13. Side section of completed double-row, post-brush dam.

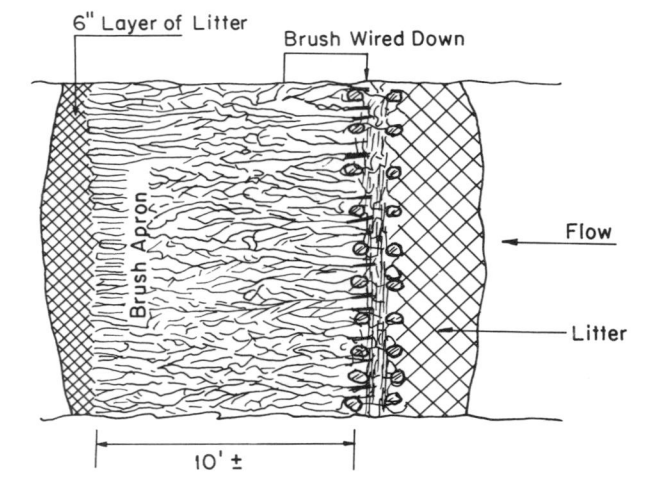

Fig. 8.14. Plan of completed double-row, post-brush dam.

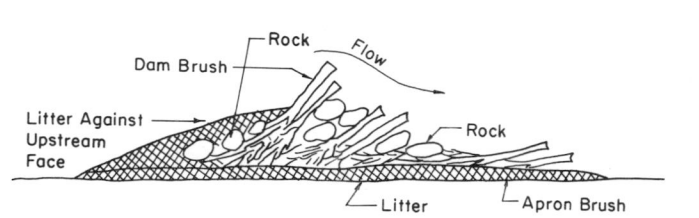

Fig. 8.16. Side section of brush and rock dam.

8.3.3 Brush and Rock Dam

Use: This is an excellent dam where rock and brush are plentiful, but considerably more brush is required than for post-brush structures. Figs. 8.15 and 8.16 show two views of such a dam just after completion.

Materials: "Apron brush," "dam brush," "litter," and rock.

Construction Procedure:

1. If banks where the dam is to be located are vertical, they should be sloped back for a distance of 12 to 15 ft as shown in Fig. 8.15. The loose earth should be thrown upstream from the dam.

2. Place a 6-inch layer of litter along the gully bottom and sides for a distance of 12 to 15 ft, as shown in Figs. 8.15 and 8.16.

3. Across the gully, on top of the downstream end of the layer of litter, place an 8-inch layer of apron brush, as shown in Fig. 8.16. The butt ends of the brush should point downstream.

4. Near the upstream end of the apron brush lay a row

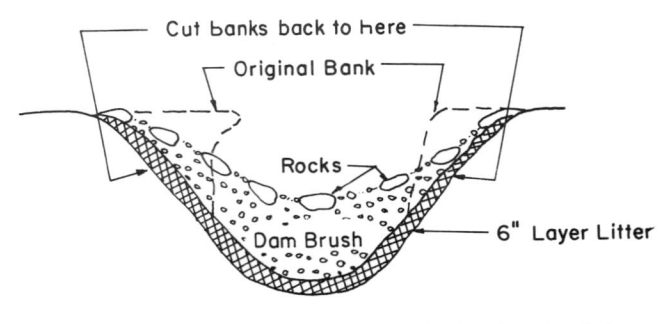

Fig. 8.15. Sectional elevation of gully showing brush and rock dam.

of rocks about 1 ft high across the gully on top of the brush. Flat rocks are superior to round rocks.

5. Place about a 4-ft layer of loose dam brush across the gully with the butt ends pointing downstream and extending just over the top of the row of rocks.

6. Lay a row of rocks across the middle of this layer of dam brush, at the same time walking on the brush to tamp it down. Flat rocks should be used if available, and the row should be about $1\frac{1}{2}$ ft high. The weight of the rocks should compress the brush until the dam is only about 2 ft high.

7. In a similar manner, place a layer of dam brush on the upstream side of this row of rock.

8. Weight this last layer of brush down with sufficient rock to hold the brush in place.

9. Place a 4-inch layer of litter against the upstream face of the dam.

8.3.4 Brush and Wire-Netting Dam

Use: This is a satisfactory dam in small gullies up to 10 or 12 ft wide where "dam brush" is plentiful, but rock is scarce.

Materials: "Dam brush," "apron brush," "litter," wire netting, stakes, and staples.

Construction Procedure:

1. If banks are vertical, slope them back to the natural angle of repose for a distance of about 6 ft where the dam is to be located.

2. Place a 4- to 6-inch layer of litter for a distance of 8 or 10 ft along the bottom and sides of the gully.

3. Cover the litter with a layer of apron brush about 8 to 10 inches thick when loose and with the butt ends pointing downstream. If necessary, dam brush can be used in place of apron brush.

4. Cut wire netting into about 18-ft lengths. Lay it over the apron, as shown in Fig. 8.17, and stake at the downstream end of the apron. The stakes should be at least 3 ft long. They should be of willow, if possible. Before the stakes are completely driven, staple the netting to them so that it will be firmly anchored as the stakes are driven the rest of the way.

5. Similarly, stake the netting down at a point 6 ft

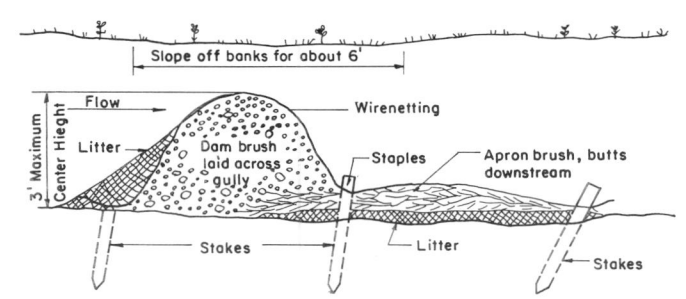

Fig. 8.17. Side section of brush and wire-netting dam.

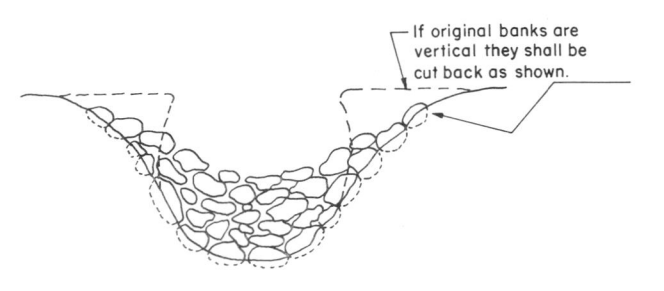

Fig. 8.18. Cross section of gully showing loose rock dam.

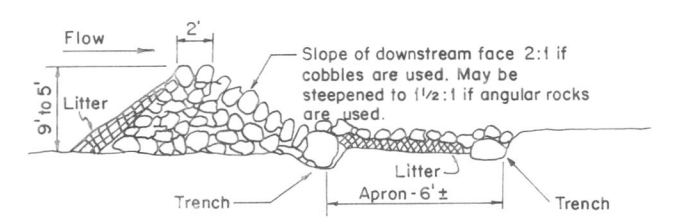

Fig. 8.19. Side section of gully showing loose rock dam.

upstream, walking on the apron so that it is more readily forced down into a compact layer. If necessary, put in additional stakes wherever the apron tends to bulk up. Fold the remaining lengths of wire netting back over the apron while the dam brush is being placed.

6. Place the dam brush in a compact interwoven mass across the gully and up the banks, building it up so that it will have a center height of about 3 ft when finally forced down by the netting. This will require that the brush be piled loosely to a height of 6 ft or more. The branches should be laid crosswise of the gully.

7. Pull the loose ends of the wire netting over the dam brush, and stake it down as shown in Fig. 8.17. The stakes should be similar to those previously used. It will probably be necessary to have one or two men stand on top of the dam while staking the netting down; otherwise the brush may not be forced into a compact mass.

8. Place a layer of litter across the upstream face of the dam when the structure is complete.

8.3.5 Loose Rock Dam

Use: This dam is suitable where there is ample rock and very little brush. Machine and/or hand labor may be used. Loose rock dams can be constructed to 9 ft (3 m).

Materials: Rock and ground litter. See general design criteria (Section 8.2.6) for guidelines on rock size and gradation.

Construction Procedure:
1. If the banks are too steep, slope them back as shown in Fig. 8.18. Throw loose dirt upstream from the dam.

2. Cut a 4- to 6-inch trench across the gully and up the sides to anchor the heavy rocks on the downstream toe of the dam.

3. Place a row of large rocks along this trench to form the downstream toe. Build back from this row. The rocks, especially on the downstream face, should be toed upward so that they will by keyed in place, as shown in Fig. 8.19. Note that the flatter rocks are used on this face.

4. About 6 ft downstream from the downstream toe of the dam cut a 4- to 6-inch trench across the gully, as shown in Fig. 8.19.

5. Lay a row of heavy rocks in this trench across the gully.

6. Place a 4-inch layer of litter in the space between this row of rocks and the row at the toe of the dam. Extend this layer well up the banks.

7. Cover the litter with a solid pavement of rock.

8. Place a thick layer of litter over the upstream face of the dam when completed.

8.3.6 Split Board Dam

Use: This dam is suitable for shallow gullies no deeper than 3 ft (1 m) in areas where split boards can be obtained from downed logs on the site or on nearby timber harvest sites (Madej et al., 1980).

Materials: Boards and stakes.

Construction Procedure:
1. Select boards long enough to span the entire width of the gully and be keyed into the banks (Fig. 8.20). Boards should be 8 to 14 inches in width, depending on the log being split. Dams may be one or two boards high.

2. Boards should be keyed (inset) into the banks to prevent lateral breaching. They should be inset into the gully side banks to an average depth of 6 inches. The bottom (lowest) board should be keyed into the gully bottom at least 2 inches in the deepest part of the gully.

3. Board may be staked for additional support as shown in Fig. 8.21.

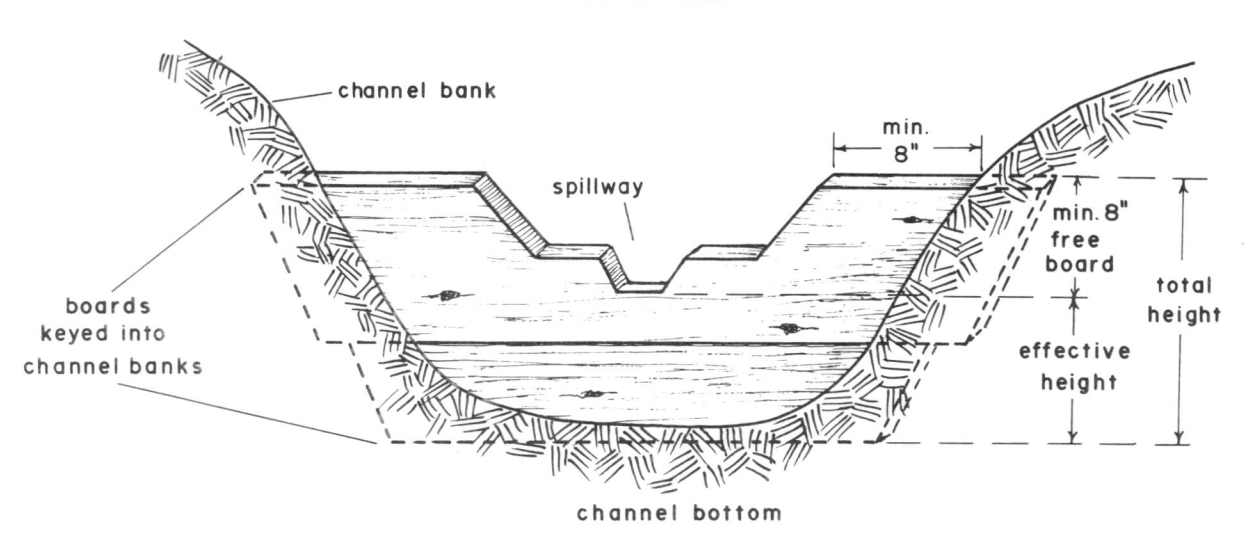

Fig. 8.20. Split-board check dam inset into channel.

4. Board dams must have an adequate spillway notch to accomodate high flows in the gully (Fig. 8.20). Low-flow spillways should be between 3 and 5 inches deep and approximately 5 to 7 inches wide. High-flow spillways have considerable flexibility to their dimensions, depending on the size of the gully, but in all cases the ends of the high-flow spillways must not be any closer than 8 inches to the point where the board goes into the gully bank.

5. Install energy-dissipation material in the gully bottom below the spillway. The energy dissipation may consist of rock, conifer or hardwood boughs, small woody slash, or a combination thereof. The dissipation material should be firmly secured to the channel bottom, located immediately below the spillway, and as wide as the width of the high flow spillway. The energy dissipator or apron must extend continuously downstream at least 14 inches from the base of the check dam.

Fig. 8.21. Redwood board check dams with trapezoidal spillway design. Boards are inset into channel and staked in place for additional support. Note willow cuttings in channel banks which have rooted and sprouted.

8.4 REFERENCES CITED

Heede, B. H. (1976). Gully development and control, *USDA For. Serv. Res. Paper RM-169,* Rocky Mtn. Forest and Range Exp. Stn., Fort Collins, Colo., 49 pp.

Heede, B. H., and Mufich, J. G. (1973). Field and computer procedures for gully control by check dams, *J. Environ. Management,* 2: 1–49.

Kraebel, C. J., and Pillsbury, A. F. (1934). Handbook of erosion control in mountain meadows, USDA Forest Service Publication, Pacific Southwest Forest and Range Exp. Stn., Berkeley, Calif., 69 pp.

Madej, M. A., Kelsey, H., and Weaver, W. (1980). An evaluation of 1978 rehabilitation sites and erosion control techniques in Redwood National Park, U. S. National Park Service, Arcata, Calif., Tech. Rept. No. 1, 113 pp.

9
Case Histories and Applications of Biotechnical Slope Protection

9.1 INTRODUCTION

In this chapter we present actual case histories of biotechnical slope protection for a variety of different site conditions and slope problems. This approach has the advantage of joining a problem to its resolution in a well-documented manner (U. S. Environmental Protection Agency, 1975). The disadvantage, of course, is that the reader may not encounter exactly the same problems. Nevertheless, the examples selected are representative of a range of slope problems and conditions that have lent themselves to biotechnical treatment. These examples and their locations include:

1. Backshore slope protection—Great Lakes shoreline
2. Watershed rehabilitation—Redwood National Park
3. Cut slope stabilization—Lake Tahoe Basin

An alternative approach to these case histories would be to present some sort of selection scheme for biotechnical methods. Several factors militate against such a procedure. In the first place the state-of-the art of biotechnical slope protection is still too fluid to codify such a selection process. More important, however, such a scheme tends to defeat the principles of biotechnical slope protection with its emphasis on fitting a solution to the site, maximizing use of indigenous materials, and utilizing locally available skills and labor.

9.2 CASE HISTORY NO. 1—BACKSHORE SLOPE PROTECTION: GREAT LAKES SHORELINE

9.2.1 Nature of Great Lakes Shoreline and Magnitude of Erosion Problem

The shorelines of the Great Lakes are largely comprised of unconsolidated glacial drift. The series of ice lobes and ice sheets that carved out the present Great Lakes basin were also responsible for the glacial sediments that now cover the region and make up a large part of the shoreline. The unconsolidated glacial deposits are comprised of clays, silts, sands, gravels, and boulders that have been eroded, transported, and deposited in varying forms by the advance and retreat of glaciers.

The shores of the Great Lakes vary greatly from place to place in their composition and landform. Major shore types that have evolved within the erodible portion of the Great Lakes and are particularly prone to erosion and mass-movement include the following:

1. *Low erodible bluffs,* ranging in height from 3 to 10 m (approximately 9 to 30 ft) and composed mainly of glacially derived gravels, sands, silts, and clays. They are found along all five of the Great Lakes, interspersed among the other shore types. Drainage and slope stability are problems commonly associated with this shore type.
2. *High erodible bluffs,* those greater than 10 m (approximately 30 ft) in height and composed of glacial materials. The Scarborough Bluffs near Toronto are among the highest of them, reaching 90 m (295 ft) above Lake Ontario. High erodible bluffs are

found on all five lakes but are most prevalent along the Lake Michigan and Lake Erie shorelines. Drainage and slope stability are likewise problems commonly associated with this shore type.

3. *Sand dunes,* which make up roughly a sixth of the Great Lakes erodible shoreline and present special considerations for development and protection. Low dunes are found on all the lakes, but high dunes reaching over 137 m (450 ft) are found primarily along the eastern Lake Michigan shoreline, where man's activity and wind erosion are the primary concerns.

The National Shoreline Study conducted by the U. S. Army Corps of Engineers (1971) provides a comprehensive review of shoreline conditions and damage caused by erosion. Of the total 3680 shoreline miles along the Great Lakes, some 1260 miles (about one-third) are undergoing significant erosion and mass-movement. About 215 of these miles are listed as "critical." Over the past century the average rate of coastline retreat or recession in many locations along critical reaches has ranged from 1 to 5 ft per year. About half of the critical shoreline erosion (104 miles) occurs in the state of Michigan.

9.2.2 Shoreline Degradation Processes

Except where bedrock is exposed or protective works are constructed, unconsolidated sediments and glacial deposits comprising the shores and backshore slopes of the Great Lakes are vulnerable to erosion and recession. The backshore slope is defined herein as the high or sloping ground rising above the beach or shore. The backshore can be acted upon by waves during severe storms, especially during periods of high water. Normally, a beach of varying width will separate the foot of the backshore slope from the water's edge.

Elevated lake levels are widely believed to be responsible for accelerated degradation and recession of backshore slopes along the Great Lakes. High lake levels which permit direct wave attack at the base of coastal bluffs are unquestionably a critical factor, but they alone do not account for all the observed damage or for the considerable variation in lateral erosion rates in many coastal areas. Degradation and retreat of the shoreline are caused in fact by both terrestrial processes (e.g., gullying, slumping, deflation, frost action, etc.) and marine processes (e.g., direct wave action, currents, and submarine landslides). A photograph illustrating the juxtaposition of these two major types of degradation along a single reach of shoreline is shown in Fig. 9.1.

Most of the shoreline damage also occurs in cycles. Periods of accelerated erosion and backshore slope

Fig. 9.1. Marine and terrestrial processes of erosion juxtaposed. Gullying and slumping are occurring on the clay bluff (top of picture) independently of wave action which is eroding the fore slope. South Haven, Michigan.

failures correspond closely to storm cycles on the Great Lakes. Undercutting of undefended coastal bluffs by large waves in severe storms may cause an entire surface of the bluff to fail, leaving a bare and denuded slope. This in turn exposes the bluff to the full brunt of terrestrial processes in succeeding years. The faster the bluff can be revegetated, the less the amount of erosion that will occur in subsequent years. Unfortunately, natural revegetation is often slow and uncertain in the high-energy environment of the coastal zone. The secret of stabilization, therefore, is to enhance and promote rapid revegetation of the face while defending the toe of the backshore slopes against future wave attacks.

9.2.3 The Rocky Gap Bluff Stabilization Project

9.2.3.1 Project Objectives. The Rocky Gap project was established by the USDA Soil Conservation Service (1940) as a demonstration project in lake bluff erosion control. The bluff selected was a high erodible bluff

composed largely of a clayey glacial till. Over the years considerable retreat of the bluff had occurred to the point where a county highway atop the bluff was endangered by encroachment of the face of the bluff. Degradation and retreat of the bluff had occurred in a cyclic manner as described previously (Section 9.2.2); wave action periodically undermined the base of the bluffs, and was followed by several years of intense surficial erosion during which time there was little chance for natural revegetation.

The objective in stabilization briefly was to get the bluff as well as the upper part of the beach covered as quickly as possible with vegetation. The expectation was that by establishing a vigorous vegetative cover on the slopes not only would surface erosion be arrested, but subsequent storms would not undercut the bluff as severely, nor would the resulting slope failures be nearly so destructive.

9.2.3.2 Project Location and Site Description.
The site chosen for the demonstration project (Fig. 9.2) was at Rocky Gap Park, 1 mile north of the City of Benton Harbor on Lake Shore Drive. The location was well

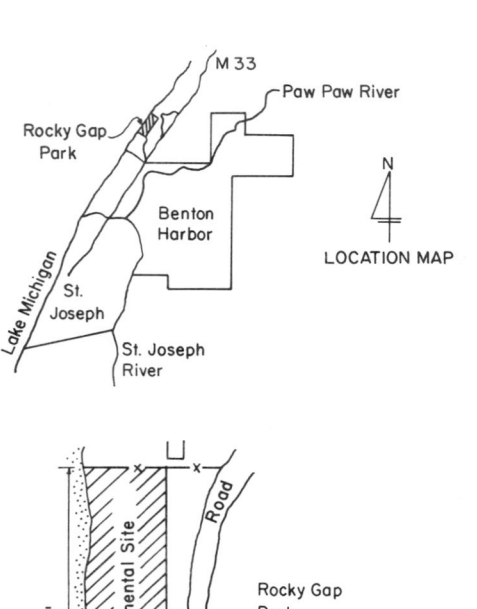

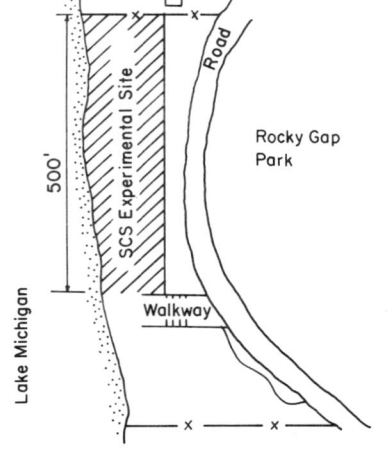

Fig. 9.2. Location of Rocky Gap lake bluff stabilization project.

suited for the project because it provided the large area of right-of-way needed for the demonstration.

The last severe storm which undercut and denuded the bluff had occurred in October 1929. The condition of the bluff in November 1937 before the start of remedial treatment is shown in Fig. 9.3. Practically no natural revegetation had occurred in the intervening 8 years. Natural revegetation was slow because during the summer months the clay slopes became dry, hard, and unproductive, whereas during the winter severe frost action tended to heave out plants and trees. The latter was especially severe where seepage emerged along the face of the bluff, a common occurrence in glacial deposits comprising the shoreline.

In order to best demonstrate and evaluate control measures under varying conditions such as slope, seepage, and amount of residual native cover, a demonstration area 500 ft long was established and subdivided into six plots. Different combinations of vegetative and mechanical control measures were used on each plot. The main features and results of a number of these plot treatments are described next.

9.2.4 Plot Treatments and Results

9.2.4.1   Plot No. 1: Post-Brush Dam and Willow Staking.
The dimensions of this plot were as follows: lake frontage 120 ft, average length of slope 160 ft, and area 2230 sq yd. Except for a small clump of willow growing at its base, very little vegetation existed on this plot. Two gullied ravines had formed as a result of the erosive action of both surface and seepage water (Fig. 9.4).

Control measures employed at this plot consisted of: a surface water diversion at the top of the slope, a post-wire-brush dam at the base, slope grading, seeding with grasses, mulching with hay, willow staking, and planting the slope with selected shrubs and trees.

A small diversion channel was constructed at a distance of approximately 10 ft from the top edge to divert storm water, which gathered from the small watershed area above. A post-wire-brush dam was built on contour across the toe of the slope. This dam consisted of willow posts set 4 ft deep in the ground, spaced on 2-ft centers and faced with 9-gage, 4 × 6-inch cattle fencing, willow brush, and straw. Live willow brush and posts were used to form a living dam (Fig. 9.5) to catch clay from the slope above and trap sand from the beach area below. The ravines and overhanging top edge were graded back, and the entire plot area was smoothed by hand grading preparatory to seeding. The average slope of the plot after grading was 60 percent.

The entire plot was seeded at a rate of 100 lb/acre with a grass seed mixture consisting of smooth brome grass, red top, alsike clover, red clover, sweet clover, and domestic

Fig. 9.3.   General condition of the lake bluff before control work was started. The picture was taken in November 1937, 8 years after the severe storm of October 1929. There was very little revegetation during that time. (*Photo courtesy of the U. S. Soil Conservation Service*)

rye grass. This high a rate of seeding was probably un-necessary to establish a grass cover. This seeding, as well as subsequent fertilizing, mulching, and so forth, was made in strips approximately 6 ft wide on contour across the plot beginning at the top edge.

The entire plot was mulched with marsh hay (*Calamo-grostis canadensis*) at approximately 4 tons/acre. The mulch was distributed to cover the ground as evenly as possible. It was held in place by laying used cattle fencing with a mesh size not greater than 4 × 6 inches over the

Fig. 9.4.   Plot No. 1 before control work was started. The gully to the left was caused by surface runoff from the area above the plot and from seepage. The shallow ravine to the right was caused by seepage. (*Photo courtesy of the U. S. Soil Conservation Service*)

Fig. 9.5.   Living barrier of willow posts, cattle fencing, and willow brush. This type of barrier was used at the toe of the bluff (Plot No. 1) to catch clay and debris washed from above.

marsh hay. The fencing itself was fastened by stapling it to the sides of live willow stakes which were driven 12 to 15 inches into the ground. These stakes, which were 1 to 2 inches in diameter, were driven so that only 4 to 6 inches remained above the surface of the ground. All willow stakes and brush as used in the post wire dam, and so on, were cut during the winter while dormant and kept moist until used.

The general planting arrangement of trees and shrubs on nearly all plots was as follows: low-growing shrubs on the upper one-third of the slope, tall shrubs or low bushy trees on the middle third, and medium tall trees on the lower third. On Plot No. 1, the upper one-third was planted to coral berry, chokecherry, and gray dogwood set 2 × 2 ft. The middle one-third was planted to red osier dogwood, lilac, and caragana set 3 × 3 ft. The lower one-third was planted to black locust set 3 × 3 ft. All shrubs and trees were planted after seeding and mulching had been completed. Shrubs and trees were fertilized at the time of planting by mixing $\frac{1}{8}$ lb 10-6-4 commercial fertilizer with the dirt in refilling each planting hole.

Work was started on this plot March 3, 1938, and completed March 20, 1938. The picture shown in Fig. 9.6 was taken April 1, 1938 and shows this plot just after control measures were put into effect. A view of the plot 4 months later with a dense, well-established cover of rye grass and some sprouting of the willow stakes is shown in Fig. 9.7.

The method used on this plot for establishment of a

vegetational cover generally proved successful. Approximately 30 percent of the willow stakes used in fastening the hold-down fencing over the hay mulch grew 12 to 14 inches during the first year. Best growth was observed on the wetter sites. On the upper one-third of the plot area, which was somewhat droughty, very few survived; however, they still served their purpose in holding the fencing in place. A better survival of willow stakes might have been obtained had a spud bar been used to make holes for the stakes.

The shrub and tree plantings on Plot No. 1 were relatively successful; some species survived better than others. Black locust obtained the best growth and highest rate of survival. Where coral berry of good nursery stock was used, it made good growth. Red osier and gray dogwood obtained next best survival but made slow growth. Chokecherry, caragana, and lilac exhibited the lowest survival and least growth.

The post-wire-brush dam at the foot of the slope (Fig. 9.5) worked successfully. The willow brush and cuttings used behind the barrier made excellent growth, but the willow posts themselves did not root and sprout. Except for one slip which exposed approximately 1 sq yd of soil in a seep area, the control measures applied to this plot were very effective.

9.2.4.2   Plot No. 6: Crib Wall and Contour Wattling.
The dimensions of this plot were as follows: lake frontage 80 ft, average length of slope 115 ft, and area 1380 sq yd.

Fig. 9.6.   Plot No. 1 immediately after control measures were applied. Marsh hay was used as a mulching material. This mulch was fastened to the ground by using cattle fencing and willow stakes. (*Photo courtesy of U. S. Soil Conservation Service*)

Fig. 9.7.   Plot No. 1, 4 months after control measures were applied. Compare with Fig. 9.6. A dense cover of domestic rye grass was quickly established. Note growth of willow stakes. (*Photo courtesy of the U. S. Soil Conservation Service*)

Very little vegetation existed on the slope face or base of the plot prior to treatment. Some seepage was observed on the slope. A nearly vertical face existed at the upper part of the plot.

Control measures employed on this plot consisted of: a crib wall and pole-brush dam constructed along the base, slope grading, contour willow wattling on the face, seeding with grasses, mulching with hay, and planting the slope with selected shrubs and trees.

A railroad tie cribbing was built across the base of the northern half of this plot. A pole-brush dam was also built across the base of the southern half so that a comparison in effectiveness could be made with the railroad tie cribbing (Fig. 9.8). The pole-brush dam was constructed by placing willow poles 2 to 3 inches in diameter horizontally in front of 6-inch willow posts set on 3-ft centers. These poles were placed as close together as possible to make a tight facing. The facing extended 1 ft below and 2 ft above the ground line. The vertical willow posts were set at least 4 ft deep in the ground and were also anchored to dead-man posts set farther back.

The vertical face of the upper part of this plot was sloped back to a grade of 69 percent (approximately 1½:1) by blasting and hand labor. The loose dirt so obtained was scaled or removed to the lower part of the slope behind the cribbing and pole-brush dam.

In an attempt to stabilize the large amount of loose fill dirt, contour wattles were used over the entire plot area. Shallow trenches were dug on contour approximately 8 inches deep. The dirt taken from these trenches was used to form a ridge along the lower side of the wattles. Willow stakes 2 ft long were driven into the ridges on 18-inch centers to within 6 inches of the stake top. The trenches were then packed with willow brush, cuttings, and loose dirt. The maximum horizontal spacing between the contour wattles was 4 ft.

The entire plot area was seeded at the rate of 75 lb/acre with a grass seed mixture consisting of orchard grass (8 lb), vetch (7 lb), sweet clover (6 lb), smooth brome grass (5 lb), and Canada blue grass (4 lb). The plot area was fertilized with 10-6-4 at the rate of 300 lb/acre. A mulch of marsh hay at the rate of 4 tons/acre was used on the northern three-quarters of the plot area, the southern one-quarter being left as a control strip (Fig. 9.8). The marsh hay was not fastened to the ground in this case as it was believed that the large number of willow stakes used in the wattles would prevent the mulch from being blown or washed away.

The upper half of the plot area was planted to buffalo berry, coral berry, caragana, Japanese barberry, and chokecherry set 2 × 2 ft. The lower half of the plot area was set to black locust and caragana spaced 3 × 3 ft. On the beach area below the plot a strip 60 ft long and 20 ft wide was planted to four rows of black locust set 3 × 3 ft next to the bluff; five rows of poplar cuttings and five rows of willow cuttings set 1 × 1 ft were also placed on the beach strip.

Work started on this plot February 25, 1938 and was

Fig. 9.8.   Plot No. 6 immediately after control measures were installed. Note that only the left three-quarters of the plot area was mulched. Railroad tie cribbing and a post–pole willow dam were used at the toe of the slope. (*Photo courtesy of the U. S. Soil Conservation Service*)

Fig. 9.9   Plot No. 6, 4 months after control measures were installed. Compare with Fig. 9.8. Note that the risers to the contour wattles on the unmulched area are not completely covered with vegetation. (*Photo courtesy of the U. S. Soil Conservation Service*)

concluded April 20, 1938. The picture shown in Fig. 9.8 was taken immediately after control measures were completed. A view of the same plot 4 months later is shown in Fig. 9.9.

Control measures employed on Plot No. 6 were generally effective in spite of problems caused by settlement and downhill movement of clayey fill material from the grading and scaling operation. Where the plot was unmulched, this movement together with seepage and runoff that accumulated in the wattle trenches caused some slippage. In some cases slips covered four to five wattle intervals. Because of this, the southern one-quarter was mulched in August 1938 with marsh hay at the rate of 4 tons/acre, in order to control the erosion on this area before its slipping could affect the stability of the northern three-quarters of the plot. Slope failure or slips on the part of the plot originally mulched were confined to a few small areas of no consequence.

As on the other plots, the best survival and growth of willow stakes was obtained on the lower portions of the plot area. In the more moist locations these willows obtained a height of more than 6 ft in two growing seasons. The cuttings and brush used in the wattle trenches, on the other hand, exhibited little growth. The brush used behind the pole-brush dam made good growth, but the poles and posts themselves did not root and sprout. Both the pole-brush dam and railroad tie cribbing effectively

held back the loose fill dirt above, but the ability of these structures to withstand and mitigate the effects of direct wave attack at the base of the bluff was never tested.

A dense cover of vetch was established on the slope early in the first growing season. By July 1938 approximately 75 percent of the surface area was covered with vegetation. Vegetation growth was heaviest in the wattle trenches, with vetch vines creeping over and covering the wattle risers (Fig. 9.9). Vegetation was densest on the lower half of the original mulched plot area, and thinnest on the part left unmulched as a test strip.

The success of the shrub and tree plantations as to survival and growth on Plot No. 6 was similar to that reported for other plots (see results for Plot No. 1). The caragana and black locust that did not survive on the lower part of the plot were replaced by Russian wild olive; Japanese barberry were planted on the upper half to replace shrubs that did not survive there. Coral berry, black locust, Russian wild olive, and buffalo berry appeared to be the most promising among the shrubs and trees planted on Plot No. 6.

9.2.5   Summary and Conclusions

The biotechnical slope protection measures employed at Rocky Gap appear to have been effective in stabilizing the clay bluffs. The bluff in the former project area is today

Fig. 9.10.   Bluffs in project area 40 years later. The bluffs are covered by a dense stand of vegetation; there is little or no evidence of erosion.

Fig. 9.11.   Bluffs just north of the project area. These untreated bluffs are still barren in places and undergoing erosion in spite of protection from beach groins.

covered with a dense stand of trees (Fig. 9.10), and there is no evidence of any erosion or slope movement. In contrast, the bluff to the north of the project area is still bare and undergoing active erosion in several places (Fig. 9.11).

A groin system was constructed along the beach in front of the bluff (Fig. 9.10) several years after the bluff stabilization project. This shoreline protection system has somewhat obscured the true role and effectiveness of the previous bluff stabilization work in stopping further degradation and retreat of the bluffs. On the other hand, the continued presence of bare, eroding bluffs (Fig. 9.11) north of the project area, which is also protected by beach groins, testifies to the effectiveness of the stabilization work in at least arresting terrestrial slope processes of erosion and mass-movement.

9.3   CASE HISTORY NO. 2—WATERSHED REHABILITATION: REDWOOD NATIONAL PARK

9.3.1   Park Setting

9.3.1.1   Geology and Soils.   The sourthern half of Redwood National Park is located in the basin of Redwood Creek, California. The Redwood Creek portion of Redwood National Park encompasses the downstream third of the 280-square-mile Redwood Creek basin. This basin has steep hillslopes that are naturally susceptible to erosion by both mass-movement and fluvial erosion processes.

Sheared and fractured upper Mesozoic Franciscan assemblages of rocks underlie most of the basin. Unmetamorphosed sedimentary rocks, together with occasional small greenstone bodies, crop out in most of the eastern half of the basin. Quartz-mica schist, which is commonly sheared and fractured, underlies most of the western half of the basin.

Hugo soils, which form on hard sedimentary rocks, are the predominant soil on the eastern side of the basin. These soils tend to occur on steep to very steep hillsides. They have a grayish brown, slightly acid, gravelly loam surface horizon and a pale brown, strongly acid subsoil horizon. Hugo soils are well drained, are moderately permeable, and exhibit moderate runoff. They are not highly erodible, but steep slopes, disrupted drainage, and removal of vegetation accentuate erosion hazards.

Atwell soils, which form on sheared sedimentary or schistose sedimentary rocks, are commonly found along the fault contact near Redwood Creek. They have a dark grayish, slightly acid loam surface horizon and a pale brown, strongly acid gravelly clay loam subsoil. Atwell soils are moderately well drained, are slowly permeable, and exhibit medium runoff. Subsoils tend to be continually moist and unstable, and are more so in the wet winter months.

These two soil series, viz., Hugo and Atwell, provide contrasting extremes of behavior with regard to their resistance to mass-movement and fluvial erosion. The most prevalent soil series in the basin (i.e., Hugo soil) possesses little cohesion and is susceptible to shallow debris slides and erosion by running water (on steep, cutover slopes). On the other hand, the Atwell soil is highly susceptible to slump-earthflow movement (Janda, 1975).

9.3.1.2   Vegetation.   The prevalent vegetation in the maritime northern third of the basin is redwood (*Sequoia sempervirens* (D. Don)) and mixed redwood and Douglas fir (*Pseudotsuga menziesii* (Mirb) Franco). In the southern parts of the basin, which are farther inland, Douglas fir predominates, and other coniferous species occur as well.

Over half of the basin has been logged, mostly within the last 25 years. Different species of brush have invaded cutover sites, for example, ceanothus (*Ceanothus* spp.), chaparral broom (*Baccharis pilularis* subsp. *consanguinea* (DC.) C. B. Wolf), and salal (*Gaultheria shaillon* Pursh.). Massive invasions of red alder (*Alnus oregona* Nutt. (Syn.: *A. rubra* Bong., not Marsh)) have occurred on cutover areas on the westside of the basin but not on the drier, east side. Native Douglas fir regenerates and thrives on cutover or disturbed sites. Young Douglas fir trees can be found growing under a range of soil, slope, and moisture conditions on cut and fill slopes along abandoned haul roads. Non-native Monterey pine (*Pinus radiata* D. Don) was planted on disturbed sites following logging operations. This tree species is targeted for eradication from the park, but it too appears to grow well and in some cases plays an important soil- and slope-protective role (Fig. 9.12).

9.3.2   Erosion and Slope Stability Problems

Steep slopes, the presence of weak unstable soils, and high rainfall combine to make mass-movement endemic in the basin of Redwood Creek. More than 30 percent of the basin is underlain by distinct erosional landforms indicative of past or present movement (Nolan et al., 1976). Field inspections of hillslopes in the basin reveal topography and/or colluvium suggestive of episodic debris slides or persistent soil creep and slow sliding. Fluvial hillslope erosion (gullying and rilling) is also common where vegetation is removed or drainage disrupted.

Against this background of inherent instability it is not surprising that timber harvesting and road construction in the basin should intensify erosion and mass-movement. Harden et al. (1978) studied the relationship

Fig. 9.12.   Monterey pine trees growing in debris fans at base of road cut. Tree roots bind and hold soil in place; stems buttress the slope; and foliage will eventually screen steep, barren cut above.

between mass-movement, storm activity, and timber harvesting in Redwood Creek basin. They concluded from their study that recent storms have initiated more streamside landslides than comparable earlier storms, which occurred prior to extensive timber harvesting.

Roughly 90 percent of the basin has been logged since 1945 (Janda, 1975). Harvesting of old-growth redwood can result in a very high proportion of ground disturbance (Fig. 9.13). Boe (1975) calculated 77 percent bare or disturbed soil following tractor clear-cutting. This extreme level of disturbance is due, in part, to the size of the timber and the equipment needed to harvest it plus the practice of bulldozing layouts on a slope to cushion the fall of giant trees.

Road construction is a specific source of soil disturbance and cause of potential slope failures. There are presently in excess of 200 miles of former logging or haul roads in the park. These roads tend to seriously disrupt natural drainage patterns by intercepting subsurface flow and by increasing or concentrating runoff. Many of these roads have slipped out, are badly gullied (Fig. 9.14), or have bare, unvegetated cuts and fills (Fig. 9.15). There are also approximately 3500 miles of old skid trails in the

park. Skid trail construction across small drainages often formed small, earth fill dams, blocking or diverting stream channels. These skid trails thus have disrupted former drainage ways, altered hillslope hydrology, and intiated serious gullying in some watersheds (Fig. 9.16).

9.3.3   Watershed Rehabilitation Program

9.3.3.1   Objectives and Scope of Program.   Enabling legislation[1] for acquisition of additional lands for Redwood National Park also mandated the preparation and implementation of a watershed rehabilitation program. The purpose of this program is to speed the recovery and reforestation of lands in Redwood Creek basin, thereby minimizing threats to the park's resources. The basic strategy of the rehabilitation program to date has been to reduce sediment discharge to Redwood Creek by concentrating erosion control work on those disturbed sites that are directly contributing sediment to perennial stream channels.

The emphasis in the rehabilitation program, which is administered by the U. S. National Park Service, has been largely on biotechnical methods. The Park Service recognized that erosion control structures alone would not provide a permanent solution to erosion problems.

---

[1]U. S. Congress Public Law 95–250, 1978.

Fig. 9.13.   Ground disturbance and erosion resulting from timber harvesting operations in Redwood National Park prior to acquisition of parkland.

Fig. 9.14.   Gullied fill in stream draw crossing. Redwood National Park.

Fig. 9.15.   Steep, unvegetated cut along main access road into Redwood National Park. Cut has remained unvegetated for years and has started to rill. This cut would be a good candidate for a ''cellular grid'' revetment (see Section 5.3.4).

Fig. 9.16.   Large gully formed in slope as a result of disrupted and diverted drainage upslope. Redwood National Park.

Vegetation also had to be firmly reestablished to provide long-term protection. Accordingly, several different techniques were employed to promote revegetation adjacent to erosion control structures. Grass seeding plus fertilization was used to promote rapid, but short-term, ground cover on disturbed sites. Transplants, willow wattles, and stem cuttings were used to provide a protective canopy and root reinforcement of the soil in a few years. Finally, redwood and Douglas fir seedlings were planted on the rehabilitation sites to promote establishment of a vigorous stand resembling the original old-growth redwood forest.

A number of revegetation and slope stabilization techniques described in preceding chapters have been employed by the Park Service in their rehabilitation work. In addition to labor-intensive work, heavy equipment (i.e., dragline cranes, crawler tractors, and rubber-tired backhoes) was also used to correct erosion problems. In general, heavy equipment was used to remove fill from disturbed drainages, to remove oversteepened fills, to reshape roads, and to help build some erosion control structures.

Removal and/or stabilization of old haul roads (Fig. 9.17) and restoration of the road right-of-way to some semblance of the original slope topography (Fig. 9.18) posed a special challenge. This restoration work involved ripping (or decompacting) the road bed, outsloping the road prism, and removing fills from stream channels—actions that required the coordinated use of heavy equipment (Figs. 9.19 through 9.22).

9.3.3.2 Site Selection.
Rehabilitation efforts were initiated in the summer of 1978 on five sites (Fig. 9.23) totaling about 230 acres. Table 9.1 summarizes results of the 1978 work. These sites represent a range of geologic, hydrologic, vegetation, and soil conditions on cutover lands. Selection of a particular site for treatment depended on a number of factors. To be selected a site had

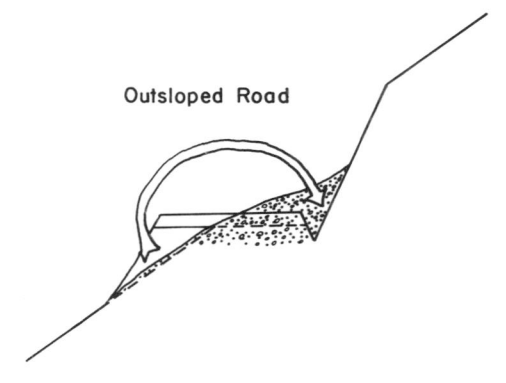

Fig. 9.18. Cross-sectional view of roadway after restoration. Fill has been pulled back against cut and road prism outsloped to conform as much as possible to original topography.

to pose an erosion problem, yet be treatable with available means. Access was also an important consideration. For the 1978 sites, a major criterion for site selection was the suitability of the site for testing various erosion control techniques.

Rehabilitation on only one of the five sites, namely Upper Miller Creek, is reviewed herein, but reference is made to related techniques and cost estimates for other rehabilitation sites as well. The Upper Miller Creek site is fairly typical of the erosion problems found in cutover slopes of the basin and of the remedies tested by the Park Service. On the other hand, this site is drier than most and

Fig. 9.19. A D-8 Caterpillar tractor decompacts roadbed with its ripper teeth. Most logging roads are surfaced with 8 to 12 inches of rock and must be disaggregated to promote infiltration and revegetation. (*Photo courtesy of U. S. National Park Service, Redwood National Park*)

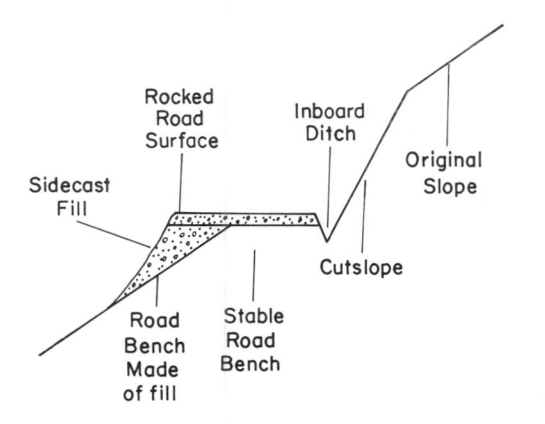

Fig. 9.17. Cross-sectional view of typical logging road. Road prism is constructed part on bench cut and part on fill.

Fig. 9.20   A dragline crane is used to lift unstable, side-cast road material and organic debris to the road bench. Dragline is well suited to this task because of long reach of its crane. (*Photo courtesy of U. S. National Park Service, Redwood National Park*)

Fig. 9.21.   Excavated fill is piled along the inboard edge of the road and against the road cut bank. A tractor grades the fill to achieve a gentle outslope on the former road alignment. (*Photo courtesy of U. S. National Park Service, Redwood National Park*)

Table 9.1.   Rehabilitation projects, Redwood National Park, 1978.

| SITE | ACRES/ROAD MILES | HEAVY EQUIPMENT | | LABOR-INTENSIVE | |
		HOURS	COST	HOURS	COST
1. Upper Miller Creek	80 acres/4000 ft	140	$14,422.00	3800	$43,000.00
2. Emerald Creek	90 acres/3170 ft	66	$2,760.00	2900	$53,557.00
3. Upper Bond Creek	51 acres/Not applicable	157	$6,025.00	4430	$19,503.00
4. Lower Bond Creek	Not applicable/1500 ft	8	$320.00	320	$3,685.00
5. C-Line Landing	2 acres/Not applicable	32	$1,760.00	400	$3,740.00

not close to a large perennial tributary. Upper Miller Creek was selected in 1978 because it was a tractor-logged site with a dead-end haul road and a good place to test methods. From an erosion hazard point of view it was not a high-priority site. The interested reader is referred elsewhere (Madej et al., 1980) for a detailed evaluation of the other rehabilitation sites and the effectiveness of erosion control techniques in Redwood National Park.

9.3.4   Upper Miller Creek Rehabilitation Test Site

9.3.4.1   Site Description.   The Upper Miller Creek rehabilitation test site includes 60 acres at the headwaters of the South Fork of Miller Creek (Fig. 9.24). The entire drainage had been clear-cut and tractor-yarded during a 2-year period beginning in 1970. Hillslopes in the area are relatively dry and generally moderate (20–40 percent) on the upslope portions of the site and steeper (50–65 per-

cent) on the downslope portions, especially below the C-10 road. The C-10 road was a rock-surfaced logging road that provided access to the rehabilitation site.

At the start of rehabilitation work in 1978, the C-10 road had been abandoned for 6 years and was the source of major erosional problems. The road disrupted natural drainage paths in several ways. Water was concentrated in the inboard ditch with only a few culvert outlets leading from the ditch. Cutbanks intercepted subsurface flow, and skid trails diverted runoff down trails and roads. No revegetation occurred on the road alignment, and infiltration was poor on the rocked and compacted surface. In addition, the road was contributing sediment into stream channels from fill slope failures, failing stream crossing, and washouts.

Fig. 9.22.   A dragline crane removes fill from a stream crossing and reshapes channel banks to a more stable configuration. (*Photo courtesy of U. S. National Park Service, Redwood National Park*)

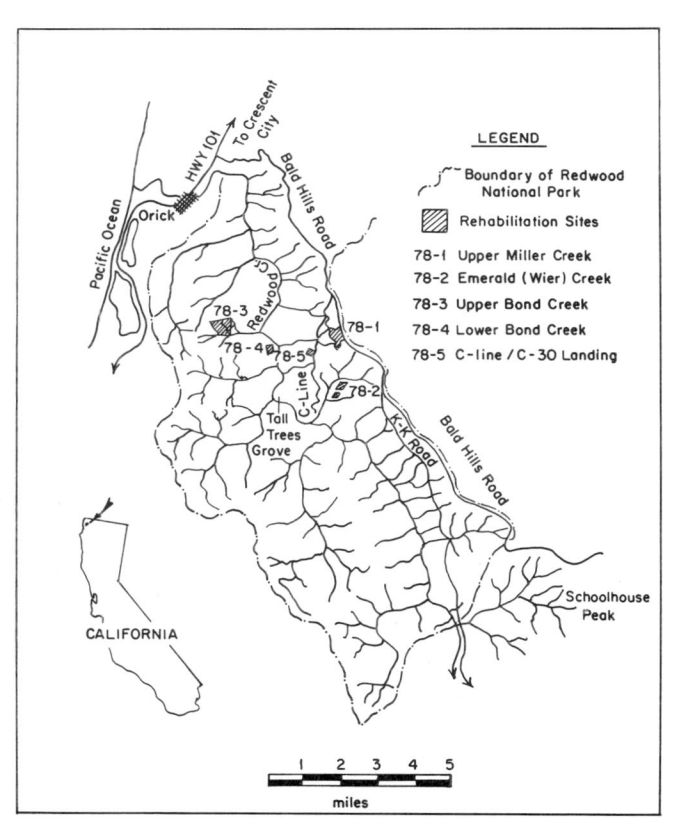

LEGEND

Boundary of Redwood National Park

Rehabilitation Sites

78-1 Upper Miller Creek
78-2 Emerald (Wier) Creek
78-3 Upper Bond Creek
78-4 Lower Bond Creek
78-5 C-line / C-30 Landing

Fig. 9.23.   Location of rehabilitation test sites in Redwood National Park.

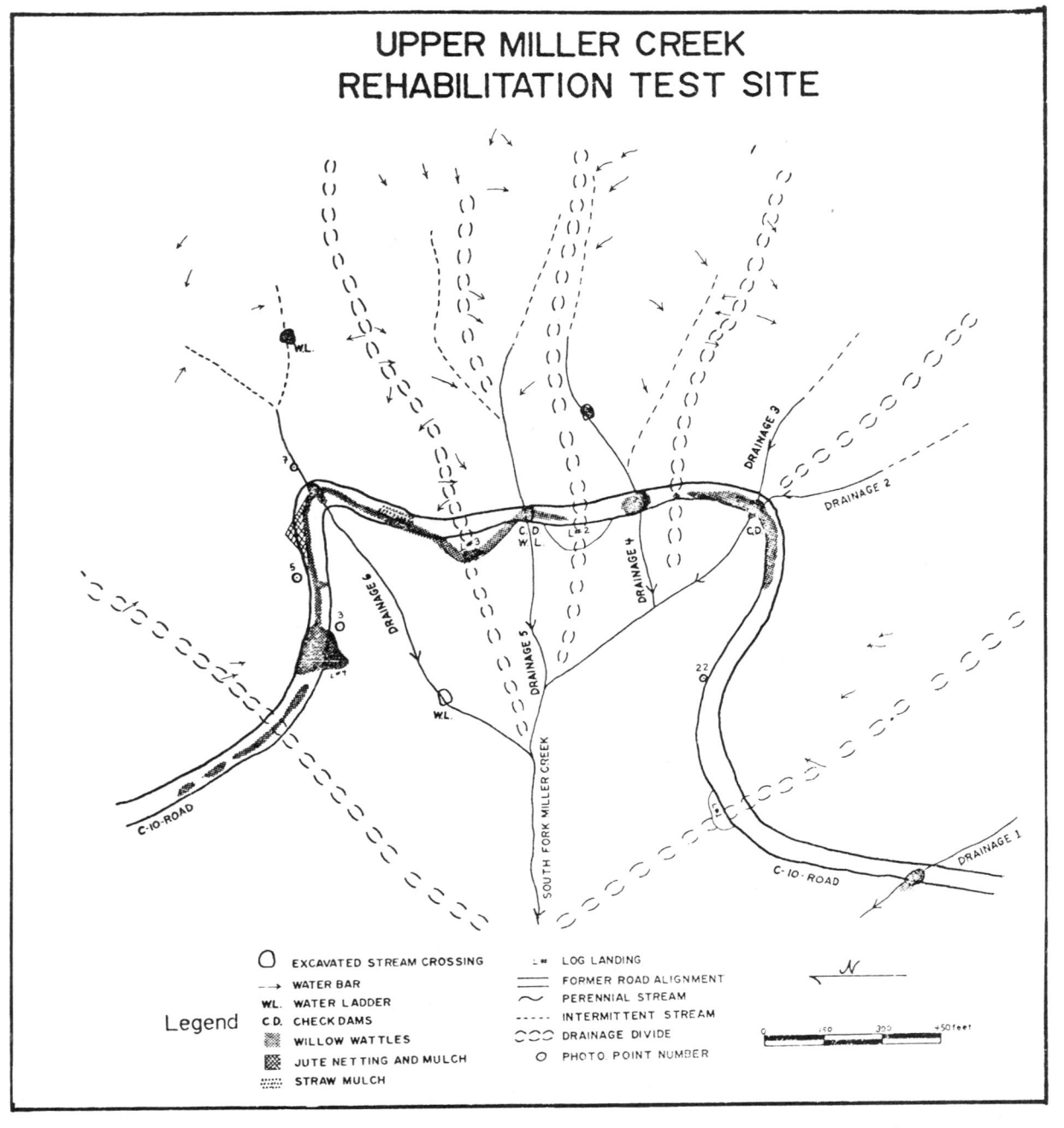

Fig. 9.24.   Map of Upper Miller Creek rehabilitation test site showing location of various erosion control treatments.

9.3.4.2   Rehabilitation Tasks.   The major task at this site was removing and stabilizing the C-10 road. This was accomplished over a 13-day period in the late summer of 1978. Initially, the road was decompacted (ripped) by a D-8 caterpillar tractor with rear-mounted hydraulic ripping teeth to increase infiltration (Fig. 9.19). Then a dragline crane excavated side-cast fill material and deposited it along the inboard edge of the road adjacent to the cutbank (Fig. 9.20). A crawler tractor outsloped this material to a gradient of 5 to 20 percent to prevent ponding or concentration of runoff (Fig. 9.21). Stream crossings on the C-10 road were excavated by a dragline crane to approximately resemble pre-road channel gradient and streambank configuration (Fig. 9.22). This work can also be accomplished by a hydraulic excavator or, for sites with smaller fill crossings, by a backhoe with extendable arm. In addition, a few fill crossings on skid trails that disrupted drainage patterns above and below the C-10 road were removed and streambanks recontoured.

After heavy-equipment work was completed, a contract was let for labor-intensive erosion control work. Component tasks of this contract included building check dams and water ladders in newly excavated channels where fill was removed, installing willow wattles on steep, unprotected slopes that were reshaped by the crane, building waterbars on skid trails, planting stem cuttings of easy-to-root species on unvegetated banks, and mulching. The locations of these erosion control measures are shown in Fig. 9.24. Estimated unit costs and times for such erosion control work, based on data for all the 1978 rehabilitation sites, are given in Table 9.2. Total labor cost for work on this site was $43,000, and 3800 person-hours were utilized (see Table 9.1). Cost of heavy-equipment work on the Miller Creek Unit was $14,422, or 25 percent of the total cost of unit rehabilitation (labor and equipment combined). Excavation costs using heavy equipment on the Miller Creek Unit ranged from $1.20 to $1.40 per cu yd of material. These excavation costs were approximately one-third to one-half those at other sites, a reflection in part of the economy of scale of earth moving and greater terrain mobility at Miller Creek.

9.3.4.3 Effectiveness of Erosion Control Measures.
Erosion control measures employed on the Miller Creek site were generally effective. Sequences of before and after treatment photos are shown in Figs. 9.25 through 9.30. Six stream channels were cleared of road fill where drainages crossed the C-10 Road. Nearly ver-

Table 9.2. Cost estimates for labor-intensive rehabilitation work, Redwood national Park.

TASK	PERSON HOURS PER TASK	CONTRACT UNIT PRICE PER TASK
Vegetative treatments:		
1. Wattling	17 hr / 1000 ft² or 0.05–0.1 hr / ft	$370–380 / 1000 ft² or $1–3 / ft
2. Sprig planting	6.2–9.1 hr / 1000 ft²	$43–80 / 1000 ft²
3. Mulching	Unknown	$185–255 / acre
4. Grass seeding	3–2 hr / acre	$43–75 / acre
5. Conifer planting	3–6 min / seedling	$0.08 / seedling
Erosion control structures:		
1. Check dams	5–16 hr / dam	$45–77 / dam
2. Water ladders	40 hr / ladder	$315–730 / ladder
3. Gully plug	unknown	$768 / plug
4. Board barriers (wooded terraces)	unknown	$20 / terrace
5. Water bars Construction Repair	3.0–4.7 hr / bar 1.5–2.4 hr / item	$29–35 / bar $14–30 / item
6. Cross road drains Ditch excavation Drain rocking	0.6 hr / ft 2.0 hr / drain	$0.85 / ft $373 / drain

Note: Cost estimates (ranges) are for all the 1978 rehabilitation sites based on contractors' work sheets. The table was compiled from the data in Madej et al. (1980).

Fig. 9.25. Fill crossing in draw *before* restoration, Channel No. 6, Upper Miller Creek test site. Culvert washout occurred at this location; note badly eroded, nearly vertical banks on the left. Photo taken summer 1978.

Fig. 9.26. Fill crossing *after* restoration, Channel No. 6, Upper Miller Creek test site. Vertical banks have been pulled back, smoothed, and wattled. Note vigorous growth of willow wattles along banks. Photo taken summer 1980.

Fig. 9.27. Stream crossing in roadway protected by check dams. Willow stakes along dams have just started to sprout. Photo taken 6 months after installation of check dams. Bond Creek rehabilitation unit 79–1, Redwood National Park.

Fig. 9.28. Check dams protecting steep reach of stream above abandoned roadway. Note vigorous growth of planted willow stakes. Photo taken 18 months after installation of check dams. Bond Creek rehabilitation unit 79–1, Redwood National Park.

Fig. 9.29.   Unstable log landing *before* rehabilitation work. Note steep leading edge and residual organic debris in landing. Photo taken Summer 1978. C-line landing rehabilitation unit 78–5, Redwood National Park.

Fig. 9.30.   Landing *after* rehabilitation work. Organic debris was removed first; landing was then graded back to stable angle. Wattles that were installed have rooted and sprouted, further stabilizing the slope. Photo taken summer 1980.

tical banks (Fig. 9.25) were pulled back to a 25–30 percent slope, smoothed, and wattled (Fig. 9.26).

Stream channels were excavated down to the estimated level of the original stream bed. Check dams were constructed to prevent additional stream downcutting in some of these restored channels (Figs. 9.27 and 9.28). Channel bed stabilization was given a high priority because channel downcutting can also lead to streambank failures as the toes of the slopes are undercut. Failure to excavate stream channels deep enough and/or to protect these restored channels with check dams appeared to be the cause of continued channel erosion and sediment delivery in a few drainage ways. Downcutting in excavated channels is probably the most significant potential source of increased sediment yield from rehabilitation projects such as the Upper Miller Creek site. Where fill material along the roadway or landing was potentially unstable (Fig. 9.29) (as indicated by tension cracks, incipient scarps, or presence of rotting organic debris), material was excavated and redeposited on stable ground along the inside edge of the landing or roadway. After excavation the slope was smoothed, wattled, and/or seeded (Fig. 9.30). No tension cracks have reappeared, nor have slope failures occurred in these excavated areas.

The Miller Creek site was broadcast-seeded with a mix of 50 percent annual and 50 percent perennial rye grass at an application rate of approximately 40 lb/acre in January 1979. Ammonium sulfate fertilizer (20-0-0) was applied at a rate of 100 lb/acre. Grass germinated about a week after seeding, but cover was generally sparse and uneven, ranging from 0 to 30 percent ground cover. It was subsequently recognized that heavy grass seeding should be carried out immediately following heavy-equipment operations when soils are generally uncompacted, and the seed can be lightly raked into the ground. Other types of grass seeding mixtures and fast-growing herbaceous covers better suited to soil and site conditions in the park are also being evaluated by the Park Service for use in their rehabilitation program.

Willow wattles were planted during the fall of 1978. The effectiveness of wattles in inhibiting erosion on disturbed slopes varied considerably with differing site characteristics. Wattles tended to work well on moist, steep sites in fine-grained soils (Fig. 9.30). They did not work well, on the other hand, on dry, rocky slopes. On these sites, dry ravel appeared to be a major surficial erosion process, and physical barriers (e.g., wooded terraces) (Fig. 9.31) were a more cost-effective mode of erosion control than wattling.

Fig. 9.31.   Slope stabilized against erosion by wooded terraces. These terraces are constructed on contour and supported by woody material (limbs, split logs, etc.) which is staked in place. Terraces can be seeded to grass as shown in the photo. Wooded terraces were found to be more cost-effective than wattling on biologically harsh (dry) sites in the Park. Site of photo is Upper Bond Creek, rehabilitation unit 79–1, Redwood National Park.

9.4 CASE HISTORY NO. 3—CUT SLOPE STABILIZATION: LAKE TAHOE BASIN

9.4.1 Location of the Project and the Erosion Problem

The Lake Tahoe Basin is located in the Sierra Nevada Mountains about 100 miles east northeast of Sacramento, California. Elevations of the planting sites were from approximately 6300 ft (near the lake level) to over 7000 ft. A site location map (Fig. 9.32) identifies these planting sites, which were on the south, west, and north sides of the lake.

Man-made disturbances of soils in the high Sierras revegetate very slowly. Highway cuts constructed 15–30 or more years ago are often devoid of vegetation and may erode at rates from 50 to 300 yards or more per acre per year (Howell, 1971). Some of the cuts involved in this project were these old cuts, and some were from more recent construction. Adverse effects of this erosion are of particular concern because of the effects on the quality of Lake Tahoe. The particulate and nutrient pollution in Lake Tahoe is degrading the water quality at an alarming rate.

9.4.1.1 Objectives of the Project.

The project had a number of objectives, three of them being to: (1) select promising plant species for revegetation of typical problem sites; (2) determine cultural requirements (including propagation) for the native species selected as suitable for revegetation; and (3) develop methods of establishing grass and woody plants to utilize the best attributes of each to stabilize disturbed areas (Leiser et al., 1974).

9.4.1.2 Soils of the Project Area.

Soils on the south and southwest sides of the lake are, for the most part, derived from decomposed granite, and those on the northwest and north are of andesite origin. Occasional occurrences of mixed alluvial and glacial deposits are encountered throughout the area. Plantings were made on all three types of soil.

9.4.1.3 Climate of the Project Area.

The planting sites are in an area of 30–45 inches annual precipitation, which occurs mostly from October to March, much falling as snow. Annual variations can be very great. Summer rains are erratic and consist mostly of scattered thunderstorms, usually of less than 0.10 inch. For example, rainfall records for 1973 at one of the Luther Pass sites showed only 3.00 inches of rain from April 1 to October 6. Of this, 1.11 inches fell in one storm on August 26–27. Three other storms accounted for 0.67 inch. In June–July there were 29, and in August–September 23 successive days with no measurable rain.

The average precipitation (in inches) for a 29-year

period of record at Tahoe City at the north end of the lake was: January, 5.84; February, 5.85, March, 3.72; April, 2.18; May, 0.95; June, 0.70; July, 0.25; August, 0.16; September, 0.50; October, 1.37; November, 2.67; December, 5.07; and annual, 29.35 (Hambidge, 1941).

Temperature records (°F) for the same period were: January average, 26.3; July average, 60.6; maximum, 94; and minimum, −15. A 24-year record gave an average frost-free growing season of 72 days, with average dates of last spring frost on June 22 and first fall frost on September 2.

The microclimates on the planting sites vary greatly because of differences in elevation, aspect, and surrounding terrain. The drought during the growing season, the short duration of that season, and the long period during which plants are subject to frost heaving contribute to the difficulty of establishing plants on these sites.

9.4.1.4 Vegetation of the Project Area.

The Lake Tahoe Basin is in an area of mixed conifer forest. There are six dominant species: Jeffrey pine, *Pinus jeffreyi* Grev. & Balf.; lodgepole pine, *P. murryana* Grev. & Balf.; sugar pine, *P. lambertiana* Dougl.; white fir, *Abies concolor* (Gord.) Lindl. ex Hildebr.; red fir, *A. magnifica* A. Murr.; and incense cedar, *Calocedrus decurrens* (Torr.) Florin (Syn.: *Libocedrus decurrens* Torr.). Six other species occur in limited numbers. There are only two deciduous tree species, with limited distribution. About 57 species of deciduous and evergreen shrubs are native in the basin. Some have widespread distribution, whereas others are relatively rare. The revegetation research was limited to these shrub species for long-term results and to introduced grass species for temporary control.

9.4.2 Preliminary Research

This project involved a geographic area and a plant spectrum where there was little or no record of past research. One mandate was that the revegetation was to be accomplished without supplemental irrigation, either at planting time or later. None of the plant spectrum was available commercially, and little information was available on the propagation or growing of these species. Some preliminary research was necessary before a revegetation plan could be developed.

9.4.2.1 Site and Vegetation Analysis.

The first step was to visit as many nonvegetated sites in the area as possible to determine the kinds of soils and the susceptibility to erosion, and to try to determine the causes of the absence of natural vegetation on these sites. Sites that had revegetated naturally were also studied for clues as to the differences between sites. Many sites were obviously

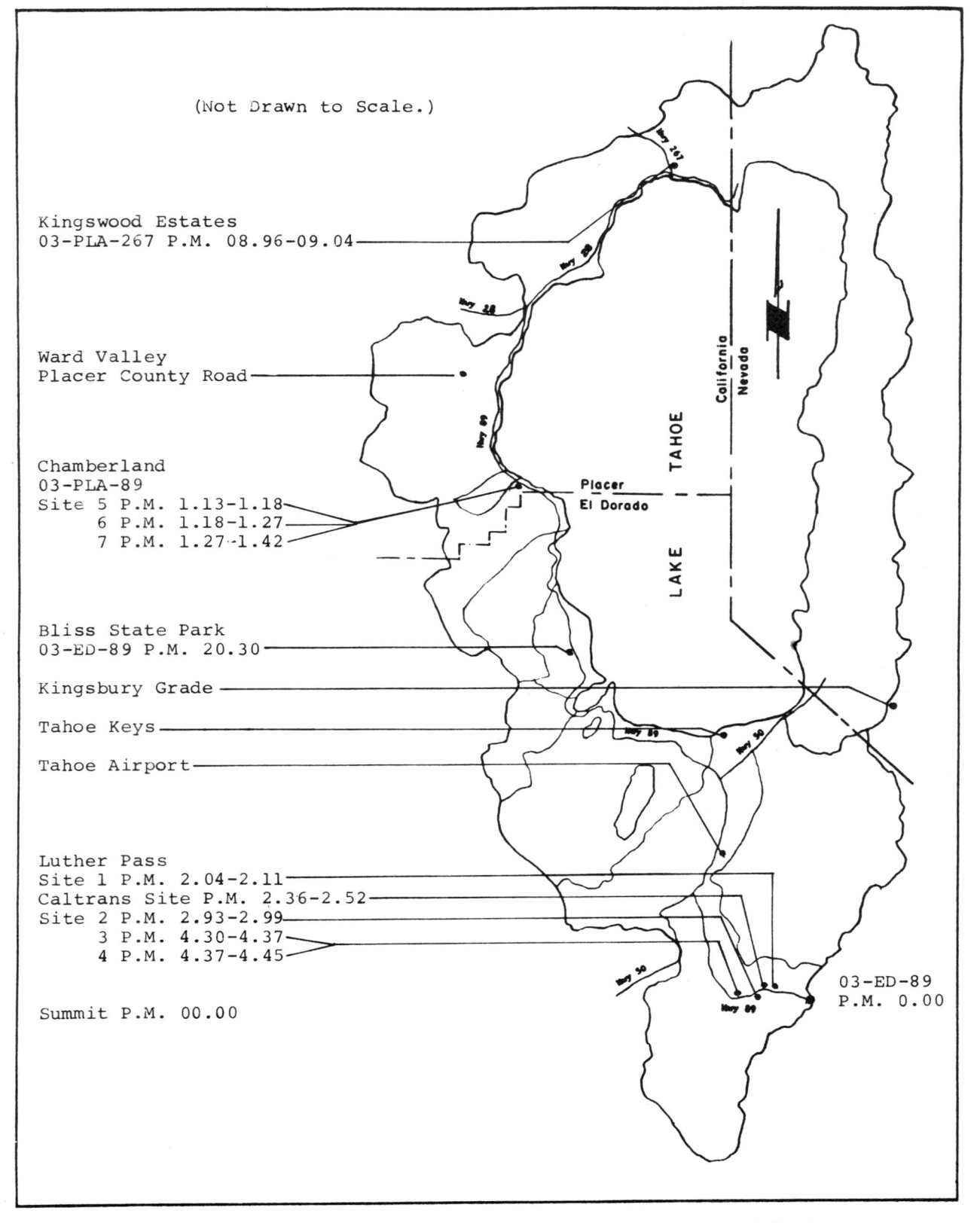

(Not Drawn to Scale.)

Kingswood Estates
03-PLA-267 P.M. 08.96-09.04

Ward Valley
Placer County Road

Chamberland
03-PLA-89
Site 5 P.M. 1.13-1.18
     6 P.M. 1.18-1.27
     7 P.M. 1.27-1.42

Bliss State Park
03-ED-89 P.M. 20.30

Kingsbury Grade

Tahoe Keys

Tahoe Airport

Luther Pass
Site 1 P.M. 2.04-2.11
Caltrans Site P.M. 2.36-2.52
Site 2 P.M. 2.93-2.99
     3 P.M. 4.30-4.37
     4 P.M. 4.37-4.45

Summit P.M. 00.00

Placer
El Dorado

California
Nevada

LAKE   TAHOE

03-ED-89
P.M. 0.00

Fig. 9.32.   Principal site locations, Tahoe revegetation plantings, Lake Tahoe Basin, California.

too steep and too unstable to retain any seeds that might fall on them. Other sites appeared to be relatively stable because of the lack of any rill or gully erosion. Trial plantings made in the fall of 1971 revealed that even these sites might erode as much as 4 inches during the winter and spring months. The majority of the plants from these plantings were found at the base of the slopes or in drainage ways the following spring. Plot stakes and plants remaining on the slopes were often exposed as much as 4 inches.

Vegetation surveys were made concurrently. Attention was focused on those species that had widespread occurrence, were found on a range of soil types, were invaders of either naturally or man-disturbed sites, and had potential for either seed or vegetative propagation. These surveys reduced the list of about 57 species to about 27, a reduction of slightly over 50 percent. As the project progressed, the list decreased further to about 12 species because of constraints of time and resources, lack of good seed crops, and difficulties of propagation or culture of some species (Table 9.3). Of these, 7 gave satisfactory results in the final revegetation plantings. The other 5 were used in limited quantities or situations, and results were inconclusive. Other species of potential value are listed in Table 9.4.

Additional time for research would undoubtedly increase the plant spectrum available. For example, subsequent research has solved the propagation problem for two other species that were not included because of these problems. These two species were judged prime candidates for revegetation on other criteria. There were many herbaceous species (forbs) that would have made good revegetation candidates. However, time constraints and the research mandate (i.e., use native woody plants) did not allow their inclusion.

9.4.2.2 Propagation Research.
The research on propagation included both seed and vegetative methods. Both methods have advantages and disadvantages. Seed propagation is often cheaper. When successful, it also permits direct seeding to be done. It may be the only way to propagate plants for which vegetative methods have not been worked out. However, many native plants only set good seed crops at intervals of several years, and seed dormancy may make it very difficult to propagate some species (e.g., *Arctostaphylos*). Some species are slow to produce planting-size stock from seed; vegetative propagation will produce planting-size stock more rapidly than will seed propagation with these species. Also, vegetative propagation is not dependent on a good seed crop. Disadvantages of vegetative propagation include difficulties of propagation and scarcity of suitable quality and quantity of cutting wood.

Propagation research on both seed and vegetative methods were conducted on candidate plant materials at the Lake Tahoe sites. Research procedures for both propagation methods are described fully in Section 6.5.3.

9.4.2.3 Interim Stabilization Research.
The overall objective of this project was to establish permanent woody vegetation for erosion control. It was recognized that grasses and other interim measures would be necessary to accomplish this objective. Considerable research was conducted with grass species and legumes and with various erosion control chemicals and mulches to determine the best methods of interim erosion control.

Erosion Control Chemicals and Mulches. In the fall of 1971 a total of 15 erosion control chemicals or mulches were compared in replicated tests at several sites in the project area. Results of those tests at Ward Valley are

Table 9.3. Woody shrub species used in Lake Tahoe Basin revegetation plantings, 1972–73.

SCIENTIFIC NAME	COMMON NAME
Alnus tenuifolia Nutt.[1]	Sierran alder
Arctostaphylos nevadensis Gray[2]	Pine-mat manzanita
Artemisia tridentata Nutt.[2]	Sagebrush. Great Basin sage
Chrysolepis sempervirens (Dougl. ex Hook.) Hjelmquist (Syn.: *Castanopsis sempervirens*)[3]	Sierra chinquapin
Ceanothus prostratus Benth.[2]	Squaw carpet. Mahala mats
Cornus stolonifera Michx.[4]	American dogwood. Red-osier dogwood
Penstemon newberryi Gray[2]	Newberry penstemon. Mountain pride
Populus tremuloides Michx.[1]	quaking aspen
Purshia tridentata (Pursh) DC.[2]	Bitterbrush. Antelope brush
Salix lemmonii Bebb[1,2]	NCN
Sambucus microbotrys Rydb.[3,4]	Mountain red elderberry
Spiraea densiflora Nutt. ex Rydb.[1]	Mountain spiraea

[1]Cuttings only. [2]Large numbers. [3]Limited numbers. [4]Cuttings and transplants.

Table 9.4. Species of potential value for revegetation in the Tahoe Basin on which additional research needs to be done.

SCIENTIFIC NAME	COMMON NAME
Chrysothamnus nauseosus (Pall.) Britt.	Rabbitbrush
Lonicera conjugalis Kell.	No common name
Nama lobbii Gray	Wooly nama
Prunus emarginata (Dougl.) Walp.	Bitter cherry
Quercus vaccinifolia Kell.	Huckleberry oak
Rhamnus rubra Greene	No common name
Ribes spp. (several species)	Currant, gooseberry
Rosa woodsii Lindl. var. *ultramontana* (Wats.) Jeps.	No common name
Rubus parviflorus Nutt.	Thimbleberry
Symphoricarpos acutus (Gray) Dieck	Sharpleaf snowberry

shown in Table 9.5. None was superior to wood fiber at 1000 lb/acre applied with seed and fertilizer (rating of 8) or to the control with seed and fertilizer alone (rating of 7). Grass stands were rated on a 1–10 basis with 1 = none, and 10 = excellent. The plastics sometimes reduced plant establishment, and they sometimes failed and peeled off the slopes in sheets (Fig. 9.33). Results varied from site to site. Numerous treatments were effective on Kingsbury Grade, whereas none was effective on Luther Pass.

Two other products, Landlock and Ecology Control, were tested later. In one test Landlock had fewer grass seedlings than wood fiber, and a crust formed that did not adhere to the slope. In a second test, both performed satisfactorily but were not superior to wood fiber.

Table 9.5. Effect of erosion control chemicals on grass establishment at Ward Valley. Seeded October 1971; evaluated June 1974.

TREATMENT	RATE	GRASS STAND*
Control A	Seed along, no fertilizer, no cover	4
Wood Fiber	Seed + fertilizer only, no cover	7
Wood Fiber	1000 lb/A, 3000 gpa water	8
Terra-Krete	180 gpa (6% in 3000 gpa water)	5
Verdyol Super	79.5 lb/A, + wood fiber 1000 lb/A, 3000 gpa water	6
Ecology Control	80 lb/A, + wood fiber 1000 lb/A, 3000 gpa water	6
Soil Seal	87.2 gpa, + wood fiber 1000 lb/A, 6000 gpa water	4
Curasol AE	90 gpa, + wood fiber 750 lb/A, 3000 gpa water	5
Terra Tack I	20 lb/A, + ground barley straw 1000 lb/A, water 1000 gpa	7
Terra Tack I	30 lb/A in 1000 gpa water applied over whole straw at 2000 lb/A	6
Terra Tack I	30 lb/A in 1500 gpa water	5
Aquatain	130 gpa in 1000 gpa water	6
Earth-Pac	1 gal/5000 sq ft in 3000 gpa water	6
SSO	10 gpa	5
Excelsior Erosion Control Blanket		7

*10 = excellent, 1 = none.

Excelsior and paper mats or blankets were included in some early trails. Initial results were promising so they were used in the final slope treatments at two locations, sites 3-4 on Luther Pass and sites 5-6-7 at the north end of the lake. Single and double thicknesses of a woven paper mat were compared to excelsior mat and to wood fiber hydromulch at 1000 lb/acre. Evaluation in July 1973 showed that no treatment was an improvement over wood fiber alone. A year later the wood fiber was superior at site 5-6-7 in two of three replications and inferior to excelsior at site 3-4 in two of three replications, for an overall average of no difference. Excelsior was only slightly better than the single paper mat. Doubling the paper mat appeared to reduce plant establishment. When the costs of the mat materials are considered, their use in the project area cannot be justified.

Herbaceous Plants for Interim Stabilization. One objective of this project was to evaluate herbaceous species for interim erosion control. Selection criteria, in addition to survival, included minimum top growth to minimize fire hazard, intrusion on the visual quality of the sites, and competition with the woody vegetation, and degree of root growth for erosion control.

Evaluation of herbaceous plants for interim erosion control in the Tahoe Basin was begun in the fall of 1970. Observations in the fourth growing season indicated there were many good, commercially available, perennial grasses but no suitable legumes among those tested. Native legumes were not tested because of lack of seed. The use of a rhizomatous grass is desirable because of its ability to spread and bind the soils. The first four grasses in Table 9.6 are rhizomatous; western wheatgrass has the most rhizomes and has the shortest top growth, while 'Oahe' intermediate wheatgrass produces much more top growth.

Small seeded bunchgrass such as crested wheatgrass, 'Sherman' big bluegrass, 'Durar' hard fescue, and orchardgrass are important because they give quick ground cover. They may later be replaced by the rhizomatous wheatgrasses. 'Potomac' orchardgrass was excellent

Fig. 9.33. Erosion control chemicals should be tested on individual sites before extensive use. Some form sheets that slough or peel from the slopes as shown in the photo. This plastic polymer tested at Lake Tahoe protected the slope from erosion initially but soon failed and actually increased susceptibility to erosion by concentrating runoff water. In many cases grass establishment is also reduced.

for this purpose; it is inexpensive and available in quantity.

Cereals (wheat and rye) gave some initial protection but have limitations. First, they may persist on the better growing sites and be very weedy. Second, they compete severely with the other species in the mix. Orchardgrass would be a better choice for quick cover.

Legumes did not survive well on these severe sites. Survival was limited to the best sites.

9.4.2.4 Fall vs. Spring Planting.

Fall planting is often recommended when plants must rely on rainfall for all their water needs. Fall planting allows a maximum time for plant establishment before periods of summer drought. Fall vs. spring plantings were compared for the three years of this project. Survival of spring plantings was higher in almost every case. At no time was fall planting markedly superior to spring planting. Transplants of *Penstemon newberryi* and willow cuttings gave approximately equal results in many cases (Table 9.7).

Comparisons of very early spring plantings (just as the snow melted) and those made in midspring (early May) indicated that the later planting dates were usually preferable.

The differences in survival among the several planting dates were attributed to at least two factors. The disturbances of the slopes in the fall or very early spring accelerated slope erosion, and frost heaving was more severe on disturbed slopes. The second factor may have been the difficulties encountered in moving plants from a relatively mild growing area to the project area. Some damage occurred to plants from freezing. In areas where

these two situations are not a factor, fall planting may be best.

9.4.2.5 Willow Cuttings.

Vegetation surveys will indicate that these species only occur on wet sites. This is so because, in nature, they reproduce from short-lived seed that must fall on sites that are moist in late spring or early summer. When propagated vegetatively they will survive and even thrive on relatively dry sites. Kraebel's work demonstrated this vividly in the dry mountains of southern California (Kraebel, 1936).

Research on willow cuttings was done with only one of the six species native in the Tahoe Basin, *Salix lemmonii*. This species was chosen because it had the most widespread distribution there.

Greenhouse trials indicated that treatment with hormone (IBA) increased speed of rooting and numbers of roots. Under the adverse conditions in the project area these differences were not apparent. Leaching of cuttings for 3 days also increased rooting in greenhouse trials, but benefits of this treatment could not be demonstrated in the field.

Cutting size has been recognized as a factor in successful rooting of willow. Trials with three sizes of cuttings, $\frac{1}{4}''$ or less, $\frac{3}{8}''$-$\frac{3}{4}''$, and $\frac{7}{8}''$ and larger, in diameter, gave best rooting with the intermediate-size cuttings. These results differ from those reported by others indicating that cuttings larger than 1 inch in diameter rooted best.

9.4.2.6 Fertility Studies.

The fertility status of some of these mountain soils was determined by

Table 9.6. Herbaceous species adaptablility for interim erosion control in the Lake Tahoe Basin. Ratings were made during the fourth growing season, with 1 = none and 10 = excellent.

SPECIES	1	2	3	4	5	6	7	8
Western wheatgrass, Colo. grown *Agropyron smithii* Rydb.	7	3	2	3	4	9	6	9
Sodar streambank wheatgrass *Agropyron riparium* Scribn. & Smith 'Sodar'	9	6	4	5	4	5	2	5
Topar pubescent wheatgrass *Agropyron trichophorum* (Link) Richt. 'Topar'	10	8	6	9	7	9	8	9
Oahe intermediate wheatgrass *Agropyron intermedium* (Host) Beauv. 'Oahe'	10	9	5	10	6	8	8	10
Norden crested wheatgrass *Agropyron cristatum* (L.) Gaertn. 'Norden'	10	8	3	6	7	9	1	6
Durar hard fesuce *Festuca ovina* var. *duriuscula* (L.) Koch 'Durar'	10	6	4	7	5	10	7	7
Potomac orchardgrass *Dactylis glomerata* L. 'Potomac'	9	9	6	5	3	8	—	5
Sherman big bluegrass *Poa ampla* Merr. 'Sherman'	6	8	8	10	6	10	10	10
Lincoln smooth brome *Bromus inermis* Leyss. 'Lincoln'	5	6	6	8	6	9	4	5
Nugaines winter wheat *Triticum aestivum* L. 'Nugains'	1	1	1	1	1	1	—	1
Tetra Petkus cereal rye *Secale cerale* L. 'Tetra Petkus'	1	1	1	1	2	1	1	1
White clover *Trifolium repens* L.	1	1	1	1	1	1	-	1
Alsike clover *Trifolium hybridum* L.	4	2	1	1	1	1	—	1
Chesapeake red clover *Trifolium pratense* L. 'Chesapeake'	4	2	2	1	1	1	—	2
Ladak alfalfa *Medicago sativa* L. 'Ladak'	2	3	—	—	—	—	—	—
Rambler alfalfa *M. sativa* L. 'Rambler'	3	5	—	—	—	—	—	—
Cicar milkvetch *Astragalus cicer* L. 'Cicar'	4	2	—	—	—	—	—	—

greenhouse pot tests (see Section 6.3.3.4 for methodology). Experience had shown that most Sierran soils are deficient in one or more elements necessary for satisfactory grass establishment. The pot tests indicated deficiencies of nitrogen, sulfur, and phosphorus. Yields, relative to the complete fertilizer controls, were approximately 7, 31, and 44 percent respectively for these elements. Potassium may have been slightly limiting on soils derived from andesite but not on those derived from granite (see Fig. 6.2).

Field tests were also conducted, and they confirmed the need for nitrogen, sulfur, and phosphorus for grasses.

Greenhouse pot tests using *Penstemon newberryi* gave large responses to nitrogen and moderate responses to phosphorus and sulfur. These tests were with a sedimentary soil of andesitic origin from Ward Valley and a decomposed granite soil from Luther Pass. Field trials were conducted using five species; *Penstemon newberryi* and *Cerococarpus ledifolius* Nutt., mountain mahogany, were planted at Ward Valley, and *Archtostaphylos nevadensis, Artemisia tridentata,* and *Purshia tridentata* at Luther Pass.

Fertilizer treatments were: control (no fertilizer); two soluble fertilizers, ammonium sulfate and ammonium sulfate/phosphate; and four controlled-release fertilizers, magnesium ammonium/potassium phosphate (MagAmp©), ureaformaldehyde (UF), sulfur-coated urea, and isobutylidiene diurea (IBDU). All were applied at 0.5 g nitrogen per plant in the bottom of the planting hole with the plant placed directly above. Additional sulfur and phosphorus were added as needed to the controlled-release fertilizers to supply adequate amounts of these elements.

Mean survival, pooling all species, was not reduced by any of the controlled-release fertilizers although, for certain species, there may have been a trend for reduced survival. Survival was lower for all species in both soluble fertilizer treatments except for *Artemisia tridentata* with ammonium sulfate.

Three species, *Arctostaphylos, Cercocarpus,* and *Purshia,* made little growth the first season; thus there were no apparent growth responses to fertilization. It could not be determined whether the lack of growth was due to low nutritional requirements of these species or the lack of water cn these sites, or a combination of these factors. The growth responses of *Artemisia* and *Penstemon* suggest that the lack of water was at least a contributing factor.

Growth of *Artemisia* at Luther Pass and *Penstemon* in Ward Valley was influenced by position on the slope (Figs. 9.34 and 9.35). In both cases growth was greatest at the bottom of the slope and least at the top for both the unfertilized controls and the complete (N, P, S) fertilizer treatments, a result that was attributed to differences in soil moisture. The differences in slopes of the regression lines indicate response to the fertilizers.

Growth and survival data for *Artemisia tridentata* for individual treatments are shown in Figs. 9.36 and 9.37. Growth data for this species are expressed as height because of the strong upright growth habit. Fertilized plants were 17 to 38 percent larger than control plants, but this response was not significant because of variations within and between replications. Survival was slightly lower, but not significantly so for the controlled-release

Table 9.7. Survival on June 4, 1974 of fall 1972 and spring 1973 plantings at four sites on Highway 89, Tahoe Basin, of five species from peat pot liners and one species of unrooted cuttings. Data are given as number surviving/number planted (S/P) and percent survival (%) and are totals of all subplots on each site. [1]

	SITE 1		SITE 2		SITE 3, 4		SITE 5, 6, 7		TOTALS	
	S/P	%	S/P	%	S/P	%	S/P	%	S/P	%
FALL 1972 PLANTINGS										
Transplants:										
Arctostaphylos nevadensis	0/50	0	0/50	0	2/150	1.3	0/148	0	2/398	0.5
Artemisia tridentata	2/50	4	0/50	0	2/50	4	0/148	0	4/298	1.3
Ceanothus prostratus	1/40	2.5	0/50	0	—	—	17/120	14.2	18/210	8.6
Penstemon newberryi	9/160	5.6	53/160	33.1	206/320	64.4	501/800	62.6	769/1440	53
Purshia tridentata	0/100	0	—	—	0/100	0	0/300	0	0/500	0
SUBTOTALS [2]	12/400	3	53/310	17.1	210/621	33.9	518/1516	34.2	793/2846	27.9
Cuttings:										
Salix lemmonii	142/300	47.3	315/600	52.5	271/600	45.2	417/1000	41.7	1145/2500	45.8
SPRING 1973 PLANTINGS										
Transplants:										
Arctostaphylos nevadensis	6/200	3	18/200	9	39/320	12.2	57/400	14.3	120/1120	10.7
Artemisia tridentata	166/280	59.3	175/280	62.5	375/480	78.1	263/560	47.0	979/1600	61.2
Ceanothus prostratus	33/600	5.5	69/600	11.5	398/1400	38.4	275/1300	21.2	775/3900	19.9
Penstemon newberryi	47/400	11.8	100/400	25	682/960	71	594/1020	58.2	1423/2780	51.2
Purshia tridentata	71/280	25.4	85/280	30.4	197/480	41	35/480	7.3	388/1520	25.5
SUBTOTALS [2]	323/1760	18.4	447/1760	25.4	1691/3640	46.5	1224/3760	32.6	3685/10920	33.7
Cuttings:										
Salix lemmonii	179/350	51.1	317/700	45.3	411/850	48.4	527/1100	47.9	1434/3000	47.8
GRAND TOTALS										
Transplants	335/2160	15.5	500/2170	24.2	1901/4260	44.6	1742/5276	33	4478/13766	32.5
Cuttings	321/650	49.4	632/1300	48.6	682/1450	47	944/2100	45	2579/5500	46.9

[1] Site locations: Site 1, Luther Pass, 03-ED-89 P.M. 2.04-2.11; Site 2, Luther Pass, 03-ED-89 P.M. 2.93-2.99; Site 3, 4, Luther Pass, 03-ED-89 P.M. 4.30-4.45; Site 5, 6, 7, Chamberland, 03-PLA-89 P.M. 1.13-1.42.
[2] Subtotal percentages of fall and spring plantings are weighted because of the large numbers of *P. newberryi* planted both seasons. This was the only species of transplants with good survival of fall plantings.

fertilizers and ammonium sulfate, but was significantly less with the ammonium sulfate/phosphate treatment.

Growth and survival data for *Penstemon newberryi* for individual treatments are shown in Fig. 9.38. Growth is expressed as area covered because of the low spreading habit. This species made more growth in every fertilizer treatment except ammonium sulfate compared to the control. Growth increases were from 60 to 100 percent, and were significant at the 95 percent level for ureaformaldehyde, sulfur-coated urea, and ammonium sulfate/ phosphate and at the 99 percent level for MagAmp© and IBDU. Survival was not reduced by any of the controlled-release fertilizers, but was significantly reduced with both soluble fertilizers.

Generalizations probably should not be made regarding the benefits of fertilizing woody plants on revegetation projects because of differences in response of woody species to nutrition and to various parameters of the microenvironment, especially soils and moisture.

9.4.3 Integrated Slope Plantings

The concluding phases of this research project involved the integrated treatment of a number of highway cuts on State Route 89 in the Lake Tahoe Basin. Treatments included engineering and biological methods of erosion control. These treatments were selected on the basis of site surveys and the results of preliminary research findings. They were both research- and demonstration-oriented. Site preparation, wattling installation, initial planting, and grass seeding were done in the fall of 1972. Final planting of cuttings and transplants were made the following spring. Some of the research treatments gave less than optimum results. For example, even though

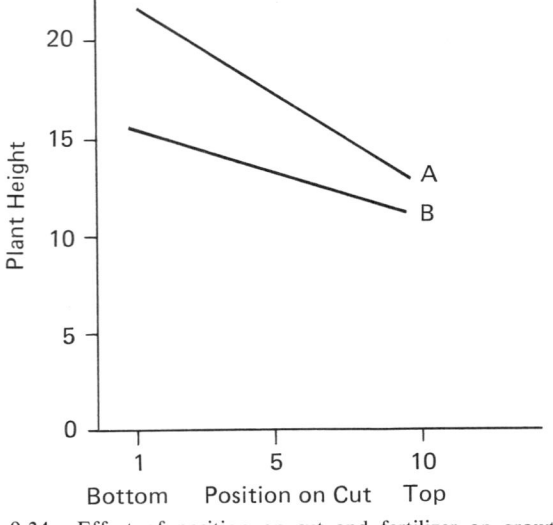

Fig. 9.34. Effect of position on cut and fertilizer on growth of *Artemisia tridentata* at Luther Pass, Tahoe Basin. A = mean of all NPS fertilizer treatments; $Y = 22.8 - 0X$, $r = -0.83$. B = unfertilized control; $Y = 16.2 - 0.54X$, $r = -0.58$.

preliminary research had indicated that spring planting was superior to fall, planting was done in both seasons to verify earlier results. About 25 percent of the plantings were made in the fall and 75 percent in the spring. Such experiments undoubtedly reduced overall success. Planting and survival data for these sites are given in Table 9.7. Only those species planted in quantity and common to most sites are included..Data for all subplots and for contiguous sites are combined. Three sites were located on Luther Pass, and one site was at Chamberland near the north end of the lake. Locations are shown in Fig. 9.32.

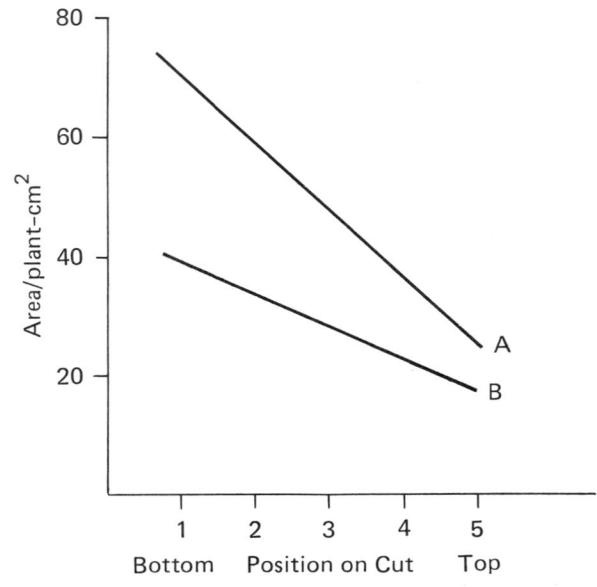

Fig. 9.35. Effect of position on cut and fertilizer on growth of *Penstemon newberryi* at Ward Valley, Tahoe Basin. A = mean of all NPS fertilizer treatments; $Y = 85.4 - 11X$, $r = -0.97$. B = unfertilized control; $Y = 46.8 - 5.8X$, $r = -0.76$.

9.4.3.1   Site 1, 03-ED-89 P.M. 2.04-2.11.

Site 1 was a south-facing cut about 420 ft long and 20 ft high with an average slope angle of 34 degrees (1.3:1). The soil was a compact, cemented sediment that appeared suitable for serrating or benching. Such benches have been useful for providing stable microsites for plant establishment, particularly in the eastern United States. Benches were cut by hand, approximately 24–30 inches wide on most of the slope (Fig. 9.39). Planting was done in three rows on each bench with additional plants on the upper part of the slope. Willow cuttings were stuck along the slope toe. A top-of-cut ditch was constructed to divert runoff from the slope above the cut. By the following spring one-half or more of each bench had collapsed, and many of the transplants were lost or buried. Willow cuttings had 47.3 percent survival.

Spring planting was done on the remainder of the benches and on the slopes between them. The slope was very unstable at that time.

Survival of the fall transplants was only 3 percent after two winters, and of the spring transplants, 18.4 percent after one winter. This was the lowest survival of any of the planting sites and appeared due to the instability of the slope resulting from the serration. Figure 9.40 shows the sparse plant stand in May 1974. Willow cuttings planted in the spring had slightly better survival, 51.1 percent, than those planted in the fall. By October 1976 (Fig. 9.41) fairly good plant cover existed on the bottom half of the slope. This cover was mainly willows and grasses.

9.4.3.2   Site 2, 03-ED-89 P.M. 2.93-2.99.

Site 2 was a cold, north-facing cut of compacted sediments that had been eroding severely. Many large boulders, up to 4 or more ft in diameter had come off the slope, and many more were exposed. The top of cut had some overhang (Fig. 9.42). Slope angle averaged 35 degrees (1.4:1) and reached 45 degrees (1:1) in some parts. The length was 320 ft, and maximum height was about 20–25 ft. A breast wall was constructed for about one-half the length of the cut to reduce the effective height and to allow a reduction in slope angle. At the downhill end of the cut the wall was about 6 ft high (Fig. 9.43). Material scaled from the top of the cut was used to backfill behind the breast wall. Willow wattling was placed in all filled areas.

Penstemon newberryi was the only species of the four planted in quantity in the fall that survived. Survival was 33.1 percent, giving overall survival for fall plantings of 17.1 percent. Survival of spring plantings was 25.4 percent overall, with some of each species surviving. Fall-planted willow cuttings had slightly higher survival than spring plantings (52.5 vs. 45.3 percent). Most bundles of wattling had some rooting. It was felt that had wattling been placed on the whole slope, stabilization and plant survival might have been enhanced. Vegetation establish-

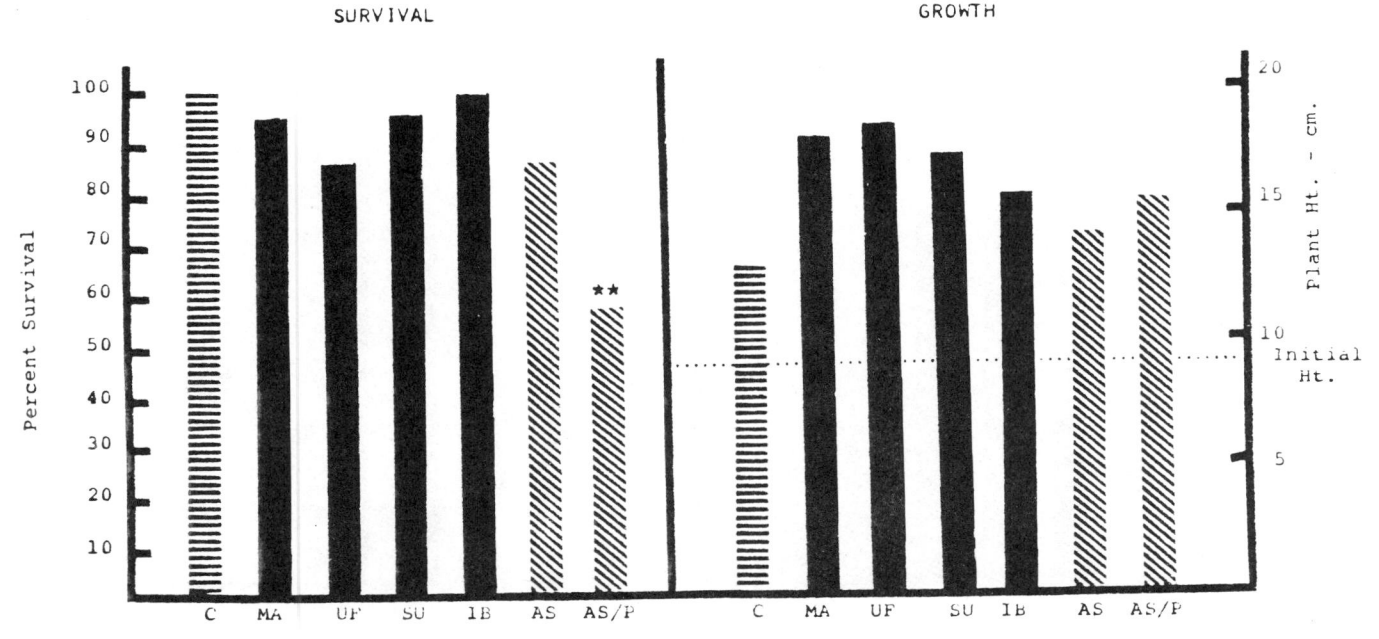

Fig. 9.36. Growth and survival of road cut plantings of *Artemisia tridentata* on Luther Pass, Tahoe Basin, as influenced by fertilizer source. Rate of fertilizer application, 0.5 g nitrogen per plant. Planted May 16, 1973; data taken September 29, 1973.

ment on the uppermost portion of the slope was not satisfactory. It had not been possible to reduce the slope angle to that desired in this portion because of right-of-way limitations. Since the original installation, fiberglass roving has been placed at the top of the cut to reduce erosion (Fig. 9.44).

9.4.3.3 Sites 3 and 4, 03-ED-89 P.M. 4.30-4.45.
Sites 3 and 4 were two contiguous southwest-facing cuts totaling 800 ft in length with a height ranging from about 6 ft at the upper end to 15–20 ft through much of its length. The slope angle was variable but averaged 35

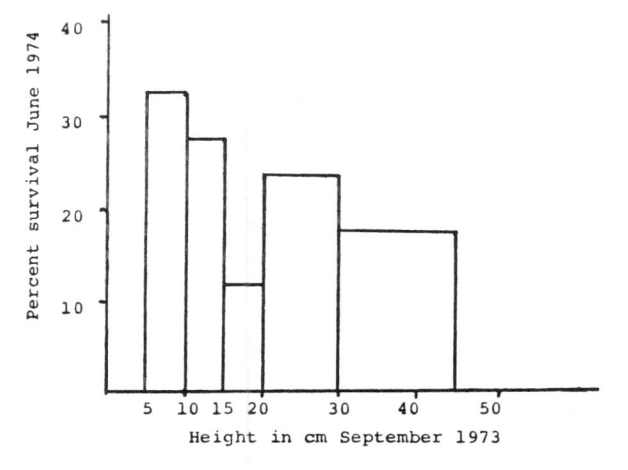

Fig. 9.37. Relation of first-year growth to first-winter survival for *Artemisia tridentata* planted May 1973, at approximately 7000 ft elevation on Luther Pass, 03–ED–89 P.M. 2.36.

degrees (1.4:1). The cut was of residual decomposed granite parent material (Fig. 9.45).

A short breast wall was constructed where the cut was highest and steepest to permit a reduction in slope angle and to prevent further undercutting of several very large rocks protruding from the cut at this point. Willow wattling was placed in several areas of loose material and around the badly eroding culvert entrance where the two cuts joined (Fig. 9.46). Project supervisors were unable to be present when this wattling was placed, and much of it was improperly installed. Rooting was poor, and many of the bundles were on top of the ground by spring (Fig. 9.47).

The principal surviving species of fall transplants was again *Penstemon newberryi*. Total survival for fall transplants after two winters was 29.2 percent, while that of spring plantings after one winter was 46.5 percent. Fall- and spring-planted willow cuttings survived at 45.2 and 48.4 percent respectively.

On this site the top of the cut was relatively stable, but the plant establishment was low. The four species thought to be most drought-tolerant had been concentrated in this area. *Penstemon newberryi* was usually planted on the lower portions of cuts where water relations were assumed to be better. In one subplot this species was planted on the top third of the cut. Survival was excellent, suggesting that this species may be more drought-tolerant than predicted (Fig. 9.48).

By the end of the third growing season the bottom two-thirds of the cut was well vegetated, and the top of the cut had fair to moderate plant cover (Fig. 9.49A,B).

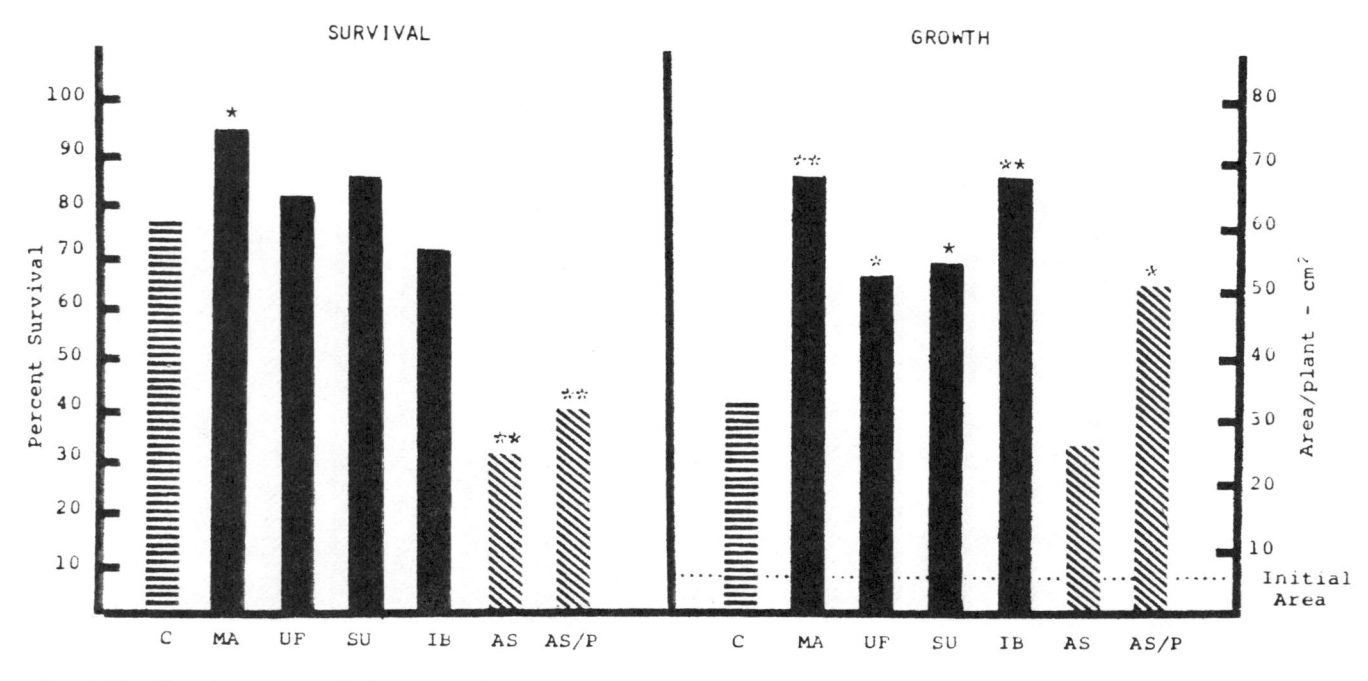

Fig. 9.38. Growth and survival of road cut plantings of *Penstemon newberryi* in Ward Valley, Tahoe Basin, as influenced by fertilizer source. Rate of fertilizer application, 0.5 g nitrogen per plant. Planted May 16, 1973; data taken September 29, 1973.

9.4.3.4 Grass Plantings, All Sites.

Various grass-planting treatments were overseeded on all sites following site prepartion, transplanting, and sticking of cuttings in the fall of 1972. The major portions were seeded with a mix of perennial grasses, wood fiber mulch, and complete fertilizer. Some subplots were left unseeded, and some had various blanket mulches applied. A typical grass mixture was 'Sherman' big bluegrass, 3#/A, 'Potomac' orchardgrass, 13#/A, 'Topar' pubescent wheatgrass, 21#/A,

and 'Oahe' intermediate wheatgrass, 20#/A. The grasses and fertilizer were applied by hydroseeding with wood fiber at 3000#/A.

Grass stands were sampled on all sites during the fourth week of July 1973 and again in June 1974. The number of grass seedlings was determined on square-foot samples taken every 3 ft from the base to the top of the slope. Counts averaged 7 plants to the square foot on both counting dates on the areas where spring planting of

Fig. 9.39. Cutting serrations or benches at Site 1, Luther Pass (03-ED-89 P.M. 2.04–2.11) in preparation for planting, October 1972.

Fig. 9.40. Condition of benches at Site 1 two years later. By May 1974 all the benches at Site 1 had failed. Survival of fall 1972 transplants was only 3% and of spring 1973 transplants, 18.4%.

shrubs was made, and 32 and 13 plants/sq ft, respectively, for 1973 and 1974 on the areas where shrubs were planted in the fall. The most obvious difference among all grass treatments was in the amount of grass on the fall shrub-planted areas as compared to the spring shrub-planted areas. The spring shrub planting obviously destroyed much of the grass stand by trampling and burying of the seed and seedlings of grasses. All grass seeding was done in the fall of 1972, following the planting of shrubs. The larger number of seedlings is desirable for erosion protection in the first year, even though they do not live through the second winter. However, the low

count in areas planted with shrubs in the spring and the reduction in grass from 32 to 13 plants/sq ft between July 1972 and June 1973 in the areas where shrubs were planted in the fall may have been beneficial to shrub establishment by reducing competition.

The effects of grass competition on woody plant survival could not be determined because of extreme site-to-site variability, variations in subplot treatments, and numbers and proportions of woody plant species from site to site. However, much of the available literature indicates that heavy stands of herbaceous plants inhibit survival and growth of woody species.

Fig. 9.41. Rooted willow cuttings and grass have given fairly good cover on the bottom half of the slope at Site 1 by October 1976. Few transplants survive.

Fig. 9.42. Site 2, Luther Pass (03–ED–89 P.M. 2.93–2.99) was a severely eroding cut, nearly vertical at the top and with scarcely any vegetation many years after construction.

Fig. 9.43. Treatment of the downhill (north) end of Site 2 (03–ED–89 P.M. 2.93–2.99) consisted of construction of a dry-laid breast wall, scaling, installation of wattling, interplanting with native woody transplants and unrooted willow cuttings, and overseeding with a grass mix.

Fig. 9.44. After three growing seasons the lower half of Site 2 was well vegetated. The steeper upper one-third had low plant survival and was treated with fiberglass roving to reduce erosion. Photographed in October 1976.

9.4.4 CalTrans Cut, 03-ED-89 P.M. 2.36-2.52

The Environmental Improvement Section, Transportation Laboratory, California Department of Transportation (CalTrans) decided to rehabilitate a large cut on Highway 89 on Luther Pass after seeing the results of wattling installed in October 1972 on the Integrated Watershed Sites (Section 9.4.3). Constraints on the project included the number of available man-hours (280, or 35 man-days) and a lack of woody plants for transplanting on the site.

The cut was 845 ft long, about 100 ft high, and had a slope angle of 34 degrees in the lower two-thirds, steepening to nearly vertical in the last 10 ft. The area was about 1 acre. Soil-forming material was residual decomposed granite. Most of the slope was smooth, dry ravel and sheet erosion accounting for much of the soil loss. Two gullies existed where water seepage occurred (Fig. 9.50A,B).

The revegetation plan adopted was to place $3\frac{1}{2}$ rows of wattling on 20-ft centers starting about 30 ft from the toe of the slope and additional rows on about 7-ft centers in the two gullied areas (Fig. 9.50A). Total wattling in-

Fig. 9.45. A portion of Site 3 (03–ED–89 P.M. 4.30–4.45) before rehabilitation. This old cut, of decomposed granite, was mostly devoid of vegetation.

Fig. 9.46.   Badly eroding culvert entrance on Site 3 was revegetated with willow wattling, native woody species transplants, and grass seeding. It was planted in October 1972 and May 1973, and photographed in June 1974.

stalled was 1140 ft. Eight thousand willow cuttings were stuck on approximately 2-ft centers. Grass was over-seeded on the slope, with half the slope receiving a recycled paper mulch and half receiving wood fiber mulch. The grass mix described in Section 9.4.3.4 was used. Construction stakes were used for the wattling installation on this cut. The top 20 ft of the cut was too steep to treat. The wattling and willow cuttings were installed the week of May 21, 1973, and the grass seeding was done the following week.

Most of the wattling bundles rooted. Willow cuttings rooted well, with some sections having 70 percent or better stands. Grass stands were best on the wood fiber mulch plots (Fig. 9.51). Erosion was virtually eliminated during the first year (Figs. 4.12 and 9.52).

Costs of this project are discussed in the next section.

9.4.5   Costs-Benefits

Cost–benefit ratios were estimated for these projects. Those for the integrated watershed plantings are given in Table 9.8, and those for the CalTrans cut on Luther Pass

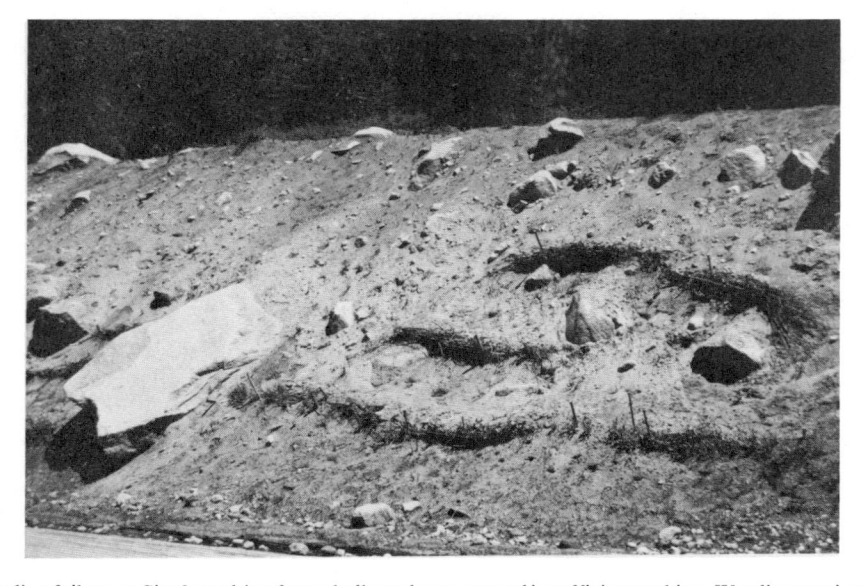

Fig. 9.47.   Willow wattling failure on Site 3 resulting from shallow placement and insufficient staking. Wattling was installed in October 1972, and photographed in June 1973.

Fig. 9.48. *Penstemon newberryi* planted in October 1972 near the top of cut on Site 3 had excellent survival. The species proved more drought-tolerant than expected. Photographed in June 1974.

Table 9.8.   Estimated costs of site preparation and planting integrated watershed plantings in the Tahoe Basin.[a]

| | SITE[b] | | | | | | | |
| | 1 | | 2 | | 3–4 | | 5–6–7 | |
ITEM	NUMBER	DOLLARS	NUMBER	DOLLARS	NUMBER	DOLLARS	NUMBER	DOLLARS
Gross labor, fall, hr	1,258		1,046		1,012		588	
Travel time, hr	186		189		192		149	
Net labor, hr	1,072		857		820		439	
Labor, @ 75% efficiency, hr	804		643		615		329	
Spring labor, hr	36		46		74		84	
Total adjusted labor, hr[a]	840	8,173	689	6,704	689	6,704	413	4,018
Loader/operator, hr	16.5	456	25	690	14	387	13	359
Trucker/operator, hr							15.5	328
Plants	2,197	769	2,800	980	4,580	1,603	5,211	1,824
Hydroseeding		102		120		200		240
Total dollars		9,518		8,479		8,894		6,769
Lineal ft slope	420		320		800		1,530	
Erosion cu yd/yr[d]	32		20		36		79	
Annual maintenance		288		180		324		711
Ten-year maintenance		2,880		1,800		3,240		7,110
Net cost, pollution control, aesthetics[c]		6,638		6,679		5,654		(341)

[a]Cost basis: Labor @ $9.73/hr, loader/operator @ $27.61/hr, truck/operator @ $21.17/hr, plants @ $0.35 each, hydroseeding @ $600/A, erosion cleanup @ $9.00/cu yd. Most fall labor was Young Adult Conservation Corps crews and is calculated at 75% efficiency.
[b]Site: 1 = 03-ED-89 P.M. 2.04-2.11; 2 = 03-ED-89 P.M. 2.93-2.99; 3–4 = 03-ED-89 P.M. 4.30-4.45; 5-6-7 = 03-PLA-89 P.M. 1.13-1.42.
[c]10-year amortization, ( ) = gain. A 20-year amortization would decrease pollution control and aesthetic benefit costs of Site 1 to $3,758, Site 2 to $4,879, Sites 3-4 to $2,413, and Sites 5-6-7 to a gain, ($7,451).
[d]Howell, Richard. 1971. Slope Erosion Transects, Lake Tahoe Basin. Interim Reports, No. M&R 657078-1, Materials and Research Department, Division of Highways, State of California, Sacramento.

Fig. 9.49A.   General view of Site 3, October 1976. Vegetation cover was good on the lower half to two-thirds of the slope and somewhat sparse on the upper one-third. There was a good mix of woody species and grasses. Willow cuttings had survived well. In spite of the sparse establishment at the top of the cut, erosion was negligible cn this cut.

in Table 9.9. Cost bases are given so that costs may be adjusted for local conditions and inflation. In both tables the erosion in cubic yards per year is based on the survey by Howell (1971). These data were determined by measuring annual sediment layers at the base of the slope, estimating sediments carried to streams, estimating sediment removal by interviewing maintenance personnel, and estimating erosion from slope overhang. It is felt that

these estimates were estremely conservative. The Cal-Trans slope, for example, had an estimated erosion of 108 cu yd per year. The area was approximately 1 acre. An estimate of erosion based on other factors, estimated time of construction, distance of slope toe from the traveled edge of the pavement, and slope angle compared to that of some other cuts on that section of highway, gave much higher estimates of erosion. The toe of the slope was over

Fig. 9.49B.   Drought-tolerant species, *Artemesia tridentata* and *Purshia tridentata,* were established on the top of cut at Site 3. Initial survival was only fair to moderate, but those that survived the first growing season continued to grow well. Photographed in October 1976.

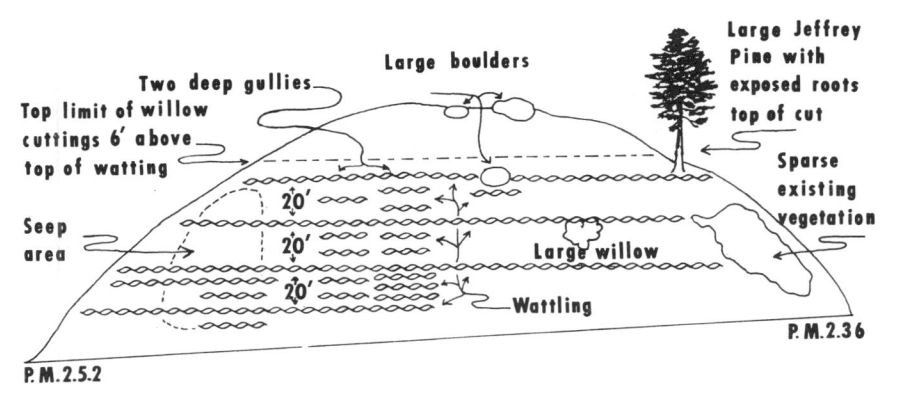

Fig. 9.50A. Cut slope face at Luther Pass, 03–ED–89 P.M. 2.4 (P.M. 2.36–2.52) showing major features and wattling placement. Slope approximately 840 ft long, 120 ft high. *Not to scale.*

15 ft from the pavement edge compared to 1 to 3 ft for many other slopes. These discrepancies in estimates of erosion would greatly affect cost–benefit comparisons.

The cost for revegetating Site 1 by using wattling instead of terracing would have been reduced. Serrations would not be recommended for this site in view of the accelerated erosion and poor revegetation that resulted from this treatment. Costs of revegetation treatment on newly constructed cuts would materially reduce the cost estimated for Site 2 and Sites 3 and 4. It was also possible to use a high proportion of mechanization on that portion needing extensive work. This also contributed to the favorable cost–benefit ratio. It is, of course, impossible to assign dollar values for the reduction in sediments in streams and lakes resulting from the revegetation.

On the CalTrans cut the costs of installing wattling were estimated at \$2.00 per lineal ft and of sticking unrooted cuttings at \$0.23 each. The project was estimated to pay costs at 4.2 years. At 10 years, a benefit of \$5,641 was estimated. This cut was estimated to have produced 36 percent of the total erosion from state highways in this watershed (Howell, 1971).

9.4.6 Summary

This case history is an example of projects where serious constraints exists, viz., limitations on the plant spectrum, use of plants about whose culture little is known, poor soils, and droughty sites with no irrigation available. The kinds of research required for successful revegetation of the sites was varied and included site and plant surveys, plant propagation and cultural practices studies, site preparation and slope treatment experiments, and revegetation plantings.

A number of conclusions were derived from this

Fig. 9.50B. Composite photograph of cut at 03–ED–89 P.M. 2.36–2.52 before revegetation. Gullied areas are left of center and just right of center.

Fig. 9.51. Highway cut 03–ED–89 P.M. 2.36–2.52, in September 1973 at the end of the first growing season. The left side of the cut (above) hydroseeded with wood fiber mulch had the best grass stand. The right side of the cut (below) was hydroseeded with recycled paper mulch.

Fig. 9.52. Highway cut 03–ED–89 P.M. 2.36–2.52, in September 1978, after five growing seasons shows a good stand of willows and grasses. Additional species are becoming established.

Table 9.9. Cost summary for revegetation of Luther Pass CalTrans site (03-ED-89 P.M. 2.36-2.52).[1]

ITEM	DOLLARS
Preparation and installation of wattling (1,140 lf)	
Labor:[1] scaling, preparation, installation, travel and down time 193 hr	1,737
Materials:[2] stakes, twine, miscellaneous	260
Equipment: chain saw, trucking, tool depreciation, transportation[1]	250
Total	2,247
Unit Costs: $2,247 ÷ 1,140 = $1.97 per lf, rounded to	2.00
Preparation and planting willow cuttings (8,000)	
Labor:[1] scaling, preparation, planting, travel and down time 173 hr	1,557
Materials:[2] twine, auxin, paint	50
Equipment: transportation,[1] tool depreciation	225
Total	1,832
Unit Costs: $1832 ÷ 8,000 = $0.229, rounded to	0.23
Total Costs	4,079
Erosion Costs 108 cu yd/yr @ $9.00/yd[4]	972
10-year costs	9,720
10-year cost/benefit	(5,641)[3]

[1]Scaling and down time due to rain (5% of total time) and crew travel time (23% of total time) and transportation Sacramento to Maryville. Labor at $7.00/hr + $2.00/hr subsistence.
[2]Willow obtained at no cost from the U. S. Forest Service.
[3]( ) = benefit; break-even point, 4.2 years.
[4]Howell, Richard, 1971. Slope Erosion Transects, Lake Tahoe Basin. Interim Reports, No. M&R 657078-1 Materials and Research Department, Division of Highways, State of California, Sacramento.

research, many of which should be applicable to other problem areas. The importance of slope preparation, scaling, and laying back is paramount. Slopes must be reasonably stable to allow plant establishment. Relatively inexpensive breast walls and willow wattling are valuable techniques to achieve this stabilization. Willow wattling is very useful on cut slopes as well as on fill slopes.

Native woody plants are well adapted to revegetation of an area, in this case benefiting little from fertilization. Spring planting was superior to fall planting in this area subject to frost heaving and erosion in the winter. Planting density should be adjusted for expected survival rates, and density should be greater near the top of cuts. In the project area, based on survival rates of experimental plantings, transplants should have been placed 2 ft on center at the bottom and 1.5 ft on center at the tops of cuts, instead of the 3-ft spacing used. Grasses were useful for interim stabilization. No mulch or matting treatments were better than wood fiber.

A number of species used in limited quantites showed potential value for revegetation. Ongoing revegetation projects should make provision for continued research on plant materials to expand the useful plant spectrum.

Demand for native plants in the project area has increased, possibly owing in part to the success of this work. Many of these plants are now available commercially. Results from this research on propagation and cultural practices for this project are now being used by commercial nurseries producing these plants.

Revegetation may be a practical and attractive alternative to continued erosion or more expensive strictly mechanical or engineering solutions.

9.5 REFERENCES CITED

Boe, K. N. (1975). Natural seedlings and sprouts after regeneration cuttings in old-growth redwood, Pacific Southwest and Range Experiment Station, Research Paper PSW-111, Berkeley, Calif.

Hambidge, G., ed. (1949). *Climate and Man,* USDA Agricultural Yearbook, Washington, D.C.

Harden, D., et al. (1978). Mass movement in the drainage basin of Redwood Creek, Humboldt County, California—A Progress Report, U.S.G.S. Open File Report 76-486, 161 pp.

Howell, R. (1971). Slope erosion transects, Lake Tahoe basin. Interim Report No. M & R 657078-1, Materials and Research Dept., Division of Highways, State of California, Sacramento, Calif.

Janda, R. J. (1975). Watershed conditions in the drainage basin of Redwood Creek, Humboldt County, California as of 1973, U. S. Geological Survey Open File Report 75-568, 267 pp.

Kraebel, C. J. (1936). Erosion control on mountain roads, *USDA Circular No. 380,* Washington, D.C.

Leiser, A. T., Nussbaum, J. J., Kay, B., Paul, J., and Thornhill, W. (1974). Revegetation of disturbed soils in the Tahoe Basin, Final Report to California Dept. of Transportation CA-DOT-TL-7036-1-75-24, University of California, Davis, Ca.

Madej, M. A., Kelsey, H., and Weaver, W. (1980). An evaluation of 1978 rehabilitation sites and erosion control techniques in Redwood National Park, U. S. National Park Service, Arcata, Calif., Tech. Rept. No. 1, 113 pp.

Nolan, K. M., Harden, D., and Janda, R. J. (1976). Erosional landform map of the Redwood Creek Basin, Humboldt County, California, U. S. Geological Survey Water Resources Investigation Open File Map 76-42.

U. S. Army Corps of Engineers (1971). Shore Protection Guidelines, National Shoreline Study, Rept. prepared by U. S. Corps of Engineers, Dept. of Army, Washington, D.C., 39 pp.

USDA Soil Conservation Service (1940). Lake bluff erosion control, Rept. prepared by U. S. Soil Conservation Service, Lansing, Mich., 81 pp.

U. S. Environmental Protection Agency (1975). Methods of quickly revegetating soils of low productivity, construction activities, EPA-440/9-75—006, U. S. EPA, Washington, D.C.

Appendices

Appendix I
Standard Designs
and Specifications
for Structural Components

A. GABION WALLS

1. Design Criteria for Gabion Walls

The *unit weight* of a filled gabion depends on such factors as the size and shape of the fill material, the method of fill placement, and the specific gravity of the fill. Generally, stone having a size range of 4″ to 8″ should be specified for filling gabions, as this size of material has the advantages of being easily handled by mechanical equipment and producing rather small voids when dumped into the empty gabions. However, based on measurements taken from a large number of tests using fill of various shapes and sizes, an average porosity of 0.30 can be used when calculating the unit weight of a filled gabion. The graph in Fig. I.1 may be used to obtain a reliable value of the unit weight for designing gabion walls.

The *coefficient of friction, f,* between the base of a gabion wall and a cohesionless soil may be assumed to be the *full value* of the tangent of the angle of internal friction of the soil. This assumption is based on the fact that the surface of a gabion is quite rough, and the foundation soil will enter the interstices between the stones in the gabions. Thus, if movement occurs, shear will take place between soil particles rather than between the soil and gabions. This conclusion may be confirmed by examining the underside of a gabion that has been torn up.

If the wall rests on clay, the resistance against sliding should be based on the full cohesive strength of the clay. If the clay is very stiff or hard, a shallow trench should be excavated where the wall will be built, and a 6″ layer of well compacted selected clean 3″ gravel placed in it.

The *angle of wall friction, ϕ_w,* may be assumed as the *full value* of the angle of internal friction of the cohesionless backfill. If no test data are available for the backfill material, a value of 30 degrees should be assumed for the angle of wall friction.

In designing gabion walls to retain clay slopes, a system of gabion counterforts is recommended. These counterforts should be spaced according to Table I.1.

Gabion counterforts are built as headers and should extend from the front of the wall to a point at least one gabion length beyond the slip circle of the bank. The counterforts serve as drains and as structural members that support the slope by friction of the bank material against the sides of the counterforts. Hydrostatic pressure in the bank is reduced by the free-draining material in the gabions. Thus, the thickness of the wall may be reduced because of this combined action of the counterforts.

For low retaining walls, elaborate theoretical calculations of earth pressure are not justified, and semiempirical methods are generally used instead. A method advanced by Terzaghi and Peck in *Soil Mechanics in Engineering Practice* (New York: John Wiley and Sons, 1948) is shown in Fig. I.2. The values of K_H and K_V are given both in units of psf per linear foot and kilograms per square meter per lineal meter, so that walls made of gabions in metric measurements may be quickly calculated.

Table I.1. Spacing of gabion counterforts.

TYPE OF SOIL	WATER CONTENT, %	COHESION, PSF	COUNTERFORT SPACING, FT
Very soft clay	40	300	13
Soft clay	35	400	16.5
Medium clay	33–30	600–800	20–23
Stiff clay	27–25	1000–1500	26–30

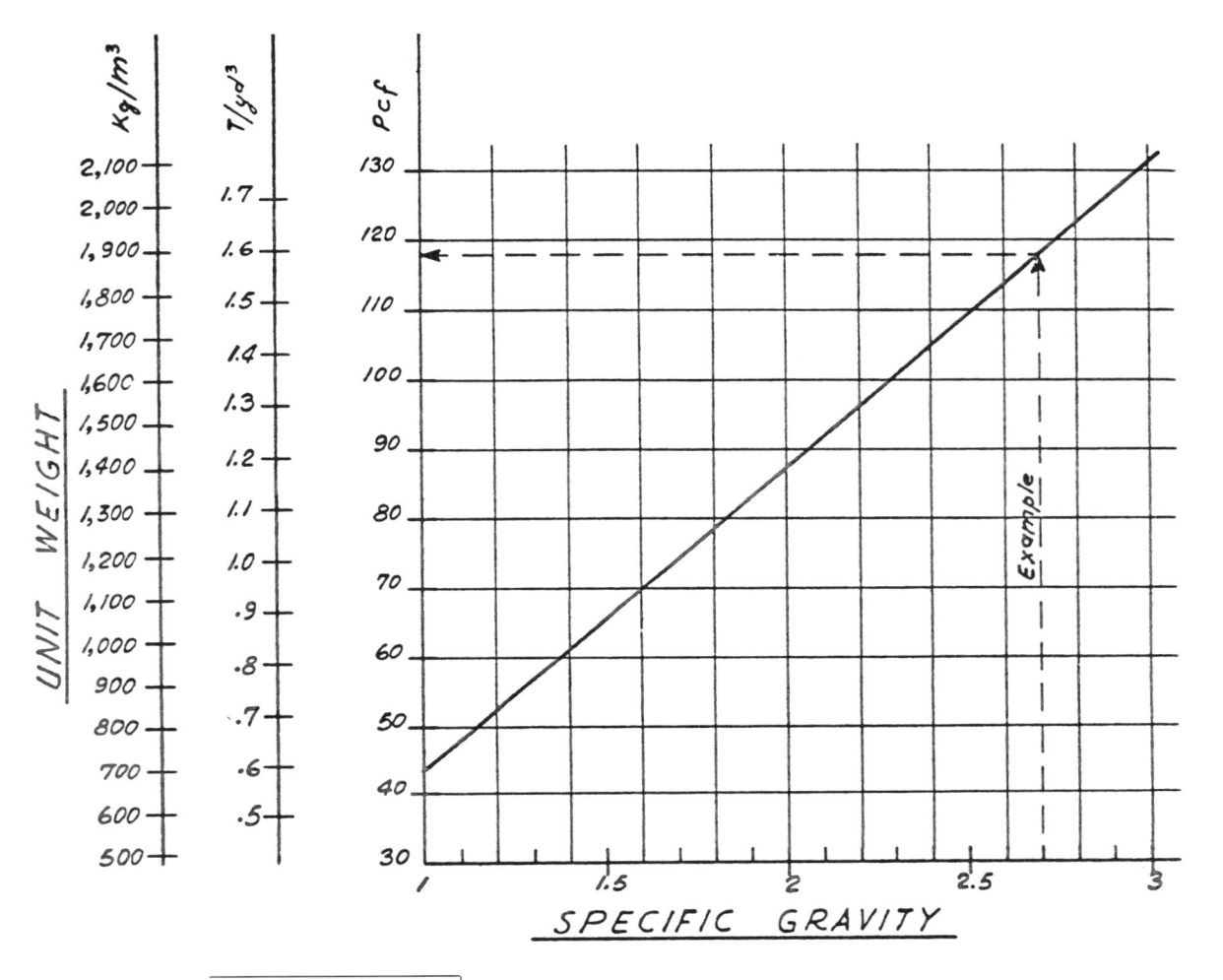

Specific Gravity of common materials	
Basalt	3.0
Brick	2.0
Concrete (broken)	2.4
Granite	2.7
Limestone	2.5
Sandstone	2.2
Trap rock	2.7

Example:
Given: Specific gravity = 2.7
Find: Unit weight in (a) pcf, (b) T/yd³, (c) kg/m³
Solution: Proceed vertically from S. G. = 2.7
to intersection of diagonal line.
Then proceed horizontally to
intersection of vertical line
and find: (a) unit weight = 118 pcf
(b) unit weight = 1.59 T/yd³
(c) unit weight = 1,890 kg/m³

Fig. I.1.   Unit weight of gabion fill (based on a porosity of 0.30).

2.   Standard Designs

The gabion walls in Figs. I.3 and I.4 are proportioned to retain soils of types 1 and 2, as shown in the legend in Fig. I.2. A unit weight of 110 psf (1760 kg/m³) has been used for both earth and gabions. If backfill of a different type is used, the wall dimensions do not apply.

The walls were designed so that the resultant is within the middle third of the base, but close to the outside edge as indicated by the arrowhead on each course. The factor of safety against overturning is at least 2.

Safety against overturning is only assured if the pressure on the soil under the toe does not exceed the bearing capacity of the soil. The walls in Figs. I.3 and I.4 are safe for soils having a bearing capacity of 2 tons/sq ft. Table 5.2 (in Section 5.1.3.1) gives nominal values of

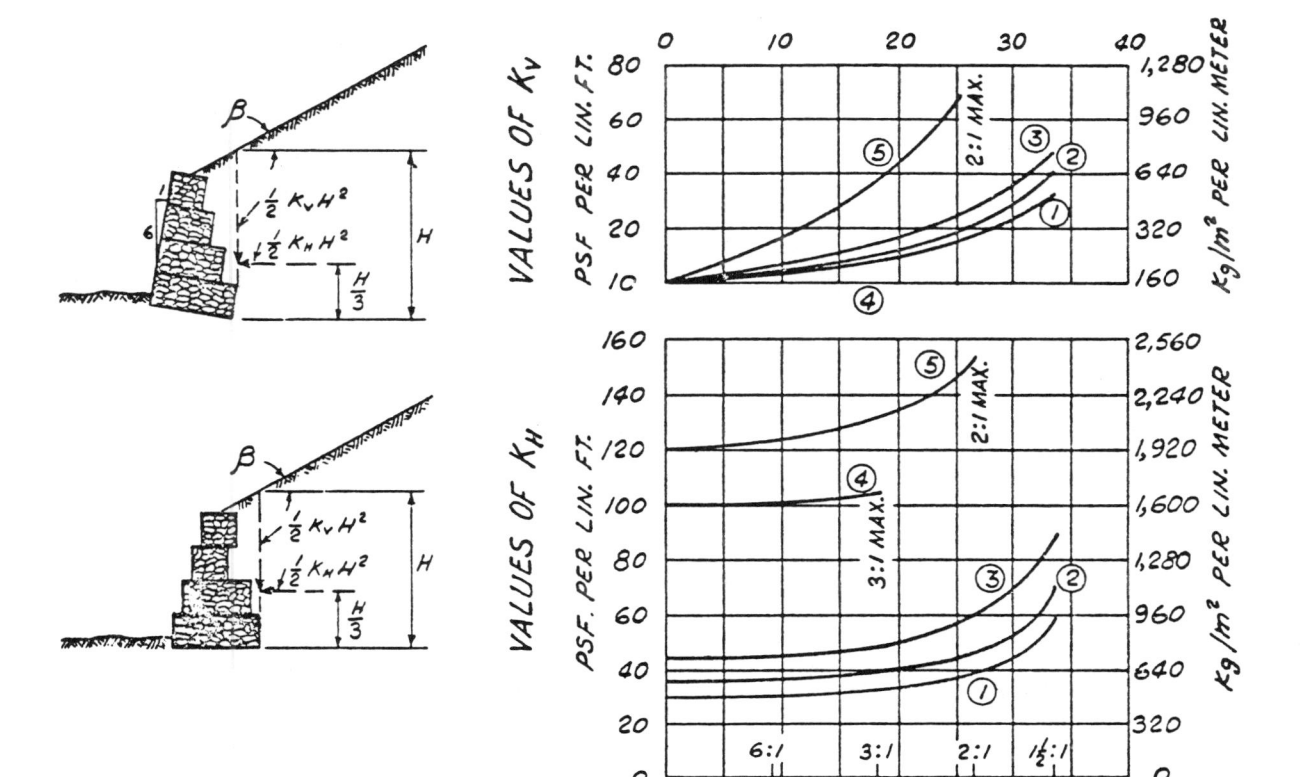

Circled numbers indicate the following soil types:
1. Clean sand and gravel: GW, GP, SW, SP.
2. Dirty sand and gravel of restricted permeability:
   GM, GM-GP, SM, SM-SP.
3. Stiff residual silts and clays, silty fine sands,
   clayey sands and gravels: CL, ML, CH, MH, SM, SC, GC.
4. Very soft to soft clay, silty caly, organic silt
   and clay: CL, ML, OL, CH, MH, OH.
5. Medium to stiff clay deposited in chunks and
   protected from infiltration: CL, CH.
For type 5 material H is reduced by 4 ft, resultant
   acts at a height of $(H - 4)/3$ above base.

Fig. I.2. Design loads for low gabion retaining walls (straight slope backfill).

bearing capacities for various soils. If the computed pressure exceeds the value for the soil in question, the toe or heel or both must be extended.

The tables accompanying Figs. I.3 and I.4 give dimensions for walls built in courses 1 m (3'3") high. Intermediate heights may be obtained by making the foundation course just $\frac{1}{2}$ m (20") high or by making the top course 12" or 20" high, or both. The foundation course should not be less than 20" high if the stepped-back wall type is used, as thinner gabions are too flexible to distribute loads effectively.

Because individual gabions encase the stone fill completely, the cross section of the wall may be reduced easily as its height is increased. A system of counterforts may be employed in some instances for further economy without sacrificing structural strength. The counterforts are made by arranging gabions alternately as headers and stretchers.

Case I: $\beta = 0°$ (Retained earth, no slope)

Note: Figures valid for soil types
1 and 2 only (see Fig. I.2) and
unit weight of 110 pcf for
earth and gabions (see Fig. I.1).

(a) Front face on 1:6 batter

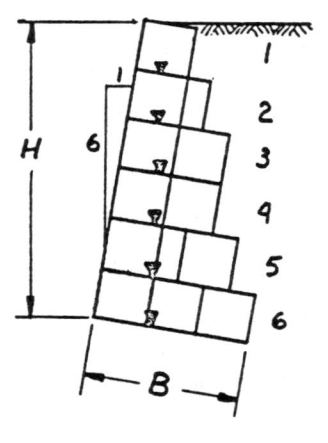

No. of courses	H	B	No. of gabions thick	Remarks
1	3′3″	3′3″	1	Front face may be vertical
2	6′6″	4′11″	1½	
3	9′9″	6′6″	2	
4	13′1″	6′6″	2	
5	16′4″	8′2″	2½	
6	19′7″	9′9″	3	

(b) Front face stepped

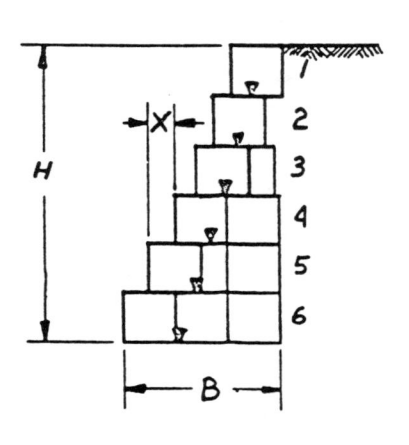

No. of courses	H	B	No. of gabions thick	X	Remarks
1	3′3″	3′3″	1	—	
2	6′6″	3′3″	1	12″	
3	9′9″	4′11″	1½	12″	
4	13′1″	6′6″	2	16″	
5	16′4″	8′2″	2½	20″	Use counterforts @ 9′9″ in course 4, see Table I-1
6	19′7″	9′9″	3	20″	

▼—Location of resultant of weight of wall and earth pressure

Figure I.3.

CASE II β = 33°41′

(Retained earth on
a 1 on 1.5 slope)

Note: Figures valid for soil
types 1 and 2 only (see Fig I.2)
and unit weight of 110 pcf
for earth and gabions.

(a) Front face on 1:6 batter

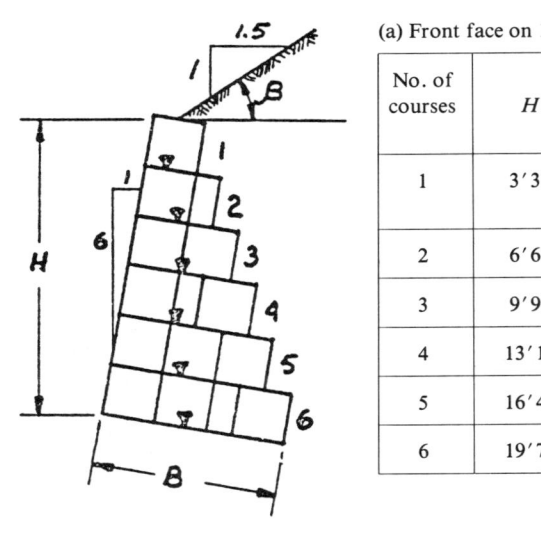

No. of courses	H	B	No. of gabions thick	Remarks
1	3′3″	3′3″	1	Front face may be vertical
2	6′6″	4′11″	$1\frac{1}{2}$	
3	9′9″	6′6″	2	
4	13′1″	8′2″	$2\frac{1}{2}$	
5	16′4″	9′9″	3	
6	19′7″	11′5″	$3\frac{1}{2}$	

(b) Front face stepped

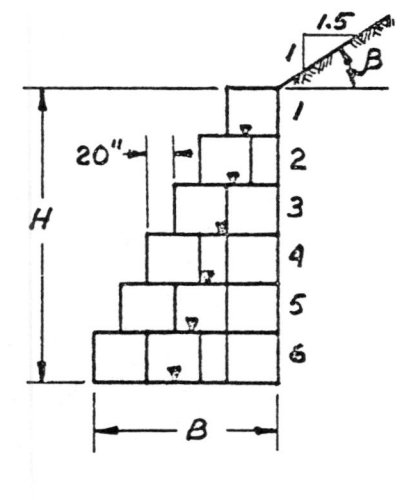

No. of courses	H	B	No. of gabions thick	Remarks
1	3′3″	3′3″	1	
2	6′6″	4′11″	$1\frac{1}{2}$	
3	9′9″	6′6″	2	
4	13′1″	8′2″	$2\frac{1}{2}$	
5	16′4″	9′9″	3	
6	19′7″	11′5″	$3\frac{1}{2}$	

▼—Location of resultant of weight of wall and earth pressure

Fig. I.4.

B. TIMBER AND LOG CRIBS

1. AWPI Pressure-Treated Timber Cribs, Standard Designs A through K

TYPE A	TYPE B	TYPE C	TYPE D
TYPE E	TYPE F	TYPE G	TYPE H
TYPE J	TYPE K		

STANDARD TIMBER CRIBBING

TYPE	MAX. HT.	BACK FILL	FACE BATTER
A	21'- 7"	1½ to 1	1 to 6
B	15'- 7"	1½ to 1	Vert.
C	29'- 0"	3 to 1	1 to 6
D	26'-10"	3 to 1	Vert.
E	30'- 0"	Level	1 to 6
F	29'- 4"	Level	Vert.
G	27'- 9"	Highway	1 to 6
H	25'- 7"	Highway	Vert.
J	21'- 7"	Railroad	1 to 6
K	20'- 7"	Railroad	Vert.

STANDARD TREATED TIMBER CRIBBING
BASIC DESIGN INDEX

| AMERICAN WOOD PRESERVERS INSTITUTE
Washington, D.C.
Portland, Oregon   San Francisco, California | SKILLING, HELLE, CHRISTIANSEN, ROBERTSON
SEATTLE, WASHINGTON
STRUCTURAL ENGINEERS |
| DATE:
Jan. 1969 | *NO SCALE* | SHANNON AND WILSON
SEATTLE, WASHINGTON
SOILS ENGINEERS |

SCHEDULE

H	D	"BOTTOM" MEMBERS			
		'A' ROWS	'A' SIZE	'B' ROWS	'B' SIZE
UP TO 8'-0"	1'-6'±	NONE REQD.		NONE REQD.	
8'-0" TO 9'-3"	1'-6'±	2	8"x8"x7'-3"	2	8" x 10" *
9'-3" TO 12'-10"	2'-0'±	2	8"x8"x9'-0"	2	8" x 12" *
12'-10" TO 16'-7"	2'-0'±	3	8"x8"x11'-0"	3	8" x 8"
16'-7" TO 21'-7"	2'-0"±	3	8"x12"x13'-0"	3	8" x 10"

* SEE NOTE ON FIGURE

NOTES:
1. BLOCK 'C' - 8"x8"x0'-7½"
2. BLOCK 'D' - 8"x8"x1'-3"
3. BLOCK 'E' - 8"x8"x0'-7½" WITH HOLE FOR ROD.

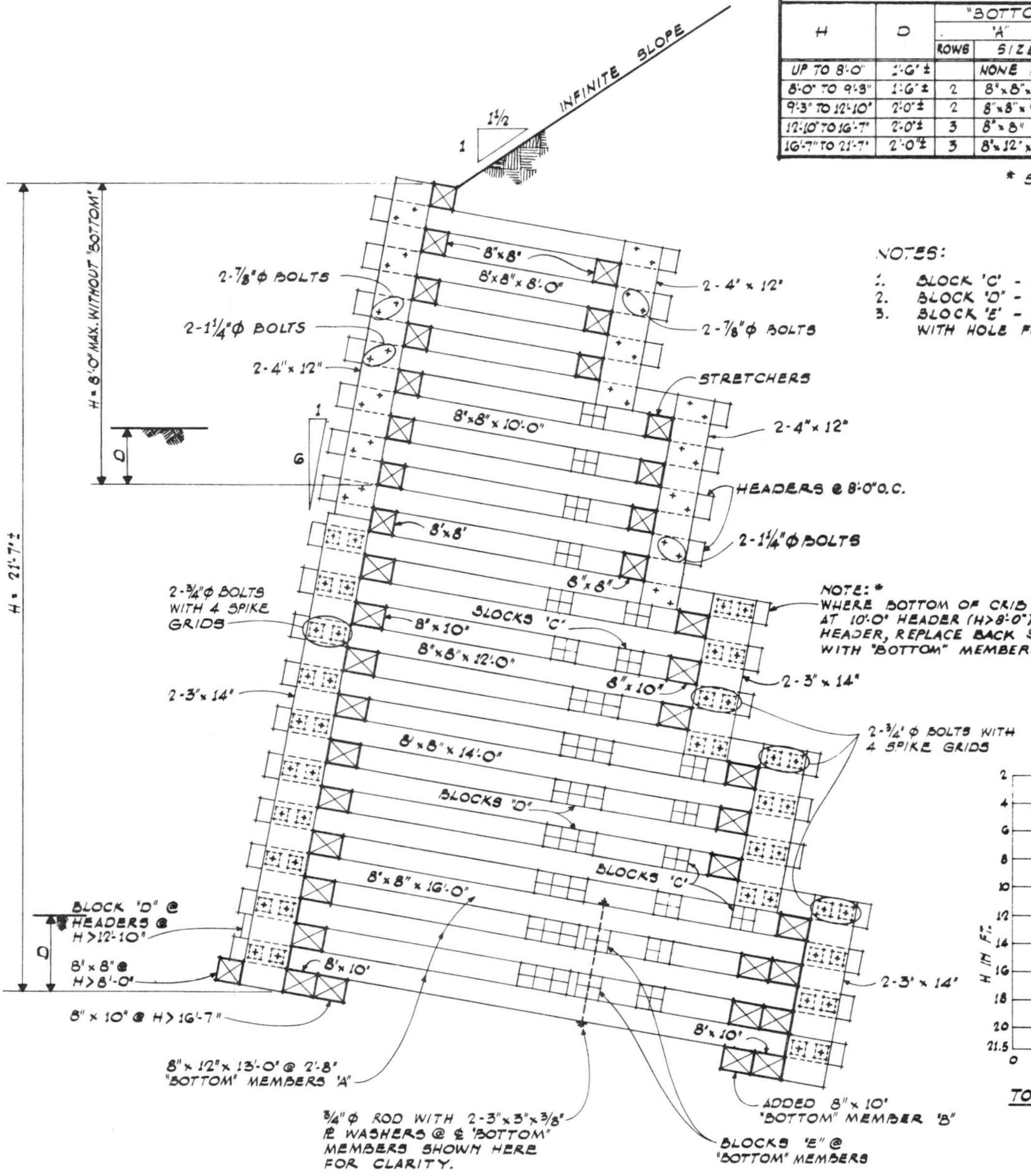

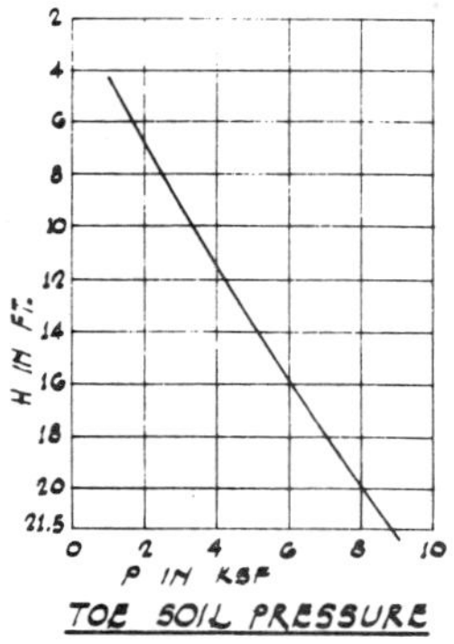

INFINITE SLOPE

1½ / 1

H = 8'-0" MAX. WITHOUT 'BOTTOM'

H = 21'-7'±

2-⅞"ø BOLTS
8"x8"
8"x8"x8'-0"
2-4"x12"
2-1¼"ø BOLTS
2-4"x12"
2-⅞"ø BOLTS
STRETCHERS
8"x8"x10'-0"
2-4"x12"
HEADERS @ 8'-0"O.C.
2-1¼"ø BOLTS
8"x8"
8"x8"
2-¾"ø BOLTS WITH 4 SPIKE GRIDS
8"x10"
BLOCKS 'C'
8"x8"x12'-0"
8"x10"
2-3"x14"
2-3"x14"
2-¾"ø BOLTS WITH 4 SPIKE GRIDS

NOTE: *
WHERE BOTTOM OF CRIB OCCURS AT 10'-0" HEADER (H>8'-0") OR 12'-0" HEADER, REPLACE BACK STRETCHERS WITH "BOTTOM" MEMBERS "B"

8"x8"x14'-0"
BLOCKS 'D'
8"x8"x16'-0"
BLOCKS 'C'
BLOCK 'D' @ HEADERS @ H>12'-10"
8"x8" @ H>8'-0"
8" x 10" @ H > 16'-7"
2-3"x14"
8"x10"
8"x12"x13'-0" @ 2'-8" "BOTTOM" MEMBERS 'A'
ADDED 8"x10" "BOTTOM" MEMBER 'B'
¾"ø ROD WITH 2-3"x3"x⅜" R WASHERS @ ℄ "BOTTOM" MEMBERS SHOWN HERE FOR CLARITY.
BLOCKS 'E' @ "BOTTOM" MEMBERS

TOE SOIL PRESSURE

(graph: H IN FT. vs P IN KSF)

SEE "GENERAL CONFIGURATION" AND "TYPICAL DETAILS" DRAWINGS FOR FURTHER REQUIREMENTS.

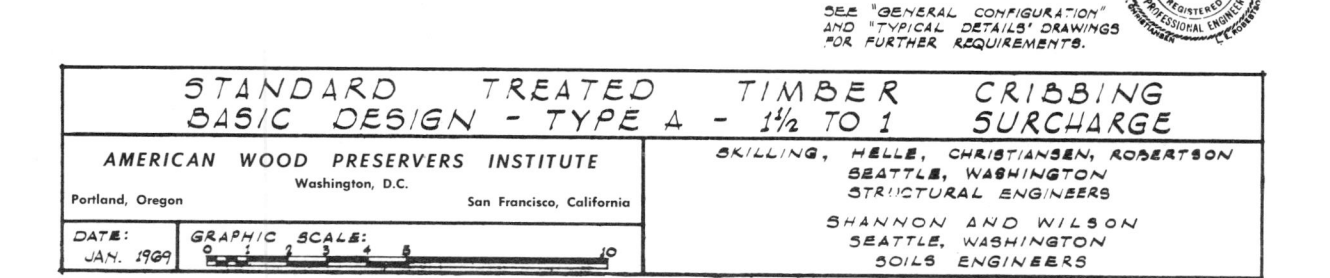

STANDARD TREATED TIMBER CRIBBING
BASIC DESIGN - TYPE A - 1½ TO 1 SURCHARGE

AMERICAN WOOD PRESERVERS INSTITUTE
Washington, D.C.
Portland, Oregon   San Francisco, California

DATE: JAN. 1969

GRAPHIC SCALE: 0 1 2 3 4 5 10

SKILLING, HELLE, CHRISTIANSEN, ROBERTSON
SEATTLE, WASHINGTON
STRUCTURAL ENGINEERS

SHANNON AND WILSON
SEATTLE, WASHINGTON
SOILS ENGINEERS

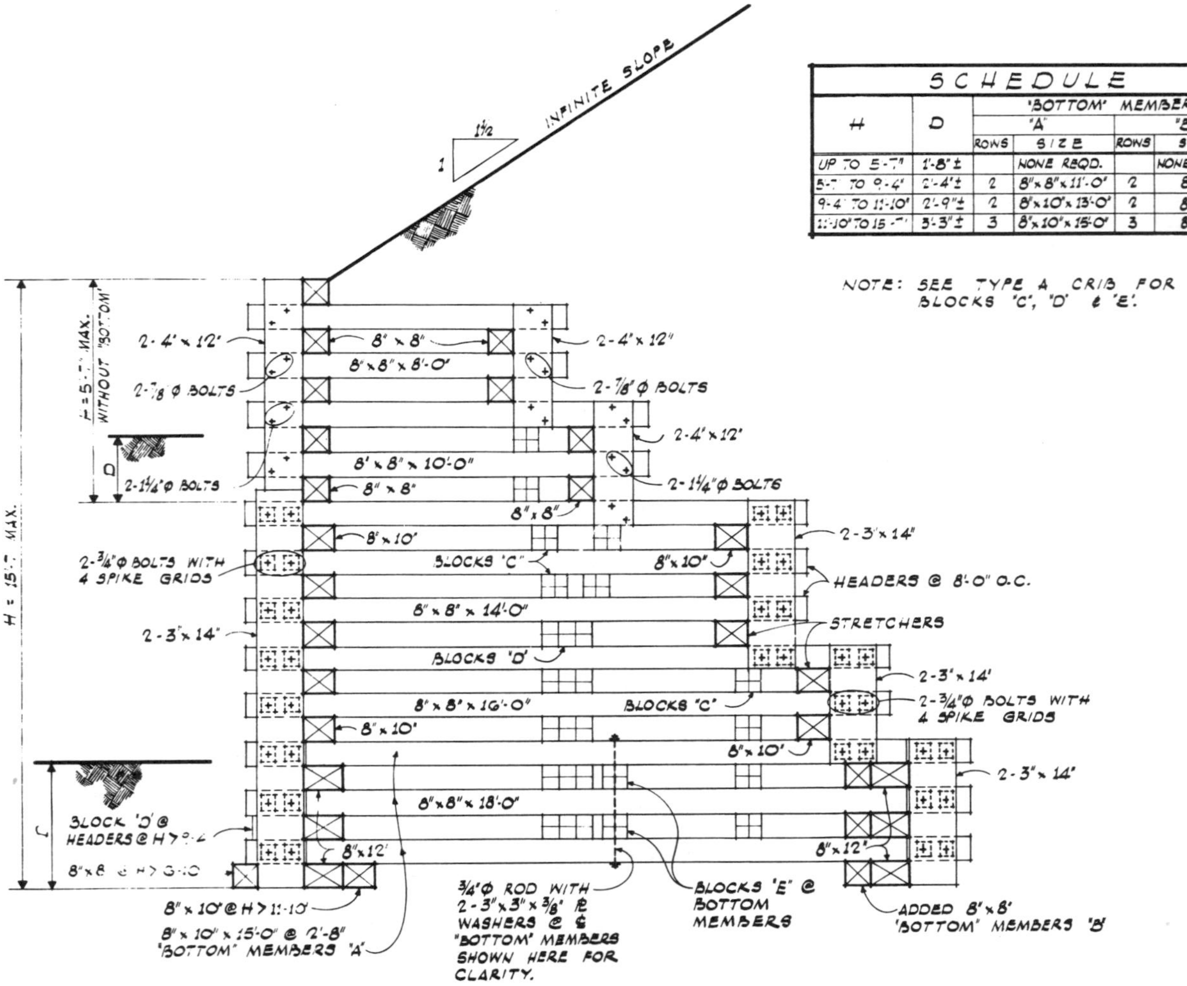

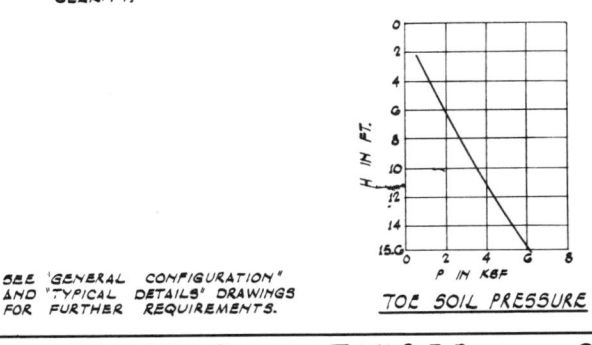

S C H E D U L E		'BOTTOM' MEMBERS			
		"A"		"B"	
H	D	ROWS	SIZE	ROWS	SIZE
UP TO 5'-7"	1'-8"±	NONE REQD.		NONE REQD.	
5'-7' TO 9'-4'	2'-4"±	2	8"x 8"x 11'-0'	2	8"x 8"
9'-4' TO 11'-10'	2'-9"±	2	8"x10"x 13'-0'	2	8'x 8"
11'-10' TO 15'-"	3'-3"±	3	8"x10"x 15'-0'	3	8'x 8"

NOTE: SEE TYPE A CRIB FOR
BLOCKS 'C', 'D' & 'E'.

INFINITE SLOPE

1½

1

L = 5'-7' MAX. WITHOUT 'BOTTOM'

D

H = 15'-7' MAX.

2 - 4' x 12'

8" x 8" x 8'-0"

2 - 7/8 Ø BOLTS

2 - 4' x 12'

2 - 7/8 Ø BOLTS

8" x 8" x 10'-0"

8" x 8"

2 - 1¼ Ø BOLTS

2 - 4' x 12'

2 - 1¼ Ø BOLTS

8" x 8"

8" x 10'

2 - ¾ Ø BOLTS WITH
4 SPIKE GRIDS

BLOCKS 'C'

8" x 10'

2 - 3' x 14'

HEADERS @ 8'-0" O.C.

8" x 8" x 14'-0"

STRETCHERS

2 - 3' x 14'

BLOCKS 'D'

8" x 8" x 16'-0"

BLOCKS 'C'

2 - 3' x 14'

2 - ¾"Ø BOLTS WITH
4 SPIKE GRIDS

8" x 10'

8" x 10'

2 - 3' x 14'

BLOCK 'D' @
HEADERS @ H > 9'-4'

8" x 8" x 18'-0"

8" x 8" @ H > 3'-0'

8" x 12'

8" x 12'

8" x 10' @ H > 11'-10'

BLOCKS 'E' @
BOTTOM
MEMBERS

ADDED 8" x 8'
'BOTTOM' MEMBERS 'B'

8" x 10' x 15'-0" @ 2'-8"
'BOTTOM' MEMBERS 'A'

¾"Ø ROD WITH
2 - 3' x 3" x ⅜' ℞
WASHERS @ ℄
'BOTTOM' MEMBERS
SHOWN HERE FOR
CLARITY.

SEE 'GENERAL CONFIGURATION'
AND 'TYPICAL DETAILS' DRAWINGS
FOR FURTHER REQUIREMENTS.

H IN FT.

0
2
4
6
8
10
12
14
15.0
0 2 4 6 8

P IN KSF

TOE SOIL PRESSURE

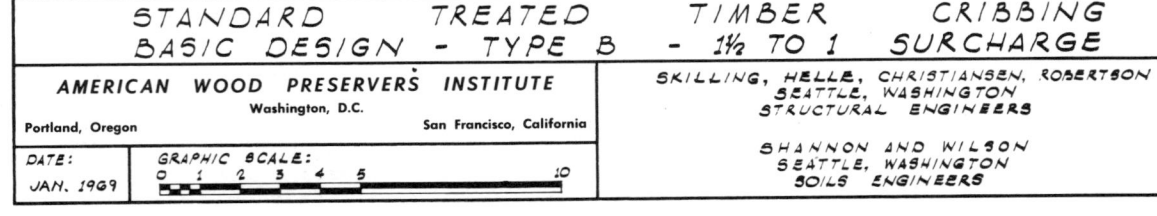

STANDARD TREATED TIMBER CRIBBING	
BASIC DESIGN - TYPE B - 1½ TO 1 SURCHARGE	
AMERICAN WOOD PRESERVER'S INSTITUTE Washington, D.C. Portland, Oregon San Francisco, California	SKILLING, HELLE, CHRISTIANSEN, ROBERTSON SEATTLE, WASHINGTON STRUCTURAL ENGINEERS SHANNON AND WILSON SEATTLE, WASHINGTON SOILS ENGINEERS
DATE: JAN. 1969	GRAPHIC SCALE: 0 1 2 3 4 5 10	

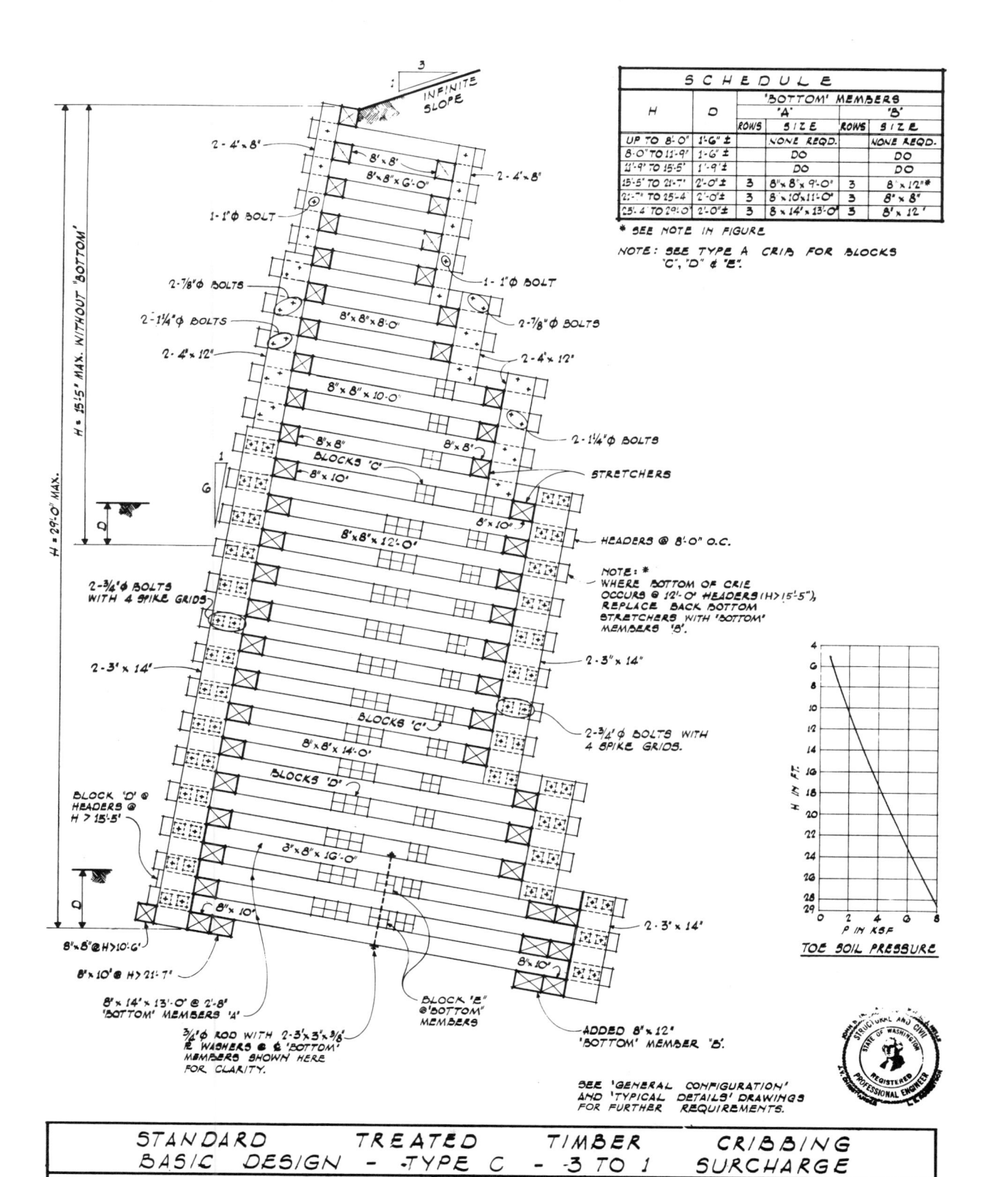

S C H E D U L E		'BOTTOM' MEMBERS			
H	D	'A'		'B'	
		ROWS	SIZE	ROWS	SIZE
UP TO 8'-0"	1'-6"±	NONE REQD.		NONE REQD.	
8'-0" TO 11'-9"	1'-6"±	DO		DO	
11'-9" TO 15'-5"	1'-9"±	DO		DO	
15'-5" TO 21'-7"	2'-0"±	3	8"x8"x9'-0"	3	8'x12"*
21'-7" TO 25'-4	2'-0"±	3	8"x10"x11'-0"	3	8'x8'
25'-4 TO 29'-0	2'-0"±	3	8 x14'x13'-0'	3	8'x12'

* SEE NOTE IN FIGURE

NOTE: SEE TYPE A CRIB FOR BLOCKS 'C', 'D' & 'E'.

STANDARD   TREATED   TIMBER   CRIBBING
BASIC DESIGN - TYPE C - 3 TO 1 SURCHARGE

AMERICAN WOOD PRESERVERS INSTITUTE
Washington, D.C.
Portland, Oregon   San Francisco, California

DATE:
JAN. 1969

GRAPHIC SCALE:

SKILLING, HELLE, CHRISTIANSEN, ROBERTSON
SEATTLE, WASHINGTON
STRUCTURAL ENGINEERS

SHANNON AND WILSON
SEATTLE, WASHINGTON
SOILS ENGINEERS

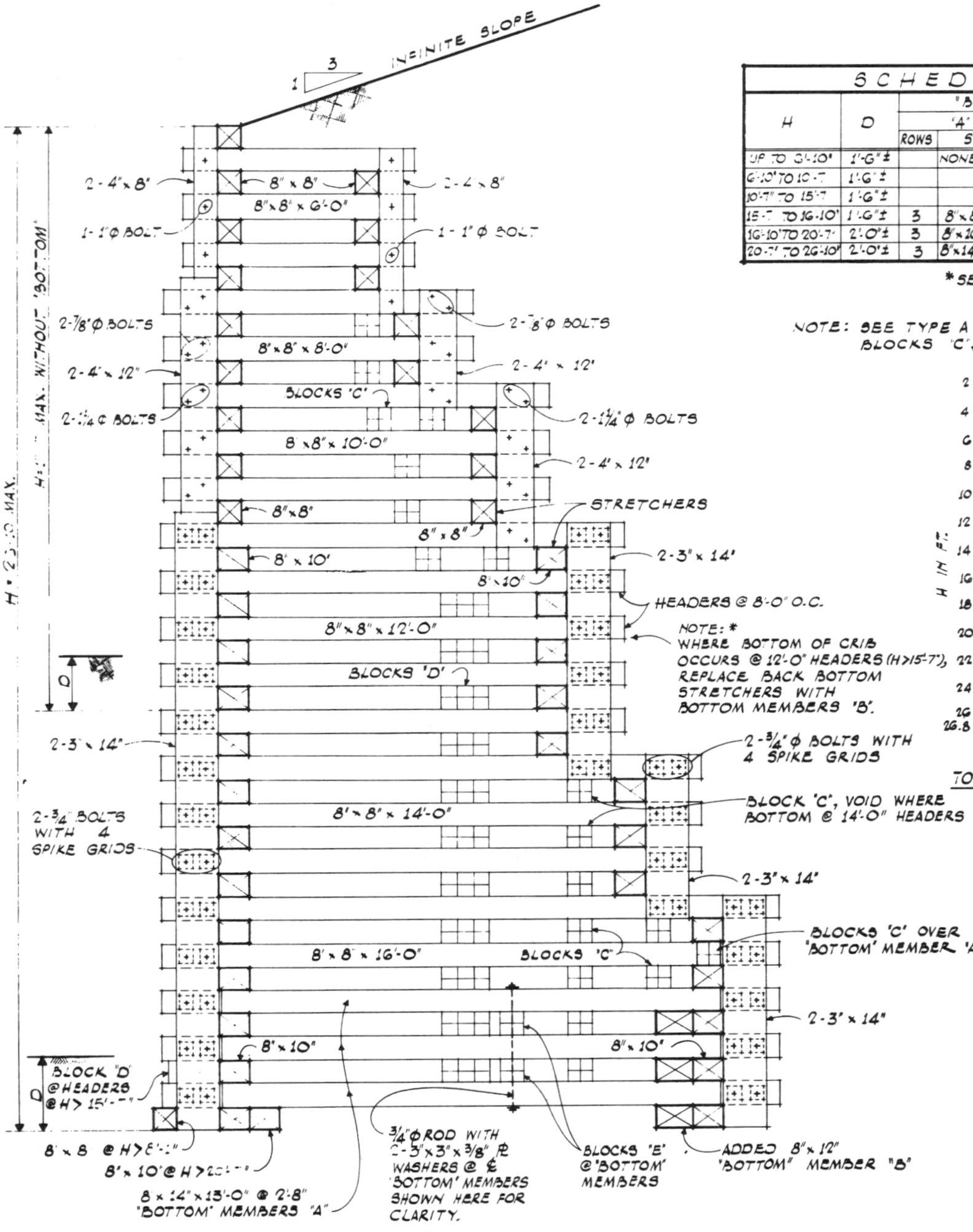

INFINITE SLOPE

1 : 3

SCHEDULE

H	D	"BOTTOM" MEMBERS			
		'A'		'B'	
		ROWS	SIZE	ROWS	SIZE
UP TO 6'-10"	1'-6"±	NONE REQD.			
6'-10" TO 10'-7"	1'-6"±	DO		DO	
10'-7" TO 15'-7"	1'-6"±	DO		DO	
15'-7" TO 16'-10"	1'-6"±	3	8"x8"x9'-0"	3	8" x 12' *
16'-10" TO 20'-7"	2'-0"±	3	8"x10"x11'-0"	3	8" x 8"
20'-7" TO 26'-10"	2'-0"±	3	8"x14"x13'-0"	3	8" x 12'

*SEE NOTE ON FIGURE

NOTE: SEE TYPE A CRIB FOR BLOCKS 'C', 'D' & 'E'.

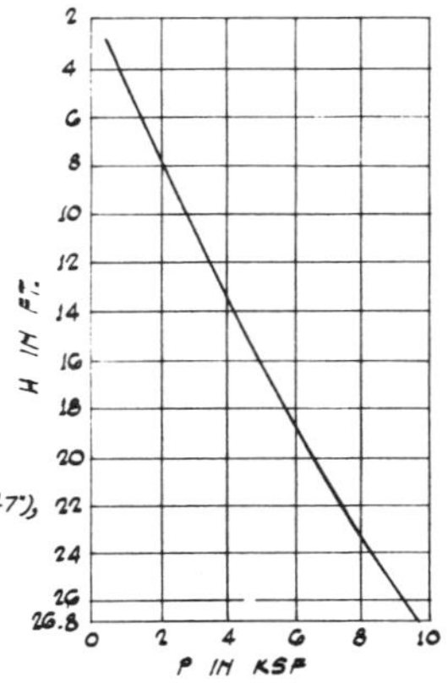

TOE SOIL PRESSURE

H IN FT.

P IN KSF

2-4"x8"
8"x8"
8"x8"x6'-0"
1-1"∅ BOLT
2-4"x8"
1-1"∅ BOLT

2-7/8"∅ BOLTS
8"x8"x8'-0"
2-7/8"∅ BOLTS

2-4'x12'
BLOCKS 'C'
2-1¼∅ BOLTS
2-1¼∅ BOLTS
8"x8"x10'-0"
2-4'x12'

8"x8"
STRETCHERS
8"x8"
8"x10'
8"x10'
2-3"x14'
HEADERS @ 8'-0" O.C.

8"x8"x12'-0"
NOTE: *
WHERE BOTTOM OF CRIB OCCURS @ 12'-0" HEADERS (H>15'-7"), REPLACE BACK BOTTOM STRETCHERS WITH BOTTOM MEMBERS 'B'.
BLOCKS 'D'

2-3'x14'
2-¾"∅ BOLTS WITH 4 SPIKE GRIDS
BLOCK 'C', VOID WHERE BOTTOM @ 14'-0" HEADERS

2-¾" BOLTS WITH 4 SPIKE GRIDS
8"x8"x14'-0"
2-3"x14'

8"x8"x16'-0"
BLOCKS 'C'
BLOCKS 'C' OVER 'BOTTOM' MEMBER 'A'
2-3"x14'

8"x10'
8"x10'

BLOCK 'D' @ HEADERS @ H>15'-7"

8"x8 @ H>6'-10"
8"x10' @ H>20'-7"
8"x14'x13'-0" @ 2'-8" "BOTTOM" MEMBERS 'A'
¾"∅ ROD WITH 2-3"x3"x3/8" ℞ WASHERS @ ℄ 'BOTTOM' MEMBERS SHOWN HERE FOR CLARITY.
BLOCKS 'E' @ 'BOTTOM' MEMBERS
ADDED 8"x12" 'BOTTOM' MEMBER 'B'

H=26'-10" MAX.

H=21'-10" MAX. WITHOUT 'BOTTOM'

SEE "GENERAL CONFIGURATION" AND "TYPICAL DETAILS" DRAWINGS FOR FURTHER REQUIREMENTS.

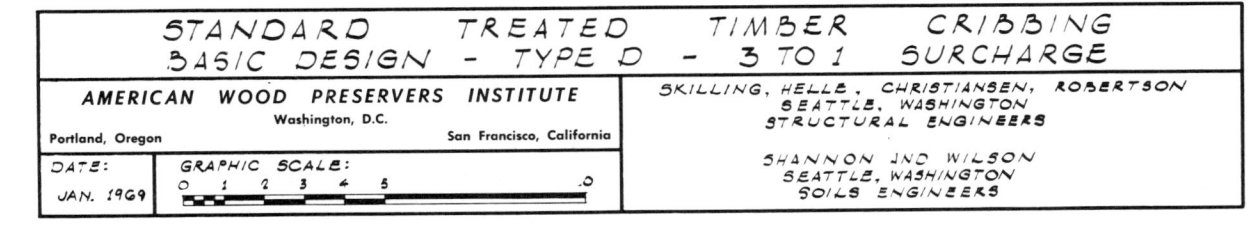

STANDARD TREATED TIMBER CRIBBING
BASIC DESIGN - TYPE D - 3 TO 1 SURCHARGE

AMERICAN WOOD PRESERVERS INSTITUTE
Washington, D.C.
Portland, Oregon   San Francisco, California

SKILLING, HELLE, CHRISTIANSEN, ROBERTSON
SEATTLE, WASHINGTON
STRUCTURAL ENGINEERS

SHANNON AND WILSON
SEATTLE, WASHINGTON
SOILS ENGINEERS

DATE: JAN. 1969

GRAPHIC SCALE:
0 1 2 3 4 5   10

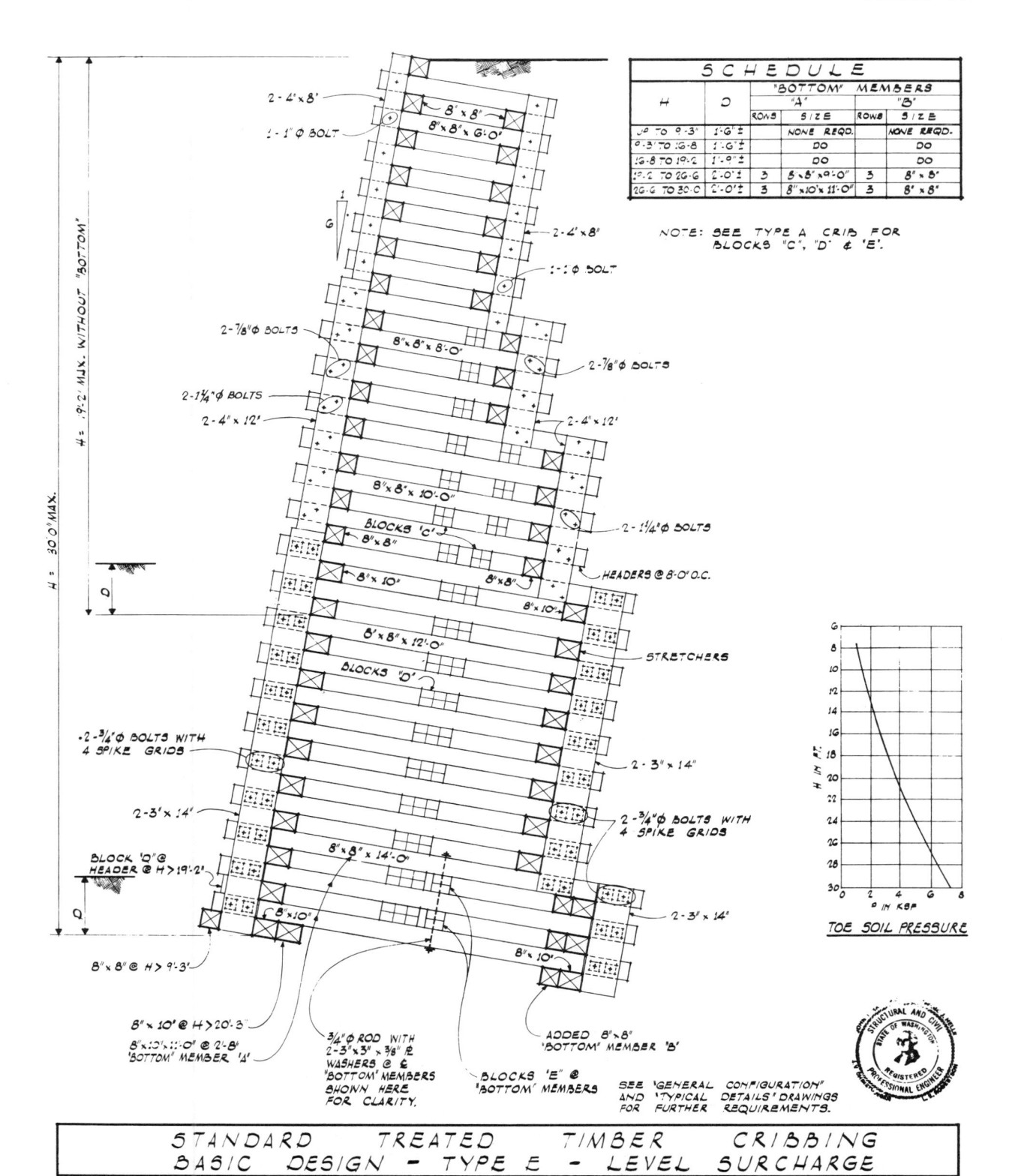

SCHEDULE

H	D	"BOTTOM" MEMBERS			
		"A"		"B"	
		ROWS	SIZE	ROWS	SIZE
UP TO 9'-3"	1'-6"±	NONE REQD.		NONE REQD.	
9'-3 TO 16-8	1'-6"±	DO		DO	
16-8 TO 19-2	1'-9"±	DO		DO	
19-2 TO 26-6	2'-0"±	3	8"x8"x9'-0"	3	8' x 8'
26-6 TO 30-0	2'-0"±	3	8"x10"x 11'-0"	3	8' x 8'

NOTE: SEE TYPE A CRIB FOR BLOCKS "C", "D" & "E".

TOE SOIL PRESSURE

STANDARD TREATED TIMBER CRIBBING
BASIC DESIGN - TYPE E - LEVEL SURCHARGE

AMERICAN WOOD PRESERVERS INSTITUTE
Washington, D.C.
Portland, Oregon   San Francisco, California

DATE:
JAN. 1969

GRAPHIC SCALE:
0 1 2 3 4 5   10

SKILLING, HELLE, CHRISTIANSEN, ROBERTSON
SEATTLE, WASHINGTON
STRUCTURAL ENGINEERS

SHANNON AND WILSON
SEATTLE, WASHINGTON
SOILS ENGINEERS

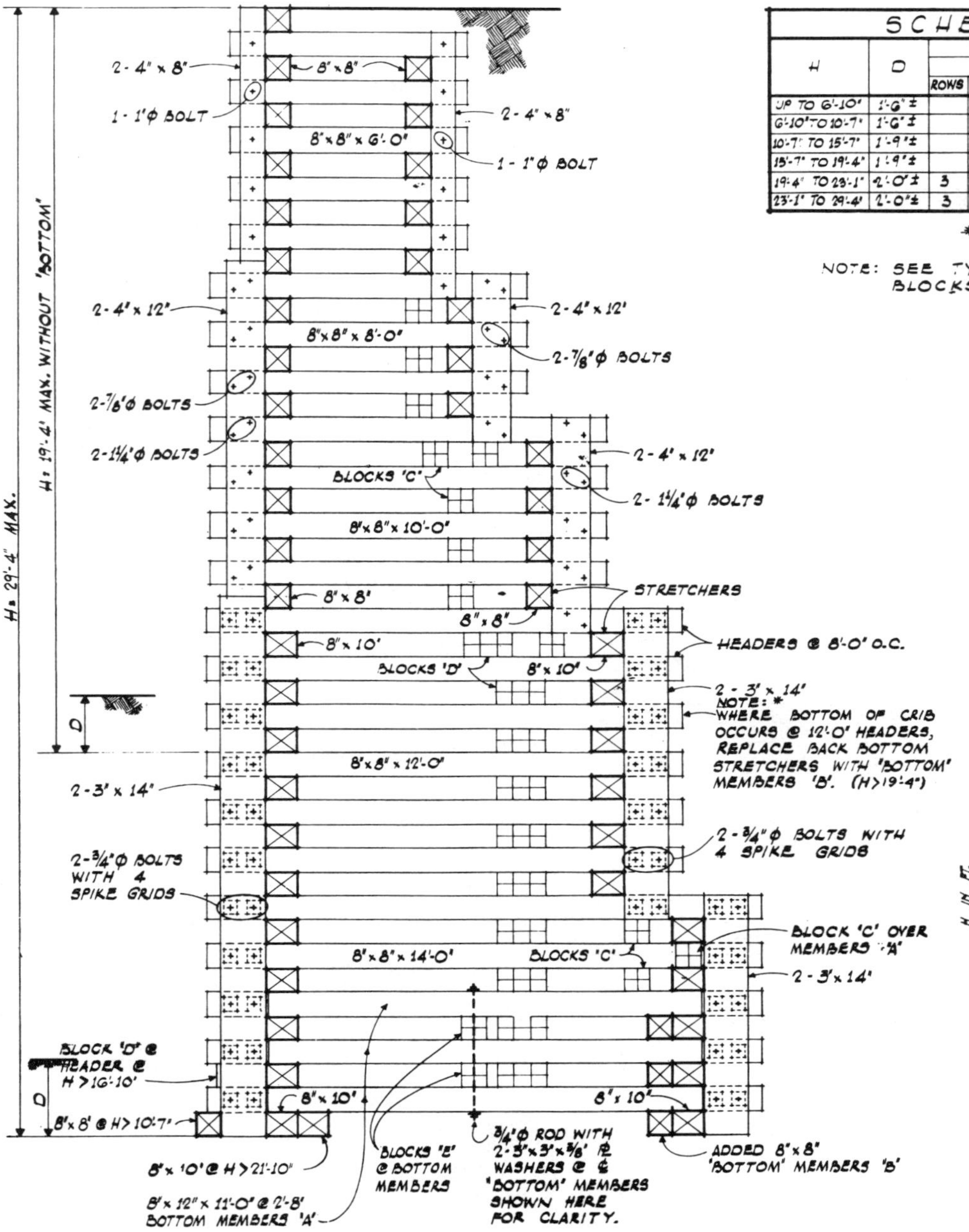

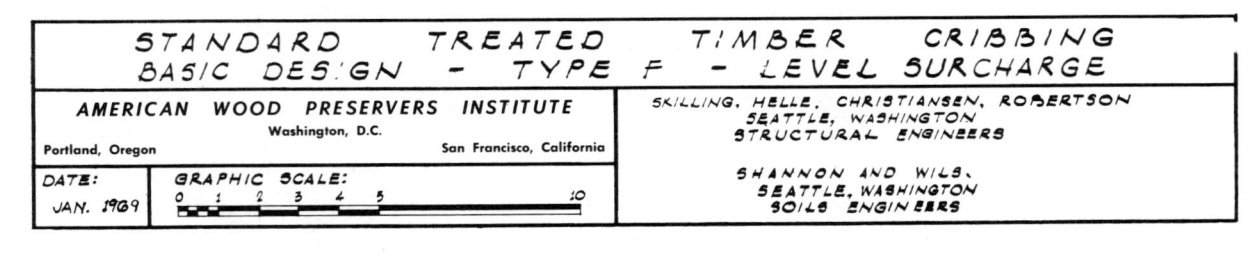

SCHEDULE						
H	D	"BOTTOM" MEMBERS				
		'A'		'B'		
		ROWS	SIZE	ROWS	SIZE	
UP TO 6'-10"	1'-6" ±	NONE REQD.			NONE REQD.	
6'-10" TO 10'-7"	1'-6" ±	DO		DO		
10'-7" TO 15'-7"	1'-9" ±	DO		DO		
15'-7" TO 19'-4"	1'-9" ±	DO		DO		
19'-4" TO 23'-1"	2'-0" ±	3	8"×8"×9'-0"	3	8"×12"*	
23'-1" TO 29'-4"	2'-0" ±	3	8"×12"×11'-0"	3	8"×8"	

* SEE NOTE ON FIGURE

NOTE: SEE TYPE A CRIB FOR
BLOCKS 'C', 'D' & 'E'.

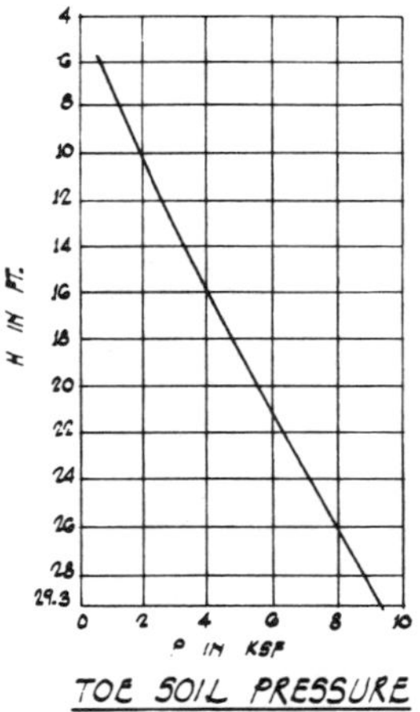

2-4"×8"
8"×8"
2-4"×8"
1-1"φ BOLT
8"×8"×6'-0"
1-1"φ BOLT

2-4"×12"
2-4"×12"
8"×8"×8'-0"
2-7/8"φ BOLTS
2-7/8"φ BOLTS
2-1¼"φ BOLTS
BLOCKS 'C'
2-4"×12"
8"×8"×10'-0"
2-1¼"φ BOLTS
STRETCHERS
8"×8"
8"×8"
8"×10"
HEADERS @ 8'-0" O.C.
8"×10"
BLOCKS 'D'
8"×10"

2-3"×14"
NOTE: *
WHERE BOTTOM OF CRIB
OCCURS @ 12'-0" HEADERS,
REPLACE BACK BOTTOM
STRETCHERS WITH 'BOTTOM'
MEMBERS 'B'. (H>19'-4")

8"×8"×12'-0"
2-3"×14"
2-¾"φ BOLTS WITH
4 SPIKE GRIDS
2-¾"φ BOLTS
WITH 4
SPIKE GRIDS
BLOCK 'C' OVER
MEMBERS 'A'
8"×8"×14'-0"
BLOCKS 'C'
2-3"×14"

BLOCK 'D' @
HEADER @
H > 16'-10"
8"×8" @ H > 10'-7"
8"×10"
8"×10"
8"×10" @ H > 21'-10"
BLOCKS 'E'
@ BOTTOM
MEMBERS
8"×12"×11'-0" @ 2'-8"
BOTTOM MEMBERS 'A'
¾"φ ROD WITH
2-3"×3"×⅜" ℔
WASHERS @ ℄
'BOTTOM' MEMBERS
SHOWN HERE
FOR CLARITY.
ADDED 8"×8"
'BOTTOM' MEMBERS 'B'

H= 29'-4" MAX.
H= 19'-4" MAX. WITHOUT 'BOTTOM'
D
D

SEE 'GENERAL CONFIGURATION'
AND 'TYPICAL DETAILS' DRAWINGS
FOR FURTHER REQUIREMENTS.

TOE SOIL PRESSURE
H IN FT.
P IN KSF

STANDARD   TREATED   TIMBER   CRIBBING
BASIC DESIGN - TYPE F - LEVEL SURCHARGE

AMERICAN WOOD PRESERVERS INSTITUTE
Washington, D.C.
Portland, Oregon   San Francisco, California

SKILLING, HELLE, CHRISTIANSEN, ROBERTSON
SEATTLE, WASHINGTON
STRUCTURAL ENGINEERS

SHANNON AND WILS.
SEATTLE, WASHINGTON
SOILS ENGINEERS

DATE:
JAN. 1969

GRAPHIC SCALE:
0 1 2 3 4 5   10

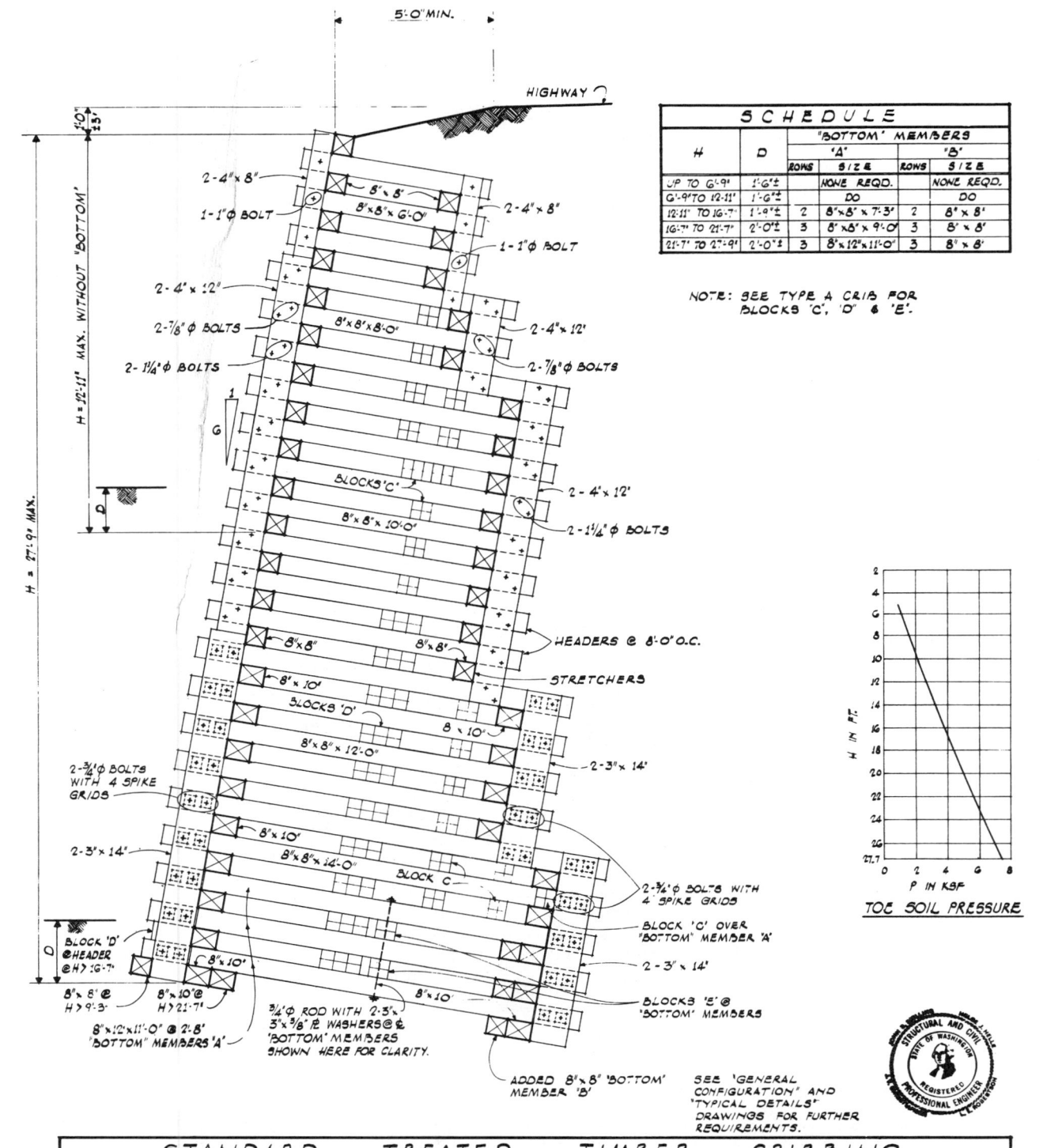

SCHEDULE

H	D	"BOTTOM" MEMBERS			
		'A'		'B'	
		ROWS	SIZE	ROWS	SIZE
UP TO 6'-9"	1'-6"±	NONE REQD.		NONE REQD.	
6'-9" TO 12'-11"	1'-6"±	DO		DO	
12'-11" TO 16'-7"	1'-9"±	2	8"x8"x 7'-3"	2	8" x 8'
16'-7" TO 21'-7"	2'-0"±	3	8"x8"x 9'-0"	3	8" x 8'
21'-7" TO 27'-9"	2'-0"±	3	8"x12"x11'-0"	3	8" x 8'

NOTE: SEE TYPE A CRIB FOR
BLOCKS 'C', 'D' & 'E'.

TOE SOIL PRESSURE

STANDARD   TREATED   TIMBER   CRIBBING
BASIC DESIGN - TYPE G - HIGHWAY SURCHARGE

AMERICAN WOOD PRESERVERS INSTITUTE	SKILLING, HELLE, CHRISTIANSEN, ROBERTSON
Washington, D.C.	SEATTLE, WASHINGTON
Portland, Oregon San Francisco, California	STRUCTURAL ENGINEERS
DATE: JAN. 1969	SHANNON AND WILSON
GRAPHIC SCALE: 0 1 2 3 4 5 ... 10	SEATTLE, WASHINGTON SOILS ENGINEERS

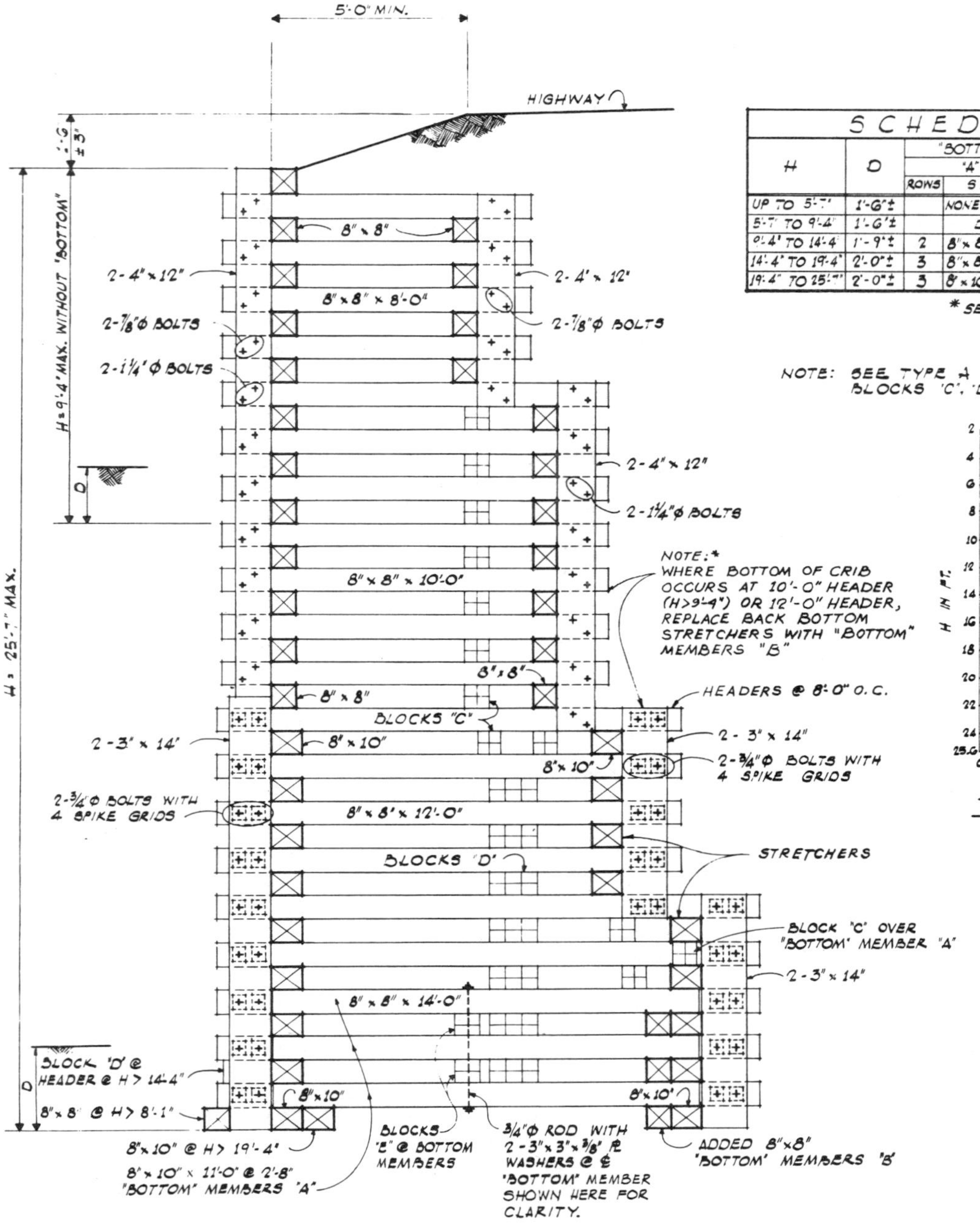
5'-0" MIN.
HIGHWAY
1'-6" ± 3"
H = 9'-4" MAX. WITHOUT "BOTTOM"
D
H = 25'-7" MAX.
8" × 8"
2-4" × 12"
2-4" × 12"
8" × 8" × 8'-0"
2-7/8"φ BOLTS
2-7/8"φ BOLTS
2-1¼"φ BOLTS
2-4" × 12"
2-1¼"φ BOLTS
8" × 8" × 10'-0"
NOTE:*
WHERE BOTTOM OF CRIB OCCURS AT 10'-0" HEADER (H>9'-4") OR 12'-0" HEADER, REPLACE BACK BOTTOM STRETCHERS WITH "BOTTOM" MEMBERS "B"
8" × 8"
8" × 8"
HEADERS @ 8'-0" O.C.
BLOCKS "C"
2-3" × 14"
8" × 10"
2-3" × 14"
8" × 10"
2-3/4"φ BOLTS WITH 4 SPIKE GRIDS
2-3/4"φ BOLTS WITH 4 SPIKE GRIDS
8" × 8" × 12'-0"
BLOCKS 'D'
STRETCHERS
BLOCK 'C' OVER "BOTTOM" MEMBER "A"
2-3" × 14"
8" × 8" × 14'-0"
BLOCK 'D' @ HEADER @ H > 14'-4"
8" × 10"
8" × 10"
8" × 8" @ H > 8'-1"
8" × 10" @ H > 19'-4"
8" × 10" × 11'-0" @ 2'-8" "BOTTOM" MEMBERS "A"
BLOCKS "E" @ BOTTOM MEMBERS
3/4"φ ROD WITH 2-3" × 3" × 3/8" PL WASHERS @ ℄ "BOTTOM" MEMBER SHOWN HERE FOR CLARITY.
ADDED 8" × 8" "BOTTOM" MEMBERS "B"

SCHEDULE					
H	D	"BOTTOM" MEMBERS			
		"A"		"B"	
		ROWS	SIZE	ROWS	SIZE
UP TO 5'-7"	1'-6"±		NONE REQD.		NONE REQD.
5'-7" TO 9'-4"	1'-6"±		DO		DO
9'-4" TO 14'-4"	1'-9"±	2	8" × 8" × 7'-3"	2	8" × 12" *
14'-4" TO 19'-4"	2'-0"±	3	8" × 8" × 9'-0"	3	8" × 12" *
19'-4" TO 25'-7"	2'-0"±	3	8" × 10" × 11'-0"	3	8" × 8"

* SEE NOTE ON FIGURE

NOTE: SEE TYPE A CRIB FOR BLOCKS 'C', 'D' & 'E'.

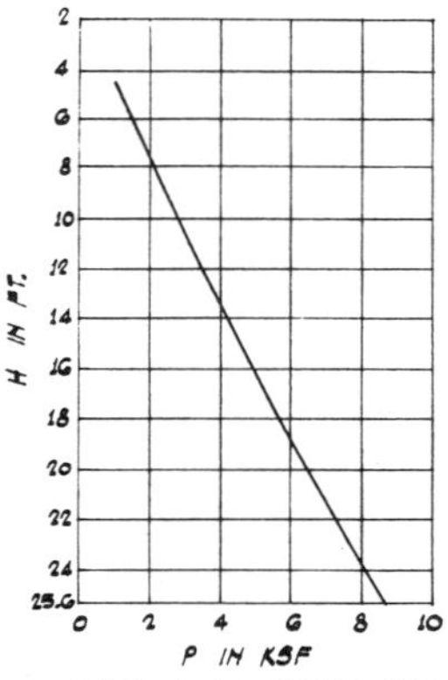
H IN FT.
2
4
6
8
10
12
14
16
18
20
22
24
25.6
0
2
4
6
8
10
P IN KSF

TOE SOIL PRESSURE

SEE "GENERAL CONFIGURATION" AND "TYPICAL DETAILS" DRAWINGS FOR FURTHER REQUIREMENTS.

STANDARD TREATED TIMBER CRIBBING
BASIC DESIGN - TYPE H - HIGHWAY SURCHARGE

AMERICAN WOOD PRESERVERS INSTITUTE
Washington, D.C.
Portland, Oregon — San Francisco, California

DATE: JAN. 1969

GRAPHIC SCALE: 0 1 2 3 4 5 10

SKILLING, HELLE, CHRISTIANSEN, ROBERTSON
SEATTLE, WASHINGTON
STRUCTURAL ENGINEERS

SHANNON AND WILSON
SEATTLE, WASHINGTON
SOILS ENGINEERS

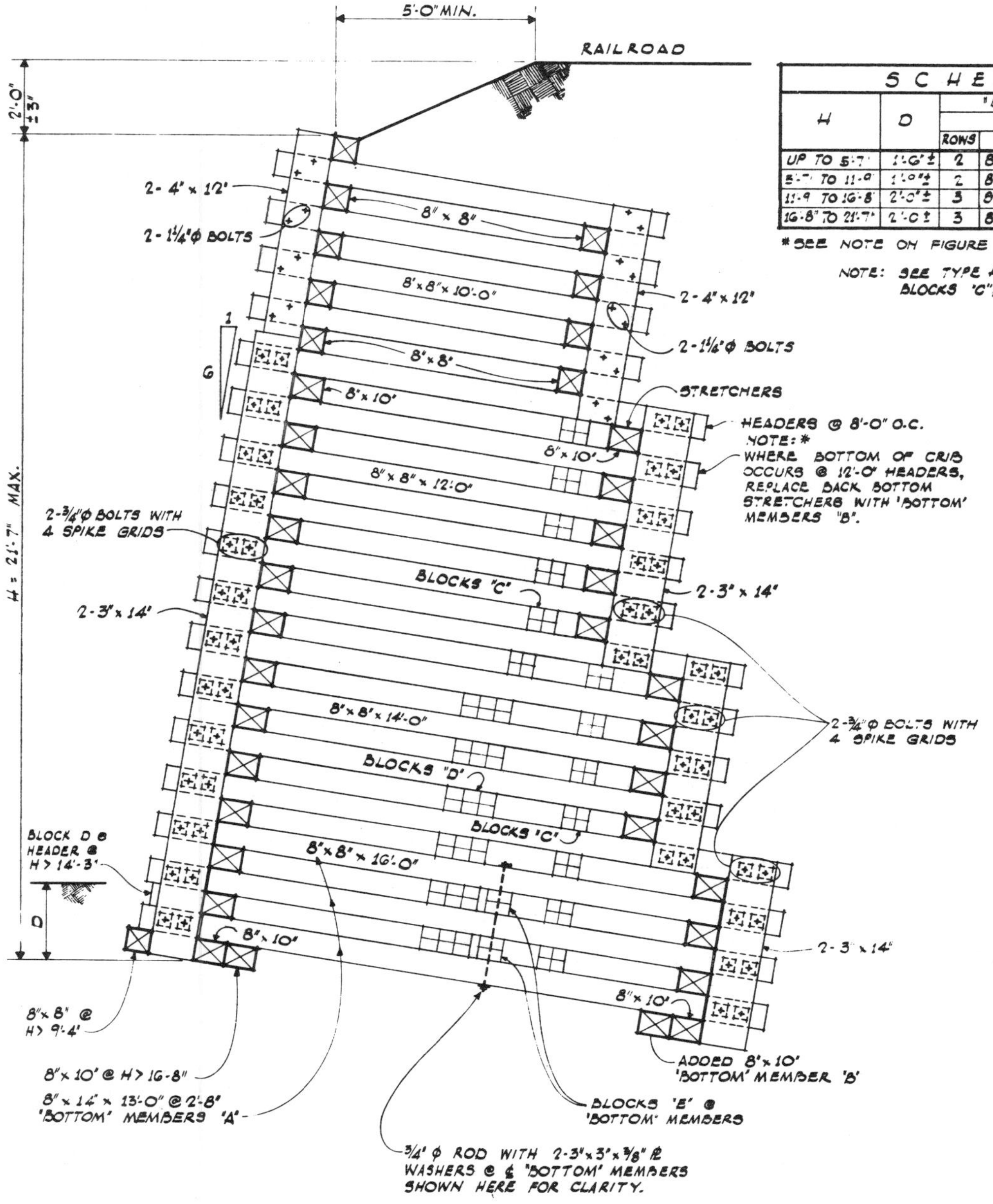

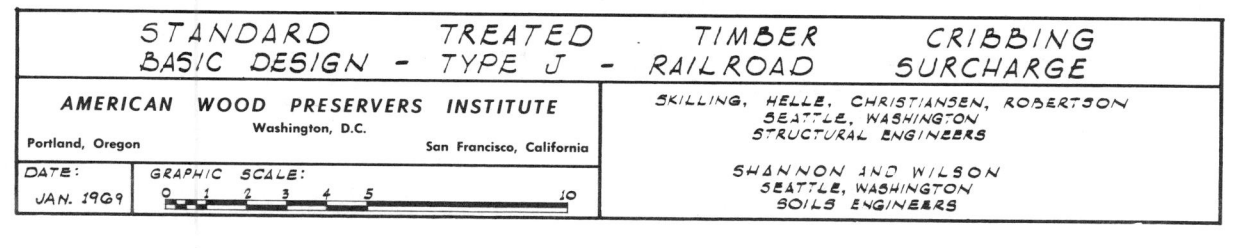

S C H E D U L E		'BOTTOM' MEMBERS				
H	D	'A'			'B'	
		ROWS	SIZE	ROWS	SIZE	
UP TO 5'-7"	1'-6"±	2	8"x 8" x 7'-3"		NONE REQ'D.	
5'-7" TO 11'-9	1'-9"±	2	8"x 8"x 9'-0"	2	8"x 12" *	
11'-9 TO 16'-8	2'-0"±	3	8"x 10"x 11'-0"	3	8"x 8	
16'-8" TO 21'-7"	2'-0 ±	3	8"x 14"x 13'-0"	3	8"x 10"	

* SEE NOTE ON FIGURE

NOTE: SEE TYPE A CRIB FOR
BLOCKS 'C', 'D' & 'E'.

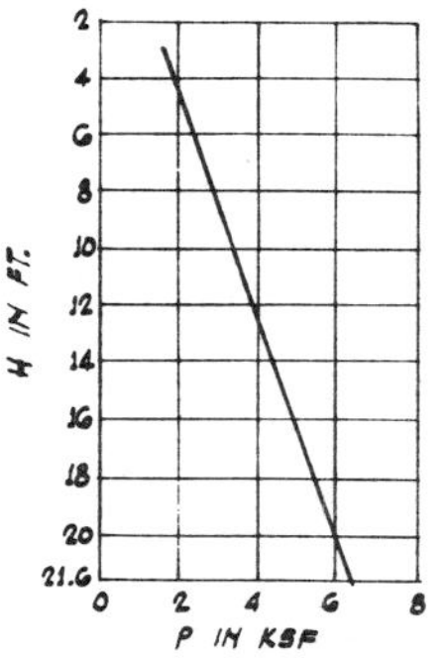

5'-0" MIN.

RAILROAD

2'-0"
+3"

2- 4" x 12"

2- 1¼" φ BOLTS

8" x 8"

8"x 8"x 10'-0"

2- 4" x 12"

2- 1¼" φ BOLTS

8" x 8"

8" x 10"

STRETCHERS

HEADERS @ 8'-0" O.C.
NOTE: *
WHERE BOTTOM OF CRIB
OCCURS @ 12'-0" HEADERS,
REPLACE BACK BOTTOM
STRETCHERS WITH 'BOTTOM'
MEMBERS "B".

6" x 10"

8" x 8" x 12'-0"

2-¾" φ BOLTS WITH
4 SPIKE GRIDS

BLOCKS 'C'

2- 3" x 14"

2- 3" x 14"

H = 21'-7" MAX.

8" x 8" x 14'-0"

BLOCKS 'D'

2-¾" φ BOLTS WITH
4 SPIKE GRIDS

BLOCKS 'C'

BLOCK D @
HEADER @
H > 14'-3"

8" x 8" x 16'-0"

D

8" x 10"

2- 3" x 14"

8" x 10"

8" x 8" @
H > 9'-4"

8" x 10" @ H > 16'-8"

8" x 14" x 13'-0" @ 2'-8"
'BOTTOM' MEMBERS 'A'

ADDED 8" x 10"
'BOTTOM' MEMBER 'B'

BLOCKS 'E' @
'BOTTOM' MEMBERS

¾" φ ROD WITH 2-3"x3"x⅜" R
WASHERS @ ₵ 'BOTTOM' MEMBERS
SHOWN HERE FOR CLARITY.

TOE SOIL PRESSURE

H IN FT.

P IN KSF

SEE "GENERAL CONFIGURATION"
AND "TYPICAL DETAILS" DRAWINGS
FOR FURTHER REQUIREMENTS.

STANDARD   TREATED   TIMBER   CRIBBING
BASIC DESIGN - TYPE J - RAILROAD   SURCHARGE

AMERICAN WOOD PRESERVERS INSTITUTE
Washington, D.C.
Portland, Oregon   San Francisco, California

SKILLING, HELLE, CHRISTIANSEN, ROBERTSON
SEATTLE, WASHINGTON
STRUCTURAL ENGINEERS

SHANNON AND WILSON
SEATTLE, WASHINGTON
SOILS ENGINEERS

DATE:
JAN. 1969

GRAPHIC SCALE:
0 1 2 3 4 5   10

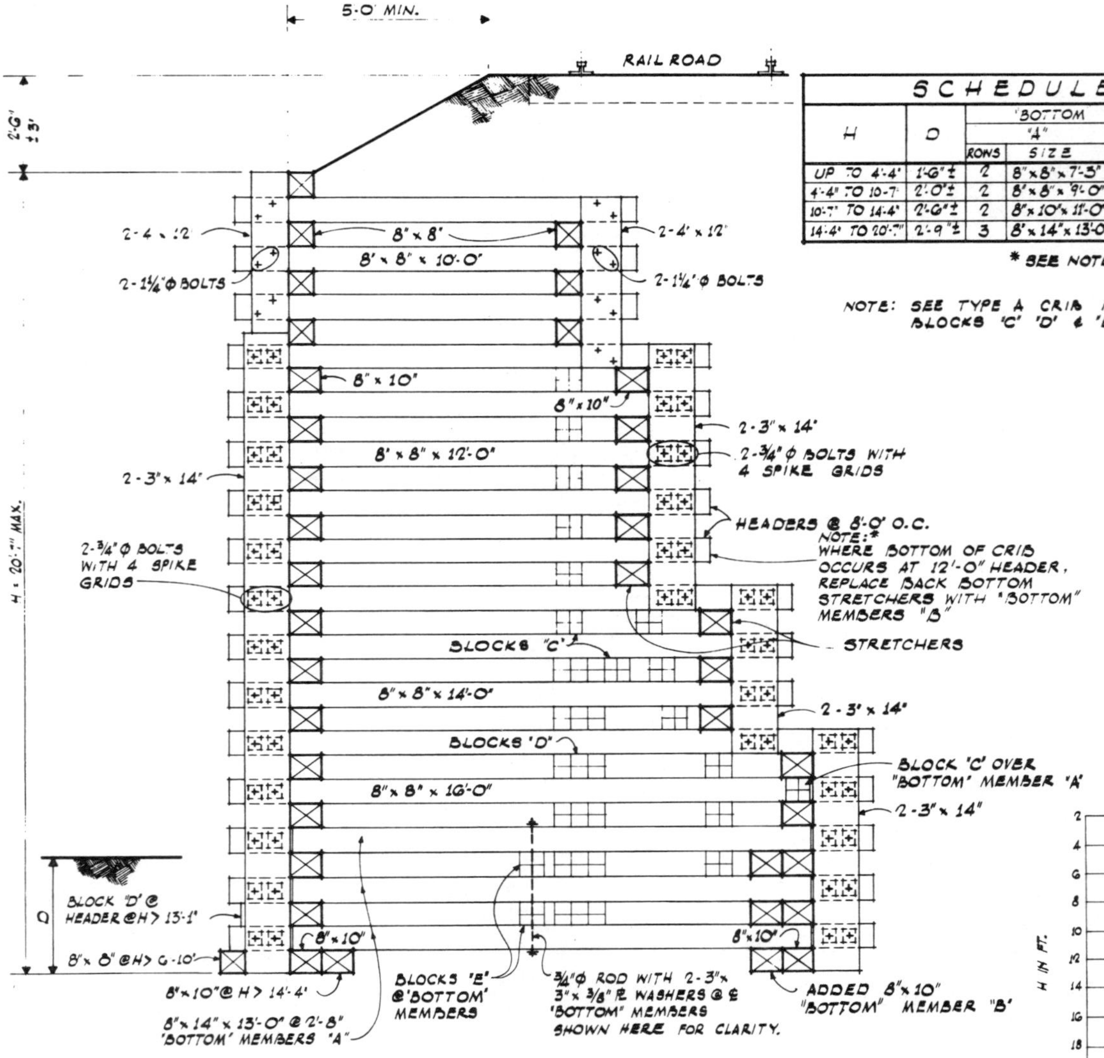

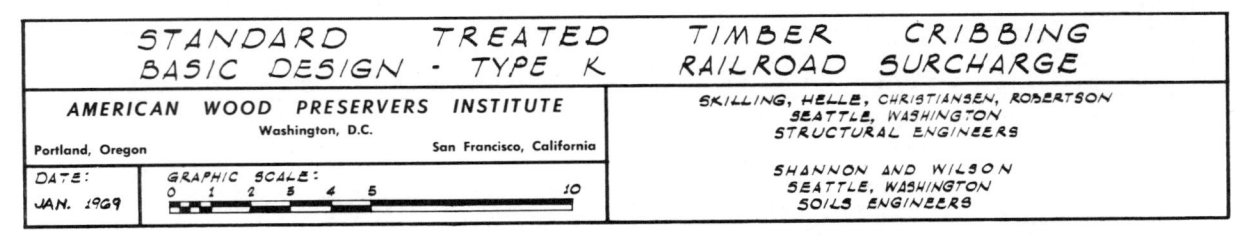

5'-0" MIN.

RAIL ROAD

2'-0" ±3"

H = 20'-7" MAX.

2-4" x 12
8" x 8"
8" x 8" x 10'-0"
2-1¼" Ø BOLTS
2-4" x 12
2-1¼" Ø BOLTS

8" x 10"
8" x 10"
8' x 8" x 12'-0"
2-3" x 14"
2-3" x 14"
2-¾" Ø BOLTS WITH 4 SPIKE GRIDS

2-¾" Ø BOLTS WITH 4 SPIKE GRIDS

HEADERS @ 8'-0" O.C.
NOTE:*
WHERE BOTTOM OF CRIB OCCURS AT 12'-0" HEADER, REPLACE BACK BOTTOM STRETCHERS WITH "BOTTOM" MEMBERS "B"

BLOCKS "C"
STRETCHERS
8" x 8" x 14'-0"
BLOCKS "D"
2-3" x 14"
8" x 8" x 16'-0"
BLOCK "C" OVER "BOTTOM" MEMBER "A"
2-3" x 14"

BLOCK "D" @ HEADER @ H > 13'-1"
8" x 8" @ H > 6'-10'
8" x 10"
8" x 10"
ADDED 8" x 10" "BOTTOM" MEMBER "B"

8" x 10" @ H > 14'-4"
8" x 14" x 13'-0" @ 2'-8" 'BOTTOM' MEMBERS "A"
BLOCKS "E" @ "BOTTOM" MEMBERS
¾" Ø ROD WITH 2-3" x 3" x ⅜" Pᴸ WASHERS @ ℄ "BOTTOM" MEMBERS SHOWN HERE FOR CLARITY.

SCHEDULE

H	D	BOTTOM MEMBERS 'A'		'B'	
		ROWS	SIZE	ROWS	SIZE
UP TO 4'-4"	1'-6"±	2	8"x8"x7'-3"		NONE REQD.
4'-4" TO 10'-7"	2'-0"±	2	8"x8"x9'-0"	2	8"x12"
10'-7" TO 14'-4"	2'-6"±	2	8"x10"x11'-0"	2	8"x8"
14'-4" TO 20'-7"	2'-9"±	3	8"x14"x13'-0	3	8"x10"

* SEE NOTE ON FIGURE

NOTE: SEE TYPE A CRIB FOR BLOCKS 'C' 'D' & 'E'.

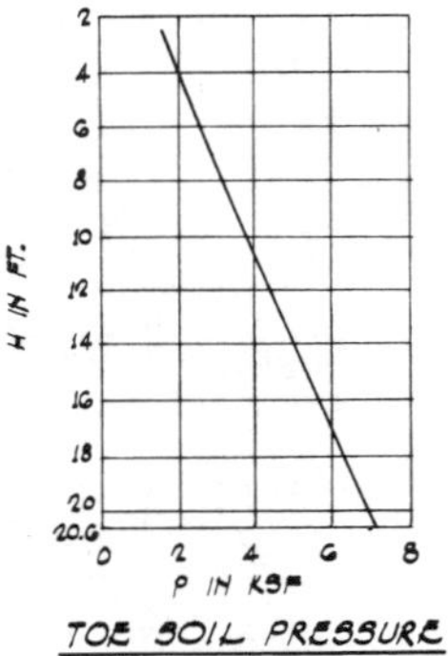

TOE SOIL PRESSURE
H IN FT.
P IN KSF

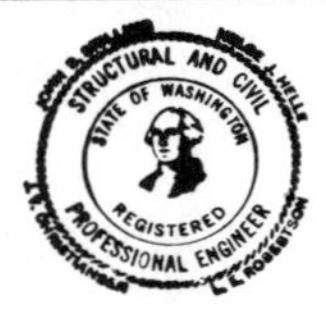

SEE "GENERAL CONFIGURATION" AND "TYPICAL DETAILS" DRAWINGS FOR FURTHER REQUIREMENTS.

STANDARD TREATED TIMBER CRIBBING
BASIC DESIGN - TYPE K RAILROAD SURCHARGE

AMERICAN WOOD PRESERVERS INSTITUTE
Washington, D.C.
Portland, Oregon   San Francisco, California

DATE:
JAN. 1969
GRAPHIC SCALE:
0 1 2 3 4 5   10

SKILLING, HELLE, CHRISTIANSEN, ROBERTSON
SEATTLE, WASHINGTON
STRUCTURAL ENGINEERS

SHANNON AND WILSON
SEATTLE, WASHINGTON
SOILS ENGINEERS

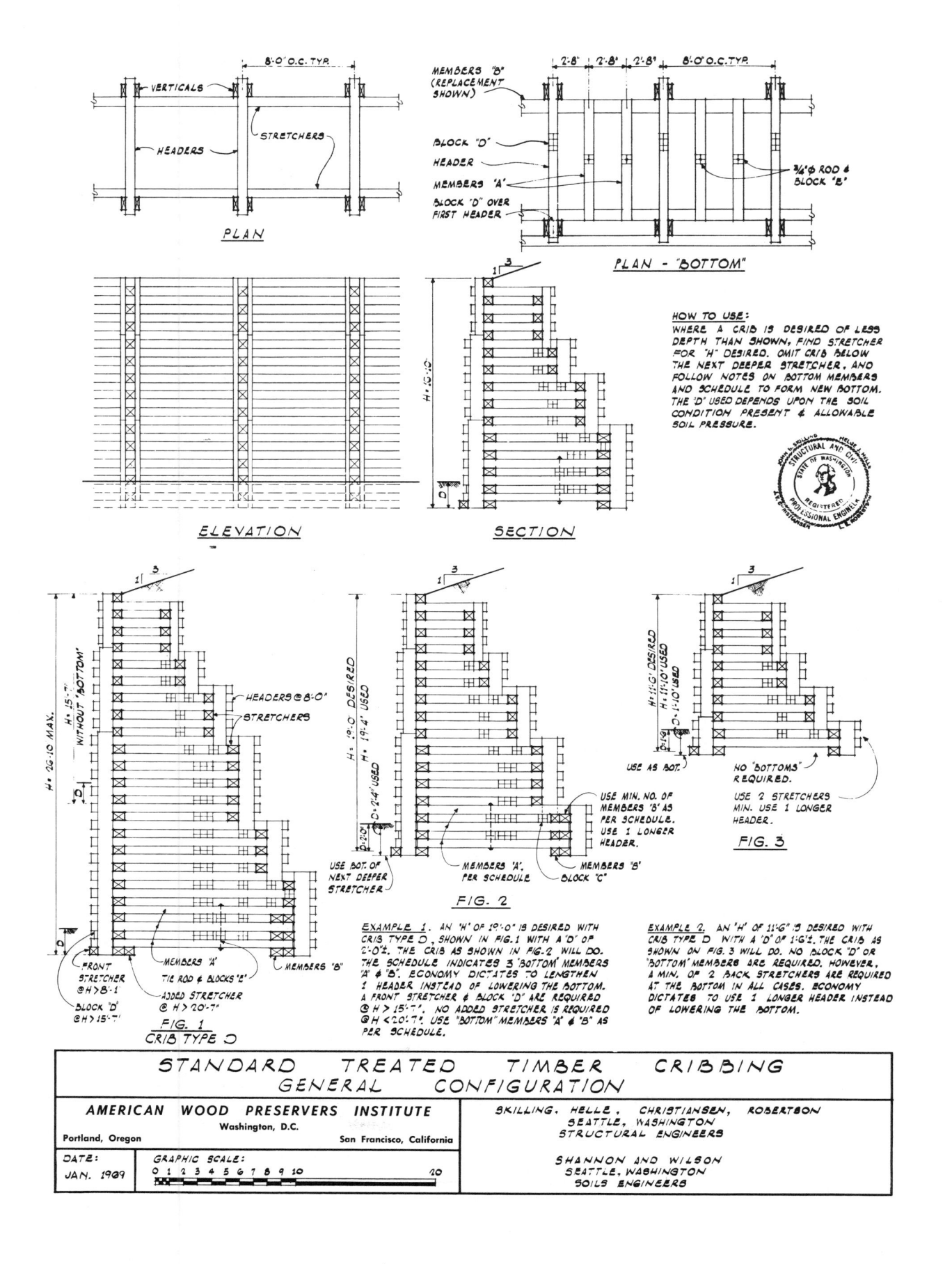

STANDARD TREATED TIMBER CRIBBING
GENERAL CONFIGURATION

AMERICAN WOOD PRESERVERS INSTITUTE
Washington, D.C.
Portland, Oregon
San Francisco, California

SKILLING, HELLE, CHRISTIANSEN, ROBERTSON
SEATTLE, WASHINGTON
STRUCTURAL ENGINEERS

SHANNON AND WILSON
SEATTLE, WASHINGTON
SOILS ENGINEERS

DATE: JAN. 1969

GRAPHIC SCALE:
0 1 2 3 4 5 6 7 8 9 10   20

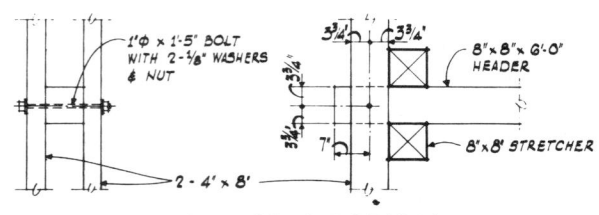

1'Ø x 1'5' BOLT
WITH 2-1/8' WASHERS
& NUT

8"x 8"x G'-0"
HEADER

8'x 8' STRETCHER

2 - 4' x 8'

1 BOLT CONNECTION

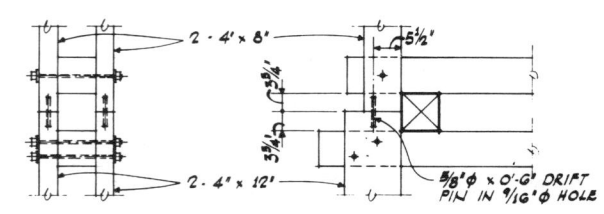

2 - 4' x 8'

2 - 4' x 12'

5/8"Ø x 0'-G' DRIFT
PIN IN 9/16"Ø HOLE

SPLICE CONNECTION

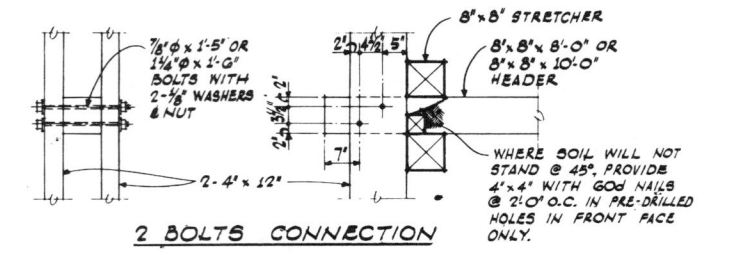

7/8'Ø x 1'5' OR
1-1/4'Ø x 1'-G'
BOLTS WITH
2-1/8' WASHERS
& NUT

8"x 8" STRETCHER

8'x 8'x 8'-0" OR
8'x 8'x 10'-0"
HEADER

WHERE SOIL WILL NOT
STAND @ 45°, PROVIDE
4'x 4' WITH GOd NAILS
@ 2'-0' O.C. IN PRE-DRILLED
HOLES IN FRONT FACE
ONLY.

2 - 4' x 12'

2 BOLTS CONNECTION

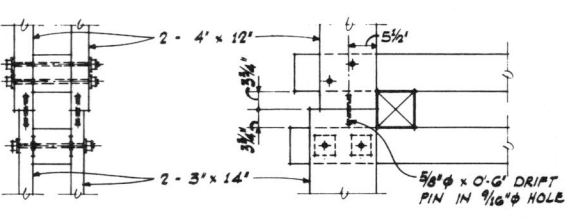

2 - 4' x 12'

2 - 3' x 14'

5/8"Ø x 0'-G' DRIFT
PIN IN 9/16"Ø HOLE

SPLICE CONNECTION

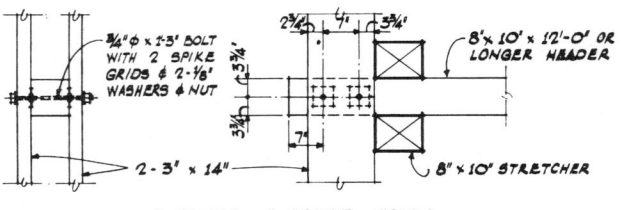

3/4'Ø x 1'5' BOLT
WITH 2 SPIKE
GRIDS & 2-1/8'
WASHERS & NUT

8'x 10'x 12'-0' OR
LONGER HEADER

2 - 3' x 14"

8'x 10' STRETCHER

2 BOLTS, 4 SPIKE GRIDS
CONNECTIONS

GENERAL NOTES

1. ALL TIMBER SHALL BE CONSTRUCTION GRADE f=1200PSI MIN. DOUGLAS FIR OR HEMLOCK (WEST COAST OR WESTERN), PRESSURE TREATED AFTER FABRICATION (SEE NOTE G). S4S

2. ALL STRETCHERS SHALL BE LAID HORIZONTALLY.

3. FASTENERS SHALL BE MACHINE BOLTS TO MATCH ASTM A-307 SPECIFICATIONS & TECO SPIKE GRID OR EQUAL. ALL HARDWARE TO BE HOT-DIPPED GALVANIZED.

4. SOIL CONDITIONS:
   FOR EACH SPECIFIC SITE AT WHICH A CRIB WALL IS TO BE PLACED, A STUDY SHOULD BE MADE TO DETERMINE THE SOIL & GROUNDWATER CONDITIONS & THE STABILITY OF THE CRIB WALL.

   THE CHARTS SHOWN GIVE PROPORTIONS & DETAILS FOR CRIB WALLS FOR THE FOLLOWING CONDITIONS:

   A. FOUNDATION CONSISTS OF SAND, SAND & GRAVEL, OR OTHER GRANULAR SOIL WHICH WILL NOT SETTLE SIGNIFICANTLY UNDER THE WEIGHT OF THE CRIB & FILL.

   B. FILL WITHIN CRIBS & BEHIND CRIBS CONSISTS OF SAND, SAND & GRAVEL, OR OTHER FREE DRAINING GRANULAR MATERIAL PLACED IN G" LAYERS & COMPACTED WITH VIBRATORY COMPACTORS.

   C. GROUNDWATER TABLE IS BELOW BASE OF CRIB.

   FOR OTHER SOIL OR GROUNDWATER CONDITIONS, THE CRIB PROPORTIONS & DETAILS SHOULD BE ADJUSTED AS NECESSARY TO PROVIDE AN ADEQUATE FACTOR-OF-SAFETY IN ACCORDANCE WITH GOOD ENGINEERING PRACTICE.

5. DESIGN ASSUMES END OF WALL TERMINATION TO OCCUR AT MAXIMUM WALL HEIGHT OF 5'-0". USE 16'-0" STRETCHERS TOE NAILED TO HEADERS @ ENDS. SPECIAL DESIGN IS REQUIRED TO TURN CORNER WITH HIGHER WALL.

G. PRESSURE TREATMENT SHALL BE OF GROUND CONTACT RETENTION EQUIVALENT TO AWPI STANDARDS LP-22, LP-33, LP44, LP55 OR LP-77 WITH PRESERVATIVE TYPE AT PURCHASERS OPTION.

STANDARD TREATED TIMBER CRIBBING TYPICAL DETAILS AND GENERAL NOTES	
AMERICAN WOOD PRESERVERS INSTITUTE Washington, D.C. Portland, Oregon San Francisco, California	SKILLING, HELLE, CHRISTIANSEN, ROBERTSON SEATTLE, WASHINGTON STRUCTURAL ENGINEERS SHANNON AND WILSON SEATTLE, WASHINGTON SOILS ENGINEERS
DATE: JAN. 1969	GRAPHIC SCALE: 0 1 2 3 G

2. Perma-Crib Walls, Types A through D

The Perma Crib Wall

Permapost Products Company has manufactured timber crib walls throughout the past decade. The design below was adopted by the U.S. Forest Service for use on several jobs in the Mt. Hood National Forest. Testing and instrumentation of the design was conducted by the University of Idaho under a contract with the U.S. Forest Service. The study and experience gained here enabled us to complete additional improvements to the design and to improve installation. During recent years this tested, proved, crib design has been utilized on many projects including several large cribs for the Colorado State Highway Dept. on Interstate highway No. 70 near Vail, Colorado. Using relatively unskilled labor and a minimum of equipment the contractor reported excellent assembly time with no problems.

Cribs are normally spaced in 8' multiples. However, special sizes, curves or tangents can be designed to suit special alignments. Standard Perma-Cribs are designed for highway surcharge.

Four types are available to cover various heights:

Type A - Up to 7' 1¼"   Type C - Up to 17' 5¼"
Type B - Up to 12' 3¼"   Type D - Up to 22' 7¼"

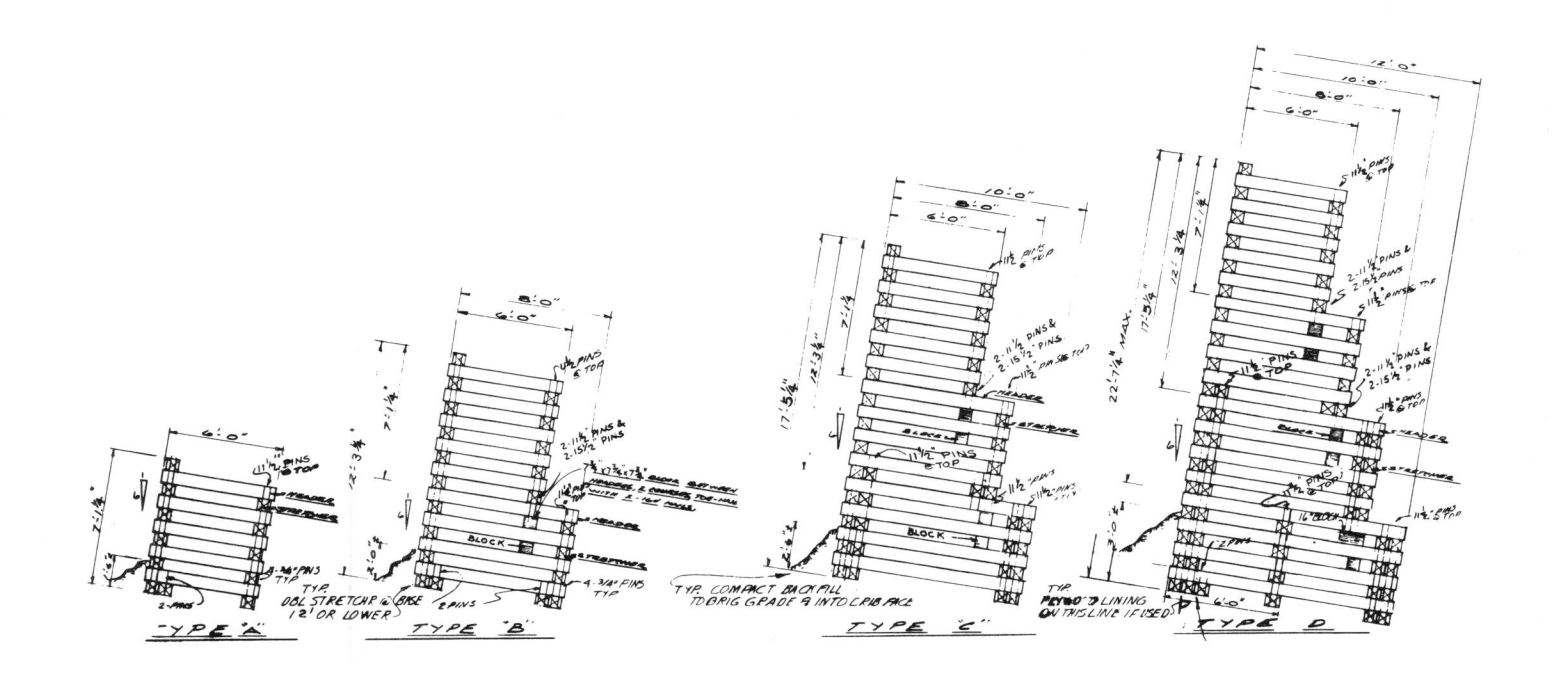

3. Washington State Department of Highways Log Cribbing

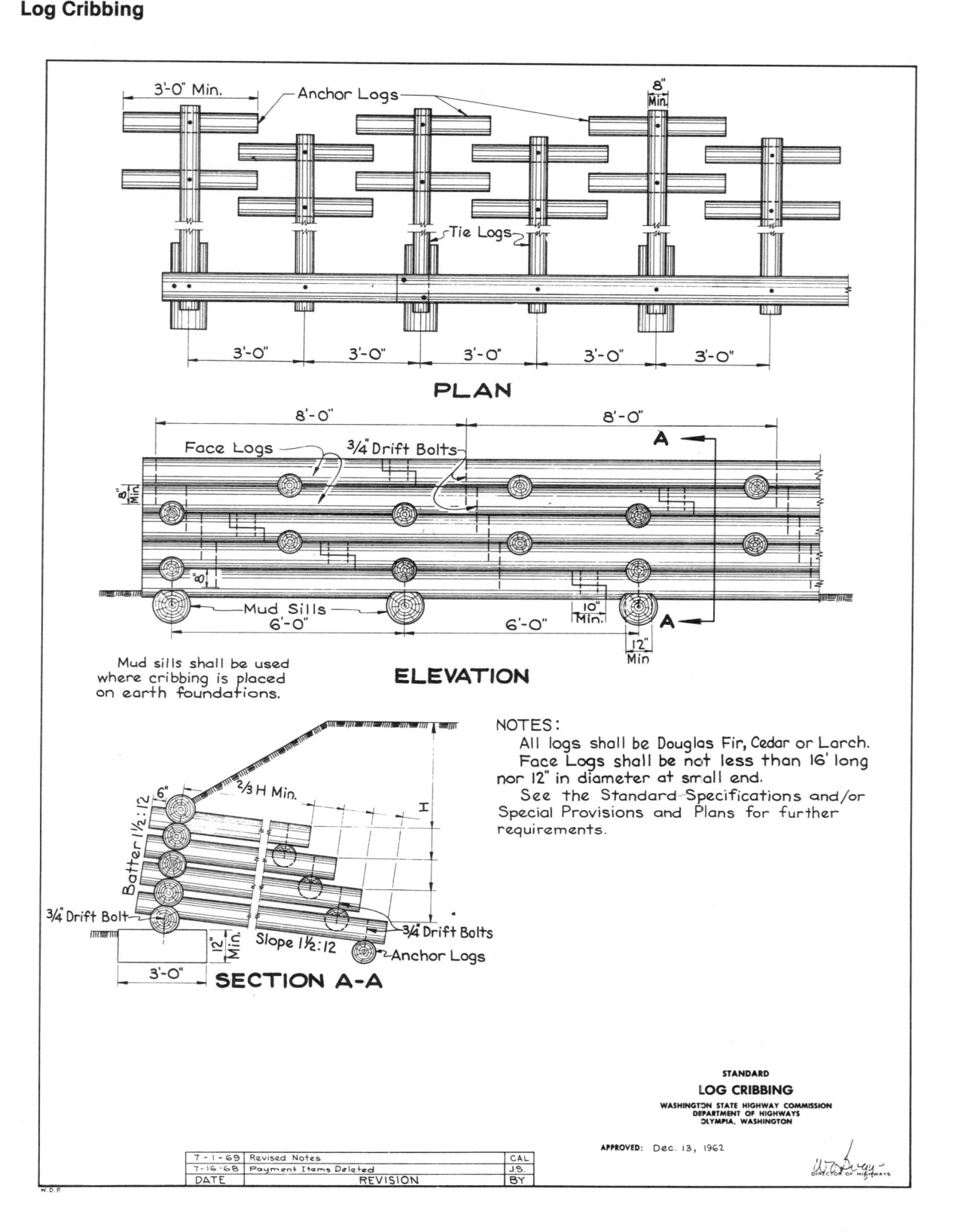

Washington State Department of Highways standard plans for log cribbing, 1973.

C. CONCRETE CRIBS

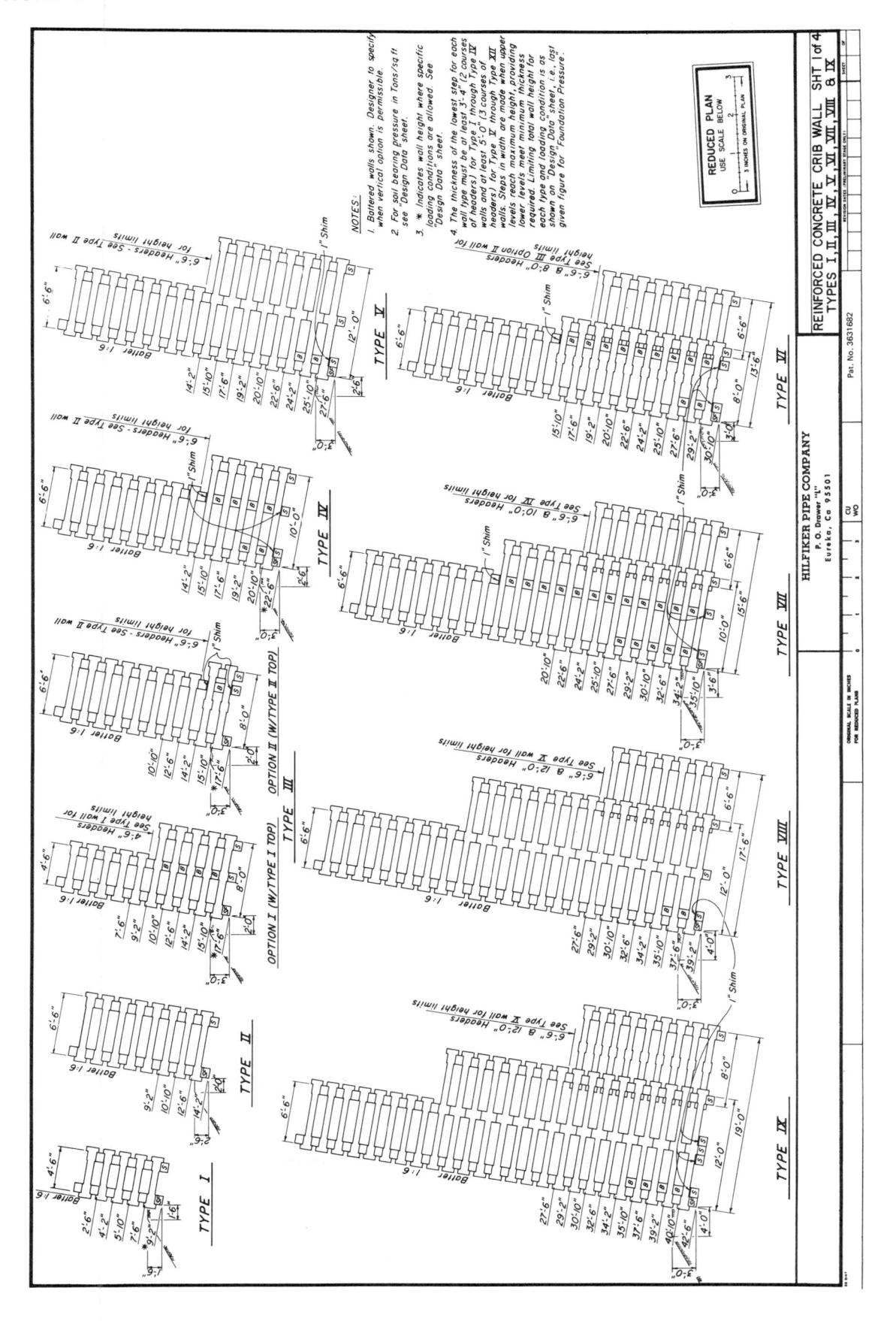

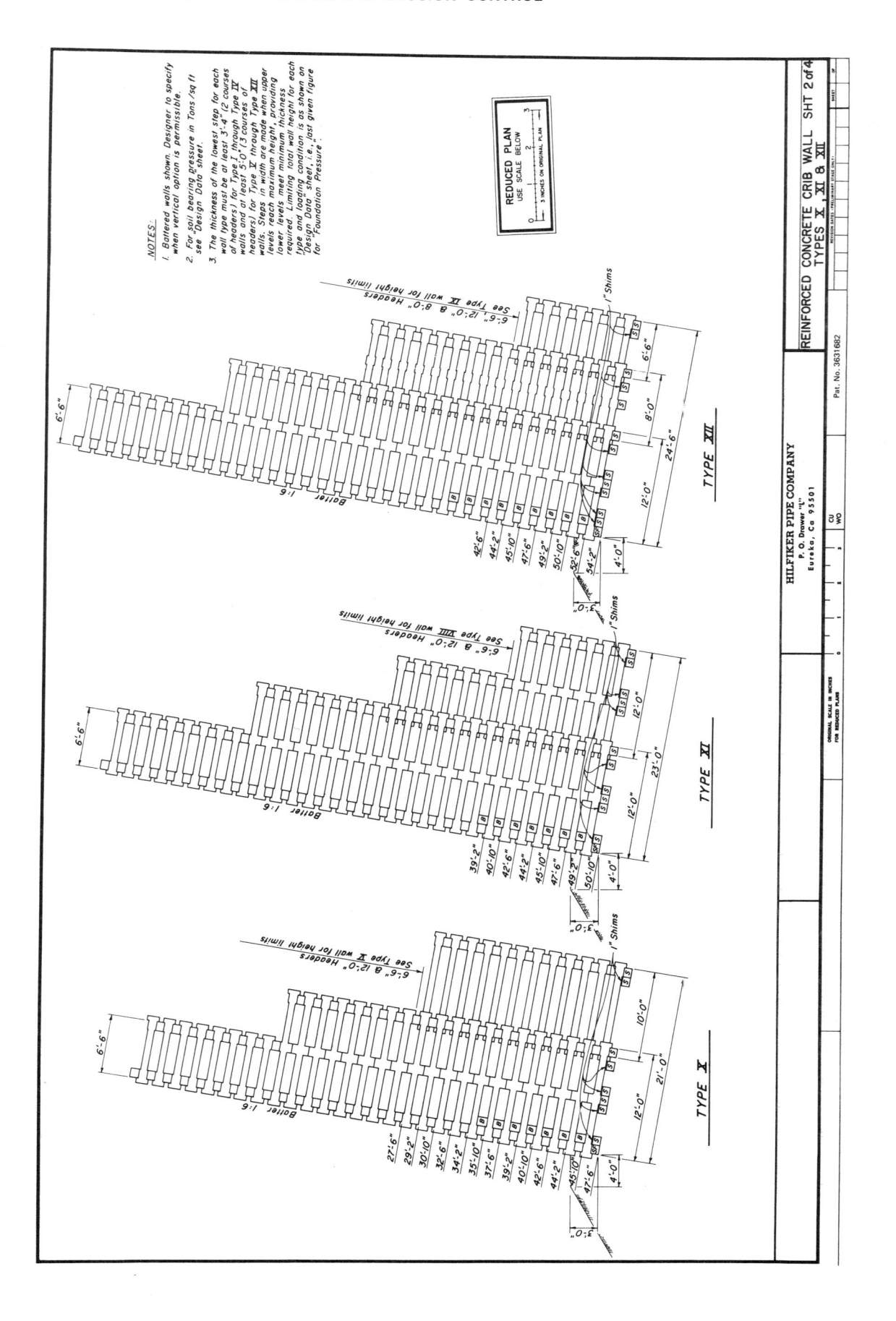

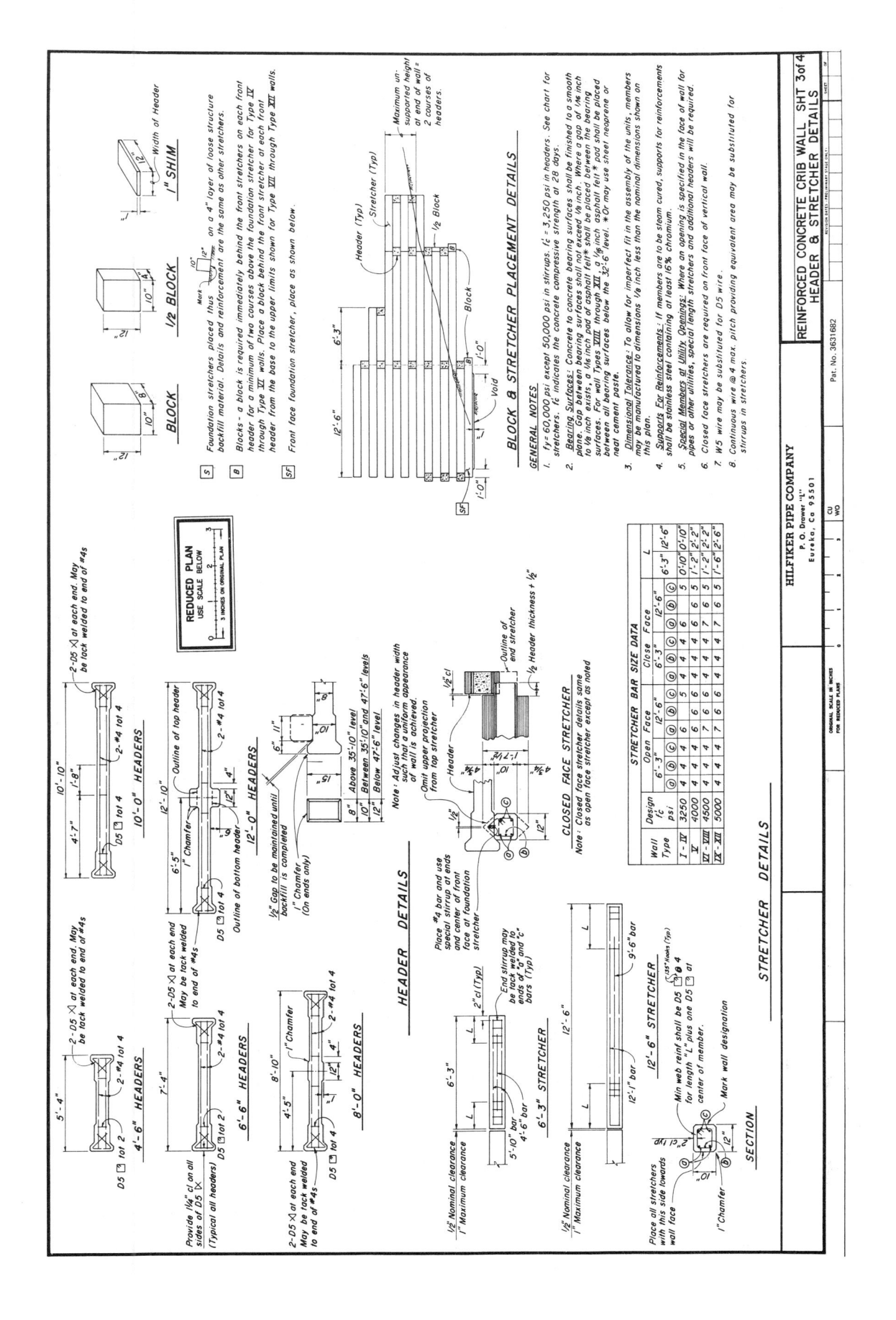

1:6 BATTER WALL

Foundation Pressure in Tons Per Sq Ft

TYPE	LOADING CONDITION	2'-6"	4'-2"	5'-10"	7'-6"	9'-2"	10'-10"	12'-6"	14'-2"	15'-10"	17'-6"	19'-2"	20'-10"	22'-6"	24'-2"	25'-10"	27'-6"
I	2S+T	0.3	0.5	0.9	1.3												
	1½:1	0.6	0.7	0.8	1.4	1.7											
	2:1	0.4	0.6	0.7	0.8	0.9											
II	2S+T	0.5	0.5	0.6	0.7	1.0	1.3	1.7	2.2								
	1½:1	0.7	0.9	0.9	1.2	1.4	1.6	2.6	3.0								
	2:1	0.5	0.7	0.8	1.0	1.1	1.2	1.2	1.5								
III-I	2S+T					1.0	1.2	1.5	1.8	2.2							
	1½:1					1.2	1.7	2.0	2.8	3.2	4.4						
	2:1					0.8	1.0	1.2	1.5	1.8	2.2						
III-II	2S+T							1.6	2.0	2.4							
	1½:1							2.6	3.0	3.3	4.6						
	2:1							1.4	1.7	2.0	2.4						
IV	2S+T									1.9	2.2	2.6	3.0				
	1½:1									3.0	3.3	4.3	4.8	6.2			
	2:1									1.8	2.1	2.4	2.8	3.2			

TYPE	LOADING CONDITION	15'-10"	17'-6"	19'-2"	20'-10"	22'-6"	24'-2"	25'-10"	27'-6"	29'-2"	30'-10"	32'-6"	34'-2"	35'-10"	37'-6"	39'-2"	40'-10"
V	2S+T	1.6	1.8	2.0	2.3	2.7	3.0	3.4	3.9								
	1½:1	2.8	3.1	3.3	4.2	4.6	5.6	6.1	7.5								
	2:1	1.5	1.8	2.0	2.3	2.6	3.0	3.4	3.9								
VI	2S+T		1.7	1.9	2.1	2.4	2.7	3.0	3.4	3.8	4.2						
	1½:1		3.0	3.2	3.5	4.3	4.6	5.6	6.0	7.2	7.7						
	2:1		1.7	1.9	2.2	2.4	2.7	3.1	3.4	3.8	4.3						
VII	2S+T					2.2	2.5	2.7	3.0	3.3	3.7	4.0	4.4	4.9			
	1½:1					4.1	4.4	4.8	5.6	6.0	7.0	7.5	8.7	9.4			
	2:1					2.4	2.6	2.9	3.2	3.6	3.9	4.3	4.8	5.2			
VIII	2S+T									3.2	3.4	3.7	4.1	4.4	4.8	5.2	
	1½:1									5.8	6.2	7.0	7.5	8.6	9.2	9.8	
	2:1									3.5	3.8	4.2	4.5	4.9	5.3	5.8	

TYPE	LOADING CONDITION	29'-2"	30'-10"	32'-6"	34'-2"	35'-10"	37'-6"	39'-2"	40'-10"	42'-6"	44'-2"	45'-10"	47'-6"	49'-2"	50'-10"	52'-6"	54'-2"
IX	2S+T	2.9	3.1	3.4	3.6	4.0	4.3	4.6	5.0	5.4							
	1½:1	5.4	5.8	6.2	6.9	7.4	8.3	8.8	9.9	10.5							
	2:1	3.2	3.5	3.8	4.1	4.5	4.8	5.2	5.7	6.1							
X	2S+T	2.6	2.8	3.0	3.3	3.5	3.8	4.1	4.4	4.7	5.1	5.5	5.9				
	1½:1	4.8	5.1	5.8	6.1	6.8	7.2	8.0	8.4	9.3	9.8	10.3	11.5				
	2:1	3.0	3.2	3.5	3.8	4.1	4.4	4.7	5.1	5.4	5.8	6.3	6.7				
XI	2S+T								4.4	4.7	5.0	5.3	5.7	6.1	6.5		
	1½:1								8.3	8.7	9.5	10.0	11.1	11.7	12.9		
	2:1								5.2	5.5	5.9	6.3	6.7	7.1	7.6		
XII	2S+T										4.8	5.1	5.4	5.7	6.1	6.5	6.9
	1½:1										9.1	9.6	10.4	10.9	11.9	12.6	13.8
	2:1										5.7	6.1	6.4	6.8	7.2	7.7	8.1

VERTICAL WALL

Foundation Pressure in Tons Per Sq Ft

TYPE	LOADING CONDITION	2'-6"	4'-2"	5'-10"	7'-6"	9'-2"	10'-10"	12'-6"	14'-2"	15'-10"	17'-6"	19'-2"
I	2S+T	0.4	0.7	1.2								
	1½:1	0.4	0.7									
	2:1	0.3	0.4	0.8	1.2	1.9						
II	2S+T	0.3	0.5	0.8	1.1	1.5	2.1					
	1½:1	0.5	0.5	1.0								
	2:1	0.4	0.4	0.6	0.9	1.3	1.8	2.4				
III-I	2S+T					1.2	1.6	2.0	2.6			
	1½:1											
	2:1					1.1	1.5	1.9	2.5	3.2	4.2	
III-II	2S+T							2.0	2.6			
	1½:1											
	2:1							1.9	2.5	3.2	4.2	
IV	2S+T									2.4	2.9	3.6
	1½:1											
	2:1									2.5	3.0	3.7

TYPE	LOADING CONDITION	15'-10"	17'-6"	19'-2"	20'-10"	22'-6"	24'-2"	25'-10"	27'-6"	29'-2"
V	2S+T	2.0	2.3	2.7	3.2	3.8				
	1½:1									
	2:1	2.1	2.6	3.0	3.6	4.2	5.0	6.1	7.4	
VI	2S+T		2.1	2.4	2.8	3.2	3.7	4.3	5.1	
	1½:1									
	2:1		2.3	2.7	3.2	3.7	4.3	5.0	5.8	6.9
VII	2S+T					2.8	3.2	3.6	4.0	4.6
	1½:1									
	2:1					3.3	3.7	4.2	4.8	5.5
VIII	2S+T									4.0
	1½:1									
	2:1									4.8

TYPE	LOADING CONDITION	29'-2"
IX	2S+T	3.6
	1½:1	
	2:1	4.4
X	2S+T	3.3
	1½:1	
	2:1	4.1

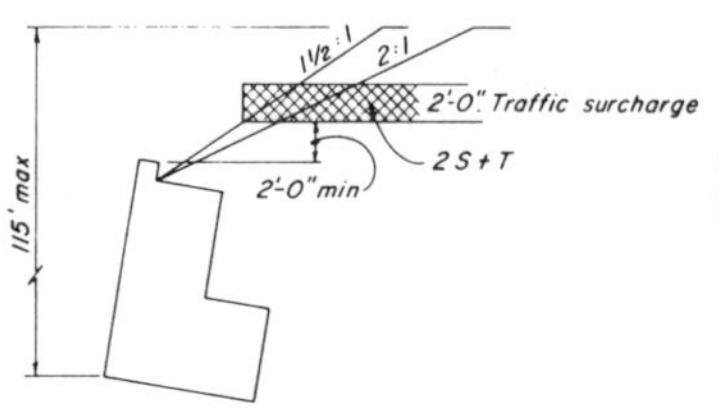

DESIGN SURCHARGE

DESIGN NOTES

1. Wall Base in Embankment: A minimum depth of 5 feet of embankment at 95% relative soil compaction is required below the base of all walls in order to constitute an embankment condition. When the foundation pressure is between 2.5 and 4.0 Tons/sq.ft., embankment below the wall shall consist of "Structure Backfill" material as set forth in Section 19-3.06 of the Standard Specifications. The limits of relative compaction (95%) shall be as set forth in Section 19-5.03 of the Standard Specifications.

2. Wall Base in Original Ground: Allowable soil pressure at toe of wall shall be determined by foundation site investigation. Walls that are to retain cut slopes shall be designed for lateral and toe pressures determined from site investigation data. Overall stability of slope with wall in place must be analyzed. If original ground slopes away from toe of wall, reduction in allowable bearing capacity due to slope must be considered.
   Walls shall not be founded in original ground having an allowable bearing capacity of less than 1.5 Tons/sq.ft.. Consideration should be given to removal and replacement of unsuitable material with "Structure Backfill" material as set forth in Section 19-3.06 of the Standard Specifications. The limits of relative compaction (95%) shall be set forth in Section 19-5.03 of the Standard Specifications.

3. Design Data: Weight of soil = 120 pcf for 2 foot level surcharge with traffic loading, an equivalent fluid pressure of 36 pcf was used. Earth pressures for 2:1 slope and 1½ slope were determined by trial wedge method with Ø = 33°42'.

4. The maximum allowable soil bearing capacity for walls founded in embankment is 4.0 Tons/sq.ft..

Legend for Chart

2S+T = 2 Foot level surcharge with traffic loading.
2:1 = 2:1 Slope above wall
1½:1 = 1½:1 Slope above wall
} 115' Max difference in elevation from toe of wall to top of slope

Heavy line indicates max allowable wall height for particular type and loading condition.

DESIGN EXAMPLES

Example No. 1
Given: Wall height 20'
2:1 Cut slope to be retained. Foundation site investigation indicates lateral pressure from material above will be equivalent to 2:1 design surcharge and the allowable soil bearing capacity is 2.5 tsf.
Select: Type V or VI battered wall. Actual H = 20'-10"

Type V or VI vertical walls can be used by increasing allowable bearing capacity of the original ground (See Design Note 2)

Example No. 2
Given: Wall height 9'
2' level surcharge with traffic loading to be retained. Base founded in embankment.
Select: Battered or vertical Type II or Type III-I. Actual H = 9'-2"

Example No. 3
Given: Wall height 10'
1½:1 Embankment slope to be retained. Base in original ground, sloping away from toe of wall at 2:1. Foundation investigation determines allowable soil bearing capacity is 3 tsf (Reduced for the effect of the slope).
Select: Battered Type II or III-I. Actual H = 10'-10". Vertical wall not allowed due to insufficient sliding safety factor.

Example No. 4
Given: Wall height 30'
2:1 Embankment slope to be retained. Base in embankment (5' depth min.)
Select: Battered Type VII, VIII, IX or X. Actual height = 30'-10". For all types foundation pressure is between 2.5 and 4.0 tsf and embankment material must be "Structure Backfill" (See Design Note 1).

REDUCED PLAN
USE SCALE BELOW
0 1 2 3
3 INCHES ON ORIGINAL PLAN

HILFIKER PIPE COMPANY
P. O. Drawer "L"
Eureka, Ca 95501

REINFORCED CONCRETE CRIB WALL SHT 4 of 4
DESIGN DATA - TYPES I THRU XII

ORIGINAL SCALE IN INCHES FOR REDUCED PLANS 0 1 2 3

CU
WO

Pat. No. 3631682

REVISION DATES (PRELIMINARY STAGE ONLY)

SHEET OF

D. WELDED-WIRE WALLS

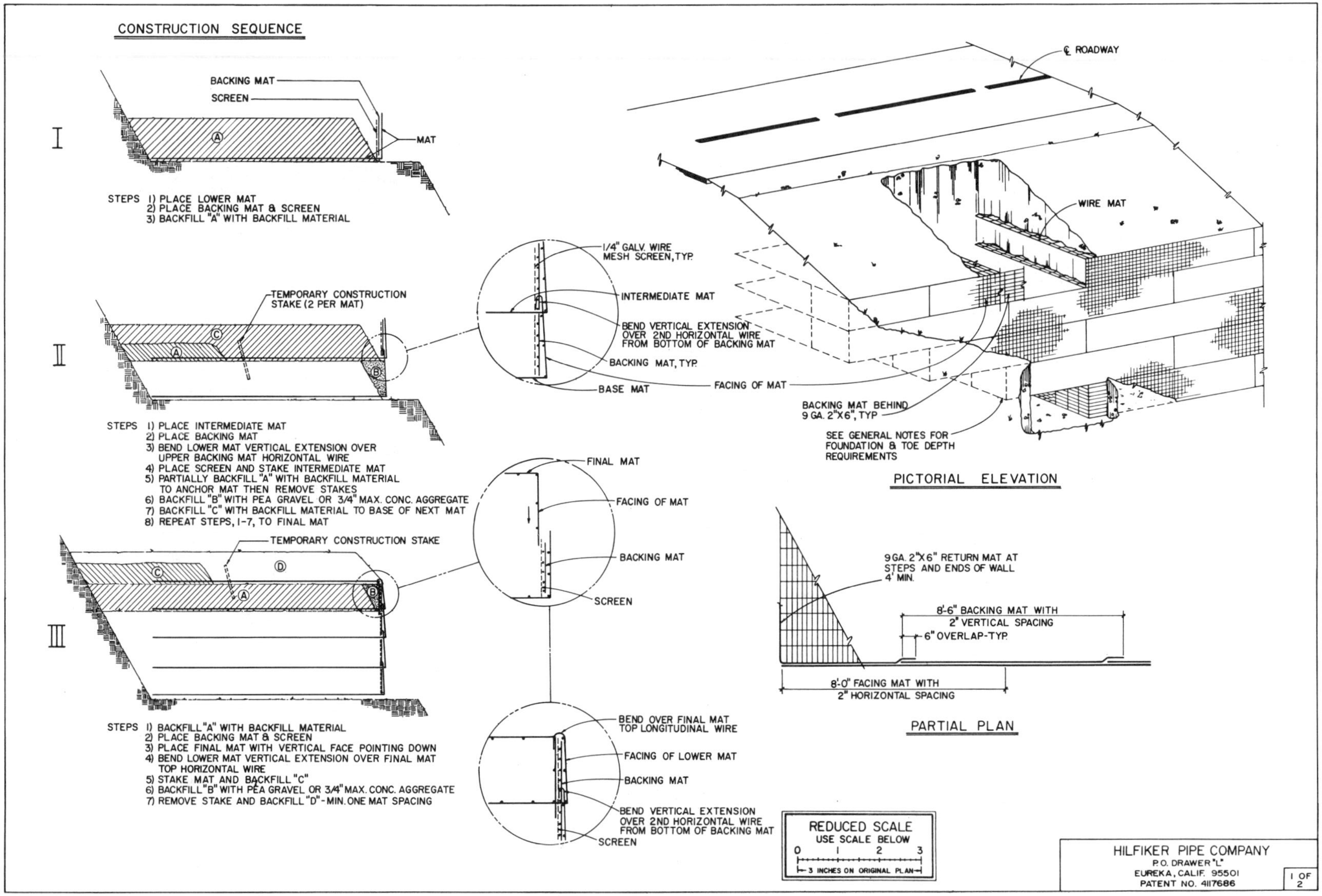

Reprinted with permission of the Hilfiker Pipe Company.

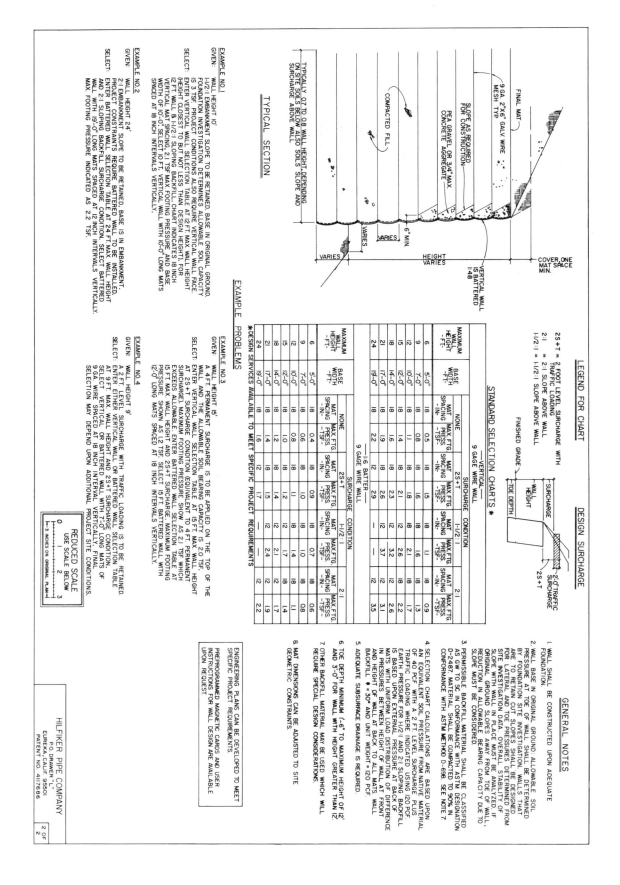

E. RIPRAP REVETMENTS: LOOSE ROCK RIPRAP[1]

1. Scope

The work shall consist of furnishing, transporting, and placing rock in the construction of loose rock riprap revetments, blankets, rock toes, crossings, and channel linings.

2. Quality of Materials

Individual rock fragments shall be dense, sound, and free from cracks, seams, and other defects conducive to accelerated weathering. The rock fragments shall be angular to subrounded in shape. The least dimension of an individual rock fragment shall be not less than one-third the greatest dimension of the fragment.

Representative samples of the rock shall conform to the following requirements:

a. The bulk specific gravity (in the saturated, surface dry condition) shall be not less than 2.5.

b. The soundness shall be such that the weight loss shall be not more than 20 percent after five cycles when tested by the sodium sulfate test method.

For all major structures, the riprap source shall be tested by a qualified materials testing laboratory.

3. Gradation

Unless otherwise shown on the drawings, rock riprap shall be well graded conforming to the following requirements:

a. Revetments

The following criteria shall be used to establish the gradation of the riprap:

(1) Stone equal or larger than the theoretical size with a few larger stones permitted should make up 50 percent of the rock by weight.

(2) The gradation of the smaller 50 percent should be selected to satisfy the filter requirements between the riprap and the filter blanket.

The theoretical stone size shall be selected from Fig. 1. Note that the impinging velocity (on outside bends directly in line with the central thread) may be assumed to be 4/3 the average stream velocity.

[1]Adapted from USDA-SCS Technical Guide, Wisconsin Construction Specifications, Section IV (1971).

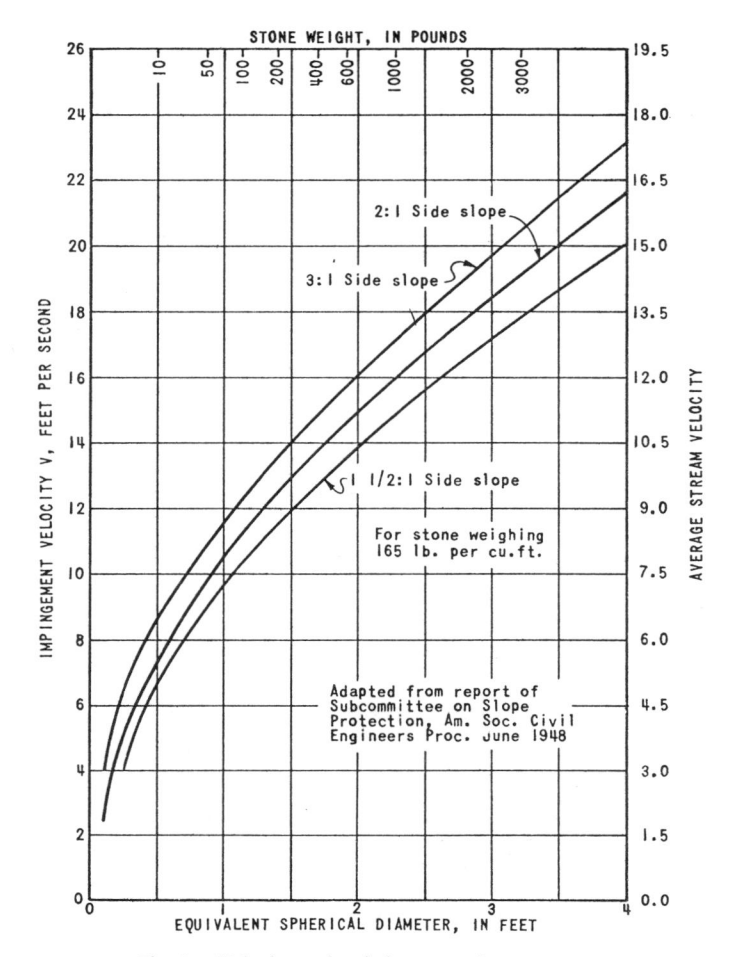

Fig. 1. Velocity and resistive stone size.

Quarry run material may be used if the material larger than 3 inches conforms to the above criteria. About 75 percent of the material (by weight) shall be 3-inch size or larger.

b. Wave Protection

The gradation of the riprap shall conform to the same criteria as established for revetment riprap. The theoretical stone size shall be selected from Fig. 2.

Stevenson's equation shall be used to compute wave height, where $h = 1.5 D^{1/2} + 2.5 - D^{1/4}$. h = wave height in feet and D = length of exposure in miles.

Table I.2 gives the values of wave height for 75 mph winds.

Table I.2. Length of Exposure, Miles.

	0.1	0.25	0.5	1.0	1.5	2.5	5.0
Wave height, ft	2.4	2.5	2.7	3.0	3.3	3.6	4.3

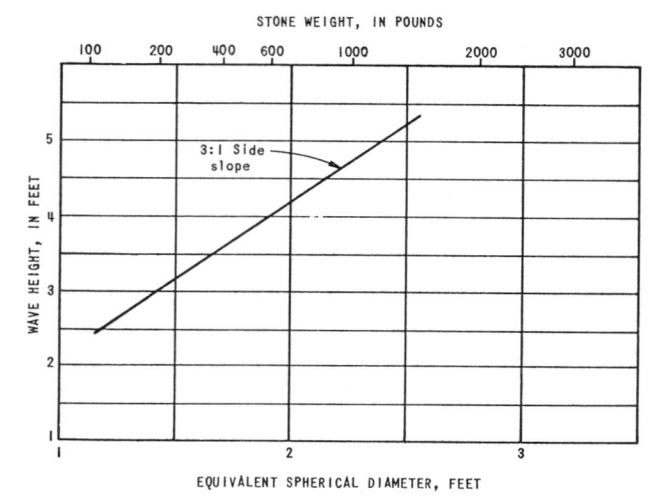

Fig. 2.

c. For Other Purposes

(1) No more than 10 percent of the total quantity (by weight) shall consist of pieces weighing less than 10 pounds.

(2) The pieces weighing 10 pounds or more shall conform to the following weight distribution:

WEIGHT OF INDIVIDUAL PIECES (LB)	% OF THE NUMBER OF PIECES THIS WEIGHT OR HEAVIER
300 or more	0–5
150–300	10–25
100–300	25–50
50–300	50–70

4. Subgrade Preparation

The subgrade surfaces on which the riprap or bedding course is to be placed shall be cut or filled and graded to the lines and grades shown on the drawings or as directed by an engineer. When fill to subgrade lines is required, it shall consist of approved materials and shall be compacted.

Riprap shall not be placed until the foundation preparation is completed and the subgrade surfaces have been inspected and approved by the engineer.

Riprap for wave protection shall extend at least 5 feet below normal pool level. Riprap shall be keyed into a berm, or large stones shall be placed at the bottom to serve as a buttress against possible undermining.

5. Bedding or Filter Layers

Unless quarry run riprap is used, a filter blanket is required. For dumped riprap, a filter ratio of 5 or less between layers will usually result in a stable condition. The filter ratio is defined as the ratio of the 15 percent particle size (D_{15}) of the coarser layer to the 85 percent particle size (D_{85}) of the finer layer. An additional requirement for stability is that the ratio of the 15 percent particle size of the coarser material to the 15 percent particle size of the finer material should exceed 5 but be less than 40. This requirement can be stated thus:

$$\frac{D_{15} \text{ (of riprap)}}{D_{85} \text{ (of bank)}} < 5 \quad < \frac{D_{15} \text{ (of riprap)}}{D_{15} \text{ (of bank)}} < 40$$

If a single layer of filter material will not satisfy the filter requirements, one or more additional layers of filter material must be used. The filter requirement applies between the bank material and the filter blanket, between successive layers of filter blanket material if more than one layer is used, and between the filter blanket and the stone cover. In addition to the filter requirements, the grain size curves for the various layers should be approximately parallel to minimize the infiltration of the fine material into the coarser material. Not more than 5 percent of the filter material should pass the No. 200 sieve.

The bedding or filter layers beneath riprap shall be spread uniformly on the prepared subgrade surfaces to a depth of 6 inches unless otherwise specified. The surfaces of the layers shall be finished reasonably free of mounds, dips, or windrows.

6. Equipment Placed Riprap

The riprap shall be a minimum of 12 inches thick or $1\frac{1}{2}$ times as thick as the maximum diameter stone, whichever is greater. If quarry run material is used to construct revetments, a filter blanket will not be required, but the riprap thickness shall be increased 6 inches.

The riprap shall be constructed to the full coarse thickness in one operation and in such a manner as to avoid serious displacement of the underlying materials. The rock shall be placed in a manner that will insure that the riprap in place shall be reasonably homogeneous with the larger rocks uniformly distributed and firmly in contact with one another. The smaller rocks and spalls shall fill the voids between the larger rocks. Riprap shall be placed in a manner to prevent damage to structures. Hand placing will be required to the extent necessary to achieve a neat appearance.

Appendix II
An Annotated List
of Selected References
for Plants for Erosion
Control

References in this appendix have been selected on several criteria. Emphasis has been placed on those references dealing with plants for unique and difficult environments and those which may not have wide distribution in libraries, e.g., government agency reports, bulletins, and circulars. A few references have been included because of wide geographic coverage. Most references are relatively recent because much of the older literature is cited in these.

Information is readily available for plants adapted to areas of adequate summer rainfall, e.g., much of the midwest, eastern and southern parts of North America, or where adequate irrigation is available. Rehder (1954) gives hardiness ratings for woody plants for much of the United States and Canada. *Sunset New Western Garden Book* (1979) gives excellent coverage of the western portion of the United States and adjacent parts of Canada. This publication has developed detailed climatic zones for these areas. Wyman, in several publications (1956, 1965, 1969, 1974, 1977), discusses plants for much of this area. Numerous other garden encyclopedias, regional garden books, Federal and State publications cover ground covers, shrubs and trees suitable for revegetation where summer water is available.

Selection of plant species for difficult sites (wet lands, dry lands, mine spoils, etc.) is not as well covered in the readily available literature. These are the citations chiefly covered here. Even these references are not meant to be all-inclusive. Some have been selected because they are general treatments, some for their special nature. Many of these citations have extensive literature citations themselves. Mine spoil revegetation research in the west is relatively new. The SEAM project will be producing more information on revegetation of these difficult sites.

Plant selection for revegetation and erosion control should not be limited to existing lists of plants. Unique problem sites will occur which will require unique solutions. Many plant species have never been adequately tested or tested at all. Lists should be used only as guides and starting points, not as ends in themselves. Observations of native and introduced species in the vicinity of the site to be revegetated should always be used in conjunction with plant lists.

Annotations briefly describe the contents and particular usefulness of these references.

Bennet, O. L., Mathias, E. T., Armiger, W. H., and Jones, Jr., J. N. (1978). Plant materials and their requirements for growth in humid regions. In: Schaller, Frank W., and Sutton, Paul, Eds. *Reclamation of drastically disturbed lands*. Amer. Soc. of Agron., Crop Sci. Soc. of Amer., Soil Sci. Soc. of Amer., Madison, Wisc. Ch. 16, pp 285–306.

Requirements and species of forbs, grasses, legumes, trees and shrubs given in text. Extensive literature citations.

Brown, Ray W., Johnston, Robert S., Richardson, Bland Z., and Farmer, Eugene E. (1976). Rehabilitation of alpine disturbances: Beartooth Plateau, Montana. In: Zuck, R. H. and Brown, L. F., Eds. *High altitude revegetation workshop No. 2*. Colo. State Univ., fort Collins, Colo. pp. 58–73. (Also as USDA Forest Svc. Res. Note INT-206-1976, Ogden Utah.)

Fourteen native and introduced grasses and sedges are listed. Natives are recommended. Five forbs are listed as active colonizers.

Brown, Ray W., Johnston, Robert S., and Johnson, Douglas A. (1978). Rehabilitation of alpine tundra disturbances. *J. of Soil and Water Cons.* (July-Aug) pp. 154–160.

Summary article citing other research. Table lists 12 grass/sedge/rush species, 17 forbs, and 5 woody species. 75 lit. cite.

Chan, Franklin J., Harris, Richard W., and Leiser, Andrew T. (1971). Direct seeding woody plants in the landscape. *AXT-n27,* Agr. Ext. Serv., Univ. of Calif., Berkeley (Reprinted 1979 as *leaflet 2577).* 12 pp.

Direct (spot) seeding results with 50 native and introduced species at numerous sites in California from seacoast to Sierras, Redding to Los Angeles. Adaptability to microsites is noted. Mostly without irrigation.

Dehgan, Bijan, Tucker, John M., and Takher, Balbir S. (1977). Propagation and culture of new species of drought-tolerant plants for highways. *Final report FHWA-CA-77-2* (NTIS PB 273-477). Dept. of Botany, U. C. Davis (for Calif. Dept of Trans.). 168 pp.

Descriptions, culture and propagation methods given for 92 California native and introduced species of relatively drought-tolerant plants.

Edmunson, George C. (1976). Plant materials study. A search for drought-tolerant plant materials for erosion control, revegetation, and landscaping along California highways. *Final Report No. USDASCS L PMC-1.* USDA SCS, Davis, Calif. (to State of Calif. Dept. of Trans., Sacramento, Calif.). 257 pp.

Research results are given for north central coast foothills, Sierra Nevada foothills, Lake Tahoe Basin and vicinity and Alturas. Appendix A lists sites and species tested, 53 grasses and forbs and 60 shrubs in foothill sites, and 34 grasses and forbs and 47 shrubs at Tahoe. Seed collection and propagation data are furnished. Appendix B lists planting methods, seed mixes and plant characteristics for 25 grasses and 12 forbs. Appendix C is a statewide list of recommended trees and shrubs for the 14 major land resource areas. Lists are applicable to many areas of adjacent states.

Environmental Laboratory (Hunt, L. Jean, compiler). (1978). Wetland habitat development with dredged material: engineering and plant propagation. *Tech. Report DS-78-16.* U. S. Army Eng. Waterway Expt. Sta., Vicksburg, Miss. 158 pp.

Table 6 lists 115 species of plants with adaptability to geographic region, pH, soils, marsh conditions (tidal, interior, water depth, etc.) and other factors. Propagules, handling, and planting techniques are in table 7. A synopsis for 28 species is in App. C. Numerous literature citations.

Everett. Richard L., Meeuwig, Richard O., and Butterfield, Richard I. (1980). Revegetation of untreated acid spoils, Leviathan Mine. Alpine County, California. *Calif. Geology.* 32:1, 3 pp.

Survival of 20–100% was obtained with 11 of 12 species tested. Mean pH was 4.1. Grass competition reduced survival.

Ferguson, Robert B. and Monsen, Stephen B. (1974). Research with containerized shrubs and forbs in southern Idaho. Reprinted from: Great Plains Abric. Counc. Publ. 68:349-358. U. S. Govt. Prtg. Off. 1974-677-093/39 Reg. No. 8.

Fourteen of 30 species of trees, shrubs and forbs gave some survival in at least one of three planting seasons. Grasshoppers caused heavy mortality. Survival ranged from 1 to 70%.

Frischknecht, Neil C. (1978). Use of shrubs for mined land reclamation and wildlife habitat. *Proc. Workshop on Reclamation for Wildlife Habitat.* Ecology Consultants, Inc., Fort Collins, Colo. 14 pp.

Text lists 10 species as suitable on oil shales in E. Utah.

Hall, V. L., and Ludwig, J. D. (1975). Evaluation of potential use of vegetation for erosion abatement along the Great Lakes shoreline. *Misc. Paper 7-75.* Coastal Eng. Res. Ctr., U. S. Army Corps of Eng., Ft. Belvoir, Va.

Methods, plant lists, 34 species from literature reviews and 33 from field surveys along south shores of Lake Superior, Lake Michigan, junction of Lake Michigan and Lake Huron, Lake Erie, and Lake Ontario. Characteristics are briefly described.

Horton, Jerome S. (1949). Trees and shrubs for erosion control in Southern California mountains. Calif. Div. For. in coop. with Calif. For. and Range Exp. Sta. (now Pacific Southwest For. and Range Exp. Sta.) USDA For. Svc. 72 pp.

A major source listing 58 native and introduced species in 3 tables according to elevation in So. Calif. mountains, further subdivided into deep and shallow soils, full sun and partial shade. Partially tested species also listed. Descriptive notes on characteristics, range and habitat, uses and planting methods. Useful in similar areas of the west.

Hoyt, Roland Stewart. (1978). *Ornamental plants for subtropical regions.* Liningston Press. Anaheim, Ca. 485 pp.

Extensive lists of herbs, shrubs, and trees by adaptation to microsites (soils, seashore, moisture regimes, *etc.*) and by landscape uses. Plant descriptions and requirements are included. Useful for much of the southwest U. S. and somewhat useful for southern and southeastern coastal states.

Hunt, L. Jean, Ford, Alfred W., Landin, Mary C., and Wells, B. R. (1978). Upland habitat development with dredged material: Engineering and plant propagation. *Tech. Report DS-78-17*. U. S. Army Eng. Waterways Exp. Sta., Env. Lab., Vicksburg, Miss.

Extensive list of 70 grasses, 112 forbs, 18 vines, and 153 trees and shrubs. Table 5 lists cultural information, range, habit, etc. Table 6 lists according to soil and regional adaptability. Many literature references.

Kaul, R. N., Ed. (1970) *Afforestation in arid zones*. Dr. W. Junk, N. V. The Hague. 435 pp.

Afforestation of various arid zones of the world is covered. Research, current methodology and plant lists and descriptions are included. Botanical index of over 600 species contains many grasses and forbs but is predominately of trees and shrubs. The sections cover the southern fringe of Europe, North Africa, the Near East, the Indian subcontinent, Central Eurasia, the American continents, and Australia. Some chapters list drought tolerant natives. Species selection is noted in text and/or tables and for most areas includes both natives and introduced species. Methods of establishment and results are included in many chapters. An excellent resource for selecting species for test plantings in a wide range of arid climates. Extensive literature references.

Kay, Burgess L. (1979). Summary of revegetation attempts on the second Los Angeles aqueduct. *Mojave Revegetation Notes No. 22*. Dept. Agron. and Range Sci., U. C. Davis, Calif. 24 pp.

Four of seven species were established by drill seeding on high elevation desert sites without irrigation.

Kimmons, J. H., Lovell, G. R., Everett, H. W., Thornton, R. B., and Dudley, R. F., (1976). Evaluation of woody plants and development of establishment procedures for direct woody seeding and/or vegetative reproduction. *Final Report No. FHWA-MD-R-76-19*. USDA Soil Cons. Svc., National Plant Materials Center, Beltsville Md. (for: Md. State Highway Adm., Brooklandville, Md.). 154 pp.

Research results given for numerous grasses, forbs, shrubs, and trees in Appalachian, Piedmont, and Coastal Plain regions of Maryland (Appendix A). Not separated as to successful and nonsuccessful species.

Knutson, Paul L. (1977). Planting guidelines for marsh development and bank stabilization. *Coastal Eng. Tech. Aid No. 77-3*. U. S. Army Corps of Eng. Fort Belvoir, Va. 21 pp.

Four species of *Spartina*, cord grass, are listed for use on Atlantic, Gulf, and Pacific Coast areas. Establishment methods are given.

Kraayenoord, C. W. S. Van. (1968). Poplars and willows in New Zealand with particular reference to their use in erosion control. Int. Poplar Commission, 13th Session, Montreal. Canada.

Reports on numerous *Populus* and *Salix* species and clones used in N. Z. for erosion control.

Kraebel, Charles J. (1936). Erosion control on mountain roads. *Circ. 380*. USDA, Washington, D.C. 44 pp.

The original work on wattling also contains (Table 2) an extensive list of native species with adaptation listed for 6 major Calif. regions, each sub-divided into 3-5 elevational (and vegetational) zones. List contains 8 grass, 36 forb, 56 shrub and 38 tree species. Regions are from north coastal to desert. Many are native or adaptable to adjacent states.

Leiser, Andrew T., Nussbaum, James J., Kay, Burgess, Paul, Jack, and Thronhill, William. (1974). Revegetation of disturbed soils in the Tahoe basin. *Final Report CA-DOT-TL-7036-1-75-25*. Depts. of Env. Hort, and Agron. and Range Sci., U. C., Davis, Calif. (To: Calif. Dept of Trans., Sacramento, Calif.) 71 pp.

Grass species and mixes (9 species eminently suitable) and 7 woody species resulting in good revegetation as transplants without irrigation are listed. These are suitable for other similar mountain areas.

McKell, Cyrus M., Blaisdell, James P., and Goodin, Joe R., Eds. (1971). Wildland shrubs - their biology and utilization. International Symposium. *Tech. Report INT-1*. Intermountain For. and Range Exp. Sta., USDA For. Svc., Ogden, Utah. 494 pp.

Section I, Continental Aspects of Shrub Distribution, Utilization and Potentials, gives extensive lists of shrubs, usually in text and by plant communities for the Indian Sub-continent, Mediterranean region of Africa, Asia, and Argentina. Many have potential for erosion control on arid sites.

Monsen, Stephen B., and Plummer, A. Perry. (1978). Plants and treatment for revegetation of disturbed sites in the intermountain area. In: Wright, Robert A. (Ed.). *The reclamation of disturbed arid lands*. Univ. New Mexico Press. Albuquerque, N. M. pp. 155-173.

Table 8.1 lists pioneer grasses (15) and forbs (17) with areas of adaptation. Table 8.2 lists 48 shrubs established by direct seeding and growing well with forbs. These are rated for growth rate, competitive adaptability and drought tolerance. A few are discussed which do best as transplants.

Naveh, Z. (1974). The ecological management of non-arable Mediterranean uplands. *Jour. of Env. Management.* 2:351–371.

Twenty species of shrubs are listed for dry, rocky, limestone slopes. Although based on Israel, these would be good for other areas with similar climates.

Plummer, A. Perry, Christensen, Donald R., and Monsen, Stephen B. (1968). Restoring big-game range in Utah. Pub. No. 68-3. Utah Div. of Fish and Game. 183 pp.

Comprehensive manual including site analysis, plant selection, methods, and plant lists. Seed mixes are given by vegetation types. Description of species from a revegetation viewpoint. Ratings of suitability to 20 characteristics, overall evaluation, and adaptation to 10 habitats are given for 56 grasses, 74 forbs, and 77 woody species. Many would be useful in much of the western U. S. Many would be good candidates for establishment by transplanting as well. Native and introduced species are included.

Plummer, A. Perry. (1970) Plants for revegetation of roadcuts and other disturbed or eroded areas. *Intermountain Region Range Improvement Notes 15(1).* USDA For. Svc. Intermountain For. and Range Exp. Sta. 8 pp.

Native and introduced plants for the Intermountain Region rated for 11 habitats, arctic alpine to desert; 23 grasses, 27 forbs and 67 shrubs and trees.

Plummer, A. Perry. (1976). Shrubs for the subalpine zone of the Wasatch Plateau. In: Zuck, R. H. and Brown, L. F., Eds. *Proceedings High Altitude Revegetation Workshop No. 2.* Colo. State Univ., Fort Collins, Colo.

Twenty shrubs, mostly natives, rated for seed and transplant establishment, natural spread, growth rates and effectiveness.

Rehder, Alfred. (1954). *Manual of cultivated trees and shrubs hardy in North America.* The Macmillan Co., N.Y. 996 pp.

Authoritative, comprehensive manual (keys and technical descriptions) of most hardy (excluding Fla. and So. Calif.) woody plants grown in No. America. Hardiness ratings are given for most by the original 10 minimum temperature zones. These may be easily converted to the more recent USDA hardiness zones.

Schiechtl, Hugo. (1980). *Bioengineering for land re-reclamation and conservation.* Univ. of Alberta Press. Edmonton, Alberta. 400 pp.

Extensive lists of plants for erosion control. Plant characteristics, adaptation to soils and climates, etc. are given. Not organized by site or environmental adaptation for easy use but it is very comprehensive, essentially world-wide in scope. Research results are chiefly European.

Shetron, Stephen G. and Carroll, Dorian A. (1977). Performance of trees and shrubs on metallic mine mill wastes. *Jour. of Soil and Water Cons.* 32:5, pp 222–225.

Nineteen woody species listed, 14 of which survived 5 years on iron tailings, 11 on copper tailings, and 11 on dikes and dumps. Michigan data.

Stark, N. (1966). Review of highway planting information appropriate to Nevada. *Bull. B-7.* Desert Res. Inst., Univ. of Nevada, Reno, Nevada. 209 pp.

Types of plantings, methods of planting. Approximately 300 native and introduced species are arranged in lists covering ten vegetation zones. Species characteristics, adaptation to soils, exposure, moisture are given. Other lists include grasses, forbs, and ornamentals for Nevada, California, and Oregon. Excellent resource applicable to much of the western U. S. Numerous literature citations.

Thornburg, A. A. and Fuchs, S. H. (1978). Plant materials and requirements for growth in dry regions. Chap. 23, pp 411–423. In: Schaller, Frank W. and Sutton, Paul, Eds. *Reclamation of drastically disturbed lands.* Amer. Soc. of Agron., Crop Sci Soc. of Amer., Soil Sci. Soc. of Amer. Madison, Wisc.

Native and introduced species of grasses, forbs, trees and shrubs (113) are listed. Adaptation to specific regions is covered in the text.

U. S. Army Corps of Eng. (1957). Dune formation and stabilization by vegetation and plantings. *Tech. Memo No. 101.* Beach Erosion Board, U. S. Army Corps of Eng., Fort Belvior, Va.

Prevalence and suitability for transplanting plants for eight coastal regions.

USDA Soil Cons. Svc. (1972). Environmental planting. In: Minimizing Erosion in Urban Areas: Guidelines, Standards, and Specifications. publ. by USDA Soil Conservation Service, Madison, Wisconsin, pp. 117–143.

Grass mixtures (Tables 14 & 15), tree selection guide by use and soils (Table 17), general shrub and vine planting guide by soil groups, use, form, *etc.* (Table 19), and general information applicable to Wisconsin and adjacent areas.

U. S. Environment Protection Agency. (1975). Methods of quickly vegetating soils of low productivity, construction activities. *EPA-440/9-75-006.* U. S. Envt. Protection Agency, Washington, D.C. 467 pp.

Case histories of revegetation in 10 areas in the U. S. Plant lists are given for: Idaho batholith, approximately 13 grasses and 35 woody species; New Mexico, 15–20 grasses; Colorado, grasses only; Mississippi, grass and forb mixes by areas; Virginia-West Virginia, grass mixes only; Massachusetts, 11 woody plants plus grasses and forbs; Alaska, grass mixes and 6 each herbaceous and woody ground covers; 17 western states, adaptation and lists of 100 grasses, 22 forbs, and 9 woody species for seed establishment.

Whitlow, Thomas H., and Harris, Richard W. (1979). Flood tolerance in plants: a state-of-the-art review. Dept. of Env. Hort., Univ. of Calif., Davis. *Tech Rept. E-79-2.* For: U. S. Army Corps of Eng., Waterways Exp. Sta., Env. Lab., Vicksburg, Miss.

Lists of flooding tolerance throughout the U. S. are given in some 30 tables. Over 10 summary tables, by geographic areas are in the appendix. Very useful for plant selection for wet and flooded areas.

Williamson, Joseph F., Ed. (1979). *Sunset new western garden book.* 4th Ed. Lane Pub. Co., Menlo Park, CA. 512 pp.

Garden encyclopedia for U. S. and adjacent parts of Canada from the Rocky Mts. west. Sunset plant climate zones (different from Rehder's and USDA's) given for all plants. Limited lists for specific micro-environments.

Wyman, Donald. (1956). *Groundcover plants.* The Macmillan Co., N.Y. 175 pp.

Groundcover plants for American gardens. A general reference.

——— (1965). *Trees for American gardens.* The Macmillan Co., New York, 502 pp.

A general reference on trees.

Wyman, Donald. (1969). Shrubs and vines for American gardens. Rev. 2nd. Ed. The Macmillan Co., New York pp.

A general reference on shrubs and vines.

——— (1974). Dwarf shrubs: maintenance-free woody plants for today's gardens. The Macmillan Co., N.Y. 137 pp.

A general reference for maintenance-free shrubs.

———. (1977). Wyman's gardening encyclopedia. Rev. Ed. The Macmillan Co., New York 1221 pp.

A general reference covering a wide range of plants, grasses, forbs, shrubs, trees and their horticulture requirements.

Addendum

Aldon, Earl F. (1973). Revegetating disturbed areas in the semiarid Southwest. Jour. of Soil and Water Conservation. 28(5):223–225.

Detailed establishment methods are given for four-wing saltbush and alkali sacaton by transplanting. Detailed methodology and limiting factors make this applicable to much of the arid southwest.

Everett, Richard L. (1980). Use of containerized shrubs for revegetating arid roadcuts. *Reclamation Rev.* 3:33–40.

Thirteen woody species native to the eastern Sierra foothills were established as containerized transplants on north and south exposures. Survival data and cover after 3 years are given for 10 of the species. Eight species on south exposures and 4 species on north exposures had more than 80% survival for at least 2 years.

Johnson, Albert G., White, Donald B., Smithberg, Margaret H., and Snyder, Leon C. (1971). Development of ground covers for highway slopes. Final Report-1971. Dept. of Hort. Sci., Univ. of Minn. for U. S. Dept. of Trans., Fed. Highway Admin., Minn Highway Dept., and Minn. Local Road Res. Board. 55pp.

Four forb and 10 shrub species are recommended, 38 forb and 17 shrub species are given limited recommendation. Several cultivars are also given for a few species. Species are mostly non-natives. Research results and cultural information is also given.

Plass, William T. (1975). An evaluation of trees and shrubs for planting surface-mine spoils. USDA For. Svc. Res. Paper NE-317. N.E. For. Exp. Sta., Upper Darby, Pa.

Fifty-five species tested on acid and alkaline sites. Survival and growth is given by site. Many gave good to excellant survival. Seventeen are listed as being especially good. Seven references are given for other midwestern and eastern sites.

Appendix III
Nomenclature and Symbols

ENGLISH NOTATION

A = shear cross-sectional area of soil

A_R = total cross-sectional area of roots (fibers) in shear cross-sectional area of soil

B = clear spacing or opening between piles

B_{CRIT} = critical clear spacing between fixed, embedded piles in a slope

C = vegetation management factor

$\overline{C}$ = average or weighted vegetation management factor

C' = climatic factor (wind erosion)

C_c = cover index for construction sites

C_s = ground surface condition factor for construction sites

C_v = average cover density factor

D = diameter of embedded pile (or tree)

$D.R.$ = dispersion ratio of soil

E = kinetic energy of rain

E_s = average suspended sediment of stream

F = factor of safety

H = height of a cut or retaining wall

H_c = critical height of cut

I = maximum 30-minute rainfall intensity

I' = field roughness factor (wind erosion)

K = soil erodibility factor (rainfall erosion)

K' = soil erodibility factor (wind erosion)

K_A = coefficient of active earth pressure

K_0 = coefficient of earth pressure at rest

L = slope length factor (rainfall erosion)

L' = field length factor (wind erosion)

L_{min} = minimum length of root (or fiber) to mobilize tensile strength of root during shear

M_O = overturning moment

M_R = resisting moment

P = erosion control practice factor

$\bar{P}$ = average or weighted erosion control practice factor

P_A = active earth force per unit length of wall

P_S = total force developed against a fixed, rigid pile (or tree) embedded in a slope

$P.I.$ = plasticity index

N_s = *stability number*

R = rainfall erosion index

R_R = concentration or density of roots in a soil

T_i = tensile strength of roots in size class i

T_R = average tensile strength of roots

X = soil loss from rainfall erosion

X' = soil loss from wind erosion

V' = vegetation cover factor (wind erosion)

a_i = mean cross-sectional area of roots in size class i

b = width of retaining wall at its base

c = cohesion intercept

c' = effective cohesion intercept

c_d = developed cohesion required for stability

c_1, c_s = cohesion along basal sliding surface

d_r = diameter of root or fiber

e = eccentricity of load

i = initial angle of inclination of fibers (roots) with respect to shear surface

h = vertical thickness (depth) of sliding or yielding mass

h_w = height of piezometric surface

k = distortion ratio ($k = x/z$)

n_i = number of roots in size class i

p = average lateral pressure or arching pressure in openings between fixed piles in a slope

q_o = uniform, vertical surcharge stress on a slope

q_{ULT} = ultimate bearing capacity of soil or ground

u = pore water pressure

s = shear strength of soil

t_R = average tensile stength of roots (or fibers) per unit area of soil

x = lateral (horizontal) displacement in shear test

$\bar{x}$ = distance from toe to line of action of normal bearing force acting on base of retaining wall

z = thickness of shear zone

GREEK LETTERS

α = angle of cut slope or batter angle of retaining wall

β = angle of natural slope or backfill

γ = unit weight of soil

γ_{BUOY} = buoyant unit weight of soil

γ_R = unit weight or density of roots

γ_{SATD} = unit weight of saturated soil

γ_W = unit weight of water

θ = angle of shear distortion

σ = normal stress on failure surface

σ_{AVE} = average bearing stress

τ = shear stress

τ'_R = maximum tangential shear stress or skin friction between fiber (or root) and soil

ϕ = angle of internal friction of soil

ϕ' = effective angle of internal friction

ϕ_1, ϕ_s = friction angle along basal sliding surface

ϕ_W = angle of wall friction

Index

Allowable bearing stress. *See* Bearing capacity
American Association of Nurserymen, 132
American Wood Preservers Institute, 96
Arching restraint, 55
    conditions for, 56
    critical spacing, 58, 59
    field evidence, 57
    theoretical models, 56
Aspect, 125

Backfill, 81
    drainage requirements, 81, 97
    gradation requirements, 81, 91
    methods of vegetating, 66, 81, 99, 107
    See also Crib walls; Reinforced Earth® walls; Welded-wire walls
Backshore slope protection, 188. *See also* Coastal slope protection
Bearing capacity, 89
    allowable, 90
    consideration in standard designs, 90, 233
    effect of eccentric loads, 90
    effect of foundation flexibility, 90
    See also Gravity retaining walls
Biotechnical approach, 1, 66, 198
    attributes of, 1
    classification, 66, 73
    cost effectiveness, 118, 120
    examples of applications, 7
    See also Case studies
Biotechnical principles, 66, 188
    compatibility requirements, 81
    elements of system, 66
    mixed construction approach, 66, 73
    role of structure, 74, 75, 76, 78
    role of vegetation, 73, 79, 80
Block revetments. *See* Revetments
Bluff stabilization. *See* Coastal slope protection
Breast walls, 66, 84, 91, 118
    backfill requirements, 91
    characteristics of, 84, 91
    construction guidelines, 92
    use with vegetation, 67, 92, 177, 220
Brush layering, 66, 71, 139, 142, 167
    advantages over wattling, 167
    function and purpose, 168
    installation procedure, 16
    use and applications, 142, 169, 170
    See also Contour wattling
Brush matting, 172, 175
    brush selection, 172

construction procedure, 173
Winooski River project, 172
See also Biotechnical approach; Streambank protection
Buttressing. *See* Arching restraint

Cascade Range, Oregon, 54, 60, 63
Case histories, 122, 124, 138, 188
    backshore slope protection, 188
    cut slope stabilization, 209
    watershed rehabilitation, 138, 197
    See also Biotechnical approach; Great Lakes shoreline; Lake Tahoe basin; Redwood National Park.
Cellular grids, 76, 112, 200
    construction guidelines, 113
    function and purpose, 112
    incorporation of vegetation, 69, 115
    ladder grids, 113, 114
    use in practice, 114, 115
    See also Revetments
Check dam construction, 182
    brush and rock, 184
    brush and wire-netting, 184, 185
    double-row post-brush, 183
    loose rock, 185
    single-row post-brush, 182, 190
    split board, 185, 186
    See also Check dams
Check dams, 77, 80, 178, 205, 206
    design criteria, 179
    function and purpose, 178
    materials, 179
    porous vs. nonporous, 178
    selection, 178, 182
    See also Check dam construction; Grade stabilization structures
Clear-cutting. *See* Timber harvesting
Coastal slope protection, 7, 171, 188
Coefficient of active stress, 88
    charts and tables for, 89
    Coulomb equation, 88
    yielding requirement, 88
    See also Gravity retaining walls
Cohesion, 30
    apparent in sands, 52, 59
    effect on factor of safety, 52
    pseudo from roots, 40, 50
    See also Direct shear tests; Shear strength
Concrete crib walls, 84, 86, 97, 118
    Hilfiker Concrib wall, 97, 98, 99
    Humes Pincrib and Minicrib wall, 99

Concrete crib walls (*Cont'd*)
  principles of construction, 84, 97
  relative advantages, 97
  standard designs, 251–254
  use with vegetation, 2, 66, 67, 99, 100, 101
  See also Crib walls
Containers, 133, 134
  biodegradability, 135
  books and blocks, 135, 136
  circling roots, 135
  deep vs. shallow, 136
  peat pots, 135
  rigid wall, 135
  selection of, 136
  See also Propagation
Contour wattling, 2, 66, 72, 139, 157, 176, 194, 205, 208
  function and purpose, 159
  installation procedure, 72, 162
    placement and covering, 161, 164, 225
    preparation of wattles, 160
    site survey, 162
    staking and trenching, 161, 163
  uses and applications, 165
    eroded slopes, 2, 144, 167, 192, 205
    road cuts, 67, 72, 139, 217, 220
    road fills, 157, 158, 165
Cost of slope protection, 114
  cost of retaining soil in place, 116, 117
  cost comparisons
    bank protection methods, 119
    erosion control on cut slopes, 120
    retaining walls, 118
  Lake Tahoe basin study, 118, 120, 223, 228
  Redwood National Park study, 203, 205
Crib fill. *See* Backfill
Crib walls, 84, 86, 91, 94, 194
  characteristics of, 94
  design as gravity structure, 84
  internal stability requirements, 91
  protection of structural members, 91
  See also Concrete crib walls; Gravity retaining walls; Timber walls
Critical height of cut, 34. *See also* slope stability analyses
Critical gradient. *See* Groundwater erosion
Cuttings. *See* Planting techniques

Dams. *See* Check dams
Debris slides, 26, 27, 63
Dewatering. *See* Water control
Dike interceptor. *See* Water control
Direct shear tests, 41
  on fiber reinforced sand, 43, 49
  on plastic fiber reinforced soil samples, 50
  on root permeated soil pedestals, 47, 48, 49
  See also Shear strength
Diversions. *See* Water control
Drainage. *See* Water control
Dry ravel. *See* Sheet erosion

Earth reinforcement, 38
  by roots and fibers, 38, 39
  with metal strips, 38
  with reticulated piles, 38
  See also Root reinforcement; Reinforced Earth® walls
Earth-sheltering, 8
Earth slumps, 26, 29, 63

Ecotypes, 130
Edaphoecotropism, 38, 81
Erodibility, 11, 12, 13, 18
  controlling factors, 11
  indices, 11
  trends, 11
  See also Soil loss predictions; Soil erosion
Erosion. *See* Soil erosion
Erosion control plantings, 129, 190, 201, 218
  grasses for interim control, 131, 201, 212
  plant lists, 131, 132, 260–264
  species mix, 130, 131, 194, 218
  use of legumes, 130, 135
  See also Plant species selection; Revegetation; Scheduling

Factor of safety, 26, 30, 88
  retaining walls, 88
  slopes, 26, 27, 52, 60
  See also Gravity retaining walls; Slope stability analyses
Failure surface, 25
  determinants of, 26
  planar, 26, 52, 59
  rotational, 26
Federal Highway Administration, 6, 91
Fertilizer requirements, 127, 146, 149, 152, 213
  chemical analysis, 127
  pot tests, 127, 128, 214
  See also Seeding methods
Fiber reinforcement. *See* Root reinforcement
Filter blanket, 109, 258
  filter cloth, 111, 112, 145
  graded aggregate, 109, 112, 144
  specifications for, 258
Friction angle, 30
  chart for determining, 33
  effect of fibers and roots, 40, 41
  effect of gradation, 33
  See also Direct shear tests; Shear strength
Frost action, 11, 13, 190

Gabion walls, 84, 86, 93, 118
  advantages, 94
  construction sequence, 93
  standard designs, 232–235
  use with vegetation, 68, 93
  See also Gravity retaining walls
Geology
  Cascade Range, Oregon, 62
  Influence on slope stability, 10, 26
  Lake Michigan shoreline, 188
  Lake Tahoe basin, 209
  Redwood National Park, 197
Grade stabilization structures, 76
Grasses and forbs. *See* Herbaceous plants
Gravity retaining walls 84, 86
  design criteria, 85
  forces acting on, 88
  safety against bearing failure, 89, 90
  safety against overturning, 88, 89
  safety against sliding, 89
  See also Bearing capacity; Retaining structures.
Great Lakes shoreline, 188
  degradation processes, 189, 190
  magnitude of erosion problems, 189

Rocky Gap stabilization project, 189
  conclusions, 195
  objectives, 190
  plot treatments, 190–194
Groundwater, 81. *See also* Soil moisture
Groundwater erosion, 16, 81
  conditions favoring, 16, 82
  critical gradient, 16
  role in gullying, 14
Growing media. *See* Propagation
Gully control. *See* Check dams; Brush layering; Contour wattling
Gullying. *See* Rainfall erosion

Hardening off. *See* Propagation
Herbaceous plants, 22, 24, 48, 66, 132, 146, 208, 214
Highways. *See* Roads
Hydro-mechanical influences, 37, 38

Idaho Batholith, 26, 52, 57
Interception, 53

Kinetic energy of rain, 13

Lake Tahoe basin, 118, 124, 138, 159, 209
  conclusions of project, 225
  integrated slope plantings, 215
    California State Route 89 highway cuts, 216–220
    CalTrans highway cut, 221, 225–227
    cost benefits, 222
  interim stabilization measures, 211
    chemicals, 213
    herbaceous plantings, 212, 214
    mulches, 212
  preliminary research, 209
    fall vs. spring plantings, 213, 215
    fertility studies, 214
    willow cuttings, 213, 219
  setting, 209, 210
Landslides. *See* Mass movement
Level spreader, 144
Live staking, 72, 173, 194, 205
  applications, 175
    check dam reinforcement, 175, 186, 206
    revetment staking, 176
    wattle staking, 161, 176
  function and purpose, 173
  planting procedure, 174, 175
  selection of species, 173, 174
  See also Contour wattling; Planting techniques; Propagation

Mass movement, 6, 10, 25, 37, 53, 63
  causes, 6, 26, 28, 54, 189, 197
  classification, 10, 25, 26
  damages, 7
  indicators, 27, 28
  in granitic slopes, 51, 52
  severity and extent, 6
  See also Slope stability analyses
Microclimate, 125
Mixed construction. *See* Biotechnical approach
Mulching. *See* Planting techniques
Mychorriza, 133, 135

Overland flow. *See* Runoff

Phreatophyte plants, 81, 125, 144
Pioneer plants, 47, 124, 130, 172
Plant lists. *See* Erosion control plantings
Plant establishment in structures, 66, 81, 99, 153
  breast walls, 66, 67, 153, 175
  crib walls, 66, 68, 99, 100, 101, 153
  gabions, 66, 68, 108, 154
  revetments, 66, 69, 107, 112, 153, 175
  tiered structures, 66, 70, 101, 105, 154
  See also Backfill; Biotechnical principles
Plant geography, 130
Plant species selection, 122, 128, 147, 190, 214
  availability, 122, 129, 132
  desirable characteristics, 129
  native vs. introduced, 129, 228
  plant succession, 130
  variation and adaptation, 130
  See also Erosion control plantings; Revegetation
Planting techniques, 122, 146, 153
  cuttings, 151, 152
  direct seeding, 145
    grasses and forbs, 145
    woody species, 147
  guidelines, 146
  mulching, 147, 148, 150, 191, 194, 218
  seed and seedling protection, 150, 151
  transplants, 133, 152
  See also Propagation; Seeding methods
Planting tools, 152
Propagation, 133, 211
  cuttings, 134, 213
  growing media, 135
  hardening off, 137
  rooting hormones, 134
  sanitation, 133
  seeds, 133
  See also Containers; Planting techniques; Scheduling

Quality standards, grasses, 132
Quasi-vegetative slope protection, 66, 157

Rainfall erosion, 10, 13
  determinants of, 11
  gullying, 10, 14, 190, 191, 199, 200
  raindrop splash, 13
  rilling, 10, 14, 200
  sheet erosion, 13, 221
  See also Soil erosion; Soil loss predictions
Redwood National Park, 2, 7, 197
  effectiveness of erosion control measures, 205
  erosion and stability problems, 198–200
  rehabilitation test sites, 203
  setting, 197
  watershed rehabilitation program, 198
Reed-trench terracing, 171
  construction procedure, 171, 172
  terrace plantings, 172
  See also Biotechnical approach; Erosion control plantings
Reinforced Earth® walls, 85, 87, 91, 104, 118
  design considerations, 91, 104
  principal elements, 104
  specifications for backfill, 104
  use with vegetation, 105, 107
  See also Retaining structures

Retaining structures, 66, 74, 83
  cost comparisons, 116, 118
  function and purpose, 75, 83
  selection criteria, 85, 91
  stability requirements, 85, 88, 91
  standard designs, 91, 232–256
  toe-wall construction, 67, 83, 84, 91
  See also Gravity retaining walls
Revegetation, 122, 154, 190, 201, 209, 228
  aftercare and maintenance, 154
  constraints and planning, 122, 221
  See also Vegetation
Revetments, 76, 107, 176
  articulated blocks, 112, 113
  cost comparisons, 119
  function and purpose, 76
  gabion, 109, 110, 111
  incorporation of vegetation, 66, 79, 80, 107, 113, 114
  types of, 107
  See also Cellular grids; Riprap
Riprap, 76, 107, 172
  effectiveness, 107
  factors limiting use, 107
  filter blankets for, 258
  gradation and size requirements, 109, 257
  placement guidelines, 110, 258
  See also Revetments
Roads, 7, 33, 61, 198
  erosion and stability problems, 15, 63, 143, 198–200, 216, 220, 221, 225
  removal and rehabilitation, 202–205
  stabilization of
    cuts, 67, 69–72, 83, 108, 115, 139, 147, 159, 218, 226
    fills, 76, 101, 105, 142, 170
  See also Critical height of cuts; Stability of road fills
Rock breast walls. *See* Breast walls
Root morphology, 41, 43, 129
  influence of hereditary factors, 43, 44
  influence of rooting environment, 43, 45
  morphological studies, 43
  of alfalfa, 47
  of beach grass, 47, 48
  of Douglas fir, 44
  of ponderosa pine, 44, 46
  tap and sinker root system, 40, 43
Root reinforcement, 30, 37, 39
  analogy of Reinforced Earth®, 38
  concept of "equivalent confining stress," 39
  concept of "pseudo cohesion," 40
  influence of fiber concentration, 40, 49, 50, 52
  influence of fiber length, 42, 50
  influence of fiber orientation, 42, 43
  influence of root morphology, 43
  in sandy, cohesionless slopes, 51
  theoretical models, 40, 42
  See also Direct shear tests; Root tensile strength
Root tensile strength, 41, 44
  decline with age, 46, 47
  influence of size, 44
  mobilization of, 41, 42
  of different plant species, 45
Root wedging, 37, 38
Rooting hormones. *See* Planting techniques
Rubble rock revetment. *See* Riprap

Runoff, 14, 142
  cause of erosion, 14
  damage to fills, 142, 144
  velocities of, 13
  See also Seepage; Water control

Scheduling plant production, 137
Sediment problems, 3–5, 203
Seeding methods, 145, 190, 194
  broadcasting, 146, 208
  drilling, 146
  fertilization, 146, 194, 208, 217, 218
  hydroseeding, 146
  spot seeding, 147
  topsoiling, 147
  weed control, 123, 149
  See also Planting techniques
Seeds, 132
  cleaning, 133
  collecting in wild, 132, 133
  dormancy, 133
  storage, 133
  See also Propagation; Seeding methods
Seepage
  effect on slope stability, 34, 52, 82, 144
  effect on soil erosion, 10, 15, 16, 144
  through check dams, 178
  See also Groundwater erosion; Water control
Serpentine soil, 126, 127
Shear strength, 26, 30, 52
  Coulomb criterion, 30
  factors affecting, 27, 28
  influence of fiber reinforcement, 39, 40, 41, 47, 51
  role in slope stability, 27
  shear strength parameters, 30, 31
  See also Direct shear tests; Cohesion; Friction angle
Site analysis, 123, 188, 197, 209
  climatic parameters, 123, 124, 209
  microsite, 125, 131
  soils, 125, 188, 197, 209
  vegetation, 124, 197, 210
Site preparation, 122, 125, 138, 228
  adjacent area protection, 145
  grading and shaping, 138, 194
    cut slopes, 139, 218
    fill slopes, 140
    restoration projects, 138
  use of engineering methods, 66, 138
  See also Retaining structures; Water control
Slope stability analyses, 29, 52, 56, 60
  approaches to, 29
  infinite slope method, 31, 52
  in terms of effective stress, 31
  in terms of total stress, 31
  limit equilibrium principles, 29, 30
  method of slices, 35
  selection of soil parameters, 33
  use of computers, 35
Slope wash. *See* Sheet erosion
Soil analysis, 125
  pH, 126
  salinity, 126
  type, 125, 189, 209
  See also Fertilizer requirements; Site analysis

Soil erosion, 3, 10, 37
  agents of, 11
  causes, 3, 189
  damages, 5, 189
  occurrence, 3, 10
  rates, 4
  types of, 10, 13, 189
  See also Rainfall erosion; Wind erosion; Soil loss predictions
Soil loss predictions, 16
  cropping management factor, 20, 22
  erodibility factor, 18, 19
  erosion control practice factor, 20, 23
  rainfall factor, 16, 17
  topographic factor, 18, 21
  universal soil loss equation, 10, 12, 16
  wind erosion equation, 21, 23
Soil loss reduction measures, 23
  computing system effectiveness, 25, 116
  evaluation formula, 23
  Factor C values for construction sites, 24
  Factor P values for construction sites, 25
Soil moisture, 52
  influence on slope movement, 53, 54
  modification by vegetation, 37, 57, 81
  stress, 53, 54, 55
Soil nutrients. *See* Fertilizer requirements
Sprigging. *See* Live staking
Stability of road fills, 33, 175, 198, 201
  equation for, 33
  failure mode, 33
  See also Slope stability analyses
Streambank Erosion Control Act, 5
Streambank protection, 8, 78, 107, 110, 172, 175
Stream channel erosion, 10, 15, 80, 175, 208
  influence of geomorphic variables, 16
  processes, 15
  severity of problem, 4
Surcharge, 37, 60
  estimates from weight of trees, 60
  influence on slope stability, 60, 61
Surface Environment and Mining (SEAM) projects, 132

Terracing of slopes, 71, 139, 208
Timber cribs, 84, 118
  basic components, 84, 95
  cribfill requirements, 97
  log cribs, 95, 250
  standard designs, 96, 97, 236–249
  wood treatment, 97
  See also Crib walls
Timber harvesting, 53, 61
  clear cutting practices, 61

field studies on effects of, 61, 62
  impact of in Redwood National Park, 198, 199
  relationship to mass movement, 39, 52, 64, 198
Toe-walls. *See* Retaining structures
Transpiration, 53, 54, 81
Transplants. *See* Planting techniques
Trees. *See* Woody plants

Unified Soil classification, 11, 90
Universal soil loss equation. *See* Soil loss predictions
U.S. Army Corps of Engineers, 4, 5, 107, 117
U.S. Environmental Protection Agency, 4, 116, 132
U.S. Forest Service, 7, 96, 116, 132
U.S. National Park Service, 7, 198
U.S. Soil Conservation Service, 17, 18, 23, 37, 132, 158, 189, 257

Vegetation, 124, 209
  control of erosion, 12, 13, 24, 37
  in biotechnical protection, 66, 73, 80, 157
  prevention of mass movement, 27, 37, 39, 51, 55, 63, 192
  See also Herbaceous plants; Revegetation; Woody plants.

Water control, 81, 125, 142, 145, 205
  groundwater, 144
    horizontal drains, 81, 125, 145
    phreatophytes, 81, 125, 144
    trench drains, 144, 145
  surface water, 142
    diversions, 142, 190
    interceptor dike, 142
    permissible velocities, 143
  See also Runoff; Seepage
Watershed rehabilitation, 8, 188, 197
Wattling. *See* Contour wattling
Weed control. *See* Seeding methods
Welded-wire walls, 84, 87, 91, 99, 118
  principles of construction, 99, 102
  relative advantages, 84, 103
  specifications for backfill, 103, 256
  standard designs, 255–256
  use with vegetation, 103
  See also Retaining structures
Willow staking. *See* Live staking
Willow wattling. *See* Contour wattling
Wind erosion, 10
  determinants, 12
  mechanics of movement, 12, 13
  See also Soil erosion
Windthrowing, 37, 38
Woody plants, 22, 38, 43, 46, 54, 56, 61, 66, 129–132, 147, 153, 172, 192, 211